# Audregnies

The Flank Guard Action and the First Cavalry Charge of the Great War
24 August 1914

Philip Watson

**Helion & Company Limited**

Helion & Company Limited
Unit 8 Amherst Business Centre
Budbrooke Road
Warwick
CV34 5WE
England
Tel. 01926 499 619

Email: info@helion.co.uk
Website: www.helion.co.uk
Twitter: @helionbooks
Visit our blog http://blog.helion.co.uk/

Published by Helion & Company 2019
Designed and typeset by Mary Woolley (www.battlefield-design.co.uk)
Cover designed by Paul Hewitt, Battlefield Design (www.battlefield-design.co.uk)



Front Cover: Picture presented by Mrs H.C. Taylor-Whitehead (Officers' Mess, The Royal Lancers (Queen Elizabeths' Own) – photo by Will Cave
Back Cover: Captain F.O. Grenfell's Victoria Cross (9/12L Museum)



ISBN 978-1-911628-97-2

British Library Cataloguing-in-Publication Data.
A catalogue record for this book is available from the British Library.

# Contents


| | | |
|---|---|---|
| List of Illustrations | | iv |
| List of Maps | | vii |
| Dedication | | viii |
| Acknowledgements | | ix |
| Foreword | | xiii |
| Preface | | xv |
| 1 | Countdown to War | 19 |
| 2 | Mobilisation | 38 |
| 3 | Loading and Embarkation | 80 |
| 4 | Crossing the Channel | 87 |
| 5 | At Base Camps | 95 |
| 6 | Rail Move to Jeumont, Obrechies and Le Pommereuil | 101 |
| 7 | Crossing into Belgium | 118 |
| 8 | Move to Mons | 129 |
| 9 | Mons | 148 |
| 10 | Audregnies and Élouges | 184 |
| 11 | Aftermath | 266 |
| 12 | Analysis | 285 |
| Appendices: | | |
| A | 9th Lancer's Casualties 24th August 1914 | 311 |
| B | British and German Casualties, 24th August 1914 | 315 |
| C | Honours and Awards, 24th August 1914 | 316 |
| Bibliography | | 318 |
| Index | | 331 |

## List of Illustrations

### Text

Mr Stuart Gruber and Spur Taylor at the 9/12L Officers' Mess, Detmold on 18th June 1972. (Mr Stuart Gruber) x
Field Marshal Sir John French. (Author's Collection) 21
Lieutenant Edward Spears. (Liaison 1914) 22
Requisitioned vehicles seen on Saturday, 1st August at the Grand Place in Mons. (Famille Houzeau de Lehaie) 24
Private Robert Sheldrake. (Norfolk Regiment Museum) 25
General Helmut von Moltke. (Author's Collection) 27
Norfolk Regiment officers c. 1913. (Norfolk Regiment Museum) 29
Generaloberst Alexander von Kluck. (Author's Collection) 41
9th Lancer's bed space in Tidworth. (Author's Collection) 44
My Daddy's a Soldier Now. (Author's Collection) 47
Captain Douglas Lucas-Tooth. (9/12L Museum) 48
SSM Hugh Durant c. 1913. (John Goodchild) 52
General Edmund Allenby. (Author's Collection) 55
Pensionnat Saint Bernard, Audregnies. (Author's Collection) 57
The Sisters of St Bernard's, Audregnies, Sisters: Saint-Martin, Félicité, Marie-Xavier, Charlotte, Bénigne, Flavie, Sylvie. Christine and Euphémie (Jean Richez, *Un Champ de Coquelicots, La Bataille d'Audregnies le 24 Août 1914*) 63
Infanterie Regiment 66 on their way to the front. (*The German 66th Regiment in the First World War*) 65
Generalleutnant Sixt von Armin. (Author's Collection) 66
9th Lancer's, Tidworth c. 1914. (Author's Collection) 69
Cheshire Regimental officers c. 1913. (Cheshire Regiment Museum) 71
General Horace Smith-Dorrien. (Author's Collection) 74
Cheshire Regiment departing Londonderry. (Cheshire Regiment Museum) 74
Lieutenant Colonel Colin Ballard. (Norfolk Regiment) 76
Lieutenant Geoffrey Pollard. (*The Bond of Sacrifice*, Vol. I) 78
C Squadron SNCOs on 16th August 1914 aboard the SS Welshman: Hollaway, West, Swaine, Gummerson, Anelay, Curtis, Praeger, Coombes, Ambrose, Pickering, Timms and Parker. (9/12L Museum) 81

Francis and Rivy Grenfell, Tidworth Officers' Mess 15th August 1914. (9/12L Museum) 82
Captain Brereton Nash-Wortham. (9/12L Museum) 83
Captain Roger Peek. (9/12L Museum) 84
Lieutenant Frederick de Vere Bruce Allfrey. (Author's Collection) 88
Lancer disembarkation. (Author's Collection) 90
Base Camp 3, 17th August 1914, Captain Peek standing. (9/12L Museum) 96
9th Lancers watering horses at Obrechies. (9/12L Museum) 107
15th Infantry Brigade "No Surrender" document. (Norfolk Regiment Museum) 112
General Sir Charles Fergusson. (Author's Collection) 113
Infanterie Regiment 26 entering Bruxelles. (*Das Infanterie-Regiment Fürst Leopold von Anhalt-Dessau (1. Magdeburg.) Nr. 26.*) 116
Nimy, the road bridge turning closed to allow the movement of barges. This is the position it was in during the Battle of Mons on 23rd August 1914. (Collection: Jean-Paul Hubens) 120
Lieutenants Charlie Garstin and Frank Crossley. (9/12L Museum) 131
Lieutenant Colonel Dudley Boger. (Cheshire Regiment Museum) 136
The Borinage. (Author's Collection) 139
Corporal R.H. 'Spur' Taylor c. 1928. (Author's Collection) 147
Élouges slag heap. (MonDour <http://www.mondour.be/>) 153
Lieutenant Colonel David Campbell. (9/12L Museum) 164
Canal Bridge Harchies. (*Infanterie-Regiment Nr. 93 im Weltkriege*) 175
Lieutenant Cuthbert Matterson. (Cheshire Regiment Museum) 188
*Infanterie Regiment 72* soldier c. 1914. (Author's Collection) 199
Flank Guard Action at Élouges. Watercolour by Captain JC Walford. (RAI) 209
Officers of Feldartillerie Regiment 40. (*Das Altmärkische Feld-Artellerie-Regiment Nr. 40 im Weltkriege 1914-1918*) 218
Lieutenant Victor Briard. (<https://www.theislandwiki.org>/) 245
Major Chetwynd-Stapylton. (Cheshire Regiment Museum) 249
Hauptmann Magnussen. (*Das 4. Thüringische Infanterie-Regiment Nr. 72*) 255
Edith Cavell. (Author's Collection) 268
Lieutenant Colonel Boger's International Red Cross POW postcard. (*Grand Guerre* <https://grandeguerre.icrc.org/>) 269
Lieutenant C.O.D. Preston's International Red Cross POW postcard. (*Grand Guerre* <https://grandeguerre.icrc.org/> ) 271
Mons, Place Leopold, c. 29-30th August 1914: British prisoners marching towards the rail station to internment camps in Germany. (Philippe Yannart) 280
Recovering the Guns. (Author's Collection) 306

**Colour Plate Section** (All images by Author)

Roman Road, Chaussée Brunehaut. i
Maréchal des Logis Louis Jules Jean Baptiste Quilico attached 4th Dragoon Guards. i
Élouges Cemetery. ii
Élouges centre. ii
L'ambulance de la Sainte Famille. iii

Line of mineral railway from the sugar factory running west to east. iii
Line of the Norfolk Company's looking north. iv
Major E. Alexander's 119th Battery's position at Élouges. Looking north from the Norfolk Regiment's HQ location. iv
Minehead at the junction between the Norfolks and Cheshires looking north. v
Norfolk Regiment Battalion HQ and B Company location. v
Sugar Factory looking south down Roman Road. vi
Thulin Railway Station, Lieutenant Charlie Garstin's location on the morning of 24th August 1914. vi
Thulin Church, Lieutenant Rivy Grenfell's location on the morning of 24th August 1914. vii
Audregnies windmill. viii
Mineral railway bridge similar to the one at the Norfolk Regiment Headquarters. viii

## List of Maps


Map 1 Cavalry Division, brigade Concentration Areas, August 1914. (*Cavalry Journal*, 1922) 104
Map 2 1st DCLI positions at Ville Pommeroeul, 22nd August 1914. (Major W.H. White DL) 140
Map 3 Cavalry Division Areas, 23rd August 1914. (*Cavalry Journal*, 1922) 149
Map 4 Communications Map, Signals 1st Cavalry Division, 23rd August 1914. (TNA WO 95/1104) 151
Map 5 Cavalry Division Areas on the evening 23rd August 1914. (*Cavalry Journal*, 1922)162
Map 6 British issue General area Map c. 1916. (QRL & NY Museum) 166
Map 7 Harchies Crossing. (*Das Anhaltische Infanterie-Regiment Nr. 93 im Weltkriege*) 176
Map 8 German *IV AK* line of advance on the 23rd-24th August 1914 – Battle of Mons. (Kluck, *The March on Paris and the Battle of the Marne 1914*) 185
Map 9 *Infanterie Regiments 26* and *66* positions at Thulin on 23rd-24th August 1914. (*The German 66th Regiment in the First World War*) 190
Map 10 *Feldartillerie 40* disposition at Élouges on 24th August 1914. (*Das Altmärkische Feld-Artillerie-Regiment Nr. 40 im Weltkriege 1914-1918*) 193
Map 11 *Infanterie Regiment 72* line of attack, 24th August 1914. (*Das 4. Thüringische Infanterie-Regiment Nr. 72 in der Flandern-Schlacht*) 202
Map 12 Detailed Map with Slag Heap of Norfolks HQ and 119th Battery position. (Author) 208
Map 13 Flank Guard and 2nd Cavalry Brigade's positions on midday on 24th August 1914. (Author) 211
Map 14 L Battery's engagement at Audregnies , 24th August 1914. (TNA WO 95/1111) 214
Map 15 Map from Captain Wright's Diary, 4th Dragoon Guards, 24th August 1914. (RDG Museum) 226
Map 16 Mounted actions of 2nd Cavalry Brigade. (Author) 231
Map 17 9th Lancers: Rough sketch map derived from memory of the Action at Audregnies. (TNA WO 95/1113/2) 232
Map 18 Cheshire Regiment's final positions at dusk on 24th August 1914. Rendered by H.F. Davis. (*Cheshire Regiment and the Miniature Colour*) 257

## Dedication

---

This book is primarily dedicated to the memory of my parents Alwyne and Margaret Watson who both sadly passed away in 2018 before they were able to read this book. Just as the book was submitted for editing, my father-in-law, Derek Davis also died which brought to an end a very difficult period of time for my family. In addition, it is dedicated to the memory of Brigadier James Mackaness MBE, who also died in 2018 and was the Commanding Officer of my Regiment. He had enough faith in me to commission me from the ranks; that changed my family's life, for the better, forever. I hope they would have all approved of my efforts to bring this story to life.

Not only during the writing of this book have I lost four important people in my life, but my Regiment also mourns the loss of three young men who lost their own battle against their demons, and who chose the time and place of their own passing. It is a timely reminder that the invisible scars are carried by soldiers and their families long after the guns have stopped firing and the armistice is signed:

**In Memoriam**

LCpl Al Winter-Hall
LCpl Matt Shillito
Tpr Tel Hopkins

**With Love**

To my wife Gill, who has had to put up with much over the last 38 years and who has shared the difficulties of 12 months. Gill married me when I was a trooper, long before I had any prospects and she has shared my life not only as a military wife, but as a mother who was left to bring up our four boys as work often took me away from home. She has had to endure endless years apart with much worry as we served and moved in an uncertain and violent world. In place of family holidays, she has had countless visits to war cemeteries, tramped over miles of battlefields as holidays morphed into battlefield tours. Also, she has seen my reference library grow to unreasonable proportions – I really do 8.23.1

## Acknowledgements

From the outset I realised I could not pull this story together on my own. This was unlike my first publication, *The Last Charges*, which was purely regimental, and came from a limited number of sources involving only a few close friends and colleagues. The aim of this book was to bring together many different stories to build up a holistic picture of Audregnies, from both Belgian, French, British and German sources. Much of my work over the last six years has been copy-typed by Mrs Celia Bokenham, and the book would have taken much longer to write without her support. She has a unique ability to read difficult and, to me, illegible handwriting. I am also incredibly grateful to my friend, Colonel Nigel Stafford CMG, for the time he spent proof reading. His contribution has elevated the quality of my work. I had the honour of being Colonel Stafford's Squadron Sergeant Major when he was a Major, so this is not the first time I find myself in his debt.

Thanks go to Mrs Angela Tarnowski, curator of the 9th/12th Royal Lancers Museum for her continued support and to the 9th/12th Lancers Museum Trust for their permission to use extracts from the diaries of Lieutenant Marden, Lance Corporal Dovey and the letters from Shoe Smith Friend and Major Alexander. Also, to my friend Captain (Retd) Mick Holtby, the assistant regimental secretary of the Royal Lancers and curator of The Queen's Royal Lancers and Nottinghamshire Yeomanry Museum for permission to use extracts from the diaries of Lieutenant Horn and Beech, but also for his company on the visit to Audregnies and Élouges in 2018, and his advice and wisdom regarding the exact position of 119th Battery's guns during the action when they required to be saved. To my friend Major (Retd) Graeme Green, the regimental secretary of The Royal Dragoon Guards for permission to use extracts from the diaries of Captain Wright and Private Dyre, and thanks to his assistant curator, Aline Staes, for correcting my French and translating the diary from Saint Bernard's. I feel the addition of the view from the perspective of the local population who wrote and viewed the day from a non-military perspective has been one of the most valuable additions. I am also most grateful to Major (Retd) Mel Tazey, the regimental secretary of The Light Dragoons for access to his website archive. Many of the German sources had already been translated by Mr Terrance Zuber, in his own publications which have been credited where appropriate, however, the account of the first RFC aircraft shot down and the first engagements at Casteau were translated by Mrs Anne-Eline Taylor, and to my knowledge these are the first time these two accounts have been published in English.

I am particularly indebted to Kate Thaxton, the curator of the Royal Norfolk Regimental Museum and The Trustees of the Royal Norfolk Regimental Museum for allowing me to read the diaries of Privates Hurrell and Sheldrake, and their subsequent usage. I am most grateful to Caroline Chamberlain, the museum officer, at the Cheshire Military Museum and Mr Geoffrey

Crump, their honorary researcher, for the production of many of the publications already written on the subject, and for helping to check my homework. The details of the map regarding the 1 DCLI positions on the 2nd August 1914 was supplied and hand-drawn by Major W.H. White DL from the DCLI Museum, for which I am most grateful.

At the heart of the book are the unpublished diaries of the officers and men who were present. The story of the Grenfell twins would not have been possible without access to the Lyttelton Family Papers held at the Queen Mary University London Archives. Without these papers, in conjunction with the unattributed manuscript (which would appear to have been written at some point by the Squadron Leader of A Squadron, Captain Douglas Lucas-Tooth) the book would have lacked much of its detail and colour. I am much indebted to Mr Malcolm Wright for the use of the A Squadron diary. The inclusion of extracts from the diary of Lieutenant Allfrey, owned by Mr Jimmy Meade, and the permission given to use extracts from Lance Corporal Hunt's diary by Mrs Marjorie MacMullen, his daughter, were again invaluable. I am also most grateful to Sir Richard Peek for allowing me to quote extracts from the diary of his grandfather Captain Roger Peek. Permission to draw on Corporal Easton's diary, held in the Liddle Collection at Leeds University was granted. Permission was also granted by Mr Richard Wells to use Private Well's diary held at the Imperial War Museum.

I would also like to take the opportunity to thank André Faehrès, a resident of Mons, who shared a beer and allowed me to view his extensive photograph collection and permission to use several examples in the book. I am also most grateful to Monsieur Jean Richez for sending me copies of his book *Un Champ de Coquelicots, La Bataille d'Audregnies le 24 Août 1914* and providing the excellent map showing the position of the slag heap at the mine at Élouges prior to its removal in the 1960s.

Mr Stuart Gruber and Spur Taylor at the 9/12L Officers' Mess, Detmold on 18th June 1972. (Mr Stuart Gruber)

I would also like to thank the Chairman of the Trustees of the Royal Lancers for allowing me to take the image for the front cover from the painting held in the Royal Lancers Officers' Mess. I am grateful to Dr Michael LoCicero for his encouragement and guidance; to Dr Jim Beach for assisting with the composition of General Allenby's intelligence section and to Dr Spencer Jones, who connected me with other authors, and who told me that the story of Audregnies was still to be told. I am flattered by his words.

Lastly, but most importantly, I would like to thank Mr Stuart Gruber, who, as an honorary member of the 9/12L Old Comrades Association since 1971, met and wrote to many 9th Lancers who were at Audregnies, long before I joined the Regiment. It was his article written in the Regimental magazine of the 9/12L, *The Delhi Spearman* in 1974, some 45 years ago, which sowed the seed for this book. It was not just the action at Audregnies, but the challenge of including the names of soldiers, as well as the officers who were present that day and whose names were in danger in being lost to the sands of time. This work had been already started by Mr Gruber and formed the foundation for Appendix A. I am indebted to him for access to his correspondence, and particularly Lieutenant Norman's letter with reference to 'wire cutting' and the additional accounts of Spur Taylor's narrow escape. The letters were all "breadcrumbs" which I followed and helped me to develop the story. I hope he, and his family, approve of my work.

## Foreword

In August and September 1914, the British Army fought one of the most gruelling campaigns in its long history. Thrown into the maelstrom of a European war for the first time in almost a century, the British Expeditionary Force unexpectedly found itself standing in the path of the German *First Army* as it drove through Belgium and into France. Outnumbered roughly three-to-one and with its flanks in the air, the BEF was forced into what became retrospectively known as the Great Retreat as the Allied armies reeled back from the German onslaught. By the time the Great Retreat ended on 5th September, the BEF had covered at least 200 miles and stood near the gates of Paris. The eventual success of the manoeuvre, which ended with the BEF turning and joining the French counterattack at the Battle of the Marne, belies the hardships and dangers faced by the army. At times, the fate of the BEF hung by the slenderest of threads.

There was no greater period of crisis than the four days from the Battle of Mons on 23rd August and the Battle of Le Cateau on 26th August. During these four days the BEF was in close contact with *First Army* and under intense pressure. The Germans sought to encircle the BEF while the British tried to fight clear of the danger. Whilst the battles which bookended this period are well known, the bitter combat on 24th August is equally worthy of study. British casualties in the rear-guard fighting on this day were higher than at the Battle of Mons, but the scattered and small-scale nature of the engagements meant that none of the actions were deemed worthy of the title 'battle' by the post-war Battle Nomenclature Committee.

The largest of these rear-guard actions took place at Audregnies. It was a small, yet bitterly fought engagement designed to protect the BEF's flank as it fell back and, although it achieved its objective, it was marred by tragedy and controversy. The 1st Cheshires were cut off and destroyed, whilst elements of 2nd Cavalry Brigade launched a chaotic cold steel charge in controversial circumstances. It was this latter incident that caught the imagination of the British public. It was lauded in the press and immortalised in popular art prints.

The emphasis on the remarkable charge obfuscated both the events and the importance of the action at Audregnies. Once press coverage had faded, the battle came to be remembered as an oddity of the early war period, cited by critics and defenders of cavalry alike, until the coming of mechanisation and the events of the Second World War rendered both sides of the argument *moot*. Its memory lived on in the battle paintings, but it was gradually forgotten by soldiers, scholars and the public. Certain questions lingered, particularly why the charge had been launched at all, but it seemed unlikely they would be answered. Even the late Professor Richard Holmes suggested historians 'would probably never know' why the cavalry had charged on that fateful day.

It is therefore especially welcome that, more a century after the action was fought, this fascinating book has arrived. It explores the background to the campaign and the events of the day in tremendous depth and, for the first time, presents a definitive account of exactly what happened. The author, Major Philip Watson, brings thorough scholarship and a soldier's eye to his analysis: this is not merely a chronicle of events, but a deep study of the British Army in 1914 and its performance in battle. It is both a valuable work of military history and a fitting tribute to the officers and men who fought and fell in those desperate days.

Dr Spencer Jones
University of Wolverhampton

# Preface

---

*From the Bottom Up*

In August 1990, I was in an instructional post at the Armour Centre in Bovington, Dorset, when we heard that one of our former instructional colleagues had been captured in Kuwait by Saddam Hussain's forces as part of the Kuwait Liaison Team. The developing situation we had been watching on the news now came a lot closer to home. During the rest of the year Britain, along with its allies, came ever closer to the possibility of war. Some of the students that came through the school, were earmarked to deploy to the Gulf and students who hitherto would not have been so attentive were now model students as they realised that the information they were learning would very soon they were about to put into practice. In the foyer of the school a notice board was created and up to date bulletins were displayed so deploying troops could keep up to date. Eventually we started to teach some of the new equipments which had been bought "off the shelf," and from the behind our desks we were safe, but felt a little jealous that, just like the Falkland's War, we were going to miss out again. For me personally, this became more acute when my own regiment was *warned-off* to go in the New Year and as we got closer to Christmas officers were taken off courses to join their regiments and deploy, but I was to remain.

My tour at Bovington had been extended slightly to coincide my family move with the Regiment's move to Germany, but the impending war had cancelled the move and I was recalled to Regimental Duty. Before I was officially told, I was receiving cryptic rumours that I was to be posted to D Squadron, the squadron due to deploy. This was something I kept from my wife, since it was only rumour. This I successfully did until another wife asked her what she thought about me "going off to war." Having explained myself, and my wish not to worry her unnecessarily, we were stood down the following day. Having been told by my father to "keep my head down," my wife asked what actually a reconnaissance soldier was?" It was at this point we established avoiding the enemy might be difficult.

I rejoined my regiment but chose to leave my wife and children in Dorset, and focussed on the matter in hand, as we had been *warned-off* again to go, and I was to be the troop sergeant of 4th Troop of D Squadron. I arrived just in time to meet the troop and we went off on exercise and to the ranges to bring ourselves back up to standard. I had been away from the Regiment for just over two years and had left as a corporal and now returned as a troop sergeant with no experience, and a little turret-rusty. The squadron went to the ranges at Castlemartin, where the gunnery instructor told me to "forget everything I had ever been taught and he was going to show me all the shortcuts and wrinkles to keep the turret firing." Once we had finished firing from a static position we practiced moving forward in bounds, but instead of side by side as usual, we were allowed to do it by caterpillaring one in front of each other, meaning the vehicle behind had its guns loaded, something we had never been allowed to do before. When we arrived in Saudi Arabia, we fired our Sub Machine Guns (SMG), and attended some *ad hoc* lectures and were introduced to plastic explosives (PE), with the intention of giving us more confidence when handling it. The instructor kept repeating P stood for "plenty" and not to be scared of it. As we detonated 1 kg balls of PE, he encouraged us to get ever closer, telling us he would let us know "when we were too close," and it is amazing how close you can get. These incidents regarding safety, and its removal were the elements of the "training gap being removed" – the difference between training and war.

After order and counter order, we flew to Saudi Arabia and joined Operation GRANBY (Desert Shield/Storm). From the minute we left to the minute we returned, every date and timing we had been given had been missed or never materialised. During the early stages of the war, SCUD missiles were fired into Saudi Arabia. Every night we went to "Air Raid Red" and put on our NBC suits and respirators and we soon realised that, at night once it's on, it stays on, and in the morning the whole process of "unmasking" now was real and not just a drill. We took over war maintenance reserve vehicles and were issued with desert pattern camouflage uniforms. The vehicles were in poor shape but we managed to build three serviceable wagons from the four we were presented with. Some of the missing critical components never materialised before the end of the war, and the main armaments was never "test fired," and to this day I will never know if it would have worked. Inside the vehicle on the wall I wrote to the previous commander "if I die in this vehicle I will come back and haunt you!" As a three-car troop we went off to war and at the end of the 100 hours, we sat in the middle of the desert on the 28th February, and heard on the BBC World Service that the Iraqi army had surrendered, and therefore we presumed we had won!

Eventually we returned to England, much towards the end of the queue of conquering heroes, and life returned to its norm, and in the spirit of Kipling's Tommy Atkins, the pubs that had suddenly been "in bounds" were "out of bounds" again. Later that year in the Warrant Officers' and Sergeants' Mess we *dined-out* one of our warrant officers on commissioning and he said in his leaving speech that he felt "every soldier should go to war at least once in their careers," and spelt out how being mobilised, and going to war, was significantly different to "going on operations."

The nature of modern conflict and operations normally means a soldier joins an operation where the political and military situation is fully understood and they know when they are to deploy, when they are expected to return and of course when their leave will be. It is these crisp dates which they and their families use to see them though the next six months, and also knowing his personal freight (MFO box) will be waiting for him/her in theatre with some of the home comforts that they could not fit into their webbing. Being mobilised to war is exactly the opposite: nothing is known, and you go to war in the kit you stand up in and if it's not in your kit or not in your head, it's all too late and you don't know when or if you are ever coming home. Soldiers and officers who had tried desperately to join the squadron found themselves on the side-lines and the bad the soldiers we took in their stead did not get any better, with predictable consequences. So, having been mobilised to war from an instructional post, being somewhat obsolete, and my reference point being one rank junior to the position I was to hold in war, I fully understand how the reservist of 1914 felt, and of course my troop who had to knock their new sergeant into shape in pretty short order. I also understood very quickly, that it did not matter how good I was at my job: it was those around me and above me who might cause me to lose my life and I just had to hope they were better at their jobs than I was at mine.

It is through this prism that I now read history: my view will always be "from the bottom up." By the end of my career I was commanding Headquarters Squadron and my *tactical* view of the world had become *operational*, with a good understanding of the *strategic*. In the beginning the books that I was reading about the Great War were the self-serving autobiographies written by senior officers, which were fine, but they were mostly "from a top down" view. This could also be said of the books written by historians and academics who had never served and could not possibly know what it was like to go to war. I noticed that films and TV programmes regarding war and soldiering rarely captured the essence of how it feels to be a soldier and it transported me to the places where I had been. They "struck a chord," showing that the director truly understood his subject and I felt "they got it!"

It is with this in mind I have chosen the style I have written, and I have included the *minutiae* of the intimate detail that only the men and women who were there could have written, whether it be in parliament, or the front line which include the thoughts, emotions, intimate details of the close friends and lovers. Some of the quotes are deliberately long so the context is not lost and their words are not reduced to a *soundbite* of history. I have always felt that if the diarists and authors been alive today, we would choose to ask them our questions instead of reading the words of other people, written in books, speculating on their motives. The stories I have used, which were carried by the press are included in full awareness that the *Defence of the Realm* (DORA) will have acted to censure the truth and the press and soldiers will always conflate. However, their inclusion does provide the alternative narrative as read at home by the wives and families and it provides an accurate timeline as to when they received information from the front in the absence of letters.

I have deliberately written the book in a diary format, with dates and times in chronologically order and it is designed to be read from the front, so the situation unfolds in the same sequence as the events presented themselves to the players in the book. I have tried my hardest to avoid historical bias, which inevitably comes with the benefit of hindsight. Before I began writing, I read as many sources (both contemporary and revisionist) as possible to try and understand the story I was trying to tell and I was prepared to be open minded as to how all the sources would 'best fit' when they were all drawn together. Naturally, in the process of writing I have selected text which illustrates the story which I think supports this. Where the story might differ from previous narratives, I have not overtly highlighted the differences and I have not deliberately set out to find errors in the Edmond's official history or discredit other authors. The official history, for the most part, although succinct and possibly understated, is reasonably accurate and I am content to let this book stand alongside it. The only observations I would make are that firstly Edmonds clearly identified that the 9L and 4DG made two separate mounted actions at Audregnies, and he does not mention the presence of wire fences, which does not mean they were not there, it possibly just means he did not see their presence as being a significant reason as to why the cavalry did not reach their objective. Clearly, the morphing of a single cavalry charge and the significance of wire fences were conflations over time, and the first draft of history was pretty good. The only error I think worth mentioning (within the context of this story) is the action at St Aybert and the action on the bridges at Hensies which prevented *Infanterie Division 8* crossing the canal on 23rd August, should be credited to the 6DG and not 1 Middlesex, as the both bridges were blown before the infantry arrived.

Finally, for ease of reading and indexing I have standardised the spelling of places and names used in the diaries and not necessarily indicated where I have done so. I have also made the time adjustment from the German diaries and used a standard time and dating system throughout. At the end of the book I have done an analysis, which is purely academic and it is done with sympathy, fully understanding, that when you go to war you do so "in the kit you stand up in and if it's not in your kit or your head, it's all too late," especially on the first action of the war! This applies to both the Germans and the allies alike.

Major Phil Watson
28th February 2019

# 1

# Countdown to War

---

*That I took my uniform with me was merely a precaution, certainly not a forecast.*

Lieutenant Edward Spears

*We are commanded to forgive those who offend us; we are not commanded to forgive those who offend against others.*

Lieutenant Colonel George Barrow

Finding themselves deployed to Belgium in the summer of 1914, Lieutenant Picard's platoon of the 2nd Lancers moved towards Stavelot.[1] He had been out on patrol since 0320, and as he looked through his field glasses from the wooded heights of his position, he was able to make out the details of the grey uniforms of the lancers on the sunlit road to the east. He sent his report by pigeon, tearing a page from his notebook he wrote 'saw a troop of Ulans [sic] in the direction of Remouchamps, 4th August, 1400.'[2] Earlier in the morning a 21-year-old soldier from 1st Squadron of the same regiment, Cavalier Antoine Fonck, had been the first Belgian soldier to lose his life in the war near Battice as the Germans started their advance south. It was exactly 44 years to the day since the invasion of the Alsace by the Prussian army in 1870.

In London, crowds had gathered outside the German consulate and the German tourists and workers were leaving London at a rate of 2000 a day. The acting-German Consul, Herr Robert von Ranke, estimated that ordinarily the German population in London was approximately 65,000 but with influx of its tourists and holidaymakers, the numbers had increased to 70,000. Herr von Ranke spoke several times from an upper window and:

1 Clayton Donnell, *Breaking the Fortress Line 1914* (Barnsley: Pen & Sword Military, 2013), p. 41.
2 George M. Thomson, *The Twelve Days, 24 July-4 August 1914* (London: Secker & Warburg, 1975). p. 194.

> Appealed to them, as sensible men, to disperse, and to make their way to Germany without further delay. "Unless you have any medical disqualification from military service, every man over 20 years of age will have to go home at once," he shouted. "We cannot guarantee that you can get through. You had better go home at once. You are only losing time here."'[3]

An hour after the Germans had crossed the Belgian border, Sir Edward Grey sent a telegram to Sir Edward Goschen, the British Ambassador in Berlin:

> We are also informed that Belgian territory has been violated at Gemmenich. In these circumstances, and in view of the fact that Germany declined to give the same assurance respecting Belgium as France gave last week in reply to our request made simultaneously at Berlin and Paris, we must repeat that request, and ask that a satisfactory reply to it and to my telegram No. 266 of this morning be received here by midnight tonight. If not, you are instructed to ask for your passports and to say that His Majesty's government felt bound to take all steps in their power to uphold the neutrality of Belgium and the observance of a treaty to which Germany is as much a party as ourselves.[4]

In Berlin, Sir Edward Goschen called on the German secretary of state that afternoon and inquired…whether the imperial government would refrain from violating Belgian neutrality. Gottlieb von Jagow at once replied that he was sorry to say that his answer must be "no," as in consequence of the German troops having crossed the frontier that morning, and Belgian neutrality had been already violated. He then pointed out to Gottlieb von Jagow that this *fait accompli* of the violation of the Belgian frontier rendered, 'as he would readily understand, the situation exceedingly grave, and asked him whether there was not still time to draw back and avoid possible consequences, which both he and I would deplore.'[5] He replied that, for the reasons he had given me, "it was now impossible for them to draw back." He then asked to see the chancellor, von Bethmann-Hollweg, as it might be, perhaps, the last time he should have an opportunity of seeing him.[6] During the afternoon the mobilisation order was received by the army commands and there had been no reply to the British ultimatum, the Foreign Office released the following statement:

> Owing to the summary rejection by the German government of the request made by His Majesty's government for assurances that the neutrality of Belgium would be respected, His Majesty's Ambassador in Berlin has received his passport, and His Majesty's government has declared to the German government that a state of war exists between Great Britain and Germany as from 2300 on August 4th.

Winston Churchill described the scene in London in the hours that led to the declaration of war:

3 *Yorkshire Post and Leeds Intelligencer*, 4th August 1914.
4 Anon., *Great Britain and the European Crisis* (London: HMSO, 1914), p. 77.
5 Sir Edward Goschen's report to Sir Edward Grey, *Great Britain and the European Crisis*, p. 78.
6 Ibid., p. 78.

> It was 2300, twelve by German time, when the ultimatum expired. The windows of the Admiralty were thrown wide open in the warm night air. Under the roof from which Nelson had received his orders were gathered a small group of admirals and captains and a cluster of clerks, pencils in hand, waiting…I walked across the Horse Guards Parade to the cabinet room and reported to the Prime Minister and the Ministers who were assembled there that the deed was done.[7]

Field Marshal Sir John French.
(Author's Collection)

In Paris, France was still waiting to hear if Britain would be coming to her aid and so was Lieutenant Edward (*Louis)* Spears, when the news arrived at last, it ended 'what seemed a frightful nightmare of suspense and sickening anxiety.'[8] Lieutenant Spears had set off for Paris on the 27th July and his presence at the *Ministère de la Guerre* was entirely unconnected with the war and he said that 'I took my uniform with me was merely a precaution, certainly not a forecast. It had been decided some months before that a British officer should be attached for a few weeks to a certain section of the French War Office, and when war suddenly loomed on the horizon it was felt that there was no disadvantage.'[9] Britain sent her ultimatum to German and 'all France heaved a sigh of relief. The people were…they concluded that although we might

7 Winston S. Churchill, *The World Crisis,* Vol. I (London: Odhams Press, 1938). p. 162.
8 Brig. Gen. Edward L. Spears, *Liaison 1914: A Narrative of the Great Retreat* (London: William Heinemann, 1930), p. 15.
9 Ibid., p. 4.

Lieutenant Edward Spears. (Liaison 1914)

not be numerous, we were at least prompt!'[10] General Lanrezac was somewhat blunter saying to Field Marshal French "Well here you are. It is just in time. If we are beaten it is thanks to you." The size and the effective role of the force to be sent by Britain had always been a moot point and its relatively small all-volunteer army could never be numerically compared to the large conscript armies of Europe. Many years before, when General Foch had been asked what the minimum force was the French would accept, he replied 'one man; and we will take good care he is killed.' General Douglas Haig felt that beyond the fighting value of an expeditionary force, the presence of British troops would give the 'French army the moral support without which they would have been overwhelmed by the demoralising memories of 1870,'[11] but what everyone had forgotten of course was the memorandum presented to the Imperial Defence Conference in London in July 1909. It was at this conference where the dominion representatives accepted Richard Haldane's proposals and a partnership for the defence of Britain was agreed. This in turn would mean that the forces of the British Empire could also be called upon if required.

Lieutenant Spears wrote, as if to mark the seriousness of the situation, that now 'Britain had declared war, I put on my uniform, "How funny you look, disguised as a dusty canary," observed the female concierge who let him in at one of the more obscure entrances to the *Ministère de la Guerre,* when she saw him for the first time in khaki.[12] 'This was disappointing, but one became used to the fact that for a long time the French thought "that to go to war in a collar and tie

10 Ibid., p. 15.
11 Brig. Gen. John Charteris, *Field Marshal Earl Haig* (London: Cassell and Company, 1929). p. 81.
12 Brig. Gen. Edward L. Spears, *Liaison 1914*, p. 16.

represented an attitude of levity quite out of keeping with the seriousness of the situation.'[13] This had been a sombre day in Paris as the funeral of Jean Jaurès had taken place. Jean Jaurès was the 54 year old leader of the *Section Française de l'Internationale Ouvrière*, (SFIO), a French socialist party. He was an ardent antimilitarist, pacifist and was openly opposed to the new French *Three-Year Service Law*. He was shot by a French nationalist at 2100 on 31st July while sitting in the Café du Croissant, 146, rue Montmartre which was located next to his newspaper *L'Humanité*. The assassin, was Raoul Villain who[14] had walked up to the restaurant window and fired two shots into Jaurès' back. Jean Jaurès had been due to attend an international conference on 9th August, in an attempt to dissuade the belligerent parties from going ahead with the war. The pacifist views of Jean Jaurès were at odds with many nationalists who saw a war with Germany as an opportunity to regains the annexed provinces of Reichsland Elsaß-Lothringen (Alsace-Lorraine) lost since 1871 and Raoul Villain was a member of the *Ligue des jeunes amis de l'Alsace-Lorraine* (League of Young Friends of Alsace-Lorraine). Paul Maze, who had just returned to Paris from Florence uneasy at the developing situation in Europe was sitting in a café in Paris 'wondering and commenting on what Britain would do'[15] when he heard the shots ring out:

> A white ambulance marked with a big red cross dramatically arrived on the scene; the corpse was brought out followed by a surging crowd; at a gallop, escorted by Republican Guards with pigtails and long black coats, the procession cut its way through the people whom the police by that time could hardly restrain. I never felt the tension created by human passion as I did at that moment; Paris seemed electrified. I had only reached my hotel with difficulty, for the street was closed at both ends by a cordon of police holding back the crowds who had come to see the departure of the German ambassador and his staff…From my hotel window I saw the whole staff get into their cars…not a murmur rose from the crowd as the cortège quickly drove away to the station.[16]

At the funeral, the red socialist banner was draped in black and the secretary of *Confédération Générale du Travail* (CGT), Léon Jouhaux,[17] who was the following day was to join his regiment said 'we take to the field with the determination to drive back the aggressor.'[18] An immense crowd had gathered for the funeral, 'but there was perfect order and all heaved a sigh of relief, France was sound to the core,'[19] and the *union sacrée* was complete. Meanwhile in Belgium, as a precaution, the government started to requisition all available civilian horses and motor vehicles.[20]

13 Ibid., p. 16.
14 Villain was imprisoned for the duration of the war and brought to trial on 29th March 1919. Subsequently acquitted by a jury still uncomfortable with Jaurès's legacy, Jaurès's widow was ordered to pay court costs.
15 Paul Maze, *A Frenchman in Khaki* (London: William Heinemann, 1934), p. 5.
16 Ibid., pp. 5-6.
17 Johaux was arrested during 1939-45 and imprisoned in Buchenwald concentration camp. He survived the ordeal and went on to be awarded a Nobel Peace Prize in 1951.
18 George M. Thomson, *The Twelve Days, 24 July-4 August 1914,* p. 193.
19 Spears, *Liaison 1914,* p. 12.
20 Footnote: Conversation with, André Faehrès on 11th November 2018.

Requisitioned vehicles seen on Saturday, 1st August at the Grand Place in Mons.
(Famille Houzeau de Lehaie)

In England that evening, at 2000, the postman arrived at Park View, the home of Mr Robert Sheldrake (which was next to the church)[21] on a bicycle from the head office at East Dereham,'[22] Norfolk, with his *mobilisation orders*. That evening he was very busy until about midnight making the final preparations and talking over family affairs with his wife Patience.[23] Robert Sheldrake had been a soldier before but had left the army and settled down as a postman in the little village of North Elmham in mid-Norfolk. They had only just moved in with their three little children (Frederick, Olive and Dolly) and with their few humble belongings, where he 'had hoped to spend a few years in peace, with 'what comfort us class that have to work for a living and exist on a small wage can expect.'[24] He was looking forward to his annual holiday in the middle of August and intended going to re-engage for the army reserve, 'as the 6d per diem is very welcome.'[25] He had anticipated his call up and had told people on his rounds, with the exception of very few who did not know he had been a soldier, because he did not have a

21 Sheldrake's daughter Patricia states that the house is on the left of The Church of St Mary the Virgin North Elmham.
22 Pte R. Sheldrake diary, p. 1.
23 Ibid., p. 1.
24 Ibid., p. 1.
25 Ibid., p. 1.

"soldier's swagger in my walk, talk or quiff." He told them that he expected to be leaving them in a few days' time, and felt so confident that he would be going, he took a part-day holiday, Bank Holiday, on the 3rd August, to gather his army papers. 'There was someone nearby who told me not to be so silly as she knew, or hoped anyway, I should not have to go.'[26]

Private Robert Sheldrake. (Norfolk Regiment Museum)

As Robert Sheldrake was packing, the King wrote in his diary, 'I held a council at 2245 to declare war with Germany. It is a terrible catastrophe, but it is not our fault. An enormous crowd collected outside the palace; we went on to the balcony both before and after dinner. When they heard that war had been declared, the excitement increased and Mary and I with David [the Prince of Wales], went on to the balcony; the cheering was terrific. Please God it may soon be over and that he will protect dear Bertie's life…serving with the Royal Navy. Bed at 1200.'[27]

Herbert Asquith had decided to appoint Field Marshal Lord Kitchener as the Secretary of State for War and gave up the role he himself had held since the *Curragh Incident*. Lord Kitchener had the distinction of being the first serving soldier to hold the post and was the first

26 Ibid.
27 George V diary, 4th August 1914.

to enter the cabinet since General Monck, during the reign of Charles II.[28] This was announced in *The Guardian* newspaper the following day. "It was officially announced last night that Field Marshal Lord Kitchener has been offered and has accepted the post of Secretary of State for War." When Herbert Asquith discussed this with Margot, his wife, she said 'I supposed he jumped at it? Herbert Asquith replied "Not he! He did not want it at all. He does not fancy taking the post, now that every detail of our plans has been made."'[29] Lord Kitchener had remarked to Lord Rosebery (former Liberal Prime Minister) that the 'cabinet deserved a Victoria Cross for declaring war in a state of such unpreparedness.[30] Lord Kitchener's appointment was little to do with his qualifications to hold the post but his presence was indispensable to 'tranquilise public feeling,'[31] and for England to go to war without Lord Kitchener 'would have been as unthinkable as Sunday without church.'[32] There had also been calls in the press for Lord Haldane to be replaced 'chiefly on the ground that he was a well-known sympathiser for Germany which was bound to make him unacceptable as a war leader to the French.'[33] Later in the year the same pressure would also be applied to the First Sea Lord, Prince Louis of Battenberg who would also need to be replaced. The following statement was issued at 10, Downing Street:

> In consequence of the pressure of other duties the Prime Minister has been compelled to give up the office of Secretary of State for War. The King has approved of the appointment of Lord Kitchener as his successor. Lord Kitchener undertakes the duties of the office for the time being in view of the emergency created by the war and his post in Egypt will be kept open.[34]

Herbert Asquith did not see this as a long-term position and wrote to Venetia Stanley, his mistress and muse, and told her that he had installed 'Kitchener there as an emergency man, until the war comes to an end.'[35] That evening when he arrived home Margot asked him 'So is it all up? Yes, it's all up, they wept,'[36] there was nothing left now left to do but wait. The 'elected Liberal government had genuinely and conscientiously grappled with the issue that confronted it and had then decided that war was the only possible step: both Conservative and Labour parties supported their decision.'[37] Britain, had had no formal alliance which had obligated it to war, in support of France. It had been debated in parliament, the only nation who had declared war to do so. The press, had gotten behind the government and the opinion of the public and

28 Barbara Tuchman, August 1914, The First Month of the First World War (London: Constable & Co., 1980). p. 193.
29 Michael Brock & Eleanor Brock (eds.), *Margot Asquith's Great War Diary 1914-1916: The View from Downing Street* (Oxford: Oxford University Press, 2014), p. 14.
30 Ibid., p. 42.
31 Arthur p. 13, op. cit. in Tuchman, *August 1914*, p. 195.
32 Tuchman, *August 1914*, p. 195.
33 Michael Brock & Eleanor Brock, *H.H. Asquith: Letters to Venetia Stanley* (Oxford: Oxford University Press, 1985), p. 152.
34 *The Guardian*, 6th August 1914.
35 Mark Bostridge, *The Fateful Year: England 1914* (London: Viking, 2014), p. 220.
36 Thomson, *The Twelve Days*, p. 198.
37 Hew Strachan, *The First World War: To Arms* (Oxford, Oxford University Press, 2001), p. 166.

government was now in step. Britain's domestic situation was such that the conditions were that Britain could go to war without the collapse of the government or civil war taking place.

At 1900, Sir Edward Goschen, the British Ambassador in Berlin, called on Chancellor von Bethmann-Hollweg for a final interview. The meeting lasted approximately 20 minutes, where he said 'that the steps taken by His Majesty's government were terrible to a degree; just for a word, "neutrality," a word which in war time had so often been disregarded just for a *scrap of paper* Britain was going to make war on a kindred nation who desired nothing better than to be friends with her.'[38] The chancellor also remarked that Britain was 'stabbing a man from behind while he was fighting for his life.'[39] The question of observing Belgium's neutrality was never treated seriously by Germany when it came to delivering the *Schlieffen or Moltke plan*s. General Erich Ludendorff, the Deputy Chief of Staff to the German Second Army said 'we were all convinced of the soundness of this plan and nobody believed in Belgium's neutrality.'[40] The 'creed of the German Governments had, since the days of Bismarck, been that victory covers all sins.'[41]

General Helmut von Moltke.
(Author's Collection)

38 Sir Edward Goschen's report to Sir Edward Grey. *Great Britain and the European Crisis,* p 78.
39 Thomson, *The Twelve Days,* p. 199.
40 Gen. Ludendorff, *My War Memories 1914-1918* (London: Hutchinson & Co, 1920), p. 25.
41 Maj. Gen. Sir F. Maurice, *Forty Days in 1914* (London: Constable and Company Ltd, 1920), p. 24.

On the morning of 5th August, the headlines in the *The Daily Mail* were 'Declaration of War by Great Britain after unsatisfactory reply to yesterday's ultimatum'. The paper dedicated its whole front page to the war which had a distinctly naval feel to it. It had a centre spread of photographs and three pages of articles relating to the war. It included articles endorsed by the Prime Minister requesting "Economy for the poor" to the prosperous should ease back on their consumption of meat to help the poor. In the same vein it suggested that Englishwomen, the paper's target audience "study economy in the matter of using gas and oil. The paper also carried requests for "motor cyclists for service with the army" and were required offering a £10 bounty for enlistment and a further £5 on discharge. Their terms of service would be for one year or as long as the war continued, There was also a broader appeal for men to enlist "The King and Country Need You" saying that every "If every patriotic young man answers her call, England and her Empire will emerge stronger and more united than ever…If you are unmarried and between 18 and 30 years old will you answer your country's call?" The paper reported that the enrolment at Scotland Yard the previous day was the "biggest since the Boer War." The paper also offered an *Overseas Daily Mirror* on a six-monthly subscription of 70-96 pages to be posted on Fridays. It also told its readers it had "completed arrangements by which it will receive a full service of photographs bearing on the war." It also reminded them about their coverage in the Balkans War, "*The Daily Mirror* which sent 11 special staff correspondents to the seat of hostilities." The rest of the paper carried its usual articles for its female readers "How to have long beautiful hair," "The Influence of a Girl, the Interesting Romance of a Love that Conquered," and "The Plaint of a Pretty Girl." The papers "thought of the day" on this historic occasion was 'Thank God every morning when you get up that you have something to do which must be done, whether you like it or not. Being forced to work and forced to do your best will breed in you, self-control.'[42]

In North Elmham, having received his mobilisation instructions the night before, Robert Sheldrake got up at about 0400 for breakfast of bacon and eggs, but could only eat the eggs at that early hour. His wife advised him to take the bacon in a sandwich, but he said he would not be bothered with it, as he could buy some food in the barracks.[43] At approximately, 0515 he 'took the painful duty of bidding farewell to my wife and walked off to the post office with something sticking in my throat. I said "I should be home again in a few weeks' time" and of course I was fool enough to believe so myself.'[44] He then went off to the Post Office to hand over his duties to a substitute, and drew a 3/- advance of pay for his travelling expenses by the War Office, and then took leave of his comrades, with their best luck and wishes. 'I boldly marched towards the railway station with another lump sticking in my throat.'[45] On his way he was passed be the parish policeman on his bicycle, who 'had been round all night calling up the Yeomanry and Territorials.'[46] When he reached the station he asked the 'worthy station-master…for a ticket to Germany, and to prove the old proverb "there is many a true word said in a joke", that is where I eventually landed for the greater part of the war.'[47]

42 *The Daily Mirror*, 5th August 1914.
43 Pte R. Sheldrake diary, pp. 1-2.
44 Ibid., p. 2.
45 Ibid., p. 2.
46 Ibid., p. 2.
47 Ibid., p. 2.

Robert Sheldrake arrived at Britannia Barracks, the depot of the Norfolk Regiment in Norwich, at approximately 0800 and passed the sentry into the barracks, the door being closed behind the caged bird. 'I went into the guardroom to report myself and received a card to present to the medical man, for him to sign fit or unfit for active service. I found about a dozen more already arrived, one or two had arrived overnight.'[48] At approximately 1030:

> The batch began passing the doctors…and answered a few questions, we marched through the mobilisation stores, leaving the opposite door with a rifle, equipment and a soldiers full fighting kit, the whole process taking but a very few minutes…The equipment had been changed for a new pattern since we were in the colour service.[49]

The mobilisation for many was also a reunion and a chance to meet up with old friends from service past,

> My comrades were continually arriving, many a hearty handshake we had that day, many a comrade I had lived with in Africa and Gibraltar and thought I might never see again turning up…my arm almost ached with shaking hands with all my old comrades, oh what greeting. Many arrived dressed in white cuffs and collars with smart cut suits, some plain and serviceable, some like navvies some like tramps and some drunken and disgraceful.[50]

Norfolk Regiment officers c. 1913. (Norfolk Regiment Museum)

48 Ibid., p. 3.
49 Ibid., p. 3.
50 Pte R. Sheldrake notebook, p. 1.

At midday they were fed and Private Sheldrake was not impressed with the provision of food for the reservists. They were given some bread and plain stewed meat for dinner in the evening and could not buy any food. He thought that the coffee shop's authorities must have been 'the only persons not expecting a war…we had some tea with neither sugar or milk.'[51] He was equally unimpressed, but forgiving by the sleeping arrangements 'one blanket for a bed on the nice hard boards, but I consider the latter is excusable, as we should have to rough it later on, so we might be getting used to it, and there would not be sufficient beds for us all in Britannia Barracks I expect.'[52] However, he continued to be unforgiving about the food at the depot and said 'I shall never forgive the Norwich Depot for the plain living consisting of bread, plain stewed meat and brown hot water for the three days I stayed there, and having money in my pocket and could not buy anything.'[53] The men who lived locally in Norwich, came up with their own solution, and 'had their relations and friends gathered round the walls to see them, bringing food and drink, and some wise men climbed the walls and went home and had another comfortable night's sleep at home.'[54]

On the 5th August, in the House of Commons, the Labour party voted to support the government's request for war credits of £100,000,000. James Ramsay MacDonald immediately resigned his chairmanship of his party and went back to his constituency in Leicester and continued to argue in the local papers for a negotiated peace. 'If this war is not to be the beginning instead of the end of wars, it is necessary, now, to get a settled public opinion as to the conditions of peace; these must be determined, not by the military men, nor by the diplomatists, but by the people.'[55] This he continued along with others opposed to the war throughout the whole of the mobilisation process. On the same day, the *Restrictions of Aliens Act* became law. It had been quickly passed by Parliament the day after war was declared on Germany. It required all foreign nationals (aliens) to register with the police, and where necessary they could be interned or deported. This act was chiefly aimed at German nationals and later other enemy aliens; however, it eventually affected all foreign nationals living in the country.[56] German citizens were required to register with their local police stations and all landlords letting properties to Germans were to report the fact to the police. Germans were not allowed to travel more than five miles from their homes without police permission and they were restricted to a period of only 24 hours away. Germans were not permitted to process: firearms, ammunition, explosives, petroleum, benzol spirit or any inflammable liquid in a quantity of more than three gallons. They were also prohibited from owning a motor car or motor cycle, homing pigeons, signalling equipment codes or cypher equipment such that secret correspondence could be made. In Leicester, 50 Germans were held by the military at the Corn Exchange while their status was established. Those who were deemed to be military reservists were classed as prisoners of war and were removed under a

51 Pte R. Sheldrake diary, p. 3.
52 Ibid., p. 4.
53 Ibid., p. 4.
54 Ibid., p. 4.
55 Malcolm Elliott, *Opposition to the First World War: The Fate of Conscientious Objectors in Leicester* <www.le.ac.uk/lahs/downloads/05_7799_vol 77_Elliott.pdf> (Accessed 4th July 2018).
56 Mark Pearsall, *Enemy Aliens in Great Britain 1914-1919* <www.blog.nationalarchives.gov.uk/blog/enemy-aliens-great-britain-1914-1919/> (Accessed 4th July 2018).

military escort to York.[57] *The Daily Mirror* reported on the 5th August that "Two Alleged Spies Arrested" and that Albert Garcia, an Italian teacher of languages, was remanded in Portsmouth the previous day and it was alleged he was "in communication with the German Secret Service and that he was about to leave Portsmouth with information in his possession when arrested." Also, Frederick Sukowski was charged under the Official Secrets Act and had been remanded for a week stating that 'the defendant had been found in the neighbourhood of the principle Tyne shipyards, and had in his possession two measuring gauges, foot rules and a map of Great Britain giving railroad and other measurements.'[58]

So, despite these measures it came as some surprise when Mrs Joan Baker, the widow of Squadron Sergeant Major Harry Baker, of the 11th Hussars, (who later to be killed near Messines on 31st October 1914), that her husband was German by birth and therefore made her German too under the conditions of the *Alien's Act!* Eventually, the situation was resolved, and she was granted a certificate of naturalisation. They had been married since 1908 and she said "I never had the remotest idea my husband was German, in fact he hated anything German. Before the war he never liked me to get any toys for our little girl that bore the words "Made in Germany." Eight months later, a Mrs Martina Leibold, a German, was prosecuted for failing to register a child.[59] The anti-German sentiment which had prevailed had caused Harry Baker to hide his true origin and it continued to play now to individuals deep seated feelings. After the cabinet meeting Herbert Asquith went to see the King who was 'a good deal relieved the war has come, he could not stand the tension of the last week. As you might expect he is becoming very anti-German.'[60] Lord Northcliffe (Alfred Harmsworth), in the *Daily Mail,*[61] later in the year said "refuse to be served by an Austrian or German waiter and if he says he is Swiss ask to see his passport." In the same month, *The Spectator* said 'the work of a waiter, since it lends itself with such particular ease to the work of espionage, should not in wartime be practised by enemy aliens,[62] but then again none of this was new and Lord Northcliffe and his papers: *The Times*, the *Daily Mail*, *The Daily Mirror*, and the *Observer* had never hidden their anti-German rhetoric.

At 1330, in Paris, Lieutenant Spears set off by liaison car for the *Grand Quartier Général* (*GQG*) at Vitry-le-François where he was to work with the intelligence section 2éme Bureau, when he arrived he was given a desk in the gymnasium at the school where the headquarters had been lodged.[63] On leaving for the war he was conscious of those they would be leaving behind and the 'indomitable women of France, who I watched them sending their men off to the war: shouldering the responsibility of all that the men were leaving behind, guaranteeing the home, the farm, the business, obstinate, brave, sturdily practical, undertaking to keep the life of France going for the men who were gone.'[64] He also felt for the old men, 'the fathers, mostly stood by, feebly silent, until the trains had left, unable to find words in which to cloak their misery.'[65]

57 Ben Beazley, *Four Years Remembered: Leicester During the Great War* (Derby: Breedon Books, 1999), p. 21.
58 *The Daily Mirror*, 5th August 1914.
59 *The Surrey Mirror*, 7th December 1915.
60 Brock & Brock (eds.), *H.H. Asquith*, p 157.
61 *Daily Mail*, 17th October 1914.
62 Mark Bostridge, *The Fateful Year: England 1914*, p. 299.
63 Spears, *Liaison 1914,* pp. 19-24.
64 Ibid., p. 18.
65 Ibid., p. 18.

In London at 1600, the *War Council* summoned by the Prime Minister 'to discuss the strategic situation,'[66] assembled at 10, Downing Street, Herbert Asquith, Sir Edward Grey, Winston Churchill, Lord Haldane, Lord Roberts, Lord Kitchener, Prince Louis of Battenberg (later Mountbatten), Sir John French, Sir Ian Hamilton, Sir John Cowans, Sir Stanley von Donop, Sir Douglas Haig, Sir James Grierson, Sir Archibald Murray, Colonel Maurice Hankey, Colonel Edward St George Gorton, and General Henry Wilson were present. The assembled group were referred to by General Haig as 'experts and amateurs'[67] at a conference where 'it was inevitable that the expression of personal opinions should predominate and exclude reasoned logical arguments.'[68] The Prime Minister sought to focus on two points: 'where the expeditionary force should be placed in the line of battle, and where it should concentrate on arrival in France.'[69] Lord Grey made a special point of Lord Haldane's strong insistence on the principle that the whole of the expeditionary force ought to be sent across the channel.'[70] Now Lord Kitchener had assumed his new appointment, he objected to the plan…and disapproved of the fact the British Army was a 'tack on'[71] to the tail of French strategy. General Wilson recorded the details of the meeting in his diary.

> Asquith said he had summoned the great soldiers at the earliest possible moment. Then a lot of platitudes on the situation and strategy generally. Sir John stated what he had arranged to do; he said that probably Maubeuge was no longer available for concentration, and then plumped for going at once and deciding later where to go to, but then he dragged in the ridiculous proposal of going to Antwerp.[72] Churchill said the Dover Straits were now completely sealed. Jimmy Grierson spoke up for decisive numbers at the decisive point. Sir John urged we should go over at once and decide destination later. I mentioned the flexibility of French railway system for switching. Haig asked questions and this led to our discussing strategy like idiots. Johnnie Hamilton plumped for going to Amiens as soon as possible. Then desultory strategy (some thinking that Liège was in Holland) and idiocy. Lord Kitchener plumped for Amiens but wanted to get in closer touch with French suggested that they should send over an officer. Sir John urged we should order the transports to be fitted at once. Decision taken to order transports for all six divisions at once. Question then arose what strength the BEF should be. Winston in favour of sending six divisions, as naval situation most favourable owing to our having had time to prepare. Lord Bobs agreed. Decision was taken that we should prepare at once for all six divisions. Lord Kitchener said one division should be ordered from India to Egypt. All agreed.

66 Brock & Brock (eds.), *H.H. Asquith*, p 157.
67 Brig. Gen. John Charteris, *Field Marshal Earl Haig* (London: Pickle Partners Publishing, 1929), p. 78.
68 Ibid., p. 78.
69 Charteris, *Field Marshal Earl Haig*, p. 78.
70 Maj. Gen. Sir C.E. Callwell, *Field-Marshal Sir Henry Wilson Bart., GCB, DSO His Life and Diaries* (London: Cassell & Co., 1927), p. 158.
71 Tuchman, *August 1914*, p. 193.
72 This was based on a 1906 Belgium option he had revisited again 1912. With landings at Zeebrugge, Antwerp and Ostend, providing a defensive line in Belgium along the coast and protecting Great Britain from German invasion.

> Slight discussion on Colonial and Ulster contingents, but no decision reached. An historic meeting of men, mostly entirely ignorant of their subject.[73]

Interestingly, the final decision for Britain going to war had not been taken by the Cabinet, but by an *ad hoc* committee convened by the Prime Minister, dominated by the military. The entry of Britain into the war had been determined by the King of Belgium. In turn, the BEF was strategically subordinated to French military strategy. Despite Britain's best efforts, it had now been drawn into alliance politics. The BEF was to be commanded by a man who was responsible for executing a strategy that was not his own, and to which he was not prepared. His own plan would have been a defensive position on the Belgian coast protecting Britain from invasion and to compound the issue both General Haig and Wilson, who were supporters of the final plan, would now be subordinated to him[74] Lord Kitchener was not happy with the arrangements and only agreed to them because there was no time to make another plan,[75] and in the cause of alliance solidarity.[76] At the end of the meeting it was decided 'to adjourn until tomorrow when we shall see a representative from the French General Staff.'[77]

In Berlin, the Kaiser made his speech from his palace and not the *Reichstag*. The Kaiser, accompanied by several generals, sat on his throne. The Chancellor was dressed in the uniform of the *Garde Dragoner*. The Kaiser, told them 'we draw the sword with clear conscience and clean hands.' He also said the war had been provoked by Serbia, with support from Russia, and then proclaimed 'from this day on I recognise no parties but only Germans, and call upon party leaders, if they agreed with these sentiments to step forward and shake his hand.'[78] At 1500, they reconvened in the *Reichstag*, and their last act before they dissolved themselves was to vote over the war credits of five billion marks. The period of suspension, was optimistically four months, or however long it took.[79] Everyone was waiting to hear what Chancellor Bethmann-Hollweg was going to say when he addressed the *Reichstag*. In his address, he fully demonstrated that he understood the international treaties they had broken, but justified them as essential in achieving their military aims, and stated that "our troops have occupied Luxembourg and perhaps are already on Belgium soil. Gentlemen, this is contrary to the dictates of international law. The wrong, I speak openly, that we are committing we will endeavour to make good as soon as our military goal has been reached."

Before Britain's ultimatum to Germany expired, a large angry crowd of people who were well-dressed and included women assembled outside the British Embassy in Berlin. Frederic Wile, a diplomat in the embassy, wrote 'while at work on my dispatches in my hotel room, it was now about 2100, I could hear Unter den Linden below my windows roaring with mob fury against Britain. *"Krämer volk!"* (Peddler nation!) *"Rassen-Verrat!"* (Race treachery!) *"Nieder mit England!"* (Down with England!) *"Tod den Engländer!"* (Death to the English!)'[80] As he tried

73 Callwell, *Field-Marshal Sir Henry Wilson Bart,* pp. 158-159.
74 Strachan, *The First World War,* pp. 204-205.
75 Tuchman, *August 1914*, p. 201.
76 Strachan, *The First World War*, p 205.
77 Brock & Brock (eds.), *H.H. Asquith*, p. 157.
78 Tuchman, *August 1914*, p. 131.
79 Ibid., p. 132.
80 Frederic W. Wile, *The Assault: Germany before the Outbreak and England in Wartime: A Personal Narrative,* (Indianapolis, Indiana: Bobbs-Merrill, 1916), p. 140.

to leave the embassy. Deeply embarrassed, profoundly apologetic, the German Foreign Office ordered mounted police to be sent to restore order and to protect the ambassador and his staff from further disturbance.[81]

> A policeman grabbed me, one pinioning my right arm, another my left, and the third gripping me by the back of the neck. All around the hotel entrance stood gesticulating Germans yelling, like Comanche Indians, *"Englischer Spion! Nach Spandau mit ihm!"* (English spy! To Spandau with him!). The policemen had now drawn their sabres to protect me, as they explained, from the murderous intentions of the mob, tossed me into the rear seat of an open taxi cab waiting at the curb. One of the policemen said to him, "the mob heard the Adlon was full of English spies, and they were waiting for you to come out. They'd have killed you on the spot if we hadn't been there to rescue you."'[82]

As the Kaiser contemplated the war that was now to come he said that "to think that George and Nicky should have played me false. If my grandmother had been alive, she would never have allowed it," which was very probably true. The following morning, the Ambassador, Sir Edward Goschen, received an apology from the Kaiser for the incident at the embassy, which was delivered verbally by an *Aide-De-Camp* at the same time, the Kaiser relinquished the British military titles he had been previously bestowed:

> The Emperor has charged me to express to Your Excellency his regret for the occurrences of last night, but to tell you at the same time that you will gather from those occurrences an idea of the feelings of his people respecting the action of Great Britain in joining with other nations against her old allies of Waterloo. His Majesty also begs that you will tell the King that he has been proud of the titles of British Field Marshal and British Admiral, but that in consequence of what has occurred he must now at once divest himself of those titles.[83]

In London, Lord Northcliffe and the *Daily Mail* were quick to style themselves as 'the paper which foretold the war.'[84] Others saw it differently, and like the Kaiser sought to blame him. Alfred Gardiner, the esteemed editor of the *Daily News* and journalist wrote 'next to the Kaiser, Lord Northcliffe has done more than any other living man to bring about the war.'[85] The *Daily News* published a "Letter to Lord Northcliffe" in which Alfred Gardner said that:

> It has always been your part to prophesy war and cultivate hate. There is nothing more tempting to the journalist than to be an incendiary. It is the shortcut to success, for it is always easier to appeal to the lower passions of men than to their better instincts. There is a larger crowd to address, and you have never deserted the larger crowd.[86]

81 Lyn Macdonald, *1914: The Days of Hope* (London; Penguin Books, 1987), p 52.
82 Wile, *The Assault*, pp. 140-142.
83 Macdonald, *1914*, p 52.
84 Brex Twells, *Scare-Mongerings from the Daily Mail 1896-1914 – The Paper that Foretold the War Dated 1915* (United Kingdom: Forgotten Books, 2017).
85 Sally Taylor, *The Great Outsiders: Northcliffe, Rothermere and the Daily Mail* (London: Weidenfeld & Nicolson, 1996), p. 143.
86 Anthony J.A. Morris, *The Scaremongers: The Advocacy of War and Rearmament* (London: Routledge & Kegan Paul, 1984), p. 1.

Lord Northcliffe did not reply to Alfred Gardner's letter, but replied to Lovat Fraser who had been the editor of *The Times* of India up to 1907 and on editorial staff of *The Times* in London:

> I do not in the least mind personal attacks, nor do I care what the public think about me. The fact that my newspapers are almost the only ones that are not shrinking rapidly at the present moment shows that my readers have faith in them. If the readers attacked me then I should begin to think that I am the wicked man, the little tradesman that Fleet Street believe me to be.[87]

The role of the press, particularly for Britain, had been a key factor in creating the conditions by which public opinion would consider going to war with Germany. Britain had no real treaties or obligations to go to war as a third party in support of another country. If this were to happen, the government of the day, in a democracy, could only do this with the public's support. The public in turn could only do this if they had an opinion, and Lord Northcliffe had shared his anti-German opinion with the British public daily for the last decade. The silken knots of the *Entente Cordiale* had now become hooks of steel.[88] For the soothsayers of war, they could now claim their prediction was correct: now it was only the length of war that was uncertain. The two war plans in place were the German plan, written by Field Marshal Alfred von Schlieffen in 1906, that was modified and delivered by General Helmuth Graf von Moltke and the French *Plan XVII,* which became effective in May 1914, designed to counter von Schlieffen's intent. It was always the intention to position the BEF on the left flank of the French Army, and had the soothsayers studied both plans together, which were known to both sides, they would have realised the strategically vulnerable location of the agreed position of the BEF at Maubeuge. Major Tom Bridges thought 'the standing army was totally inadequate to fulfil our obligations while our reserves in men and material were insignificant.'[89] The five infantry and one (oversized) Cavalry Division was never designed to be the solution to any perceived military problem and General Wilson himself had said "there was no military problem to which the answer was six divisions." Likewise, the size of the Cavalry Division was also questioned as being far too large for one man to command as it consisted of four brigades of three regiments, which was twice the size of the German and French Cavalry Divisions. When asked the question regarding its size, General Haig's reply was 'you must have four for the charge. Two brigades in the first line, one in support and you must have one in reserve.'[90] His opinion, reflected a return to older ideas and the new renewed confidence of the cavalry since the retirement of Field Marshal Roberts. However, the overall size of the Army was smaller, as it was all that Britain could afford and man without significantly changing the budget, without affecting the manning of the troops in the empire or introducing compulsory (conscription) military service. Lord Haldane knew that the nation would only accept this in time of war five years before, in 1909, he stated:

87 Ibid., p. 1.
88 Lt. Gen. Sir Thomas Bridges, *Alarms and Excursions, Reminiscences of a Soldier* (London; Longmans Green and Co., 1938), p. 68.
89 Ibid., p. 68.
90 Marquess of Anglesey, A *History of the British Cavalry 1914-1919*, Vol. 7 (London: Leo Cooper, 1986), p 64.

> Compulsion may be necessary if we have to fight for our existence during a great war, but compulsion in war is quite a different thing from compulsion during peace when recruiting for the first line ought to be the paramount consideration and nothing should impede it. In war the government would take powers to keep the men serving with the colours in the ranks while the war lasted…and the change can only be made with safety when the government has the powers which would be accorded it in the event of a major war.[91]

It is said that 'hindsight is the first refuge of the historian' and it is only natural that after the war that was about to begin, that history would look at what could have, or should have happened had events played out differently.[92] Europe would "willingly" move towards war and there was nothing or anyone collectively strong enough to bring the process to a halt. No single organisation could either unite or produce a coherent argument against going to war, and everyone felt that *in extremis* it was acceptable to do so as they considered how it might facilitate their own ends. Had the information regarding the *Schlieffen Plan* that was sold to the French by *Le Vengeur*[93] in 1904 been taken seriously or the study of German military organisation had not been specifically forbidden in Britain,[94] both France and Britain may have understood that the placing of the BEF on the left flank of the assembled French army, would place them at the *schwerpunkt* of the planned German encircling action. Industrially and economically, war made little sense. Those who predicted a short war were either poorly militarily informed or were basing their opinion on fiscal prudence. This being the case, would the socialists of Europe conspire collectively to bring their nations to a halt as England had in the period of *great unrest,* or had the assassination of Jean Jaurès not poleaxed the European socialists at the point of crisis. The womenfolk of Europe had much to lose, and even though they had been emboldened by the suffragettes, who were to be the widows and mothers of their menfolk, they did not unite to bring their nations to a standstill. In fact, they did the opposite and called a truce to support the war effort. In support of the recruiting campaign to come in 1914, "Your King and Country Needs You" was a British popular song, with both words and music by Paul Rubens. It was written as a woman's recruiting song to be sung with the intention of persuading men to volunteer to fight in the war. The profits from its sale were to be given to "Queen Mary's Work for Women Fund". The song raised over half a million pounds for the fund, and it contained the words:

> *Oh! we don't want to lose you, but we think you ought to go*
> *For your King and your Country both need you so;*
> *We shall want you and miss you but with all our might and main*
> *We shall cheer you, thank you, kiss you when you come back again.*

At the end of August, *The Order of the White Feather* was founded by Admiral Charles Fitzgerald. It encouraged women to give out white feathers to young men who had not joined the British

91 Frederick Maurice, *Haldane 1856-1915* (London: Faber & Faber, 1937), p. 273.
92 David Ascoli, *The Mons Star: The British Expeditionary Force 1914* (Edinburgh: Birlinn, 2001), p xi.
93 Le Vengeur was a disgruntled German officer who sold *Schlieffen Plan* documents to the French for 60,000 Francs. The purloined papers showed the German intention to move through neutral Belgium.
94 Brig. Gen. Sir J.E. Edmonds, *Military Operations France and Belgium 1914*, Vol. I (London: Macmillan & Co., Limited, St Martin's Street, 1937), p. 11.

Army. Initially, he enlisted 30 women in Folkestone to distribute white feathers to men not in uniform. Many of the suffragettes now turned their energy to assisting with recruiting and became *white feather girls.* Mrs Pankhurst toured the country, making recruiting speeches. Her supporters handed the white feather to every young man they encountered wearing civilian dress and appeared at Hyde Park meetings with placards: "Intern Them All." The campaign was also supported by Field Marshal Kitchener and *The Daily Mail* which reported the activities of the *Order of the White Feather*, hoping that it 'would shame every young slacker'[95] into enlisting. The following year *The Times* carried the following message 'Jack FG. If you are not in khaki by the 20th I shall, cut you dead. Ethel M.'[96] However, the *white feather girl's* actions were sometimes ill-placed. Chief Petty Officer George Samson was celebrating the 110th anniversary of Nelson's victory in Trafalgar Square in civilian clothes and was given a white feather, just two weeks after he had received the Victoria Cross at Buckingham Palace.

The collective churches and religions did not unite or try to intervene. The Catholic church which covered the whole of Europe, in the absence of their sick Pope, who had been ill since his heart attack in 1913 and had never recovered. It was said that he was a shadow of his former self and was not strong enough to intervene. The declaration of war sent the 79-year-old Pope into a "state of melancholy." It was the same for the Anglican Church in that they also failed across Europe, to unite their churches and bring the war to a halt. The blood ties of the monarchy, in the absence of Queen Victoria, could not prevent the three cousins from antagonising each other. This perpetuated the public's prejudices and the presses' use of stereotypes, which in turn created the conditions where the possibility of war became likely. The delay in the ultimatum from Austria to Serbia after the assassination of the archduke had caught out the main political and monarchic influences as they went about their summer holidays. Europe was drifting to war and there was no one at the helm strong enough to steer it to safety. This was compounded by politicians and soldiers on all sides who all had their own agendas and failings. They knew either nothing of soldiering or little of politics. How could anyone predict what was to happen, when it had never happened before and with a government which had 'specially charged with the promotion of the cause of peace, and'[97] despite the economic concerns and warnings of the City?

95 *The Daily Mail*, 30th August 1914.
96 *The Times*, 8th July 1915.
97 David Lloyd George op. cit. in Cameron Hazlehurst, *Politicians at War, July 1914-May 1915: A Prologue to the Triumph of Lloyd George* (New York: Alfred Knopf, 1971), p. 115.

# 2

# Mobilisation

*To understand the problem of mobilising a modern continental army, it is important to realise that the whole process is a race against time.*

Lieutenant Edward Spears

On the subject of continental mobilisation, Spears wrote with clarity and understanding:

> If the mobilisation is delayed or slow, the enemy will be able to advance with a fully equipped army against an unprepared one, which would be disastrous...Mobilisation is in itself manoeuvre at the end of which the armies must be ready to strike according to the pre-arranged plan.[1].

Britain, France and Germany all had mobilisation plans in the event of war. *The War Book,* written by General Wilson and the French *Plan XVII* were mobilisation documents designed to deliver the armies to where they needed to be, and considered the 'mobilisation, concentration and deployment of their armies.'[2] The subsequent *Plan XVII,* despite being the seventeenth iteration of a plan designed to protect France from another German invasion had an inherent flaw in that it failed to *fully* recognise the possibility of being invaded through a non-common border and the 'German strategy had little in common with what the French imagined it to be.'[3] This had been rectified by the acknowledging its possibility and making adjustments regarding the position of the Fourth and Fifth Armies. However, the most critical mistake made by the French was their assumption to what extent the Germans would use its reserves in the initial phase of the war. The French had convinced themselves that their integration would not be significant, and this was purely base on the 'low opinion of the quality of its own reserves.[4]

1 Spears, *Liaison 1914,* p. 35.
2 Hew Strachan, *The Outbreak of the First World War* (Oxford: Oxford University Press, 2004), p. 194.
3 Spears, *Liaison 1914, A Narrative of the Great Retreat,* p. 57.
4 Hew Strachan, *The First World War,* p. 186.

Copies of *Plan XVII,* had been issued to army commanders on 7th February and the final draft was ready by the 1st May. The document contained a statement that the Germans were expected to concentrate the bulk of their army on the Franco-German border and might cross before French operations could begin. The instruction of the Commander-in-Chief was that:

> Whatever the circumstances, it is the Commander-in-Chief's intention to advance with all forces united to the attack of the German armies. The action of the French armies will be developed in two main operations: one, on the right in the country between the wooded district of the Vosges and the Moselle below Toul; the other, on the left, north of a line Verdun–Metz. The two operations will be closely connected by forces operating on the Hauts de Meuse and in the Woëvre.[5]

To achieve this, the initial deployment positions of the 'French armies were to concentrate, ready to attack either side of Metz–Thionville or north into Belgium, in the direction of Arlon and Neuf Château.'[6] An alternative concentration area for the Fourth and Fifth Armies had been specified, in case the Germans advanced through Luxembourg and Belgium but an enveloping attack west of the Meuse but was not anticipated and the gap between the Fifth Army and the North Sea was covered by territorial units and obsolete fortresses.[7]

The German plan, written by Field Marshal von Schlieffen was completed in the year he retired, in 1906. The *Schlieffen Plan*, inherited by his successor, was the genesis for the plan to be delivered by General von Moltke. The *Schlieffen Plan* was supposed to be a complete plan for the whole campaign, not just mobilisation, in which the Field Marshal had only allowed six weeks (39 days) to defeat France, a time which was commensurate with his estimate as to how long he thought it would take the Russians to be fully mobilised. It addressed the unique German geographical problem of possibly having to fight a war on two fronts, in both the east and west against France and Russia simultaneously. The first phase of the plan was to defeat France as quickly as possible so that troops could be moved to the east to fight Russia separately. To what extant General von Moltke inherited a complete plan is disputed, but if nothing else Field Marshal von Schlieffen at least bequeathed a concept, to which General von Moltke could continue to develop as his own plan. General Wilhelm Groener, the head of the German railways, wrote that Field Marshal von Schlieffen had left a legacy to 'point his successor on the path to victory in the battle of Germany against an enormous superiority in numbers.'[8] However, the concept still remained the same, and was born out of the teachings of Clausewitz. To win, it would need to be 'a quick victory through a decisive battle.'[9] Field Marshal von Schlieffen also studied Hannibal's victory at the Battle of Cannae on 2nd August 216 BC and said 'that the principles of strategy remain unchanged. The enemy's front is not the objective. The essential thing is to crush the enemy's flanks…and complete the extermination by attack

5 Edmonds, *Military Operations France and Belgium 1914,* Vol. I, p. 446.
6 Robert A. Doughty, *Pyrrhic Victory: French Strategy and Operations in the Great War* (Cambridge, Massachusetts: Harvard University Press, 2008), p. 37.
7 Edmonds, *Military Operations France and Belgium 1914,* Vol. I, p. 17.
8 Strachan, *The Outbreak of the First World War,* pp. 163-164.
9 Tuchman, *August 1914*, p. 32.

upon his rear.'[10] To achieve the quick victory over France, the German Army would advance through neutral Belgium and sweep in a large encircling movement using the flat plains of Flanders using the captured roads and railways. The inclusion of the violation of neutral Belgium had been included in the *Schlieffen's Plan* since 1899. The extent of the encircling right flank grew larger with each revision until by 1905 it had moved to the east of the River Meuse and would cross Belgium from Liège to Bruxelles before it turned to move south.[11] General Sir Frederick Maurice, GOC 3rd Infantry Division thought the plan:

> In conception bold, simple, and based upon a careful abstract study of war. It was at the same time utterly ruthless and immoral in its cold-blooded contempt of national pledges… it was not in any sense a rigid plan, or that the direction and objective of the great enveloping movement was fixed at the time when the march into Belgium began. The Germans are too good soldiers to commit a stupidity of that kind…Moltke had always taught that the preparation of a plan of campaign in detail should not be carried further than the first contact with the opposing troops…he once said to his staff in criticism of a military exercise: "Gentlemen, I have observed that there are always three courses open to the enemy, and that he usually takes the fourth."'[12]

General von Moltke, had owned the plan since 1906 and his revisions were significant enough for it to be *The Moltke Plan*. By 1913 the German General Staff consisted of 650 officers and 'theirs was a continuous task of analysis and revision: for this there was an annual cycle incorporating staff rides and war games. Whatever was planned in 1906 was specific to that year…and was an incremental evolution from the plans the previous year…and was not a definite statement intended to remain unchanged…there was no single solution, no one plan.'[13] Over the period of evolution, *The Moltke Plan* had firstly altered the course of an advance by the armies on the right (northern) wing, to avoid the Netherlands, retaining the country as a useful route for German imports and exports. He also considered their vulnerability once they had advanced into France 'that a hostile Holland at our back could have disastrous consequences for the advance of the German Army to the west.'[14] By only advancing only through Belgium, this meant that the German armies would lose the railway lines around Maastricht and have to squeeze the 600,000 men of the *AOK 1* and *AOK 2* through a gap 19 kms wide. This made it vital that the Belgian railways were captured quickly and intact. In 1908, the General Staff devised a plan to take the fortified position of Liège and its railway junction by day 11 of the mobilisation, this was seen as the *coup de main* if the plan was to succeed. Subsequent changes reduced the time allowed to five days.[15] Also Field Marshal von Schlieffen said the right wing should be set at 7:1 to ensure it could overwhelm the French, but in 1909 General von Moltke reduced this ratio to 3:1 by deploying two armies to defend Alsace and Lorraine. The strength of the right wing was

10 Ibid., p. 32.
11 Ibid., p. 32.
12 Maurice, *Forty Days in 1914*, pp. 16-18.
13 Strachan, *The Outbreak of the First World War*, p. 164.
14 Paul Kennedy, *The War Plans of the Great Powers 1880-1914* (London: Allen & Unwin, 1979), p. 212.
15 Robert T. Foley, *German Strategy and the Path to Verdun: Erich von Falkenhayn and the Development of Attrition, 1870-1916* (Cambridge: Cambridge University Press, 2005), pp. 77-78.

reported to have been the subject of Field Marshal von Schlieffen's final words to General von Moltke on his deathbed, "keep the right wing strong," but as this was *Moltke's Plan* which he and his staff had been working on for seven years it had been adjusted to take into account the prevailing political situation and current German military thinking.

Generaloberst Alexander von Kluck. (Author's Collection)

Each nation had now mobilised and each of them had to stick rigidly to their plans. Britain, had a considerably smaller force to mobilise and move than the Germans and French, they did have to cross the English Channel. Time had been lost by the delay in the decision to mobilise and send the BEF. General Wilson's plan needed to be adjusted to take account of the reduced size of the planned BEF. This was something he had anticipated which enabled time to be made up, and the 'moves originally fixed for the 13th day were carried out on the 12th day, and those for the 14th on the 13th day.'[16] Despite the congestion to civilian traffic caused by the August bank holiday, railway movements were accomplished without major disruption. During the period of mobilisation '1800 special trains ran, and they arrived at Southampton every three minutes for 16 hours a day. [17] The embarkation began on 9th August and was accomplished by 17th August. By 20th August, the concentration at Maubeuge was complete and the speed of the mobilisation would ultimately see all countries embark upon war before they were fully

16 Archibald Hurd, *The Merchant Navy*, Vol. II (London: John Murray, 1924), p. 82.
17 Strachan, *The First World War*, Vol. 1, p 206.

mobilised. The Germans had mobilised and concentrated their active corps of their *Westheer* and were in position by 12th August, and the reserve corps by the 14th. All the railways in Germany came under military command. Each corps required 6,010 wagons, organised into 140 trains, to complete its movement. As they started to mobilise and move their troops one train crossed the Rhine over the Hohenzollern Bridge at Köln every 10 minutes.'[18] The ersatz divisions were in position four days later on the 18th. The composition of the German force was seven armies formed in 78 divisions consisting of 1,318,82 men:[19] the *AOK 1* (von Kluck, 164 battalions) and the *AOK 2* (von Bűlow, 159 battalions) were grouped on the Belgian frontier opposite Liège. The *AOK 3* (Hausen, 104 battalions) and *AOK 4* (Albrecht, Grand Duke of Württemberg, 123 battalions) faced the Ardennes, down as far as Luxembourg: The *AOK 5* (Crown Prince Wilhelm of Prussia, 147 battalions) was in the Thionville-Metz area of Lorraine, and north of the *AOK 6* (Crown Prince Rupprecht of Bayern, 131 battalions). The *AOK 7* (von Heeringen), the weakest of all at 108 battalions, was echeloned back and to the south, from Strasbourg down the east of the Rhine.[20]France's mobilisation had gone well and 'the concentration was completed by 18th August and of a total of 4,278 trains used,[21] only 20 were late.[22] The mobilised numerical strengths of France and Germany were comparable, each of the armies having approximately two million men each. The French had 1,108 battalions to German's 1,077. Both figures included their reserves. With both forces being so closely balanced (in the west) it meant 'that manoeuvre and concentration, operational and tactical ability, might well be decisive.'[23]

For *Infanterie Regiment 66* in Magdeburg of *Infanterie Brigade 13*, from Generalleutnant Johannes Riedel's *Infanterie Division 7,* the waiting was over, and the barracks became a hive of activity as reserves arrived, equipment was issued and training started:

> The feverish tension was broken at 1845 on 1st August by the order for general mobilisation. The following days were strenuous. The arriving reservists were assigned to companies and issued their combat uniforms, weapons and equipment, down to first aid dressings and identity disks. Ammunition was brought out of the bunkers, vehicles out of the sheds and horses requisitioned for wagon teams and mounted men. The war-strength companies (250 men) conducted road marches and combat training. In these days, one task followed the next, until every man was strained to breaking point. The regimental Adjutant, the three battalion Adjutants, the purser (property clerk), the regimental clerk, the battalion clerks, the company first sergeants and their clerks, the armourers and the orderlies did not get a moment's rest. The mobilisation calendar, carefully prepared with exactitude, did not need to be altered[24].

18 Strachan, *The Outbreak of the First World War*, p. 207.
19 Dr Robert Foley, 'Baptism of Fire: Germany's Lost Victory in 1914: Why the Germans lost the First World War in 1914', WFA presentation 2015.
20 Ibid., p. 207.
21 Spears, *Liaison 1914,* p. 35.
22 Strachan, *The Outbreak of the First World War*, p. 206.
23 Ibid., p. 207.
24 Otto Korfes, *The German 66th Regiment in the First World War* (Stroud: History Press, 2016), p. 21.

The mobilisation of the British Army was conducted in accordance with the *Regulations for Mobilisation 1912*.[25] These regulations covered both mobilisation at *home* and *abroad,* and both *general* and *partial* mobilisation. These came into immediate effect on the order for mobilisation. On 1st January 1914, the standing Regular Army in Britain was 138,497 troops and an army in the Empire (India, Egypt and the colonies) of 117,517. The actual strength of the two combined armies against its establishment of 252,458 which meant that the army was understrength by approximately 64,000 men. The priority manning was to units posted in India. This meant that the army based in Britain bore the brunt of the under manning and of the serving soldiers at home only 4,192 had 15 or more continuous years of service, 46,291 had less than two years' service.[26] The impact was not only numerical and General Maurice recorded that 'the necessity for keeping up our foreign garrisons having long turned our army at home into a feeder for the army abroad, it was in consequence normally below strength, and contained a large number of young recruits, who, not being qualified either by age or training to take the field, had to be left at the depots on mobilisation.'[27] This would mean that the British Army was heavily dependent on the *reserve.*[28] These were soldiers who had served in the army, and had left at the end of their engagement, but were still liable to mobilisation in time of war. The reserve element for the BEF would make up 61.8 percent of its total on mobilisation and was always intended to be an integral part of the Army. It was instigated as part of the Haldane reforms. The reserve was required to bring the army up to its war time establishment and each regiment was allocated +10 percent of its establishment to account for initial casualties.[29] The cavalry was understrength by 768 men, and for the reservists who were to report to the 9th Lancers, each reservist was given instructions to report to the barracks in Tidworth. On arrival, each soldier was given an initial medical, and providing he was 'capable of bearing arms and was sufficiently trained, over the age of 20 and fit for service abroad,'[30] they joined the Regiment. Private Arthur Gibb of the 9th Lancers described his room in Tidworth:

> The barrack rooms were long and whitewashed, a stove in the middle, rows of iron beds down either side to take 20 men in peace times. As it was, we late-comers slept on "biscuits", square hard mattresses, laid down between the iron bunks, and mustered nearly 40 in a room…over each bed was a locker (without a lock, of course) where each man kept his small kit, razor, towel, toothbrush, blacking and his personal treasures. Those who had no bed had no locker and left things beneath the folded blankets of the beds. How one missed one's household goods! One learnt to live like a snail, with everything in the world upon one's person, everything in the world cut down to the barest necessities, pipe and baccy, letters, a photograph, knife, fork and spoon, toothbrush, bit of soap, tooth paste, one towel, and one extra pair of socks.[31]

25 It is believed that this was the edition used. The 1914 edition may have been written in November 1914.
26 *Official Digest of Statistics 1913/1914* op. cit. in Ascoli, *The Mons Star,* p. 8.
27 Maurice, *Forty Days in 1914*, p. 77.
28 The estimate for the number of reserves required to bring the BEF up to its war time establishment was 30% for the cavalry and 50-70 percent for the infantry.
29 HMSO, *Regulations for Mobilisation 1912*, para. 172.
30 Ibid., para. 40.
31 Maj. A. Hamilton Gibb, *Gun Fodder, The Diary of Four Years of War*, pp. 15-16.

9th Lancer's bed space in Tidworth. (Author's Collection)

All surplus men or those not fit for overseas service in the cavalry were sent to the Reserve Regiments of Cavalry,[32] or sent to other corps such as the Army Veterinary Corps (AVC) and Army Service Corps (ASC). The Regiment was also required to report the number of additional horses required to bring the Regiment up to its war establishment. It was also presumed on mobilisation that 10% would be unfit for service.[33] Lieutenant Trevor Horn, the Machine Gun Officer of the 16th Lancers, wrote that horses over 14 years of age could be caste but despite their age, some of the older horses that 'were considered to be the best and under any conditions they were kept. Troop leaders had their dislikes for one reason or another, shy feeders, kickers…minor cases of lameness were exaggerated.'[34] The shortfalls in the numbers of horses was met by requisition, effected under powers conferred by the *Army Act*. Detailed instructions for the collection and distribution of animals on mobilisation will be laid down in the *Remount Manual*.[35] 'Complete *turn-outs* of horses, harness and vehicles will be requisitioned

32 HMSO, *Regulations for Mobilisation 1912*, para 30.
33 Ibid., para, 47.
34 Lt T.L. Horn, 'Diary of the Regiment: 16th (The Queens) Lancers, 4th August-18th October 1914', p. 3.
35 Ibid., para, 45.

when impressing horses, harness and vehicles for transport.'[36] The instructions required all Commanding Officers to maintain a party and transport for the collection of their horses and the exact numbers were based on an average requirement "at the rate of one man to every two animals," and provision had to be made for 'a proper proportion of officers and NCOs, and of shoeing smiths when available. Men accustomed to horses should, as far as possible, be selected to take over animals.'[37] The instructions were specific and very detailed taking into consideration the equipment required and the quarantine arrangements associated with adding new horses to the stables:

> These animals will not be brought into the proximity of army horses until passed by the veterinary officer, as free from contagious diseases. He will arrange for harness and saddlery to be fitted as soon as possible, and for animals to be marked under regimental arrangements. Swords and sword-bayonets sharpened.'[38]

The numbers of horses required by the BEF was nearly 200,000 against its actual holding of 25,000. On the first day of the mobilisation, magistrates sat early 'hurriedly signing warrants to authorise the seizure of vans, cars and horses…within 12 days the army had successfully, impressed 165,000 of them, each would require clipping, veterinary inspections, and to be re-shod[39] and this also included a spare set of shoes making before they could go to war. The horses to be selected were to be aged between six and 10 years old and be between 15.2 and 16 hands high.[40] The impact of losing horses to the war and its impact on the country to continue to go about its daily business and still continue to support the war had all been considered. The large haulage companies, larger department stores and municipalities were among the major suppliers of horses, but the railway companies had secured exemption of their animals from compulsory purchase on the grounds that they would be of greater assistance to the war effort in transporting the soldiers and their equipment to railway stations.[41] However, it was not the same for some of the smaller owners and farmers were forced to do without their finest animals, and had to rely on their breeding mares for work in the fields thereby reducing the numbers and quality of the next generation of animals.[42] The War Office issued price 'guidelines for the purchase of horses which indicated that £70 was an appropriate price for an officer's charger, but in a number of cases of an *extravagant nature* more than double that sum was paid. An average working-horse could go for as little as £35.[43] In Ireland at the Curragh, which had been turned into a remount depot the 16th Lancers were paying similar prices with officer's chargers costing £60 and troop horses fetching £40. Some unscrupulous owners realised it was possible to leave the racecourse with their horse once they had been paid and would then change the horse's appearance and bring it back in for a second time. It took

36 Ibid., para, 45.
37 Ibid., para. 50.
38 Ibid., para. 226-227.
39 Marquess of Anglesey, *A History of the British Cavalry, 1914-1919*, Vol. I, p. 58.
40 Horn, 'Diary of the Regiment', p. 3.
41 Bostridge, *The Fateful Year*, p. 217.
42 Ibid., p. 217.
43 Ibid., p. 217.

two or three days before this was realised. To prevent this happening again, horses were 'branded on the hoof. This of course stopped the practice.'[44] Hallie Miles witnessed this going on and wrote 'I saw a sad procession yesterday of the dear horses being marched through the streets, even they have to take their share. I believe the big stores have had all their van horses commandeered.'[45] On the evening of each day of mobilisation, brief reports were dispatched to the War Office by GOCs stating the progress made during the day and each GOC-C was required to telegraph to the War Office as soon as a unit reported its mobilisation complete.[46] A unit was 'considered to be mobilised when its personnel and animals have been completed to war establishment, and the whole of its war outfit has been received, its horses shod and its harness and saddlery fitted.'[47] Clear guidance was also given for the issue of rations for both men and horses and the provision of ammunition:

> If mobilisation is for service abroad, service small arm's ammunition will not be distributed to individuals, unless orders to the contrary are issued, until the port of disembarkation is reached[48]' In addition to the unexpended portion of the ration for the day of entertainment, each man will carry on his person, on leaving the place of mobilisation of his unit for the port of embarkation, two days preserved rations for use in case of delay in embarkation or during the voyage. Similarly, 6 lbs of oats will be carried in the nosebag of each horse. The above supplies will, if not otherwise available when mobilisation is ordered, be bought locally by the officer in charge of supplies.[49]

Provision was made for officers and soldiers who were on leave in Britain from their units in the Empire when war was declared, the 'warrant officers, non-commissioned officers and men on furlough from stations abroad will be ordered by the officer in charge records to report themselves in person at the nearest military station whence, in the absence of special orders, they will be dispatched to the depot of their regiment or to the nearest depot of their corps.'[21] The officers and soldiers from the 21st Lancers (the 9th Lancers paired regiment) who were on leave and courses from their Regiment which was stationed at Rawalpindi (Punjab, India) would have been included in this instruction and sent to Tidworth. The 7th Reserve Regiment of Cavalry in Tidworth was commanded by Lieutenant Colonel Forrester Farnell Colvin who had previously commanded the 9th Lancers from 1900-1901.[50] Private Albert Otton, who had enlisted a 21st Lancer, had been called up to the 9th Lancers and was subsequently transferred to the AVC,[51] and he estimated 'that the 9th are composed of about 50% of our reservists.'[52] Captain Gerald Reynolds of the 21st Lancers had been an instructor at the Cavalry School, Sangor, in India, and had relinquished his post on the 1st June.[53] This would have had an added significance as when he arrived at the 9th Lancers

44 Horn, 'Diary of the Regiment', pp. 3-4.
45 Hallie E. Miles, *Untold Tales of Wartime London: A Personal Diary* (London: Cecil Palmer, 1930), p. 15.
46 HMSO, *Regulations for Mobilisation 1912*, para. 74.
47 Ibid., para 75.
48 Ibid., para 83.
49 Ibid., para 85.
50 Footnote: 7th Reserve Regiment of Cavalry.
51 Medal Index Card for 741 (L-13629) Private Albert Otton.
52 *The Vadette*, 31st March 1915, p. 14.
53 *Army and Navy Gazette*, 1st August 1914.

My Daddy's a Soldier Now. (Author's Collection)

for duty it would have been the Adjutant, Captain Guy Reynolds, his younger brother, to whom he would have reported. The two Reynolds brothers were now serving together in Tidworth, but they also had an older brother Alan, serving with the 12th Lancers, who was mobilising in Norwich as part of the 5th (Independent) Cavalry Brigade. As well as Gerald Reynolds, another officer from India who was in England at the time of mobilisation was Lieutenant William Fraser[54] from the 21st King George's Own Central India Horse. Both he and Gerald were attached to C Squadron under the experienced command of Major Eustace Abadie DSO. The 9th Lancers, along with the rest of the brigade, started to prepare for war on the 28th July.[55] The declaration of war, which for many came as no surprise, was greeted with different emotions. The 34 year old Grenfell twins, Francis and Riversdale (Rivy) saw it as an opportunity after their own personal financial situation had changed three months earlier when their business interests, which Rivy was managing, failed.[56] Out of choice both of them would have followed the family tradition of joining the Army, but after the premature death of both their parents, their guardian and uncle Field Marshal Francis Grenfell had said 'one of them must choose a more lucrative calling, and the duty fell to Rivy, as having entered the world a few minutes later than his twin…in this assignment

54 Later Major General William Archibald Kenneth Fraser, CB, CBE, DSO and Bar, MVO, MC.
55 Maj. E.W. Sheppard, *The Ninth Queen's Royal Lancers 1715-1936* (Aldershot: Gale & Polden, 1939), p. 233.
56 "They had lost their combined fortune when their brother's business had failed." See John Buchan, *Francis and Riversdale Grenfell: A Memoir*, (London: Thomas Nelson & Sons, 1920), p. 183.

Francis was the luckier, for he was born for the Army. Indeed, both were, for it is hard to believe that Rivy had any aptitude for high finance:'[57]

> What to most people was like the drawing in of a dark curtain was to the twins an opening of barred doors into the daylight. For Francis, the career which had seemed at an end was to be resumed upon an august stage and for Rivy the chance had come to redeem private failure in public service…Rivy was determined to go out with Francis…Every moment of his time was devoted to sitting at his brother's feet and learning what he could teach him about the art of war and buying his equipment in feverish haste. The twins decided to take six horses between them, and they borrowed an additional groom from the Duke of Westminster.[58]

Captain Douglas Lucas-Tooth. (9/12L Museum)

On the 4th August, Captain Douglas Lucas-Tooth[59] wrote that 'everything went very smoothly, though the necessity of getting a *flying column*[60] ready interfered a little with the progress, also the inoculation against typhoid, which caused many men to be disabled daily, handicapped the work somewhat.'[61] Everything had gone well despite the disruptions and the regular brigade parades and the arrival of reserves and horses.[62] Private Tom Caselli, one of Captain Lucas-Tooth's soldiers, wrote to his wife Alice in Huddersfield, about their inoculations:

57 Ibid., p. 19.
58 Ibid., pp. 187-188.
59 Captain Douglas Keith Lucas-Tooth, DSO, died of wounds, 14th September 1914, buried Moulins New Communal Cemetery, Aisne, France.
60 Advance Parties left for France on 7th August 1914.' Anglesey, *A History of the British Cavalry, 1914-1919*, Vol. 7, p. 55 '
61 TNA WO 95/1113/2, 9th Lancers War Diary, 4th August 1914
62 Ibid., p. 1.

> I have all been inoculated today, all the regiment has got to be done before we proceed to the continent. Poor old Ted is beginning to be knocked up with it, and my arm is beginning to become swollen and stiff, tomorrow we shall be incapable of doing any work, it takes about three days before one is fit for anything after being inoculated. It is supposed to prevent one from catching enteric fever or cholera, which is always prevalent amongst armies in foreign countries.[63]

Lance Corporal Thomas Veness of B Squadron wrote home from Tidworth to his sister telling her of the soldier's high spirits, and told her that one day she might be proud of him and tell their mother Annie not to worry:

> I suppose you know that we are mobilised and ready to move to the front at any minute. Everybody is in the highest spirits over it. No one would think to look at the faces of the soldiers down here that we are expecting to go to war. Will you please tell mother not to worry about me, for, after all, what did I join the army for, and what is the use of being a soldier if we shirk the work we are trained to do. You may be sure that I will take great care of myself if we have to go, and perhaps you will have cause to be proud of your brother soon.[64]

The 9th Lancers thought themselves lucky in having a lecture from Major Bridges of the 4th Dragoon Guards, who had just relinquished his post as Military Attaché at Bruxelles, and was able to give them 'the most up to date information as to the country, the Belgian Army, and the way the campaign was likely to develop.'[65] For at this point the British Army's understanding of German tactics for most officers and soldiers was virtually non-existent since the study of German military organisation and methods was specifically forbidden at war games, staff tours, and intelligence classes,[66] before the outbreak of war. All of these would 'have provided the best opportunities for such instruction,'[67] unless, like Francis Grenfell in 1911, individuals had had the opportunity to attend and observe German manoeuvres. The visit of Major Bridges had been arranged by Brigadier Henry de Beauvoir De Lisle, the 2nd Cavalry Brigade commander, and the subject to be discussed was the fortresses that lay in the path of the German advance. Major Bridges gave an estimate on the holding power of Liège.

> I was invited to give a *résumé*, of the position and its probabilities. Liège, I said, could hold out for a fortnight or until heavy howitzers could be brought up for the attack...I gave it 10 days. The French entrenched camp of Maubeuge, which I had once visited with Henry Wilson,

63 Postcard in author's collection.

64 *Hastings and St Leonard's Observer*, 14th November 1914, op. cit. in Andrew Thornton, *Old Contemptibles: Men of the British Expeditionary Force on 1914. The Cavalry:* Vol. 1 (United Kingdom: CreateSpace Independent Publishing Platform, 2016), p. 23.

65 Anon., 9th Lancers War Diary, 4th August 1914, p. 1.

66 Edmonds, *Military Operations France and Belgium 1914,* Vol. I, p. 11.

67 Ibid., p. 11.

> and which he described as a "waspish place." I said it would cover our concentration and hold out for at least a fortnight. When asked by the Brigadier how long the war would go on, I said I had not the faintest idea, but speaking at random would give it six months. I understood that there were financial reasons why the *Great Powers* could not continue for long. I had had this from the Prime Minister who told me that Lord Haldane had told him so. De Lisle, however, in an able summing up, used these words: "make no mistake, gentlemen, we are in for a long and bitter war."'[68]

On the day that war was declared, Private (Shoeing Smith) Jack Friend in C Squadron of the 9th Lancers started his letter home to his mother in Torquay telling her not to worry, while at the same time expressing his own concerns. As a shoe smith he was involved in the regimental party responsible for collecting and shoeing the mobilised horses. The buying officer for horses, for the Regiment was Major Henry Ricardo, a retired artillery officer. He had been made responsible for the Regiment's horses and also some for the ASC. To date they had collected 100 horses from the Stroud Brewery Company which had been subsidised by the government. [69] In Cheltenham, Lieutenant Lennox Harvey collected 40 horses purchased for the Regiment. As a 'well-known steeplechase rider...we thought them a very high-class of cavalry horses...the Cotswold Hunt, who have brought in really good horses and sold them at a nominal price.'[70] Even at this early stage they thought it would all be over by Christmas. It would appear Jack Friend added to his letter over the coming days.

> Just a few hurried lines in answer to yours after a long time hoping this will find you and all at home in the best of health as it leaves me at present. Well dear mother I hardly know what to make of this terrible affair, I know one thing it makes bags of work, what with travelling the country fetching horses and working half the night shoeing them. If this is getting ready for war, I don't want it to happen very often as we have not had a minute peace since it started, but there I am happy enough and it's no use cribbing. Dear mother don't worry too much as I heard today although England has declared war if they go out fighting the same as they have been doing the British Army will not be wanted. I hope that will be the case as I am not anxious to go to Germany as most of the fellows are, and regards Tom he won't leave England as the ferries are our home defence which go right around the coast to guard there so you have no need to worry about him it will do him the world of good along the sea front with bags of fresh air. Dear mother do not worry about me as you can trust your humble to dodge anything if he has half a chance. However, I don't think it will last very long I should say about three months at the most.[71]

Captain Grenfell was keen that his twin brother Rivy would be able to come to with him to war. Francis was very well connected and tried every possible avenue to ensure it would happen as Rivy went off to rejoin his Yeomanry regiment, the Bucks Hussars, at Wycombe. Francis wanted to obtain permission that he be formally attached to the 9th Lancers; the Commanding

68 Bridges, *Alarms and Excursions,* p. 7.
69 *Gloucestershire Echo*, 5th August 1914.
70 *Cheltenham Chronicle*, 8th August 1914.
71 Shoe Smith J Friend, Letter to Mother, 4th August 1914.

Officer and the Brigade Commander, had applied for him to be attached as a special *reserve officer*. On about the 6th August, Francis started to get together all the equipment he thought he would need and went back to London to 'arrange his things, and with the aid of J. and L. and to buy what was necessary.[72] While they were in London they found that when the Bank of England had re-opened on the 6th August, a new legal tender of *treasury notes* had been issued. The Bank of England had issued black £1 notes and red 10-shilling notes, and this was the first time the government had issued paper money since the 17th century.[73] Gold could no longer be withdrawn.

Francis's Squadron Sergeant Major was SSM Hugh Durant. He was an Olympic pistol shot and specialised in the .455 Webley Scott Automatic pistol and had won two Bronze medals in Stockholm in 1912. The Commanding Officer and other officers had already seen the effectiveness of this new weapon and had bought their own personal pistols. SSM Durant had even purchased a second pistol just before embarkation. Both Francis and Rivy were also impressed, 'we both got Webley Scott Automatic pistols, and during the rest of the mobilisation period we used to ride out together to practice at the targets which were situated on the firing range; in the afternoons and in the evenings, we practiced at the revolver ranges. Both gained a great deal of confidence with our new weapons.'[74] After mastering his new pistol, the next priority for Francis was learn how to be a Squadron Leader. 'Immediately after mobilisation we had brigade parades regularly, which helped me a good deal as I had not handled a squadron before.'[75] He had previously been the Adjutant and he assumed his appointment as B Squadron Leader from Major Victor Brook. When Rivy returned to Tidworth, Francis managed to use him as a *galloper*, as he otherwise would have remained in the rear of the troops. Rivy's job was to sort out their horses for the war, and thanks to him they obtained some excellent horses from the remount at Leighton Buzzard. 'I chose out two for ourselves. We decided to take the following horses between us: *Ginger*, *Joe Boy*, *Pearl of Price*, *No. 36*, a black from Leighton, a Chestnut from Leighton, a nice thorough-bred horse, which we renamed *First Favourite*. Rivy took over the management of all the horses, and we took on Bell, one of the reserves as a groom, which turned out a very good move. Matthews and Clark also arrived, and Bendor [The Duke of Westminster] sent us a spare groom.'[76]

On the 6th August, Lord Kitchener threw himself into his new job as Secretary of War with 'great energy.'[77] As Lord Haldane handed over the appointment of Minister of War to Lord Kitchener, the subject of raising a reserve was something that Lord Haldane had always planned as part of his reforms since 1908. The reserve and support to the Regular Army was to come from the Territorial Army and to be increased through the *county associations*,[78] led by the Lord Lieutenants and supported personally by King Edward VII. At a meeting on 23rd October 1907 he said:

72 Capt. F.O. Grenfell, Grenfell Family Papers (within Lyttelton Family Papers), 5th August 1914, p. 2.
73 Bostridge, *The Fateful Year*, p. 206.
74 Grenfell, Grenfell Family Papers, 5th August 1914, p. 2.
75 Ibid., p. 2.
76 Ibid., p. 3.
77 Brock & Brock (eds.), *H.H. Asquith*, p. 158.
78 Richard B. Haldane, *Richard Burdon Haldane: An Autobiography* (London: Hodder & Stoughton, 1929), p. 279.

SSM Hugh Durant c. 1913.
(John Goodchild)

> I have summoned you…to acquaint you with the new duties and responsibilities which will now devolve upon you…Henceforth my Yeomanry and my volunteers are to form the Territorial Army, over the destinies of which you and your *county associations* are to watch; so to you are now delegated the duties of raising, equipping and maintaining that portion of this force of the Imperial Army of the second line which lies within the shores of this Kingdom.[79]

Lord Haldane tried to persuade Lord Kitchener to follow his plan but despite his efforts 'was unable to prevail.'[80] Lord Kitchener had been opposed to the plan from its creation.[81] A flaw in the plan was that a territorial was not liable for overseas service unless as a volunteer,[82] which was an 'unalterable dictum'[83] that had been laid down by the Duke of Wellington. Therefore, it was Lord Kitchener's plan to raise completely new 'Kitchener Armies,'[84] that would be made up of volunteers who would enlist for a short period of service. Lord Kitchener said 'we must be prepared to put armies of millions into the field and maintain them for several years.'[85] His challenge was to preserve enough of the current Regular Army to provide the core of professional officers and men for his new one.

79 Maurice, *Haldane 1856-1915*, pp. 213-214.
80 Haldane, *Richard Burdon Haldane*, p. 279.
81 Ray Westlake, *Kitchener's Army,* (Staplehurst: Spellmount, 1989), p. 9.
82 Ibid., p. 9.
83 Tuchman, *August 1914*, p. 194.
84 Haldane, *Richard Burdon Haldane*, p. 279.
85 Tuchman, *August 1914*, p. 193.

While Lord Haldane was handing over to Lord Kitchener, the advancing German Army were now on the outskirts of Liège. It was a night that General Erich Ludendorff would never forget: 'it was cold and as I had left my kit behind, Major von Marcard gave me his cloak. I was very anxious and listened feverishly for the sound of fighting. It was all quiet and the suspense was unbearable.'[86] At sea the first actions had also taken place between the British and German navies just off the English east coast. Herbert Asquith wrote to Venetia telling her about the sad sinking of *HMS Amphion*, 'who did so well yesterday, has been blown up by mines today, apparently no one saved.'[87] *HMS Amphion,* with a flotilla of destroyers, had sunk the *Königin Luise*, a Hamburg-Amerika vessel fitted as a minelayer which the previous day which had laid 180 mines off Harwich and Southwold. When returning from the action, she ran into one of the mines and was sunk. The information Herbert Asquith had at the time was incorrect and her Captain, 16 officers and 135 men had been saved.

In the morning, General Ludendorff went forward to establish what was happening, only to find the *Infanterie Brigade 14* commander, General Friedrich von Wussow's orderly leading the General's horse, which had an empty saddle. The orderly said that the General had been killed by machine gun fire on the road ahead.[88] General Ludendorff took command of the Brigade and ordered Hauptmann Ott with a company of Jägers to seize the bridges over the Meuse. The company reached the bridges unopposed. After daybreak, General Emmich ordered the town to be entered. The *advance guard* commanded by Oberst von Oven and was followed by the rest of the *Infanterie Brigade 11* and General Emmich and his staff. Thinking that Oberst von Oven was in position, General Ludendorff [89]went with the brigade Adjutant in a commandeered car to the citadel. When he arrived, there were no Germans present, and the citadel was still occupied by approximately 100 Belgians, 'I banged on the gates which were locked. They were opened from the inside…they surrendered at my summons.'[90] Although the citadel had been taken easily, the city of Liège had not been taken and it was still holding out defiantly. In Bruxelles, the previous day, under a flag of truce, Hauptman Brinckman, the former German attaché, spoke to General Leman, who he knew. He threatened him that, if Liège did not surrender and let the Germans through, it would be bombed. General Gérard Leman, declined and on 6th August the Zeppelin Z VI was sent from Köln and dropped 13 bombs[91] on the city which killed nine civilians.[92]

In Herbert Asquith's letter to Venetia that day he told her 'we had our usual cabinet meeting this morning and decided with much less demur than I expected to sanction the dispatch of an expeditionary force of four divisions.'[93] Both he and Lord Kitchener had their own reservations and concerns about sending all six infantry divisions with the BEF. Herbert Asquith was concerned over civil unrest and a result of the loss of overseas trade resulting in large-scale unemployment. Lord Kitchener was concerned about home defence and retaining a nucleus

86 Ludendorff, *My War Memories 1914-1918,* pp. 36-37.
87 Brock & Brock (eds.), *H.H. Asquith*, p 158.
88 Tuchman, *August 1914,* p. 174.
89 Ludendorff was awarded the *Pour le Mérite* for his actions.
90 Ludendorff, *My War Memories 1914-1918,* p. 37.
91 Converted artillery shells.
92 Tuchman, *August,1914*, p. 175.
93 Brock & Brock (eds.), *H.H. Asquith*, p. 158.

of an army large enough to build another. It was decided to initially keep two divisions back, eventually a fifth division was released with a sixth division to follow in early September and a seventh would be formed from troops released from South Africa to follow on in the middle of the same month.[94] He also told her about the decision to abort the decision to conduct offensive operations against the German colonies in an attempt to deprived Germany of coaling stations and wireless stations for her navy.[95] 'We also discussed a number of smaller schemes for taking German ports and wireless stations in East and West Africa and the China Seas were discussed with some gusto: indeed I had to remark that we looked more like a gang of Elizabethan buccaneers, than a meek collection of black-coated Liberal ministers.'[96] The decision to send four infantry divisions and a Cavalry Division had been made when the *War Council* had met for the second time that evening. General Wilson had told the council that the expeditionary force would not be ready for general action for 20 days. The council arrived at the decision that the 1st, 2nd, 3rd and 5th Infantry Divisions along with the Cavalry Division would embark, and the 4th Infantry Division would follow on later. All of the units to initially embark would come from the United Kingdom, with the majority being in England and Scotland, with the exception of the 5th Infantry Division and the 3rd Cavalry Brigade which were stationed in Ireland. The general allocation of ports of embarkation were: Southampton, Dublin, Glasgow, Queenstown, Belfast, and Jersey for troops and horses. Newhaven was used for stores, Liverpool for mechanical transport and frozen meat; and Avonmouth for mechanical transport and petrol. The movements were worked on the ferry system, with some vessels making a single voyage and some making a maximum of nine voyages during the period. The whole embarkation was completed in 570 trips with a daily average of 13 sailings.[97] The first day of embarkation would be Sunday, 9th August.[98] On the same day, Prince Louis of Battenberg, the First Sea Lord, and the French Deputy Chief of Staff of the Navy, Antoine Schwerer, signed a convention in London on the division of responsibilities between the two navies. The convention confirmed the terms of the *Entente Cordiale*, and placed France in command of all naval operations in the Mediterranean. Malta and Gibraltar would both be treated as French naval bases. In the event that Austria entered the war, France would act against its naval forces.[99]

The BEF would deploy to France in the same two armies as it had done in the 1912 Army Manoeuvres, but they would be retitled as *corps* to conform to the French nomenclature and they would be commanded by the same men as in 1912, with Lieutenant General Haig commanding I Corps, and Lieutenant General Grierson commanded II Corps. Both Corps Headquarters were expected to be conduits for the passage of command direction from GHQ and were not intended to serve as commanding headquarters.[100] General Allenby, who had been the Inspector General of Cavalry since 1910, would command the Cavalry Division, but the force he was about to command was considerably larger than anything he had commanded operationally

94 Hew Strachan, *The First World War,* pp. 205-206.
95 Brock & Brock, *H.H. Asquith*, p. 159.
96 Ibid., p. 158.
97 Hurd, *The Merchant Navy,* Vol. II, Vol. 2, p. 82.
98 Callwell, *Field-Marshal Sir Henry Wilson Bart.*, p. 159.
99 *Charles Koburger, The Central Powers in the Adriatic, 1914–1918: War in a Narrow Sea, (Greenwood, 2001), pp. 31-32.*
100 Spencer Jones, 'Command Amidst Chaos: Leadership in the BEF', WFA Presentation 2015.

before. Despite being a Commanding Officer and the Commander of the 4th Cavalry Brigade, the largest force he had commanded operationally was columns of 2000 men during the anti-guerrilla operations in 1902 in South Africa. General Allenby, like many, polarised his peers and subordinates opinions. Some thought 'his soldierly talents were considered to be 'worthy rather than outstanding and had an unenviable reputation for being a *martinet*...and showed no outstanding talent and performed indifferently when his Cavalry Division was attached to General Haig during the 1912 Army Manoeuvres.[101] However, Field Marshal Wavell said that 'he was no *martinet*, and maintained discipline...rather by the force of his personality[102]...such was the penalty in reputation that his brusqueness in manner, the result largely of a natural shyness, had brought him[103]...the orders he insisted on had all a reason of good common sense.'[104] However, Brigadier Gough noticed that General Allenby was easily perplexed and, in his uncertainty, followed Haig's procedures, often an unwise course and Brigadier Sir James Edmonds came to a similar conclusion that General Allenby was at heart "a good sort who was forced to play-act a role for which he was not suited."[105] His reputation had earned him the nickname "The Bull" amongst the officers. To the men, he was later known as "Tin Hat."'[106] That said, Field Marshal French had never operationally commanded more than a cavalry division before he assumed command of the BEF.[107]

General Edmund Allenby. (Author's Collection)

101 Lawrence James. *Imperial Warrior, The Life and Times of Field Marshal Viscount Allenby 1861-1936, p. 49.*
102 Gen. Sir Archibald Wavell, *Allenby, a Study in Greatness: The Biography of Field-Marshal Viscount Allenby of Megiddo and Felixstowe,* (London, George G Harrap, 1940), p. 111.
103 Ibid., p. 123.
104 Ibid., p. 297.
105 Ibid., p. 46.
106 Marquess of Anglesey, *A History of the British Cavalry, 1816-1919, vol. 7: 1914-1919*, p. 74.
107 Ibid., p. 55.

The reason for not sending the whole BEF centred on Lord Kitchener's concern regarding the threat of invasion. General Haig thought the expeditionary force should only be 'be regarded as an advance party'[108] and that the reason for only sending four infantry divisions was as a result of "a marked deficiency of equipment…at most not more than four divisions could be fully equipped." He attributed this to 'the government's economy campaign of the last few years.'[109] Major Bridges was more scathing and bitter regarding the situation, which he felt could have been avoided with compulsory military service and others would now have to pick up the pieces. 'This short-sighted and spineless policy was the terrible wastage of the best of the nation. How many officers like myself who took over ill-trained and ill-equipped troops after long months of precious time wasted, did not curse and curse again the apathy and weakness of successive governments which turned a blind eye to the writing on the wall.'[110]

That evening in Holywood Barracks, in Belfast, the canteen had been opened to welcome the reserves who had arrived from Norfolk. 'It became one glorious reunion that is judging by their behaviour that night and the next morning.'[111] The *Belfast News Letter* reported their arrival '700 reservists for the Norfolk Regiment at Holywood will arrive by special boat today, and another batch will be brought in on Saturday morning.'[112] The reserves had been met at the station by the band and 'played-in…they all began singing as we marched along, trying no doubt to forget what they had left behind.'[113] At Norwich the depot had 'paraded on the square in our war array and 500…to join the 1st Battalion stationed at Holywood, Ireland.[114] They had crossed during the night having left 'Heysham just before midnight, and crossed on the usual passenger boat. It was a stormy night and I felt a bit of a headache, so I coiled up in my coat on deck.'[115] During the night, Private Sheldrake's personal feelings regarding the suffragette movement were challenged 'I felt sorry for the lady passengers on deck, but perhaps it was only a waste of sympathy, as they may have belonged to that class that consider they are equal to a man.[116] On their arrival they 'were soon told off to our different companies and received some bread with butter on, and tea with milk and sugar.'[117] After the difficult crossing and conditions before their departure from Norwich, Sheldrake on arrival in Belfast 'found things much better here than at Norwich Depot.'[118] Some of their reserves that arrived and who had previously served in the battalion had gone on to be professional footballers. These included William Fiske, Nottingham Forest's goalkeeper, who had only just joined the club from Blackpool for a large fee. He had been called up on the 1st August, the same day as he had signed his contract and on the same evening had to leave to join the colours. William Fiske left his wife Bessie and child in Blackpool.[119] Later

108 Brig. Gen. John Charteris, *Field Marshal Earl Haig*, p. 79.
109 Ibid., p. 78.
110 Lt. Gen. Sir T. Bridges, Alarms and Excursions, *Reminiscences of a Soldier*, p. 68.
111 Pte R. Hurrell, *Log of Round the World Cruise, Autobiography*, p. 2.
112 *Belfast News Letter* dated Friday 7th August 1914.
113 Ibid., p. 2.
114 Pte R. Sheldrake notebook, (1915), p. 3.
115 Pte R. Sheldrake diary, p. 5.
116 Ibid., p. 5.
117 Ibid.
118 Ibid., p. 6.
119 *Sheffield Daily Telegraph*, 22nd August 1914.

on he would also be joined by Burnley's Sam Gunton[120] who had previously served in the Army from 1899 to 1909. William Fiske would never play for Nottingham Forest as he was killed in action on 27th May 1918.

During the day of the 6th August at *Le Pensionnat Saint Bernard pour Jeunes Filles (*Saint Bernard's Boarding School for Young Girls*)* in Audregnies, a small village west of Mons in Belgium *Madame la Supérieure* had spoken to *Madame la Prieure* (the Prioress) about the setting up of a temporary military hospital (*L'Ambulance*) at the *Pensionnat.* It had been decided that the hall, study rooms, meeting room, cloakroom and small infirmary would be used. The following morning, the doctor arrived who placed himself at their full disposal and the day was spent setting up beds. Their aim was to set up a facility of 75 beds, but they were unsure if it was achievable. François Jaspar was sent to Mons for medical supplies, but many items were unavailable. Daily life in the *Pensionnat* was being affected by the war. Butter had not been available for days and *Madame la Supérieure* had said that sugar and tablecloths would also now not be available.

Pensionnat Saint Bernard, Audregnies. (Author's Collection)

On the 7th August, the day that the *Flying Column* had left Tidworth for France, the staff of the German *AOK 1* was ready to leave Stettin by rail for Grevenbroich. The rail transport to the western front 'was carried out with a remarkable punctuality.'[121] The send-off for the soldiers was well publicised and supported. The civilian population came out in their numbers

120 *Burnley News*, 8th August 1914.
121 Alexander von Kluck, *The March on Paris and The Battle of The Marne, 1914*, p. 5.

'and food given to the troops by the population and by the indefatigable Red Cross workers considerably exceeded their needs.'[122] The staff were now able to settle down to hard work, which was an uninterrupted life of conferences, important decisions, and examination of intelligence; recreation was cut down to an absolute minimum and the composition of the staff seemed a most happy one.'[123] In Tidworth, Jack Friend added the details of the Regiment's departure to his letter, and expressed no regrets on enlisting and hoping to make his family proud:

> Dear mother, up to now our orders are we leave here on Sunday morning early for Southampton where we embark on Monday for Belgium where we stop for a day or so. We have everything ready and our wills made. Dear mother, I have never been sorry that I enlisted. The only time I ever regretted was the first six months that I joined the Army and even at this terrible time I am glad it has happened as I shall see what others have had to go through and managed to get through quite safe and by God's help, I hope I shall do the same. In any case, I shall go out with a good heart knowing that I am fighting for my King and country although it is very hard to leave behind those whom I love dearly. Dear mother, father, brothers and sisters a dear sweetheart whom I love with all my heart, but we soldier's must not look on the dark side of it but must look forward to the return journey with flying colours and then you will be proud of your soldier son.[124]

On 7th August, as the first element of the Expeditionary Force were leaving, Lord Kitchener's call to arms was published:

> "Your King and Country need you." The requirement was for an additional 100,000 men to join his Majesty's Regular Army as an immediately necessary in the present grave national emergency. Lord Kitchener is confident that this appeal will be at once responded to by all those who have the safety of our Empire at heart. The terms of service were for a period of three years or until the war is concluded and the age of enlistment was between 19 and 30. All the information could be obtained from the post office or any military depot.[125]

Before the Expeditionary Force had left, Lord Kitchener had anticipated that the war would last at least three years and he would have to be prepared to replace virtually the whole of the force. He also issued an *Army Order* for the "Pardon for Deserters" for the widest distribution. The *Singapore Free Press and Mercantile Advertiser* carried the following article having received it on the 8th August 'His Majesty the King has been graciously pleased to approve of pardons being given to soldiers who were in a state of desertion from the regular forces on 5th August 1914, and who surrender themselves in the United Kingdom on or before the 4th September 1914, or at any station abroad where are regular forces on or before 4th October 1914.'[126] On the promise of a pardon H/2471 Private Timothy McHale of the 18th Hussars handed himself in at Warwick on Saturday 8th August to the care of the local authorities who said "he was

122 Ibid., p. 5.
123 Ibid.
124 Shoe Smith J Friend, *Letter to Mother.*
125 Edmonds, *Military Operations France and Belgium 1914,* Vol. I, p. 497.
126 *Singapore Free Press and Mercantile Advertiser,* 8th August 1914, p. 20.

quite willing to go back and fight for his country." He was remanded to await an escort. The mayor remarked that there was an official notice pardoning all deserters.'[127] He was returned to his regiment in Tidworth just in time to embark with them to France, eventually being demobilised on 23rd January 1919.[128] Even Private Harold Spiers of the Worcester Regiment who had deserted in Llanelli in 1911 during the riots, when his battalion had shot and killed two rioters, rejoined the army on the outbreak of war. Private Spiers, technically was not a deserter as he was subsequently charged on a lesser charge *of absence without leave* after the intervention of the Home Secretary.

Mr Reginald McKenna, made an announcement on the same day regarding the suffragettes. Since the outbreak of war, they had proclaimed a truce,[129] he said that the government 'would release all suffrage prisoners who would give an undertaking "to not to commit further crimes and outrages,"...few days later, after pressure, Home Secretary announced in the House of Commons that it was the intention of the government, within a few days, to release unconditionally, all suffrage prisoners.'[130] Emmeline Pankhurst wrote, 'so ends, for the present, the war of women against men,'[131] and all remaining suffragettes were released from prison on 10th August.

As the 9th Lancers and the BEF were still in the early stages of mobilising, the German Imperial Army had already completed its preparations of collecting horses and processing reservists. The *Infanterie Brigade 13,* commanded by Generalmajor Georg von Schüßler in Magdeburg were about to hold their final church services and make the last adjustments to their structures. On Thursday, 6th August, *Infanterie Regiment 66* had completed its mobilisation and on the afternoon the Regiment assembled on the Schroteplatz training area for an 'unforgettable, sombre holy communion.'[132] The Regiment had lost:

> A lieutenant colonel, five captains and seven lieutenants who were also transferred... primarily to staff the reserve regiment. On Saturday, 8th August, the Regiment marched to the station and loaded onto rail cars at the Magdeburg. The battalion's march through the city was like a triumphal procession, past the citizens who thickly lined both sides of the street, mothers, women and brides waved to the warriors going to the field with tears in their eyes and accompanied them to the gates of the station. Fifes and drums played over the noise of the crowd and flowers decorated the uniforms. The long row of rail cars waited at the station.[133]

At the same time *Infanterie Regiment 66* was holding its service of holy communion on its training area, the 9th Lancers were attending church in Tidworth. Francis wrote 'we both went to early service at Tidworth, after I had attended a parade service in the open air at 0700. All this time I was very busy with the Squadron, sorting out horses and reservists. I received a

127 *Leamington Spa Courier*, 14th August 1914.
128 Thornton, *Old Contemptibles*, p. 22.
129 Emmeline Pankhurst, *My Own Story* (New York: Hearst International, 1914), Foreword.
130 Ibid.
131 Ibid.
132 Korfes, *The German 66th Regiment in the First World War*, p. 21.
133 Ibid., p. 21.

great deal of help from the troop leaders.[134] Rivy had a lot to learn and it 'amused Captain Mark Porter and me by his preference to sleeping on the valise on the floor in my room in order to get accustomed to it. He did everything he possibly could to learn in a few days and accustom himself in a few hours 'to habits which had taken soldiers years to master.'[135] He amused him 'by desiring to have repeated rehearsals of what he should carry, and how everything should be packed. He was really of course quite right, as, even at the last minute, in spite of his precaution, we found a few things did not fit on the saddle.'[136]

In Belfast, the Norfolk Regiment had marched to St Anne's Cathedral to 'deposit the Regimental Colour…this was a very great ceremony.[137] The band had played at the cathedral and on the way Private Reginald Hurrell 'noticed some people were crying, no doubt thinking that we were then going to the front that day.'[138] When they arrived at the cathedral they were surprised to be met by a guard of the 'Ulster Volunteers who, lined each side of the street with rifles at the present.'[139] The *Belfast Telegraph* reported that it was difficult to tell the difference between the volunteers and the soldiers 'when, as one old lady said, "ye cudn't know who is the sojers."'[140]

After the short service they marched back to barracks, which was about five miles. The band played most of the way as they marched back in the rain. That evening in Tidworth the Commanding Officer of the 18th Hussars received a phone call telling him that Her Majesty the Queen intended to come to Tidworth the next day to bid farewell to her Regiment before its departure for France.'[141] The following morning on 8th August the Commanding Officer Lieutenant Colonel Burnett met Her Majesty and Princess Mary at Bulford Station and escorted them to Tidworth where the Regiment had been paraded by the cricket ground ready for Her Majesty's inspection. On her arrival Generals Sir W.P. Campbell and De Lisle were also present to receive her. 'After a short time, the Regiment marched past complete for war in every detail, together with its first-line transport, and forming up again advanced at *the charge* to within a few paces of where Her Majesty stood.'[142]

While the Queen had been visiting the 18th Hussars in Tidworth, parliament had also been busy looking at the legislation that might be needed as they went to war. On Saturday, 8th August, the *Defence of the Realm Act* (DORA) became law just four days after Britain had entered the war. The reasons behind the haste and the passing of the DORA was as a result of the government becoming concerned about security. That had its origins a decade earlier over the lack of control over the press during the Boer War and 'the indiscriminate publication at home of military information which should have been unquestionably kept secret. The Boers were well informed, not only of the strength of the force sent against them, but in many cases

134 Grenfell, Grenfell Family Papers (within Lyttelton Family Papers), 9th August 1914, p. 3.
135 Ibid., 9th August 1914, p. 3.
136 Ibid., 9th August 1914, p. 4.
137 Pte R. Hurrell, Notebook, p. 2.
138 Pte R. Hurrell, Log of Round the World Cruise, p. 3.
139 Ibid., p. 3.
140 *Belfast Telegraph*, 14th August 1914.
141 Ibid., p. 15.
142 Ibid., p. 15.

of movements which were actually pending'[143] They obtained this information from Lorenzo Marques in the Portuguese territories without 'let or hindrance.'[144] The proclamation stated: 'we strictly command and enjoin our subjects to obey and conform to all instructions and regulations which may be issued by us or our Admiralty or *Army Council*.'[145] The DORA would touch the lives of every British citizen for the next four years. The Act itself was designed to help prevent invasion and keep morale high at home. It gave the government wide-ranging powers, such as the authority to requisition buildings needed for the war effort, or by creating new criminal offences. It also contained a variety of social control measures. The two main themes included press censorship and the requisitioning of land by the government:

> No civilian could: talk about naval or military matters in public places, spread rumours about military matters, buy binoculars, trespass on railway lines or bridges, melt down gold or silver, light bonfires, fireworks or fly a kite, give bread to horses or chickens, use invisible ink when writing abroad, buy brandy or whisky in railway refreshment rooms, ring church bells during periods that lighting restrictions were in force. If anyone broke these rules, they could be arrested, fined, sent to prison, or even executed. A total of 11 'German spies' were executed under the regulations. This would ultimately affect the Press's ability to report factually on the war.[146]

On the same day as the DORA became law, Herbert Asquith met with Lord Kitchener and had him read his instructions to Sir John French to him and thought them 'quite good.'[147] They outlined the government's reason for going to war which was 'furtherance of the *Entente* which exists between this country and France, His Majesty's government has decided, at the request of the French Government, to send an expeditionary force to France,'[148] and it limited him to 'assist the French Government in preventing or repelling the invasion by Germany of French and Belgian territory and eventually to restore the neutrality of Belgium, on behalf of which, as guaranteed by treaty.'[149] It also considered the size of the force and Britain's ability to reinforce the expeditionary force, in that 'it must be recognised from the outset that the numerical strength of the British Force and its contingent reinforcement is strictly limited, and with this consideration kept steadily in view it will be obvious that the greatest care must be exercised towards a minimum of losses and wastage.'[150] The level of support he was able to offer had been seriously limited:

> The gravest consideration will devolve upon you as to participation in forward movements where large bodies of French troops are not engaged and where your force may be unduly exposed to attack. Should a contingency of this sort be contemplated I look to you inform

143 Lloyds News, *Lloyds ABC of the War: A Complete Reference Book of Facts and Figures which all should Know* (London: Hodder & Stoughton, 1914), p. 77.
144 Ibid., p. 77.
145 *London Gazette Supplement* 28859.
146 *London Gazette* <https://www.thegazette.co.uk/> (Accessed 4th July 2018).
147 Brock & Brock (eds.), *H.H. Asquith*, p. 161.
148 Edmonds, Hurrell, *Military Operations France and Belgium 1914,* Vol. I, p. 499.
149 Ibid., p. 499.
150 Ibid., p. 499.

> me fully and to give me time to communicate to you any decision His Majesties government may come in this matter. In minor operations you should be careful that your subordinates understand that risk of serious losses should only be taken where such risk is authoritatively considered to be commensurate with the object in view.[151]

The command relationship with his French allies was made very clear in that:

> I wish you distinctly to understand that your command is an entirely independent one, and that you will in no case come in any sense under the orders of any allied general. In minor operations you should be careful that your subordinates understand that risk of serious losses should only be taken where such risk is authoritatively considered to be commensurate with the object in view.[152]

Lord Kitchener also understood the limitation and experience of the officers and men particularly regarding the type and nature of any experience that they might have gained previously. 'A high courage and discipline of your troops should, and certainly will, have fair and full opportunity of display during the campaign, but officers may well be reminded that in this their first experience of European warfare, a greater measure of caution must be employed than under former conditions of hostilities against an untrained adversary.'[153] Kitchener's orders reflected his concerns over the plan which the BEF had subscribed to and the temperament of the man who was to command it. It placed specific limitations which he hoped would reduce the British casualties long enough for him to raise another army and use the nucleus of what remained to provide it with experience. Herbert Asquith clearly did not consider that he and Venetia were bound by the DORA as he said in the same letter, 'I have told him [Kitchener] to send me a full statement of the composition of the force, regiments etc and this I will show or send to you. I love and prize you with all my heart.'[154]

On 8th August, James Ramsey MacDonald continued his opposition to the war and addressed members of the Labour group at the Leicester Trade Hall. He made the first of many of his public speeches outside the Commons decrying Britain's involvement in the war. His speech prompted a swift response from the other political parties and a hastily arranged public meeting was held in Leicester Market Place on the 9th August to demonstrate cross-party support that rejected James Ramsey MacDonald's views before a large crowd of townspeople.[155] This demonstration was happening just as the first troops were embarking and General Haig was moving his corps headquarters into the Dolphin Hotel in Southampton.[156]

On the 8th August in Belfast, the Norfolk Regiment continued their training. They now needed to integrate their reserves who had just arrived and needed to be brought up to standard as quickly as possible:

151 Ibid., p. 499.
152 Ibid., p. 499.
153 Ibid., p. 500.
154 Brock & Brock (eds.), *H.H. Asquith*, p. 161.
155 Beazley, *Four Years Remembered*, p. 15.
156 Charteris, *Field Marshal Earl Haig*, p. 82.

> So, there was more marching, practising with the reserves, getting their feet hardened up, and also by carrying the fully loaded pack and rifle besides other forms of necessary training, including lectures on military tactics. If they were not marching then they were signing wills, allotting pay, signing papers, drawing knives, emergency rations, 150 leaden pills, got a half sovereign pay the only one I have drawn.[157]

During one of these marches, Private Sheldrake had 'passed by that notorious anti-Home Rule famed house, Craigavon. The Irish poor around that part looked the same as I had read about and expected to see, namely dirty and shoeless, quite a contrast to the many well fed and clothed dashing about in motor cars.'[158] The former-postman from Norfolk was well informed and had clearly arrived in Ireland with an expectation of what he might find.

In Audregnies they had been praying a lot and were trying to remain brave, but all the signs from the priest were pessimistic. The role of the *L'Ambulance* had been confirmed by the Red Cross in Mons, so *Madame la Supérieure* designated which sisters were to act as nurses: Asceline, Hildegarde, Odilon, Marie-Gertrude, Jules, Marie Edouard, Marie-Geneviève, Marie-Félix,

The Sisters of St Bernard's, Audregnies, Sisters: Saint-Martin, Félicité, Marie-Xavier, Charlotte, Bénigne, Flavie, Sylvie, Christine and Euphémie. (Jean Richez, *Un Champ de Coquelicots, La Bataille d'Audregnies le 24 Août 1914*)

157 Pte R. Sheldrake diary, p. 6.
158 Ibid., p. 6.

Concorde and Euphémie. The remainder were to continue in their 'obedience' while at the same time conducting cooking and sewing duties.[159]

On the 10th August, Generaloberst von Kluck drafted his first *Army Order* while on the 49 hour railway journey from Stettin to Grevenbroich, and he issued it after their arrival in the concentration area, fully understanding what he was asking his troops to do. He was of pains that they should not violate the Netherlands. That had been one of the General von Moltke's key amendments to *Schlieffen's Plan:*

> The *AOK 1* will deploy on the extreme right wing of the armies. As soon as the assembly in the concentration area is completed, the army will be closed towards Aix-la-Chapelle, and, avoiding Dutch territory, will hold itself in readiness on the roads north of Liège leading across the Meuse between Vise and Herstal. The movement of the army on Aix-la-Chapelle and its passage across the Meuse must be carried out rapidly. The concentration in a very narrow area and the length of the columns during the advance will need careful organisation and preparation. Great demands will be made on the marching power of the troop.[160]

Generaloberst von Kluck also issued some tactical guidance notes with the orders and in them he gave clear instructions on maintaining the fighting efficiency of his army:

> There are countless ways of raising and maintaining the fighting power of an army. They depend on the character and energy of its leaders. Thus, particular attention must be paid to keeping the marching capacity of the men at the highest pitch, by guarding against the many insidious influences that may affect it, especially sore feet and other internal and external injuries caused by long marches, ill-fitting boots, etc. Again, a constant watch should be kept over the supply of food and ammunition and over the medical care of all ranks, including the army staff. Neglect of any of these matters will diminish the fighting strength of the army. All wastage of manpower must be jealously guarded against, as every possible rifle must be available at the decisive moment of the operations. In our present military situation, this is a matter of hard and absolute necessity.[161]

Generaloberst von Kluck's *AOK 1* waited at their assembly on the left bank of the Rhine north east of Aix-la-Chapelle, with its main base at Dusseldorf. It would wait there until Liège had been taken and they would be able to advance with the other two German Armies. Their anticipated date to move was the 10th August, but due to the situation at Liège the move of the *AOK 1* was changed to the 13th. At 0630 on 12th August, the *Infanterie Regiment 66* marched towards Aachen. The Regiment bivouacked at Broich and in the surrounding villages, with the battalions closely packed together, and the countryside was thick with troops.[162] The afternoon was spent

159 *Annales du pensionnat Saint Bernard à Audregnies*, p. 39, op cit. in Jean Richez, *Un Champ de Coquelicots, La Bataille d'Audregnies le 24 Août 1914.*

160 Alexander von Kluck, *The March on Paris and The Battle of The Marne 1914* (London: Longmans, 1920), p. 9.

161 Ibid., p. 8.

162 Korfes, *The German 66th Regiment in the First World War*, p. 23.

Infanterie Regiment 66 on their way to the front. (*The German 66th Regiment in the First World War*)

checking equipment, writing letters home and saying goodbye to the cheerful German population. `Everyone, soldiers and civilians alike, was in a serious, solemn mood. It was evident in the faces of all that they were completely prepared to give everything for the Fatherland. All day long we heard the sound, like far-away thunder, of the guns at Liège.'[163] Early on the morning of 13th August, the division assembled and marched 'in burning heat to Aachen, arriving in the city just before noon, dusty and sweaty, but in perfect formation.'[164] They were surprised by the reception they received 'our reception by the population was indescribable: general jubilation, extravagant masses of flowers, refreshments and bread, sweets and fruit, given to the soldiers by pretty girls and women. No one expected this, the most wonderful reception that *IV AK* ever experienced.'[165] On their arrival in the city the Regiment marched past in review order in front of the Corps Commander, Generalleutnant Friedrich Sixt von Armin. 'His quiet and serious face looked with satisfaction on the elite of the province of Sachsen.'[166] The Regiment knew that on the far side of

163 Ibid., p. 24.
164 Ibid., p. 24.
165 Ibid., p. 24.
166 Ibid., p. 24.

Generalleutnant Sixt von Armin. (Author's Collection)

the city was the valley which led to the Belgian border and as they waited 'another world appeared. Lorries drove past from Liège, loaded with wounded, also Belgian prisoners. Our first view of the seriousness of war.'[167]

As *Infanterie Regiment 66* marched towards Aachen, the advance party of the British Cavalry Division was unloading from the *Combrie Castle* at Le Havre, having sailed from Southampton the previous day. General Allenby was only just drawing his new headquarters together. Unlike the headquarters of his brigades, his own had not formally been established in peace time and had to be drawn together on mobilisation in Aldershot. The appointment of Inspector General of Cavalry had not attracted any staff support. It is not clear if General Allenby ever raised his concerns regarding mobilising to war with an untrained and exercised headquarters, but his predecessor had done in 1907.[168] General Wavell thought,

> It was a serious blot on our otherwise admirable preparations for war that the formation likely to take first contact with the enemy should be so unhandily organised and so freshly staffed…Allenby must share it for his acquiescence. But the real fault lay in the false financial economy which insists on the limitation of staffs in peace to the bare minimum required for peace-time routine. The limitation of the peace strength of units is a grave

167 Ibid., p. 24.
168 Gen. Sir Archibald Wavell, *Allenby: A Study in Greatness* (London: Harrap, 1941), p. 119.

disadvantage in training for war, but the limitation of staffs is an even more dangerous economy. The starved body can more quickly and easily be recuperated than the starved brain.'[169]

The Cavalry Division Headquarters consisted of Colonel John Vaughan, from the Cavalry School, a well-known horseman, (which along with the Inspector General of Cavalry was a war-time position tied to the post[170]) as the GSO1 and Major Archibald 'Sally' Home[171], of the 11th Hussars, who had spent a "weary year" as an instructor at the Staff College but as a result it "brought its reward " as the GSO2. Unusually for an army officer he spoke both French and German.[172] Captain Henry Howard, of the 16th Lancers, came from an appointment at the War Office. He had no operational experience at all and was appointed the GSO3.[173] The chief administrative staff officer was Colonel Edmund Ludlow, from the Army Service Corps, who had come from a staff appointment in the Northern Command at York,[174] and the cashier was Ravenhill.[175] A valuable addition to the staff was made during mobilisation in the person of Lieutenant Colonel George Barrow, an Indian Army officer from the 35th Scinde Horse, 'a short genial little man'[176] who General Allenby had met in the corridors of the War Office. Lieutenant Colonel Barrow, was on leave from India when war was declared, and he immediately made his way to the War Office hoping to find an appointment with the BEF. His intention was to use the influence of the 'best two soldier-friends' he had Generals Wilson and Robertson. They both assured him a place could be found, and he was told it was likely to be an intelligence appointment, so was sent for instruction in cipher with Colonel Macdonogh. The following day he met General Allenby in one of the passages, a man he hardly knew, and who said to him 'I heard you were in England, I want you to come along with me.'[177] Since there was no existing appointment he could give him, he appointed him as his Intelligence Officer. Lieutenant Colonel Barrow 'was allowed to organise a small intelligence section.'[178] He referred to as the 'illegitimate child of an army organisation,'[179] and was even more *ad hoc* than the rest of his headquarters. The intelligence section consisted of Mr George Darrock,[180] an employee of the London & North Western Railway and a civil engineer and aviation pioneer. Lieutenant Thornhill was another Indian Army officer. A Dutchman and a Swede (Knut Otto Waldenstrom, a London businessman of Swedish extraction[181]) were selected for their

169 Ibid., pp. 118-119.
170 Gen. Sir George de Symons Barrow, *The Fire of Life*, (London: Hutchinson & Company Limited, 1942), p. 140.
171 Medal Index Cards reads, embarkation 13th August 1914.
172 Brig. Gen. Sir Archibald Home, *Diary of a World War 1 Cavalry Officer* (Tunbridge Wells: Costello, 1985). Dust jacket notes.
173 Marquess of Anglesey, *A History of the British Cavalry 1914-1919*, Vol. 7, p. 77.
174 Wavell, *Allenby*, p. 128.
175 Home, *Diary of a World War 1 Cavalry Officer*, p. 13.
176 Anglesey, *A History of the British Cavalry 1914-1919*, Vol. 7, p. 77.
177 Gen. Sir George de Symons Barrow, *The Fire of Life*, (London: Hutchinson, 1942), p.140.
178 Ibid., p. 141.
179 Ibid., p. 143.
180 George Richard Sutton Darrock (1880-1959) gained his flying certificate on 14th February 1911.
181 Special thanks to Dr J.M. Beach, Senior Lecturer in Twentieth Century History, Faculty of Education & Humanities, University of Northampton.

knowledge of foreign languages. There were also two police detectives with bicycles, and later two Englishmen Theodore Clarke[182] and Arthur Capel[183] with cars, who were subsequently added early in the retreat. [184] Arthur "Boy" Capel was 'a personal friend of Allenby.'[185] In the obituary of one of Arthur Capel's daughters, he was described as 'an intellectual, politician, tycoon, polo-player and the dashing lover and sponsor of the fashion designer Coco Chanel.'[186] Arthur Capel tragically died in a car crash in 1919 and it is said that it was while he was travelling to see Coco for a Christmas rendezvous. After his death, Coco began wearing black during her grieving process and she told a friend that the world would mourn with her which is where the *little black dress* (LBD) evolved from.[187] The two Englishmen were joined by a territorial officer Captain Bertrand Stewart[188] from the Queen's Own West Kent Yeomanry who had famously been arrested when he had volunteered to pose as a tourist and spy on German naval activities. He was caught in possession of a German code book and betrayed by a German double agent and was sentenced in January 1912 to three and a half years in jail[189] during which time 'he had acquired a lively hatred of the Germans.'[190] One might consider that the way in which the Cavalry Division was going to command itself and process intelligence pre-war had been given little or no consideration, and Lieutenant Colonel Barrow's small intelligence department was as *ad hoc* as it was colourful!

The small advance party from the Cavalry Division had consisted of just the GSO1, RQMG and the cashier. They arrived at about 1530, and Major Archibald Home wrote 'on the way only met a couple of torpedo boats, the first passed within 50 yards…we met surprisingly very little shipping…we made a triumphant entry into Le Havre itself…the men on the deck sang the *Marseillaise*, where they had learnt it heaven only knows…we made fast opposite the wharves of the German Hamburg-America line, now quite deserted, and the disembarkation began.'[191] However, not all went to plan as Major Home was informed that their 'car (a beautiful six cylinder Siddeley limousine) could not be sent on'[192] as there was a shortage of petrol. The horses were unloaded and sent to the supply depot for the night as they 'had suffered a good deal on the ship on account of the heat.'[193]

The following morning as the advance party of the Cavalry Division were on the train *en-route* to Maubeuge, the Commanding Officer of the 9th Lancers, at 1400 on Thursday, 13th held a dismounted parade in Tidworth to present the prizes of the *troop competition* and addressed his Regiment.

182 Medal Index Cards reads embarkation as 15th September 1914.
183 Medal Index Cards reads embarkation as 19th August 1914.
184 Barrow, *The Fire of Life*, p. 142.
185 TNA WO339/55790.
186 *The Daily Telegraph*, 4th October 2006.
187 *Arthur Capel: The Man Who Shaped Chanel* <https://www.menstylefashion.com/arthur-capel-the-man-who-shaped-chanel/> (Accessed 4th November 2018).
188 Medal Index Cards reads embarkation as 12th August 1914 – 1st class agent (Intelligence).
189 *Charles Emmerson, 1913: The World before the Great War (New York: Random House, 2013), p. 13.*
190 Ibid., p. 142.
191 Home, *Diary of a World War 1 Cavalry Officer*, p. 13.
192 Ibid., p. 13.
193 Ibid., p. 13.

The colonel made a splendid speech in which he recalled all the great deeds in the past which had been performed by the 9th; how in the mutiny the Regiment had carried out its duties and several officers obtained VCs, with such distinction that when it left India the viceroy gave orders that it should be saluted by 41 guns. This had never been done before and has never been done since. In Afghanistan, it had been greatly praised by Lord Roberts and in South Africa, it fought for two years with the greatest distinction and had received most complimentary messages from all its commanders, the one from Sir John French being particularly complimentary. He also reminded us Lieutenant Macdonald had on one occasion fought till every man of his troop and himself had been killed[194]. He reminded the Regiment we were now going forth to the war with the greatest traditions to uphold. Nothing could have been finer than his speech or could possibly have appealed more to the officers and men. I was very sorry Rivy did not hear it.[195]

9th Lancer's, Tidworth c. 1914.
(Author's Collection)

The orders for the *AOK 1* to cross into Belgium were issued the following day. The march of the *AOK 1* to its position of deployment abreast of Liège by the roads mentioned in the deployment orders will begin at once and the *IX AK* will still be under the orders of the commander of the *AOK*

194 The Hon. Archibald Ronald Armadale Macdonald, killed in action Eelenburg, South Africa, 17th April 1901.
195 Grenfell, Grenfell Family Papers (within Lyttelton Family Papers), 13th August 1914, p. 5.

*2*. On the arrival of the *AOK 1* will clear its front.'[196] Detailed orders were given to ensure the movement of over 200,000 troops with all their baggage through the defile formed by a town only 2,000 yards wide:

> The march through the town will, so far as can be foreseen, take place by three roads. The commandant of Aix-la-Chapelle will mark the line of these roads through the town, avoiding any mention of what corps are to use them, and will block the side roads; he will send a sketch of the road sections allotted to each of the corps as soon as the order for the advance is given. He will also ensure that the march through the town proceeds smoothly and without interruption, and that the troops use no other roads than those allotted to them. The troops themselves will be ordered to carry out any instructions that he may give; any disorder is to be I immediately suppressed with the utmost rigour. The well-ordered execution of the march through Aix-la-Chapelle is a preliminary essential for the success of the movement of the army across the Meuse, which will take place immediately afterwards.[197]

The *AOK 1* march formations had consisted of a deep column of two corps on each of the three roads, which did not greatly diverge between there and the Meuse, north of Liège, and beyond. Early in the morning *Infanterie Regiment 66* crossed the border into Belgium and immediately noticed the change. As they entered the villages, they felt deserted and either the inhabitants had fled or were in hiding. They noticed that the troops before them had had to remove the roadblocks made from trees across the road. The regiment marched in oppressive heat until, 1600, when it reached Dahlem. It quartered there and in the surrounding area. On their arrival, they conducted a search of the local houses which revealed weapons.[198] The *friendly passage* that the Germans had requested and had been denied was now manifesting itself and the Belgian newspaper *Bugerwelzyn* on the 14th August reported that as the German troops had approached the outskirts of Liège at the village of Herstal 'men, women and children were described as having fought the Germans in an action which the newspaper found praiseworthy.'[199] This would now inevitably slow down the German advance and put von Schlieffen's proposed time line for reaching Paris in jeopardy.

As the Germans were moving through Belgium, there was a steady stream of reports making their way back to England, and these notes were distributed amongst the Commanding Officers. On 13th August, the 15th Infantry Brigade issued eight bullet points to the Cheshires that had been picked up during the engagements around Liège.

> Masses of men can be swept away by steady fire of much smaller numbers. Keep cool don't lose their heads and don't waste ammunition. When on the move do not crowd together. Artillery, while alarming, will do little harm unless the men are crowding. Germans apparently hate cold steel, if therefore we get the chance of using the bayonet, go in with real vigour and we are bound to win. Army officers should be picked off. German soldiers have remarkably little power of initiative and lose their heads when their officers have

196 Kluck, *The March on Paris and The Battle of The Marne, 1914*, p. 12.
197 Ibid., p. 13.
198 Korfes, *The German 66th Regiment in the First World War*, p. 24.
199 Zuber, *The Mons Myth: A Reassessment of the Battle,* (Stroud: History Press, 2010), p. 88.

> fallen. The main principle rubbed into them being to advance in masses and obey their officers. Such large numbers will be difficult to feed, hence every opportunity should be taken of shooting or capturing their convoys. Especially impress on all ranks that the 5th Infantry Division never surrender, we fight to the finish, everyone to the last man.[200]

General Haig and the rest of his staff, having established their HQ in the Dolphin Hotel finally arrived along with the staff of I Corps and General Grierson. Colonel Eugen 'Micky' Ryan, the I Corps Chief Medical Officer, wrote to his wife 'here is the last for some time from the shores of old England. Sir Douglas and all his crowd are here, and we start this evening. All full of courage and hope. Personally, I am feeling splendid…this place is full of soldiers one day and practically empty the next. Nearly all the Aldershot troops have gone through…'[201]

Cheshire Regimental officers c. 1913. (Cheshire Regiment Museum)

The following morning for the 9th Lancers, Friday 14th August was their last day in barracks. In the morning 'the whole of the 2nd Cavalry Brigade…paraded in marching order for inspection by the Brigade Commander…he wound up the inspection by ordering the Brigade to execute

200 NWHRM: 12/8.
201 Eugene Ryan, *Haig's Medical Officer, The Papers of Colonel Eugene 'Micky Ryan* (Barnsley: Pen & Sword, 2013), p. 13.

a *charge* in line with drawn swords.'[202] Captain Archie Wright of the 4th Dragoon Guards wrote after the *charge* that 'the regiments presented a fine appearance and De Lisle told us that he never wanted to command a more efficient or highly trained brigade. The reservists had all flocked to the colours on the announcement of war with Germany and the esprit of the whole army is extraordinarily good.'[203] After the inspection there were no other parades, so Captain Grenfell spent it 'in making final preparations. While I attended to my squadron, Rivy went up to the stables. Rivy and I dined alone, and Porter helped us to get the dinner. In the evening, we finished off our papers and were ready to march next morning.'[204] The strain of waiting to know if the Expeditionary Force would really be sent had been very great, but now that the certainty had come, a spirit of "real but quiet enthusiasm" as Captain Grenfell expressed it, 'pervaded all ranks. All had toiled unceasingly to fit the Regiment for this supreme moment, and the greatest confidence was felt in its leaders and in its power to uphold its traditions.'[205] Private (Shoeing Smith) Jack Friend concluded his letter to his mother:

> Dearest mother I pray and hope by the time I come back dear old dad will be himself again and working. I hope Alf found him much better when he saw him. Well darling mother do not think too much about it just think of the day I return wearing a medal for fighting for King and country. Roll on when it's over. Dear mother I must close now I will write again before Sunday if possible. Good-bye for the time being with love to all.[206]

While the 9th Lancers were preparing to leave, Field Marshal French and his two Corps Commanders were already on their way. At 1400, the Field Marshal had departed from Charing Cross by special train for Dover, and embarked on the *Sentinel*, sailing just before 1600. They landed in Boulogne at approximately 1730, where he was met by the governor, commandant and port officials. He took the opportunity to visit the rest camps and found the 'officers and men looked fit and well and full of enthusiasm and cheer.'[207] Later that evening at 1930, he left for Amiens to meet the commander of the lines of communications and Brigadier Sir David Henderson who was also commanding the aviation. The two Corps Commanders Generals Douglas Haig and Grierson had also departed Southampton that day, sailing on the *Combrie Castle* for Le Havre. The ship was the same vessel which had taken the advance party of the Cavalry Division over the day before. The vessel was not fitted with passenger accommodation, so the ships officers gave up their cabins to the generals and their chiefs of staff, with the rest of the staff bivouacking on deck.[208] The ship was also unable

202 John M. Brereton, *A History of the 4th and 7th Royal Dragoon Guards and Their Predecessors 1685-1980* (Catterick, Published by the Regiment, 1982), p. 306.
203 Capt. A. Wright Diary, RDG Museum, August 1914, p.1.
204 Capt. F.O. Grenfell, Grenfell Family Papers (within Lyttelton Family Papers), 14th August 1914, p. 5.
205 Anon., 9th Lancers War Diary, 14th August 1914, p. 2.
206 Shoe Smith J. Friend Letter to Mother, Property of 9/12L.
207 Field Marsh Viscount French of Ypres, *1914,* p. 32.
208 Brig. Gen. John Charteris, *Field Marshal Earl Haig,* p. 83.

to provide any food for the 13 hour crossing so some officers had hastily collected a picnic in Southampton. General Haig was more fortunate as Lady Haig 'with practical forethought had provided him with a well-stocked luncheon basket.'[209]Colonel Ryan quantified the overcrowding in a letter to his wife Sadie. 'They packed over 2000 troops and 100 officers and 43 nursing sisters on board a ship which accommodates five officers, and 130 at other times…had to sleep on deck, down came the rain at about 2400. I stuck it for an hour but was drowned out so I upped and scouted and got what shelter I could.'[210] General Haig, unlike most, did not get wet but wrote in his diary about the unsuitability of the vessel, 'I understand that it was a mistake our being put on board such a small uncomfortable steamer. The one intended for us had been delayed in the fog.'[211] As they left, Great Britain was truly going to war: its commander and his chief of staff was English, its two Corps Commanders (Haig and Grierson) were born in Scotland, and the Sub-Chief of Staff (Wilson) was born in Ireland.

General Wilson, who had been the Director of Military Operations (DMO) on the outbreak of war, was initially offered the appointment of Brigadier General of Operations but as he was already a Major General he negotiated that the appointment should be called Sub-Chief of Staff.[212] In the preceding decades none of them could have realised that they would go to war taking their own personal baggage regarding their previous dealings with each other with them. Field Marshal French had borrowed a large sum of money from General Haig (who was from the Haig whisky family and very wealthy) and had never repaid it. General Smith-Dorrien (an infantryman) had taken over from General French (a cavalryman) as GOC Aldershot and had reversed some of the changes he had made and at the same time 'had criticised the cavalry for their indifferent musketry,'[213] which along with differences regarding cavalry training resulted with them being no longer on speaking-terms. Field Marshal French had had General Grierson removed from post as his COS in 1913 and replaced him with General Murray. General Haig also did not have a high opinion of Field Marshal French and told the King: "I had great doubts however, whether his temper was sufficiently even or his military knowledge sufficiently thorough to enable him to discharge properly the very difficult duties which will devolve upon him. In my own heard I know that French is quite unfit for this great command in time of crisis." It was not an ideal start!

That night in Belfast, the Norfolk Regiment received their orders to embark the following day. Private Hurrell, of the band, made his final preparations and 'handed in his instrument together with red tunic and all spare gear.'[214] However he sent his 'bicycle and private box to some friends in Belfast.'[215] In the evening, lots of 'girlfriends came to the barracks to say goodbye. Of course, we all expected to be back with them again in a few weeks, thus making the parting easier. The scenes around the barracks reminded one of Hyde Park in summer. I shall never forget that day and night. Sleep was entirely out of the question.'[216] The rest of 15th Infantry Brigade,

209 Ibid., p. 83.
210 Ryan, *Haig's Medical Officer*, p. 14.
211 Ibid., p 14.
212 Keith Jeffery, *Field Marshal Sir Henry Wilson: A Political Soldier*, (Oxford, Oxford University Press, 2006), pp. 132-133.
213 Edward Owen, *1914 Glory Departing*, (London: Buchan & Enright, 1986), p. 32.
214 Pte R. Hurrell, Log of Round the World Cruise, p. 4.
215 Ibid., p. 4.
216 Ibid., p. 4.

General Horace Smith-Dorien.
(Author's Collection)

Cheshire Regiment departing Londonderry.
(Cheshire Regiment Museum)

commanded by Brigadier Gleichen, were *en-route* for Belfast docks. The Cheshire and Bedford Regiments had left their barracks early in the morning from Londonderry and Mullingar by train and the Dorsets and Cheshires were both already garrisoned in Belfast.

The whole process of mobilisation had gone well in all respects and the brigade had been practically ready since the 9th August, just waiting on some 'machine guns or two and some harnesses which were late arriving from Dublin.'[217] The process of mobilisation had been practised as usual in the early summer. The Brigade got its initial order to embark on the 8th August with the detailed instructions arriving on the 11th informing them they were to leave Belfast on the 14th August. When the Brigade arrived in Belfast the brigade was to embark on two ships; the *SS Massilia* of the Anchor Line and the *SS Oronsa*. The battalions and the Brigade Headquarters were divided between the two ships. The Brigade Headquarters, the Dorsets and half the Norfolks were on the *SS Massilia* and the Cheshires and the other half of the Norfolks and the Bedfords were on the *SS Oronsa*. The *SS Massilia* had been 'provisioned for India so while aboard the men were fed like fighting cocks.'[218] By the time the Brigade was ready to embark there was 127 officers and 3,958 men, 258 horses and 74 vehicles. The battalions had grown 'to unheard of sizes.'[219] Just as they were about to leave a Captain's wife 'unclasped a bracelet from her wrist, and fastened it upon the wrist of her husband.'[220]

In Belfast, Private Robert Sheldrake and the Norfolk Regiment had woken up at approximately 0400 and were to march to the docks at 0600.[221] The Regiment was ready to depart except for those who would remain behind consisting of a 'few medically unfit and drummer and tailor boys, including the bandmaster.'[222] The battalion's numbers had swelled to 1,021 officers and men and they had marched down to the York Dock in two parties. The first arrived at 0700 and the second at 0745. In addition to the men, the battalion took 58 horses, five wheeled vehicles, three, four wheeled limbers (which included a signal limber), nine carts and 12 bicycles. The Cheshire Regiment had been a little more lenient with the rules. 'Even the youngest drummer boys pleaded hard to accompany their older comrades to the front, but only two: W.F. Woods and Andrews were allowed.'[223] The main issue had been Woods' age as he 'was only 17 years of age, the medical officer told him he was too young to go, but the youth pleaded so hard, even threatening to desert from the Regiment unless allowed to go that the doctor gave way, saying "you are a plucky lad, you shall go."[224] Lieutenant Colonel Colin Ballard gave the word of command "the battalion will move off in columns of fours from the right, A Company leading". The order of march was alphabetical 'A, B, C, D and transport in the rear and the music was provided by the bugle, fife and drum band. Once they were on the march 'the word came from the front to march at ease. We put our rifle in any position to suit one's convenience, (see picture

217 Brig. E. Gleichen, *Infantry Brigade 1914, The Diary of a Commander of the 15th Infantry Brigade, 5th Division, British Army, During the Retreat from Mons,* (Driffield: Leonaur, 2007), p. 9.
218 Frank Simpson, *Cheshire Regiment the First Battalion at Mons and the Miniature Colour. Cheshire Regiment the First Battalion at Mons and the Miniature Colour* (London: W.H. Evans, Sons & Co, 1929). p. 10.
219 Gleichen, *Infantry Brigade 1914,* p. 9.
220 *Belfast News Letter*, 4th September 1914.
221 Pte R. Sheldrake diary, p. 7.
222 Pte R. Hurrell, Log of Round the World Cruise, p. 5.
223 Frank Simpson, *Cheshire Regiment the First Battalion at Mons and the Miniature Colour*, p. 13.
224 Ibid., p. 13.

on page 74) then we could talk, sing or do as we please except smoke or get out of step.'[225] Private Hurrell struck up a conversation with a man next to him who was an elderly man who had nearly finished his 12 years' service. He thought this was hard luck as he told him he had a nice comfortable job on the railway at Diss and was very, very sorry to leave his wife and four children behind and he felt certain in his own mind 'he'd never see them again.'[226] As they marched to the docks one lady came up and gave Private Hurrell a small bottle of best brandy and she said in broad Irish, "Here boy, take this perhaps you'll need it later on."'[227] After waiting several hours whilst the transport baggage was put on board, the Norfolks 'finally embarked at 1430 on the *Massilia* of Glasgow. There were no special quarters allotted and they put their gear wherever they could. 'After all were aboard and some more weeping and farewells with those leaving their wives and sweethearts in Ireland.'[228] Private Reginald Hurrell was glad there was no one to see him off, 'some women burst through the ranks clinging to their respective husbands and sweethearts. They had even brought their own children, which didn't improve the embarrassing situation. Personally, I felt thankful that no one was present who belonged to me. It was indeed sufficiently painful.'[229]

Lieutenant Colonel Colin Ballard. (Norfolk Regiment)

225 Pte R. Hurrell, Log of Round the World Cruise, p. 6.
226 Ibid., p. 6.
227 Ibid., p. 6.
228 Ibid., p. 6.
229 Ibid., p. 7.

This was not the case for all those soldiers and their loved ones who were parting, C Squadron of the 12th Lancers who were posted away from the Regiment at the Equitation Centre at Weedon in Northamptonshire had a double move as they first had to rejoin the main body of the Regiment in Norwich. The *Northampton Mercury* reported:

> One soldier's sweetheart, determined to give her boy a last kiss, and defying the warning shouts of the railway officials as a fast train was approaching, dash across to the opposite side to where her boy was standing, threw her arms around his neck and gave him a smacking kiss. Then she blushingly returned to her original position amid the sympathetic cheers of both soldiers and spectators. The young soldier, not at all embarrassed, joined his comrades, who all looked as if they envied his luck.[230]

Private Hurrell's ship started to move at 1730, 'and what a noise, cheers, shouting. As soon as we had left the dock side things became much quieter, except for ships whistles blowing.'[231] As the ship left, Private Hurrell climbed 'into one of the ships lifeboats in order to get a good view of all that was going on. On our way up the river we passed the great ship yards of Harland & Wolff, where the largest ship in the world was being built called the *Britannic* for the White Star Line.'[232] As they passed, the 'men working on board cheered…it was truly a wonderful sight to see men perched on top of her huge funnels. They just looked like flies.'[233] As they went up the 'Belfast Lough we could just see little Holywood with a few of its inhabitants standing on the shore waving goodbye. An hour afterwards we were completely out of sight.'[234] On the *SS Massilia* an officer of the Cheshires wrote that 'we have been awfully lucky in getting this boat, as she was loaded with three months provisions for a voyage to India when she was commandeered by the government and consequently we have been having first-class food provided by the company free, whereas the other three or four boats have had to fend for themselves.'[235] He was aware that 'there's been something exciting in the North Sea during the last week for certain, [*HMS Amphion* incident] but no information, or details are to hand…we have passed, and been called up, by several warships. This morning a French cruiser, destroyer, and three submarines came and examined us.'[236] By the time they had rounded the 'Lizard and Land's End shortly before sunset on 15th August the *SS Massilia* found herself in a procession of nine ships conveying troops. 'On the starboard side as they sailed towards the Scilly Islands, a solitary British cruiser beat up and down keeping silent watch and guard. She signalled the convoy and the sailors waved their arms; and as the line of crowded troopships passed by, each, in turn, dipped her ensign.'[237] Amongst the ships sailing that day was also the *Minneapolis* with General Allenby and the rest of his staff. The General's war had not gotten off to a good start when his best set of dentures was lost in the post. He wrote a letter to his wife Adelaide telling

230 *Northampton Mercury*, 7th August 1914.
231 Pte R. Hurrell, Log of Round the World Cruise, p. 6.
232 Ibid., p. 8.
233 Ibid., p. 8.
234 Ibid., p. 8.
235 Simpson, *Cheshire Regiment the First Battalion at Mons and the Miniature Colour*, p. 13.
236 Ibid., pp. 13-14.
237 Simpson, *Cheshire Regiment the First Battalion at Mons and the Miniature Colour*, p. 14.

her to claim compensation from the Post Office. After telling her about his dentures he wrote, 'I shall write when I can; but henceforth my letters will, as you know, will probably be few and scrappy. It is a lovely calm day, and the Solent is full of big steam yachts. God bless you, my dear love, and Michael, too.'[238] Sadly Michael, his only son joined the Royal Horse Artillery and was to be killed in action in 1917, at the age of 19, having already won the Military Cross.[239]

At the Curragh, Lieutenant Geoffrey Pollard from 119th Battery RFA wrote home to say that he had paid all his bills with the exception of two small ones, which he was unable to get to. He also told his parents what he wished to be done with his small belongings, and asked them earnestly "that if he died in any honourable way that no one who cared for him should be put on mourning" and thanked his mother and father 'for helping him to go off to war, as I do with a light heart.' The letter was written during a thunderstorm and his immediate worry was that the horses might stampede.'[240] The following day he would march to Dublin and then on to Le Havre.

Lieutenant Geoffrey Pollard. (*The Bond of Sacrifice*, Vol. I)

Lieutenant Spears, having left Paris, arrived at Rethel, the French *GQG*. He had received orders that he would be 'working under the direct orders of the head of the British intelligence, Colonel

238 Gardner, *Allenby*, p 67.
239 Lieutenant Horace Michael Hynman Allenby, MC, killed in action 29th July 1917 age 19.
240 Alfred Pollard, *Two Brothers: Accounts Rendered* (London: Sidgwick and Jackson, 1917), pp. 20-21.

George Macdonogh,'[241] and in 'my first few days at Rethel my duties were almost exclusively concerned with the organisation of our intelligence in this area.'[242] Their initial task was to try and build up a picture of the German advance by 'attempting to lay a net along the probable line of a German advance, a net of eyes and ears to watch and listen for the enemy.'[243] This included a number of intelligence officer in Belgium where 'individuals had to be found who would be prepared for patriotic or other reasons to run the great risks involved in collecting information.'[244] This information proved invaluable 'since besides air reports we had practically nothing else, for the French cavalry, in spite of the exhausting marches it was called upon to carry out, brought in little or no information of value.'[245] However, soon Lieutenant Spear's role would change 'I soon found that a great deal of work not connected with duties...was expected of me. Our own people kept asking me questions concerning the plans and intentions of the French...Colonel William Bowes from the operations section was more especially charged with the duty of keeping in touch with the Fifth Army...from August 20th onwards [he only] occasionally came over from GHQ.'[246] As a result he 'had to devote more and more attention to operations work...the fact that I was the only British officer permanently attached to the Fifth Army, and the pressure of entirely unforeseen events, forced me to assume the role of a liaison officer dealing with operations.'[247] Meanwhile, Major Home, having been separated from his car at Le Havre, finally arrived by train in Maubeuge at 0900 after the overnight journey. It was here that he met the French officers to be attached to the Cavalry Division, and he thought 'them very kind and did everything for our comfort.' After lunch at 1200 they went off to visit the Division's billeting area. On his journey he noticed 'there are no men in France now, the population is women and children. Every road, bridge and railway is guarded by the old men, day and night, they shoot on sight unless the motor stops at once. The harvest lies on the ground, the men are at war.'[248]

241 Spears, *Liaison 1914,* p. 44.
242 Ibid., p. 44.
243 Ibid.
244 Ibid.
245 Spears, *Liaison 1914,* p. 45.
246 Ibid., p. 45.
247 Ibid.
248 Home, *Diary of a World War 1 Cavalry Officer,* pp. 13-16.

# 3

# Loading and Embarkation

*We leave very quietly as if marching on manoeuvres, but a more magnificent regiment never moved out of barracks for war. Everyone is full of enthusiasm.*

Captain F.O. Grenfell

On Saturday, 15th August, which turned out to be a drizzly morning, the 9th Lancers started the process of embarkation under the upmost secrecy and with incredible organisation. This was in stark contrast to the departure of the German units in Magdeburg a week earlier. The Regiment's was to *trek* from Tidworth, via Amesbury, to Southampton. The plan was to load the Regiment in two parties with the main party sailing on the 15th August consisting of 30 officers (five attached), 588 other ranks and 613 horses. Before leaving, the Regiment had received significant reinforcements from the Reserve Regiment of Cavalry and soldiers from its sister regiment of the 21st Lancers, which had increased its numbers to its wartime establishment from the 19 officers and 404 it paraded in August 1912 for the Army Manoeuvres. On the 15th, the Regiment moved along with the Brigade Headquarters and entrained on four trains at Amesbury, *en-route* for Southampton which was reached about 1500. The headquarters 2nd Cavalry Brigade, headquarters 9th Lancers, A and B Squadrons, embarked on SS *Welshman* and C Squadron, with others troops of the brigade, were on the SS *Armenian*.'[1] Corporal Harry Easton had left the Regiment in Canterbury and been mobilised while working for the police in Maidenhead. He had rejoined the Lancers in Tidworth. When he boarded the SS *Welshman*, he thought the name was highly appropriate 'with the Regiment with a march past of the *Men of Harlech*.'[2] The second party was scheduled to follow them six days later on the 21st August when a further two officers and 49 men were to follow on.[3] Before the Regiment had departed Tidworth, five officers had been detached from the Regiment to undertake staff appointments

1 TNA WO 95/1113/2: *War Diary 9th Lancers*, 15th August 1914.
2 Cpl. H. Easton Diary, p. 37.
3 Sheppard, *The Ninth Queen's Royal Lancers 1715-1936*, p. 234.

with the BEF,[4] and of those officers who went to war with the Regiment there were four pairs of brothers, the: Grenfells, Reynolds, Harveys and the Taylor-Whiteheads.[5] Captain Francis Grenfell and his squadron were in the first party to leave Tidworth. He 'got up at 0500, wrote a few letters and made final arrangements for things to be left behind, and for servants.'[6] One of the letters Francis wrote was to his uncle and guardian, Lord Grenfell, and he told him of both his, Rivy's and the Regiment's enthusiasm to which they unassumingly and silently went to war. 'We leave very quietly as if marching on manoeuvres, but a more magnificent regiment never moved out of barracks for war. Everyone is full of enthusiasm. Rivy goes with me and it is a great thing having him…I have had the happiest possible life and have always been working for war and have now got into the biggest [war] in the prime of life for a soldier.'[7]

C Squadron SNCOs on 16th August 1914 aboard the SS *Welshman*: Hollaway, West, Swaine, Gummerson, Anelay, Curtis, Praeger, Coombes, Ambrose, Pickering, Timms and Parker. (9/12L Museum)

4 Major H.M. Durrant, Major F.W.L.S.H. Cavendish, Captain L.W. de V Sadler-Jackson, Lieutenant G.H. Phipps-Hornby and L.W. Diggle.
5 Sheppard, *The Ninth Queen's Royal Lancers 1715-1936*, p. 379.
6 Grenfell, Grenfell Family Papers (within Lyttelton Family Papers), 15th August 1914, p. 5.
7 Buchan, *Francis and Riversdale Grenfell*, pp. 188-189.

Before they left 'Rivy went up to the stables early to see if everything was all right. They had breakfast at 0900 and parade at 1000. Everything was a 'rush and our pack saddles did not quite fit. A photographer came up to photograph us both standing in the door way of Tidworth Barracks just as we were about to start.'[8] Francis paraded his squadron and 'marched very quietly in drizzling rain out of the barracks at 1015 and left Rivy behind with our servants and pack saddles as they were not quite ready.'[9] The Regiment marched over the downs to Bulford, and halted at the artillery barracks where they fed and watered the horses. It was here that Rivy caught up with Francis and they marched together to Amesbury. At Amesbury they loaded the horses onto the trains. 'The troop leaders arranged to entrain the horses. This was carried out satisfactorily and took about 40 minutes. The train left at 1350 and we arrived at Southampton about 1600. Rivy and I travelled in one compartment with Captain [Brereton] Nash-Wortham and wrote letters on the way.'[10] The detail and secrecy of the Regimental move is best captured by Captain Lucas-Tooth:

Francis and Rivy Grenfell, Tidworth Officers' Mess 15th August 1914. (9/12L Museum)

> It would have been hard to find a more finely mounted body of men than the 9th Lancers… No one knew of the Regiment's departure although the last squadron did not leave till 1000

8 Grenfell, *Grenfell Family Papers (within Lyttelton Family Papers)*, 15th August 1914, p. 5.
9 Ibid., 15th August 1914, p. 6.
10 Ibid., 15th August 1914, p. 6.

in the morning. No crowds were there to cheer, no waving of farewell. All good byes had been said in quarters. The march over the downs took the Regiment to Amesbury, where it entrained. There was no one at all at the station, and when later on I went down into the town to get some drinks for the officers to have with their lunch in the train, nobody in the town had any idea that a regiment was leaving, and tried to pump me as to which regiment it was. The Regiment was entrained squadron by squadron, the men were in tearing spirits, and the horse's fresh and looking simply magnificent. It was the first time I had seen many of the men since Potchefstroom days, and it made saying "Good bye" even more poignant having to greet the men and talk with them of the three and a half years we had spent in South Africa and saying "God-speed" all in the same breath. Nobody knew where they were going to not even the engine driver or the transport officer. The latter was very kind and did his best to try and find out for me. Having eventually seen the train going out, everybody was singing and cheering.[11]

Captain Brereton Nash-Wortham. (9/12L Museum)

Despite all the secrecy of the move, Mrs Wood, turned up with an 'enormous luncheon hamper which incidentally lasted about three days.'[12] This was shared amongst the A Squadron officers 'Captain Lucas-Tooth, Captain Wood, myself [Peek], Lennox Harvey, Marden, Bunny Taylor-Whitehead, and Douglas Harvey.'[13] Captain Lucas-Tooth had arrived at Southampton and was surprised to find nobody was expecting them and Lieutenant Basil Marden of A Squadron

11 Anon., 9th Lancers War Diary, 15th August 1914, p. 3.
12 Capt. R.G. Peek diary, 15th August 1914.
13 Ibid., 15th August 1914.

wrote that they had to 'amuse ourselves as best as we can on the dock until the flowing morning. Peter, who is the Regimental Transport Officer (RTO) at Southampton, spends the afternoon with me on the dock, which we cannot leave as the boat may arrive at any moment. I have some dinner at an eating house in the town and settle down to sleep on the iron stairs of the dock shed.'[14]The train journey went well and took about 13 hours, once the Regiment was at Southampton, they 'detrained in one of the docks. All was carried out very smoothly, a good deal of hanging about however took place as a sheep and cattle boat had arrived eight hours late and was not properly fitted for horse accommodation. '[15] For some soldiers, like Corporal Percy Snelling of the 12th Lancers, this was the first time they had ever seen the sea.[16]

Captain Roger Peek.
(9/12L Museum)

The adaptation of both ships for the carriage of horses had been hastily carried out. In fact, it was only by continuous work throughout the night that the carpenters just kept ahead of the loading with the erection of fittings.[17] When it came to rationing, there were also some issues. 'There was ample forage and water for all the horses, but some shortage of rations for the personnel,[18] so while they were waiting, during the afternoon Rivy and Francis, Frank Crossley,

14 Lt B.J.N. Marden diary, 15th August 1914.
15 Grenfell, Grenfell Family Papers (within Lyttelton Family Papers), 15th August 1914, p. 6.
16 Ascoli, *The Mons Star*, p. 32.
17 *The Delhi Spearman,* 9th March 1928 p. 7.
18 Sheppard, *The Ninth Queen's Royal Lancers 1715-1936*, p. 234.

Ian Straker, Charlie Garstin, and Henry Mather-Jackson went and had tea at a small public house in Southampton.[19]

This was about at the same time Field Marshal French had arrived in Paris, having left Amiens in the morning. When he arrived, he experienced large crowds which had assembled outside the British embassy and where they were 'received with tremendous greetings by the people…their welcome was cordial and extreme.'[20] He dined at the embassy where he was joined by the British Ambassador, the French President, the Prime Minister and the Minister of War. The situation was fully discussed and he 'was much impressed by the optimistic spirit of the President.'[21] The President had *playfully* discussed the possibility of there being 'another battle being fought by the British on the old field of Waterloo.'[22]

On arrival of the 9th Lancers in Southampton, Lance Corporal William Hunt of 2nd Troop C Squadron was *warned-off* for fatigues which sounded 'nice and comforting after our railway journey. This fatigue, by the way, was packing horses and I was on from 1600 to 2300. Then I left in the time worn fashion and regaled myself with tea and buns.'[23] The process of loading the horses was long and laborious as all the horses had to be *slung* on board, which caused much delay. Captain Grenfell's squadron 'did not start shipping their horses till about 2300 at night which lasted till about 0300.'[24] While all this was going on 'Rivy went on board the cattle boat and wisely secured himself a berth in the Purser's cabin, and also arranged for a berth'[25] for Francis with the chief officer.

While the 9th Lancers were sorting themselves out, the Norfolk Regiment were still at sea having left Belfast the day before, 'We were still steaming round the Irish Channel near Land's End. It was a nice journey, not too rough at all, so most of us enjoyed it very much. We spent most of the day singing, cleaning up, there was a letter from the King read out to us, wishing us good luck telling us to look after ourselves and so on.'[26] After the message had been read out 'Lord Kitchener's message was given out to us which was little slips of paper.'[27] The night spent on board had not been a comfortable one as "we didn't get much sleep in the night owing to a good strong wind which was coming from the south being rather draughty on deck." When they woke in the morning, they 'passed an English cruiser who came very close to us no doubt making sure who we really were. It was quite easy to see England, the Needles was quite plain.'[28]

On the day the 9th Lancers had moved from Tidworth to Southampton and the Norfolks were at sea, *Infanterie Regiment 66* had crossed the Meuse at Argenteau on a pontoon bridge built by *Pioneer Battalion 4*. They could see the iron bridge that had been destroyed by the Belgians sticking up out of the water. The crossing over the pontoon bridge went without incident. As they crossed, they could still hear the fire from the isolated forts at Liège that were still holding out. That evening, the Regiment reached Millen and Genoeis-Eldern where the troops were

19 Grenfell, Grenfell Family Papers (within Lyttelton Family Papers), 15th August 1914, p. 6.
20 Field Marshal Viscount French of Ypres, *1914* (London: Constable, 1919), p. 33.
21 Ibid., p. 33.
22 Ibid., p. 33.
23 LCpl W. Hunt diary, p. 1.
24 Grenfell, Grenfell Family Papers (within Lyttelton Family Papers), 15th August 1914, p. 6.
25 Ibid., 15th August 1914, p. 6.
26 Pte R. Hurrell Notebook, p. 7.
27 Ibid., p. 7.
28 Pte R. Hurrell Notebook, p. 8.

fed from the 'mobile field kitchens: with meat, vegetables and potatoes requisitioned from the surrounding area. There was seldom any bread.'[29] That evening Field Marshal French dined in the Paris Ritz with Lieutenant Colonel Brinsley Fitzgerald, his private secretary, and they observed how the French capital 'had put on the sombre garb of war. The buoyant, optimistic nature of the French people was apparent in the few we met; but there was no bombastic over-confident tone in the conversation around us, only a quiet grim determination which fully appreciated the tremendous difficulties and gigantic issues at stake.'[30]

29 Korfes, *The German 66th Regiment in the First World War*, p. 24.
30 Viscount French of Ypres, *1914*, p. 34.

# 4

# Crossing the Channel

*Slept on deck. We spend a lot of time below, looking after the horses. One could cut the atmosphere with a knife. Smooth crossing.*

Lieutenant B.J.N. Marden

The 16th August for the BEF would be the penultimate day of embarking and disembarking as it was intended that this should be complete by the 17th August. Each regiment had departed under different circumstances but had encountered the same enthusiastic and optimistic crowds. When each of them arrived at the base camps they would find the bell tents had already been erected by the *flying columns*. The German armies advance was crossing the internal border in Belgium between Flanders and Wallonia and they too would see a difference in their reception. Liège, which had staunchly held out, was on the verge of falling, and the German battalions which had been on the march adjusted their manning to take into account the limitations of some of the reserve soldiers and the necessity to now guard the valuable captured Belgian railways. The fact that the city had fallen did not mean the resistance had stopped and a local newspaper carried a story regarding the attacks on the German headquarters of the Liège garrison and that 'from a neighbouring apartment building civilians armed with pistols fired on the German soldiers.'[1] Above all it was a Sunday, for the advancing Germans it was the opportunity to have their first mass away from home, for the BEF, the Sabbath seemed to go unnoticed. In anticipation of the arrival of the Cavalry Brigades, the Cavalry Division issued the 'GS instruction for moves to billets.'[2]

After the loading of the 9th Lancers horses on the SS *Armenian* it sailed at about 0400 and the SS *Welshman* about an hour later. After a smooth and uneventful crossing, they arrived at Boulogne about 12 hours later in the early evening. Lieutenant Marden was not impressed with the troopship and feelings below deck were tense. 'We embarked at 0400 on the *Welshman*, very bad horse accommodation, merely a converted cattle boat. Slept on deck. We spend a lot

1 Zuber, *The Mons Myth*, p 88.
2 Home, *Diary of a World War 1 Cavalry Officer*, p .16.

Lieutenant Frederick de Vere Bruce Allfrey. (Author's Collection)

of time below, looking after the horses. One could cut the atmosphere with a knife. Smooth crossing.'[3] Marden's fellow squadron officers found somewhere to sleep on board but were equally uncomplimentary. 'Lucas, Wood and self, slept in a very curious little cabin. The *Welshman* was a filthy cattle boat, and this was the painter's store I should think.'[4] Francis and Rivy 'spent most of the day in the Purser's cabin reading up about Belgium and a few of my notes. I assisted him but also had to attend to my duties of looking after the men and horses.'[5] Lieutenant Frederick de Vere Bruce Allfrey[6], the Machine Gun Officer was slightly more complimentary of the *Welshman*. His initial observation was a "dirty tramp steamer" and having sailed on it he said it was 'a good sea-boat.'[7] Lance Corporal Hunt, who was sailing aboard the *Armenian*, also recorded a good crossing and the fact that aboard his transport the Commanding Officer had read out the message from King George V. 'We sailed at 0400 on Sunday morning. Very calm crossing, had church parade and the Colonel read out the King's farewell message.'[8]

> You are leaving home to fight for the safety and honour of my Empire. Belgium, whose country we are pledged to defend, has been attacked and France is about to be invaded

3 Lt B.J.N. Marden diary, 16th August 1914.
4 Capt R.G. Peek diary, 16th August 1914.
5 Grenfell, Grenfell Family Papers (within Lyttelton Family Papers), 16th August 1914, pp. 6-7.
6 Killed in action 7-9-1914, buried in Frétoy, Seine-et-Marne.
7 Lt F. de V.B. Allfrey diary, 16th August 1914.
8 LCpl W Hunt, *Diary of Lance Corporal William Hunt MM*, p. 1.

> by the same powerful foe. I have implicit confidence in you my soldiers. Duty is your watchword, and I know your duty will be nobly done. I shall follow your every movement with deepest interest and mark with eager satisfaction your daily progress, indeed your welfare will never be absent from my thoughts. I pray God to bless you and guard you and bring you back victorious.

The 4th Dragoon Guards were on the *Ivini Gredia.* They were woken by Lieutenant Colonel Mullens at 0330 who had found their destination was to be Boulogne. The saddles were put on and decks washed down. They disembarked at 0700 where they were joined by four French officers and NCOs. Their many coloured uniforms 'afforded much interest and amusement to the men.'[9] At 1130 they marched into the rest camp and Captain Wright wrote, 'we expect to be entrained for the front tomorrow and are all pleased at being one of the first regiments to go.'[10] Prior to the arrival of the BEF, Monsieur Felix Adam, the Mayor of Boulogne, issued a poster which set the tone of the public reception for the British troops, 'My dear Citizens, this very day arrive in our town the valiant British troops: who come to cooperate with our brave soldiers to repel the abominable aggression of Germany. Boulogne, which is one of the homes of the *Entente Cordiale*, will give to the sons of the United Kingdom an enthusiastic and brotherly welcome.'[11] He also requested they 'decorate the fronts of their houses with the colours of the two countries.'[12] Whether the welcome they received was spontaneous or orchestrated, clearly Field Marshal Kitchener had anticipated the risks in the guidance he issued to the British troops before their departure.

The reception they received as they arrived in France compared to their secret and silent departure could not have been in more marked contrast. Captain Grenfell wrote 'after a beautiful voyage, we reached Boulogne about 1700 and disembarked before a cheering crowd on the quay. It was very interesting suddenly finding ourselves among French people. The arrangements for disembarking were very good; various interpreters met us. We formed up on the quay and then marched off to a camp about three miles away, which we reached in darkness, having left little Garstin behind to help to unload the ship. It was about 2230 before we had finished.'[13] Lance Corporal Hunt had wished he had paid more attention in French lessons at school: 'very enthusiastic reception, large crowd clamouring for "souvenirs" I left my shoulder numerals with a charming French girl (why was my French so sadly neglected?).'[14] The soldiers of the 21st Lancers who had been attached to the 9th Lancers were equally generous with their adopted regiment's badges and numerals:

> We all wear our own badges and numerals, although we were issued with the 9th Lancers, but all the French and Belgium lasses possess them now and I am a barefaced lancer. So do

9 Capt. A. Wright diary, 14th August 1914, p.1.
10 Ibid., p. 1.
11 John Terraine, *Mons: Retreat to Victory* (London: Leo Cooper, 1991), p. 26.
12 Ibid., p. 26.
13 Grenfell, Grenfell Family Papers (within Lyttelton Family Papers), 16th August 1914, p. 7.
14 LCpl W. Hunt diary, p. 2.

send me a cap badge and a set of numerals, I do not want to wear the 9th, and want to let some of the other regiments know that there are some 21st Lancers having a go.[15]

Lancer disembarkation. (Author's Collection)

Prior to departing, Lieutenant Marden put together a phonetic phase book for his troop. His soldiers put it to good use immediately on their arrival in Boulogne, 'the little book of which I am the proud author of French and German phonetic phrases scores its first success. All my troops bombard an embarrassed French damsel with cries of "Kell Bell Jurn Fee."'[16] As the 9th Lancers were arriving in Boulogne, the 15th Infantry Brigade were landing at Le Havre and were about to receive the same enthusiastic reception as the Lancers. Private Sheldrake wrote that at approximately '1600 we sighted land and were soon disembarking in the lovely harbour of Le Havre, and some of my comrades were soon making comrades with the French soldiers, doing duty in the docks, by helping them to eat their dinners. I was just going to make up for my lost time on the boat by eating a tin of bully beef and some teeth crackers but got orders to march off.'[17] Once they had unloaded, they marched through the middle of the town 'thronged with people, showering flowers, rosettes, wines, cigars, fruits etc. on us. The advanced troops had cemented the *Entente Cordiale* by making love to the girls as almost all we saw in the town had a sweetheart on their arm. We could tell the regiments that had been through the town before us, as they had left plenty of badges behind.'[18] This had now started to cause an issue of security 'as by the time my regiment arrived in Belgium, there was not many cap badges or

15 *The Vadette*, 31st March 1915, p. 15.
16 Lt B.J.N. Marden diary,16th August 1914.
17 Pte R. Sheldrake diary, pp. 6-7.
18 Ibid., p. 7.

county names left. This incurred the wrath of our colonel, saying the men would be severely punished who gave them away in future.'[19] As they left the 'men, accompanied by a flute, sang the popular song, which was true just then: It's a long long way to Tipperary.'[20]

As the ships were unloading at the ports, Major Home undertook a reconnaissance to Belgium by car and was held up on his journey for an hour by a "crusty old man armed with a rusty gun." This was as a result of the rumours that German officers were supposed to have made reconnaissances dressed as British and French officers. On his journey he noted the 'country very much wired and very like England in many places.'[21] Major Home was very much ahead of the game as the Cavalry Divisions Intelligence Officer, Lieutenant Colonel Barrow had only just arrived in Le Havre and was staying overnight in the Continental Hotel and he would not start his own information gathering process 'from the French or any other sources that might be of service,'[22] until the following morning. It had taken Lord Kitchener's personal intervention to get Lieutenant Colonel Barrow's released for service with the BEF after the Indian Army had initially refused permission and sent him his sailing orders to return to India. Despite this he made his way to Southampton where he met General Allenby who told him 'I hear they are after you, you better get on board and hide.' Lieutenant Colonel Barrow required "no second bidding" and lay low on board until land was out of sight. As a result of this somewhat clandestine departure, General Allenby often used to speak of him as the "stowaway."'[23]

While Major Home was on his reconnaissance to Belgium, the 15th Infantry Brigade had remained at the docks until about 1930 when it began to trek up to No. 8 Rest Camp, about six miles away, on the hills above Le Havre. They arrived at the camp, a huge place at the top of a long and steep hill, that evening about midnight.[24] After the long sea journey, Private Sheldrake was glad to be ashore but was 'very hungry after living practically on sea air, and sicking that up again for two or three days, but managed to climb up the camp (misnamed rest camp) up a very steep hill, up to our knees in slush, as it has been raining the previous night.'[25] When he finally arrived he thought it was 'a very gloomy place to arrive at in the twilight of an evening but we borrowed some linseed straw corn for a bed and passed away the night after a little feed by sleeping in a tent once more.'[26] Private Hurrell noted that when they arrived, the 'tents were already pitched, and...how dreadfully damp it was. They detailed 14 men to each tent, which meant that we were very cramped, too much to be healthy, being only small army bell tents. Once more we began to realise that after all, this is war time and perhaps this will be the last tent we shall see (and it was).'[27] For some, the night would be much longer as those with the brigade transport had still not arrived and had to take an alternate route as a result of the mud on the roads. The Brigade Headquarters camp was not located with that of the Brigade and the Brigade Commander had "immense difficulty in finding" it. The camp was quite a long way from the other battalion's camps which were 'dotted on the open fields at some distance from

19 Ibid., p. 7.
20 Ibid., p. 7.
21 Home, *Diary of a World War 1 Cavalry Officer*, p. 16.
22 Barrow, *The Fire of Life*, p. 142.
23 Ibid., p. 142.
24 Simpson, *Cheshire Regiment the First Battalion at Mons and the Miniature Colour*, p. 14.
25 Pte R. Sheldrake diary, p. 7.
26 Ibid., p. 7.
27 Pte R. Hurrell, Log of Round the World Cruise, p. 14.

each other and pitched in no particular order.'[28] It was approximately 2300 before the Brigade Commander had found his bearings. His was as just as uncomfortable as his men's as 'there was of course no baggage, nor anything to sleep on except the bare ground under the tents, with our saddles for pillows.'[29]

It was about 0200 by the time the last of the Brigade reached the rest camp as they had difficulty getting the Brigade and regimental transport up the hill 'and the horses being released, were led up to the camp.'[30] This was only achieved 'after considerable labour, some confusion and *language*. As the camp was in total darkness, the horses were picketed and the men, went to sleep among the corn stooks. Towards dawn something frightened them and horses stampeded.'[31] In the morning, the Norfolk Regiment were awakened to more civilians trying to get souvenirs[32] and 'found our farmer friend raging about his precious corn being spoilt after he had gathered it in and stacked it. It was rather hard on him but I have seen much worse since.'[33]

As the 9th Lancers and 15th Infantry Brigade were arriving in France and receiving an enthusiastic welcome from the local population, the German *AOK 1* had just crossed the internal border between the two different regions of Belgium, from Wallonia (French speaking) to Flanders (Dutch speaking) and they immediately noticed the difference in how they were received. In Wallonia as the Belgian Army withdrew, the German *AOK 1* continued to be engaged by small pockets of *franc-tireurs* (irregular civilians) of the Walloons who fired from behind hedges 'an act of daily occurrence.'[34] The Germans saw these acts as an act of murder as some of these were Belgian soldiers dressed as civilians.[35] Ironically, the invading Germans soldiers considered that this was against 'international law!'[36] The Germans tried to put an end to the practice by issuing proclamations and warnings threatening the population to stop these incidents but it had no effect. The advancing Germans therefore began 'a severe and inexorable system of reprisals which had to be applied by the commanders on the spot; to put an end to this state of things.'[37] The Germans had initially hoped for clear passage through Belgium as part of the request for *friendly neutrality*, and had asked for it, knowing that any delay in reaching France would mean that the Allies would be better prepared. As they halted each night they could not sleep soundly or safely and 'it was advisable, whether in or out of quarters, to have a rifle handy, even for the divisional and other staffs some way behind the front. Each quarter occupied by the Army Commander had to be guarded by a battalion of infantry, with machine guns and single field guns, ready for action.'[38] The punishments under martial law allowed for the 'shooting of individuals, and the burning of houses,'[39] and this became prevalent along the

28 Gleichen, *Infantry Brigade 1914,* p. 11.
29 Ibid., pp. 10-11.
30 Simpson, *Cheshire Regiment the First Battalion at Mons and the Miniature Colour,* p. 15.
31 Ibid., p. 15.
32 Pte R. Hurrell, Log of Round the World Cruise, p. 15.
33 Pte R. Sheldrake diary, p. 7.
34 Kluck, *The March on Paris and The Battle of The Marne, 1914*, p. 25.
35 Ibid., p. 25.
36 Ibid., pp. 25-26.
37 Ibid., p. 26.
38 Ibid., p. 26.
39 Ibid., p. 26.

front, but did little to stop it happening. As the German Army advanced, the stories of the burning of property and shooting of civilians put fear into the villages of France and Belgium on the path of the German advance. As the advancing army passed through the villages behind its lead troops, they read the signs on the doors left by their predecessors 'we took fire from this house and this house must be protected.'[40] The reprisals against the civilian population were brutal. Even General Moltke was 'shocked by his armies excesses.'[41] General von Kluck justified his soldier's actions by stating that the actions of the *franc-tireur* 'ate into the very vitals of the army…the communications and the country in the rear of the army and its reserves had to be protected…in a most thorough manner so as to prevent their repetition against troops following later.'[42] As the German Army advanced, its reputation preceded it and a wave of refugees moved south leaving their homes and farms with the crops still in the fields behind them.

For the Germans, it came as some relief as they crossed the country's internal border into Flanders. *Infanterie Regiment 66* noticed 'the inhabitants made an open and willing impression. We did not speak to each other in French but were able to use *Plattdeutsch* (the north German dialect similar to Dutch).'[43] Hauptmann Walter Bloem recorded the change in attitude and dialect:

> Whenever I spoke to any of the villagers, they now answered in a language that was more familiar to me, more reminiscent of my frequent visits to Belgium, and then it struck me that, of course, we had passed through the Walloon half of the country and were now in that part of it that spoke the Flemish dialect. That expression of hatred and suspicion on every face had gone, and when questioned they replied fearlessly and at their ease, laughing whenever I attempted to make myself better understood in their own dialect. Major von Kleist, the battalion commander, noticing my frequent conversations with the local inhabitants, told me I was to act in future as his interpreter[44]

For *Infanterie Regiment 66,* the Sunday brought an unexpected rest day which, 'after the exertions of the last week, was greeted with great joy.'[45] The day of rest taken by *IV AK* was to allow the following two reserve corps to close up on the four (*IX, III, IV* and *II)* first line corps. At 1600, the Regiment held its first field church services in enemy territory. 'The Regimental band then played patriotic tunes, and we all sang along.'[46] The long marches had started to take their toll on the soldiers and on the rest day the battalions used the opportunity to adjust their establishment and this allowed the 100 or so *limited-duty* men from *Infanterie Regiments 26* and *66* to be formed into a company to perform rail security under Hauptmann Knaths who had commanded 8 *Kompanie* up until this point on the advance and on the assumption of his

40 Korfes, *The German 66th Regiment in the First World War*, p. 24.
41 Gen. Helmut Moltke, *Erinnerungen, Brief Dokemente, 1877-1916*, op. cit., David Ascoli, *The Mons Star, The British Expeditionary Force 1914*, p. 43.
42 Kluck, *The March on Paris and The Battle of The Marne, 1914*, p. 26.
43 Ibid., p. 25.
44 Walter Bloem, *The Advance to Mons, The Experiences of a German Infantry Officer* (Solihull: Helion & Company, 2004), p. 28.
45 Korfes, *The German 66th Regiment in the First World War*, p. 25.
46 Ibid., p. 25.

new role, he handed command to Leutnant Reich (Martin).[47] The adjustment of the troops meant that for the advancing Germans there was no overall loss in effective manpower and the men were now employed in roles that they were able to effectively carry out. Additionally it provided protection to the railway system which would be critical in bringing supplies forward, the further the German Army was from German border.

In Liège, 11 out of the 12 forts had fallen, with now only Fort de Loncin holding out, under the command of General Gérard Leman. The fort had been bombarded for three days, when on the 16th August the magazine, which held 12 tons of explosives, was hit by a shell.[48] The explosion destroyed the heart of the fort, killing 350 of the 550 man garrison. Fort de Loncin was the only fort which did not surrender. The fort's commandant, Victor Naessens, wrote that 'under the effect of this titanic volcano, what remained of the concrete massif was dislocated and the greater part of the garrison was crushed by blocks of concrete, burned alive or asphyxiated.'[49] When the Germans entered the city they found the body of General Leman, pinned beneath a block of masonry. The Adjutant stood guard over his body and remarked, "respect the General he is dead." However, the General was not dead. He was alive but unconscious. He was revived and carried to General von Emmich, where he was to surrender his sword. General Leman told General Emmich, to ensure in his dispatches to say, 'I was taken unconscious.' General von Emmich returned his sword and said your "military honour has not been violated by your sword, keep it.'"[50]

47 Ibid., p. 25.
48 Clayton Donnell. *The Forts of the Meuse in World War I* (Oxford: Osprey, 2007), p. 51.
49 *La Libre.be* <www.lalibre.be/regions/liege/le-fort-de-loncin-livre-ses-secrets-51b8994ce4b0de6db9b1d4d7> (Accessed 3rd July 2018).
50 Barbara Tuchman, *August 1914*, p. 191.

# 5

## At Base Camps

---

*We make our way to our bivouac to the east of the town where bell-tents are provided. I hope I shall be equally comfortable throughout the war?*

Lieutenant B.J.N. Marden

In Britain on the morning of the 17th August, a press release was published in some of the morning papers with the headline: "The Secret is Out" – the British expeditionary army has landed safely on French soil'[1] and was be carried in most papers the following day. Any speculation regarding the BEF's involvement by the Germans should now have been put to rest. This was the first day in France for the 9th Lancers, who had left Tidworth in such secrecy and arrived in Boulogne to a welcome which surprised them. For the alliance, it was going to be a day that would shape the relationship between the two allied commanders. The barrier of the different languages would come into sharp focus as the two commanders tried to communicate and more interpreters arrived for the Lancers. Meanwhile, the German advance continued and elements of the *AOK 1* had crossed the Meuse and saw the transition between Wallonia and Flanders as it advanced through Belgium towards the French border. Both sides were eager to make contact. The tempo of the German advance was being controlled by General Bülow and the flank towards Antwerp needed securing. At this stage, neither Field Marshal French, nor General Bülow or Generaloberst Kluck, were aware of each other's dispositions.

Finally, after their long journey which had remarkably taken less than 48 hours, the 9th Lancers arrived for their first night on French soil at No. 3 Base Camp. This was a tented camp at Pont de Briques. Lieutenant Marden was both naively optimistic and impressed by the tented accommodation. His view was possibly coloured by having previously spent two uncomfortable nights on the docks at Southampton and on the boat. He wrote 'amid scenes of inconsolable enthusiasm, we make our way to our bivouac to the east of the town where bell-tents are provided. I hope I shall be equally comfortable throughout the war?' [2] The tents had

1 *Liverpool Echo*, 17th August 1914.
2 Lt B.J.N. Marden diary, 17th August 1914.

Base Camp 3, 17th August 1914, Captain Peek standing. (9/12L Museum)

been pitched, the rations were ready and the horse lines had been laid. This was the hard work of 'Sergeant Wilson and his party of men who had been the *Flying Column* who had departed from Tidworth ahead of the Regiment some days before.'[3]

The 17th August was the first full day in camp and "was an idle one" the preparations for the war to come began. The horses had spent the best part of two days in cramped conditions and being loaded and unloaded from trains and ships. This would have come as a shock to many of them as a large number had only been *impressed* in the short period since war was declare and had not experienced this process before. Captain Roger Peek wrote: 'there was a good deal of trouble to get the horse lines down as the *impressed horses* of course could not understand what was happening to them.'[4] At this early stage of the war it was the expectation that the BEF was here to push the Germans back into Germany and all the mapping was issued for this task. These maps anticipated moving in the direction of Berlin 'had the fortunes of war not led it in the exactly opposite direction, for which there were few, if any, maps available.'[5] The maps 'arrived in innumerable boxes, and everyone was issued with a very large pocketful from which, given the time and space to spread them out and fit them together, it was possible to trace every step of the victorious march of the allies from any point on the coast of France and Belgium to

3 *The Delhi Spearman,* March 1928, p. 7.
4 Capt. R.G. Peek diary, 16th August 1914.
5 Sheppard, *The Ninth Queen's Royal Lancers 1715-1936,* p. 234.

Berlin and beyond.'[6] Along with the maps, interpreters started to arrive at the base camp and they were allocated to the squadrons. They 'arrived in cabs, taxis, on bicycles and on foot, and kept on arriving in ever increasing numbers and all required horses. The following names can be remembered: Messieurs M Leclercq,'[7] 'De Pas, Paul Fort, Walleart and the two brothers Lecrouge. There were others including the most gallant Monsieur Lettory [Letoré] who remained with the Regiment through all the hardships and setbacks of the opening weeks of the campaign.'[8] Before the war he had been the French master at Blundells.[9] Rivy went off to make friends with a lady who lived nearby and she gave him some eggs and milk and chickens. 'She told him that all her relations were out at the war.'[10] Private Alfred Wells, who had been mobilised as a reservist and who had been in Woolwich training since the 7th August reported to Tidworth to rejoin the Regiment to find it had already left and it would take him another five days to catch his Regiment up.[11]

During the day, there was opportunity to explore the local area and sample the local food and wine. They also knew that their stay there was only for a short time. Lieutenant Marden took the opportunity to wander about the town all day and noticed that the 'Hotel Christal et Bristol was being used as the headquarters. He dined at a café near the bivouac.'[12] The orders for the move that night from Boulogne were received at midday.[13] Lance Corporal Hunt managed to get out in the afternoon with his friends having heard about their next move and sampled the local wine and he heard that 'we are going up country by train tonight. Chenby, Wyatt, Humby, Reeves and I explored the village in the afternoon, tasted red and white wine and absolutely shocked the good lady by asking for sugar with it.'[14] Captain Peek's diary recalls the efforts of the officers to make themselves comfortable and how the duties continued. It almost has the feel of a peacetime routine being conducted on the brink of going to war, 'we all slept well, and I took the squadron out for an hour's exercise. Very few unfit to go. At one very pretty house I passed the family came and gave us lovely flowers and a tricolour flag. I finally fixed up the messes and got Bently to run ours. Everyone cleared off to Boulogne and bathed etc., but as I was orderly officer could not.'[15] The 4th Dragoon Guards had an equally easy day. They had paraded at 0830am and they marched to the sea, about four miles from the rest camp. Captain 'Pat' FitzGerald the Machine Gun Officer, 'swam a long way out. When he returned to the shore, he found everybody else already dressed, and several beautiful French ladies watching him with much interest. Poor Pat, very much embarrassed, signalled to his servant for his clothes and made a hasty but very public toilet at the water's edge.[16]

While the 9th Lancers were sorting themselves out one of the most important meetings of the war (for the BEF) was about to take place at Rethel, at General Lanrezac's Headquarters.

6 *The Delhi Spearman*, March 1928, p. 8.
7 Lt B.J.N. Marden diary, 19th August 1914.
8 *The Delhi Spearman*, March 1928, p. 8.
9 Lt B.J.N. Marden, *Diary of Lieutenant Basil Marden*, 19th August.
10 Grenfell, Grenfell Family Papers (within Lyttelton Family Papers), 17th August, p. 7.
11 Pte Wells diary, p. 1.
12 Lt B.J.N. Marden diary, 17th August 1914.
13 *9th War Lancer Diary*, 17th August 1914, p. 5.
14 LCpl W. Hunt diary, p. 2.
15 Capt. R.G. Peek diary, 17th August 1914.
16 Capt. A. Wright diary, 17th August, 1914, p.1.

Lieutenant Spears along with the rest of the staff understood the importance of the meeting and all were curious to see what Field Marshal French looked like. `The orderlies, even the escort, were curious to see the great man, the leader of the strange islanders who were coming from over the sea, from their mysterious foggy land, to fight against the Germans.'[17] The questions that were going through their minds were:

> How would those armies cooperate? Would it be possible for them to work together almost as if they were under one commander? Would the special qualities of each compensate for differences in training and in temperament? It depended on these two men more than on any other factor. No one present doubted the good that would come of this interview, the only matter open to question being that of degree, and of the capacity for cooperation the two generals would show. All guessed the difficulties that might arise between allies speaking a different tongue and with a totally different tradition and mentality.[18]

They met at the headquarters at about 1000 and it was immediately obvious that the two men were visibly different as General Lanrezac met Field Marshal French and they walked off together.

> Sir John stepped out of his car looking very spick and span. He was a good deal shorter than General Lanrezac, who came out to greet him. The two men stood for a moment in strong contrast to each other, Lanrezac large, swarthy, revealing his Creole origin (he was born in Guadeloupe), Sir John ruddy-faced, his white moustache drooping over the corners of his mouth. His clear penetrating blue eyes, his very upright bearing and quick movements, made him infinitely the more attractive personality, and gave him the appearance of being by far the more soldierly of the two. The two men walked into General Lanrezac's sanctum together, the one short, brisk, taking long strides out of proportion to his size, the other big, bulky, heavy, moving with short steps as if his body were too heavy for his legs.[19]

The two commanders went into General Lanrezac's office. We knew that Lanrezac spoke no English, and Sir John, though he understood a little French, at that time could hardly speak it at all. In fact, he never mastered it,[20] but more to the point even if General Lanrezac had spoken English, the Field Marshal's `was not of a kind readily intelligible to a Frenchman.'[21] The discussion was therefore carried out mainly through General Wilson, acting as an interpreter.

> Field Marshal French stepping up to a map in the 3éme Bureau, took out his glasses, located a place with his finger, and said to Lanrezac *"Mon General, est ce que"* His French then gave out, and turning to one of his staff, he asked "How do you say to cross the river in French?" He was told and proceeded; *"Est ce que les Allemands vont traverser la Meuse d—d"* Then he fumbled over the pronunciation of the name. *"Huy"* was the place, unfortunately

17 Spears, *Liaison 1914,* p. 71.
18 Ibid., p. 72.
19 Ibid., p. 73.
20 Ibid., p. 73.
21 Callwell, *Field-Marshal Sir Henry Wilson Bart.,* p. 164.

> one of the most difficult words imaginable to pronounce, the "u" having practically to be whistled. It was quite beyond Sir John, "Hoy," he said at last, triumphantly. "What does he say? What does he say?" exclaimed General Lanrezac. Somebody explained that the Marshal wanted to know whether in his opinion the Germans were going to cross the river at Huy? Lanrezac shrugged his shoulders impatiently, "Tell the Marshal" he said curtly, "that in my opinion the Germans have merely gone to the Meuse to fish." General Wilson somewhat diplomatically translated the reply as. "He says they're going to cross the river, sir," and the conference ended with the usual compliments and bowings and handshaking.[22]

Evidently his conversation with Sir John had put him in a bad mood 'and he did not hesitate to show it by being deliberately rude.'[23] It was the opinion of Lieutenant Spears, that the only reason for General Lanrezac's rudeness to Field Marshal French was that 'he was already rattled.'[24] The meeting had not gone well and neither of the two commanders had come away from the meeting with a feeling of mutual respect. In fact, Field Marshal French wrote 'having heard such eulogies, probably coloured in his favour, but looking back, I remember that his personality did not convey to me the idea of a great leader. He was a big man with a loud voice, and his manner did not strike me as being very courteous.'[25] At the beginning of the day Lieutenant Spears had written 'today all is still well.'[26] By the end, that was clearly not the case.

On the 17th, the *AOK 1* were clear of the Meuse defiles and was organised in two groups of four corps in front and two in reserve. The Belgian Army withdrew before contact with the advancing *AOK 1.* The retirement of the Belgian centre was carried out in good time, and no French troops had been observed with the Belgians.[27] The withdrawal of the Belgian Army led to the conclusion that, at the moment, it felt that in Flanders at least, the Germans had the superiority of numbers. During the day, the *AOK 1* had continued its advance while the *AOK 2* had halted. This allowed the two armies to come together and align. At 0500 on 17th August, the *Infanterie Regiment 66* marched through Tongres, reaching Aiken at 1600 where it quartered. Now the Regiment was in Flanders, and they like those who had passed before them 'found the inhabitants made an open and willing impression'[28] and spoke in *Plattdeutsch* instead of French. Late in the afternoon, the *Infanterie Regiment 66* unsuccessfully shot at an enemy aircraft. The German aerial reconnaissance reported strong Belgian forces behind the Gette River, 'so we had to assume we would soon engage the enemy. Everyone was eager to come to grips with him. The war had begun, but we had not yet seen combat.'[29]

On the evening of the 17th August at 1630 the following order arrived from the *OKH* that General von Moltke had subordinated the *AOK 1* and the *Heereskavalleriekorps 2* (*HKK 2* - High Cavalry Command) to General Bülow in an attempt to regulate the speed of advance:

22 Ibid., p. 164.
23 Spears, *Liaison 1914,* p. 74.
24 Ibid., p. 75.
25 Viscount French of Ypres, *1914*, p 36.
26 Ibid., p. 73.
27 Kluck, *The March on Paris and The Battle of The Marne 1914*, p. 25.
28 Korfes, *The German 66th Regiment in the First World War*, p. 25.
29 Ibid., p. 25.

> The First and Second Armies and the II Cavalry Corps (Marwitz) will be under the orders of the commander of the Second Army (Bülow) during the advance north of the Meuse. This advance will begin on the 18th August. It is most important that the enemy's forces reported to be in position between Diest-Tirlemont-Wavre should be shouldered away from Antwerp. It is intended to initiate further operations of both armies from the line Bruxelles-Namur, and measures must be taken to secure the flank against Antwerp.[30]

While the two generals of *AOK 1* and 2 were digesting the impact of their new orders, the 15th Infantry Brigade at Le Havre had rounded up its horses. It was, however, still struggling to get its transport up the hill to their base camp as they were having to use an alternative steep and narrow road which was the only alternative to the blocked one. They eventually ended up bringing up all the supplies by hand.[31] The Cheshires had expected that they would remain at the camp for another night, 'but at 1415 orders were received to "move off" by train that night. At 2300 the battalion paraded and marched to the station. About 0200 they entrained for some unknown destination; after waiting in the train three hours they were told, about 0500 that they were about to start on an 18 hour journey by rail.'[32] At 1800, the Norfolks 'received orders to move off.'[33] Private Hurrell packed a small ham, together with other food stuffs, fastening the parcel on top of his pack making it very heavy![34] After about two hours they arrived at the station,[35] and 'laid in the yard till nearly midnight.'[36] Once it became time to entrain, eight men were detailed off to each compartment. That was quite sufficient with all their 'stuff including rifle etc, and we were packed in like sardines.'[37] The French system for entraining units allowed for four hours. The Brigade Headquarters only took about 40 mins of which the brigadier's charger *Silver* took about 30 as he was very 'bobbery as usual and it took a good half-hour to persuade him to enter the truck. Once in, he slept like a lamb.'[38] On the sides of some of the carriages was written *40 hommes et 8 chevaux.*[39] It was these precise figures that General Wilson had used for his *War Book* and his calculations.

30 Kluck, *The March on Paris and The Battle of The Marne, 1914*, p. 21.
31 Gleichen, *Infantry Brigade 1914*, p. 11.
32 Simpson, *Cheshire Regiment the First Battalion at Mons and the Miniature Colour*, p. 15.
33 Pte R. Hurrell, Log of Round the World Cruise, p. 16.
34 Ibid., p. 16.
35 Ibid., p. 16.
36 Pte R. Sheldrake diary, p. 7.
37 Pte R. Hurrell, Log of Round the World Cruise, p. 10.
38 Gleichen, *Infantry Brigade 1914*, p. 11.
39 'Horses were in trucks holding eight a piece and men were in carriages.' See TNA WO 95/1134/2: 5th Lancers War Diary.

# 6

## Rail Move to Jeumont, Obrechies and Le Pommereuil

*The train stopped at different stations where people gave them apples, pears, cigarettes, tied flowers on the carriage doors thus receiving every kind of welcome possible.*

Private R. Hurrell

The journey of the Norfolk Regiment overnight had not been too comfortable along the Nord railway.'[1] Private Hurrell slept having a 'sitting doze, and occasionally a good shaking till daybreak arrived.'[2] Now it was light, he could see out of the carriage and noticed that 'we were amongst some very good crops of corn, wheat and oats mostly, and some good beetroots, the country being dotted with several sugar beet refineries. We passed through the pretty towns of Rouen and Amiens. Some French field guns were being entrained there, covered with flowers they looked more like going to a battle of flowers, than to the devil's work.'[3] He also noticed that 'the farmers do not cut the clover for the cows here, but stake them out to cut on their own, and they leave their manure behind them. I thought it a good idea. Also, the milkmaids take a dog drawing a cart with milk cans to fetch the milk home instead of driving the cows the double journey.'[4] At about 0900[5], the train pulled into a siding so that they could brew tea, have a wash etc. To make tea, the hot water had to be obtained from the engine.[6] Along the route the train stopped at different stations where people gave them 'apples, pears, cigarettes, tied flowers on the carriage doors thus receiving every kind of welcome possible.'[7] 'It was noticeable that there no active young men anywhere. They had all gone to defend their country.'[8]

1 Pte R. Sheldrake diary, p. 7.
2 Ibid., p. 8.
3 Ibid.
4 Ibid.
5 Pte R. Hurrell notebook, p. 11.
6 Pte R. Hurrell, Log of Round the World Cruise, p. 17.
7 Ibid., p. 17.
8 Pte R. Sheldrake notebook, p. 3.

Eventually, at 1800, the Norfolks arrived at Le Cateau where they detrained and at 1900 'formed up into line, and…we marched through the town receiving another welcome from its inhabitants. I must say that this was a very pretty little place.'[9] Private Sheldrake's company, D, 'was left in charge of the baggage wagons and owing to a broken harness we had to stop for some time.'[10] During this time, he had his first taste of French beer, and had been warned of the difference of the wines and spirits in France 'which I drank and found quite harmless. It's not so strong as our English beers, but of course we must beware of the wines and spirits, they are both cheap and strong here I believe.'[11] The Norfolks 'marched about four miles' to Le Pommereuil where 'the whole regiment were scattered all over the village putting a few men at each house where possible, the landlady, or landlord as the case may be, being responsible for eating and sleeping of every soldier.'[12] Private Hurrell made himself comfortable in 'a little old barn or outhouse with plenty of straw for a bed, however after having some eats, wash, smoke and etc. finally anchored ourselves down to sleep, most of us being very tired. Some said that during the night rats and mice were running all over us. I was evidently too tired to notice anything, so slept through it.'[13]After the long journey from North Elmham, in Norfolk, to the depot in Norwich and then on to Belfast, followed by the sea crossing to Le Havre, Private Sheldrake was glad of the rest. 'I was one of a dozen in a small farmstead and slept on some nice hay in a barn, and I spent three good nights there.'[14] The village of Le Pommereuil was not just playing host to the Norfolk Regiment, but the Cheshires too. During the train journey to Le Pommereuil, the train the Cheshires was on stopped at the railway station at Busigny, where Lieutenant Elliot of A Company, got off. Shortly afterwards he returned with a quantity of fruit. The Lieutenant was popularly known to his brother officers by the name of *Winkerpop*.[15] Knowing this his platoon sergeant asked him what name he had used to sign for the fruit? Lieutenant Elliot replied 'Oh I signed it George Robey,[16] the Cheshire Regiment!'[17] The rest of the Brigade and the Headquarters were billeted in the village of Ors.[18] It was on the way to Ors that Brigadier Gleichen was met by a motorbike with a 'cipher telegram,' but was not able to decode it as he had not yet reported to the Divisional Headquarters for the 'local field cipher-word.'[19] On the road, Brigadier Gleichen saw a car coming in his direction with some "brass hats" so he stopped it with 'a view to getting the key.'[20] However, to his "horror," the car contained Field Marshal French and his chief of staff General Murray. When Brigadier Gleichen showed Field Marshal French the message, he was told it was not important and we

9 Pte R. Hurrell, Log of Round the World Cruise, p. 17.
10 Pte R. Sheldrake diary, p. 8.
11 Ibid., p. 8.
12 Pte R. Hurrell, Log of Round the World Cruise, p. 17.
13 Ibid., p. 18.
14 Pte R. Sheldrake diary, p. 8.
15 Pte Schofield op. cit., *Chester Chronicle* dated Saturday 24th October 1914.
16 Contemporary British comedian and one of the greatest music hall performers of the late 19th and early 20th centuries.
17 Simpson, *Cheshire Regiment the First Battalion at Mons and the Miniature Colour,* p. 17.
18 Gleichen, *Infantry Brigade 1914,* p. 12.
19 Ibid., p. 12.
20 Ibid., p. 12.

'could disregard it as they knew what it was about, and it was of no particular importance by this time.'[21]

Having stayed overnight at Base Camp No. 3, it was the plan for the 9th Lancers to move by rail from Boulogne on Monday 17th August and arrive at Jeumont on Tuesday 18th August, which for them was still an unknown destination. They left Base Camp No. 3 at 2345 and they started to load up just before midnight on the 17th August. They departed early in the morning having spent all night loading the horses onto three trains. The journey from base camp to the railway did not go entirely smoothly when Private Charles Winter[22] broke his leg when he fell from his horse while riding through Boulogne, and was left in hospital there. He was possibly 'the most disappointed man in the expeditionary force.'[23] The first squadron to load was B Squadron which entrained at 2100. Captain Lucas-Tooth thought 'it was a slow process owing to the necessity of using ramps, and of these only a few were provided, and the horses kicked a good deal in the new boxes. The French method of putting horses into trains was also new to the men.'[24] The Regiment was briefed by a French colonel and they were given their 'entraining orders and timetables were given out of the various halts which were from five to 10 minutes.'[25] Lieutenant Marden thought the process was 'a long and weary job and got some coffee and bread and butter at the station café[26] which showed foresight since the journey they were about to take would last for 14 hours. The train left at midnight, and, after passing through Amiens, Vusigny and Maubeuge, the Regiment reached Jeumont at 1400.[27] During the journey, provision had been made for the washing and the feeding of both men and horses *en-route* as well as could be managed.[28] They washed in buckets during the halts and fed and watered the horses.[29]As the journey continued, staff officers and interpreters met the train at the different stations. The Regiment finally detrained at Jeumont under the personal supervision of Brigadier De Lisle[30] who had been travelling on the same train.[31] Rumours and reliable information poured in at every station on the journey until the most generally believed possibility was that things were shaping up for the world's greatest battle at Waterloo again. When passing through Busigny, where Lieutenant Elliot had masqueraded as George Robey, 'a French battalion was drawn up to cheer the Regiment as the trains passed and it was here that 1911 Private Sidney Perkins in his efforts to express his *fraternité*, fell out of one of the horse trucks. However, he was none the worse and rejoined his squadron at Obrechies two days later.'[32] It was not just the 2nd Cavalry Brigade that was moving, but the whole of the Cavalry Division. Major Home wrote: 'another day with trains, saw many old friends as regiments of cavalry coming through all day, otherwise a very monotonous proceeding. Moving to sudden orders'[33]

21 Ibid., p. 12.
22 No 4488.
23 *The Delhi Spearman*, March 1928, p. 8.
24 Anon., 9th Lancers War Diary, 17th August 1914, p. 5.
25 Ibid., 17th August, p. 5.
26 Lt B.J.N. Marden, *Diary of Lieutenant Basil Marden*, 18th August.
27 Anon., 9th Lancers War Diary, 17th August 1914, p. 5.
28 Ibid., p. 5.
29 Grenfell, Grenfell Family Papers (within Lyttelton Family Papers),17th August 1914, p. 8.
30 Ibid., 17th August 1914, p. 8.
31 Anon., 9th Lancers War Diary, 17th August 1914, p. 6.
32 *The Delhi Spearman*, March 1928 p. 8.
33 Home, *Diary of a World War 1 Cavalry Officer*, p. 16.

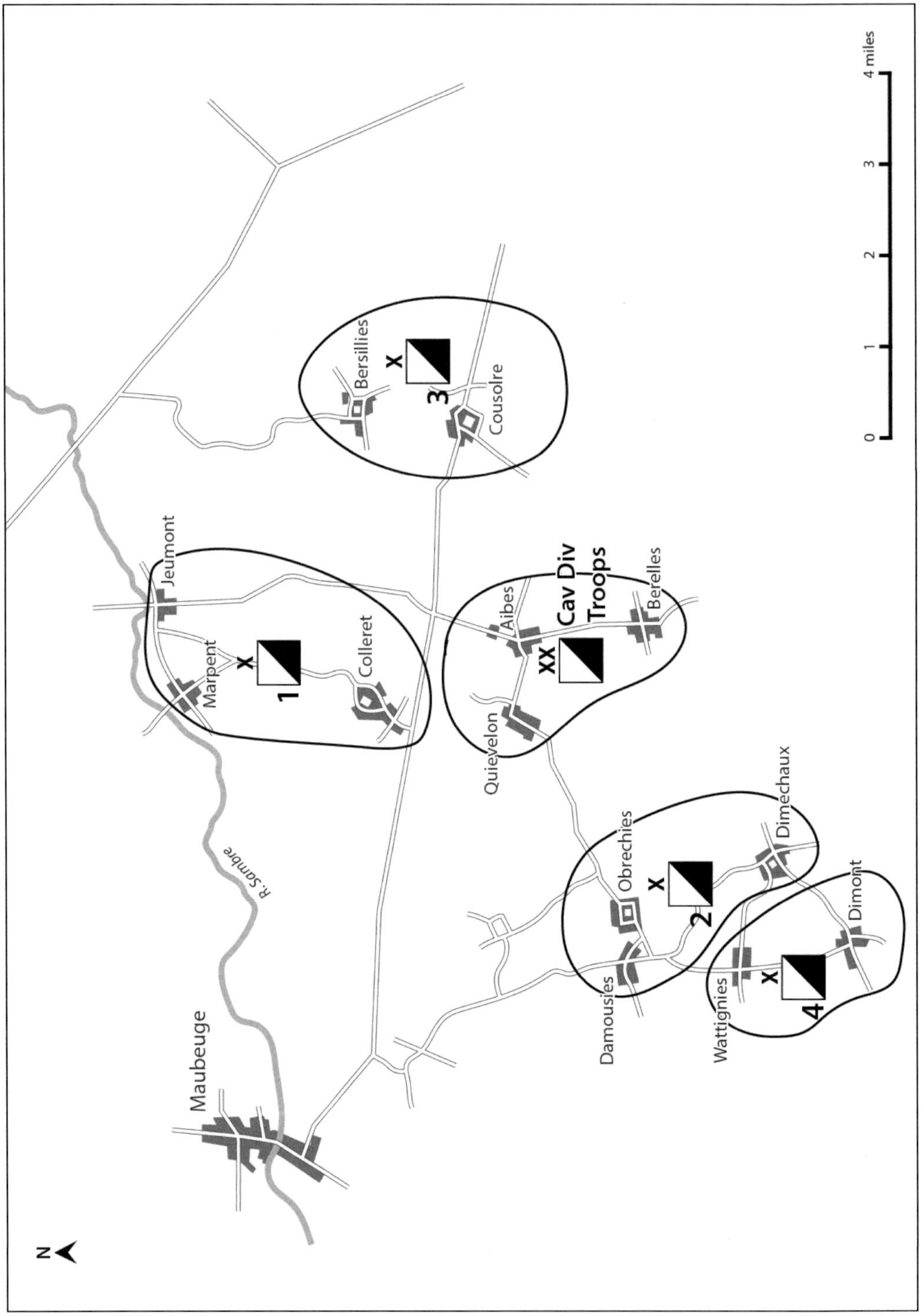


Map 1 Cavalry Division, brigade Concentration Areas, August 1914. (Cavalry Journal, 1922)

While the 9th Lancers and 15th Infantry Brigade had been loading and leaving their base camps, the German *AOK 1* had continued its advance south and had met slight resistance as the French withdrew and the position of the Germans on their right flank became clearer. The *AOK 1* received information regarding the advance of the French forces on their right flank moving from Charleroi towards Gembloux.'[34] There was also a report that 'the French 5th Cavalry Division had retired from near Pervez, with heavy loss, under the fire of Marwitz's 4th and 9th Cavalry Divisions.'[35]

It was during the train journey that Captain Peek and the Regiment heard the sad news of the death of General Grierson. 'Lennie and I had a compartment to ourselves. A sort of half coach at the end of the train. We heard the sad news of the death of Grierson on the way up.'[36]General Douglas Haig was also travelling by train from Le Havre to Amiens when he was called to the phone at a wayside station at Sergueux, where he was told of the General's death. He 'had died suddenly in the train immediately following his own.'[37] There were various rumours as to the cause of his death, such as being shot by an enemy spy, and that he had broken a blood vessel, and he had died from heart failure.[38] The official press bureau release was 'General Grierson died this morning of heart failure while travelling in the train.'[39] Captain James Dunn, a Scottish physician who was the Regimental Medical Officer to the 2nd Battalion the Royal Welch Fusiliers, recorded:

> I was summoned early to the lines of communications HQ and told that General Grierson, commanding II Corps, had died suddenly on the train…I have the best of reasons knowing that he died from the bursting of a blood-vessel, probably brought on by the heat and a heavy meal. He was a man of full habit, the weather was torrid, and the staffs of higher formations were at that time living exclusively on hampers supplied by Fortnum and Mason.[40]

At Amiens, Colonel Ryan was ordered to see General Grierson by General Haig. He noted that 'he had died of apoplexy.'[41]

It was Major Henry Fraser of the 21st Lancers, who was a staff officer to the late General Grierson, who took the General's body back to England.[42] Back in England, General Horace Smith-Dorrien had also heard the news. He wrote 'little did I think, on receiving the news, how his death would affect me.'[43] Once they arrived at Jeumont, the 9th Lancers began to detrain. This was supervised by the Brigade Commander who "became a little fussy" and interfered with the detraining. This occurred when Rivy's and Francis's pack horses took a long time to saddle

34 Kluck, *The March on Paris and The Battle of The Marne, 1914*, p. 29.
35 Ibid., p. 29.
36 Capt. R.G. Peek diary, 18th August 1914.
37 Charteris, *Field Marshal Earl Haig*, p. 84.
38 Simpson, *Cheshire Regiment the First Battalion at Mons and the Miniature Colour*, p. 16.
39 Ibid., p. 16.
40 Capt. J. Dunn, *The War the Infantry Knew 1914-1919* (London: Abacus, 1988).
41 Ryan, *Haig's Medical Officer*, p. 19.
42 *The Globe*, 24th August 1914.
43 Gen. H. Smith-Dorrien, *Memories of Forty-Eight Years' Service* (London: John Murray, 1925), p. 375.

up, which delayed everybody 'and annoyed the General.'[44] Lieutenant Crossley's troop were the *advance guard* for the day and the Regiment set off for Obrechies. The local population turned out again and greeted the Lancers with their now customary hospitality of gifts of food and 'we had the honour of being the first British squadron to arrive. We were accorded a great reception.'[45] 'All the peasants cheering and women giving us flowers, looked rather comical to see troops riding along carrying huge bouquets, of course, as soon as we got out of the village the bouquets went over a hedge. One place had a triumphal arch of flowers and laurels with "Hurrah for England" in the centre, kiddies running along shouting for souvenirs. The Regiment billeted on a farm at Obrechies about four miles from the Belgian frontier'[46] which had been pre-arranged by staff officers.[47] The Regiment arrived at approximately 1700 and 'the women of the town were most generous and gave the men coffee, milk, bread and butter.'[48] The Regiment bivouacked on the green[49] by a local pub[50] not far from the railway station.[51] Lance Corporal Hunt 'went out in the evening and got some decent food, four fried eggs. The worthy shopkeeper could understand all the English coinage, bar a half a crown, which I produced. Didn't know what change to give me, however, after a delay an old schoolmaster came in and interpreted for us.'[52] Earlier, when the Regiment had arrived at Jeumont, the Commanding Officer sent Lieutenant Marden to make contact with the French at Recquignies[53] and, despite the official nature of his task, he managed to take full advantage of the situation. 'I take Private Buck, we are accorded a hearty welcome after drinking *'a Berlin'* in the château. I return, tho' Buck is with difficulty torn away from a charming damsel who has been treating him to the local champagne. Slept in a pub after a square meal.'[54] When the Regiment arrived at Obrechies, Francis sent off Rivy to discover what was going on. Rivy reported to the French officer in command at Ferriere-la-Petite that the first English cavalry regiments were arriving that evening, and to give him the dispositions of the 2nd Cavalry Brigade. On arrival his arrival he was met by Colonel Beauchime of *2nd Regiment Territorial*, and at once surrounded by French territorial soldiers 'who greatly admired *mon cheval, "oh! Qu'il est beau!"*'[55] The Colonel asked Rivy 'if the English were keen to fight, what force we were sending over, and was greatly elated when he told him how anxious the men were to kill a German. He told him of the dispositions round Maubeuge, which he described as "impregnable." He also then showed Rivy 'how to eat a raw egg, by making a hole at each end, and sucking it, a tip which has proved invaluable to me since.'[56] When Rivy returned he rejoined his brother where they slept in a peasant's cottage. 'The noise of guns was heard. This was

44 Grenfell, Grenfell Family Papers (within Lyttelton Family Papers), 17th August 1914, p. 8
45 Ibid., NL/GRE/16/9; Francis Grenfell account of First World War, 17th August 1914, p. 1.
46 LCpl W. Hunt diary, p. 3.
47 Anon., 9th Lancers War Diary, 17th August 1914, p. 6.
48 Ibid., p. 6.
49 LCpl W. Hunt diary, p. 2.
50 Lt B.J.N. Marden diary, 18th August 1914.
51 TNA W O95/1113/2: 9th Lancers War Diary. 18th August 1914.
52 LCpl W. Hunt diary, p. 2.
53 Lt B.J.N. Marden diary, 18th August 1914.
54 Ibid.
55 Lt R.N. Grenfell, Grenfell Family Papers (within Lyttelton Family Papers, 17th August 1914, p. 2.
56 Ibid., p. 2.

reported to be the making of clearances for the field of fire in front of the forts of Maubeuge.'[57] Rivy and the soldiers were learning quick and adapting to their new situation especially when it came to eating and breakfast. 'At first, we followed the old British habit of having our own food cooked by indifferent men in the squadron, but soon tumbled to the French practice of getting the women in the houses to cook for us, and give us *café au lait* at reveille. For Rivy this made 'all the difference. As you know, every French or Belgian woman is an expert at *café*, and they nearly all gave us our *café* for nothing, and also to the men.'[58]

9th Lancers watering horses at Obrechies. (9/12L Museum)

The 18th was the first day that Field Marshal French had managed to assemble the Corps Commanders and their staffs. The meeting was held at GHQ at Le Cateau at 1200. Their reports regarding their mobilisation 'were highly satisfactory.'[59] At the end of the discussion and a 'brief appreciation of the situation,'[60] he told them, 'when our concentration is complete, it is intended we should operate on the left of the French Fifth Army, the 18th Corps being on

57 Anon., 9th Lancers War Diary, 17th August 1914, p. 6.
58 Lt R.N. Grenfell, Grenfell Family Papers (within Lyttelton Family Papers, 17th August 1914, p. 2.
59 Viscount French of Ypres, *1914*, p. 40.
60 Ibid., p. 40.

our right. The French Cavalry Corps of three divisions will be on our left and in touch with the Belgians.'[61] However as 'a preliminary to this, we shall take up an area north of the Sambre, and on Monday, the heads of the allied columns should be on the line Mons-Givet, with the cavalry on the outer flank. Should the German attack develop in the manner expected, we shall advance on the general line Mons-Dinant to meet it.'[62] After the meeting, they had lunch and Major Home got back to his own headquarters at about 1600 to find he had received two letters from home. As a result of the strict censorship, he acknowledged them by postcard. It was also a day where his knowledge of the French language would prove useful as he tried to teach his servant the French for toothbrush, an item he required, despite the "most comic" affair. He then went out and bought him one. More seriously there was tension between the British and French officers 'I think there will be some problem with French officers. We do not know how to treat them at all. Hope it will blow over. It is, to my mind, of utmost importance to keep friends with them. I dislike R, but he is no worse than many of our own people, the British officer is very insular.'[63]

Back in England, General Smith-Dorrien had received a telegram telling him that he was to replace General Grierson as II Corps Commander and was to report to Lord Kitchener immediately. On his arrival he was told by Lord Kitchener that in effect Field Marshal French had requested someone else to replace General Grierson:

> Lord Kitchener's first words to me, when in response to his order I entered his room at the War Office on the 8th of August, 1914, expressed grave doubt as to his wisdom in selecting me to succeed the late General Grierson in command of the II Corps; he explained that the Chief of Staff, General Sir Charles Douglas, had just told him that it would be putting me in an impossible position, as Sir John French had shown great jealousy of, and personal animus towards me for some years, and that such was well-known to the Army Council. On my replying that I had no such feelings towards Sir John and that I felt sure I could, by serving him loyally, overcome his dislike, Lord Kitchener adhered to his decision to send me.'[64]

Imposing the appointment of General Smith-Dorrien and not conceding to Field Marshal French's request, one might reasonably assume that Field Marshal Kitchener had decided to take the earliest opportunity to impose his own authority as Secretary of State over Field Marshal French.[65] Equally, Field Marshal French might have expected as the commander of the BEF to be at least consulted as he certainly knew the situation far better than Field Marshal Kitchener, given that all his service had been colonial and he had never commanded anything in England. Lord Kitchener had never served in the War Office and was not familiar with its

61 Ibid., p. 42.
62 Ibid.
63 Home, *Diary of a World War 1 Cavalry Officer*, p. 16.
64 Smith-Dorrien, *Memories of Forty-Eight Years' Service*, p. 375.
65 Ascoli, *The Mons Star*, p. 40.

processes and had not studied the plan for mobilisation.[66] That said, Field Marshal French accepted his appointment 'without demur'[67]

General Smith-Dorrien only had two days to prepare himself to take over his Corps, which had already embarked and arrived in France. He was replacing a man for whom he had a lot of professional respect for 'the man who was heart and soul a soldier, who, once *persona grata* with the Kaiser, and a welcome guest in the German Army, had of late years seen through their wily machinations, and devoted himself to preparing the army and himself for the day when the Germans should unmask.' He also felt that by his early death, that he and the country had in some way been cheated, '*Der Tag* had arrived, and Grierson landed in France, bursting with enthusiasm and thirsting for the fray, when the cruel blow fell and the nation lost an unrivalled leader in the very hour of her need.'[68]

On the day that the 9th Lancers moved to Obrechies, *Infanterie Regiments 26* and *66* would have their first taste of war. The Belgian Army had dug-in behind the River Geete where they waited for French support. Generaloberst von Kluck decided that he would attack the Belgians in front with his forward three Corps. The *IV AK* objective was Haelen and early in the morning, all the troops were ready to march. The Division set off in column, and the lead battalion was *Infanterie Regiment 66* who acted as the *advance guard*. The Brigade gave the order to deploy from the line of march east of Rummen; II Battalion was to march on the Rummen-Hulsbeck road, with III Battalion to the south of the road, and I Battalion was held as the Corps Reserve. Two battalions of *Infanterie Regiment 26* would advance on their left. The move out began at 0800 with *Hussar Regiment 10* who rode out ahead of the lead *kompanie* of II Battalion. The lead *kompanie* acting as the *advance guard* was 6 *Kompanie* commanded by Oberleutnant Holscher and the point section was led by Leutnant Hermens. The section 'advanced towards the Geete on a wonderful, arrow-straight road with deep roadside ditches, marching magnificently in the bright early morning sun which rose behind it. Left and right the road was lined with high poplars, whose crowns provided a shady roof. To both sides of the road were meadows, lined with wire to form individual enclosures.'[69] As he advanced, he thought 'it looked like home, the Altmark north of Salzwedel.'[70] As the *advance guard* and hussars were seen they were immediately engaged from their front. The hussars raced back to the rear and the column halted and took cover in the ditches. The battalion commander, Major Knauff, took control of the situation and 'stood quietly and easily on the road and gave his orders: "we will attack! Initially, 6 *Kompanie* will continue towards the Geete; 5 *Kompanie* will deploy to the left and cover the flank and attack; *7* and *8 Kompanie* will follow on both sides of the road.'[71]

Leutnant Hermens section was reinforced to platoon strength and "advanced by bounds against an invisible enemy," the other two platoons of *6 Kompanie* commanded by Reserve Leutnant Koebbling and acting officer Westphal, followed in support. Heavy rifle fire came from the forest and bushes that lined the far side of the River Geete. As they advance a broad water-filled ditch blocked their way and could only be crossed by a road bridge. Leutnant

66 Brig. C.R. Ballard, *Smith-Dorrien*, (London: Constable, 1931), p. 146.
67 Ibid., p. 153.
68 Smith-Dorrien, *Memories of Forty-Eight Years' Service*, p. 375.
69 Korfes, *The German 66th Regiment in the First World War*, p. 26.
70 Ibid., p. 26.
71 Ibid.

Hermens led his men forward and the platoon closed to within 200m of the enemy and opened fire. While attempting to advance again, Leutnant Hermens was severely wounded by a bullet to the head and fell into a water-filled ditch. He was pulled out by Landwehr Feldwebel Feldmann, who carried him to cover. Trumpeter Wieblitz was killed by a bullet through the heart, the first fatal casualty of the Regiment. As Feldwebel Ullmer assumed command from Leutnant Hermens, who was wounded four times by rifle fire and was unable to continue. The supporting *kompanie*s continued their advance. 5 *Kompanie* under Leutnant Kartes moved up level and joined 6 *Kompanie* and provided covering fire diagonally from their position. 7 and 8 *Kompanie*s continued their advance and were receiving very little in the way of rifle fire. Leutnant Kortes crossed the water-filled ditch with his *kompanie* where they suddenly they saw movement in the enemy position as the Belgian defenders withdrew west. When the *kompanie*s reached the river 5 and 6 *Kompanie*s crossed using tree trunks, then 7 and 8 *Kompanie*s followed on using the bridge. III Battalion crossed to the south, at Geete-Beetz, under very little fire. When they arrived on the defender's position, they found 'weapons and pieces of uniforms of various Belgian units in the abandoned Belgian position. The first battle was over. On the horizon, a Belgian cavalry regiment could be seen disappearing over a ridge.'[72] Once the *Infanterie Regiment 26* had reached the Dierst-Tirlemont rail line, which was the limit of advance, it occupied an assembly area at the foot of the high ground. This was situated on the west side of the River Geete to cover the construction of a bridge. Once in their assembly area, soldiers were sent out to find water but returned with 'red wine and champagne. 'The inhabitants said that the position had been held by 200 guides (cavalry), which had relieved the Belgian 4th Infantry Regiment the previous day.'[73] The assessment was that 'enemy force had abandoned the Geete position, so that *IV AK* was opposed only by *rear guards* without artillery.'[74] This was the first taste of action for the Regiment. Resistance was light but they suffered their first casualties of the war. The position of the enemy was identified by the hussars, and the *advance guard* crossed and secured the river. The whole operation was conducted without artillery support, and once the high ground had been secured, the *pioneers* constructed a bridge. It is not clear if it was intended to conduct the operation without artillery support, but it is likely that if artillery had been used, that the position would have been vacated earlier and their casualties as light as they were, might have been completely avoided.

On Wednesday 19th August,[75] B Squadron of the 9th Lancers was ordered to make a reconnaissance to the Belgian frontier. They went out first thing in the morning and were to be back by the afternoon. This was the first opportunity to exercise in the French countryside and integrate the *reservists* who had been *called up* and were out of practise. Captain Grenfell (who prior to embarkation had been the Adjutant) had only just taken command of B Squadron as they deployed. While on their patrol he felt it necessary to re-establish some old standards back to his squadron which he had felt had started to slip. 'I had reason to find fault with the turn-out of the men, boots and spurs having been allowed to get rusty; so I formed up the squadron and told them I insisted on the turn-out being good throughout the campaign, as it was proverbial that the best

72 Korfes, *The German 66th Regiment in the First World War*, p. 27.
73 Ibid., p. 27.
74 Ibid., p. 28.
75 There is no reference to this taking place in the War Diary. Captain Grenfell records the event on 18th August and Rivy records it as occurring on the 19th and 20th.

turned-out troop was nine times out of 10 the best fighting one.'[76] He told them that just 'because the men were on active service, there was no reason why they should imagine that they had ceased to be in the Ninth and become colonials. I ordered the few men whose turn-out was very bad to march two miles on foot on the way home.'[77] He also warned them that if it was to happen again 'any man who was reported to me badly turned out would have his horse taken from him and be made a *tramp*. I am certain that this had a great effect on the squadrons.[78] Once the inspection and the reprimand was completed they 'marched about 10 miles, a very hot day.'[79] During the march '*advance guards* were practised for the benefit of the reservists and on reaching the frontier, a short conference of officers and NCOs on *advance guard* work was held and various points which had been done wrongly were pointed out.'[80] Francis had 'great difficulty getting the men to realise they were on active service and to send men out far enough to the front and flanks.'[81]

This was also the day of the first aerial reconnaissance flights by the Royal Flying Corps (RFC). They were carried out by Captain P.B. Joubert de la Ferte of No. 3 Squadron, in a Bleriot, and Lieutenant G.W. Mapplebeck of No. 4 Squadron, in a BE. They started out at 0930 and flew without observers. Captain Joubert de la Ferte was to reconnoitre Nivelles-Genappe in order to report what Belgian forces were in that neighbourhood and Lieutenant Mapplebeck was to find out whether enemy cavalry was still in force in the neighbourhood of Gembloux. The machines flew together as far as Nivelles, so that if one was required to descend the other could report its whereabouts. Both the pilots lost their way and lost each other. Lieutenant Mapplebeck eventually found himself over a large town which he did not recognise as Bruxelles. Later he picked up his position at Ottignies, and soon found Gembloux, where he could see only a small body of cavalry moving in a south easterly direction.[82] The flights had not been entirely successful, but they had learnt much regarding navigation and observation in a countryside they were not familiar with, and they had identified cavalry.

While Captain Grenfell was out with his squadron, the Norfolks awoke in their new billet. It was Private Hurrell's 21st birthday and it was the first time he had heard from home since they had embarked. There was nothing 'to do but lounge around waiting for orders.'[83] On the barn door orders were posted 'that we were on no account to leave the place and await further instructions.'[84] For his birthday breakfast he had 'two nice boiled eggs, fresh bread and butter, with milk. I paid the landlady a little extra, she was as pleased as I was myself, must say I enjoyed it very much.'[85] After his breakfast he 'took a walk round the orchard, helping himself to plums, apples etc. He 'managed to get a nice store of big lovely plums like peaches and then asked the landlady to stew them which she did. They were lovely, having sufficient for another

76 Buchan, *Francis and Riversdale Grenfell* notes (p. 190) that this diary entry was for 18th August but refers to an incident prior to the move from Jeumont to Obrechies.
77 Ibid., p. 190.
78 Ibid.
79 Grenfell, Grenfell Family Papers (within Lyttelton Family Papers), 17th August 1914, p. 10.
80 Anon., 9th Lancers War Diary, 18th August, p. 6
81 Capt. F.O. Grenfell, *Grenfell Family Papers (within Lyttelton Family Papers)*, 18th August, p. 10.
82 Walter Raleigh, The *War in the Air* (Oxford: Clarendon Press, 1922), p. 300.
83 Pte R. Hurrell, Log of Round the World Cruise, p. 19.
84 Ibid., p. 18.
85 Ibid., p. 18.

meal.'[86] For lunch, Private Sheldrake 'found some potatoes and onions and made some good stew with our tinned beef.'[87] His hostess made them hot coffee in the mornings for when they awoke 'and had it with the whisky bottle waiting for us…I felt sorry I could not thank her in French.'[88] Later in the day, General Sir Charles Fergusson, GOC 5th Infantry Division, paraded the Brigade battalions and addressed them each in turn. In addressing the 1st Battalion, Cheshire Regiment at Le Pommereuil, he spoke of its past records, its shooting and marching reputation on leaving for the front and concluded by saying, 'remember that if you have no ammunition, you have your bayonets. If your bayonets get broken, you have your fists. Fight to the last man, and I myself will be with you to die in the last ditch if necessary; but remember! No surrender for the 5th Infantry Division. Men we are up against it.'[89] This was a stirring message and instruction which would stay with the battalion and shape the outcome in days to come. The message also contradicted the direction Lord Kitchener had given to Field Marshal French 'that that the greatest care must be exercised towards a minimum of losses and wastage…in minor operations you should be careful that your subordinates understand that risk of serious losses should only be taken where such risk is authoritatively considered to be commensurate with the object in view.'[90]

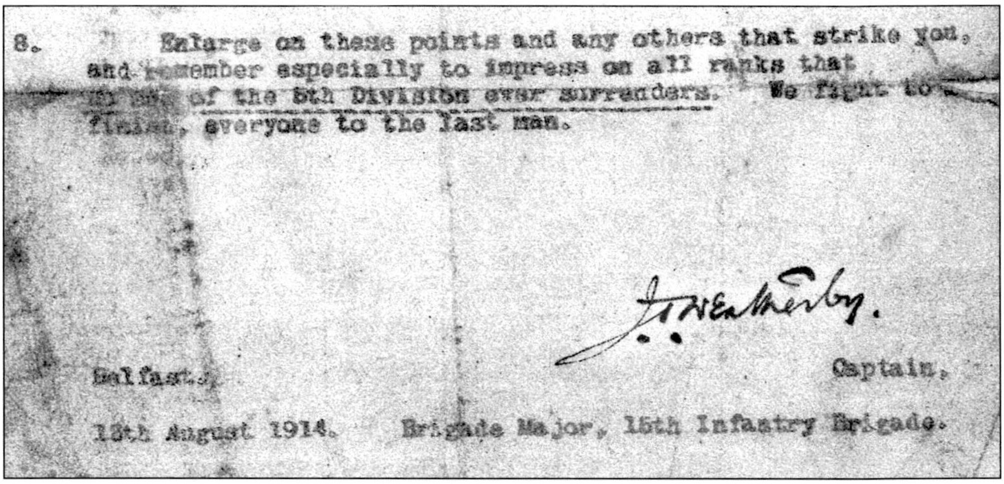

8. Enlarge on these points and any others that strike you, and remember especially to impress on all ranks that [illegible] of the 5th Division ever surrenders. We fight to [illegible], everyone to the last man.

Belfast.

Captain,

13th August 1914. Brigade Major, 15th Infantry Brigade.

15th Infantry Brigade "No Surrender" document. (Norfolk Regiment Museum)

In London, *The Times* that day carried the news of General Smith-Dorrien's appointment 'Sir H. Smith-Dorrien's new command. Successor to General Grierson. The King on the recommendation of Field Marshal Earl Kitchener, Secretary of State for War has approved the appointment of

86 Ibid., p. 18.
87 Pte R. Sheldrake diary, p. 8.
88 Ibid., p. 8.
89 Col. A. Crookenden, *The History of the Cheshire Regiment in the Great War,* (London: W H Evans & Co, 1938), pp. 17-18.
90 Edmonds, *Military Operations France and Belgium 1914,* Vol. I, p. 499.

General Sir Horace Smith-Dorrien GCB, DSO, to command an army corps of the British Expeditionary Force, in succession to Lieutenant General Sir J.M. Grierson KCB, CVO, CMG, *Aide-De-Camp*, General to the King.'[91] Lord Kitchener, far from the front, 'felt anxiety and foreboding…He telegraphed Sir John French that the German sweep north and west of the Meuse, about which he had warned him, seems 'definitely to be developing.'[92] Meanwhile the Germans continued their advance south. On the 19th, the *AOK 1* had not advanced as far as they had intended. This was a result of the long marches it had conducted since they crossed the Belgian border and they were now experiencing difficulties with the supply chain due to the distances involved. As a result, a request was also made that a shorter march might be ordered for the army on the 21st, 'as the rear division had to push up to the head of the column to relieve the leading division.'[93] For the BEF, every delay in the advance of the German Army would mean they would be better prepared and in position.

General Sir Charles Fergusson.
(Author's Collection)

For the 9th Lancers, this was their first night away from the organised billeting of the rest camp and they therefore had to 'learn how to billet.'[94] Lieutenant Marden, however, preferred to sleep outside as the cottages were 'somewhat high I erected my bivi in a field.'[95] At the end of the

91 *The Times*, 19th August 1914 op. cit., Frank Simpson, *Cheshire Regiment the First Battalion at Mons and the Miniature Colour*, p. 19.
92 Barbara Tuchman, *August 914, The First Month of the First World War*, p. 267.
93 Kluck, *The March on Paris and The Battle of The Marne, 1914*, p. 31.
94 Lt B.J.N. Marden diary, 19th August 1914.
95 Ibid.

squadron reconnaissance, B Squadron returned about 1500 and 'were billeted in a small cottage. Our troop, including our horses, was billeted in a farm, owned by a fine, buxom woman who at once made friends with our men, and supplied them with milk and quite excellent coffee.'[96] During the afternoon there was much amusement for the soldiers when, after the horses had been turned loose in a field to graze, a large stallion broke into the field, being 'hotly pursued by the buxom lass calling "*Nini, viens ici* (Nini, come here)."[97] In the evening, the B Squadron officers Francis, Rivy, Frank Crossley, Straker and Charles Garstin bathed in the stream.'[98] Like B Squadron, the A Squadron officers also took the opportunity to bathe in the river. 'Have a swim in a local river with Bunny, Lenny and Douglas, muddy.'[99] Once they had retired for the evening, Captain Peek was woken 'with the *joyful news* of a brigade parade.'[100]

On Thursday 20th August, back in England just as the 2nd Cavalry Brigade was about to conduct its first exercise, General Smith-Dorrien along with his staff Major Hope-Johnstone, AMS, and Captain W.A.T. Bowly, *Aide-De-Camp*, had set off for Boulogne. At 0900,[101] the 9th Lancers paraded and moved out for brigade training. When they arrived the 'General assembled us and told us the latest news and that we would soon be moving forward.'[102] The Brigade was to conduct an '*advance guard* action to a place named Cousobre, and a *rear guard* action back.'[103] The Regiment 'practiced covering retirement, the different methods of retiring by bounds.'[104] The 9th Lancers practised a *rear guard* exercise, and 'it was noticeable that the junior officers did not study their maps sufficiently, when suddenly called upon to go somewhere they had no idea of their present position on the map which caused delay.'[105] Also Captain Grenfell admits he also did not get it exactly right. 'I made the mistake of not getting in close enough touch with my colonel and warning him that owing to my fear of exposing Abadie's flank I had not retired as quickly as he expected me to.'[106] Despite the clear indication that they still had much to learn the exercise did not go down well with the officers and soldiers. 'The brigadier's insistence on doing a large-scale brigade exercise was universally voted ill-timed and unnecessary.'[107] Captain Peek's opinion of the exercise had not improved from his opinion the night before: 'all very angry and bored to tears.'[108] Lieutenant Marden was equally unimpressed 'everybody is fed up, useless fatigue of horseflesh after a tiring journey. Lance Corporal Hunt had gotten off lightly as he was not involved in the exercise and detailed with 'a corporal and three other chaps, directing post on some cross roads. Cooked our food at the local *estaminet* and were supplied with wine.'[109] All of these negative comments came from A and C Squadrons. The fact that B Squadron had

96 Grenfell, Grenfell Family Papers (within Lyttelton Family Papers 19th August 1914, p. 2.
97 Ibid., 19th-20th August 1914, pp. 2-3.
98 Ibid., 18th August, p. 10.
99 Lt B.J.N. Marden diary, 19th August 1914.
100 Capt. R.G. Peek diary, 19th August 1914.
101 Only Grenfell records this for 19th August, all other related diaries denote 20th August.
102 Anon., 9th Lancers War Diary, 19th August 1914, p. 7.
103 TNA WO 95/1113/2: 9th Lancers War Diary, 19th August 1914.
104 Cpl. R.H. Taylor, Letter of Sergeant 'Spur' R.H. Taylor, p. 1.
105 Ibid.
106 Grenfell, Grenfell Family Papers (within Lyttelton Family Papers), 19th August 1914, p. 11.
107 Maj. E.W. Sheppard, *The Ninth Queen's Royal Lancers 1715-1936*, p. 234.
108 Capt. R.G. Peek diary, 19th August 1914.
109 LCpl W. Hunt diary, p. 3.

already had the opportunity to practice squadron movement during their reconnaissance, and had identified their shortfalls, might have contributed to the lack of negative comments from Captain Grenfell's men.

In the afternoon the Regiment returned to their billets about 1500 and the officers who were to be attached as interpreters arrived: 'Lord Blackwood, Mr Julian Martin-Smith, Captain Joseph Montgomery (7th Dragoon Guards), and Mr Addison. Lord Basil was attached to the headquarters, Mr Smith to A Squadron (sic) Mr Addison to C, and Mr Montgomery to B Squadron.'[110] However, Captain Grenfell records that Mr Julian Smith was attached to his squadron' and 'I attached him to Ian Straker's troop.'[111] That evening, General Smith-Dorrien arrived in Boulogne and was 'impressed by the lack of excitement, the general cheerfulness and efficient arrangements at that busy port.'[112] At Obrechies, after dinner, Captain Grenfell got his troop leaders together. He 'held a lecture to explain some of the literature we had received and make sure all the troop leaders thoroughly understood the necessity of perfection.'[113] Captain Peek's day improved when 'one of our French interpreters is excellent and raided the cellar and produced some really passably good wine.'[114] Later that evening the Regiment received its orders to march at 0500. It was another long day and late night and 'Rivy and I went to bed at 1100 or 1200.'[115]

During the 20th August, Bruxelles had fallen and Generaloberst von Kluck had been expecting to find the BEF with the Belgian Army. Both he and the press, were uncertain as to where the BEF were, as according to the Belgium newspaper *La Patriote*, 'a British expeditionary force had landed in France on the 19th August, however their position was not known.'[116] It is likely that this headline came from the same story carried in the British press from the previous two days. The German *Army Order* of the 20th August, issued at 2000 that evening, reported that 'the *IV AK* entered Bruxelles today, without opposition. A great part of the Belgian Army has apparently retired on Antwerp: one infantry division is reported at Termonde. It is believed that the disembarkation of the BEF was conducted in French harbours on the 18th August; the direction of its advance is unknown.'[117] On the 20th August, General von Moltke informed Generaloberst von Kluck that 'it is reported at Boulogne their advance from about Lille must be reckoned with. It is believed that disembarkation of troops on a large scale had not yet taken place.[118] So, as Generaloberst von Kluck continued his advance he still had no clear understanding of exactly where the BEF was, but at least he now knew it had arrived.

That evening at 1930, General Allenby issued his first set of orders, for the first moves at 0615 the following morning as a result of receiving *Operation Order No. 5* from GHQ. The four brigades were to move to the area of St Symphorien, Harveng, Vieux Reng, Grand Ring and Fauroeulx. They were to be positioned to the east of 3rd Infantry Division. The 5th (Independent) Cavalry Brigade was to move to Binche and the 3rd Cavalry Brigade were to send a squadron

110 Anon., 9th Lancers War Diary, 19th August 1914, p. 7.
111 Ibid.
112 Smith-Dorrien, *Memories of Forty-Eight Years' Service*, p. 376.
113 Grenfell, Grenfell Family Papers (within Lyttelton Family Papers), 19th August 1914, p. 11.
114 Capt. R.G. Peek diary, 19th August 1914.
115 Grenfell, Grenfell Family Papers (within Lyttelton Family Papers), 19th August 1914, p. 12.
116 Korfes, *The German 66th Regiment in the First World War*, p. 38.
117 Kluck, *The March on Paris and The Battle of The Marne, 1914*, p. 35.
118 Ascoli, *The Mons Star*, p. 30.

to Binche at 0530 to establish if the town was still in the possession of the Belgians. General Allenby's headquarters was to move to Givry and all the brigades would remain under his command. As the GOC, this was the only time he personally commanded his whole Cavalry Division. *Operation Order No. 5* gave the movement tables for the two corps for the next three days up until the 23rd August and the moves were to be covered by the Cavalry Division.[119]

Earlier that day, just as the 9th Lancers had been returning to their billets after the brigade exercise at about 1500, the German *IV AK* entered the Belgian capital, Bruxelles, led by *Hussar Regiment 10,* followed by *Infanterie Regiment 26*'s band which followed the battalions of the Regiment. Before they entered the city, the barricade which had been erected at its entrance by the inhabitants had to be cleared away. As they entered the corps passed in review as it had in Aachen, before its commander, General Sixt von Armin. The troops marched through the city in 'squad column, with fixed bayonets, singing, and to the sound of Prussian march music, the streets thickly lined with people. The populace was calm, and the Belgian national colours were frequently seen. Marching in step for 16 kms through the city in the burning August heat was fatiguing but exhilarating.'[120] The local population turned out to watch the Germans march through their city. 'Thousands of astonished people turned out to witnessed the rare spectacle.

Infanterie Regiment 26 entering Bruxelles. (*Das Infanterie-Regiment Fürst Leopold von Anhalt-Dessau (1. Magdeburg.) Nr. 26.*)

119 'Operation Order No. 5', August 1914 quoted in Edmonds, *Military Operations France and Belgium 1914,* Vol. I, pp. 452-456.

120 Korfes, *The German 66th Regiment in the First World War*. 29.

Bruxelles, the seat of the Belgian Government, the intellectual and financial centre of a prosperous country, a city of 650,000 inhabitants, was in German hands…a huge, highly visible moral victory!'[121] At the end of the day, *III Battalion* of *Infanterie Regiment 66* remained as the garrison of Bruxelles and was attached to the *Infanterie Brigade 16*. I Battalion was quartered in Waasbroek and II Battalion was responsible for finding outposts for the night south west of Bruxelles on the road to Hal. Hauptmann Bloem asked his hosts at Hal why they had continued to fight and 'offered this senseless and useless resistance to our overwhelming superiority? "You must think of our self-respect, Hauptmann, "said Monsieur P, "and what the rest of the world would have thought of us if we had just let you pass through. But now we have done enough, I think, to preserve our honour, and we all hope that our gallant young King will make a reasonable peace with you.'[122] On the day that Bruxelles fell, Pope Pius X died. Coincidentally the 4th August, the day Britain had declared war, was the 11th anniversary of his being appointed to the Vatican. Not only did his death coincide with the fall of Bruxelles but also a solar eclipse [the Papal Eclipse] of the Sun. Some saw these as a sign of divine *intervention and displeasure* and as Generaloberst von Kluck turned in for the night he was still no closer to knowing where the BEF were!

121 Robert Dunlop, Holger Robert Dunlop & Holger Puttkammer (eds.), *The Battle of Mons: The official German Account.* (New York: Robert Dunlop, 2015). p. 15.
122 Bloem, *The Advance to Mons*, p. 36.

# 7

# Crossing into Belgium

*The only black spot is that the British will probably have on top of them very superior German forces, so that they may be forced to beat a hasty retreat, which would compel me to follow suit as quickly as possible.*

General Charles Lanrezac

On the morning[1] of 21st August, General Joffre issued his orders to Field Marshal French and General Lanrezac in *Ordre Particulier 15*. It contained his first instructions to the BEF and articulated the support to the French Fifth Army. The tone spells out the relationship between Field Marshal French and General Lanrezac, in that he is "asked to cooperate."

> The Fifth Army, resting on the Meuse and the fortress of Namur, will take as its objective the enemy northern group. The Commander-in-Chief of the British forces is asked to cooperate in this action, on the left of the Fifth Army, directing at first his main bodies in the general direction of Soignies. The line of demarcation between the zones of march of the Fifth Army and the British will be fixed by mutual agreement between the British Commander-in-Chief and the Commander of the Fifth Army. The information obtained by the Cavalry Corps and generally by the Fifth Army will be communicated to British GHQ and *vice versa*.[2]

At 1230, General Lanrezac replied to *Ordre Particulier No. 15* and specifically asked if he was to cross the Sambre:

> The Fifth Army has its *advance guards* on the Sambre from Namur to Thulin. It is ready to cross the Sambre, but it is obliged to leave one army corps on the Meuse between Givet and Namur, to guard its flank, so long as the Fourth Army has not crossed the Meuse, at

1 Spears, *Liaison 1914*, p. 125.
2 Ibid., p. 126.

> least with its *advance guards*. The British Expeditionary Force has announced that it will have its heads of columns on the front Mons-Erquelinnes on the 23rd. If the Fifth Army debouches tomorrow and, on the left bank of the Sambre (diminished by the I Corps, left on the Meuse), it may be exposed to giving battle alone. If it is to act in liaison with the British Army, it must wait until the 23rd or perhaps the 24th. The general commanding the Fifth Army has the honour to ask whether he is to cross the Sambre tomorrow.[3]

General Lanrezac would have to wait until late in the evening for a reply from General Joffre. Meanwhile, as *AOK 1* and *2* continued their advance south, Generaloberst von Kluck's *AOK 1*, had been subordinated to General Bülow's *AOK 2,* which the former felt would hinder the "envelopment" of the allies. He was instructed by the following *Army Order* issued on the 21st August:

> *AOK 2* will advance on the 22nd to the line Binche-Jemeppe, and, by crossing the Sambre on the 23rd, enable the *AOK 3* to cross the Meuse. The *AOK 1*, whilst observing Antwerp and holding Bruxelles, will so conform to this movement that, if needed, it will be able to operate west of Maubeuge in support of the *AOK 2* after it has invested the north and north east fronts of that fortress.[4]

The BEF were still in the process of complying with *Operation Order No. 5* issued the previous day. The Cavalry Division had set off early in the morning at 0500[5] and was ordered to be clear of Maubeuge by 0900 and to be clear from Bonnet by 1200,'[6] with the rendezvous for the supply columns railway station on the French side of the Belgian frontier between Valenciennes and Mons.[7] The cavalry were to take up positions on a line from Mons to Binche with the 5th (Independent) Cavalry Brigade arriving in Binche at about 0800.[8] General Allenby sent his GSO2, Major Home to Fontaine L'Sogne [sic] to see General Sordet, the commander of the French Cavalry Corps. When they met, he thought him very "polite and punctilious." When he saw their horses, he wrote that they 'were very tired. They have been having a good doing.'[9]

The orders for the 2nd Cavalry Brigade would see Brigadier De Lisle send out patrols from the 4th Dragoon Guards and 9th Lancers to both sides of the Mons-Condé Canal from Maurage to Obourg, with German patrols being seen but not engaged at Obourg and Nimy bridges.[10] For the 9th Lancers, reveille was early as they prepared to move to Harmignies which would involve crossing the frontier into Belgium in accordance with the movement tables.[11] After

3 Ibid., p. 127.
4 Kluck, *The March on Paris and The Battle of The Marne 1914*, p. 37.
5 Home, *Diary of a World War 1 Cavalry Officer*, p. 16.
6 Edmonds, *Military Operations France and Belgium 1914,* Vol. I, p. 509.
7 Grenfell, Grenfell Family Papers, (QMUL, within Lyttelton Family Papers); NL/GRE, letter "Dear Lily letter, Near Paris," 21st August 1914.
8 Home, *Diary of a World War 1 Cavalry Officer*, p. 16.
9 Ibid., p. 16.
10 Edmonds, *Military Operations France and Belgium 1914,* Vol. I, p. 50.
11 'Cavalry Division Operation Order No. 1'.

Nimy, the road bridge turning closed to allow the movement of barges. This is the position it was in during the Battle of Mons on 23rd August 1914. (Collection: Jean-Paul Hubens)

reveille at 0300, Captain Grenfell found his brother and 'saw all the men get up.'[12] They paraded at 0600 and the men were given coffee by the French women of the town. When the Belgian frontier was crossed, the Regiment again received a warm reception from the inhabitants who 'welcomed them as the forerunners of the English force who had at last come to succour the sorely pressed Belgium army.'[13] As usual 'presents of food, matches and tobacco were pressed on the men from all sides. This of course was greatly appreciated by all concerned it being awfully thirsty travelling along the dusty roads.'[14] Rivy and Francis rode together. 'Rivy rode *Pearl of Price* and Francis rode *Joe Boy* 'this march had been announced as a preparatory march so most of the Regiment had not got their maps, or their rifles charged.'[15] They were now moving to the BEFs initial deployment positions, passing through Aibes, Jeumont, Grand Ring, Rouveroy and Givry.[16] When they reached Givry, they were warned to prepare for action. Rivy 'could not help noticing a tightening of lips, and a sort of increased tension through all ranks. We had a triumphal march through all the above towns. Some of the people had scarcely seen soldiers

12 Grenfell, Grenfell Family Papers (within Lyttelton Family Papers), 21st August, p. 12.
13 Anon., 9th Lancer War Diary, 21st August 1914, p. 7.
14 Cpl. R.H. Taylor letter of Sergeant 'Spur' R.H. Taylor, p. 1.
15 Grenfell, Grenfell Family Papers (within Lyttelton Family Papers), 21st August 1914, p. 12.
16 Grenfell, Grenfell Family Papers (within Lyttelton Family Papers, 21st August 1914, p. 3.

before, and, behold, here were their benefactors, the English, coming to their rescue!'[17] It was here that the Regiment came into touch with the other brigades of the Division.[18] The whole Cavalry Division passed through, taking over two hours to pass. The head of the column passed at 0700, and the 9th Lancers reached Grand Ring at 0900. They finally reached Harmignies at 1200 and remained saddled for four hours until they went into their billets at 1800. That night, the B Squadron officers 'slept in a very comfortable house, where the owner and his wife were exceedingly kind to us and put their very best rooms at our disposal, and also their cooking.'[19] The scouts of the 4th Dragoon Guards came in touch with the enemy, who were said to be advancing in great force towards Soignies and Ath, with the main body around Brillecourt. 'The high dumping ground covering Mons was to be held until the infantry could come up… For the first time everyone was tingling with expectancy.'[20] The 4th Dragoon Guards arrived in Harmignies at approximately 1300. The Regiment was then sent to hold La Bout en Haut, where they remained until relieved by the 1 Middlesex who, when they arrived, looked very dusty and tired. While Captain Charles Hornby was out on patrol, A Squadron was holding the bridge over the canal and Captain Wright:

> Spent a very cold night in a cart, part of a barricade, no blanket nor coat, there were no alarms that night, the country about Mons, five miles from the canal, appeared to be fire of the enemy, early next morning we strengthened our position, dug small trenches and put wire entanglements across the roads. The people in a château near were very good to us and fed us man and beast.[21]

During the march, Lieutenant Marden had heard about 'the fall of Bruxelles and the presence of a very large German force north of Mons,'[22] and he also heard that 'the general promises the DSO or DSM [sic] to the first officer or NCO who 'sticks' an opposing patrol leader.'[23] The news of the fall of Bruxelles was also heard at Saint Bernard's which did not come as a surprise as from the morning, they 'had been expecting a disappointment: they announced the breaking of communications between Mons and Bruxelles and the storming of the capital city. In Bruxelles, the newspapers didn't get published and those from yesterday were already published with big blanks, articles deleted by censorship.'[24]

When the 9th Lancers arrived at their billets, Captain Peek was more than happy with his troop's arrangement. 'My farmer was a good fellow and I supplied my men with a good dinner and the horses with plenty of hay.'[25] Lieutenant Allfrey wrote that they were aware of how close the Germans were and possibly as a consequence slept fully clothed. 'Heard there was a German army camp about seven or eight miles away…billet, quite comfy, but not allowed to undress…

17 Ibid., 21st August, p. 3.
18 Grenfell, Grenfell Family Papers (within Lyttelton Family Papers), 21st August 1914, p. 12.
19 Ibid., 21st August 1914, p. 12.
20 Anon., 9th Lancer War Diary, 21st August, p. 8.
21 Capt. A. Wright diary, 21st August 1914, p.2.
22 Lt B.J.N. Marden diary, 21st August.
23 Ibid.
24 *Annales du pensionnat Saint Bernard à Audregnies*, p. 42, op. cit., Jean Richez, *Un Champ de Coquelicots, La Bataille d'Audregnies le 24 Août 1914.*
25 Capt. R.G. Peek diary, 21st August 1914.

slept on a table.'[26] Captain Grenfell went to bed at about 2300 and was woken up at midnight by Rivy with a message which later he completely forgot he had received although he had signed it![27]

The patrol that Brigadier De Lisle had ordered the 9th Lancers to send a patrol forward to a bridge a mile and a half north of Mons. It was commanded by Lieutenant Eric Smith from C Squadron. While they were there, they saw a few German patrols. The troop was finally relieved about 2300 by troop from the 11th Hussars.[28] Lance Corporal Hunt of C Squadron wrote:

> I had a fine reception of fruit, eggs (I put two in my cap and they fell out), cigars. Outside Mons about four miles we halted and loaded our rifles. I was smoking a long cigar, couldn't realise we were on active service, of course someone let off a round and got *straffed* by the Squadron Leader. Then our troop went on in front advance troop to the brigade, went and made good a wood just outside Mons, the Germans we were told were only two miles in front and am just getting excited. Went forward into Mons and relieved the Belgian Civic Guard on the big canal bridges, the Mons people were good. I stayed in the small lawn of a gentleman's house with about six horses and everytime I started slackening their girths or getting their nosebags on, this good old chap would immediately rush up with a big jug of beer. In the finish, what with the girths and nosebags, I was feeling rather jolly with myself.[29]

C Squadron of the 4th Dragoon Guards commanded by Major Bridges, was sent out 'to get in touch with the enemy in the neighbourhood of Havre and Thien, and to keep touch during the night.'[30] Major Bridges was in action again as a 43 year old Squadron Leader, 14 years after his action at the Relief of Mafeking, and pushed forward on the afternoon of the 21st to try to make contact with the enemy. All his operational experience started to come back to him, and his gut started to tell him something did not feel right:

> We halted in a little village and sent forward patrols to get information. This all pointed to the Germans streaming south on every road from Bruxelles, and one retired Belgian officer, visited in his château, estimated them at 450,000, but still no enemy were seen, and fugitives reported them bivouacked for the night 15 miles to the north. We made ourselves comfortable in a field outside our hamlet, keeping standing patrols out on all approaches and continuing to reconnoitre. But I soon took a dislike to our village. Too many young men had been seen leaving it on bicycles for the north, so after dark I moved across the main Bruxelles road into a wood on a hill that I had noted. From this point, I hoped to ambush the enemy's *advanced guard* and get some prisoners.[31]

26 Lt B.J.N. Marden diary, 21st August 1914.
27 Grenfell, Grenfell Family Papers (within Lyttelton Family Papers), 21st August 1914, p. 13.
28 TNA WO 95/1113/2: 9th Lancers War Diary, 21st August 1914.
29 LCpl W. Hunt diary, p. 3.
30 Bridges, *Alarms and Excursions,* p. 76.
31 Ibid., p. 76.

Private Ben Clouting who was with 4th Troop, C Squadron 4th Dragoon Guards had a sleepless and nervous night. 'Our troop was in a cornfield, along the back of which ran a wood. A screen of sentries was sent out, allowing those not on standby to eat something or catch up on some sleep. Everything was still and quiet; everyone was tense. We tied the horses' reins round our wrists, while those too nervous to rest talked to each other in whispers.'[32]They were very much aware of their isolated position and 'we were warned that for all we knew we might already be surrounded and that we mustn't speak to anyone. A few of us slackened our horses' girths to let them breathe freely. But silence was the order and, as horses were prone to play with their loose bit bars, we held or tied handkerchiefs around the bars to muffle any sound.[33]

The information being gathered by the 4th Dragoon Guards and 9th Lancers was still to be passed back from the Cavalry Brigade. In the absence of any information from the divisional cavalry, General Allenby sent his intelligence officer, Lieutenant Colonel Barrow, accompanied by Captain Stewart, into Mons "to exercise a novel plan" and try and get an understanding of the German movements and to the 'extent of the great left wheel he was evidently about to make.'[34] With the consent of the French authorities, they took possession of the Mons railway telephone office:

> I sat all day and far into the night ringing up all possible and impossible places in Belgium not known yet to be in German hands – Soignies, Braine-le-Comte, Hal, Tubize, Lens, Ath, Ghislenghien, Lessines and many others. Replies took the following forms: "No signs of enemy here, but rumours they are in A" "Germans are five miles distant on road to B." Have just received message from C that enemy close to town; we are closing down." A German voice or failure to get contact told that the enemy had already arrived. It was easy from these replies to get a fairly accurate picture of the German line of advance.[35]

With this information, General Allenby was one of the first in the BEF 'to grasp the reality of the BEF's situation. 'It was laying athwart the line of advance of a formidable German Army… not only were the British outnumbered by at least three to one, but they were in danger of being outflanked and cut-off from any line of retreat to the coast.'[36] The reconnaissance flights of the RFC had struggled with the weather and found observation difficult. The weather in the morning was too foggy for observation and, in the afternoon, was rainy and misty. The three reconnaissance flights made during the afternoon showed that the country immediately in front of the British was very quiet, but in the wood one mile south of Nivelles, Lieutenant Corballis reported a large body of cavalry[37] with some guns and infantry. He also reported another body of infantry moving south on Charleroi and at Pont-a-Celles on the Charleroi canal, south of Nivelles, and three villages were seen to be burning.[38] This information was sent on to GHQ as

32 Richard Van Emden, *Teenage Tommy: Memoirs of a Cavalryman in the First World War* (Barnsley: Pen & Sword, 2013). p. 39.
33 Ibid., p. 39.
34 Barrow, *The Fire of Life*, p. 143.
35 Ibid., p. 143.
36 Lawrence James. *Imperial Warrior, The Life and Times of Field Marshal Viscount Allenby 1861-1936* (London: Weidenfeld & Nicolson, 1993), p 58.
37 This was later identified as the German 9th Cavalry Division.
38 Walter Raleigh, *War in the Air*, p. 301.

it showed that the German right extended much further west than had been suspected. Field Marshal French had learnt during the Manoeuvres of 1912 that information from the RFC needed to be corroborated by another source. As just because the RFC reported the absence of an enemy did not necessarily mean they were not there. Confirmation was normally done by the cavalry. However, the majority of the Cavalry Division (four brigades) were on the western flank ready to advance north and the 5th (Independent) Cavalry Brigade were doing the same task on the eastern flank. Therefore, technically, Field Marshal French had no real strategic cavalry assets, no screen had been deployed forward to provide the BEF with *protective reconnaissance* and the four squadrons of divisional cavalry of the 15th and 19th Hussars were providing reconnaissance patrols for the four infantry divisions. The chosen deployment and use of the cavalry limited this process of corroboration and without the flow of information from the Belgian and French armies, Field Marshal French's intelligence picture was only *operational* at best.

When General Allenby informed GHQ of the information he had collected, the reply signed by General Wilson said that 'the information which you have acquired and conveyed to the Commander-in-Chief appears to be somewhat exaggerated. It is probable that only mounted troops supported by *Jägers* are in your immediate neighbourhood. In no circumstances, however, does the Commander-in-Chief wish the Cavalry Division to be seriously engaged.'[39] At 1545 he was ordered to close the gap that was forming to the east of Mons and the French and that the 5th (Independent) Cavalry Brigade under command of Brigadier Philip Chetwode was to take up a position to the left of General Sordet's French Cavalry Corps in front of Binche.[40]

Field Marshal French later wrote that 'the intelligence reports which constantly arrived, and the results of cavalry and aircraft reconnaissance, only confirmed the previous appreciation of the situation, and left no doubt as to the direction of the German advance, but nothing came to hand which led us to foresee the crushing superiority of strength which actually confronted us.'[41] The entry in Field Marshal French's diary for the 21st read 'Lanrezac says that eight German Corps and three Cavalry Divisions are now north of the Meuse. I doubt there are more than six, but time will tell.[42] Lanrezac's estimate was off by two corps, but the location was correct, and he had correctly appreciated the German's intentions. Field Marshal French's estimate was out by four. It would appear that Field Marshal French was suffering from *cognitive dissonance* where he had been guided by his preconceptions and chose to believe the advice from General Wilson, over the information being provided by his intelligence section and General Lanrezac. General Wilson's calculation was wrong but by now he had become Field Marshal French's *Svengali*, and while waiting for corroboration of the conflicting reports, no planning was being done to effect a possible retirement.

This scenario had been anticipated by General Douglas Haig who said General Murray was an 'old woman,'[43] and 'might acquiesce too readily in the proposals of the Commander-in-Chief, even when he disagreed with them.'[44] This was possible as a consequence of seeing what happened

39 Marquess of Anglesey, *A History of the British Cavalry 1914-1919*, Vol. 7, p. 111.
40 Edmonds, *Military Operations France and Belgium*, Vol. I, pp. 51-52.
41 Viscount French of Ypres, *1914*, p. 43.
42 Diary of Field Marshal French, 21st August 1914, op. cit. in Ascoli, *The Mons Star*, p. 48.
43 Tuchman, *August 1914*, p. 200.
44 Charteris, *Field Marshal Earl Haig*, p. 82.

when the previous Chief of Staff during the Army Manoeuvres of 1913 when General Grierson had pointed out the 'impracticability of some of his proposals.'[45] He had been removed from post at once but had been replaced by himself. This was bound to induce some natural caution. General Haig also did not have a high opinion of General Wilson. Although he respected his intellect, "he did not trust his judgement." He felt that he had 'fallen under the influence of the French General Staff Officers, and indeed of the French nation…his temperament was almost Latin, and he was well aware of the personal ambition which dominated his mind…his career at the War Office had thrown him into close contact with politicians and he had begun to apply political methods, savouring always of opportunism, to military problems.'[46] As a known Francophile, he was known to his intimates as Henri.'[47]

General Allenby had done remarkably well, as he and his staff were using their flair and initiative to deliver one of their core functions, providing information, which is somewhat ironic, since the Cavalry Division had not been established for an intelligence officer on mobilisation and Lieutenant Colonel Barrow's appointment was only made possible because he was unable to rejoin his regiment in India on the outbreak of war. While the cavalry and RFC were trying to build up an intelligence picture to their front the infantry were moving north from their concentration areas. The 15th Infantry Brigade had spent three days at Le Pommereuil and Ors and now marched northwards about 20 miles to Gommignies to their new billets. This march was to be a challenge, for everyone, as the day was hot and the roads were hard. The Norfolks 'took to the road and were soon sweating, and they found their packs very heavy and the sun very hot.'[48] Private Hurrell found the roads 'very rough indeed making one's feet very sore,' but it was the reservists who felt it the most and they 'felt every inch a big pull, or shall I say a drag on their reserve energy, which meant that some simply had to fall out long before we arrived at the destination.'[49] The Brigade Commander had watched his men fall by the roadside, and wrote 'many, all of them reservists who had not carried a pack for years. They had every intention of keeping up, of course, but they simply could not.'[50] When he spoke to them to 'urge them along… the answer was always the same, "oh, I'll get along alright, sir, after a bit of a rest, but I ain't accustomed to carrying a big weight like this on a hot day…to do them justice they practically all did turn up.'[51] Numerous orders had been issued regarding the fitting and greasing of boots and these were not the issue, 'except in a very few cases.'[52] When the Norfolks finally got to their billets there was a wedding going on in the village at the house where Private Sheldrake was billeted. They were invited to the proceedings and they 'drank the health of the bride and bridegroom in beers, wines and spirits, the bridegroom having to leave shortly for the war. Our hostess put several men into her bedrooms, the remainder of us sleeping in an outhouse.'[53] After the long hot march and the wedding, Private Sheldrake did not sleep well as he felt 'sick from the effects of the fruit, drinks and the heat of the day. He felt so unwell he decided to go outside

45 Ibid., p. 82.
46 Ibid., pp. 82-83.
47 Anglesey, *A History of the British Cavalry 1914-1919*, Vol. 7, p. 73.
48 Pte R. Sheldrake diary, p. 9.
49 Pte R. Hurrell, Log of Round the World Cruise, p. 19.
50 Gleichen, *Infantry Brigade 1914*, p. 15.
51 Ibid., p. 15.
52 Ibid., p. 15.
53 Pte R. Sheldrake diary, p. 9.

and leave his billet. The other men were laying 'so thick I had to crawl over their heads, feet and all sorts to get out, and dare not venture back again, so I coiled up in my coat outside, it being the first night I had spent outdoors for a few years.'[54] Private Hurrell's billet was in a barn attached to a house which had plenty of straw, because the 'cows and horses were occupying the same place.'[55] Eventually he became accustomed to the smell and 'one didn't seem to mind that after a while.'[56] Private Hurrell was also ill that night 'probably due to eating so much fruit which the inhabitants of the various villages offered while passing through.'[57] During the day, Brigadier Gleichen had met a French patrol of *Chasseurs â Cheval* who were wearing light blue tunics and shakos. He told him that they had seen "Uhlans" somewhere to the north of them, and he duly passed the information back to 5th Infantry Division. However, the Brigadier had no overall understanding of the operational picture as to where the enemy was:[58]

> We did not know in the least what was happening elsewhere, beyond the fact that the 3rd Infantry Division was somewhere on our right, and that the French cavalry was believed to be covering our left front. We did not know at this period what the movement was about or where the Germans were supposed to be. We trusted our superiors to do what was necessary and plunged blindly into the *fog of war.*[59]

Brigadier Gleichen's memory of the countryside they were marching through would have been described by 'novelists as "smiling" pretty, in a mild sort of way: clean, green, with tidy farmhouses and cottages, and fields about ripe for harvest. Plenty of orchards there were too, with lots of fruit trees alongside the roadside, and the people offering us fruit and milk and water and coffee as we went along,'[60] and it was in Gommignies that he had been acquainted with the excellent 'penny cigar of the country.'[61]

Late that evening at 2000, General Joffre replied to General Lanrezac's earlier communication regarding *Ordre Particulier No. 15:* 'I leave you absolute judge of the moment when your offensive movement should begin. This evening the Fourth Army should reach the front Bievre-Paliseul-Bertrix-Neuf Château. I will keep you informed daily of the line reached by the Fourth Army – Joffre.'[62] Later in the evening, Field Marshal French's GHQ issued their own Operation Orders on receipt of *Ordre Particulier No. 15.* At 2135, General Wilson issued specific instructions to General Allenby and said that 'in no circumstances, however, does the C-in-C wish the Cavalry Division to be seriously engaged until he is ready to support it. Cav. Div. HQ will move to Quiévrain.'[63] At 2355, Colonel G.M. Harper, on behalf of Field Marshal French, issued *Operation Order No. 6* which complimented *Operation Order No. 5* issued the previous day, giving the details of the locations of the outposts. The Cavalry Division were:

54 Ibid., p. 9.
55 Pte R. Hurrell, *Log of Round the World Cruise, Autobiography,* p. 20.
56 Ibid., p. 20.
57 Ibid., p. 20.
58 Gleichen, *Infantry Brigade 1914,* pp. 15-16.
59 Ibid., p. 16.
60 Ibid., p. 17.
61 Ibid., p. 18.
62 Spears, *Liaison 1914,* p. 127.
63 Edmonds, *Military Operations France and Belgium 1914,* Vol. I, p. 514.

> To remain in their present position until the outposts of the II Corps are in position. They will then move to the area Thulin-Quiévrain-Baisieux- Audregnies-Élouges (on the left of 5th Div). GOC II Corps will send a Staff Officer to Cav. Div. to lead the division across the billeting area of the corps. Cav. Div. HQ to Quiévrain and outposts. II Corps. The line Givry inclus- Harmignies-Bois la Haut all by 12 noon. Nimy and the line of the canal westward, as far as bridge S. of OE in Pommeroeul inclus. Not later than 1300 Cav. Div. from left of 2nd Corps along line of canal to Condé sur Escaut.[64]

The canal that the BEF was to concentrate on was the Mons-Condé Canal which was a canal 16 ¼ miles long, of which 12 ¼ miles was in Belgium. It ran from east to west. The canal was 64 feet wide and its maximum depth was seven feet. It was crossed by 18 bridges, all of which, with the exception of the railway bridges east of St Ghislain and at Les Herbieres, were swing bridges.[65] The initial deployment positions of the BEF would be to the south of the canal. Field Marshal French described the II Corps area to the west of Mons as:

> The valley of the Haine forms a long, low plain, covered with meadows, through which the river meanders in broad bends as far as the Scheldt. Numerous water ditches, cut in the peaty soil and marked out by poplars and willows, drain the land and render the movement off the roads of any troops but infantry quite impracticable. On the northern boundary of the valley of the Haine, a belt of sand gives rise to a tract of rough uncultivated land which is in many places covered with woods. On its southern boundary the ground rises steeply on the east, and more gently on the west.[66]

This meant, for both British and Germans alike, the roads and the bridges were going to be key for both advancing and retreating. Now the scene was set. These were the last operational orders Field Marshal French would issue until *Operation Order 7* on 24th August. The BEF was asked to cooperate in this action, to the left of the Fifth Army, directing at first his main bodies in the general direction of Soignies and the moment for the commencement of the offensive moment was left in the hands of General Lanrezac by General Joffre. The British cavalry would form a screen around the BEF with General Allenby's Cavalry Division to the left of the 5th Infantry Division south of the Mons-Condé Canal in anticipation of covering the BEFs left flank as they advanced north east towards Soignies. Brigadier Chetwode's 5th (Independent) Cavalry Brigade were to guard the right flank of the I Corps. To the front was a thin cavalry screen of the 15th and 19th Hussars from the divisional cavalry. General Wilson wrote in a letter home on the 21st, 'today we start our forward march, and the whole line from here to Verdun set out. It is at once a glorious and an awful thought, and by this day week the greatest action that the world has ever heard of will have been fought. I am full of confidence, but nothing is certain in war.'[67] General Smith-Dorrien had arrived from England just in time to be briefed by Field Marshal French and he "explained the general situation as far as he could, for the *fog of war* was peculiarly dense at that time." He was told "that we were to move on the morrow to the general

64 Ibid., p. 457.
65 Viscount French of Ypres, *1914*, p. 49.
66 Ibid., p. 49.
67 Callwell, *Field-Marshal Sir Henry Wilson Bart*, p. 165.

line of the Mons-Condé Canal, the I Corps on the right, my corps on the left, the latter's position to be along the line of the canal from Mons westward."'[68] That however 'was only to be a preliminary step to a further move forward which would take the form of a slight right-wheel into Belgium, the British Army forming the outer flank, pivoting on the French Fifth Army.'[69] On arrival at his headquarters at 2300, he 'approved of the orders for the move next morning, and turned in.'[70]

Prophetically, General Lanrezac wrote in his diary that day 'The only black spot is that the British will probably have on top of them very superior German forces, so that they may be forced to beat a hasty retreat, which would compel me to follow suit as quickly as possible.'[71]

68 Smith-Dorrien, *Memories of Forty-Eight Years' Service,* p. 376.
69 Ibid., p. 376.
70 Ibid., p. 376.
71 Lanrezac, op. cit. in Spears, *Liaison 1914,* p. 128.

# 8

## Move to Mons

*The whole action can't have lasted much more than three minutes and as the fighting abated, the order was given to cease fire and withdraw."*

Private Ben Clouting

On Saturday 22nd August Field Marshal French woke early at 0500 full of optimism. 'I awoke, as I had lain down to sleep, in high hopes. No evil foreboding of coming events had visited me in dreams.'[1] This day would see the BEF move to its long pre-arranged start position on the left of the French Fifth Army in support of General Lanrezac with the intention of advancing and pushing the Germans back. Field Marshal French was not aware that Lieutenant Spears was travelling in the opposite direction to meet him. The general position of the BEF at Mons had General Haig's I Corps to the east, General Smith-Dorrien's II Corps to the west along the Mons-Condé Canal and the Cavalry Division of General Allenby to the west in support of II Corps. On the morning of the move, Smith-Dorrien believed he was not ready to move. 'The corps deployed despite not being ready and the concentration not being complete. This was at the insistence of the French who wanted the BEF to move to cover their left flank.[2] At this point, his corps was still 'short of guns, field hospitals, and engineers.[3] They had also been short of drivers, as was the BEF but 25 volunteer motorists from the Royal Automobile Club Volunteer Force (RACVF) had been sent from London by the War Office with their cars to drive officers of the GHQ staff at the front. They had just had arrived at Le Havre.[4] However, despite not being completely ready, Field Marshal French, on hearing the Germans had left Bruxelles and were marching west and south, decided to go without them. The move saw II Corps move 12 to 15 miles to the line of the canal:

1 Viscount French of Ypres, *1914,* p. 56.
2 Smith-Dorrien, *Memories of Forty-Eight Years' Service,* p. 379.
3 Ibid., p. 379.
4 Frederic Coleman, *From Mons to Ypres with French, A Personal Narrative, From Mons to Ypres with French, A Personal Narrative,* (London: Sampson Low, Marston & Co., 1916). p. 1.

> Where in accordance with orders we took up a line of outposts extending from Pommeroeul (five miles east of Condé) round the north side of Mons to Nimy and thence to Givry, 21 miles in all. The 3rd Infantry Division went into billets round Mons in the area of Nimy-Ghlin-Frameries-Spiennes, and were there by 1300, whilst the 5th Infantry Division rather later occupied the canal on their left from Jemappes to Pommeroeul. During this day they saw nothing of the enemy, and their general news of the enemy was very vague, but the general opinion was that considerable German forces were moving towards us and that contact on the morrow was almost a certainty.[5]

For the 9th Lancers, it was going to be a very long day with reveille sounded at 0200, but even before reveille Captain Grenfell's day did not get off to a good start. At 0100, a messenger came and woke both him and Rivy up,[6] Rivy was sent to see what was wanted, and the messenger had said "an officer was wanted on the telephone at a station, a mile away." Both of them were suspicious and they were not sure if the messenger was genuine or not, but the patron of the house in which they were staying said he knew him.[7] As they set off for the station Rivy told the messenger to walk in front of him, at the same time he turned his torch on him, and pointed his pistol at his head, 'and warned him that if anyone shot at me, I would shoot him at once. As it transpired, he turned out to be a very peaceful Belgian, and was much frightened.' [8] When he got to the station, he spoke on telephone to Captain R.K. McGillicuddy,[9] who told him that there had been a phone conversation between the station he was guarding and Mons had been suddenly cut off. He reported this fact to Brigadier De Lisle's *Aide-De-Camp*.'[10] Finally, when Captain Grenfell got up at 0230, he went around to the men in their billets and was not impressed with what he found:

> Was annoyed to find some of the officers had undressed and had found that some of the ammunition had not been issued, nor had the men received any hot food. The exception was 4th Troop, commanded by Lieutenant Charlie Garstin, who by 0300 were all saddled up and the men had had hot coffee and bread and seemed to be comfortable. The horses too had likewise been carefully looked after.[11]

Captain Grenfell's squadron was *turned out* at 0345 but eventually at 0430 they were told to *turn in* again, but to remain ready at any moment. The situation that Captain Grenfell had found at reveille was sufficiently serious and he was so "very annoyed" he reported the matter to the Commanding Officer, who most sensibly advised him to deal with it himself 'and not to bring it to his notice.[12] Captain Grenfell having been given direction by the Commanding Officer,

5 Smith-Dorrien, *Memories of Forty-Eight Years' Service,* p. 380.
6 Grenfell, Grenfell Family Papers (within Lyttelton Family Papers), 22nd August 1914, p. 13.
7 Grenfell, Grenfell Family Papers (within Lyttelton Family Papers, 22nd August 1914, p. 4.
8 Ibid., p. 4.
9 B Squadron 4th Dragoon Guards.
10 Grenfell, Grenfell Family Papers (within Lyttelton Family Papers, 22nd August 1914, p. 4.
11 Ibid., 22nd August, p. 14.
12 Ibid., 22nd August, p. 14.

which clearly articulated where he thought the Squadron Leader's responsibilities lay, gathered his troop leaders together for a moment of perspective:

> At 0500 I assembled all the troop leaders in a small room and gave them a straight talking to and told them it was impertinence to say they were tired, as sentries who did not do their duty and gave the excuse of being tired were sentenced in South Africa to four years' imprisonment; I also told them that up to now I had given them a very *free hand* which apparently did not work successfully and, in the future, I should be very much stricter. I told them that any officer who disobeyed any order in future I would send to the base immediately. I was very annoyed and perhaps said a little too much, but it had the effect of moving all to tears and assuring me that they had made a mistake which would not occur again. I told them that what especially annoyed me was that I had given orders, with the enemy at out gates that nobody was to undress, and I found that they had disobeyed me. I brought forward all the mistakes I had found on going around, and how I noticed that all officers took nearly half an hour to get to their men. I think it had a very good effect. It gave me a chance I had been waiting for to establish myself as commander of the squadron and to let them see I was going to have no nonsense from anybody. Every commander must, at some moment, put his foot down. Little Garstin and Frank Crossley afterwards came to me and said they had never worked so hard in their lives as they had for me and hoped I would realise how hard they had tried to please me.[13]

Lieutenants Charlie Garstin and Frank Crossley. (9/12L Museum)

13 Ibid., 22nd August, pp. 14-15.

While Captain Grenfell was dealing with his troop leaders, at about 0630 Major Bridges squadron of the 4th Dragoon Guards moved from their night location and started to water the horses when reports from the locals came in that there were German cavalry in the vicinity. The cavalry units were from *Kavallerie Brigade 13* from *Kavallerie Division 9* of the *HKK 2*. A patrol from Kűrassier *Regiment 4*, had been sent out south at dawn in the direction of Mons, via Notre Dame, Louvignies, Cambron, Casteau to Ormeignies in the southern part of Ath.[14] As they advanced south from Soignies they joined another patrol from *Husaren Regiment 8*[15] (Ewald Squadron) which had had been given the same mission, so together they advanced down the road south towards Mons. Halfway, and 'in the middle of the town of Casteau, a squadron of British cavalry appeared from a side street, which forced the patrol to beat a hasty retreat.'[16] Private Clouting observed:

> At about 0630, we arrived at a farm on the corner of a staggered crossroads and began watering our horses in a trough. There were already a few people about and as we waited, a farm worker came in saying he'd seen four Uhlans coming down the road. Once this was confirmed, there was a flurry of action, and a plan was hatched to capture the patrol as it passed. Four men from 4th Troop were dismounted and ordered to fire a volley of shots into the patrol at close quarters. This would be followed by 2nd Troop charging forward and bagging the remainder. I, along with the rest of 4th Troop, was placed out of sight, mounted, waiting with drawn sword. I believe a man was sent out behind a hedge to signal when the Germans were about to arrive, but in his excitement, he ran to grab his horse and gave the position away. 1st Troop of C with Hornby at their head went after them, and the rest of the squadron followed on in support, with drawn swords. Our troop officer, Lieutenant Swallow, led the troop at a fast canter, everyone was highly excited and I recall looking round to find our saddler sergeant major, not with a sword, but with a cocked .45 in his hand.[17]

The chase was given by 1st Troop 'down the hard, high road, which was wide for about a mile and a half'[18] and caught up with the German patrol in the village and chased them through to the far side, where they met with another German patrol, dismounted and the first shots of the war were fired. The Uhlans carrying lances had been hampered and a good number of them threw them away.[19]

> As the Germans retired into the village, they met up with a larger group of Uhlans, and, owing to the congestion, were soon caught by the 1st Troop. A fight immediately broke out. However, we arrived after the Germans had scattered, with the main body splitting off and carrying on up the main road. We continued to give chase, our horses slipping all

14 Heinrich Glasmeier, *Geschichte des Kürassier-Regiments von Driesen Nr 4,* (Oldenburg: Stalling, 1932), p. 54.
15 *Husaren-Regiment Kaiser Nikolaus II von Russland (1. Westfèalische) Nr. 8.*
16 Terence Zuber, *The Mons Myth: A Reassessment of the Battle* (Stroud: History Press, 2010). p. 119.
17 Van Emden, *Teenage Tommy*, pp. 39-40.
18 Bridges, *Alarms and Excursions,* p. 77.
19 Ibid., p. 77.

> over the place as we clattered along the square-set stones. Our chase continued for perhaps a mile or more, until we found ourselves flying up a wide, rising road, tree-lined on both sides. The Germans, reaching the road's crest, turned and, though they were still mounted, began firing back down the hill. "Action front, dismount," rapped Hornby, "Get the horses under cover." In one movement, the troop returned their swords, reached for their rifles· and dismounted, dashing for cover, lying flat on their stomachs behind the trees. Glancing up the hill, I saw several Germans filling the road. They made a perfect target, and Thomas, the first into action, shot one from his horse.[20]

Fred Bulmer remembered that 'it was a wide cobbled road with tramlines and a couple of our horses lost their footing and came down. I remember we galloped past a riding stable, later we found that the owner was an Englishman and he gave us a good old cheer!'[21] This was the first shot fired in anger on continental Europe since 1815.[22] Private Clouting did not take part directly in the dismounted action as he was a 'designated horse holder, I did not come into action...the troop had been riding in fours, and being number three, it was my job to take the reins of the two horses on my left and those of the one on my right.'[23] The first action and shots of the war was over quickly, "the whole action can't have lasted much more than three minutes and as the fighting abated, the order was given to cease fire and withdraw." After the engagement 'we never knew the extent of German casualties...as far as I am aware, we came out of the action with three prisoners, all suffering from sword wounds.'[24] After the action there was much talk amongst the squadron especially about, the squadron's fencing champion, 1st Troop's SSM Sharpe, who had faced one Ulan, parried the German's lance thrust before swinging his sword, and chopped all the Ulan's fingers off.[25] By the time Major Bridges had arrived on the scene the skirmish was over and the chase was brought to an end by sharp rifle fire from a battalion of cyclists in position on the crest and Major Bridges was keen to capitalise on this first contact with the enemy:

> A convenient château with a walled garden gave us cover and a fire position, and I now withdrew Hornby's two troops and sent a message back to say what had occurred, suggesting that a flanking movement by fresh squadrons, while we held up the head of the German column, might be productive of good results. But other plans had already been made and the whole of the cavalry were now to move across to the left flank for the Battle of Mons. No doubt the German *advanced guard* had had a shake-up for we withdrew unmolested.[26]

The patrol from *Kűrassier Regiment 4* was led by Leutnant Lothar Grafen von und zu Hoensbroech. The contact with the 4th Dragoon Guards was reported immediately and the message was delivered by Kűrassier Küster from the 3rd Squadron. The ride to Kavallerie

20 Ibid., p. 77.
21 Ascoli, *The Mons Star,* p. 53.
22 Thornton, *Old Contemptibles,* p. 27.
23 Bridges, *Alarms and Excursions,* p. 77.
24 Ibid., p. 77.
25 Ibid., p. 77.
26 Ibid., p. 77.

*Division 9* took him 75 minutes and as soon as he arrived the report was immediately passed up the chain of command. At 1250 it was with the *OKH* at Löwen. A report from the *HKK 2*, radio message: "A unit of the *Kűrassier Regiment 4* have unequivocally detected an English squadron at Casteau, north east of Mons."'[27] The unit report said that:

> In the unit the great circumspection, calm and bravery of Feldwebel Kotz from the 3rd Squadron stood out. In the first encounter with the enemy, the unit lost four men, of whom one, the previously freed Schuer, escaped again, and reached the division in the evening. The three others were taken prisoner by the English, who had much fresher horses. Only one of the unit's horses was injured by being lightly grazed by a bullet.[28]

The arrival back of the 4th Dragoon Guards with their prisoners (three prisoners, two badly wounded, at Bois la Haute[29]), escorted by Sadler Corporal Edward Regan of C Squadron, caused much excitement and an increase in morale as the prisoners were escorted back to the Brigade Commander and then to Colonel Richard Mullens.[30] This was witnessed by the 9th Lancers who had been again *turned out* at 1100. Captain Grenfell missed the arrival of the prisoners but reported that a 'few prisoners…were brought in amidst the excitement of the men and were closely inspected. I personally did not see them, but to all who did it gave them morale of 50% increase.'[31] Although Captain Grenfell did not see the prisoners Lieutenant Marden and Captain Lucas-Tooth did and were 'cheered up by seeing numerous batches of prisoners. The 4th Dragoon Guards draw first blood, chasing and scuffing an Ulan patrol,'[32] and on 'seeing the prisoners, raised their morale and made them even more eager to get into action. The eyes of all had been refreshed by the sight of the first German prisoners, captured by a squadron of the 4th Dragoon Guards under Major Solly-Flood [sic]…the first sight of captured Germans sharpened the desire of all to meet the enemy.'[33] Lieutenant Grenfell was more interested in their equipment 'the 4th Dragoon Guards sent in three very tired prisoners, two of whom they had wounded. Much interest in examining their lances, saddlery.'[34] The 'stack of lances were brought in by a 4th Dragoon Guards sergeant major in a buggy and were bought past the whole division.'[35] Lieutenant Grenfell also heard the story of how they had been captured:

> The 4th Dragoon Guards had seen an advance party of Germans advancing. They waited behind a wall to ambush them, but, as usual, one man, not realising, showed himself, and the Germans turned and fled, pursued by two troops, Butcher Hornby got the first spear! He pricked a man slightly in the back, who, at once surrendered. Three were taken prisoner, and the rest drew our force on to the crossroads, where infantry was entrenched, luckily, our men saw it, and stopped. We afterwards found this is a regular plan of theirs, to run

27 Ibid., p. 77.
28 Glasmeier, *Geschichte des Kürassier-Regiments von Driesen Nr 4,* p. 55.
29 Private H. Dyre diary, 22nd August 1914, p. 2.
30 *The News of the World,* op. cit. in Thornton, *Old Contemptibles,* p. 27.
31 Grenfell, Grenfell Family Papers (within Lyttelton Family Papers), 22nd August, p. 16.
32 Lt B.J.N. Marden diary, 22nd August.
33 Anon, *9th Lancer Diary*, 22nd August, p. 9.
34 Lt R.N. Grenfell, *Grenfell Family Papers (within Lyttelton Family Papers,* 22nd August, p. 4.
35 Lt Gen. Sir T. Bridges, *Alarms and Excursions, Reminiscences of a Soldier,* p. 78.

> away, and draw the cavalry on to their infantry. Tom Bridges thinks his men killed and wounded one officer, and about 10 men, all with the sword.[36]

The promise that Lieutenant Marden had heard about the General promised the DSO to the first officer who "sticks" an opposing patrol leader was honoured and Hornby was awarded the DSO for his brush with the Germans having been…the first British officer to kill [sic] a German with the new 1912 Pattern Cavalry Officer's Sword.[37] During the rest of the day as they waited for their anticipated move to the west, the 2nd Cavalry Brigade stayed in the village and the General took up a position at an inn in the middle of the town. It remained saddled there for the rest of the day. As they waited they could hear the heavy firing to the north and north east. Unperturbed, 'Captain Grenfell and Rivy went to a small cafe and had some raw eggs and bread and butter and Francis wrote to his uncle to ask him to check that Rivy was properly attached to the *special reserve*.'[38] While the Regiment waited, Lance Corporal Hunt took advantage of the time in the village and expectation remained high. 'We stood ready all day and didn't move off. J Granger and myself went around the village buying handkerchiefs etc…just heard we march as soon as it gets dark and attack the flank on 'von Kluck's' army at dawn.'[39] Later they would pass through the infantry brigades as they made their way to the western flank of the BEF. For the 9th Lancers the day concluded as one of only tension and expectancy.

The 15th Infantry Brigade were on the move again, with the destination being Boussu and Dour. Brigadier Gleichen wrote 'off at cock crow, the country got uglier and blacker, and more thickly populated…by the time we had crossed the Belgian frontier, we felt indeed that we were in another land.'[40] As he crossed the border he noticed that unlike France, in Belgium the 'streets were crowded by men who, we felt most strongly, ought to have been fighting in the ranks.'[41] During the march the Brigade had halted in the Bois de Boussu, to allow the 2nd Cavalry Brigade 'to pass through…they crossed at a trot, men and horses both looking very fit and workman like, and disappeared westwards through the haze of the factories; anymore impossible country for cavalry, except perhaps the London Docks, I have never seen…the whole countryside was one vast straggling town, it was impossible to say where one town ended and the other began.'[42] The Brigade received its orders that they were to billet in the Bois de Boussu, about half a mile short of Boussu.[43] Lieutenant Pollard from 119th Battery, which was supporting the 5th Infantry Division, wrote home again to his parents to say that 'he was on active service, by the roadside.' He told them that he was in the best of health and spirits and was pleases to find that his fluency in French (he had qualified as an interpreter) was contributing to the comfort of his battery.[44]

36 Grenfell, Grenfell Family Papers (within Lyttelton Family Papers, 22nd August 1914, p. 4.
37 Bridges, *Alarms and Excursions*, p. 78.
38 Grenfell, Grenfell Family Papers (within Lyttelton Family Papers), 22nd August 1914, p. 16.
39 LCpl W. Hunt diary, p. 4.
40 Brig. E. Gleichen, *Infantry Brigade 1914*, p. 18.
41 Ibid., p. 18.
42 Ibid., p. 19.
43 Ibid., p. 19.
44 Pollard, *Two Brothers: Accounts Rendered*, p. 21.

By midday the Cheshires, who had been on the march since 0300 the previous day, finally arrived at the Bois de Boussu where they were billeted in the area of some factories. They arrived in good order on what had been another hot day for the reservists. During the march, 'Lieutenant Elliot, of A Company, organised singing, and made his best section march behind to prevent stragglers and cheer them up when…the intense heat, they were almost exhausted…it was a severe test for the reservists who composed more than half of the battalion…a number of the men fell out temporarily, but with the exception of four, all rejoined in billets.'[45] Lieutenant Colonel Dudley Boger, along with the other 'mounted officers walked to save their horses, and it was no uncommon sight to see officers carrying the kit, or rifle, of exhausted men in addition to his own kit weighing about 50 pounds.'[46]

Lieutenant Colonel Dudley Boger. (Cheshire Regiment Museum)

The Cheshires were 'acknowledged to be one of the best marching Regiments in the British Army. In the Army Manoeuvres of 1910, the Regiment had marched 33 miles and fought for 12 hours; and in the Irish command manoeuvres of 1913 they continued to hold the record for marching.'[47] When the battalion arrived at Boussu, 'the order came to enter and barricade

45 Simpson, *Cheshire Regiment the First Battalion at Mons and the Miniature Colour,* p. 20.
46 Ibid., p. 20.
47 Ibid., p. 20.

the factory just behind them. With crow-bars and chisels they made loopholes in the walls.'[48] Corporal Walter Crooke[49] 'was quite proud of the loophole he made, it was so obviously according to regulations. A good broad V-shaped hole with but a small opening at the outer side of the wall. He sighted his rifle through it and found that he had a good wide field of fire.'[50] To ensure he did not lose it 'he wrote his number, rank, name, regiment and the date above it.'[51]

The Norfolk Regiment was to be billeted in Dour. As they crossed the border into Belgium, Private Hurrell saw a board printed "Welcome to old England." When they arrived in Dour, they halted at a 'large coal mine and, when the people found that we were stopping there, the girls and boys rushed and got our tea pails off the wagon and, getting water from the town helped to make the dinner and tea for us.'[52] For Private Hurrell, despite the closeness of the war, there was time for a romantic interlude. He was sitting on a sack of straw when 'a very nice young lady began talking to me in very broken English and after a while we both walked out together. We finally arrived at her house, a very large hotel, where she introduced me to her parents and sister.'[53] After 'a nice dinner she took me around the shops, showing me the sights. On parting we promised to see some more tomorrow, but tomorrow never came for us.'[54] That evening Private Sheldrake 'could see large fires coming from…the front line…all sorts of rumours began to pour in from the front. The first was that Liège and Namur forts had fallen to the Germans and they were advancing very rapidly.'[55] That night two of the 'companies went out that night on outposts a few miles northward guarding our left flank. Private Hurrell remained at the mine but did not get much sleep 'owing to so much noise, there were troops moving past all night and with the rattle of the guns,'[56] unfortunately he 'was chosen for regimental guard on the gates, so I never had much sleep that night.'[57] During the evening, Private Hurrell saw several planes overhead which he thought were 'both German and English. Several bombs were dropped,'[58] which made 'the inhabitants rush indoors and close all windows.'[59]

During the move of the cavalry, Brigadier Gough had received reports that the Greys had come into action at Givy, so to clear up the situation a patrol from A Squadron of the 16th Lancers was sent out commanded by Lieutenant Charles Tempest-Hicks. His patrol was to cover the high ground between Bray and Peronnes, and he was then to reconnoitre the village of Peronnes itself. When his patrol reached the high ground, they found it was 'strongly held by infantry.'[60] Private Reginald Betts wrote:

48 Cpl. W. Crooke, Twenty Fourth August 1914 (An Impression).
49 This J.N.C.O. has two Medal Index Cards (the same person) with alternate spelling of surname 'Crooks.'
50 Cpl. W. Crooke, Twenty Fourth August 1914 (An Impression).
51 Ibid.
52 Pte R. Hurrell Notebook, p. 16.
53 Pte R. Hurrell, Log of Round the World Cruise, p. 22.
54 Ibid., p. 22.
55 Ibid., p. 22.
56 Pte R. Hurrell notebook, p 18.
57 Pte R. Hurrell, Log of Round the World Cruise, p. 22.
58 Ibid., p. 22.
59 Ibid., p. 22.
60 TNA WO 95/1153/2: 3rd Cavalry Brigade War Diary, 22nd August 1914.

> There were several corn stooks in a field and the Germans tried to take cover behind them, but we were going at a fair gallop and they didn't have much chance. To give them credit they stood their ground, though they hadn't any time to make a run for it and we speared quite a number on the way through and some more on the way back…I aimed at a jerry but he dodged me and my point went into the ground. Luckily the lance shaft broke or I would have been fetched out of the saddle.[61]

During the engagement Lieutenant Tempest-Hicks had his horse shot from under him and two other horses were also killed, with two men wounded.[62] The Germans attempted to cut off the patrols retreat by sending a platoon down on Bray but their attempt was 'frustrated by some well-directed shells from E Battery[63] and the Regiment sent C Squadron to cover his retirement.[64] Lieutenant Horn's account of the action at Peronnes indicated that he thought that the patrol of Lieutenant Tempest-Hicks had got 'rather ambushed.'[65] The battery that fired in support of Lieutenant Tempest-Hicks was the same battery that had fired the BEF's first artillery rounds of the war earlier in the day at 1100.[66]

During the afternoon, the Cavalry Division was given orders to move to the far left of II Corps. 'By 1500 the main bodies of the three leading cavalry brigades were on the line Binche-Bray-Villers-St Ghislain and at 1600 the infantry of II Corps relieved the cavalry who by then had made the long night march of about 15 miles to the area Thulin-Quiévrain-Baisieux-Audregnies-Élouges.'[67] At approximately 1600, the 9th Lancers moved out into a field and remained *en masse* there ready to move out. While they were waiting at 'about 1800 nearly all the Cavalry Division passed. Most of them had had a brush with the enemy and a few experiences. Rivy and I stayed in the field and after eating raw eggs and bread and butter called out to our friends as they passed by. These included Jack Woodhouse, Geoffrey Brooke, General Gough and also the 4th Hussars.'[68] At approximately 1930, the 9th Lancers received their orders to continue their march to Thulin, the whole way being on cobble stones. They passed the 4th Hussars just outside Harmignies. Captain Grenfell wrote that "everyone was very tired and slept while sitting on our horses." They passed through the south of Mons, the provincial capital of the *Borinage* in the region of Hainaut which was the mining and manufacturing district of Belgium, and it seemed as if they 'were going through one perpetual town.'[69] The ride was one of the longest many could remember ever having done.

The area of the Mons-Condé Canal directly north of the 9th Lancers at Thulin was occupied by troops from 1 DCLI, who were from the 13th Infantry Brigade of the 5th Infantry Division. They had moved and occupied their position while the cavalry was also moving and the 1 DCLI found themselves on the extreme left of the BEFs line with only a troop from the 6DG watching

61 Ascoli, *The Mons Star*, p. 54.
62 Lt T.L. Horn, Diary of the Regiment, 16th (The Queens) Lancers, 4th August – 18th October 1914, p. 9.
63 TNA WO 95/1153/2: War Diary, 3rd Cavalry Brigade War Diary, 22nd August 1914.
64 TNA WO95/1134/2: *5th Lancers War Diary*, 22nd August 1914.
65 Lt T.L. Horn, Diary of the Regiment, 16th (The Queens) Lancers, 4th August – 18th October 1914, p. 9.
66 John Hutton, *The Gunners of August 1914: Baptism of Fire* (Barnsley: Pen & Sword, 2014), p. 42.
67 *The Cavalry Journal* Vol. XII, January-October, (London, Royal United Service Institute, 1922)., p. 28.
68 Grenfell, Grenfell Family Papers (within Lyttelton Family Papers), 22nd August 1914, p. 16.
69 Ibid., 22nd August 1914, p. 17.

The Borinage. (Author's Collection)

Lock No. 5 to their left. 1 DCLI had left their billets at Pissotiau shortly after 0500 and, after a long march, reached Sardon, a small village just south of La Haine river, a mile south of the Condé-Mons Canal. At about 1600, the 14th Infantry Brigade had been ordered to hold the line of the canal from the bridge a quarter of a mile south of Pommeroeul to the railway bridge at Les Herbieres. The battalion had A Company under Major Price on the southern bank of the canal on the left of the East Surreys towards the west and one platoon of B Company, commanded by Captain Romilly, continued the line to the bridge at Le Petit Crépin. The remaining three platoons dug in to form a bridgehead in a semicircle around the buildings of Le Petit Crépin [Map 2]. In total, approximately 12 trenches were made on the northern side of the canal. All were well-constructed for fire standing and excellently concealed. The field of fire was good with trees, dykes and wire obstructing the advance of the enemy should he attack the battalion. Difficulty, however, would be experienced in bringing fire to bear upon the long straight road from Ville Pommeroeul: this was the weakest point in an otherwise excellent position.[70] North of Le Petit Crepin the railway line crossed the road, the railway siding being full on the eastern side with passenger rolling stock and, on both sides, there were rows of trees. 1 DCLI positioned one machine gun to secure the road from Ville Pommeroeul. The two remaining companies, C and D, were detailed as the reserve and were positioned to the south between the La Haine river and Sardon. "We put out outposts," wrote Lieutenant A.C. Acland, 'dug ourselves in and waited for the Germans.'[71]

70 Everard Wyrall, *The History of The Duke of Cornwall's Light Infantry 1914-1919* (London: Methuen & Co., 1932), p. 13.
71 Ibid., p. 13.

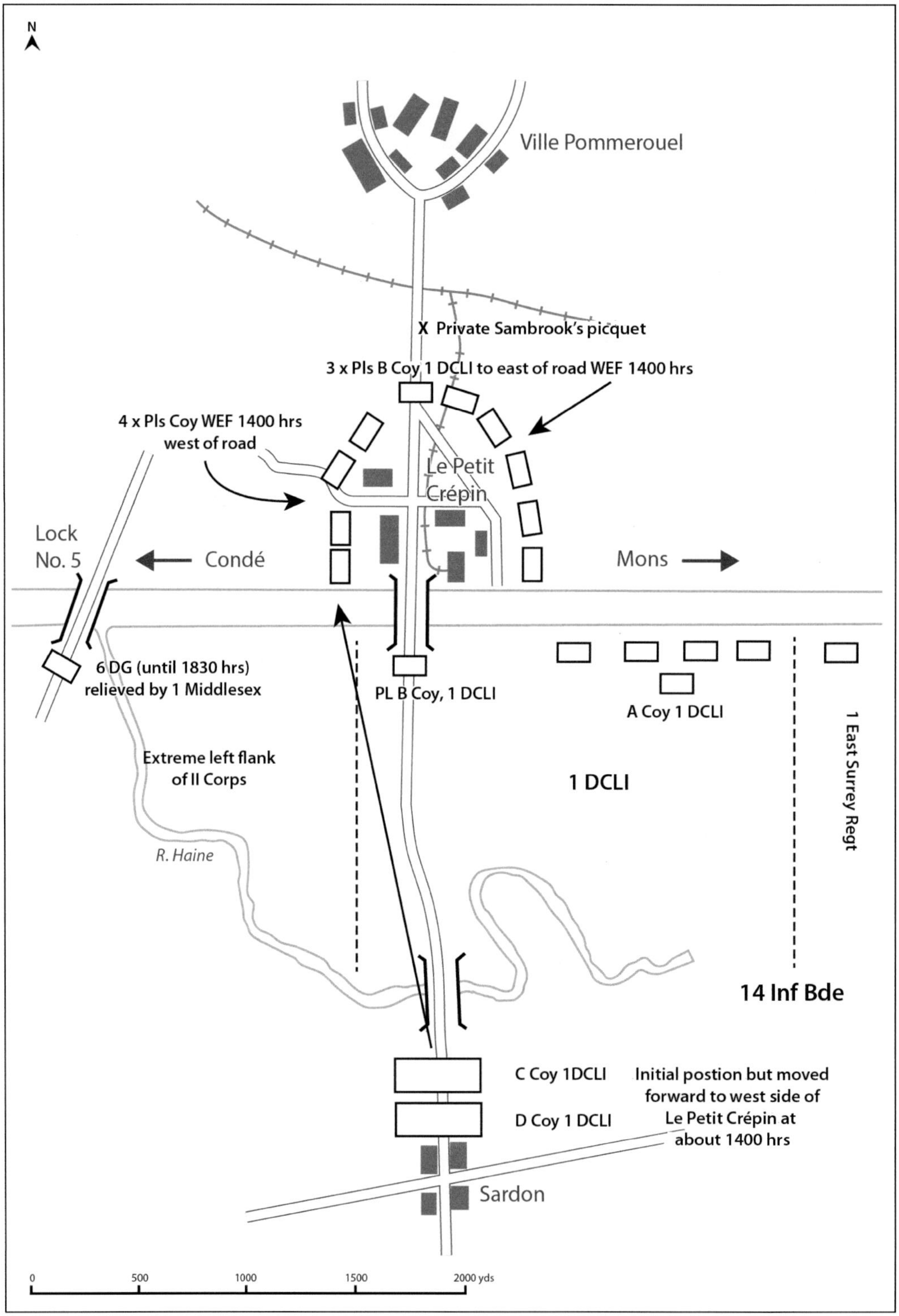


Map 2 1 DCLI positions at Ville Pommeroeul, 22nd August 1914. (Major W.H. White DL)

In the small, quiet, village of Audregnies the beginnings of the battle and war to follow started to shatter their quiet lives as the first element of the BEF arrived and the headquarters of the Cavalry Division was looking for billets for the night:

> This morning, around 0900, the village, which had been paralysed by a deathly silence for 15 days, was all of a sudden full of agitation. We heard women run and talk, that a regiment had arrived by the Chaussee and crossed the train tracks by the station. They were English, so tired, poor chaps were marching from Le Havre...We brought them fruits, milk...The priest gave them cigars. Most of all, they would have needed to refresh their poor sore feet, but they didn't stay here. Children came back happy to have been able to talk to them in their language, to have seen Irish with rosaries around their necks...Even Evelyse forgave the Commanding Officer for having called her in a friendly way: "Little Ginger"...Several airplanes flew over Audregnies in the afternoon. We learned later that one of them was German. A second regiment passed by at 1700. *Madame la Supérieure* said that troops were lodging in the village and that we had 20 officers to accommodate. The quartermaster was waiting to see the room...We made, in a rush, two English flags, one for the hallway, the other for the students' dining room: "Very good, said again the officer, it looks like it was made for us and that you sent your students home just to welcome us". Supper was eaten on beautiful white tablecloths. Around 2000, the mayor asked us if we could have another 30 men, we replied that beds were available but that we didn't have any food. But as the quartermaster didn't want to put them in the same room as the officers, so we haven't been able to accommodate them. The first group arrived around 2100.[72]

The soldiers who had arrived were from the 1st Cavalry Brigade. Lieutenant A.R.J. Lamb of the 2nd Dragoon Guards wrote 'arrived at our destination Audregnies south west of Mons at 1230. Horses were bivouacked in a large field, and all the officers of the Regiment went into billets in a *pensionnat*. The officers' room consists of a dormitory with a small stage at one end, beds all round and a long table down the centre.'[73]

While the BEF were taking their positions Field Marshal French's day was to slowly unfold and had he known at the beginning of his day the direction it was about to take it is unlikely that the move of the BEF would have taken place in the way that it did, but the wheels had been set in motion. It was not his intention to have a second meeting with General Lanrezac and he had to be persuaded to by his staff. He was somewhat reluctant after the unproductive meeting they had had on the 17th August. The Field Marshal met with Lieutenant Spears who told him that General Lanrezac was not in his *GQG*:

> I started by motor in the very early hours of a beautiful August morning to visit General Lanrezac at his *GQG* in the neighbourhood of Philippeville. Soon after entering the area of the Fifth French Army, I found my motor stopped at successive crossroads by columns of infantry and artillery moving south. After several such delays on my journey, and before I had gone half the distance, I suddenly came up with Captain [sic] Spears of

72 *Annales du pensionnat Saint Bernard à Audregnies*, pp. 42-43, op. cit., Jean Richez, *Un Champ de Coquelicots, La Bataille d'Audregnies le 24 Août 1914.*
73 Lt A.J.R. Lamb diary, 22nd August 1914 (Property of the 1st Queen Dragoon Guards).

> the 11th Hussars, who was the liaison officer at General Lanrezac's GQG. There is an atmosphere engendered by troops retiring, when they expect to be advancing, which is unmistakable to anyone who has had much experience of war. It matters not whether such a movement is the result of a lost battle, an unsuccessful engagement, or is in the nature of a strategic manoeuvre to the rear. The fact that, whatever the reason may be, it means giving up ground to the enemy, affects the spirits of the troops and manifests itself in the discontented, apprehensive expression which is seen on the faces of the men, and the tired, slovenly, unwilling gait which invariably characterises troops subjected to this ordeal. This atmosphere surrounded me for some time before I met Spears and before he had spoken a word. My optimistic visions of the night before had vanished, and what he told me did not tend to bring them back.[74]

Lieutenant Spears described travelling to Le Cateau to meet Field Marshal French to tell him of the news from the French *GQG* at the crossroads on the main Chimay, Avesnes, Landrecies road east of Avesnes:

> I passed the British Commander-in-Chief's car followed by another one. He signalled to me to stop, and he and his staff got out. I well remember the place; quite a number of French soldiers, a couple of companies perhaps, were halted on either side of the road, and stared suspiciously at these strange, khaki-clad, red tabbed officers. There was a small house by the roadside, a kind of combined cottage and estaminet, into which we all trooped. There was a table under a window to the left of the door, piled high with dirty plates and cups these were cleared aside and a map spread out. Sir John bent over it and asked me for my news. I began to speak, but in spite of my best endeavours could not make myself heard. The lady of the house, who had watched our intrusion with a wide-open mouth from which no sound came, had noisily resumed washing up her dishes in a tub. Captain Guest persuaded her, not without difficulty, to postpone this important operation so that I might proceed with my report![75]

Lieutenant Spears 'reported that the guard and 7th German Corps had since daybreak advanced on the Sambre in the neighbourhood of Frenière and had attacked the Tenth French Corps which was holding the river. The advance troops had driven the Germans back; but he added that 'offensive action was contrary to General Lanrezac's plans.'[76] Lieutenant Spears pleaded with the Field Marshal to continue his journey and meet with General Lanrezac, but once the Field Marshal had learnt that General Lanrezac was at a meeting at Mettet, he thought this too far away. Lieutenant Spears was left with a feeling of personal failure that he was unable to persuade the Field Marshal to continue, but he was adamant. 'Perhaps I was not emphatic enough. I was only a subaltern and much intimidated at having to deal with such important people. The glamour of the great still dazzled me, and I failed to gain my

74 Viscount French of Ypres, *1914,* p. 57.
75 Spears, *Liaison 1914,* p. 11.
76 Viscount French of Ypres, *1914,* p. 57.

point.'[77] General Wilson wrote in his diary the same day 'I wish I could have got Sir John to go and meet Lanrezac. It is of great importance that they understand each other.'[78]

The RFC made 12 reconnaissances on the 22nd, one of which revealed the presence of large bodies of troops moving in the direction of the British front. The first aircraft to return came in soon after 1100. This was piloted by Captain G.S. Shephard, with Lieutenant I.M. Bonham-Carter as observer. They had landed at Beaumont (approximately 12 miles east of Maubeuge) to refuel. While refuelling they were informed that the French cavalry had encountered German infantry north of the Sambre canal on the previous afternoon and had had to fall back.[79] The afternoon reconnaissances added little that was new except to report that there were cavalry and infantry in the area north of the Mons-Condé Canal. As each of the reports came in, they were analysed, and the information contained in one report was immediately recognised as being so significant that Brigadier Henderson took it personally to GHQ. It stated that:

> A long column, whose strength was estimated to be that of an army corps, was moving westward on the Bruxelles-Ninove road. At Ninove, the column continued south west towards Grammont. This was von Kluck's Second Corps [sic], and the report seemed to show an attempt at an enveloping movement. The same report confirmed what had already been seen, the presence of enemy troops moving along the great Chaussee on Soignies. This column was taking advantage of the trees on either side of the road to shield its movements.[80]

This was also a landmark day for the RFC as it was the first day on which an aircraft had failed to return from a reconnaissance flight. Lieutenants Vincent Waterfall and Charles Bayly, of No. 5 Squadron, had been on a reconnaissance patrol at 1016 flown in an Avro 504. The bringing down of this aircraft gave the Germans their first proof that the BEF had landed. The observer's report, so far as he had written it, was picked up near the machine wreckage by Belgian peasants, and it eventually found its way to the War Office in London.[81] Leutnant Freytag of *Infanterie Regiment 26* witnessed the downing of the aircraft:

> Several planes chased around above us, but we barely paid attention to them. But towards midday one appeared which had a strange colour and it seemed suspicious. Out with the binoculars, true it did not sport an iron cross, therefore an enemy plane. It approached quite high, ferociously fast, we dropped to the ground, the distance to the plane was quickly estimated, and our fire rang out in the air for several minutes. In spite of this, calmly and without allowing itself to be deflected, the plane flew over our column. From behind came the sound of shooting, the main troop was firing on him too. Suddenly, we could not believe our eyes, he did a loop, came down to about 300m and returned towards us, such effrontery had never happened to us before. We started firing again. At once he stopped, a jubilant cry rose from our lines: like a wounded bird the large machine wavered and plummeted towards the ground. For a moment it once again succeeded in straightening up,

77 Spears, *Liaison 1914,* p. 135.
78 Callwell, *Field-Marshal Sir Henry Wilson Bart,* p. 166.
79 Raleigh, *War in the Air*, p. 301.
80 Ibid., p. 303.
81 Ibid., p. 303.

> then the tail end soared upwards and the plane hurtled to the ground, where it crashed in a cloud of smoke 200m from 3 *Kompanie*. The machine was in a thousand pieces, the men in it, two British officers, were shattered and unrecognisable. The regimental account says accordingly to the *kompanie* who were marching with the main troop, the unit had downed the plane. But 6 *Kompanie* also claimed the credit because they were marching in a lateral direction and opened fire on the plane in a well ordered and well directed manner, during which the plane began to waver and then suddenly crash.[82]

On his return from his unsuccessful visit to Fifth Army and his chance meeting with Lieutenant Spears, Field Marshal French sent General Lanrezac the following massage which articulated his concerns of now being in advance of the French Fifth Army and felt unprepared, which he had previously told him:

> I am waiting for the dispositions arranged for to be carried out, especially the posting of French cavalry corps on my left. I am prepared to fulfil the role allotted to me when the Fifth Army advances to the attack. In the meantime, I hold an advanced defensive position extending from Condé on the left, through Mons to Erquelinnes, where I connect with two reserve divisions south of the Sambre. I am now much in advance of the line held by the Fifth Army and feel my position to be as forward as circumstances will allow, particularly in view of the fact that I am not properly prepared for offensive action till tomorrow morning, as I have previously informed you.[83]

It became apparent towards the end of the day that Lieutenant Spear's fears had been correct and the BEF had deployed with the expectation and instructions to expect to advance on the day the French had started to withdraw. It now fell to Lieutenant Spears to inform the Field Marshal:

> If I were mistaken in my deductions or in my observations the result might be terribly serious. Yet the situation, if I understood it rightly, was so perilous that I felt I must convince Sir John of two things that General Lanrezac was not going to attack whatever happened, and that the position of the Fifth Army was dangerously exposing the British. It seemed to be my plain duty to inform the Commander-in-Chief that I was sure of this, whatever might be the consequences if I proved to be wrong, for if, as had appeared probable in the early afternoon.[84]

When Lieutenant Spears arrived at GHQ, dinner was running very late. He was met by Colonel Macdonogh who gave him half a bottle of champagne! Lieutenant Spears waited for him standing in the drawing room and on his arrival explained the situation as he understood it to the Field Marshal and General Murray:

82 Wolfgang von Vormann, *Infanterie-Regiment Fürst Leopold von Anhalt-Dessau (1. Magdeburg.) Nr. 26.* (Oldenburg: Verlag Stalling, 1926).
83 Viscount French of Ypres, *1914,* p. 59.
84 Spears, *Liaison 1914,* p. 148.

> I pointed out that, quite apart from the danger on the right, the intelligence reports of the Fifth Army tended to confirm that the threat to the left flank of the British was no less serious. This was confirmed by Colonel Macdonogh, who gave the Commander-in-Chief the information he possessed regarding the enemy, emphasising once more the importance of the news brought in by the airman already referred to, which showed a whole German corps marching down on the extreme left of the British line.[85]

Field Marshal French stood and listened in silence to his report, looking occasionally at a map spread out on a table by his side. General Murray looked grim. When Lieutenant Spears had finished speaking, he made no comment and the young officer was told to leave the room. As he sat outside waiting, Lieutenant Spears realised the magnitude of the consequences of the information he had just delivered:

> Then followed one of the most painful experiences of my life. A sickly feeling came over me as I realised that they were discussing a plan, evidently already decided upon, for a general advance upon the following day…I thought of the ill-fated Nolan who had brought the order to charge to the Light Brigade at Balaclava. We waited for what seemed to be centuries but was really only about 20 minutes. Then the door opened suddenly, and General Murray stood framed against the dark hall. Looking at the officers sitting round the table, he said "You are to come in now and see the Chief. He is going to tell you that there will be no advance. But remember there are to be no questions. Don't ask why, there is no time, and it would be useless. You are to take your orders, that's all."[86]

For Field Marshal French, the day concluded with "*disappointment and disillusionment,"* when at 2300 Colonel Huguet, the head of the French Military Mission brought a French staff officer to the headquarters who had come direct from General Lanrezac. His report confirmed the information given to him by Lieutenant Spears earlier. The purpose of the visit was to ask if the BEF 'would attack the flank of the German columns which were pressing him back from the river.'[87] At the same time Colonel Macdonogh informed Field Marshal French that 'the intelligence department believed there are three German army corps marching on us, the west corps being as far as Ath. In view of this information I would hold my present forward position for 24 hours.'[88] Sometime during the night of 22nd-23rd August GHQ were informed by the military attaché at the Haig that 100,000 Germans had passed through Liège on the 20th August.[89] Field Marshal French decided that 'in view of the most probable situation of the German Army, as it was known to both of us, and the palpable intention of its commander was to effect a great turning movement round my left flank…that such an operation as he suggested was quite impracticable for me,'[90] and he informed General Lanrezac's emissary that he would retain his current position for another day; but after that, the BEF would withdraw to the

85 Ibid., p. 147.
86 Ibid., p. 149.
87 Viscount French of Ypres, *1914*, p. 58.
88 Diary of Field Marshal French dated 23rd August 1914 op. cit. on David Ascoli, *The Mons Star*, p. 59.
89 TNA WO 95/1 (GHQ), 21st August 1914, op. cit. in James. *Imperial Warrior*, p.58.
90 Ibid., p. 59.

Maubeuge position, which he recorded in his diary 'I must consider whether the movement against my front and the French retreat did not render it necessary for me to retire again to the Maubeuge position.'[91] The BEF now found itself on its own and Lanrezac's Fifth Army were now nine miles to their south.

On the evening of 22nd August, the German *IV AK* completed its day march and stopped with the *Infanterie Division 7*, commanded by Generalleutnant Johannes Riedel near Silly and the *Infanterie Division 8* commanded by Generalleutnant Georg Karl August Hildebrandt near Ollignies, but they were still 25 to 30 kms from the Mons-Condé Canal. It was here at Ollignies that Sister Julie from the *pensionnat* at Audregnies had come, only two days earlier, to celebrate the festival of Saint Bernard's, and had been fortunate to leave before the Germans had arrived.[92] At 2100, Generaloberst von Kluck issued his orders for the following day from the *OKH* in Hal which showed for the first time he knew where the BEF was, and they contained the overall intent and the specific instructions for his leading corps to cross the canal. He also moved the *OKH* to the Château Brison on Rue de la Station[93] at Soignies.[94] He said:

> A squadron of British cavalry[95] was encountered today at Casteau, north east of Mons, and a British aeroplane coming from Maubeuge was shot down near Enghien.[96] The *AOK 1* will continue its advance tomorrow to the area north west of Maubeuge, masking that fortress, and the *II AK* will reach La Hamaide, marching from Ninove through Grammont; the *IV AK* will march to Basecles and Stambruges by Ath and Chievres; the *II AK* will reach St Ghislain and Jemappes by Lens and Jurbise. The rising ground on the southern side of the canal is to be occupied. The *IX AK* will cover the movement of the army towards Maubeuge, and for this purpose will advance across the line Mons-Thieu towards the north and north western front of Maubeuge, keeping its main force on its right flank. The line Ath-Roeulx will be crossed by the leading troops of the *IV, III,* and *IX AK* by 0800.[97]

The situation facing both Field Marshal French and Generaloberst von Kluck was gradually becoming clearer, but neither were fully aware of each other's size and dispositions. The BEF had obligated itself to hold its position for 24 hours to cover the withdrawal of the Fifth French Army to their east, with the overall intention to retreat. Unaware of this, however, the 9th Lancers at 1500 along with the cavalry continued their movement to the western flank of the BEF ready to cover the flank as it advanced, it was a most *dismal experience* as the Regiment clattered through the streets paved with cobblestones.[98] Lance Corporal Hunt said 'We marched and it was about the longest march I have ever been on, went through several large towns Be-2-Jer (can't spell it but it sounds something like that). All the people came down in

91 Diary of Field Marshal French dated 22nd August 1914, op. cit. in Ascoli, *The Mons Star,* p. 56.
92 *Annales du pensionnat Saint Bernard à Audregnies*, p. 41, op. cit., Jean Richez, *Un Champ de Coquelicots, La Bataille d'Audregnies le 24 Août 1914.*
93 Jack Horsfall & Nigel Cave, *Mons 1914* (Barnsley: Pen & Sword, 1999). p. 141.
94 Kluck, *The March on Paris and The Battle of The Marne, 1914*, p. 45.
95 C Squadron, 4th Dragoon Guards.
96 Lieutenants Vincent Waterfall and Charles Bayly of No. 5 Squadron.
97 Kluck, *The March on Paris and The Battle of The Marne, 1914*, p. 45.
98 Anon., 9th Lancer War Diary, 22nd August 1914, p. 9.

Corporal R.H. 'Spur' Taylor c. 1928. (Author's Collection)

their night attire, some amusing sights, gave us coffee and wine whenever we halted.'[99] The 9th Lancers finally arrived at Thulin at 0300 and Captain Grenfell wrote 'we bivouacked in a field very very tired and taking up our lines with some difficulty in the dark. Rivy lay on some hay close to our lines and went to sleep there. I took my valise and went into an empty house where I slept until 0800.'[100] Lance Corporal Hunt thought the location was less than ideal, 'we bivouacked the night at Thulin, well we got there at 0400, my troop were unlucky and we were in a marsh, and we were nearly all suffocated.'[101] Corporal 'Spur' Taylor reported that 'they had arrived without any signs of the enemy although we had been warned that their patrols were in the vicinity. Our Commanding Officer issued orders to the effect that every man was to obtain as much rest as he possibly could. Of course, it did not take long to settle down in dreamland.'[102] So, as the day concluded as the 9th Lancers slept in a less than ideal location, in a damp field south of Thulin, 1 DCLI held the bridge to their north with their outposts forward of the Mons-Condé Canal all expecting to advance towards Soignies in support of the French Fifth Army, which was exactly where Generaloberst von Kluck had located his *OKH*.

99 LCpl W. Hunt diary, p. 4.
100 Grenfell, Grenfell Family Papers (within Lyttelton Family Papers), 22nd August 1914, p. 17.
101 LCpl W. Hunt diary, p. 4.
102 Cpl. R.H. Taylor letter of Sergeant 'Spur' R.H. Taylor, p. 1.

# 9

# Mons

*Local inhabitants told Husaren Regiment 3 that 30,000 British soldiers had been seen on 22nd August marching towards Mons from the area south of St Ghislain.*

The morning of the 23rd August was a Sunday. After a misty and rainy start it turned out to be another warm day. The church bells rang and the inhabitants of the villages near the canal were seen in their best attire going to worship as if war was utterly distant from them.[1] The trains were still running, taking people to the holiday markets in Mons. The position of the BEF was that I Corps were now facing east, whilst II Corps halted along the line of the Mons–Condé Canal facing north and was in the process of wheeling into line to face north east on a line from Binche to Lens, with the intent to support General Lanrezac's left flank as he advanced.[2]

The German Army started their march on a broad front in a south westerly direction, in accordance with orders issued the previous evening. The corps spread their divisions along two or more parallel march routes. As they advanced, 'every step was taken to reconnoitre the canal crossings. By the end of the day Generaloberst von Kluck's troops on the outer flank of the sweeping advance would have marched 150 miles in 11 days, which for a body of troops of its size was 'a remarkable achievement in the early days of a campaign.'[3] There were early encounters with the advancing Germans from 0600 along the BEFs line from Binche-Bray-Havre-Obourg and Nimy, westwards to 1 DCLI and 6th Dragoon Guards on the left of the line. By 1000, the Cavalry Division had established its headquarters in Quiévrain and the 1st Signal Squadron, Royal Engineers had laid cable from a Sunbeam car all the way to Lock No. 5 on the far-left flank for the use of the 4th Cavalry Brigade. The Brigade was commanded by Brigadier Cecil Bingham and consisted of the 6th Dragoon Guards (Carabiniers), the 3rd (King's Own) Hussars and, on mobilisation, the Brigade was brought up to its full strength with the addition of the Household Cavalry Composite Regiment. Telephone and later telegraph communications were established to GHQ at Le Cateau and telephone communications to

1 Brig. Gen. Sir James E. Edmonds, *Military Operations France and Belgium 1914,* Vol., p. 67.
2 Ascoli, *The Mons Star,* p. 52.
3 Maurice, *Forty Days in 1914*, p. 76.

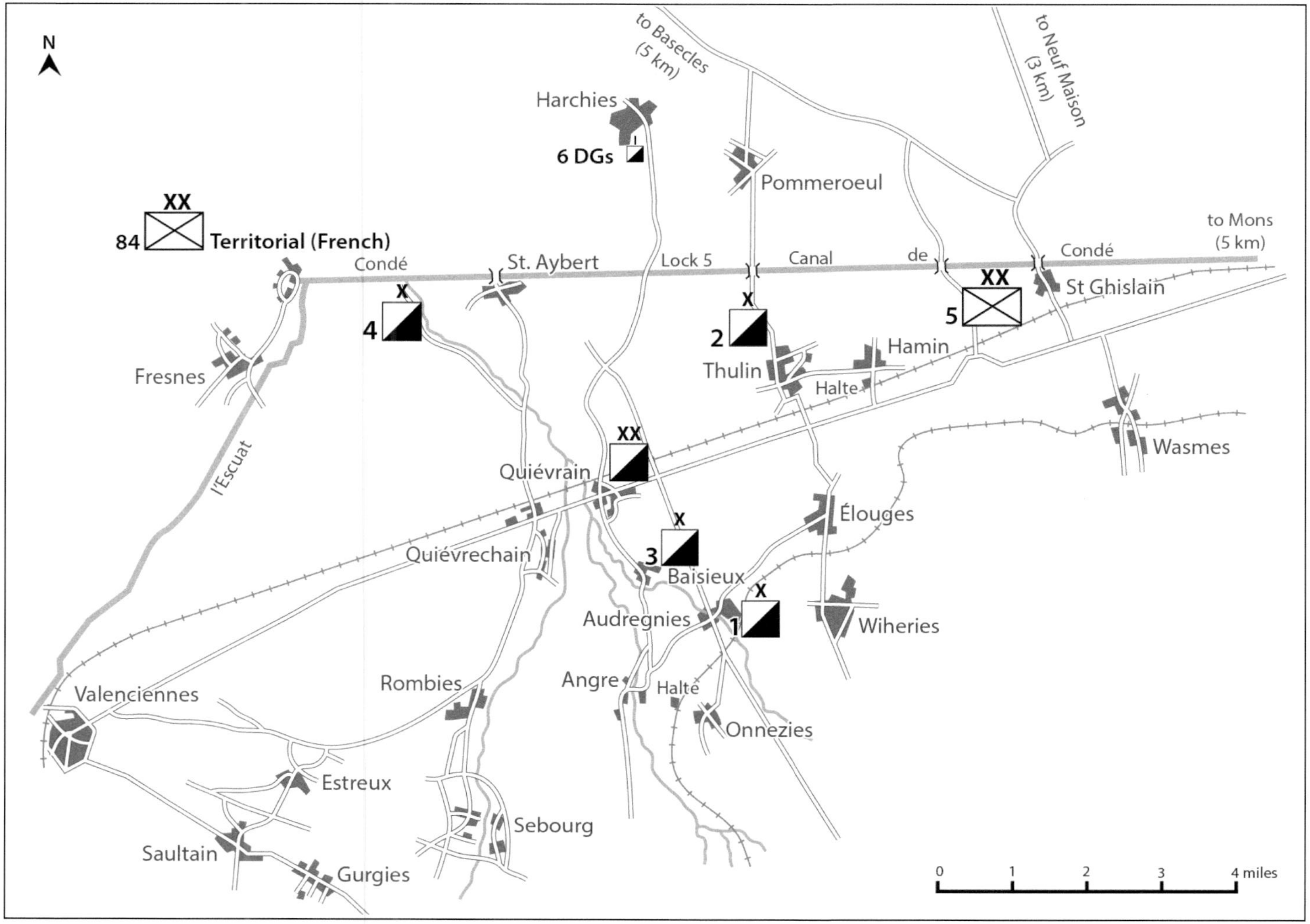


Map 3 Cavalry Division Areas, 23rd August 1914. (Cavalry Journal, 1922)

Thulin from the railway station wireless office [See Map 4].[4] They had been given the use of a Rolls-Royce car by Mr Raoul Edwards,[5] [Don Raúl Edwards MacClure].[6] Interestingly, GHQ only had telephone communications with I Corps, and none with II Corps 'and the staff had not taken care to have a direct wire laid...Reports took a long time to come in;' orders took a long time to go out, and precious hours were wasted.'[7] The last time the British had fought on these fields, the Duke of Wellington overlooked the whole battlefield and could see the French columns advancing against him and he needed no reports from his subordinates. He made his decision based on what he could see with his own eyes. For Field Marshal French, this was not the case as his GHQ was 35 miles to the rear.[8]

The bridges at Obourg and Nimy started to receive artillery fire at 0900. Lieutenant Lamb of the 2nd Dragoon Guards who had billeted at the *pensionnat* of Saint Bernard's in Audregnies, had a far more relaxed affair and he wrote in his diary 'slept until 0730. Breakfast-boiled eggs, coffee and jam provided by the nuns at 0800. Then I walked down to where the horses are bivouacked and went around my horses. Nothing special in the afternoon.'[9]

For General von Moltke, the exact dispositions of the British and French had become no clearer overnight and, in the morning, the *OKH* in Hal received a message from the *HKK* stating that a major detraining of troops had been taking place in Tournai, east of Lille,[10] and had been since the 22nd August. This perpetuated the unresolved question concerning the location of the BEF. It was understood that the BEF had landed, but exactly where was still unclear, and it was quite possible that they were detraining at Lille. However, there had been reliable reports that the BEF had been identified by *AOK 1* in the Mons area. Since at this stage only cavalry forces had been identified for certain, these may not have constituted the main force. None of this had been confirmed before the day's march had begun as aerial reconnaissance in the morning failed to produce any results because of the mist.

Therefore, against this unclear picture, the *AOK 1* continued to advance according to the orders issued the previous day, but with an additional responsibility to protect the right flank against the possibility of the BEF advancing from Lille. The army command was still concerned about the unidentified build-up of troops to the west and therefore ordered the lead elements of *IV, III* and *IX AK* to halt, in order to prepare the army for a turn to the west. The corps received specific orders not go beyond the Leuze–Mons–Binche road. *IV AK* had to specifically cover and reconnoitre towards Tournai as well as maintain contact with the *HKK 2*.[11] Soon the clarity regarding the identity of the troops in Tournai became clearer and the position and strength of the BEF in Mons also became known. This was when the local inhabitants told *Husaren*

4 1st Signal Squadron Royal Engineers, 1st Cavalry Division War Diary.
5 Wyrall, *The History of The Duke of Cornwall's Light Infantry, 1914–1919,* p. 15.
6 *The Times*, 21st January 1924: A dispatch received by mail says that on December 17, at the British Legation in Santiago de Chile, Don Raoul Edwards, received the 1914 Star from Mr Arthur Grant Duff, British Minister in Chile. He is the only Chilean to whom this medal has been given. Three Chilean generals and members of the British colony were present at the ceremony. He joined the ASC in March 1917.
7 Brig. C.R. Ballard, Smith-Dorrien, p 161.
8 Ibid., p. 161.
9 Lt A.J.R. Lamb diary (Property of the 1st Queen Dragoon Guards), 23rd August 1914.
10 Dunlop, Dunlop & Puttkammer (eds.), *The Battle of Mons,* p. 22.
11 Ibid., p. 22.

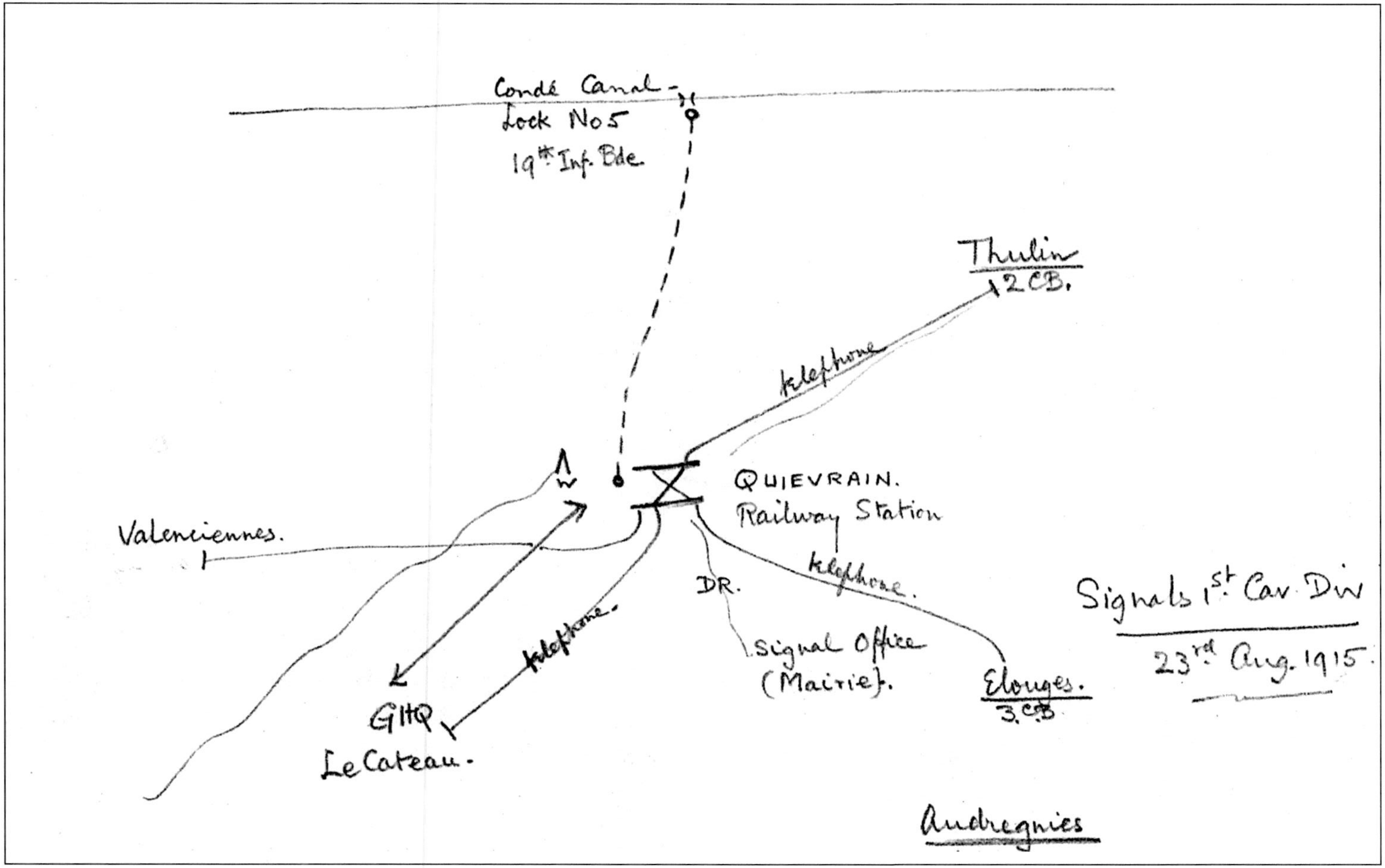


Map 4 Communications Map, Signals 1st Cavalry Division, 23rd August 1914. (TNA WO 95/???)

*Regiment 3* that 30,000 British soldiers had been seen on 22nd August marching towards Mons from the area south of St Ghislain. This information was corroborated by an intercepted private letter which indicated a strong British Army presence south of Mons.[12] Early in the morning, a patrol from *Husaren Regiment 8* reached the railway yard at Ville Pommeroeul where it was immediately engaged losing one man (possibly Hussar Rohde)[13] and a horse killed. The patrol took cover behind a garden hedge, observed and sent back its report.[14] All of these reports confirmed where the BEF was deployed and once the concern over the troops to the west and been satisfied, the army resumed its advance.[15] As the engagement of *III AK* developed, and as it fought for the bridges around St Ghislain and Jemappes, this prompted Generaloberst von Kluck to set *IV AK* on the move in the afternoon once more. Its mission was to capture the southern canal bank and thereby support *III AK. IV AK* had already received an order at 1300 hours to march towards Hensies and Thulin but this had been postponed by a subsequent *army order* to stop and rest[16] while the question of the location of the BEF was resolved. *IV AK* started its day's march, and *Infanterie Division 7's advance guard* of the day was 3 *Kompanie* of *II Battalion, Infanterie Regiment 26*[17] which along with *Infanterie Regiment 26* had set off at 0700 with II Battalion leading in the direction of Chievres-Pommeroeul, some 15 kms west of the centre of Mons.[18] The *Infanterie Brigade 13* was marching towards the Mons-Condé Canal and it was still 25 to 30 kms before they would reach the canal. [19] The two infantry divisions advanced along two or more parallel march routes. As they advanced, pontoon bridging equipment was brought forward and incorporated into the marching columns.'[20] At 1500, *Infanterie Regiment 66* received the report 'that the British held the Condé Canal north of Thulin. The division continued the march so as to engage the British that day.'[21]

The Cavalry Division had moved to and occupied overnight positions from the bridge north of Thulin where they were in touch with the 5th Infantry Division and to the east, at Condé, they were liaising with the French 84th Territorial Division Garrison at Valenciennes. The 13th and 14th Infantry Brigades were deployed forward along the line of the canal and the 15th Infantry Brigade was the Divisional Reserve to their rear.[22] General Allenby positioned his brigades with the 2nd and 4th Cavalry Brigades forward (in Thulin and St Aybert) and the 1st and 3rd Cavalry Brigades in support (in Audregnies and Élouges). On his arrival in Élouges Lieutenant Rowland Beech from A Squadron of the 16th Lancers wrote, 'eventually arrived at Élouges, south west of Mons, about 0300. Put the horses in an orchard, got some food and slept till about 0800. Spent the day here. In the afternoon we got on to a high shale-heap [slag heap]

12 Ibid., p. 24.
13 *Onlineprojekt Gefallenenden Kmäller* <http://www.denkmalprojekt.org/verlustlisten/vl_hus-reg_von_ziethen_brandenb_nr_3_wk2.htm> (Accessed 16th August 2018).
14 Zuber, *The Mons Myth,* p. 163.
15 Approximately a delay of 1 hour.
16 Dunlop, Dunlop & Puttkammer (eds.), *The Battle of Mons,* p. 50.
17 Vormann, v. Infanterie-Regiment Fürst Leopold von Anhalt-Dessau (1. Magdeburg.) Nr. 26, pp. 42-48.
18 Korfes, *The German 66th Regiment in the First World War*, p. 31.
19 Zuber, *The Mons Myth,* p. 162.
20 Dunlop, Dunlop & Puttkammer, *The Battle of Mons,* p. 22.
21 Korfes, *The German 66th Regiment in the First World War*, p. 31.
22 Gleichen, *Infantry Brigade 1914,* p. 20.

near the town, but there was not very much to be seen except shells bursting, and an odd village or two burning. Saw an aeroplane being shelled, but with no effect.'[23] The forward regiments of the 2nd Cavalry Brigade had the 18th Hussars on the left and the 9th Lancers on the right with the centre line being the railway station at Thulin. The 6th Dragoon Guards were covering the locks and bridges at St Aybert. The arrival of the 9th Lancers at Thulin had attracted much attention, and when they *stood to* at 0800,[24] thousands of people came around to watch our movements. 'It was naturally a great chance to exchange washing and have a thorough dig out.'[25] Ammunition was issued and the Commanding Officer and Brigade Commander had ridden forward and had come under rifle fire. It would be *Infanterie Division 7* of *IV AK* on its current line of advance that would first make contact with 14th Infantry Brigade from II Corps of the BEF in the area along the canal:

Élouges slag heap. (MonDour <http://www.mondour.be/>)

The 14th Infantry Brigade had been ordered to hold the line of the canal from the bridge a quarter of a mile south of Pommeroeul to the railway bridge at Les Herbieres. This line was divided into two sections, one extending from the railway bridge (inclusive) to the crossing a quarter of a mile south of La Hamaide which the 1 East Surreys were to hold, the other from the crossing south of La Hamaide to the bridge a quarter of a mile south of Pommeroeul allotted to 1 DCLI. One section of RE was attached to each battalion. The

23 Lt R.A.J. Beech diary, 23rd August 1914.
24 Grenfell, Grenfell Family Papers (within Lyttelton Family Papers), 23rd August 1914, p. 17.
25 Cpl. R.H. Taylor l*etter of Sergeant 'Spur' R.H. Taylor*, p. 2.

> remaining units of the 14th Infantry Brigade billeted in Hannity with the exception of a troop of the 2 Life Guards [sic] watching Lock No. 5 and other bridges, on the left of 1 DCLI. The latter were the extreme left of the British line.[26]

As the infantry battalions took up their positions along the canal, the cavalry took up their positions to the rear. The exception was the position on the British left flank at St Aybert, which was still held by the 4th Cavalry Brigade. The 6th Dragoon Guards sent out reconnaissance patrols to St Aybert and were told to hold the lock and bridges. There were several mounted attacks against German *Kűrassier* carried out by A Squadron before the Regiment withdrew across the two bridges at St Aybert. Preparations were made to defend the bridges and Lock No. 5, which was about a mile to the east, and blow them if necessary. The bridge at Lock No. 5 and another bridge over the branch canal about 600 yards to the front were held by Lieutenant W.T. Gill's troop, later assisted by another troop from B Squadron.[27]

The 15th Infantry Brigade at Bois de Boussu and Dour started to dig trenches and the commanders studied the ground looking at the approaches to the brigade position. The Brigade Commander along with Lieutenant Colonel Tulloch, who was the Divisional Engineer Commander, went around the brigade positions in a car. Brigadier Gleichen wrote 'such a hopeless place. There was no field of fire anywhere except to the left, just where the railway crossed the Boussu road…little roads over ground composed of a bewildering variety of slag heaps 40 to 150 feet high intersected with railway lines, mine heads, chimneys, industrial buildings, furnaces, and *usines* of all sorts.'[28] Paul Maze thought that the 'high chimney-stacks shone like minarets among the dark slag heaps of the coal mines rising like pyramids.'[29] This resulted in the situation that 'nowhere could a continuous field of fire be obtained.'[30] The position of the battalions was that the 'Norfolks were on the left at the station and eastwards down the line…and the Cheshires a bit thrown back, in beastly close countryside for the most part.'[31] It appeared that 'one of the big slag heaps seemed to offer a good command, but to our disgust it was so hot we could hardly stand on it…other heaps again seemed to give a good position, and they were fairly cool, but there was always something wrong. The problem was that there were more slag heaps in front which blocked the view, or the heap ran to a point and there was not enough room for more than two men…or it faced the wrong way…it was a nightmare of a place.'[32] The Dorsets and Bedfords were pretty well together and occupying some trenches on a high railway embankment.[33] The Brigade Commander had ordered that two companies of each battalion should prepare positions to their front and the remaining companies were to support them.[34]

26 Wyrall, *The History of The Duke of Cornwall's Light Infantry 1914-1919*, p. 12.
27 Lt. Col. L.B. Oatts, *I Serve Regimental History of the 3rd Carabiniers* (London: Published by Home Headquarters 3rd Carabineers, 1966), p 202.
28 Gleichen, *Infantry Brigade 1914,* p. 21.
29 Maze, *A Frenchman in Khaki*, pp. 14-15.
30 Brig. E. Gleichen, Infantry Brigade 1914, *The Diary of a Commander of the 15th Infantry Brigade, 5th Division, British Army, During the Retreat from Mons,* p. 21.
31 Ibid., p. 22.
32 Ibid., p. 23.
33 Ibid., p. 23.
34 Ibid., p. 22

Privates Hurrell's and Sheldrake's companies (B and C[35]) were both out digging trenches. Private Hurrell did not go with his company as he was kept behind on guard duty. During the day, troops continued to file past and he watched another British aeroplane fly over the German lines and return successfully. In the afternoon artillery 'a little in the rear, every once in a while they would shoot making a terrific explosion, shaking the whole town…the poor inhabitants were scared. They screamed, running here and there. Most went indoors, closing all doors and windows and pulling all blinds down. I must say I felt sorry for them, especially those with young babies.'[36] In Private Sheldrake's platoon, small rifts started to form between the old reservists who had colonial experience and the regular peace time soldiers who had none, unlike Private Sheldrake who had served in Natal in 1907.[37] The previous day on the march his zealous captain who "did not realise he was really on active service," had put 30 of the company in front of the Commanding Officer for drinking water, while they were resting on the roadside, that they had been given by a passer-by. They knew that they were not to drink on the march as it threw the step out. However, they were not aware this applied to them when they were resting as well. To Private Sheldrake this did not make any sense, 'for there was all us old reserve men who had done several years of service in the colonies and since have filled the responsible positions of being fathers to the rising generation, and now have to ask the officer if we can drink from our water bottles, and having a drink was 'ruled by his own mood.'[38] He also found out that his platoon sergeant only had about three years' service, 'on me making inquiries I gained the information that he had been an instructor on the square, and had not done any field training, or very little anyway. The lance corporals were also lads of under one year's service and afraid to give an old reservist an order.'[39]At approximately midday, Private Sheldrake's company 'marched out to a railroad and dug some trenches as the enemy were drawing nearer the town. There was a rumour going around that our cyclist scouts were all captured or killed, but this luckily proved to be a false report. It appeared that only one[40] was killed.'[41] The story was that the scouts had been north of the canal and had 'narrow escapes, swimming across the canal with bullets following them. No doubt that this was the first Norfolk soldier to be killed in this war.'[42] At approximately 1600, Private Hurrell's company returned to the coal mine, "all looking as black as coal and very tired. They had been digging all day, making temporary trenches for emergency." Throughout the day, Brigadier Gleichen had been watching his battalions digging in and so had the local population 'and all the miners were loafing about with nothing to do.'[43] The Brigade Commander 'got hold of the best-dressed and most authoritative looking men and showed them what needed to be done…the idea caught rapidly caught on and soon they were hurrying off for their tools.'[44] That night Private Hurrell was sent out on outpost duty. 'A few

35 TNA WO 95/1571/1: 1st Cheshire Regiment War Diary.
36 Pte R. Hurrell, Log of Round the World Cruise, p. 25.
37 Pte R. Sheldrake diary, p. 10.
38 Ibid., p. 10.
39 Ibid., p. 10.
40 The battalion lost Pte William Porter on the 22nd and Pte William Chapman on the 23rd August 1914.
41 Ibid., p. 10.
42 Ibid., p. 10.
43 Gleichen, *Infantry Brigade 1914*, p. 22.
44 Ibid., p. 22.

of us had to go out a few miles to outposts. That increased our thoughts of soon coming into contact with the enemy. On our arrival, we were told there were no troops of our own on the left, so keep a sharp lookout for the enemy, challenge whoever approaches and fire if the answer is unsatisfactory.'[45] From their position they could see on the skyline villages or woods burning that had been bombarded during the day.[46] That evening, just after dinner, Brigadier Gleichen received further orders. The Brigade Commander and his Brigade Major, Major[47] 'Weatherby cantered down to the Divisional Staff to learn details…to the effect that the Norfolks and Cheshires were to be left under the direct command of the Divisional Commander and that the Brigade Headquarters was to be at Pâturages by sunrise on the morrow, and to hold that with our other two battalions on the right.'[48]

As the 15th Infantry Brigade secured their position to the rear, the battalions of the 14th Infantry Brigade had taken up their positions along the canal. The canal crossing at Ville Pommeroeul to the north of Thulin was the bridge covered by 1 DCLI and the 2 Manchesters covering the bridge to their south on the La Haine river where 59 Field Company, Royal Engineers had built another bridge across the river, deeming the current bridge insufficient,[49] using one pontoon and one trestle. 59 Field Company had arrived in Hanin, east of Thulin, on the 22nd August and had been detailed to strengthen the outpost line of the 14th Infantry Brigade. On the 23rd August, No. 1 Section had been sent to Mons to prepare the bridges for demolition. At 1000 on 23rd August they received orders that the bridges on Thulin-Pommeroeul road and the road bridge on the La Haine should be prepared for demolition. No. 3 Section was detailed with the task, but when they arrived at the Thulin–Pommeroeul road bridge they found that it had already been done so they prepared the bridge over the La Haine only.[50] To their south, the 9th Lancers were in Thulin. To their front, the Germans had already started their advance and the scouts from *Hussar Regiment 10* who were leading the advance ahead of the main body had reached the railway station at Ville Pommeroeul, just to the north of Thulin, at 0600.

At 0500, Field Marshal French set off for a meeting with his Corps Commanders and went to Sars-la-Bruyere (headquarters of II Corps), and arrived at 0600. There he met Generals Haig, Smith-Dorrien, and Allenby. Major Home had promised himself "a long lie" after the long overnight move to Quiévrain, a journey of about 15 miles over paved roads which he thought was 'the worse march I have ever done.' He was very disappointed to be woken at 0300 for a 0430 departure with General Allenby.[51] At the meeting, Field Marshal French shared with his commanders his concerns and gave them an estimate of the size of the German force facing them 'of that little more than one, or at most two, enemy corps, with perhaps a Cavalry Division, were facing the BEF.'[52] The information the cavalry had so far provided did not overly worry him and he preferred to wait for further information from the RFC in the morning before deciding on a plan. At this point a retreat was already being considered:

45 Pte R. Hurrell, Log of Round the World Cruise, p. 27.
46 Ibid., p. 27.
47 Simpson, *Cheshire Regiment the First Battalion at Mons and the Miniature Colour,* p. 23.
48 Gleichen, *Infantry Brigade 1914,* p. 24.
49 Horsfall & Cave, *Mons 1914,* p. 188 and Wyrall, *The History of The Duke of Cornwall's Light Infantry 1914-1919*, p. 18.
50 TNA WO 95/1535, 59th Field Company, Royal Engineers War Diary.
51 Home, *Diary of a World War 1 Cavalry Officer,* p. 16.
52 Smith-Dorrien, *Memories of Forty-Eight Years' Service,* p. 382.

> I told the commanders of the doubts which had arisen in my mind during the previous 24 hours and impressed on them the necessity of being prepared for any kind of move, either in advance or in retreat. I discussed exhaustively the situation on our front. Allenby's bold and searching reconnaissance had not led me to believe that we were threatened by forces against which we could not make an effective stand...They all assured me that a quiet night had been passed and that their line was firmly taken up and held. The air reconnaissance had started at daybreak, and I decided to await aircraft reports from Henderson before making any decided plan. I instructed Sir Archibald Murray, my Chief of Staff, to remain for the present at General Smith-Dorrien's headquarters at Sars-la-Bruyere and gave him full instructions as to arrangements which must be made if a retreat became necessary.[53]

General Smith-Dorrien's recollection of the meeting shows that at this stage it was unclear as to what the plan was going to be, but the preparation of the bridges for demolition shows doubts were setting in. He remarked that both he and Field Marshal French had slept well "blissfully ignorant" of the developing situation. General Smith-Dorrien thought 'Sir John was in excellent form and told us to be prepared to move forward, or to fight where we were, but to get ready for the latter by strengthening our outposts and preparing the bridges over the canal for demolition.'[54] General Haig took 'the opportunity of emphasising the weakness of his general line and the danger of holding on to the Mons salient, remarking that he was issuing orders for the preparation of a retired position south-west and clear of the town of Mons to cover, should a retirement become necessary.'[55] He also told the Field Marshal that 'the advanced troops at Nimy and Obourg would have to fall back behind Mons, as soon as things got hot rather than risk being cut off. The chief expressed himself in agreement and approved my action.'[56]

General Douglas Haig, *en-route* to the meeting, had noticed that the peaceful scene had begun to change. A few miles northwards shells were beginning to fall; the stream of refugees, which was to be a constant companion of the army, had begun to flow. When Lieutenant Colonel Barrow saw the refugees for the first time he wrote:

> Those sad crowds of refugees impeding the roads, old men, and women young and old, little children; on carts, on donkeys, on foot; drawing hand-carts, pushing perambulators and wheelbarrows; leading dogs drawing carts, carrying in wagons and every sort of vehicle as much of furniture, bedding and household goods as could be piled upon them; leaving almost all they possessed, together with their hearts, in the farms and cottages that had meant home to them and to the generations of their forbearers.[57]

Paul Maze, interpreter with the Scots Greys, had also seen the flow of refugees and the start of the French withdrawal:

53 Viscount French of Ypres, *1914*, p. 61.
54 Smith-Dorrien, *Memories of Forty-Eight Years' Service*, p. 382.
55 Ibid., p. 382.
56 Ibid., p. 382.
57 Barrow, *The Fire of Life*, p. 144.

> The sight of the enemy had an immediate repercussion on the crowd. Women started to wail, and rushed for home, followed by the men, while children, torn by curiosity, lagged behind turning to see. At once the atmosphere changed, in a few seconds all these civilians were fleeing along the roads…a peasant's cart squeaked along the road; from inside the lit-up hood rose the pathetic wail of a newly born child; the shadow of the mother projected against the canvas. Then started a solemn procession of convoys of wounded, followed by the infantry retiring.'[58]

The conference had 'bought no reassurance to Haig. The fears that he had entertained from the day of mobilisation of the different personalities who controlled the operations at the GHQ appeared to be realised.'[59] Firstly there was a "sharp division in opinion" between the intelligence and operations sections regarding the large troop movements in and through Tournai.'[60] This had been reported by agents and air reports and German troops were moving westwards, but Field Marshal French 'would not accept these reports.'[61] General Haig had noticed that General Murray, his Chief of Staff took 'little part in the discussion, nor did Sir John French appear to consult or attach any importance to his views.'[62] General Haig attributed this to the strength of the relationship between the Field Marshal and his sub-Chief of Staff General Wilson, 'which had become close during Sir John French's tenure of office on the General Staff in London, and which had been strengthened during the Ulster crisis, led him to rely on the opinions of Wilson, and Wilson could not free his mind from the optimistic view of the French General Staff.'[63] General Haig felt that 'it was sufficient for Wilson, that the French were about to attack. Success was assured. The German centre would be broken.'[64] He was also of the opinion that "in war, we tend to believe what we wish for." At the end of the conference, Field Marshal French had accepted General Wilson's view and in his summary of the situation 'made no reference to the information supplied by his own intelligence department, which emphasised the facts which supported the view of the French General Staff.'[65] The meeting with Field Marshal French and his Corps Commanders had left them confused. The plan for the day had been to advance from their start position on the canal, and now there was to be no move for 24 hours, and they were to prepare to stand and fight where they were or to retreat. These were three different operations and as such the current position and the supporting troops behind were echeloned for an advance. To defend their current locations which was a *thin line* of outposts of 21 kms with little or no reserves was going to be hard and to retreat would be even more difficult. With General Murray now attached to II Corps, Field Marshal French was waiting to corroborate the information he had from both the RFC and cavalry. His sole counsel was now General Wilson.

The *advance guard* from *Infanterie Division 7, Infanterie Brigade 13* made contact with the BEF south of Ville Pommeroeul. The three battalions of *Infanterie Regiment 26*[66] were advancing on

58 Maze, *A Frenchman in Khaki*, pp. 19-25.
59 Charteris, *Field Marshal Earl Haig*, pp. 88-89.
60 Ibid., p. 88.
61 Ibid., p. 88.
62 Ibid., p. 88.
63 Ibid., p. 88.
64 Ibid., p. 88.
65 Charteris, *Field Marshal Earl Haig*, p. 88.
66 *Infanterie-Regiment Fürst Leopold von Anhalt-Desseu (1 Magdeburgisches) Nr. 26.*

Ville Pommeroeul. The battalions were ordered forward with III Battalion, with two machine gun platoons, deployed against Ville Pommeroeul and the canal, while II Battalion with a machine gun platoon attacked on the right towards the railway embankment, I Battalion followed behind III Battalion.[67] *Infanterie Regiment 66* was also in support, and reconnoitring out to their front were the cavalry patrols of *Husaren Regiment 8*. 1 DCLI were waiting in position covering their bridge on the canal at Ville Pommeroeul and they also had a position north of the canal which had a clear view to their north. They first saw the reconnaissance scouts of *Husaren Regiment 8* at 0600:

> 2nd Lieutenant Savile was occupying a trench with a section of No. 6 Platoon (B Company). At a bend in the road about a couple of 100 yards to his front, a sentry post of three privates had been established. All unconscious of danger and taking no military precautions, riding along in close order, laughing and talking, a strong officer's patrol of German dragoons [sic] rode towards the sentry post. The three men withheld their fire, though their fingers must have itched to press the triggers of their rifles. They were all concealed and, crouching low in their ditch by the roadside, waited until the Germans were practically abreast of them. Then suddenly the German officer saw them and began to fumble with his revolver. He was, however, too late, for Private Sambrook, one of the three Cornishmen, shot him at point-blank range. The patrol wheeled about and Sambrook's comrades then fired at them with effect: the officer fell forward on to the neck of his horse, but one of the German dragoons seizing the reins, led the animal away still bearing the inert body of the officer.[68]

Gustav Schubert a medical orderly with *Infanterie Regiment 26* wrote:

> A group of 10 hussars come riding up and stop on the other side of the road. Suddenly with a sssssssing infantry shots whiz way over our heads. Nobody knows where they are coming from…a few hussars have dropped to the ground; and a man with a bad leg, who was resting on the field kitchen, is shot dead. The hussars ride back into the wood to reach cover.[69]

This engagement initially halted the reconnaissance patrols, but the Germans continued their advance and returned about half an hour later by which time 1 DCLI had adjusted their position and the outpost of Private Sambrook had withdrawn back to 2nd Lieutenant Savile's position. The patrols were then engaged again:

> The patrol advanced along the by-road to within 100 yards of 2nd Lieutenant Savile and his section of No. 6 Platoon, who were so admirably concealed as to be almost invisible. The first intimation of danger the Germans received was a hail of bullets in their ranks which caused them, or rather the survivors, to beat a hasty retreat. How many were killed

67 Zuber, *The Mons Myth*, p. 163.
68 d Wyrall, *The History of The Duke of Cornwall's Light Infantry 1914-1919*, p. 16.
69 Gustav Schubert, *In Frankreich Kriegsgefangen, meine Erlebnisse auf dem Vormarsch der 1. Armee durch Belgien und Frankreich sowie in der Französischen Kriegsgefangenschaft* (Magdeburg: Reinecke, 1915), p. 37.

> or wounded could not be ascertained, but the villagers brought in a number of trophies in the form of arms, equipment and clothing, and several dead horses were left on the road.[70]

Later that morning at about 0800 one of the German dragoons [sic], who had been badly wounded in the head, was brought in by the villagers. This gave 1 DCLI their first close look at their enemy. From the information gained by the medical officer, it was clear that the extended German advance meant that as far as the reconnaissance patrols were concerned their rations were not getting through. The German soldier's expectation on capture indicated had clearly been briefed that he would be roughly handled:

> He was, however, quite sensible and able to stand, but was in abject fear, crying and begging for mercy. He apparently expected to be shot at once and could not understand being treated kindly. He was put on a stretcher and carried back to the reserve of the outpost. An interesting sidelight on the strenuous nature of the German advance, the Medical Officer reported that from this man's vomit his stomach was absolutely empty save for some oats which he had evidently been sharing with his horse.[71]

The German advance continued and another mounted patrol came from the direction of Ville Pommeroeul.

> The German lancers had ridden towards the Cornwall's…like their dragoon comrades, were apparently all unconscious of the danger in front of them. Again, the Cornwalls, with a machine gun already trained on the Germans, reserved their fire, until suddenly someone on the left unable to control his excitement opened fire prematurely when the enemy was about 700 yards away. It was a foolish thing to do, for whoever fired the shot must have had a very poor field of fire. The patrol turned sharply about and galloped off, only one horse (as far as could be ascertained) being killed. Later, the rider of this horse was brought in uninjured. He also was in an abject state of fear, crying and begging for mercy as he was led away, as if he had fallen into the hands of savages who massacred their prisoners.[72]

This first encounter had been witnessed by General Smith-Dorrien as he was assessing the positions of his corps north of the canal 'as far as I recollect, about 0900.'[73] I motored to the left of my outpost line at Pommeroeul, and leaving the car crossed the bridge and saw an interesting scrap between the Cornwalls and German scouts. [74] The hussars lost one soldier and had another wounded. The remaining patrol withdraw back and took cover behind a garden hedge and remained in a position of observation and sent back their report. [75] In total the German cavalry made three reconnaissance patrols against the 1 DCLI position.[76] At approximately

70 Ibid., p. 16.
71 Ibid., p. 17.
72 Ibid., p. 17.
73 Edmonds, *Military Operations France and Belgium 1914,* Vol. I states 'between 6.30 and 7.00am,' p. 67.
74 Smith-Dorrien, *Memories of Forty-Eight Years' Service,* p. 384.
75 Zuber, *The Mons Myth,* p 163.
76 Ibid., p. 161.

the same time,[77] Field Marshal French went on to Valenciennes to see General Drummond (commanding the 19th Infantry Brigade) and the French Commandant at Valenciennes. When he met General d'Amade, (who met him at the station) he inspected some of the entrenchments which were under construction, and the disposition of the Territorial troops which had been detailed to guard his left flank. Field Marshal French arrived at 19th Infantry Brigade just as 2 Argyll and Sutherland Highlanders were completing its detrainment. It was at this point he placed General Drummond under command of General Allenby.[78]

As the 9th Lancers woke after their long ride and the difficult night in a bog, if they were not aware in the change in their surroundings they woke to a completely different landscape and were now listening to the first engagements of the war around them. 'Instead of the wide rolling downs of their dreams, our cavalry now found themselves called on to fight in a land full of little smoky villages and coal mines, towering slag heaps, railway embankments and endless wire fences, and a population as dense as that of a Black Country town at home.'[79] All ranks were now wondering how they would operate in this new landscape and were unclear what was happening now to their front. 'The officers were puzzled to know how cavalry could operate here, and all ranks were equally puzzled as to the plan of campaign and as to what was going on in front of and all around them.' [80] This was not just the observation of the Lancers but the 4th Dragoon Guards had also contemplated how they might operate as mounted cavalrymen and felt that traditional mounted action would be out of the question. 'The terrain was a maze of slag heaps, sugar beet fields, scattered buildings. Fences, sunken roads, railway lines and other hazards calculated to make any mounted action seem out of the question.'[81]

Rivy had chosen to sleep on some hay close to the squadron lines and had woken before reveille, 'rather cold at 0630 to find my horse had eaten away my bed!'[82] Captain Grenfell had slept in an empty house in his valise and had woken about 0800. On getting up, he 'went around the lines and inspected each horse and all shoes. 'After stables, the Colonel had a conference with officers at 1000, after which we went away and got some food and arranged about ammunition etc., being given out. Rivy went I think, to a small inn and lay down to sleep and write some of his diary.'[83] Later that day at 1300, a small group of officers and interpreters dined in the inn for lunch. After lunch the two twins went back to the house and had a bath in the back kitchen in the bucket used for the milk in the garden. [84]

> For the 9th Lancers, it felt that this was going to be the first real day of their war, as ammunition was given out during the morning and this meant business. The likelihood of a fight seemed to be *imminent* for a squadron of the 19th Hussars passed through having been engaged with the enemy.[85] During the afternoon, General Smith-Dorrien drove round the outposts

77 At 0900. See Ascoli, *The Mons Star*, p. 75.
78 Viscount French of Ypres, *1914*, p. 65.
79 Sheppard, *The Ninth Queen's Royal Lancers 1715-1936*, p. 235.
80 Ibid., p. 235.
81 John M. Brereton, *A History of the 4th and 7th Royal Dragoon Guards and Their Predecessors 1685-1980* (Catterick: Published by the Regiment, 1985), p. 312.
82 Grenfell, Grenfell Family Papers (within Lyttelton Family Papers, 23rd August 1914, p. 5
83 Grenfell, Grenfell Family Papers (within Lyttelton Family Papers), 23rd August 1914, p. 17.
84 Ibid., p. 17.
85 Anon., 9th Lancer War Diary, 23rd August 1914, p. 10.

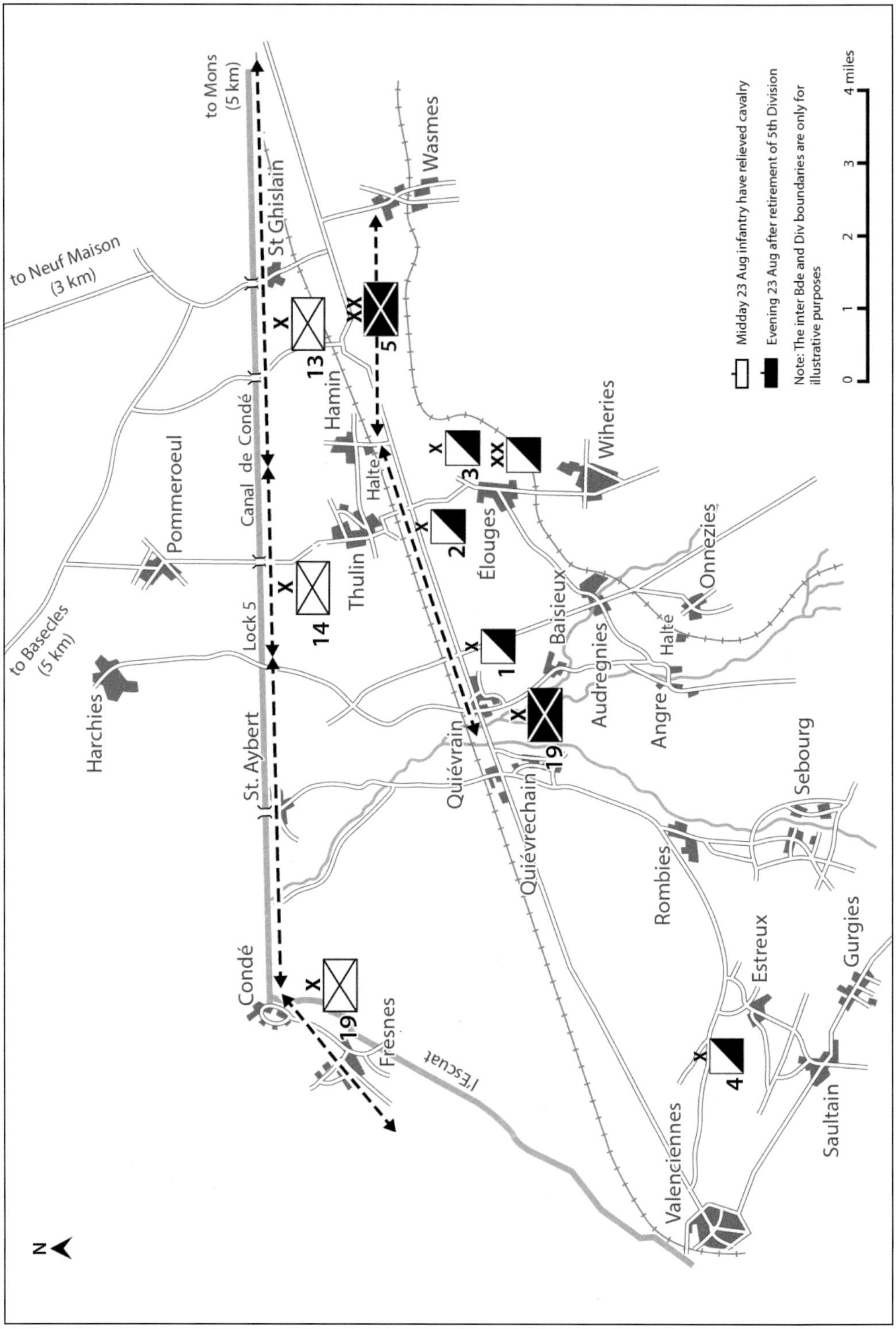


Map 5 Cavalry Division Areas on the evening 23rd August 1914. (Cavalry Journal, 1922)

and reconnoitered the positions and considered his options and falling back from the line of the canal was a serious possibility. His observations on the industrial landscape presented the same challenges for a defensive battle as it would for a cavalry engagement. It might be considered that the ground for the next day might be less than ideal and not one of first choice:

> In my hasty survey, I had come to the conclusion that, from a fighting point of view, our position was a very difficult one. The ground on the enemy's side of the canal commanded it from comparatively short ranges, and was densely wooded, giving them the advantage of a covered approach. Any idea of fighting a serious action on the outpost line was therefore out of the question, although such a thing in any case would have been impossible in view of the enormous extension of the corps, covering as it did 21 miles with only two divisions. I came to the conclusion that our only hope, if attacked in force, would be to hold a less extended position in rear on which the outposts could fall back. This, however, was not very encouraging, as although the ground rose considerably on a general line some two to three miles south of the canal it was so broken up by the pitheads and wired enclosures, and so thickly covered with houses, that any organised effective defence must involve great risks.[86]

At midday, General Fergusson's Divisional Reserve, the 15th Infantry Brigade, 'was ordered to dig in on a defensive position which had been selected by the Brigadier that morning, and on which trenches had already been started by the impressed labour of Belgian miners.'[87] The brigade position was in the area of Wasmes in and around the railway embankment. 'The Norfolks was allotted the left sector, from Wasmes station eastwards; the Cheshires were on its right (but thrown back a little in very enclosed country); while the Bedfords and Dorsets occupied some trenches on a high railway embankment further to the east.'[88] The selected position was far from suitable for infantry, 'but there was no better alternative for miles.'[89] While the brigade was in position, the Brigade Commander had visited the Cheshires during the day and had informed Lieutenant Colonel Boger 'that the army was establishing a line of strongpoints, or '*points d'appui*' and that the French were about to attack, or reinforce between them.'[90] The Cheshires situation on the right was:

> A and B Companies to go and dig trenches, and C and D Companies to advance and hold a crossroads about five miles ahead. The scouts of C and D under Captain Jackson, led the way and arrived at the position without hindrance. The scouts went on to try and locate the enemy and shortly came in touch with a German picket. This was immediately reported to Major Chetwynd-Stapylton who was in command at the crossroads, and the scouts continued to keep in touch with the German picket until dawn, when, without being discovered, they withdrew to Petit Wasmes…British aeroplanes buzzing about. One more venturesome than the rest appeared just over the trench but was immediately fired on by the German guns on the other side of the canal. It was pretty to see the shrapnel bursting round it, but it got away without receiving, so far as could be seen, any damage. It brought

86 Smith-Dorrien, *Memories of Forty-Eight Years' Service,* p. 381.
87 Crookenden, *The History of the Cheshire Regiment in the Great War,* p. 4
88 Ibid., p. 4.
89 Ibid.
90 Ibid.

the trench diggers under fire, but luckily no one was injured. They had to man the trenches for about an hour, after which they continued digging until it was dark. A vivid sunset gave colour to a strange scene. To the north were several villages ablaze. Everywhere in trench, or covered position, were lines of eager, anxious men standing to their arms awaiting that first great collision of armies [91]

Lieutenant Colonel David Campbell. (9/12L Museum)

About 1300, Lieutenant Colonel David Campbell of the 9th Lancers sent for his 'Squadron Leaders and told them that six corps of German infantry and three Cavalry Divisions were advancing against the BEF, and that the plan was for us to 'retire and fight a *rear guard* action.'[92] Captain Grenfell 'went back and worked this out with Nash-Wortham and explained it to Rivy. Firing in the meanwhile was going on northeast of Thulin and had gotten very heavy in the afternoon.'[93] 'The rest of the day was spent in deep mystification.'[94] What the 9th Lancers could hear was the actions of 1 DCLI at Ville Pommeroeul, to their north. After the initial contacts in the morning of the German Hussar reconnaissance patrols 1 DCLI consolidated their position. Then moved most of the battalion south of the river relocated the machine gun and built some *ad hoc* defences, fully expecting to being attacked and having to withdraw:

91 Simpson, *Cheshire Regiment the First Battalion at Mons and the Miniature Colour,* p. 21.
92 Grenfell, Grenfell Family Papers (within Lyttelton Family Papers), 23rd August 1914, p. 17.
93 Ibid., 23rd August, p. 18.
94 Buchan, *Francis and Riversdale Grenfell,* p. 192.

> At about 1400, the garrison at the bridgehead was strengthened by the addition of C Company. The latter occupied all the trenches to the west of the main road, while B Company (less one platoon still flanking the trenches from the south bank of the canal) held those on the east. The machine gun was withdrawn altogether…as it was doubtful whether, in the event of attack and under heavy fire, the position could be maintained. In its place, however, a breastwork was constructed across the main road by removing the paving stones (of which it was made) and building them into a wall. This work was garrisoned by 10 rifles under the supervision of the OC Post, whose orders were 'to hang on until the place becomes untenable owing to attack by too superior numbers and then to retire.'[95]

At 1500, the 19th Infantry Brigade, released from their *lines of communications* duties, relieved the 4th Cavalry Brigade on the canal to the west of the 14th Infantry Brigade. However, the 6th Dragoon Guards were still in place and were not relieved until 1830 when they withdrew to Estreux.[96] The 1 Middlesex, commanded by Lieutenant Colonel Bertram Ward, had entrained at Le Havre on the 22nd and had reached Valenciennes early on the 23rd. On detraining the battalion marched via Quiévrain to St Aybert. The positions on the canal were held with 1 Middlesex on the right, next to 1 DCLI, and 1 Cameronians on the left. 1 Middlesex deployed B Company to hold Lock No. 5 on the right and A Company the St Aybert bridge on the left,[97] with the 2 Royal Welsh Fusiliers and 2 Argylls in reserve.[98] 19th Infantry Brigade was placed under command of General Allenby's Cavalry Division. This final brigade now brought a total of nine and half infantry battalions along the line of the canal in the II Corps area.[99]

During the afternoon, confusion and rumours occupied the thoughts of the 9th Lancers in the absence of any clear information. There was a strong rumour that German cavalry had crossed the canal and the movement of 1 DCLI was premature. 'At about 1600 a company of the Cornwall Light Infantry passed through us which caused rather a scare as we were still off-saddled and understood that they held the line in front of us. They were immediately ordered back, as apparently they had retired through some mistake.'[100] They told the 9th Lancers that they 'had left a few for us.'[101] The reports of the German cavalry cause huge excitement and gave Lieutenant Rivy Grenfell his first insight as to the *fog of war* and the accuracy of information they were hearing. Lieutenant Grenfell was 'suddenly told to saddle up at 1640. I rode *No. 36*, and Francis rode *Ginger*.'[102] 'We scoured the country, but found no one, and got back to Thulin at 2100. This gave us our first insight of human nature on active service, for though we had a troop out in front of us a very excited gunner sergeant major told us a lot of Germans were in action behind the house quite close to us.'[103] Later the sergeant major returned 'and told us a German

95 Wyrall, *The History of The Duke of Cornwall's Light Infantry 1914-1919*, p. 19.
96 TNA WO 95/1135, War Diary, 4th Cavalry Brigade War Diary.
97 Zuber, *The Mons Myth,* pp. 164-165.
98 Ascoli, *The Mons Star*, p. 59.
99 Ibid., p. 59.
100 Grenfell, Grenfell Family Papers (within Lyttelton Family Papers), 23rd August 1914, p. 18.
101 LCpl W. Hunt diary, p. 4.
102 Grenfell, Grenfell Family Papers (within Lyttelton Family Papers, 23rd August 1914, p. 5.
103 Grenfell, Grenfell Family Papers (within Lyttelton Family Papers), 23rd August 1914, p. 18.

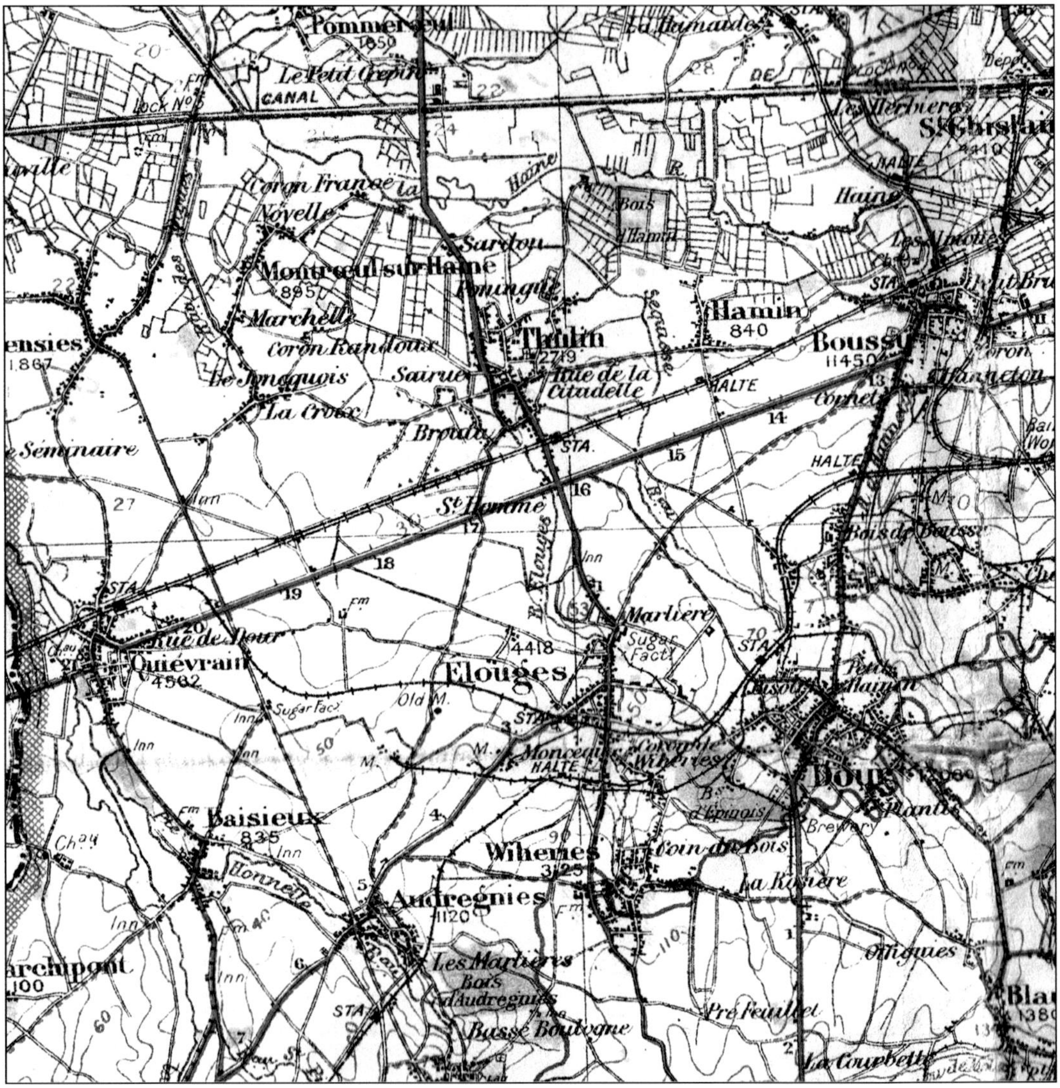


Map 6 British issue General area Map c. 1916. (QRL & NY Museum)[104]

104 The map issued to Lieutenant Colonel Ballard was dated 1909, but is identical to the map illustrated.

cavalry regiment was in a wood quite close to us, absolutely mad with excitement, and although we formed for an attack, soon found the enemy a phantom one. Porter was sent off with some scouts on the right flank.'[105]

At approximately 1545, the Germans started their attempt to cross the canal in front of 1 DCLI.[106] Their orders were that 'in the event of being forced to retire 1 DCLI will retire to Sardon-Thulin, thence by the 'E' of Marlière [see Map 6.] 2 Manchester Regiment will cover their withdrawal and retire by the same route.'[107] As the Germans advanced, 1 DCLI were shocked at the tactics they saw as the enemy began moving along the road southward from Ville Pommeroeul towards the canal:

> They presented an extraordinary appearance, mounted men preceded by jägers, all in close order, marching slowly and deliberately forward in one solid mass and occupying the entire roadway. The OC Post waited until the head of the advancing enemy reached the level crossing the range of which was known to be exactly 750 yards. Then, with combined sights at 750 and 800 yards fire was opened. The number of rifles was all too few, but every shot must have taken effect. The result upon the enemy was miraculous. In a moment, the road was clear except for a few skirmishers at the level crossing who opened fire at so long a range as to be absolutely harmless. From our trench, a few long-range shots were fired at the mass of cavalry at Ville Pommeroeul, but we failed to find the range. The OC Post was now wondering how to interpret his orders. The enemy had been effectually checked in enormously superior numbers, but the post had not yet become in any way untenable. Apparently, therefore, it was his duty to "hang 'on" for the present. At that moment, Major Petavel, appeared from nowhere with orders for the two companies to fall back to the south side of the canal. B Company accordingly vacated its trenches and retired over the bridge, the range of which the enemy had not yet found, while C Company went across country and crossed the canal by means of two barges...that had been moored together as an alternative line of retreat. These barges were successfully unlashed, unmoored and cast adrift after the last man had crossed.[108]

On their arrival at the village, *Infanterie Regiment 26* found 1 DCLI were holding the railway embankment south and southeast of the village. III Battalion, *Infanterie Regiment 26* was the *advance guard* regiment, with 10 *Kompanie* in the lead. At 1650, as the company left the woods north of Ville Pommeroeul, it received *unexpectedly* received heavy fire from the town at close range. *10 Kompanie* deployed to the right against a railway embankment, 9 *Kompanie* to the left of the road, *12 Kompanie* to the right, with I Battalion *Infanterie Regiment 26* in reserve. The terrain felt very familiar and the commander of III Battalion, Oberleutnant Faelligen, felt that the 'deployment of the battalion on terrain that was completely flat meadow, crisscrossed with ditches and hedges, was conducted like on the Anger (the local training area in Magdeburg). It was a joy to see the dash and aggressiveness of our men, in spite of the heavy enemy fire, most

105 Ibid., 23rd August 1914, p. 18.
106 Zuber, *The Mons Myth*, p. 162.
107 Everard Wyrall, *The History of The Duke of Cornwall's Light Infantry, 1914-1919*, p. 19.
108 TNA WO 95/1564/1 op. cit. in Wyrall, *The History of The Duke of Cornwall's Light Infantry, 1914-1919*, p. 19.

of which was fortunately too high.'[109] On the right, I Battalion moved through a railway yard, the boxcars still containing British equipment. A platoon leader, Leutnant Freytag a platoon commander in 1 *Kompanie*, said:

> The troops conducted themselves well during their baptism of fire. The platoon used the boxcars for cover, but the cars had been uncoupled and there were open spaces between them. The British watched these spots well, and each time the platoon crossed the open areas, with very large intervals between the men, the British opened fire. Thank God they almost always fired too high.'[110]

The German platoon moved through the railway yard and consolidated behind a pile of coal, and made a short 50m bound to a factory building that was on the canal, they saw a 1 DCLI trench 500m south of the canal. The platoon moved laterally behind a hedge to a house on the north side of the bridge. All of this movement by *Infanterie Regiment 26* was undertaken without any artillery support as the initial position of *Feldartillerie Regiment 4*[111] with I Battalion, a quarter to the left of the road and II Battalion to the right, along the south tree line.[112] The battalion commander found the position was unsatisfactory. 'It was open to the enemy while at the same time had poor observation of the canal. British artillery fire landed near the exit from the woods, and it took some time to get the guns into a position of observation so they could provide covering fire. The II Battalion moved through the woods to avoid this fire, which caused a delay and it finally succeeded in bringing IV Battalion into position by 1715.[113] At 1830, II Battalion of *Infanterie Regiment 66* was committed and deployed east of the road. The battalion advanced in the growing darkness on a broad front from the rail line south of Ville Pommeroeul.[114] The battalions was supported by the machine gun platoon of Reserve Leutnant Seldte. The battalion had to 'wade through several broad and deep water-filled ditches. For the smaller men, loaded with equipment, this wasn't easy, as the water came to their necks. The heavy machine gun and rifle fire from the front fortunately all went too high, and there were no casualties.'[115] The final position of the German artillery was still not suitable and so the artillery regimental commander, Oberstleutnant Sigismund von Eisenhart-Rothe reconnoitred further positions and ordered *Feldartillerie Regiment 4* to move forward. I Battalion moved south of the railway line and west of the road, and II Battalion set up on the railway embankment east of the road but the 'observation was still limited by trees and it was becoming dark, so the two batteries never fired from these positions. The regimental commander therefore ordered a platoon from II Battalion to manhandle two guns right up to the bridge site and destroy a British machine gun at 200m range. The effect was immediate: the machine gun ceased fire and the farm the British occupied burst into flames.'[116]

109 Zuber, *The Mons Myth*, p. 163.
110 Ibid., p. 163.
111 *Feldartillerie-Regiment Prinz-Regent Luitpold von Bayern (Magdeburgisches) Nr. 4.*
112 Rübesamen (Hauptmann/Bartels (Oberleutnant), *Feldartillerie-Regiment Prinzregent Luitpold von Bayern (Magdeburgisches) Nr. 4*, Pt. 1, pp. 57-58 cited and translated by Zuber, *The Mons Myth*, p. 163.
113 Zuber, *The Mons Myth*, p. 163.
114 Korfes, *The German 66th Regiment in the First World War*, p. 31.
115 Ibid., p. 31.
116 Zuber, *The Mons Myth*, p. 164.

During the afternoon a squadron of the 19th Hussars passed through, the position of the 4th Dragoon Guards and said they had lost a patrol under Lieutenant Horn.[117] At approximately 1700, Captain Wright wrote the Manchester Regiment:

> Suddenly started retiring on to us much to our alarm, as our horses were unsaddled in their lines. The 2 Manchester's were ordered back to their positions and we reinforced them. The firing became heavy at this time and Captain FitzGerald was sent up with his two Maxims, Gallagher supporting him with a troop. The Regiment remained in reserve on the left. On receiving orders from Major Hunter to connect up with the infantry right flank, I took a patrol of one corporal and three men and galloped across country, we had a rough ride all of us taking several falls in the dykes which divided the fields, Private Ward's horse was shot under him and the corporal was nearly drowned through his horse falling on him, only Private Carter (my servant) arrived with me. I found there was a gap between the two infantry regiments on the canal,and went up to the firing line on foot to report it to the officer commanding the 2 Manchester's. I then rejoined my squadron.[118]

At 1830,[119] no sooner had 1 DCLI fallen back across the canal to the La Haine river position than the two guns of *Feldartillerie Regiment 4* engaged the bridge but they failed to prevent the Royal Engineers finishing their dangerous work:

> Lieutenant Robert Flint[120] of 59 Field Company was working on it with his men to fix the charges; the bridge could safely be blown as all the British troops were over the river. To deal with the danger caused by the gun whilst he and his men worked at their task, he posted a man to shout a warning whenever he saw the flash from the gun's muzzle. The men would drop into the ditch before the shell arrived. This extremely risky business did result in the bridge being blown.[121]

III Battalion, *Infanterie Regiment 26*'s attack had made good progress until it came up to the canal bridge, which they found had been destroyed. A standing firefight developed, with both sides using houses and the canal embankment for cover.[122] By 2010 contact between *Infanterie Regiment 26* and *Infanterie Regiment 66* along the canal had been established at the *Zuckerfabrik* (sugar factory). Reserve Leutnant Seldte brought his machine gun into position on the roof of a farm building near the canal. At 2100, I Battalion (which had been the divisional reserve) was moved forward to the north side of the sugar factory and 'in spite of their exhaustion, the troops were burning to get at the British.'[123] However, the advance came to a halt while they waited for the divisional bridge train and *Pioneer Battalion 4* to be brought forward. In their eagerness to

117 This action is not mentioned in Horn, *Diary of the Regiment.*
118 Capt. A. Wright diary, 14th August 1914, p.1.
119 Horsfall & Cave, *Mons: 1914,* p. 103.
120 Lt R.B. Flint DSO (killed in action 23rd January 1915) is buried in Dranouter Churchyard, West-Vlaanderen, Belgium.
121 Horsfall & Cave, *Mons: 1914,* p. 103.
122 Zuber, *The Mons Myth,* p. 164.
123 Korfes, *The German 66th Regiment in the First World War,* p. 32.

cross the canal some of the troops while waiting for the *pioneers* to arrive started to construct a makeshift footbridge which was completed despite the enemy's machine gun fire and was ready by midnight.

When the German soldiers reached the trenches which had been dug by 1 DCLI and which they had vacated in haste, a soldier wrote an account which was published in the *Kölnische Zeitung*:

> They had left some excellent equipment behind. We noticed in particular their long-handled shovels. Also, some good pickaxes fell into our hands. We found eatables, especially corned beef, and back packs containing many letters, from which we able to determine which regiment lay before us. All the young ladies wrote that they wished to see their soldiers soon again "in your red coats." In these letters there was no mention of Germans, let alone any hatred of them. We continued over the canal…three of our men set to work whilst we covered them, and they threw planks over the remains of the destroyed bridge.[124]

The first to cross over the shaky planks to the far bank was Leutnant von Reuß with NCOs and men from *10 Kompanie*. Leutnant Schacht followed behind with a machine gun platoon.[125] Leutnant Freytag also used *10 Kompanie's* planks to cross the canal.[126]

> Shortly before our advance, English troops had arrived and hearing our approach, moved back a short distance to the canal. They have blown the bridge up behind themselves, have built barricades 400 yards back from it, and behind these have set up two machine guns which control the road. The houses beyond the canal are provided with loopholes and are prepared for defence…the 11 *Kompanie* [sic] reaches the canal, whose half-metre high embankment grants good cover to us…Both English machine guns are now in action and continually plaster the street as well as the remains of the destroyed bridge. We must reach the canal in order to silence the two machine guns, but how to get there? A comrade from my company drags a long board over to it. Happily, he succeeds in throwing this across the footings of the destroyed bridge without being wounded in the process. Already the first man is over and when on the other side of the cover finds cover against the gable wall of the houses on the left. Two brave souls jump up after him, but they make only a few steps forward; they sink, shot down before they reach the board. From the left side of the road some more jump up, with rifle in hand, crouching down as they race across the wobbling narrow board, happily they reach the protection of the house, where they press themselves firmly against the wall, so as not to offer a target to the Englishmen shooting from the windows…When I have made it across, happily some 60 men probably have made the rush through the storm of bullets; some have swum over. Behind a barn we gather to reorganise ourselves.[127]

124 Joachim von Delbrück, *Der Deutsche Krieg Feldpostbriefen*,, Vol V), p. 40 op. cit., Matthew Richardson, *1914: Voices from the Battlefields* (Barnsley: Pen & Sword, 2013), pp. 37-38.
125 Dunlop, Dunlop & Puttkammer, *The Battle of Mons*, p. 51.
126 Zuber, *The Mons Myth*, p. 164.
127 Schubert, *In Frankreich Kriegsgefangen, meine Erlebnisse auf dem Vormarsch der 1. Armee durch Belgien und Frankreich sowie in der Französischen Kriegsgefangenschaft*, p. 37.

It was now dark and Leutnant Freytag, on his own initiative. He continued his advance straight down the road to Thulin towards a burning building. He moved his platoon off the road to the left. The terrain to the left of the road looked negotiable but after 10 steps he encountered a ditch, beyond which was an orchard. Moving quietly through this, he deployed his platoon on line and had them fix bayonets. As they advanced, the platoon cut through a wire fence, crossed two ditches and reached the farm, which was not occupied. The platoon began to take both enemy and friendly fire, so it lay down in the farmyard and waited for daylight.[128] The final positions were '*Infanterie Regiment 66* on the left of the *Infanterie Regiment 26*.'[129] At 2200 'Musketeer Hermann Voigtlander swam the canal and established that the British had gone.'[130] The bridge train and *Pioneer Battalion 4*[131] arrived and temporary repairs were made to the bridge, III Battalion and parts of I Battalion managed to cross while it was dark. Later II Battalion, *Infanterie Regiment 66*[132] and 'II Battalion, *Infanterie Regiment 26* were ferried across on pontoons from the divisional bridging train. The two battalions entrenched themselves either side of the roadway, about 400m south of the canal. The uncertain situation and the darkness ruled out an immediate continuation of the attack.'[133] After the 25 km march from Silly, *Infanterie Brigade 13* had successfully crossed the canal and had established themselves in a position approximately 400m south. The successful crossing of the canal cost *Infanterie Regiment 66* only a few casualties and *Feldartillerie Regiment 4* had one man killed and three men wounded.[134] 1 DCLI were aware that the canal to their north had been crossed and both sides continued to engage despite the fact that they could not see each other:

> Long after darkness had set in, an incessant fusillade and artillery fire continued. Several machine guns also opened fire upon both sides. The shrapnel fire of the enemy had no effect whatever, except upon the trees. On neither side could the infantry see one another and the expenditure of ammunition by the enemy was out of all proportion to its effect. After nightfall, both combatants endeavoured to enfilade the lines of their opponents with machine gun fire, by taking advantage of the bends in the river line. Our men acquired very poor opinion of German musketry and a still poorer one of their artillery fire. As a result of several hours' fire we had one man killed [Private Gow] and five wounded. We withdrew without any difficulty at 2300.[135] At about 2300, the bridge over the La Haine river went up.[136]

The whole of the 14th Infantry Brigade retired on Dour. The withdrawal was effected from the outer flank, the 2 Manchester Regiment and 1 DCLI extending. D Company (Captain Woodham) of 1 DCLI was the last to retire.[137] Their casualties for the day had been four soldiers

128 Ibid., p. 164.
129 Ibid.
130 Ibid.
131 Ibid.
132 Korfes, *The German 66th Regiment in the First World War*, p. 32.
133 Dunlop, Dunlop & Puttkammer, *The Battle of Mons*, p. 51.
134 Zuber, *The Mons Myth*, p. 164.
135 TNA WO95/1564/1 op. cit. in *The History of The Duke of Cornwall's Light Infantry 1914-1919*, p. 21.
136 Wyrall, *The History of The Duke of Cornwall's Light Infantry 1914-1919*, p. 21.
137 Ibid., p. 21.

killed and one officer and 12 men wounded.[138] As they retired they witnessed the consequences of war and its effects on the civilian population. The battalion was no longer 'greeted with the welcome cheers and cries of *"Vive L'Angleterre," "Vivent les Anglais;"* on all sides there were nothing but tears and mourning. The advance of the dreaded Germans was now certain. Throughout the night, there passed a continuous stream of fugitives, old and young, men and women, each bearing a bundle containing their worldly possessions, all fleeing for safety.'[139]

On the first day of action along the Mons-Condé Canal, the Germans tried to cross in numerous places. Some crossings were successful, and as the reports came in from the front at 1900, General Smith-Dorrien received the first reports that the Germans had crossed in places. His concerns now grew for the gap between his two divisions and the threat to his flank:

> At about 1900, a report came in saying that the enemy had penetrated the line near Frameries and were swarming through that village. I had no troops left, and all I could do was to request the 5th Infantry Division to push out to their right, which they did by sending the 1 Bedfords from 15th Infantry Brigade to Paturages. Knowing the gap was appreciable, owing to the left flank of the 3rd Infantry Division in retiring having failed to join up with the right flank of the 5th Infantry Division, and that if the Germans realised it there was nothing to prevent their pushing through in large numbers and rendering our position untenable.[140]

However, he was generally happy with how the day's fighting had gone: He wrote in his diary 'I was quite happy after the result of the days fighting, and of what I had heard of the men's spirit, and from the number of Germans killed, and that we had held our own well so long as our flanks were not turned.'[141] At 1915, General Smith-Dorrien sent in his report to GHQ highlighting the danger and asked for permission to withdraw his corps back should there be a threat of him being *pierced*:

> To GHQ, G 271, August 23rd. 3rd Infantry Division report at 1847 the Germans are in front of his main position and are not attacking at present, they are, however, working round 3rd Infantry Division on left flank. If it should appear that there is a danger of my centre being *pierced*, I can see no course but to order a general retirement on Bavai position. Have I your permission to adopt this course if it appears necessary? From II Corps, 1915 (Signed Oxley, Colonel).[142]

He then went to General Haig's headquarters at Bonnet, which was about four miles away, and asked if he 'would allow Haking's 5th Infantry Brigade, which was on the road about two and a half miles from Frameries, to push on and cover the gap.'[143] When he arrived at General Haig's

138 Zuber, *The Mons Myth*, p. 165.
139 TNA WO 95/1564/1 op. cit. Wyrall, *The History of The Duke of Cornwall's Light Infantry 1914-1919*, p. 22.
140 Smith-Dorrien, *Memories of Forty-Eight Years' Service*, pp. 384-385.
141 Diary Gen. H. Smith-Dorrien, 23rd August 1914 op. cit. in Ballard, *Smith-Dorrien*, p. 160.
142 Smith-Dorrien, *Memories of Forty-Eight Years' Service*, pp. 384-385.
143 Ibid., p. 385.

headquarters, he also found Lieutenant Colonel F.B. Maurice, General Hubert Hamilton's GSO 2 from 3rd Infantry Division on the same quest. General Haig was happy to offer support and Lieutenant Colonel Maurice went off to inform Brigadier Haking. It would now appear from the developing picture that the Germans would attack that evening or the following morning, so at 2040, Field Marshal French made the decision to 'stand the attack on the ground now occupied by the troops. You will therefore strengthen your positions by every means possible during the night.'[144] The Field Marshal wrote in his diary 'we live from hour to hour. The most contradictory reports are circulated. The fog of war hangs heavily over us. According to Joffre we may tomorrow be attacked in our present forward positions by two and a half army corps and one Cavalry Division. Aeroplane reconnaissances do not tally with this.'[145] The figure was in fact three corps: (*III, IV and IX AKs*) with a fourth about to enter the battle (*II AK*).

After the fruitless search for German cavalry, the 9th Lancers retuned to Thulin at about 2130.[146]As a result of the infantry including 1 DCLI withdrawing back from the canal, the cavalry adjusted its position slightly to the south and provided a screen behind the infantry. It was at this point that many of the local villagers decided to leave their homes, and those that remained were told they had to leave. 'We had to clear all the villagers out. Very pitiful sight as most of them wouldn't leave their homes.'[147]

The crossing to the west of Thulin took place while the second crossing of *IV AK* was being undertaken by *Infanterie Division 8* north of Quiévrain. This was a more complex operation than at Ville Pommeroeul as this was a double canal crossing. The *advance guard* of the division was *Infanterie Regiment 93* from Generalmajor Paul von Reichenau's *Infanterie Brigade 15*. Their reconnaissance patrols reported that the canal was strongly defended by the 6th Dragoons. *Infanterie Regiment 93* was ordered to seize a crossing over the canal. To do this the Regiment would also need to take the bridge Canal d'Antoing at Rivage as well. At 1620, the regimental commander Oberst Louis von Arnim, issued his attack order. He said "that an enemy force of unknown strength held the bridge over the canal 4 kms south of Harchies. II Battalion would attack frontally against the bridge over the Mons-Condé Canal, I Battalion would seize the bridge over the Canal d'Antoing at Rivage and attack the Condé Bridge from the west." The lead company of the battalion was *8 Kompanie* which moved forward quickly with two platoons. A Leutnant with a small group of men few men ran over the bridge, which then was raised behind them, cutting them off. A *feldwebel* and a soldier climbed up the bridge and lowered it with their weight. Once the bridge was secure, *8 Kompanie* stormed across. The enemy, an estimated platoon, withdrew to the Mons-Condé, 800 metres to the south. [148] As the Regiment reached the south of Harchies, fierce house-to-house fighting broke out between the machine gun company and the BEF. Hauptmann Thũmmel, the company commander, was killed while leading his men and Leutnant Freiherr von Ledebour was also killed, having urged his men on to greater efforts with the words "above all, victory must be ours."'[149] The battalion soon

144 Edmonds, *Military Operations France and Belgium 1914*, Vol. I. p. 84.

145 Field Marshal French diary, 23rd August 1914, op. cit., Ascoli, *The Mons Star*, p. 48.

146 Grenfell, Grenfell Family Papers (within Lyttelton Family Papers), 23rd August 1914, p. 19.

147 LCpl W. Hunt diary, p. 5.

148 Trützschler von Falkenstein, *Das Anhaltische Infanterie-Regiment Nr. 93 im Weltkriege*, pp. 33-37 cited and translated in Zuber, *The Mons Myth*, p. 165.

149 Dunlop, Dunlop & Puttkammer, *The Battle of Mons*, p. 51.

captured the bridge with the support of Oberst Konrad von Hippel's *Feldartillerie Regiment 74* who had unlimbered south of Harchies and fired on the houses.[150] Once the bridge over the Canal d'Antoing had been taken the Regiment continued its advance south to the Mons Canal Bridge. This second crossing would prove more problematic and although they continued their advance it was halted by heavy rifle and machine gun fire from farm buildings on the far bank. 'It was not possible to continue the attack because of nightfall and the lack of artillery support.'[151]

As the Regiment approached the canal, the BEF evacuated the houses and blew up the bridge and the canal could not be crossed without bridging material. The attack was therefore broken off. The 6th Dragoon Guards reported that:

> The road leading to the crossing from the north was dead straight for at least 300 yards, so that when the German infantry advanced down it they were given an extremely hot reception…The bridge over the canal was a drawbridge, with its hinges on the northern side. The German method of crossing, or attempting to cross, was to pull it up to an angle of 45 degrees, to act as a shield and then let it down with a bang in the hope that the soldiers would have time to take cover on the far side before being shot down…Having held the main bridges all day, the 6th Dragoon Guards were relieved by the Middlesex Regiment at 1900, but the bridges were blown before they left. Lieutenant Gill's troop had been in action at close range for over three hours, suffering its first casualty of the war while it was withdrawing after being relieved, when Sergeant Ernest Huxtable was killed.[152]

Lieutenant Gills' troop at the lock 'were attacked by 500 infantry and were heavily shelled. They waited until they were 600 yards off and opened fire on them when in columns of four. They claimed to have killed 100.'[153] When 1 Middlesex Regiment arrived to take over from the 6th Dragoon Guards, they were ordered to hold a bridge over the Mons-Condé Canal and Lock No. 3 towards Condé. A Company was ordered to hold the bridge and C Company the lock: B and D Companies were in reserve. A and C Companies, having had dinner, proceeded to dig themselves in to make the best of the position. At 1700 [sic] a heavy attack was made on B Company, which successfully held the enemy at bay until the Germans mounted a machine gun in a house commanding the buildings at the bridge. The latter was blown up by an NCO of a cavalry regiment, just in time to deprive the enemy of the use of it. The buildings, on the southern side, however had to be abandoned, though the 1 Middlesex held the enemy in check. Hostile rifle fire gradually died down and later, as darkness fell, ceased altogether. During the night the Germans launched another attack, but it was easily driven back. The 1st Battalion had had very few casualties with one man, Private Gow killed and five wounded.[154]

150 Hippel K, von Erinnerungsblatt des ehem. *Königl. Preuß. Torgauer Feldartillerie-Regiments Nr. 74*, pp. 30-31 cited in Zuber, *The Mons Myth,* p. 166.
151 Ibid., p. 166.
152 Oatts, *I Serve,* p 202.
153 TNA WO 95/1135: 4th Cavalry Brigade War Diary, 23rd August 1914.
154 Everard Wyrall, *The Die-Hards in the Great War: Vol. 1,* (Naval & Military Press, 1926), pp. 18-19.

Canal Bridge Harchies. (*Infanterie-Regiment Nr. 93 im Weltkriege*)

I Battalion from *Infanterie Battalion 93,* which had successfully crossed the Canal d'Antoing, had found movement 'slow due to numerous deep and swampy ditches and barbed-wire fences'[155] and in the process, took fire from their right. It finally reached 'II Battalion only after dark and on their arrival, I Battalion took over security on the canals and II Battalion bivouacked to their rear.'[156] They would now have to wait until the morning to complete their crossing of the Mons-Condé Canal and the *Pioneer Battalion* would need to construct a new crossing point. The attack on the two bridges cost *Infanterie Regiment 93* three officers and 11 killed and one officer and 24 soldiers wounded and in support of the action *Feldartillerie Regiment 74* had fired a total of 157 rounds of ammunition.[157]

155 Hippel K, von Erinnerungsblatt des ehem, *Königl. Preuß. Torgauer Feldartillerie-Regiments Nr. 74*, pp. 30-31 cited in Zuber, *The Mons Myth,* p. 166. Ibid., p. 166.
156 Ibid., p. 166.
157 Ibid.

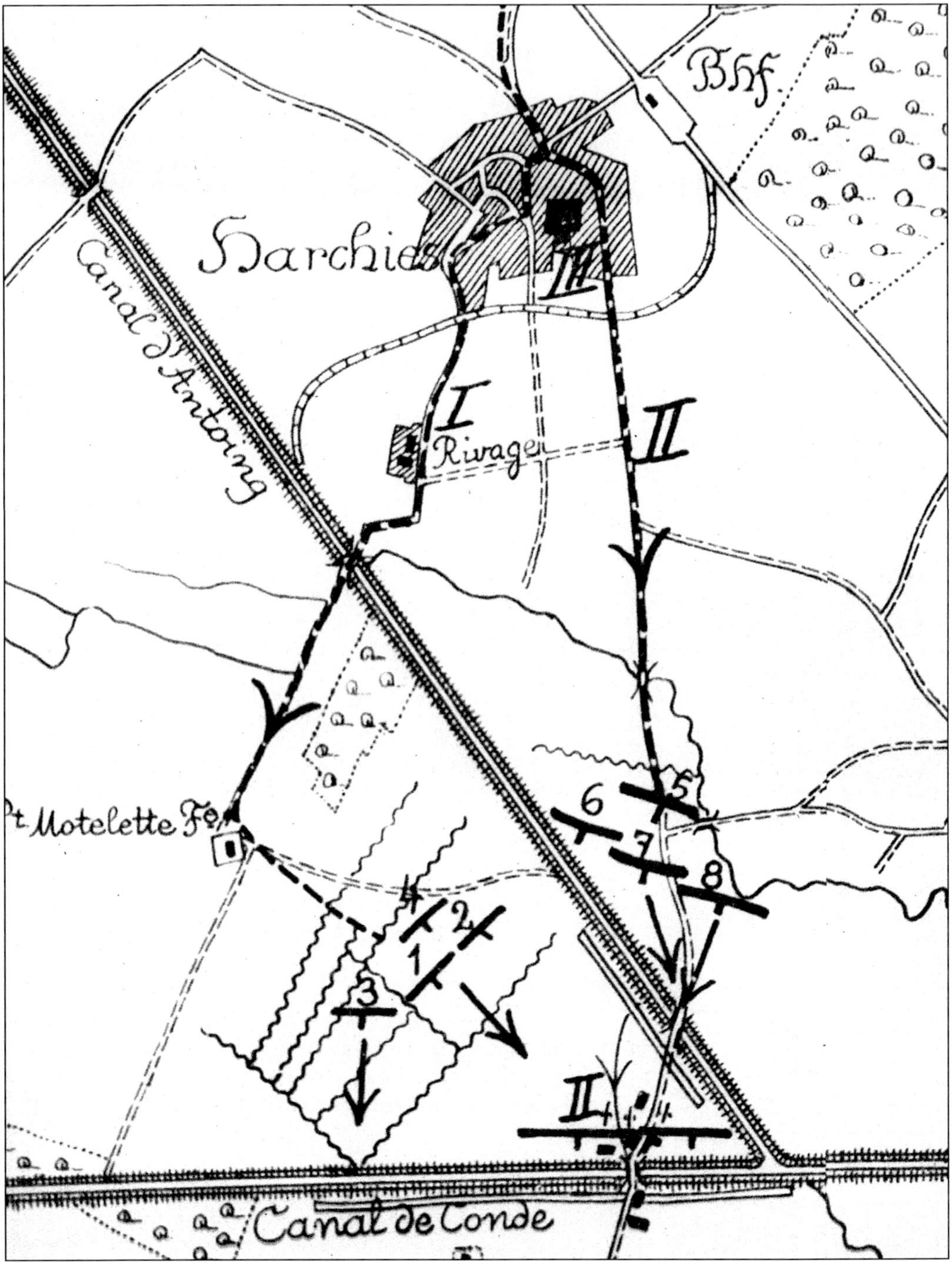


Map 7 Harchies Crossing. (Das Anhaltische Infanterie-Regiment Nr. 93 im Weltkriege)

Roman Road, Chaussée Brunehaut.

Maréchal des Logis Louis Jules Jean Baptiste Quilico attached 4th Dragoon Guards.

Élouges Cemetery.

Élouges centre.

L'ambulance de la Sainte Famille.

Line of mineral railway from the sugar factory running west to east.

Line of the Norfolk Company's looking north.

Major E. Alexander's 119th Battery's position at Élouges. Looking north from the Norfolk Regiment's HQ location.

Minehead at the junction between the Norfolks and Cheshires looking north.

Norfolk Regiment Battalion HQ and B Company location.

Sugar Factory looking south down Roman Road.

Thulin Railway Station, Lieutenant Charlie Garstin's location on the morning of 24th August 1914.

Thulin Church, Lieutenant Rivy Grenfell's location on the morning of 24th August 1914.

Audregnies windmill.

Mineral railway bridge similar to the one at the Norfolk Regiment Headquarters.

Earlier in the afternoon, General Joffre had asked General Lanrezac, the Commander of the Fifth French Corps, his opinion of the situation. He also enquired of him what he understood to be Field Marshal French's opinion. At 2100, General Lanrezac answered the Commander-in-Chief's enquiry by the following telegram: 'The Third Corps attacked at 1600, did not hold its ground and has fallen back to Walcourt. The enemy threatens my right on the Meuse; an infantry detachment which crossed the river north of Hastifcre has succeeded in occupying Onhaye. Givet threatened, Namur carried. In view of this situation and the *delay of the Fourth Army have decided to withdraw army tomorrow* [author's italics] to the front Beaumont-Givot.'[158] It was at this point that the intentions and dispositions of the French army and the BEF were at odds, and since the BEF was on the left flank of the French Army, in support, it would be inevitable that Field Marshal French would have to decide to withdraw, retire or retreat at some point. Time, from this point, was critical as darkness had now fallen and all these adjustments would be best done out of contact with the enemy and before first light. Unbeknown to the BEF, they continued to adjust their positions for the following morning they expected to attack or advance. At approximately the same time, the 9th Lancers had returned to Thulin after their fruitless search for the German cavalry.

At 2330, the 9th Lancers received their orders 'to entrench ourselves on the railway south of Thulin, for an attack at dawn.'[159] The Regiment was to take up the line of entrenchment 1500 yards along the line supported on its right by infantry and on the left by the rest of the Cavalry Division. After conducting a reconnaissance, Captain Grenfell was concerned about the exposed nature of the location he had been given, and that 'the position allotted to me seemed to be an almost impossible one and I rode out to get in touch with the infantry on my right and found they had fallen back to some high ground and were therefore in the rear of us. I came back and reported this to the Colonel who was at Thulin station.'[160] The issue around the siting of the 9th Lancers location was 'that as the position afforded no field of fire, the enemy could creep up and line the opposite embankment with complete impunity.[161] After the Colonel had vigorously represented the situation he got leave to select a better position. A withdrawal was made to the ridge near *Élouges* to the south of Thulin.'[162] Captain Grenfell was given orders "to hold the little station and take up a position on the road to the south of it," so he left Lieutenant Garstin at the railway station and sent Captain Nash-Wortham to give him a hand. They did everything they could to barricade the road with wire while we in the rear of him prepared a position as best we could in the dark to receive an attack.[163]

> Not altogether the role of cavalry. We got some spades with difficulty, chose a position with some infantry on our left, and were about to begin, when another order came not to entrench, but to barricade, and hold the station, and also the crossroads, south of Thulin. We found some carts, wire, bricks and faggots in a farm, and barricaded a fairly good position, as best we could in the short time. Meanwhile, the inhabitants of Thulin, who

158 Spears, *Liaison 1914,* p. 174.
159 Grenfell, Grenfell Family Papers (within Lyttelton Family Papers), 23rd August 1914, p. 5.
160 Grenfell, Grenfell Family Papers (within Lyttelton Family Papers), 23rd August 1914, p. 19
161 Anon., 9th Lancer War Diary, 23rd August 1914, p. 11.
162 Ibid., p. 11.
163 Grenfell, Grenfell Family Papers (within Lyttelton Family Papers), 23rd August 1914, p. 19.

> had been very civil to us, were ordered to leave down the road we were guarding, a rather pathetic sight. Two came blubbering up, and said they had forgotten one of their children at the far end of the town, could they go and fetch them? We had to refuse, and put one under supervision, as the story sounded rather impossible, and we thought their children might turn out to be full grown German soldiers.[164]

Corporal Taylor was moved by the sight of the families being turned out of their houses at a moment's notice 'gathering what articles they could and having to seek refuge elsewhere. It was a terrible sight to see children tugging at their mothers and crying painfully. This sight touched us immensely. Those that witnessed it and saw worse still on the following day when the enemy occupied the town. They set it on fire to it, levelling it to the ground.'[165]

B Squadron, with Captain Grenfell, were the forward squadron of the Regiment. To his rear A and C Squadrons were entrenched across the road which they dug during the night.[166] On the 9th Lancers left was the 18th Hussars and they had infantry on their right. 'Julian Smith connected us with the 18th Hussars, and we had intended using the French interpreters to keep me in touch with the infantry on the right, in spite of him saying that his *"mission was trés dangereux."'*[167] During the night, there had been much confusion as thousands of refugees tried to escape through Thulin in the pitch dark, Captain Grenfell had trouble finding the first line transport wagons,[168] and was still unclear who was to his front.[169] To the rear, in A Squadron's location, Lieutenant Marden's day did not seem quite so eventful 'after a slack day in which I restock stores and return to Thulin and retire southwards.'[170] Lance Corporal Hunt's night was longer than most: 'went to Thulin station and waited in a field all night. One man holds five horses, the other four sleep if possible. I was 2nd relief and Asplin's horse, a big impressive hunter knocked my pipe out of my mouth, and of course I could not find it. To add to this Lackey Woods who should have relieved me could not be found. I was "Jimmy Green," a double sentry and lost my pipe.'[171] Corporal Taylor recognised the night 'as the worst I have ever spent.'[172]

At approximately the same time as the 9th Lancers had received their orders to dig in on the railway, the easy day of the 2nd Dragoon Guards in Audregnies was shattered when at about 2200;

> We got an order to saddle up just as we were going to bed (I had actually taken some clothes off). The Brigade marched about 2300 northward to Quiévrain where a lot of civilians had been obtained with lanterns and shovels. All the squadrons with the help of these men made a line of trenches from Quiévrain Station to a point about 1 kilometre east along the railway where we joined with the 5th Dragoon Guards. My machine gun section remained

164 Grenfell, Grenfell Family Papers (within Lyttelton Family Papers), 23rd August 1914, pp. 5-6.
165 Cpl R.H. Taylor letter of Sergeant 'Spur' R.H. Taylor, p. 2.
166 Lt B.J.N. Marden diary, 23rd August 1914.
167 Ibid., 23rd August 1914, p. 22.
168 Ibid.
169 Ibid.
170 Lt B.J.N. Marden diary, 23rd August 1914.
171 LCpl W. Hunt diary, p. 4.
172 Cpl. R.H. Taylor letter of Sergeant 'Spur' R.H. Taylor, p. 2.

> during this time in the station square, and those of us who felt tired enough, slept on the flag-stones! Very cold but we were very tired.

The arrival of the civilians with lanterns did concern some of the soldiers. Private William Clarke of the 2nd Dragoon Guards wrote in his diary:

> When we got there, we found that a lot of miners and peasants were waiting for us, all set to help us to dig trenches across the bank of the railway cutting. They got in our way a bit, though they did help, but what frightened us was that the locals had brought lanterns to work by and we feared that it might draw fire from the other side of the canal, but it was alright.[173]

During the late afternoon and evening very "disquieting reports" had arrived at French's GHQ as to the situation on his right flank.[174] This had also been picked up by Lieutenant Spears who made another trip to French's Headquarters, but the telegram arrived ahead from the French *GQG*, which arrived at 2330:

> From *GQG* at 2330 on the 23rd: 1. Namur fell this day. 2. The Fifth French Army had been attacked all along their front by the 3rd German Corps, the Guard, the 10th and 7th Corps, and was falling back on the line Givet-Philippeville-Maubeuge 3. Hastiere had been captured by the Germans on the 23rd. 4. The Meuse was falling rapidly and becoming fordable in many places, hence the difficulty of defence.

It was now clear that the calculations made by General Wilson were at best optimistic and the conflicting reports from the French and RFC were the accurate version of events. General Wilson recorded in his diary:

> I made a careful calculation, and I came to the conclusion that we only had one corps and one Cavalry Division (possibly two corps) opposite us. I persuaded Murray and Sir John that this was so, with result that I was allowed to draft orders for an attack tomorrow by Cavalry Division…they were ready by 2000. Just as they were ready, a wire came from Joffre to say were had two and half corps opposite us. This stopped our attack, and at 2300, news came that the Fifth French Army was falling back still further. Between 2300 and 0300 we drafted orders and made arrangements for retirement to the line Maubeuge-Valenciennes.[175]

However, these orders would not contain the specific instructions for the withdrawal of the two corps but would appear to have concentrated on clearing the routes and roads which they would require. Field Marshal French had held on to the belief that the advance would go ahead as planned until the arrival of the telegram. During the day, Lieutenant Spears had earlier come to the same conclusion. For Field Marshal French, the realisation finally set in and he could no

173 Pte W. Clarke diary, 23rd August 1914.
174 Terraine, *Mons*, p. 8. Lanrezac had decided to retire at 2100 and made no provisions to inform the hard-pressed BEF.
175 Callwell, *Field-Marshal Sir Henry Wilson Bart,* p. 167.

longer delay the issue of the order that the BEF was going to have to retreat as a result of the withdrawal of the French Fifth Army, which now left his right flank exposed:

> It clearly showed that our present position was strategically untenable; but this conclusion had been forced upon me much earlier in the evening when I received a full appreciation of the situation as it then appeared at French *GQG*. General Joffre also told me that his information led him to expect that I might be attacked the next day by at least three German corps and two cavalry divisions. Appreciating the situation from the point of view which all reports now clearly established, the order for the retreat was issued. My last hope of an offensive had to be abandoned, and it became necessary to consider an immediate retreat from our present forward position. I selected the new line from Jerlain (south east of Valenciennes) eastwards to Maubeuge. This line had already been reconnoitred. The corps and divisional staff officers who were called into headquarters to receive orders, especially those of the II Corps, thought our position was much more seriously threatened than it really was and, in fact, one or two expressed doubts as to the possibility of effecting a retirement in the presence of the enemy in our immediate front. I did not share these views, and Colonel Vaughan (Chief of the Staff of the Cavalry Division) was more inclined to accept my estimate of the enemy's forces on or near the canal than the others were. His opportunities of gauging the enemy's strength and dispositions had been greatly enhanced by the fine reconnoitring work done on the previous two or three days by the Cavalry Division. However, I determined to affect the retreat, and orders were issued accordingly.[176]

At approximately 2300, General Smith-Dorrien received a message from GHQ to send his chief of staff to GHQ at Le Cateau, 30 miles away. Brigadier Forestier-Walker returned sometime after 0300 on the 24th with fresh information and told General Smith-Dorrien "that Field Marshal French had decided that instead of standing to fight, the whole BEF was to retire. I naturally asked him for the plan of retirement, and was told that GHQ were issuing none, though he had gathered that the idea was for the I Corps to cover the retirement of the II, but that I was to see Haig and arrange a plan with him."'[177] Brigadier Johnny Gough, the I Corps Chief of Staff[178] had already received its instructions over the phone and had issued its instructions at 0200 and had already started its withdrawal. General Haig took personal control of the situation and felt that providing flank protection to II Corps while he was in the act of withdrawing was he thought *'clearly impracticable.'*[179] There were only two hours left before dawn, and by dawn it was reasonably certain that the Germans would begin their attack. Within those two hours General Haig decided to set his own troops in motion:

> To make arrangements to resist any attack by the Germans thereby gaining time for the retreat of his main columns; and to adjust the order of retirement with the II Corps, substituting some practical solution for the impractical orders of GHQ. 'It was never Haig's custom to rely on consultations with his staff officers in a time of crisis. He took personal

176 Viscount French of Ypres, *1914,* pp. 63-64.
177 Smith-Dorrien, *Memories of Forty-Eight Years' Service,* p. 387.
178 Ibid., p. 388.
179 Charteris, *Field Marshal Earl Haig,* p. 90.

> and immediate control. Within five minutes a staff officer [it is unclear if this happened] was on his way to General Smith-Dorrien to co-ordinate the retreat.'[180]

General Haig, although content with his own plan, remained concerned that Field Marshal French had not fully grasped the situation. The situation that was now unfolding was one he had previously exercised in India:

> Though Haig had every reason to be satisfied with the situation of his own corps, he still doubted whether the Commander-in-Chief fully realised the seriousness of the wide outflanking movement of the Germans. He himself had a clear conception of what he now believed to be the immediate task of the British Army. It was the same problem which he had thrashed out in his Staff Tours in India. A retreating army could not afford to risk battle: its first duty was to disengage itself from the enemy, to take advantage of the opportunity which its shortening lines of communication afforded it to disengage itself, and then await a suitable chance for resuming the initiative.[181]

Considering General-Smith-Dorrien and the corps headquarters were all just getting to know each other, the task fell to Brigadier Forestier-Walker to extract II Corps, something he took in his stride:

> Forestier-Walker was of inestimable value to his chief, taking all the routine labour from his shoulders. He wanted no long explanations – a couple of words about the general intention would be enough, and a few minutes later he had worked out all the detail and drafted the orders. He was quite imperturbable; no time was wasted in lamenting over unfavourable news or in gloating over reports of success. In fact, all reports were received with the same calm.... He would spend half a minute in thought, while he lit a fresh cigarette, and then turn to his table.[182]

By the time II Corps was aware of the requirement to withdraw, I Corps had already started, and the German *IV AK* was about to cross the canal at Thulin and Hensies. Any chance to break contact and withdraw under the cover of darkness had gone. II Corps was now presented with the problem of withdrawing two divisions which were still in contact with the Germans down very limited roads which were already congested with refugees and elements of Allenby's cavalry. Also, as a result of the withdrawal of I Corps, the borrowed 5th Infantry Brigade which had been covering the gap between the 3rd and 5th Infantry Divisions had withdrawn along with the rest of I Corps which now left General Smith-Dorrien's right flank completely exposed.

At about 0100 on the 24th, Lieutenant Spears visited Field Marshal French again and told him that the French 'were seriously checked all along the line. The Third and Fourth French Armies were retiring, and the Fifth French Army, after its check on Saturday, was conforming to the general movement.'[183] General Smith-Dorrien recorded in his diary that about 0300 he

180 Ibid., p. 90.
181 Charteris, *Field Marshal Earl Haig,* p. 91.
182 Ballard, *Smith-Dorrien,* p. 155.
183 Spears, *Liaison 1914,* p. 172.

'received an order from GHQ that in consequence of the French on our right having fallen back instead of advancing both our flanks were exposed…it would be necessary to retire.'[184] As a result of not sending just the simple order to withdraw the corps, much planning time had been lost. All this would have been best done under the cover of darkness, while breaking clean from the enemy, with the withdrawing infantry been screened by the cavalry and supported by the artillery. General Smith-Dorrien thought:

> There must have been some very good reason why four or five hours of valuable time had been lost by sending for staff officers instead of sending the order and plan for retirement directly the chief had decided on it. It must be remembered that we had prepared for continuing the fight and our fighting impedimenta, such as ammunition columns, were close behind the troops and blocking the roads, and before a retirement could commence, these would have to be cleared away; also, that it would take a long time to get the change of orders to the troops, and lastly that I had to find out what Haig was going to do. All this could have been done and the retirement actually begun before dawn had we known in time. As it was, daylight was already breaking when the order reached me and some hours must elapse before the retirement could commence, by which time we should be in deadly grips with the enemy and would have to carry out one of the most difficult operations in war, namely, breaking off a fight and retiring with the enemy close on the top of us.[185]

From the German point of view, when the evening came to an end the *AOK 1's* engaged corps were fighting along the general line of the canal from north of Hensies 1 km north of Thulin, north of St Ghislain, the southern edge of Mons, to St Symphorien. At the end of the day they concluded that the *AOK 1* had engaged strong British forces. The fighting had been tough, especially against III Corps. It was likely that the enemy would take advantage of the high ground south of Mons and would continue to resist strongly next day.[186] Generaloberst von Kluck felt that his *AOK 1* had had a successful day and that the British opposition on the canal had been "obstinate" and "fought excellently" in a battle where both sides had suffered heavy losses and he felt that *IV AK* had done particularly well. 'By the evening the *IV AK* had advanced to immediately north of the line Hensies-Thulin; showing a praiseworthy grasp of the situation, they had pushed on beyond the appointed end of the day's march and crossed the canal between Condé and St Ghislain.'[187] '*IV AK* had managed to get troops from *Infanterie Division 7* over the bridge at Ville Pommeroeul, but *Infanterie Division 8* were yet to cross north of Quiévrain.'[188] The pressure of the German advance onto the canal had resulted in the BEF withdrawing from its original position on the canal by approximately 5 kms. By midnight II Corps had withdrawn to 'prepared positions'[189] on the high ground after 36 hours of continuous fighting and was in line with I Corps. The casualties for the first day for the two British Corps

184 Ballard, *Smith-Dorrien,* p. 163.
185 Smith-Dorrien, *Memories of Forty-Eight Years' Service,* pp. 387-388.
186 Dunlop, Dunlop & Puttkammer, *The Battle of Mons,* pp. 52-53.
187 Kluck, *The March on Paris and The Battle of The Marne, 1914,* p. 48.
188 Ibid., p. 48.
189 Horsfall & Cave, *Mons: 1914,* p. 105.

had been 1,571 killed in II Corps and only 40 in I Corps.[190] The expectation was that they were to advance again from these positions in support of the Fifth French Army advance to their east, but in truth both British corps had begun the retreat. Whilst the situation to the front had been clarified as a result of the day's engagements, the German *OKH* was still totally unclear as to what was on its right flank. The *HKK 2* was operating to the right of *AOK 1* and had not encountered any enemy forces. So, it seemed that there was no imminent danger to the army's right flank. Based on this information:

> Generaloberst von Kluck decided to continue the attack the next day against the enemy force to his front, enveloping its left wing. The aims were to prevent the enemy from disengaging to the west and to push them towards Maubeuge. The front-line army corps were given axes of advance for a general half-right sideways move, in order to avoid bunching up towards Maubeuge.[191]

At Saint Bernard's at Audregnies that evening before the Cavalry Division headquarters departed and after dinner, General Allenby and his HQ thanked *Madame la Supérieure* for her hospitality.

> They left in small groups. Where are they going? What was the tactic?...From 2300 we could hear gunfire, probably around Mons, and we might have some casualties tonight,'[192] for the rest of the soldiers later that night a 'telegram was received that changed the plans and all of a sudden, the soldiers had to leave. It was around 2230. For 45 minutes, feverish comings and goings, rush, and the long march of horses and cars. Finally, everything calmed down. If we had to fear a surprise, we were protected only by God.[193]

For the *Westheer*, for the most part the mobilisation and deployment had gone as planned, despite the time necessary to take Liège. However, the six weeks allowed for Russian mobilisation, which was originally anticipated by Field Marshal von Schlieffen, but understood to be insufficient by General von Moltke, was now becoming a reality. Time was becoming critical for the allocation of troops in the west to support the *Ostheer*. During the Franco-Russian military convention in 1913, the French had pressured the Russians to agree to conduct military operations on the 15th day after mobilisation. Generaloberst Hans von Plessen wrote in his diary on the 23rd August "but east Prussia, the Russians are burning and laying waste to everything! We must contrive to be finished in the west as quickly as possible to come to the aid of the east."[194]

190 Smith-Dorrien, *Memories of Forty-Eight Years' Service*, p. 386.
191 Dunlop, Dunlop & Puttkammer, *The Battle of Mons*, p. 53.
192 *Annales du pensionnat Saint Bernard à Audregnies*, p.44, op. cit., Jean Richez, *Un Champ de Coquelicots, La Bataille d'Audregnies le 24 Août 1914*.
193 Ibid., p. 44.
194 Strachan, *The First World War*, p. 191.

# 10

## Audregnies and Élouges

---

*I saw more Germans in that one first moment than I ever set eyes on during the rest of the war.*

Lieutenant Colonel C.R. Ballard

The morning of the 24th August was the anniversary of the eruption of Mount Vesuvius and the destruction of Pompeii in AD 79. For some elements of the BEF, it was to be just as cataclysmic. The general situation that morning was that, in the German *Infanterie Division 7* sector, both elements of *13 Infanterie Brigade*: *Infanterie Regiment 26* and *Infanterie Regiment 66* had crossed the canal in the early hours and dug in 400 metres to the south of Thulin. *Infanterie Division 8* to the west had crossed the first of their bridges, at Canal d'Antoing at Rivage, but were still held north of the canal, 4 kms south of Harchies and north of Quiévrain. Overnight, the BEF had retired to positions 5 kms to the south of the canal. The 5th Infantry Division had issued its orders the night before. The 13th Infantry Brigade received its orders at 1930 to retire at 2100[1] to Wasmes; the 14th Infantry Brigade including 1 DCLI to the north of the 9th Lancers received its orders to retire at 1945[2] to the area of Dour and was in the area of Bois du Boussu by 0100. The 15th Infantry Brigade had moved to become the Divisional Reserve and the Cheshires and Norfolks were now under command of the Divisional Commander. The 19th Infantry Brigade on the far left of the line was told at midnight to withdraw to Élouges, which it did leaving at 0200 via Hensies and Quiévrain.[3] Effectively, they had given up their positions in the Mons Salient and the 5th Infantry Division was on 'a line from Paturages through Wasmes, Hornu, and Boussu with reserves at Dour.'[4] This move had effectively reduced the II Corps frontage to 12 miles, which General Smith-Dorrien still felt that 'it was still far too large for the troops I had and every man was practically in the front line, so that a

1 TNA WO 95/1548/1-7: 13th Infantry Brigade War Diary.
2 Ibid.
3 Edmonds, *Military Operations France and Belgium 1914,* Vol. I, p. 95.
4 Smith-Dorrien, *Memories of Forty-Eight Years' Service,* p. 389.

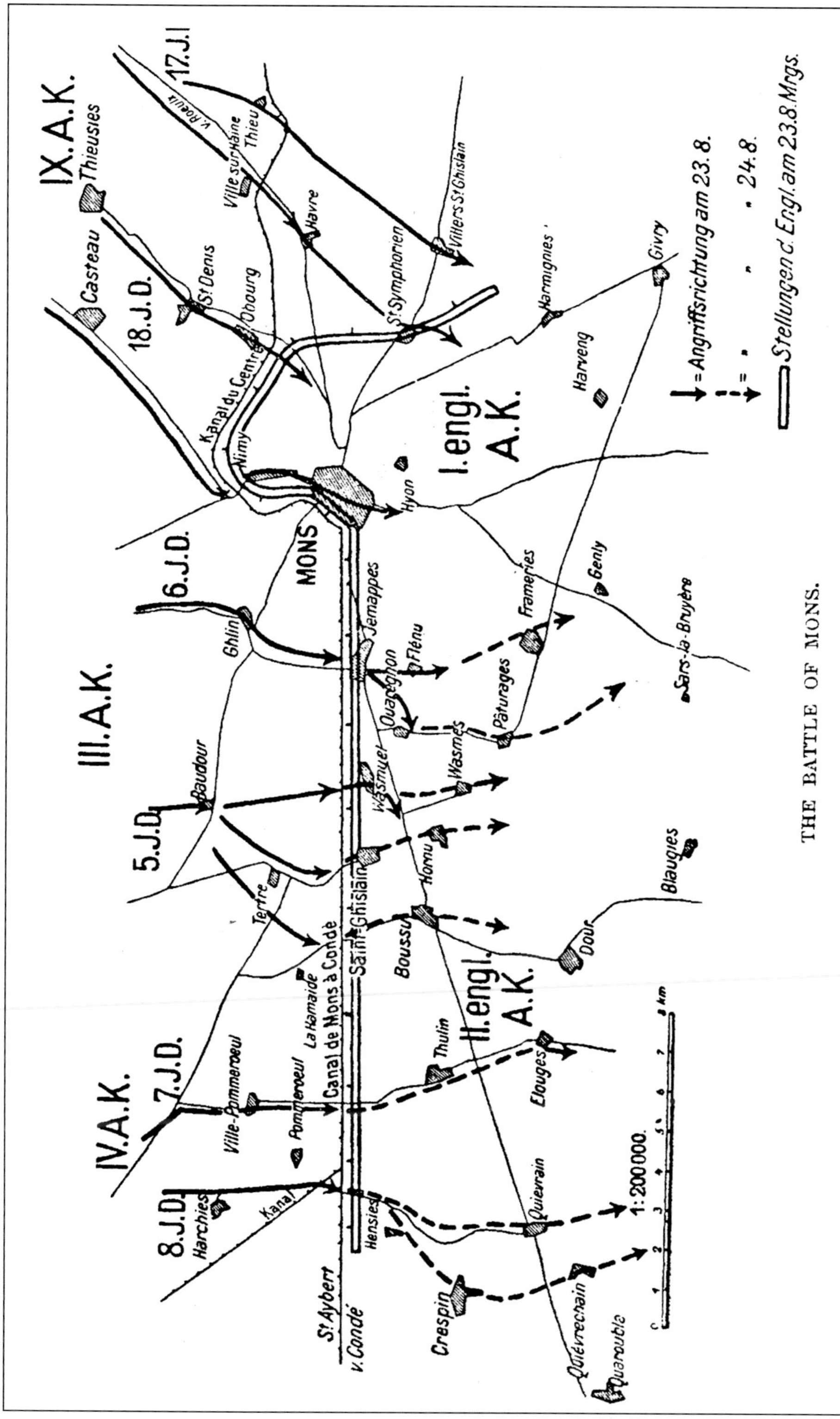


Map 8 German *IV AK* line of advance on the 23rd-24th August 1914 – Battle of Mons. (Kluck, *The March on Paris and the Battle of the Marne 1914*)

breakthrough, with no reserves to meet it, must have entailed retreat.'[5] The French Fifth Army to the east were now 15 miles to the south and General d'Amade's 84th Territorial Division to the west had started its retirement from Valenciennes towards Cambrai. This meant the BEF was now in front of its French allies. Both its flanks were exposed and in danger of being outflanked on both sides.[6] Whilst the aerodromes were changing location (which was becoming a daily occurrence) and No. 4 Squadron were moving from Maubeuge to Le Cateau, Captain Shephard and Lieutenant Bonham-Carter were airborne. By 0400 they were watching General von Kluck's right wing.[7]

2nd Cavalry Brigade had fallen back from Thulin to Marlière on the evening of the 23rd August and were 'holding the line of the railway one mile to the north with two regiments,'[8] the 18th Hussars and the 9th Lancers. The Cavalry Division headquarters had left Quiévrain at short notice at 0100 on the 24th, and on leaving destroyed the telephone exchange and removed all the instruments from the railway station. They relocated to Élouges and by 0230 had re-established telegraph communications from the railway station via Bavai to Le Cateau.[9] Early in the morning in Élouges, Lieutenants Beech and Reggie Davies were up early to find breakfast for their soldiers and 'went round the houses collecting coffee and bread. Every room contained about 15 people, all sitting round and talking. They all wanted to know "*Yat-il de danger*?" to which we said no.[10] They also heard the rumour that the Germans had crossed the canal at Thulin and the detail of how the opposing subalterns (Leutnants von Reuß, Schacht and Freytag) had achieved it was very accurate. 'Left Élouges at 0400. Saw Leny, who told me how the Germans had succeeded in crossing the canal under very heavy fire; each man brought up a single plank, and nine out of ten of them were shot, but some of the planks fell in the right place, and eventually they had enough to cross.'[11]

At first light General Allenby became aware that the Germans were in great strength to his left so decided to withdraw some distance, he sent a message to General Fergusson to that effect. However, on hearing that the 5th Infantry Division were to hold their ground he agreed to cover his flank and ordered that the roads in the areas Élouges, Audregnies, Angre and Roisin left clear for their withdrawal. General Allenby's Cavalry Division had stayed in position well after the time GHQ had ordered the infantry to retire at 0600.[12] General Allenby had sent a staff car with three officers to try and ascertain if the 5th Infantry Division had started its withdrawal, but as yet they had not returned. However, the cavalry started its slow move south and the 2nd Cavalry Brigade acted as the rear guard.[13] The 19th Infantry Brigade were ordered further back to Rombies while the three other cavalry brigades withdrew back in succession on the same line.[14] For some time General Allenby had not been convinced that the planned advance of the BEF would take place and early that morning had 'filled the wallets of his saddle with all the

5 Ibid., p. 389.
6 Ascoli, *The Mons Star*, p. 73.
7 Raleigh, *War in the Air*, p. 307.
8 Brig. Sir H. De Lisle, Account of Audregnies.
9 1st Cavalry Division, 1st Signal Squadron Royal Engineers War Diary.
10 Lt R.A.J. Beech diary, 24th August 1914.
11 Ibid., 24th August 1914.
12 *The Cavalry Journal Vol. XII*, p 30.
13 Edmonds, *Military Operations France and Belgium 1914*, Vol. I , p. 96.
14 Ibid., p. 95.

maps of the country towards Paris on which he could lay hands and with spare handkerchiefs, in anticipation of the baggage being out of touch.'[15] Unbeknown to 5th Infantry Division and II Corps, I Corps had already started to retire and soon they would have to do the same, but some three hours later and in daylight. At GHQ, tension was high, and the significance of the French retirement on the right of the British Force was sinking in. Frederick Coleman encountered a number of officers from time to time who openly criticised "a retirement, the strategical needs of which had not been explained to them, and the plain necessity of it not as yet having become apparent." General Wilson borrowed Frederick Coleman's car to drive slowly and carefully over the road in order to reconnoitre the surrounding country. He explained to Frederick Coleman[16] 'his dislike of the best available ground in that vicinity as a defensive position.'[17] It is unclear what the purpose this reconnaissance was as General Wilson recorded in his diary 'drafting orders for an attack tomorrow by Cavalry Division 19th Infantry Brigade and II Corps to north east, pivoted on Mons.'[18] By the end of the day, Mons would be occupied by the Germans, but still General Wilson was wedded to *Plan XVII.*

Early in the morning at Audregnies, the refugees started to arrive from Thulin seeking safety at Saint Bernard's *Pensionnat* which had been turned into a temporary military hospital, *L'Ambulance.*

> At 0130, there was a big commotion in the village, shouting, talking and finally someone rang the door...They were refugees from Thulin. The *sauve-qui-peut* (state of panic) happened during the night and they arrived half-dressed. It was dreary, a little child didn't have any shoes. We welcomed them in the hallway, gave a bed to each of them, men on one side of the room, women on the other side. Then we left them there and went back to bed. At 0430, the doorbell rang again. This time, it was to tell us that the German cavalry has arrived. Straight away, *Madame la Supérieure* raised two *L'Ambulances* flags. A family from Thulin asked to be sheltered, offering money in exchange for them and their dog. *Madame la Supérieure* made them understand that it was not possible and we had to send everyone out of the *L'Ambulance,* and it had to be available for possible casualties. We made them breakfast but they didn't quite enjoy their bread without any butter, but we couldn't give them what we didn't have. After which, they went on their way again.[19]

By 0500, the intermittent firing of the morning had turned simultaneously into fighting across the whole front.[20] As the 9th Lancers awoke, the bridges to their north had both been blown. The infantry who had been guarding them, the 2 Manchesters and 1 DCLI, had withdrawn and the Germans were now 400m south of the canal. The position of the 9th Lancers at Thulin was 'on the road with a ditch in front of it, and covering the railway and the exits over it,'[21]

15 Wavell, *Allenby,* p. 132.
16 An American citizen who was a member of the Royal Automobile Club Volunteer Force.
17 Coleman, *From Mons to Ypres with French,* p. 4.
18 Diary of General Wilson dated 24th August 1914, op. cit. in Ascoli, *The Mons Star,* p. 70.
19 *Annales du pensionnat Saint Bernard à Audregnies,* p.44, op. cit. in Jean Richez, *Un Champ de Coquelicots, La Bataille d'Audregnies le 24 Août 1914.*
20 Dunlop, Dunlop, Puttkammer (eds.), *The Battle of Mons,* p. 55.
21 Grenfell, Grenfell Family Papers (within Lyttelton Family Papers), 24th August 1914, p. 22.

Captain Grenfell left "little Garstin to hold the railway station and the level crossing over the railway commanding the main street of the town." A further two troops were covering him further back with another in reserve.[22] A patrol came in at 0330 reporting they had been fired on by a large force of advancing Germans, so Captain Grenfell sent out another patrol of four men commanded by Corporal Bulk[23] [sic] to confirm the report. On his return, Corporal Bulk reported that he had seen no troops so Captain Grenfell then left him and his patrol to help protect the railway.[24] Captain Grenfell also made a patrol of the area and afterwards placed 'Crossley on the road, Straker on the right, Lieutenant Mather-Jackson on the left, and sent out patrols along the railway.'[25] For the Cheshires to the east during the night, they too had been curious, to what was to their front. Lieutenant Cuthbert Matterson and Corporal Tunnicliffe went as scouts across the Mons-Condé Canal to the enemy lines and brought back useful information.

Lieutenant Cuthbert Matterson. (Cheshire Regiment Museum)

22 TNA WO 95/1113/2: 9th Lancers War Diary. 'Lt Harvey with one troop of A Squadron was about 500 yards in rear.'
23 There is no Bulk on the embarkation roll, it is likely to be 1430 L Cpl Frederick Bolke (later RFC) who embarked with B Squadron.
24 Grenfell, Grenfell Family Papers (within Lyttelton Family Papers), 24th August 1914, p. 19
25 Anon., 9th Lancers War Diary, 24th August 1914, p. 12.

As the battalion woke, they were greeted by a beautiful morning but the first signs of war were in evidence:

> Dawn revealed a weirdly beautiful scene. Our aeroplanes were reconnoitring, each ringed with bursting shrapnel, tinged pink by the rising sun. A long cloud low on the horizon was reported to be a Zeppelin. Several villages were still ablaze to the north. Guns and gunners peered forth from behind slag heaps and cover. To the west a church steeple was burning, having been hit by a German shell. Our field guns opened fire overhead, bodies of troops withdrew through the position, and apparently to clear the front, and all seemed to give promise of a great battle.[26]

The 18th Hussars, like the 9th Lancers, had also been given permission the previous evening to fall back to a better position on the ridge which ran parallel to the Mons-Valenciennes road. They occupied a sunken road to the south, separated, and deployed their Maxim guns and contacted their flanking units:

> Leveson's and Thackwell's Squadrons were on the left and right respectively, and held a sunken road which ran north, north west and south, south east about half mile to the north west of Élouges, Stewart's Squadron was quarter mile to the left rear. One machine gun was with Leveson, headquarters were with Stewart, and Stobart's troop of C Squadron (Thackwell's) and one machine gun under Holdsworth were posted in a small house at the crossroad by the 17 kms stone on the Mons-Valenciennes road. A sunken road also ran from the position occupied by the forward squadrons to where Stewart's squadron was posted. On the left we were in touch with the 1st Cavalry Brigade and with the 9th Lancers on our right.[27]

As the sun rose, at 0415, and the mist cleared, Captain Grenfell received new orders at dawn[28] that he was 'to make a reconnaissance through the town and see what was going on beyond it,'[29] and see why the enemy had not advanced during the night.[30] It was Captain Grenfell's squadron which was fulfilling the 9th Lancers role as the rear guard to the Cavalry Brigade, which in turn was covering the retirement of the 5th Infantry Division. As he woke and was 'feeling its forward to Thulin,'[31] he would have been unaware of the importance of his mission.

At 0400, II Battalion of *Infanterie Regiment 66* 'crossed La Haine river and attacked towards Thulin. Leutnant Wincker and Reserve Leutnant Borchert from *8 Kompanie* and Leutnant Fricke from *7 Kompanie* led the troops.'[32] *Infanterie Regiment 26* were the lead regiment of the brigade and they had *Infanterie Regiment 66* and Oberstleutnant Adolf Büstorff's *Feldartillerie Regiment 40* in support. The initial limit of exploitation for the day was the railway line south

26 Simpson, *Cheshire Regiment the First Battalion at Mons and the Miniature Colour*, p. 23.
27 Account of the Action at Élouges by Lieutenant Colonel Charles Burnett 18th QMO Hussars.
28 Anon., 9th Lancer War Diary, 24th August 1914, p. 12.
29 Grenfell, Grenfell Family Papers *(within Lyttelton Family Papers)*, 24th August, p. 20.
30 Ibid., p. 12.
31 Edmonds, *Military Operations France and Belgium 1914*, Vol. I, p. 95.
32 Korfes, *The German 66th Regiment in the First World War*, p. 32.

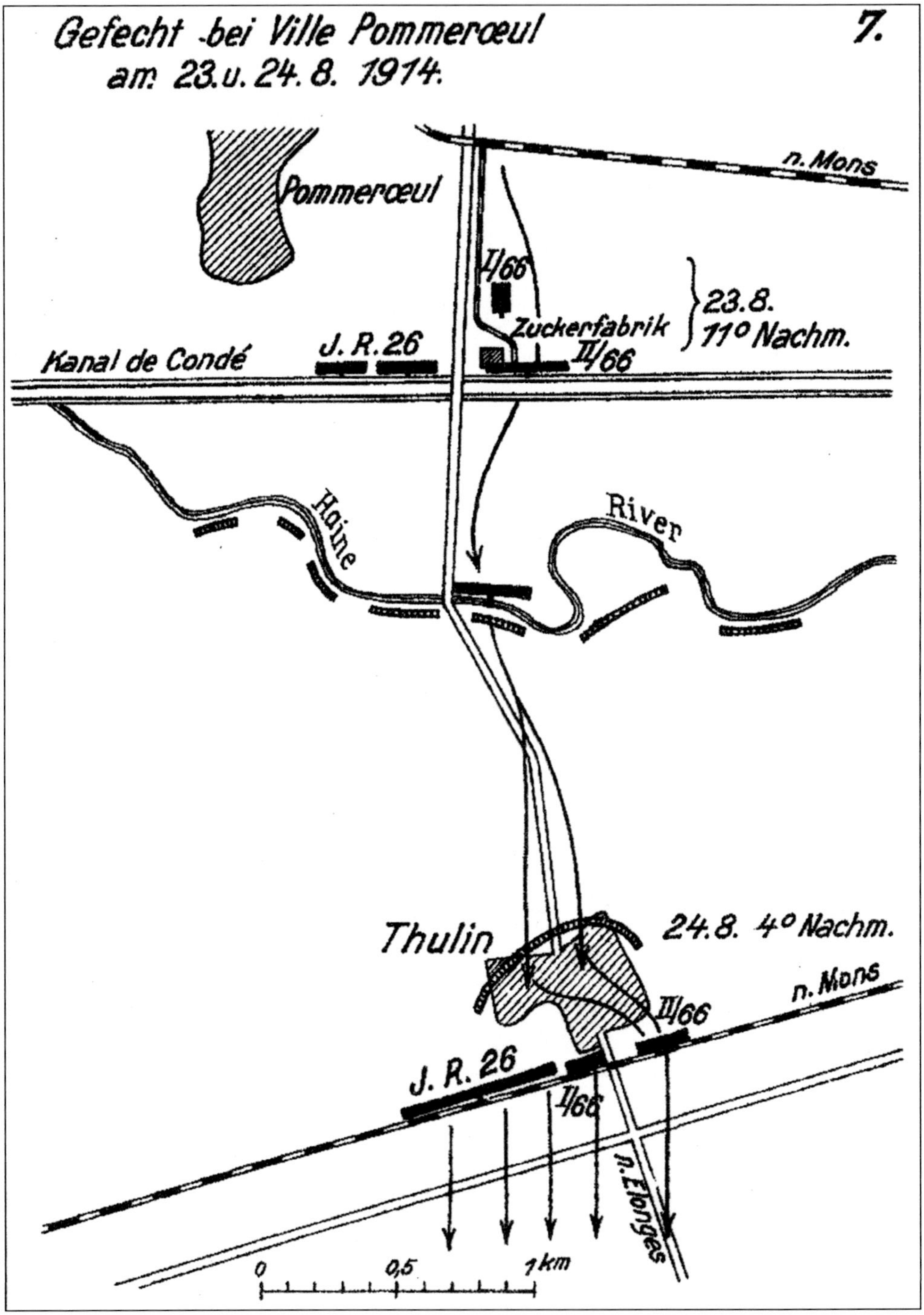


Map 9 *Infanterie Regiments 26* and *66* positions at Thulin on 23rd-24th August 1914. (*The German 66th Regiment in the First World War*)

of Thulin (Lieutenant Garstin's overnight location). Once Captain Grenfell had roused his squadron and given them orders he moved forward with *caution*, and he deployed his squadron. 'To carry this out I sent patrols around the town and penetrated it myself, sending patrols down each side of the streets blocking them, and leaving Lieutenant Garstin in my rear to cover my retirement.'[33] He also sent his brother to the church to see if he could get a view of the enemy.[34] Captain Grenfell's troops advanced through the town in bounds keeping one mounted for emergencies. When he got approximately three quarters through the town they met some RAMC orderlies who told them that there were 11th Hussars to their front. This now meant Captain Grenfell was unsure who was actually in front of him.[35] The lancers started to receive heavy fire so Captain Grenfell, with Lieutenant Ian Straker and Sergeant Major Durant 'who is the pluckiest man in the Army,'[36] went forward to verify the enemy's strength. "As we approached a sort of farm I suddenly heard a strange noise and a lot of shouting and the familiar "crack crack" of South Africa. A heavy fire was opened on us which caused us to turn about rather sharply." Lieutenant Grenfell 'thought his brother's orders to go back to Thulin 'rather a stupid thing, as we had only withdrawn from it at 2230 the previous evening.'[37] He went to the church in the town square where he and the squadron second-in-command Captain Nash-Wortham 'woke up a fat priest and asked if I could go up the steeple to look out through my glasses.'[38] When he got to the top, he watched his brother go into action for the first time, leading the reconnaissance patrol through the town:

> Francis went down the street leading north. When three quarters of the way through the town, a shot was fired, so Francis ordered the "two points" to go through the street and see what it was. As they hesitated, he went himself with Ian Straker. They were received by heavy fire at short range and had to beat a hasty retreat. Meanwhile, firing broke out down the street I was in[39], but we could only see one or two Germans. One of our aeroplanes passed over the enemy, who fired a volley, and soon showed us they were in some force, so we retired to the railway station, south of Thulin. *Ginger* had been shot through the stomach and was bleeding profusely. We took him behind a wall, and plugged it up, and, luckily, ran across another horse for Francis.[40]

Captain Grenfell's patrol held the end of the street for some time. Francis had lost his cap during the engagement so he went back for it and he thought his sergeant major acted with "great coolness." In fear of being outflanked Francis, returned to the railway station with three troops and sent Straker back to hold a position at the rear.[41] As they withdrew, Private William

33 Grenfell, Grenfell Family Papers (within Lyttelton Family Papers), 24th August 1914, p. 12.
34 Anon., 9th Lancer War Diary, 24th August 1914, p. 13.
35 Ibid., p. 13.
36 Grenfell, Grenfell Family Papers (within Lyttelton Family Papers), 24th August 1914, p. 23.
37 Grenfell, Grenfell Family Papers (within Lyttelton Family Papers), 24th August 1914, p. 6.
38 Ibid., p. 6.
39 Grenfell, Grenfell Family Papers (within Lyttelton Family Papers), 24th August 1914. 'Here they had rather a curious experience as the priest locked them in and they only got out by blowing off the lock with their revolvers.'
40 Grenfell, Grenfell Family Papers (within Lyttelton Family Papers), 24th August, p. 6.
41 Anon., 9th Lancer War Diary, 24th August 1914, p. 13.

Reynolds was shot in the head and was believed to be dead. Sergeant Major Durant, despite the time pressure of the advancing Germans, went forward and recovered his body at considerable danger to himself, which was most fortuitous for Private Reynolds as later he made a full recovery[42] after a period in hospital, and Sergeant Major Durant's most 'gallant action was rewarded.'[43] Rivy withdrew from the church and rejoined his brother. Captain Grenfell made his report, 'I sent a message back to the Colonel to say we had met about 50 of the enemy in the town and they were advancing.'[44] 'We had not been at the railway station long before we saw a mass of troops at the end of the street. They, in the faint light, greatly resembled ours…luckily, one man's helmet was uncovered, and so we opened a heavy fire with Lieutenant Garstin's troop. Garstin took a rifle and was sure he shot three himself. It caused a good deal of commotion, and they, in return, opened a heavy rifle fire on us.'[45] This was the first time the twins would stand together under rifle fire which did not 'disconcert them.'[46] Once on the road, Captain Grenfell 'sent Lieutenant Straker to ride on my right flank and Lieutenant Mather-Jackson on my left; we held on for some time but as the enemy approached and out flanked us we were obliged to fall back to the next position at the cross roads.[47] Otherwise they would have 'lost our horses as it was I retired a little bit late and we lost 12 men, and Lieutenant Nash-Wortham was wounded,'[48] shot through the chest,[49] a glancing shot, and, we think, not serious…A trooper was shot dead[50], and several wounded. Francis was lucky and was only shot through his boot.[51] Rivy went back to the Commanding Officer to inform him of the situation to the south of Thulin and was then sent across to tell the 4th Dragoon Guards to retire. His horse was stone cold, having been going all night, so he 'changed on to Nash's and then on to *Pearl of Price*, my polo pony, which my servant was riding in the ranks. This little pony did wonders during the next 12 hours and seemed indefatigable.'[52] Captain Grenfell's squadron pulled back and rejoined the Regiment.

As the 9th Lancers withdrew, Thulin was occupied by *7* and *8 Kompanie*s of *Infanterie Regiment 66*, from II Battalion. They reported that Thulin was vigorously defended by a small force. They 'took fire from almost all the houses, especially from a church on which hung a Red Cross flag,'[53] and 'after a short fight, in which Reserve Leutnant Borchert and elements of *8 Kompanie* distinguished themselves, the town was taken.'[54] The taking of Thulin had not come without cost as Reserve Feldwebel Kunzmann was killed on his birthday.[55] Once the town had been taken

42 4064 Pte W Reynolds died on 26th May 1915 and is buried in Hazebrouck Communal Cemetery.
43 *The Delhi Spearman*, March 1928, p. 7; M.I.D. *London Gazette* 20-10-1914; *Medaille de Militaire, London Gazette* 2nd September 1914.
44 Anon., 9th Lancer War Diary, 24th August 1914, p. 14.
45 Grenfell, Grenfell Family Papers (within Lyttelton Family Papers), 24th August 1914, p. 7.
46 Ibid., p. 21.
47 Ibid., p. 7.
48 Anon, 9th Lancer War Diary, 24th August 1914, p. 14.
49 Lt B.J.N. Marden diary, 24th August 1914.
50 1090 Sadler Cpl Thomas Denslow was buried in Thulin Municipal Cemetery before his remains were relocated to Cement House Cemetery, West-Vlaanderen, Belgium in February 1954.
51 Grenfell, Grenfell Family Papers (within Lyttelton Family Papers), 24th August, p. 7.
52 Ibid., 24th August 1914, p. 7.
53 Korfes, *The German 66th Regiment in the First World War*, p. 32.
54 Ibid., p. 32.
55 Ibid., p. 32.

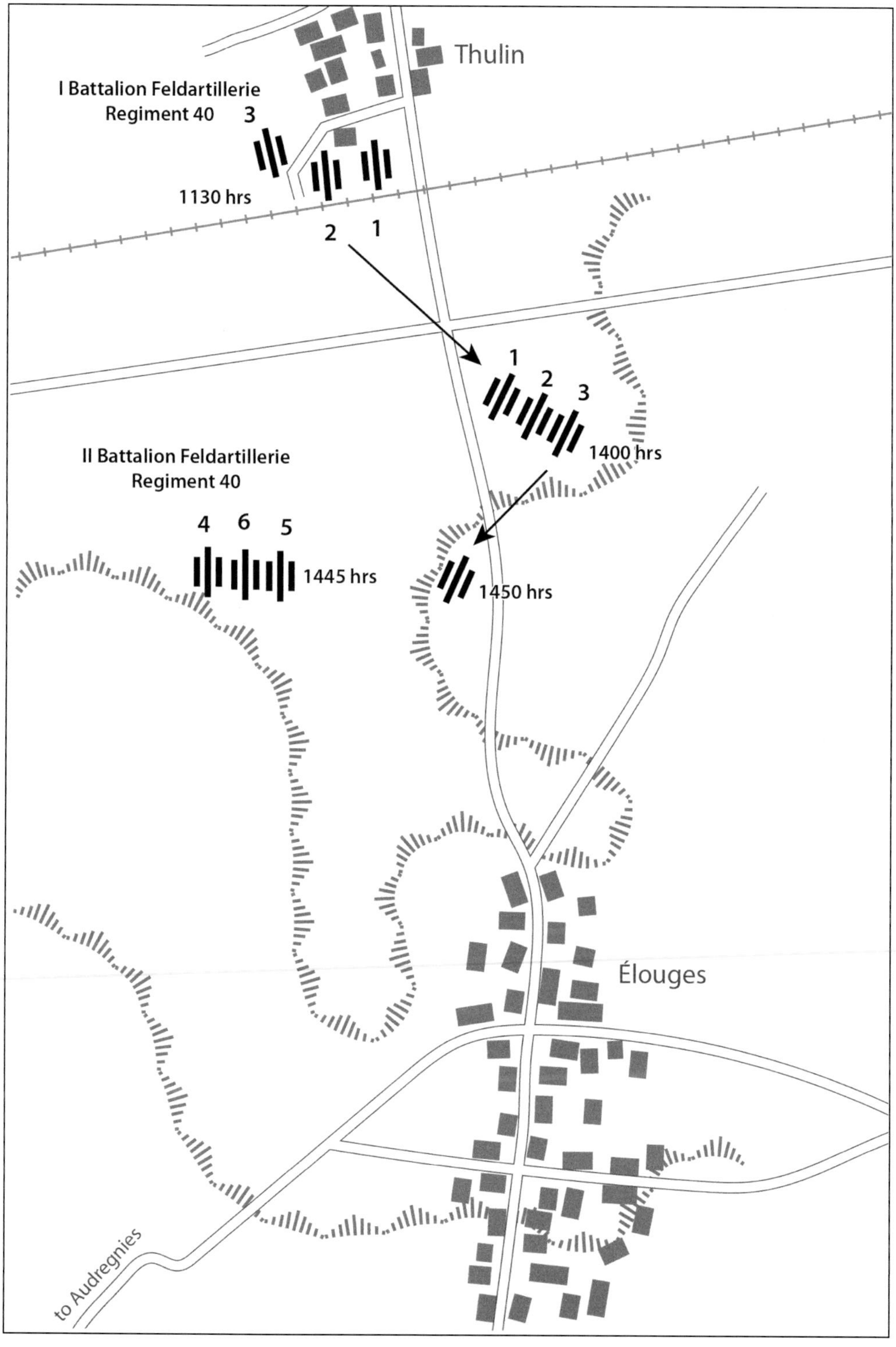


Map 10 *Feldartillerie 40* disposition at Élouges on 24th August 1914. (*Das Altmärkische Feld-Artillerie-Regiment Nr. 40 im Weltkriege 1914–1918*)

they 'continued under heavy fire to the rail embankment…the brigade limit of advance.'[56] Once at the railway, the *Infanterie Regiment 66* rested behind the embankment. By now *Infanterie Regiment 26* had moved up on their right, as they had moved out at '0540 and by 0600 had also reached the railway line. Once the two regiments had reached the Mons-Valenciennes road, they were joined by their supporting artillery of two battalions of *Feldartillerie Regiment 40* and 'deployed its II Battalion east of the road and I Battalion west of it and men and horses were fed.'[57] From their position on the west of the town they could see Thulin which, as a result of the house to house fighting, was now partially in flames.[58] *Infanterie Brigade 13* had reached its objective. Thulin had been taken and the BEF had withdrawn and they were now waiting for further orders to continue their advance south.

As *Infanterie Regiment 26* were reaching the railway line, Captain Shephard and Lieutenant Bonham-Carter were returning from their aerial reconnaissance 'with news of extensive movement about Ath and Leuze. They reported a broken column nearly 10 miles long with its head pointing at Peruwelz. The column branched off the main Ath-Tournai road at Leuze. This was part of von Kluck's *AOK 2,* and its line of march would take it to the west of the extreme western flank of the British army.'[59] The news was not reassuring and in the absence of the French 84th Territorial Division, this would bring General von Kluck's wheeling force directly into the exposed left flank of the BEF and the 5th Infantry Division. As a consequence, General Smith-Dorrien issued orders for a retreat.

Meanwhile B Squadron of the 9th Lancers were still engaged in Thulin and A and C Squadrons were the reserve for the 9th Lancers. Lieutenant Norman of C Squadron had been ordered to dig in and clear the wire fences to their front ready to advance while sending out patrols to their flanks to understand what was happening around their position.

> I myself was detailed with a party of about a dozen NCOs and men to go out to our front and cut gaps in the wire fences on a front of about 30 yards to make a passage across the country wide enough for the Regiment to move forward on a one troop frontage: We all had wire cutters, strong and efficient for cutting ordinary round steel wire barbed or plain, but the Belgian farmers had not used this sort of wire. Their wire was in the form of steel ribbons one inch or more wide. Instead, therefore, of cutting the wire with one strong snip it took several snips to cut one wire. What was needed was a powerful pair of shears rather than the cutters with which we were provided. This made it a slow and laborious job…The sound of the infantry battle to our front and left flank continued as well as some patrolling. We then came under some rather long-range shrapnel and rifle fire from our front and occupied our trenches.[60]

The issue of wire was not just local to the 9th Lancers, as on the same day further to their west, Lieutenant Harry Owens, the Medical Officer of the 3rd Cavalry Field Ambulance, saw 'two or three regiments of cavalry, some lancers come into a field and begin cutting the wire fences

56 Ibid., p. 32.
57 Zuber, *The Mons Myth,* p. 191.
58 Korfes, *The German 66th Regiment in the First World War*, p. 32.
59 Raleigh, *War in the Air*, p. 307.
60 Lt C.W. Norman letter to Mr Stuart Gruber, 29th March 1973.

in their line of retreat.[61] One of these was the patrol of Lieutenant Jack Riddell from the 16th Lancers at Wiheries who 'was out with a patrol, wire cutting, and was coming back, with the Germans coming on pretty fast.'[62]

Major Abadie sent out another patrol to look at the flanks commanded by Lieutenant Fraser of the Central India Horse, Corporal Taylor was his troop corporal 'and was despatched to a map reference point…and link up with the nearest cavalry regiment, which happened to be the 16th Lancers and report any movement of the enemy.'[63] Corporal Taylor wrote:

> My troop who was under the command of an officer belonging to the Central India Horse were ordered to act as right flank patrol. Myself being sent out farther to the right to reconnoitre a village and make fast time. On returning was informed by the inhabitants that a party of villains were in the vicinity and had chased a party of our regiment which I have gathered since were my own troop. Of course, expected to meet the enemy and naturally took precautionary measures. But we did not see them. Having been cut off from my troop returned to the place where they were last seen when I was sent forward and luckily met the 4th Dragoon Guards whom I anchored myself to for the time being.[64]

Meanwhile, C Squadron, were holding the posts and 'barricades which had been erected along the road, and were subjected to long range rifle fire.'[65] From his position with C Squadron, Corporal Easton could see the Germans from *Infanterie Regiment 26 and 66* and they engaged them as they got to the railway south of Thulin. 'They were head and shoulders exposed above the long railway sleeper fence but after a few seconds they disappeared and, later, a scout galloped in and said we were being outflanked from our right.'[66] Lance Corporal Hunt, also with C Squadron, did not engage the Germans although came under fire for the first time and said:

> Being under fire, I thought it was just like marking up at the butts, only you didn't have the trouble of signalling the shots. They retreated, none of us fired a shot. We got the order to mount and I saw young Evans, just having a joke with him and we heard that one of B Squadron fellows was killed and also that about five were wounded among them Captain Nash-Wortham.[67]

When they got the order to retire,[68] the man to his right of Corporal Easton was killed. He and another corporal attended to him and Harry got hold of his horse just as the Germans were arriving:

61 IWM 4788: Private Papers of Captain Henry Barton Owens, 24th August 1914.
62 Lt R.A.J. Beech diary, 24th August 1914.
63 Cpl. R.H. Taylor to Mr Stuart Gruber, 11th January 1973, p 2.
64 Cpl. R.H. Taylor letter of Sergeant 'Spur' R.H. Taylor, p. 3.
65 Anon., 9th Lancer War Diary, 24th August 1914, p. 20.
66 Cpl. H. Easton diary, 24th August 1914, p. 37.
67 LCpl W. Hunt diary, p. 5.
68 Lt B.J.N. Marden diary, 24th August 1914 states approx. 0800.

> Quickly got into a galloping retreat, across a couple of fields and on to a road, when a bullet hit my right-hand man in the back of his head and he was dead. I stopped intending to get his identity disc and pay book. I took his horse while another corporal searched and took his pay book and identity disc, and we left him and galloped after our troops and caught up with them in another village just ahead of another German column which we engaged and had to get out fast. So it went on till my troop dismounted, our horses in a nearby hollow, we saw the Germans advancing on to a field 600 yards away, so we opened fire.[69]

The 9th Lancers withdrew south towards Audregnies 'on a ridge and this field had recently been harvested and the corn in stooks,'[70] and watered and fed.[71] The German infantry and artillery reached the Mons-Valenciennes road at 0700[72] and L Battery RHA came into action having joined the 2nd Cavalry Brigade from Wiheries at first light. The battery deployed south of Élouges and east of the E in Élouges [see Map 6] and shelled the small numbers of dismounted troops debouching on the railway line south of Thulin at a range of 1800 yards[73] when a German aircraft:

> Sailed overhead, circled round, and went back to the German lines. Everyone watched it with naive curiosity, but in a very few minutes with a bang and a whizz a German shrapnel burst overhead. The aeroplane had lost no time in reporting the Regiment's whereabouts. The first shell was followed by others, and it was necessary to move off hastily. Even so, two or three men, including Major Beale-Browne's trumpeter [Reeves], were hit and a few horses[74].

Captain Porter, who was scouting from the top of a haystack, was also wounded.[75] Lance Corporal Hunt along with others shot at the aircraft 'but of course nothing happened,'[76] and just as they were engaging the aircraft 'a shell came over and Jack Reeves got hit.'[77] Lieutenant Marden attributed the presence of the aircraft and the artillery fire as being connected, 'shelled, aeroplanes directing, Mark [Porter] wounded, shrapnel in thigh, flesh only, fire at German planes with no success.'[78] As a result of the incoming artillery fire, Lieutenant Allfrey's 'Maxim gun horses stampeded, one wagon which luckily turned over and stopped.'[79] The aircraft that had directed fire onto the lancers had also found L Battery's guns as well, so they retired 'four

69 Cpl. H. Easton diary, 24th August 1914
70 Ibid.
71 LCpl W. Hunt diary, p. 5 – field (mangol).
72 De Lisle, Account of Audregnies. p. 1.
73 TNA WO 95/1111: L Bty., RHA War Diary.
74 Sheppard, *The Ninth Queen's Royal Lancers 1715-1936,* p. 236. 'Captain J.G. Porter and several men were wounded, and a shell killed Major Beale-Browne's charger, which he had left for a moment to be held by a trumpeter.'
75 Anon., 9th Lancer War Diary, 24th August 1914, p. 21.
76 LCpl W. Hunt diary, p. 5.
77 Ibid., p. 5.
78 Lt B.J.N. Marden, 24th August 1914.
79 Lt F. de V.B. Allfrey diary, 24th August 1914.

guns followed by two and they moved west with the rest of the 2nd Cavalry Brigade through Audregnies towards Angre'[80]

At 0700, the first of the casualties started to arrive in Audregnies at Saint Bernard's. The first casualty had a:

> Bullet went through his arm, but he managed to stay on his horse. About 10 others followed: English and Scottish. Two were badly wounded, a Scottish officer had a broken leg, a soldier was losing a lot of blood from a gunshot injury on his arm. We took care of them, put some bandages on the wounds and some of them laid down. Around 0900, an *Aide-De-Camp* and a French interpreter arrived and told them to put their uniforms on, some cars were on their way to pick them up. We were sad to see them leave as we were thinking that we would have had to take care of them. They thanked us by gesturing with their hands, but they looked like they were in a rush to leave this place. The poor officer got back to his stretcher and slowly, he wanted to shake the Dames and Soeurs' hands who were there to assist their departure. *Madame la Supérieure* asked discreetly the officer why this order to leave: "we want our wounded men to stay safe," "then, are we in danger?" The officer didn't reply but he did give an intense look to *Madame la Supérieure*, with a vague gesture that told a lot. The order has been widespread through the village to take off all wire fences that separated the meadows to allow easier troops movements.[81]

At about 0800 the 18th Hussars received orders to retire to a second position, which they had already reconnoitred. This was not straightforward as they 'got shelled a good bit during this retirement as we were ascending the ridge all the time; we were also hampered a good deal by Belgian refugees, who, poor people, were at their wit's ends to know what to do.'[82] It was the bicyclists who were the greatest trouble, 'as we couldn't let them through without passes, and naturally they had not been able to obtain such formalities, but nevertheless they had to be turned back, as it was quite possible their interests might be with our enemy, and having probed our position they might have hid and then retraced their steps.'[83] The 18th Hussar's final position[84] was on the 'left two troops of A Squadron were posted near a mine shaft a mile south east of Quiévrain and the other two troops of A on a mound[85] about 300 yards south west of the level crossing on the Audregnies-Thulin road.'[86] On the right, 'B Squadron were in a large cutting, through which a mineral line from a spot about a mile south west of Élouges ran to

80 TNA WO 95/1111: L Bty., RHA War Diary.

81 *Annales du pensionnat Saint Bernard à Audregnies*, p.44, op. cit. in Jean Richez, *Un Champ de Coquelicots, La Bataille d'Audregnies le 24 Août 1914.*

82 Lieutenant Colonel Charles Burnett 18th QMO Hussars account of the Action at Élouges .

83 Ibid.

84 Burnett's report: 'On the left two troops A Sqn in a sugar refinery, the centre two troops A Sqn on a mound about 300 yards south of the level crossing which lay about half a mile W of Élouges, the right B Squadron a little retired in a large cutting on a mineral line which led from the sugar refinery to Élouges station. C Squadron and machine gun in support near the western end of the same line. The whole position lay just S of the word Élouges.

85 The mound (slag heap) is no longer visible. It is this statement which accurately identifies where the mound used to be.

86 Account of the Action at Élouges by Lieutenant Colonel Charles Burnett 18th QMO Hussars.

*Monceaux Halte.* C Squadron and machine guns were in support at the western end of the same line.'[87] The 18th Hussars waited patiently for the infantry *rear guard* so they could withdraw. The delay did not come without cost as Sergeant Sutherland, Corporal O'Melia and two others were wounded[88] and four horses were also killed during this retirement:

> Retiring from the canal, took a long time to get back to the rising ground on our right or east flank, so Stobart could not withdraw his men and uncover their flank and the enemy in many places gained a footing on the railway and were almost on the top of him. It was then about 0600, [sic] the troop had its horses hidden behind the wall of the little house, but immediately this friendly cover was left a long open stretch had to be crossed before our cutting could be reached. When it was impossible to hold on any longer the troop mounted and galloped for safety under heavy fire from a German machine gun which had been brought up to the railway embankment.[89]

Meanwhile, to the rear of the 5th Infantry Division, the newly created Divisional Reserve was now, converging on the Divisional Headquarters, having handed over their positions. The Cheshire's trenches had been completed by 0700 'much to the satisfaction of the men… In the meantime, a staff officer (Major Wetherall, Brigade Major, 15th Infantry Brigade) in a fast motor car delivered to the Commanding Officer, Lieutenant Colonel Boger, a despatch, ordering him to hand over his trenches to 2 Manchester Regiment as soon as they arrived, and to proceed to Dour railway station and to report to Divisional Headquarters. The 2 Manchester Regiment arrived about 0800 and took over their trenches.[90] The Norfolks had been relieved much earlier at 0430 by the Suffolks and were also ordered back to Dour. Private Hurrell and his outpost were oblivious to the change of plan and battalion move until he was having his breakfast which he carried in his haversack having 'got a little hot water from a house very near and made a little drop of tea.'[91] At about '0800, we met the battalion coming along the road. We marched another mile or two then joined our company and stopped on a [pea[92]] field just outside Dour. The Cheshires also joined us on the same field, and as our battalion hadn't had any breakfast, they made a little coffee in one of the houses close by and issued it out, about a small cup per man besides a few ration biscuits.'[93]For the soldiers of the Cheshires, this retirement 'was bewildering to those who were not aware of the reasons which necessitated it. The entrenching of a position had suggested a stand of some duration, and it is probable that all ranks pictured a fight there to the last man and the last round, as conjured up by Sir Charles Fergusson's speech a few hours before'[94]

In the *Field Service Regulations Part 1 of 1909,* the passage of information regarding retiring was quite specific and it limited those in the chain of command who were to know, understanding

87 Ibid.
88 Both died later.
89 Account of the Action at Élouges by Lieutenant Colonel Charles Burnett 18th QMO Hussars.
90 Simpson, *Cheshire Regiment the First Battalion at Mons and the Miniature Colour,* p. 24.
91 Pte R. Hurrell notebook, pp. 20-21.
92 Cpl W. Crooke, Twenty Fourth August 1914 (An Impression).
93 Pte R. Hurrell notebook, p. 21.
94 Crookenden, *The History of the Cheshire Regiment in the Great War*, p. 4.

the effect this would have on the men's morale.'[95] 'Orders for a possible retreat should always be thought out beforehand in case of need, but they should not be communicated to the troops before it becomes necessary to do so. They may be communicated beforehand, confidentially, to the higher commanders when considered advisable, but this should be rare.'[96] For the Cheshires 'there was no hint, either at this time or later, that a withdrawal was contemplated...and therefore, in complete ignorance of the true situation, that Lieutenant Colonel Boger led that battalion to Divisional Headquarters and reported to General Fergusson.'[97] Further to the west *Infanterie Division 8,* which had been held north of the canal the previous evening, crossed the canal at 0900 after *3 Kompanie, Pioneer Battalion 4* had prepared a new crossing. The action the day before had resulted in the brigade formations being disrupted and had been re-organised. *Infanterie Regiments 72 and 93* advanced south from Hensies towards Quiévrain.[98] At 0815 *Infanterie Regiment 72* was ordered to take Quiévrain. It deployed and entered the town, which they found had been prepared for defence, but when they arrived the BEF had left. 'Up to the tricks of the trade from their experiences of small wars, the English veterans brilliantly understood how to slip off at the last moment.'[99] *Feldartillerie Regiment 74* moved across the canal at 0730 and by 0835 and the II Battalion was in a position to overwatch the movement

*Infanterie Regiment 72* soldier c. 1914. (Author's Collection)

95 Ibid., p. 4.
96 *Field Service Regulations 1909,* Part 1, p. 32, para. 14.
97 Crookenden, *The History of the Cheshire Regiment in the Great War*, p. 4.
98 Dunlop, Dunlop & Puttkammer (eds.), *The Battle of Mons,* p. 55.
99 Hauptmann von Brandis, op. cit. in Edmonds, *Military Operations France and Belgium 1914,* Vol. I, p. 115.

of *Infanterie Regiment 72*. As the infantry battalion advanced, the I Battalion of *Feldartillerie Regiment 74* moved forward to the Quiévrain-Mons road.[100]

The defences *Infanterie Regiment 72* had found were those prepared by the 1st Cavalry Brigade who had arrived late the previous night from Audregnies and had prepared their defences with the help of the local inhabitants. Private Clarke wrote 'we didn't get much rest that night though. Then we were on the move again and fell back with many stops and starts to Angre.'[101] Lieutenant Lamb recorded 'my machine gun section remained during this time in the station square, and those of us who felt tired enough, slept on the flagstones! Very cold but we were very tired.'[102] However by the morning, along with the Cavalry Division headquarters, they had moved before the Germans had arrived. The consequence of the Cavalry Division leaving was that there was now no communications with the troops at St Aybert and Lock No. 5. The cable had been laid, but now there were no British troops in Quiévrain for them to inform as to what was happening on the left flank of the BEF.

Once the 9th Lancers had moved back with the rest of the 2nd Cavalry Brigade to the south of Audregnies,[103] 'we then seemed to break off action and after a bit of wandering about went to water our horses. It was rather like manoeuvres, where one stops for an hour.'[104] While the 9th Lancers had been engaged at Thulin and the general withdrawal was taking place of II Corps, the delayed move of 5th Infantry Division had caused the timing of the move of Allenby's cavalry and the 19th Infantry Brigade to become uncoordinated with the general movement, General Fergusson became concerned that his left flank was becoming exposed as the 5th Infantry Division did not begin its withdrawal until 0900 and 'hardly had the 13th and 14th Infantry Brigades begun their retreat, when Sir Charles became aware…that his left flank was seriously threatened.'[105] At 1100 General Fergusson tasked part of his reserve to protect his flank. This flank would also require the assistance of General Allenby's cavalry who would need to return to positions they had just vacated. Lieutenant Grenfell, who had been galloping for Brigadier De Lisle, found Allenby about 1130. He told Brigadier De Lisle "to go back and take the ridge from which we had been fired at in the morning, but not to get too heavily engaged." Brigadier De Lisle took his brigade back and sent the 18th Hussars about a mile north along the Roman road (*Chaussée Brunehaut*), to a sugar factory and went there himself accompanied by Lieutenant Grenfell.[106]

Brigadier De Lisle had already received this information from his Aide-De-Camp. A lieutenant from the 10th Hussars, Lieutenant Pat Armstrong had been dispatched an hour earlier from the Brigade Headquarters to the 5th Infantry Division and had returned with the information that the 5th Infantry Division required support from the Cavalry Division on the left flank to enable it to retire. At this point, the frictions between General Allenby and Brigadier Gough started to manifest themselves again and despite the fact that the whole of the Cavalry Division was now deployed, Brigadier Gough felt that they 'had deployed without

100 Hippel pp. 31-32 cited in Zuber, *The Mons Myth*, p. 185.
101 Pte W. Clarke diary (Property of the 1st Queen's Dragoon Guards), 23rd August 1914.
102 Lt A.J.R. Lamb Diary (Property of the 1st Queen Dragoon Guards), 23rd August 1914.
103 TNA WO 95/1113/2: Lt. Col. D.G.M. Campbell, Account of Audregnies. p. 1
104 Anon, *9th Lancer Diary*, 24th August, p. 21.
105 Edmonds, *Military Operations France and Belgium 1914*, Vol. I, p. 99.
106 Grenfell, Grenfell Family Papers (within Lyttelton Family Papers), 24th August, p. 38.

any of the Brigade Commanders knowing the scheme of operations...Was this how they were meant to operate?[107] By now it was about midday and General Smith-Dorrien had finally found the time to discuss his plan of action for the retirement of the two corps, with General Haig's at his headquarters at Bonnet but by the time he had arrived the plan for I Corps to cover the retirement of II Corps was 'ably planned and in full swing.'[108] In his diary, General Smith-Dorrien wrote 'I saw Haig, and we settled on a course of action, as we both realised that we were in for a heavy day's fighting and that the operation of withdrawal in the face of such numbers was a very serious and difficult one.'[109]

General Allenby, in response to General Fergusson's request, ordered the 2nd and 3rd Cavalry Brigade back to the high ground north of Audregnies. The 2nd Cavalry Brigade moved to the north of Audregnies and the 3rd Cavalry Brigade moved north west towards Baisieux and Angre.[110]

The 2nd Cavalry Brigade received its new orders and, after watering, was ordered to assemble in a mass on the hill.'[111] It was here Corporal Taylor rejoined the Regiment having become detached from his patrol earlier in the morning:

> I also met Captain Reynolds, our Adjutant, who informed me that they were all going to enjoy a brief rest. I found the Regiment and of course had to give an explanation to my Squadron Leader of my reconnaissance and how I dodged the enemy. They naturally thinking I had been captured. I should imagine we had rested for about two hours when suddenly ordered to mount and move out immediately.[112]

Corporal Taylor remembered that his escape from the German patrols and return journey to the Regiment was 'the hardest and longest that'[113] he could recall.

The Regiment then 'moved up to a hill,'[114] the Commanding Officer having received orders from Brigadier De Lisle 'to move through the village and take up a position just to the north west of the village with a view to being ready to support the 18th Hussars should this be necessary.'[115] As the Regiment passed through Audregnies, it was 'full of people; it seemed so incredible to pass through a populous village with cornfields all round, to or from a fight, two miles off.'[116] Brigadier De Lisle then sent L Battery to the high ground between Audregnies and Élouges. He joined the battery and ordered Major Hon. Walter Sclater-Booth to take up a good fire position and support the brigade.'[117]

107 Anthony Farrar-Hockley, *Goughie: The Life of General Sir Hubert Gough* (London: Harper Collins, 1975), p. 125.
108 Smith-Dorrien, *Memories of Forty-Eight Years' Service*, p. 388.
109 Ballard, *Smith-Dorrien*, p. 163.
110 *The Cavalry Journal Vol. XII, January to October*, p 30.
111 Grenfell, Grenfell Family Papers (within Lyttelton Family Papers), 24th August 1914.
112 Cpl. R.H. Taylor letter of Sergeant 'Spur' R.H. Taylor, p. 3.
113 Cpl. R.H. Taylor letter to Mr Stuart Gruber, 11th January 1973, p 2.
114 Dunlop, Dunlop & Puttkammer (eds.), *The Battle of Mons*, p. 57.
115 TNA WO 95/1113/2: Lt Col D.G.M. Campbell, Account of Audregnies, p. 1.
116 Grenfell, Grenfell Family Papers (within Lyttelton Family Papers), 24th August, p. 37.
117 TNA WO 95/111: L Bty., RHA War Diary, p. 3.

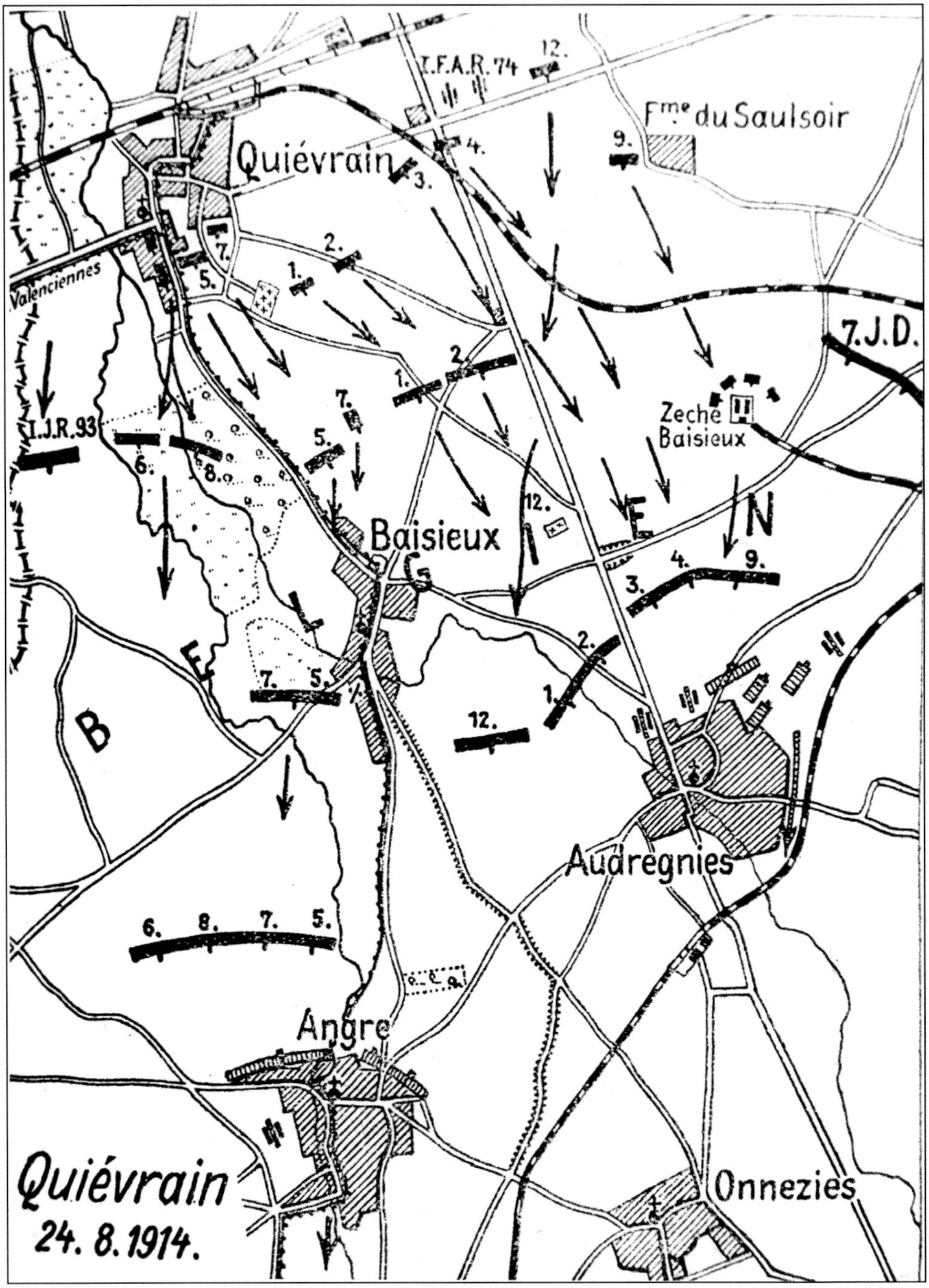


Map 11 *Infanterie Regiment 72* line of attack, 24th August 1914. (*Das 4. Thüringische Infanterie-Regiment Nr. 72 in der Flandern-Schlacht*)

> The battery galloped into action in a field south east of Audregnies losing two wagons on the way, one from shell fire and the other upset crossing a sunken road. Fired on infantry advancing in closely formed lines from Quiévrain and east of that town, a very clear target, range 2000-2300 yards. Enemy broke and retired losing heavily, came on again and broke... The battery continued firing on hostile infantry (enemy guns which kept up continuous fire could not be located.)[118]

The sisters at Saint Bernard's knew exactly where the BEFs cavalry and artillery were and the precarious position they were in when, at 1100, the cavalry 'passed back running through the wood. They had a battery in Madame Hottois' field, another one on the train tracks behind our field. We were caught between fire, Germans gunning from Baisieux and coming from Angre and Élouges. They had a battery in Monsieur Duquesne's garden. The English were in the wood behind us.[119] From his position, Lieutenant Colonel Campbell could see large columns of smoke in the direction of Quiévrain and presuming this to be the likely presence of enemy sent out patrols to the west and south west[120] but the patrol had not been gone long before it encountered three Uhlans.[121] It was during one of these patrols that *Husaren Regiment 10*, from *Infanterie Division 7,* lost its Rittmeister, Hans von Puke, near Thulin. He was their second casualty having lost Hussar (Trumpeter) Kaczmarek, the previous day.[122] After reporting this to the Brigadier, Lieutenant Colonel Campbell:

> Could see long lines of infantry advancing east from Quiévrain. I at once ordered one squadron to take up a fire position and fire was shortly after opened on us, the range to the nearest troops being 1200 yards. I now ordered a second squadron to come into action keeping one squadron in reserve; at this time the fire from the enemy was fairly heavy. I was once sent to report the situation by Lord Blackwood to Brigadier De Lisle.[123]

At Dour, Lieutenant Colonel Boger found himself as one of several officers who had been summoned to the 5th Infantry Division Headquarters, along with Lieutenant Colonel Colin Robert Ballard, the Commanding Officer of the Norfolks. After some delay, General Fergusson called up Colonels Ballard and Boger, and, having ascertained that Lieutenant Colonel Ballard was senior, placed the Cheshires and the 119th Field Battery, RFA, under his command. Not only was Ballard senior to Boger but he was a little younger, aged 46. He also had more operational experience than Ballard, having served in Burma 1891-92, the Northwest Frontier in 1895 and during the Boer War where he was the Adjutant of Robert's Light Horse taking part in operations at the Relief of Kimberley, Paadeberg, Poplar Grove, Driefontein, the Transvaal and Orange River. After the Boer War, he stayed in east Africa from 1903-04 taking part in

118 Ibid., p. 3.
119 *Annales du pensionnat Saint Bernard à Audregnies,* p.45, op. cit. in Jean Richez, *Un Champ de Coquelicots, La Bataille d'Audregnies le 24 Août 1914.*
120 Sheppard, *The Ninth Queen's Royal Lancers 1715-1936*, p. 236.
121 TNA WO 95/1113/2: Lt Col. D.G.M. Campbell, Account of Audregnies, p. 1
122 Oberstleutnant Albert Benary, *Königlich Preußisches Magdeburgisches Husaren Regiment Nr. 10 im Weltkriege 1914/1918,* (Berlin: Verlag Bernhard & Graefe, 1934).
123 Ibid., p. 1.

operations in Somaliland. Lieutenant Colonel Boger was nearly 50 and had only just taken command of the battalion on the 26th June. He had nearly 30 years' service but had little operational experience, only seeing service during the Burmese Expedition in 1885, where he had been the *Aide-De-Camp* to the General in Command. During the Boer War he had missed out having been the Adjutant of the 3rd (Volunteer) Battalion, Welch Regiment, from 1898 to 1903 and from December 1904 to November 1906, he was attached to the intelligence staff at the War Office. After two years, he was posted to Malta in charge of musketry duties until he was promoted to major in 1907[124] and took command of the depot at Chester.[125] On balance, the decision as to who should command the *flank guard* was correct as this fact in itself placed Lieutenant Colonel Boger in an unfortunate minority amongst his peers, as he was the only one of the 19 Commanding Officers of the 157 infantry battalions of the BEF who had no Boer War experience.[126] It was nearly 30 years since his last operational deployment.

The GOC then passed Lieutenant Colonel Ballard on to a staff officer to receive his orders and Lieutenant Colonel Boger was told to rejoin his battalion. He was not present when Lieutenant Colonel Ballard was being given his orders.[127] While Lieutenant Colonel Boger was with the Divisional Commander, Brigadier Gleichen, the Brigade Commander made a speech to the Cheshires, somewhat similar to that of General Fergusson at Le Pommereuil, adding 'a German is no good with fists in a tight corner.'[128] The orders he was given were 'to make a *counter stroke* to the north west. Though no Germans could be seen at the moment there was little doubt we should soon be up against them.[129] We were put out in line formation *quarter column*,[130] and the two battalions had moved approximately half a mile[131] and the battalions had just extended to sweep forward when new orders were received. Colonel Romer, of the Divisional Staff, came up hurriedly with entirely fresh orders and Lieutenant Colonel Ballard said he was told that 'my little force was now to be moved south west to take up a defensive position covering Élouges and Audregnies.'[132] The specific instructions were to 'to occupy a position near Élouges facing north west to form left *rear guard* to the force.'[133] General Fergusson had actually issued orders for the 'Divisional Reserve, consisting of the Norfolks and Cheshires with the 119th Battery, under Lieutenant Colonel Ballard of the Norfolks, ordered to act as a *flank guard.*[134] Although similar, these are two completely different operations a *flank guard* 'may be required to hold its own without support until the main body and transport have passed,'[135] and is clearly defined as a temporary and facilitation task. A *rear guard* 'carries out its mission best by compelling

124 *The Oak Tree*, 1935, p. 381.
125 *Army & Navy Gazette*, 12th September 1914.
126 Peter Hodgkinson, WFA Presentation, 'The Battalion Commanders of the BEF', 5th April 2015.
127 Crookenden, *The History of the Cheshire Regiment in the Great War*, p. 5.
128 Frank Simpson, *Cheshire Regiment the First Battalion at Mons and the Miniature Colour*, p. 24.
129 Lt. Col. C.R. Ballard, Account of Audregnies, p. 10.
130 Crookenden, *The History of the Cheshire Regiment in the Great War*, p. 5.
131 Maj. J.H. McGuinness, The Cheshire Regiment Forty Years on from Mons, *Oak Tree Journal*, 1954, p. 170.
132 Lt. Col. C.R. Ballard, Account of Audregnies, p. 11.
133 Lt. Col. C.R. Ballard, Account of Audregnies, Rough War Diary, pp. 2-3.
134 Hussey & Inman, *The Fifth Division in the Great War*, p. 7.
135 *Field Service Regulations 1909, Part 1* p. 94 para 2.

the enemy's troops to halt and deploy for attack.[136] It is not clear where this confusion arose whether it might be the instruction given by Colonel Romer was different to that which General Fergusson had ordered, or it may have been due to Lieutenant Colonel Ballard's understanding of the difference between the requirement of a *flank guard* and a *rear guard.*

Lieutenant Colonel Ballard informed Lieutenant Colonel Boger that the orders for a *counter attack* had been annulled, and that Lieutenant Colonel Boger was to follow him with his battalion to another position some distance to the left, on the north side of Élouges.'[137] The march from Dour 'to the Élouges-Audregnies position was about six miles over cobblestones and rough roads. The soldiers had hardly slept for 24 hours and the march was made with 'great exertions',[138] as both battalions had already marched from the area of Wasmes to Dour previously, which was approximately three miles. Lieutenant Colonel Ballard 'understood that a copy of the Divisional Orders for the withdrawal, which explained the role of the two battalions, had been given to Lieutenant Colonel Boger at the same time as he himself had received his own.'[139] This was not the case and Lieutenant Colonel Ballard had not 'mentioned the words *rear guard'*[140] or *flank guard* to Lieutenant Colonel Boger. The battalion war diary written by Captain Shore at the end of the day clearly states:

> The GOC 5th Div gave Col Ballard, 1st Bn Norfolk Regt orders to take the 1st Bn Cheshire Regt, 1st Bn Norfolk Regt and 119th Bty RFA and take up a position facing north west along the Élouges-Audregnies road and act as a *flank guard* to the 2nd Bn Manchester Regt and the troops entrenched round Wasmes in their retirement.[141]

The Divisional Commander had ordered a *flank guard* Colonel Romer had told Lieutenant Colonel Ballard he was to conduct a *rear guard.* The Cheshire's battalion HQ thought it was to conduct a *flank guard.* Lieutenant Colonel Boger was not present when the orders were given and did not have sufficient information to understand the role of his battalion as part of the overall military situation and he only had a confused and ill-defined understanding in his mind as to what his battalion was to do as part of Lieutenant Colonel Ballard's small force. However, a mind-set of the divisional "no surrender" policy made on the 13th August by the Brigade Major before they had embarked, subsequently reinforced by the two speeches made by General Fergusson and Brigadier Gleichen, were foremost in his mind before the battalion would go into action for the first time. Despite the importance of the task, the command of the mission had been delegated to Lieutenant Colonel Ballard who was ultimately responsible for the *flank guard* and its planning had not been undertaken by the 15th Infantry Brigade staff. Lieutenant Colonel Ballard was thus presented with two options:

136 Ibid., p. 96 para 2.
137 Simpson, *Cheshire Regiment the First Battalion at Mons and the Miniature Colour,* p. 25.
138 Ibid., p. 25.
139 Ibid., p. 6.
140 TNA WO 95/1571/1: 1st Cheshire Regiment War Diary, 24th August 1914. 'Along the Élouges-Audregnies road and act as a flank guard to the Manchesters and the troops entrenched around Wasmes in their retirement.'
141 TNA WO 95/1571/1: 1st Cheshire Regiment War Diary.

> He could make up a separate headquarters by withdrawing personnel from the units under his command, thereby disorganising them, or could exercise the dual function of detachment and battalion commander through his normal battalion staff. The position was aggravated by the fact that most of the signal personnel of battalions had already been withdrawn to form a brigade section. Lieutenant Colonel Ballard chose the latter of the two alternatives.[142]

The two battalions set off, with the Norfolks leading. Lieutenant Colonel Ballard thought 'the ground seemed perfect for defence. A smooth and open slope led down towards Quiévrain, 3000 yards away. Though there was no time for entrenching, the front companies found some rough cover.'[143] Both battalions would now have to accept battle on ground which they had never seen before and which was unsuitable for developing small arms fire power, upon which they depended for security.[144] Corn stooks and slag heaps masked most of the ground, and, besides offering ranging marks to the enemy, added to the difficulty of locating the companies once they had left the road.[145] It was difficult for any definite orders to filter down to the rank and file.[146] On arrival at the Élouges-Audregnies road, Lieutenant Colonel Ballard distributed his own companies at intervals along it from the Élouges-Quiévrain railway to the colliery and by 1215 were beginning to deploy.[147] He then met Lieutenant Colonel Boger near the mineral railway bridge south of Élouges on the road and told him:

> To take up a position as quickly as possible, in prolongation of his left, as far as a spot he indicated on the map, close to Audregnies (rather more than a mile of front for my battalion) and to protect the road against an advance of the enemy. You will be all right, our cavalry [18th Hussars] are in front. We came under fire immediately on arrival on the ground.[148]

The area allocated to the Cheshires had not been seen by either Commanding Officer, and Lieutenant Colonel Ballard, upon delegating this task, had no idea if Lieutenant Colonel Boger and his battalion had enough men to cover their piece of ground. As the Norfolks moved into position, the Germans were already to be seen moving along the Mons-Valenciennes road and mistook them for their own left wing, which was swinging round south in the direction of Wiheries and did not deploy or open fire. Lieutenant Colonel Ballard made his headquarters at the place just south of where he had met Lieutenant Colonel Ballard at the bridge where the mineral railway crossed the road. When they arrived there, Lance Corporal G. Holland reported that the remainder of the battalion were lying under cover of bank near a railway bridge. A civilian who had been sitting on the railway bridge "scuttled off" immediately when

142 Crookenden, *The History of the Cheshire Regiment in the Great War*, p. 5.
143 Lt. Col. C.R. Ballard, *Account of Audregnies,* p. 10.
144 Crookenden, *The History of the Cheshire Regiment in the Great War*, p. 7.
145 Ibid., p. 7.
146 Ibid.
147 Lt. Col. C.R. Ballard, Account of Audregnies, pp. 10-11.
148 Lt. Col. D.C. Boger, Mons, The Original Report of Lt Col DC Boger, p. 1.

he found he was being watched.[149] Lance Corporal Holland was from B Company which had been kept as a reserve where the *sunken road*, was nearly 20 feet deep and offered the company good protection.[150] A dressing station was established at a house near the bridge and the first line transport was sent back to Élouges with Lieutenant G.C. Lyle of C Company.[151] 200 yards to their rear, four guns of 119th Battery RFA also had a good cover from view.[152] This was approximately the same location that L Battery had used earlier in the morning to engage the elements of *Infanterie Regiment 26* and *66* as they had reached the railway line south of Thulin. The Norfolks second-in-command, Major Orr 'went along with the Cheshires, and reported back that they were in position and in touch with the 2nd Cavalry Brigade on their left.[153] As the companies went 'off to watch our right'[154] it was the last time the Commanding Officer would see his Second-in-Command 'and I saw no more of him.'[155]

The Germans quickly discovered that the troops on their flank were the BEF and deployed from the road to meet the threat. When they reached the road, the German artillery to the south could see the British cavalry brigade, the infantry battalions and artillery deploying to protect General Fergusson's flank. With the absence of an effective screen to their front were unaware that the Germans has crossed the canal and were now south of Quiévrain. The Germans reported that '1000 metres to the left, a dismounted cavalry squadron practiced flag signals towards the south; in the valley large groups of cavalry with horse artillery and a battalion of infantry moved back and forth apparently at random. Their conduct was so unconcerned and peaceful that we could not believe that they were enemy; in any case they had no idea that we were in the immediate vicinity.'[156] The interpretation of what they were seeing was in fact the reporting of their movements by using semaphore and the deployment of the 2nd Cavalry Brigade, the Cheshires, Norfolks and the two batteries of artillery as the *flank guard*. The Germans observed that the cavalry did not carry lances like themselves and therefore they suspected that they were enemy but were refused permission to open fire in case they were *HKK 2* or the cavalry of *III AK*. To resolve the issue, the section commander sent Leutnant Thiele of II Battery, *Feldartillerie Regiment* 74 'forward on an officer's patrol, who quickly established and reported that the troops were British.'[157] Unlike the German cavalry, it was not only the Uhlans but other mounted cavalry which also carried lances. They had seen the hussars and dragoons to their south and were not familiar with what they were observing.

There had been no time for reconnaissance as speed was of the essence and the Cheshires needed to get quickly into position. As they marched south down the Élouges–Audregnies road, Lieutenant Colonel Boger had no alternative but to drop his companies at intervals along the road in the same way as the Norfolks had done. He started to drop off the first of his companies at the 4 km stone[158] and by the time the Cheshires had reached the windmill (north

149 *Belfast News Letter*, 12th November 1914 p. 6.
150 Lt. Col. C.R. Ballard, Account of Audregnies, p. 11.
151 Lt. Col. C.R. Ballard, Account of Audregnies Rough War Diary, p. 3.
152 Francis Loraine Petre, *The Norfolk Regiment 1685-1918*, Vol. II (Norwich: Jarrold & Sons, 1924), p. 4.
153 Lt. Col. C.R. Ballard, Account of Audregnies, p. 10.
154 Ibid., p. 10.
155 Ibid., p. 10.
156 Hippel pp. 54-58 op. cit. in Zuber, *The Mons Myth*, pp. 186-187.
157 Zuber, *The Mons Myth*, p. 187.
158 TNA WO 95/1571/1: 1st Cheshire Regiment War Diary.

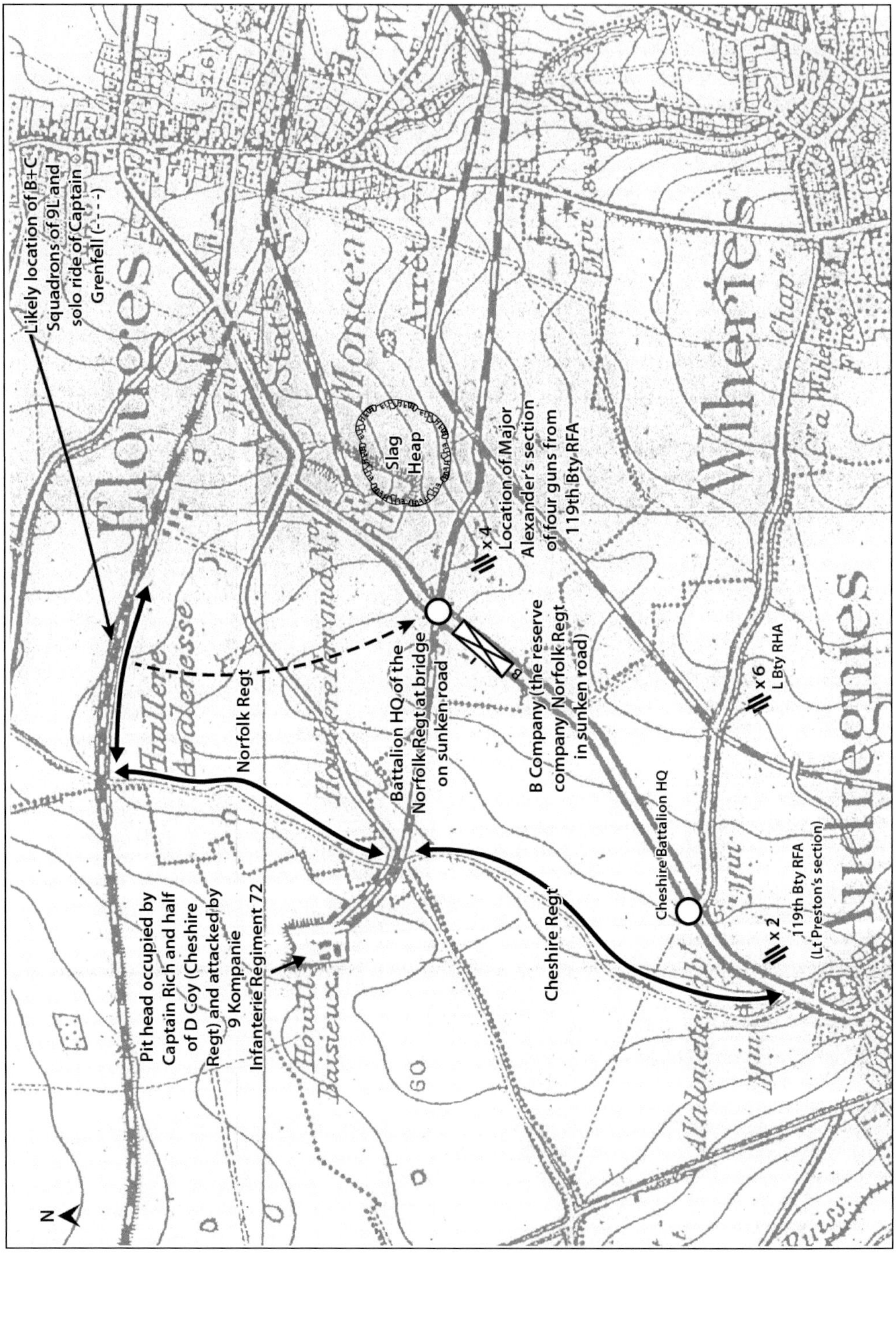


Map 12 Detailed Map with Slag Heap of Norfolks HQ and 119th Battery position. (Author)

Flank Guard Action at Élouges. Watercolour by Captain JC Walford. (RAI)

of Audregnies), the companies were fully deployed and lined the road south east of the cross roads at the colliery at *Houillères Baisieux* and Audregnies facing north west. Once in position Lieutenant Colonel Boger ordered his company commanders to give depth to the battalion position by 'pushing forward out two platoons each, west of the road and hold their ground at all costs.'[159] The general position of the Cheshires was the battalion in two lines of defence just a few hundred yards apart and with no reserve. The company locations were: Captain Shore and half of B Company in Audregnies, and the remaining half of B Company with Captain Jolliffe, to his right. A *deserted cottage*[160] on the Élouges-Audregnies road served as the boundary between B and A Companies. A Company, with Captain Dyer in command, occupied a front of 200 yards, with its left on the cottage. His firing line was approximately 150 yards north of the road, in the corn field, and their supports on the road behind and [161] their position covered the junction of the Wiheries-Audregnies, Élouges-Audregnies roads.[162]C Company were in the centre with Captain Dugmore in command with Captain Jackson and his second-in-command. D Company, under Captain Jones, prolonged the line to the right of C Company,[163] astride the mineral railway.[164] All the companies had considerable gaps between them, and owing to

159 Maj. J.H. McGuinness, The Cheshire Regiment Forty Years on From Mons, p. 171.
160 It was later discovered that the cottage was not deserted, and the family were hiding in the well – Frank Simpson, *Cheshire Regiment the First Battalion at Mons and the Miniature Colour,* p. 40.
161 Simpson, *Cheshire Regiment the First Battalion at Mons and the Miniature Colour,* p. 26.
162 Crookenden, *The History of the Cheshire Regiment in the Great War*, p. 6.
163 Simpson, *Cheshire Regiment the First Battalion at Mons and the Miniature Colour,* p. 26.
164 Crookenden, *The History of the Cheshire Regiment in the Great War*, p. 6.

the undulating ground were unable to see each other. The battalion machine guns, under the command of Lieutenant Randall, were placed on the main road, one on either side of the *deserted cottage* located between B Company and A Company using the low bank in front as cover. As they moved into position, German aeroplanes flew above the Cheshires location trying to locate the machine gun positions. The Cheshires engaged the aircraft without success as they flew too high to be reached by their gun fire.[165] To the rear, the battalion headquarters was established behind the *deserted cottage* on the roadside.[166] The flanks which were the most vulnerable had D Company in the north on the right of the line while the companies of the Norfolk Regiment, had their right flank on the railway from Élouges to Quiévrain.[167] To the south was the village of Audregnies was held by the 2nd Cavalry Brigade, (less the 18th Hussars who were to their front) and half of B Company of the Cheshires.

On the initial deployment, Captain Shore and half of B Company had been detailed to act as the battalion *flank guard* as the battalion had to deploy to its positions along the road at right angles to the direction of the enemy's approach march.[168] Once Captain Shore had completed his first *flank guard* task, he halted and went to get orders from the Commanding Officer. The Adjutant gave him orders to come in on the left to the line on the left of A Company and on moving along the road to the house on the right of the road.[169] Captain Shore moved his company down the hill to the village of Audregnies, but on moving along the road to the house on the right of the road several men were struck by rifle fire,[170] including the Company Sergeant Major, Sergeant Fred Meachin, who was wounded in the head. On arrival at Audregnies, the Commanding Officer of the 4th Dragoon Guards ordered them to hold the village facing north west and placed them in a walled garden (referred to by the men as the cloisters[171]). This position was later supported by Lieutenant Newson's platoon making the position approximately 50 strong and the Vickers machine gun of the 4th Dragoon Guards was located to the right of the garden wall.[172] This movement meant Captain Shore had the longest march to his position and would find himself on the far-left flank of the Cheshires and the most difficult to communicate with. The road was already getting congested. However, this position did offer more protection than the rest of the company locations. This move was not before the road became a seething mass of cavalry horses with shell and rifle fire coming down on it. [173]

The first company of the Cheshires to get into position was D Company on the right flank to the north adjacent to the Norfolks. Captain Jones placed himself in the centre and sent Captain Rich to the far-right flank to make contact with the Norfolks east of the colliery and the small group of houses at the crossroads. Captain Jones, advanced about 300 yards from the road and took up a position in the cornfield, leaving the CQMS with the two transport men and the ammunition mules on the road, to the rear of the last platoon.[174] Captain Jones, in line with the

165 Simpson, *Cheshire Regiment the First Battalion at Mons and the Miniature Colour*, p. 27.
166 Crookenden, *The History of the Cheshire Regiment in the Great War*, p. 7.
167 Simpson, *Cheshire Regiment the First Battalion at Mons and the Miniature Colour*, p. 26.
168 Crookenden, *The History of the Cheshire Regiment in the Great War*, p. 7.
169 TNA WO 95/1571/1: Capt. J.L. Shore, Amplified Account, 24th August 1914.
170 Ibid.
171 Simpson, *Cheshire Regiment the First Battalion at Mons and the Miniature Colour*, p. 26.
172 TNA WO 95/1571/1: Capt. J.L. Shore, Amplified Account, 24th August 1914.
173 Ibid.
174 Frank Simpson, *Cheshire Regiment the First Battalion at Mons and the Miniature Colour*, p. 28.

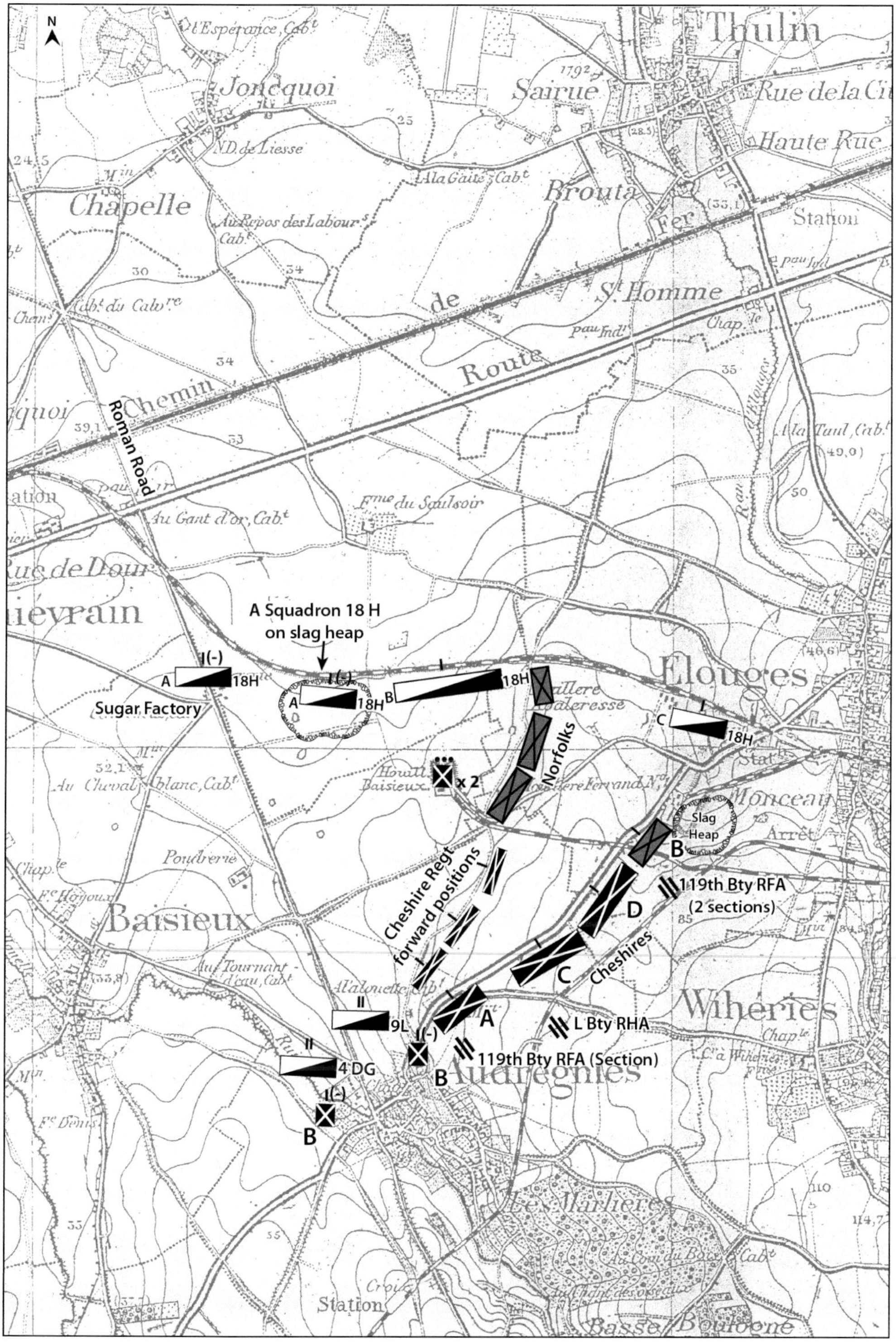


Map 13 Flank Guard and 2nd Cavalry Brigade's positions on midday on 24th August 1914. (Author)

direction to add depth to the position sent two platoons under Captain Rich from the firing line to reinforce his right flank. Captain Rich took up a position on the extreme right of the battalion and advanced his men into position by sections about 800 yards forward. The position was on a cart track and formed a natural trench, and the two leading platoons advanced as far as the railway terminus, at the colliery, half mile north west of the 4th milestone [see Map 6].[175] Despite the cover it provided, it was a poor fire position as a large colliery stood almost opposite their fronts. To overcome this, Captain Rich posted his men on either side of the building; No. 14 Platoon on the left at 10 paces interval, and No. 13 Platoon moved over to the right and linked up with the firing line of the Norfolk Regiment by the area of the colliery. This force of Norfolks had been commanded by Major Orr who was shortly afterwards severely wounded.[176] The bank of the mineral railway in front of D Company gave very good cover for the advanced platoons of the company which now engaged the German infantry as they advanced towards their position. As they got into position, they immediately took several casualties from heavy artillery fire 'including Lieutenant Bolton (posted from the 3rd Battalion Special Reserve) who was in command of No. 13 Platoon and who was wounded in the leg, Private F. Thorpe was also severely wounded.'[177]

The Norfolks moved into position before the Cheshires, having had a shorter distant to march. They moved into position without seeing the enemy or being seen. Lieutenant Colonel Ballard was standing with Major Done, (2IC) Captain C.E. Luard (OC C Company) and Captain Francis Cresswell (Adjutant) near the railway bridge of the mineral railway from which they could see west along the front as far as Quiévrain. However their view was limited due to a slight rise in the ground between them and the Cheshires and he had a large slag heap to his right and rear, which also obscured his view. However, notwithstanding this limited observation, he dictated a message to the Adjutant to inform the Brigade Commander that he was in a strong position and everything seemed quiet on this flank.[178] Captain Cresswell had only been with the battalion since 1912 having obtained a commission from the militia. At 31 years of age, he had already served during the Boer War and had served with the King's African Rifles from 1908-1911, so had arrived at the battalion with a wealth of experience.[179]

It was at this point the Cheshires had moved down the Audregnies-Élouges road and Lieutenant Colonel Campbell of the 9th Lancers was aware that he had infantry on his right flank and 'their head being close to my squadrons in action.[180] The soldiers of *Infanterie Brigade 13* who had taken Thulin took the opportunity to rest once they had reached the brigade objective of the railway embankment, but at 1000 the brigade received an order from General Sixt von Armin that 'the attack was to continue towards the high ground near Élouges, where the enemy had been located. *Infanterie Brigade 13* was to proceed on both sides of the road, deploying a strong right flank to drive the enemy south east if possible.'[181] The advance started at 1220, with I and II Battalions of *Infanterie Regiment 66* taking over from II Battalion who had taken

175 TNA WO 95/1571/1: Capt. J.L. Shore, Amplified Account, 24th August 1914.
176 Simpson, *Cheshire Regiment the First Battalion at Mons and the Miniature Colour,* p. 33.
177 Ibid., p. 27.
178 Lt. Col. C.R.Ballard, Account of Audregnies, pp. 11-12.
179 *Army and Navy Gazette*, 12th September 1914, p. 14.
180 TNA WO 95/1113/2: Lt Col. D.G.M. Campbell, Account of Audregnies, p. 1
181 Dunlop, Dunlop & Puttkammer (eds.), *The Battle of Mons,* p. 56.

Thulin moving south down the west side of the Thulin-Élouges road were III and I Battalions of *Infanterie Regiment 26* on the east side. The battalions advanced in widely spaced skirmish lines and were well supported by artillery fire.[182] The 9th Lancers assembled *en masse* on a low hill north of Audregnies, with A and B Squadrons dismounted and engaging *Infanterie Regiment 72* as they advanced south from Quiévrain at a range of 1200 yards with C Squadron being kept in reserve.[183] At 1200, Lieutenant Allfrey deployed his Maxim guns on the flank of 119th Battery RHA, [184] which was Lieutenant C.O.D.[185] Preston's section. This section had just moved down the Élouges-Audregnies road from east to west in full sight of the advancing Germans:

> The section had been detached from the main battery to 500 m east where it subsequently moved from a *half cock* position north on the Wiheries-Audregnies road as he was unable to command his section by voice, even with a chain of orderlies as a result of the noise so was determined to move his position and called up his teams. By this time, he had already received several casualties. The section moved by road in front of the other two sections towards the left in the direction of Audregnies in full view of the enemy and was heavily shelled and the Cheshires were lining the embankment. Lieutenant Preston's section moved south west along the road until they came into action in the open just alongside the end house of the village where two field tracks met in a fork, heavy ploughed land. They had arrived at Audregnies under very heavy shell fire and one of the lead horses was shot so Sergeant McCartney dismounted and cut it out. After going for about half a mile Lieutenant Preston halted his section and brought it into action against German cavalry. [186]

Lieutenant Grenfell and Lord Blackwood were sent to report the new situation to Brigadier De Lisle. To their north, the 9th Lancers could see the lead battalions of *Infanterie Regiment 72* making their advance south. Captain Grenfell's squadron joined A Squadron where there was cover from a house and dismounted his squadron and opened fire at 1200 yards.[187] Once B Squadron had dismounted, 'all the troop leaders behaved splendidly and Straker, Garstin, Mather-Jackson, and Crossley dismounted their troops and opened fire with great calmness as if firing at landscape targets, repeatedly checking the men and altering the range.'[188] Captain Grenfell's appreciation of the situation was positive. 'I am sure we could have put up a very pretty fight, but unfortunately at this moment my colonel said he had received orders to *charge*. I at once reconnoitred the ground with my glasses and saw there was a good deal of wire.'[189]

While Captain Grenfell was looking to his front and Leutnant Thiele was trying to establish the identity of the troops to his front, the sisters at Saint Bernard's prayed and then *Madame la Supérieure* suggested they 'sing for the rest of the soul of Pope X. His death occurred last Thursday but has been overlooked in the middle of these gloomy events. The shooting seems to

182 Korfes, *The German 66th Regiment in the First World War*, p. 32.
183 Anon, 9th Lancer War Diary, 24th August 1914, p. 21.
184 Lt. F. de V.B. Allfrey diary, 24th August 1914.
185 IRC POW record reads 'Preston, Classon OD'.
186 Hutton, *The Gunners of August 1914*, p. 61.
187 Grenfell, *Grenfell Family Papers (within Lyttelton Family Papers)*, 24th August 1914, p. 24.
188 Ibid., p. 24.
189 Ibid., 24th August 1914, p. 24.

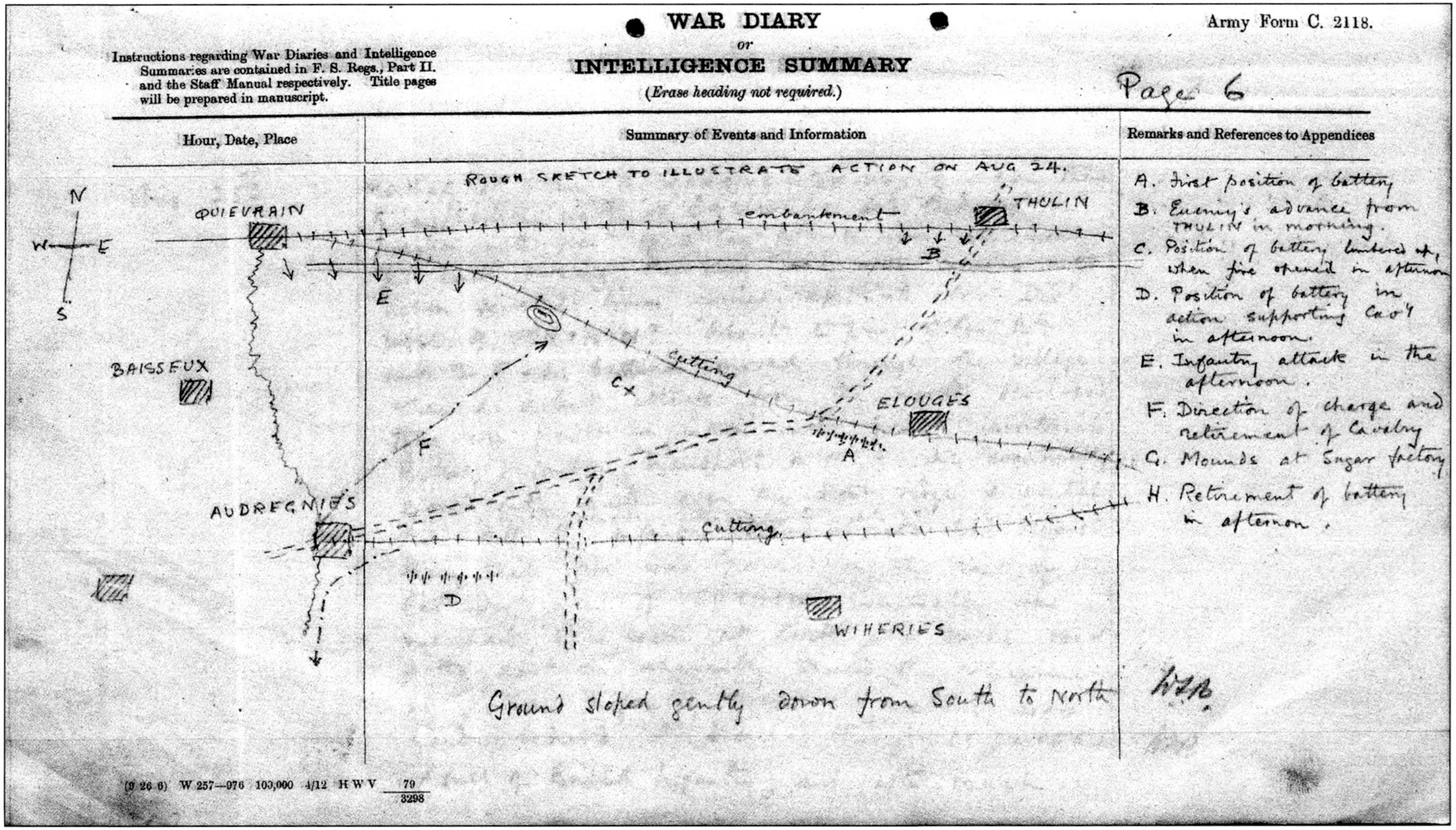


Map 14 L Battery's engagement at Audregnies , 24th August 1914. (TNA WO 95/1111)

have calmed down, "is that it finally?" From inside the *pensionnat,* the sisters could not see the developing situation.[190] Leutnant Thiele had still not returned when *Feldartillerie Regiment* 74 started to position its guns:

> The guns of I Battalion had been brought forward at a walk, in order not to draw attention or stir up clouds of dust. There was no time to lay telephone lines from the Battery Commander's observation post to the guns so the fire commands would be done by voice. The space on the road was tight but 'I and II Battalions managed to deploy in a covered position, but there was not enough room for III Battalion in the same location, so they had to set up behind some hayricks and tall poplars lining the road. The Section Commander stood on his observation ladder near a railway man's house.[191]

While the supporting artillery of *Infanterie Division 8* was deploying, the Germans found that the BEF had vacated Quiévrain. '*Infanterie Regiment 72* drew water from the wells'[192] and then the Regiment deployed once again south with 5 *Kompanie* and 7 *Kompanie* on the south side of the town, 1 *Kompanie* and 2 *Kompanie* in an open field, with 3 *Kompanie* and 4 *Kompanie* echeloned to the left along the Valenciennes road on both sides of the railway line, and with 6 *Kompanie* and 7 *Kompanie* in the town. III Battalion was tasked with guarding the artillery.'[193] At 1230, Leutnant Thiele made his report, and opened fire on his own initiative.'[194] As soon as *Infanterie Regiment 72* began its advance south, the gunners of L Battery RHA and 119th Battery RFA engaged the lead German companies, from the north side of Audregnies and opened fire. The Regiment continued its advance with *5* and *7 Kompanies* moving directly south, while *1* and *2 Kompanies* advanced on Audregnies.[195]

From his position by the railway bridge to the west, Lieutenant Colonel Ballard saw the advance of *Infanterie Division 8*. At that moment Major H.R. Done of A Company shouted "great Heavens, Colonel, look over there!" Through glasses he could see a mass of Germans moving in dense columns over open ground just north of Quiévrain. 'We could see at least 4000-5000 and knew that there must be many others out of sight...I saw more Germans in that one first moment than I ever set eyes on during the rest of the war.'[196] Lieutenant Colonel Ballard sent a message at once to the Brigade Headquarters and to the Cheshires which had to be delivered by hand as he was not in communication with either. Before *Infanterie Regiment 72* started to advance 'there was a terrific burst of shell fire from six German batteries which had lined up along the main road east of Quiévrain. Lieutenant Colonel Ballard could see the flashes and count the guns...that line of guns offered a beautiful target to the 119th Battery but I sent orders to Major Alexander to hold his fire until the German infantry came within range in the open.'[197] No sooner had the artillery barrage started than 'big columns began to deploy on both

190 *Annales du pensionnat Saint Bernard à Audregnies, p.46,* op. cit. in Jean Richez, *Un Champ de Coquelicots, La Bataille d'Audregnies le 24 Août 1914.*
191 Hippel op. cit, in Zuber, *The Mons Myth,* p. 187.
192 Zuber, *The Mons Myth,* p. 187.
193 Ibid., p. 187.
194 Ibid., p. 187.
195 Ibid., p. 187.
196 Lt. Col. C.R. Ballard, Account of Audregnies, p. 13.
197 Ibid., p. 14.

sides of Quiévrain, moving straight towards us; for a little distance. They were hidden by a fold of the ground, and were still out of rifle range.'[198]

D Company of the Norfolks was possibly the first company to get into position as it was on the far right of the line. Private Reginald Hurrell was in No. 13 Platoon of D Company, Norfolks commanded by Lieutenant E.F.V.[199] 'Victor' Briard,[200] from Jersey. His section commander was Sergeant R.J. Lemmon. Their position was on the Norfolks right flank and, as they deployed, he was aware of the position of the cavalry and artillery. They could already see the German infantry advancing. Suddenly, 'orders were passed around to *advance in line formation*. That meant one man every 15 yards, perhaps a little less, running as quickly as possible a few yards, then laying down, allowing a small space of time between these periodic rushes.'[201] When they halted 'we soon found ourselves in the centre of this big field with no one in the rear, but in front the cavalry and four field guns of our own, and on the skyline 1000s, yes 1000s, of Germans.'[202] No sooner had they stopped:

> There was a terrific burst of fire which sounded like 100 machine guns firing at once and falling on us like hailstones. It was shrapnel. The results were very deadly. Our section commander was the first, Sergeant Lemmon shot or hit, having his left ear blown completely off. He rolled over just like a shot rabbit. Next came the fellow on my right. He just shouted to me "they've got me Reg." They were his last words. My pal Bill on the other side came running over asking me to bandage his finger. Oh, what a gash it was. I said "you fool, keep down until this fire ceases." It was what they call *sweep fire*, where every square inch is covered by fire. However, we managed to get his finger patched up. After this fire died down a bit, the whistle blew to continue the advance. Unfortunately, many remained where they were, either motionless or wounded. Thus, a very thin line moved up. During this short sprint we lost the officer in command with many others. In this spot we stayed for quite a while, waiting for the next sprint.[203]

As *Infanterie Regiment 72* continued its advance south and crossed the Mons-Valenciennes road, 3 and 4 *Kompanie*s to the east of Quiévrain moved south east towards A and C Companies of the Cheshires. Hauptmann Huber, the *kompanie* commander of 9 *Kompanie*, III Battalion, who had been protecting the artillery wrote:

> To the left rear east of Quiévrain decided to take the mine head to his front. 9 *Kompanie* was a superbly trained company, and its commander an outstanding tactician. The 3 Platoon moved out by bounds in two lines, in a very open formation with 10 pace intervals between the skirmishers, covered by the fire of the rest of the *kompanie*. Such an attack maximised supporting fire. The dispersion required troops who were willing and able to advance on

198 Ibid., pp. 11-12.
199 Ernest Felix Victor, known as Victor.
200 Pte R. Hurrell notebook, p. 1.
201 Pte R. Hurrell, Log of Round the World Cruise, p. 28.
202 Pte R. Hurrell notebook, p. 24.
203 Ibid., pp. 24-25.

> their own initiative, towards the mine head at the colliery. 1 and 2 Platoons followed on behind using the same formation.[204]

At the same time *Infanterie Division 8* at Quiévrain had moved south of the Mons-Valenciennes road with its advancing infantry supported by the artillery. On the road, *Infanterie Division 7* was doing the same south of Thulin:

> At 1220, I and II Battalions of *Infanterie Regiment 66* moved off from the western side of Thulin-Élouges road, with III and I Battalions of *Infanterie Regiment 26* on the eastern side. These start positions conformed to the final disposition having crossed the canal at Ville Pommeroeul and taking Thulin. As the regiments advanced, they used 'widely spaced skirmish lines were used to make the push towards the heights of Élouges…They were well supported with artillery under General Karl von Stumpff's command, which was positioned behind the railway embankment.[205]

II Battalion of *Infanterie Regiment 66* was given the objective of Élouges.[206] The terrain in the *Infanterie Regiment 26* sector contained a large number of mounds of coal and slag which led to bitter close-range infantry combat.'[207] As *Infanterie Regiment 26* were moving forward artillery started to engage 119th Battery and the machine guns of the Norfolk Regiment. A leutnant in 4 Battery wrote 'we galloped into position under British infantry fire. We scored great numbers of hits on British artillery and machine guns using direct fire. Hauptmann Meufel stood on the observation ladder and I observed standing on his wagons.'[208] 'The commander of *Feldartillerie Regiment 40*, Oberstleutnant Büstorff, was riding with and even in front of the forward line of infantry and the attack initially won ground quickly. 'Hurrah, finally it starts. We gallop past the lead infantry elements and go into battery; first the bullets sail over our heads and smack against the gun shields.'[209] It then ran into stiff resistance from the Norfolks on the Mons-Valenciennes road. The casualties in 2 Battery were so high that 1 Battery was sent forward to reinforce it.'[210] As soon as the artillery opened fire, 3 Battery, *Feldartillerie Regiment 40* 'immediately took counter battery fire from Élouges-Audregnies and suffered heavy casualties in men and material. The hayricks that were being used as camouflage were set on fire by direct hits and two ammunition wagons caught fire. Shells were being 'fired at a prodigious rate and soon every available man was bringing ammunition to the guns under fire.'[211]

After the initial success, *Infanterie Division 7* lost momentum but at 1245, the infantry attack picked up steam again, moving forward in short bounds. The three batteries of *Feldartillerie Regiment 40* came into line when 2 Battery and 3 Battery came on line with 1 Battery.'[212] While 119th Battery was engaging, they had been observed by *Feldartillerie Regiment 40* which had

204 Zuber, *The Mons Myth,* pp. 188-189.
205 Dunlop, Dunlop & Puttkammer (eds.), *The Battle of Mons,* p. 57.
206 Korfes, *The German 66th Regiment in the First World War*, p. 32.
207 Zuber, *The Mons Myth,* p. 191.
208 Ibid., p. 192.
209 Ibid., p. 192.
210 Ibid., p. 191.
211 Terence Zuber, *The Mons Myth: A Reassessment of the Battle,* p. 187.
212 Ibid., p. 191.

Officers of Feldartillerie Regiment 40. (*Das Altmärkische Feld-Artellerie-Regiment Nr. 40 im Weltkriege 1914-1918*)

detected 'a long line of British artillery, south west of Élouges,[213] four to five batteries, which were firing at *Infanterie Division 8* at Quiévrain, offering their flank to *Feldartillerie Regiment 40*, which opened a withering fire, without receiving any counter fire in return.'[214] The counter battery fire on 3 Battery *Feldartillerie 74* resulted in many casualties but they 'kept up the fire. All the officers in 3 Battery save one were wounded; an officer from the regimental staff brought an order to the section and stayed to direct the fire of the battery.'[215] During the day, *Feldartillerie Regiment 74* fired 1,340 rounds of ammunition.[216] The advance east from Thulin by *Infanterie Regiments 26* and *66* supported by *Feldartillerie Regiment 40* were moving towards Élouges and the Norfolk's positions. Private Robert Sheldrake's company took up a position in the hollow of a railroad and as he was marching up, he saw his first dead soldier, a cavalryman, who was 'being carted down on a stretcher, his horse lying dead nearby.'[217]

213 Ibid.
214 Ibid.
215 Ibid., p. 187.
216 Ibid., p,.190,
217 Pte R. Sheldrake diary, p. 12.

> About midday, the terrible battle began. All I can describe it by is a terrible roaring of cannon, with innumerable shells and bullets singing through the air, mingled with the terrible rat-tat-tat of the machine guns brigaded together, mowing down troops like corn before the scythe, I laid between the two fires, we being sheltered in the hollow of the railroad both from view and fire. We crawled up the bank and fired occasionally. I fired 20 to 30 rounds where I thought there appeared to be some men moving about amongst some corn sheaves 700 to 800 yards away. So, I cannot say I hit anyone, it is more likely to be the opposite.[218]

As *Infanterie Regiment 66* were getting closer to Private Reginald Hurrell's position he wasable to engage the Germans for the first time, but by then most of his officers and senior non-commissioned officers had been killed or wounded. The ammunition was running short and no more was being brought forward:

> The enemy [Germans] were about 800 yards away, so for the first time we were able to use our rifles. This had to be done at our own discretion, having lost all commanders even to the lance corporal. And with having stayed in this one position so long, ammunition was exhausted, with no supplies coming up. Thus, the only thing left was to get it from those already shot. This was successful up to a point, because one had to keep low in passing one to the other. Apart from that, there was the thoughts of poor old so and so laying there with his head or arms or legs blown away. One fellow of the company had a shell pass completely through his stomach, which set him on fire. I found the best thing to do was to lay beside each one, use all his ammunition and go to the next and do likewise.[219]

On the D Company main position, it was difficult to see from the road what was going on in front due to the tremendous volume of enemy shell and rifle fire poured onto this crest of road. This meant that the soldiers had to keep close to whatever little cover could be found. CQMS Pitt of D Company passed word along to Lieutenant Campbell who was, at that time, the only officer with whom he was in contact as 'to the advisability of taking the mules into the open when the company advanced. Before any reply could be received a section of the 119th Battery RFA galloped up the road at a terrific pace and on reaching the rear of D Company transport received the full force of concentrated shrapnel.'[220] This was Lieutenant Preston's section moving to Audregnies.

The advancing German infantry was *Infanterie Regiment 72* who were advancing south from Quiévrain. The machine gun "crews moved forward just like in training" and the commander of I Battalion, Major Semeral, motioned that they should join him in a copse. From that position they opened fire on an artillery piece at 900 metres range:

> I saw our troops to the right of me advance. I went forwards with Elias' platoon's baptism of fire. We were receiving very heavy artillery fire, but had no infantry to shoot at, so we went forwards, almost without firing. An enemy battery stood in the direction of the

218 Ibid., p. 12.
219 Pte R. Hurrell notebook, pp. 34-35.
220 Simpson, *Cheshire Regiment the First Battalion at Mons and the Miniature Colour*, p. 30.

> church steeple at Audregnies. I approached to within 700 metres, but only a squad followed me into the sunken road. Shells flew over our heads. I decided to storm the battery, which probably consisted of two guns. We advanced without stopping. Our great hope was that we will get them! Lots of dead horses. They attempted to get the guns away. We were almost there and began shooting again, when a gun pulled by a nag went into the town.[221]

It was Lieutenant Preston's isolated position that had attracted the attention of the machine guns and artillery supporting *Infanterie Regiment 72*. Despite getting into action and firing most of his ammunition, the fire from the advancing Germans was most effective, resulting in his being wounded, losing men, horses, and an ammunition wagon. The section stayed until the ammunition wagons were almost exhausted and the ground was littered with empty cartridge cases and then sent for the teams to come up.[222] Major Bridges of the 4th Dragoon Guards saw Lieutenant Preston's 'two British guns firing away at the advancing German hordes as steadily as if they had been on the range at Okehampton.'[223] The German infantry and machine guns waited until they got within 800 yards of the guns. Lieutenant Preston sent one gun out of action and was again wounded. Sergeant McCartney took his gun under cover and then rode back to assist Lieutenant Preston to get the other away. The wagon of this sub-section was found not to be following the gun and Lieutenant Preston went back to try to get it away but was unable to do so as most of the horses had been killed. Altogether he was wounded four times, twice severely. He was put in an ambulance and Sergeant McCartney brought the section away. The other four guns with Major Alexander at Élouges remained in action longer.[224] Lieutenant Preston wrote 'by this time the enemy had worked forward and was playing very prettily on my section with machine guns. I had several casualties but got away both guns and one ammunition wagon. I then hurried after my teams to catch up the guns and got a bullet through my knee while doing so but managed to clamber on an ammunition wagon.'[225]

As a result of the heavy fire, the D Company mules stampeded and, with other loose animals, dashed down the sloping road followed by the CQMS plus two transport men[226] who cautiously made their way after their mules. They found them at the bottom of the hill where the mineral railway crossed the road diagonally by a fairly wide bridge. They found a confusion of loose horses, wounded men, and stretcher bearers. CQMS Lyons of C Company, whose mules had also stampeded under the effects of the artillery and small arms fire, was also there. As CQMSs Pitt and Lyons returned to their company positions, halfway up the slope they were met by a staff officer shouting that "the road must be kept clear," and he refused to allow the Cheshire men to proceed any further up the road and ordered them back. As they halted, a Captain of the Norfolks appeared on the scene with a small party. They were then joined by six of the Cheshire's stretcher bearers and the company transport had also attached themselves to the CQMSs. As they waited, they were informed that the Germans had already reached

221 Zuber, *The Mons Myth*, p. 188.
222 Hutton, *The Gunners of August 1914*, p. 62.
223 Bridges, *Alarms and Excursions*, p. 82.
224 Hutton, *The Gunners of August 1914*, pp. 61-62.
225 Ibid., p. 62.
226 Lt. Col. D.C. Boger, Mons: The Original Report of Lt Col D.C. Boger, p. 3, 'Privates Woodier and Thorp'

the road, so they decided to retired to the railway halt at Audregnies and made a stand on the railway lines.

At approximately 1200, while the Norfolks were being engaged to their front by *Infanterie Regiments 26* and 66, Captain Dugmore of C Company, the Cheshires ordered his second-in-command, Captain Jackson, to move forward with two platoons one of which was No. 9 Platoon and take up a position approximately 300 yards in advance of the road. This was to fill the gap between himself and D Company to his left. The new position was a corn field that had been cut and the corn stood in sheaves. Either side of the corn field were fields of turnips. It was during this move that the Germans opened up with artillery fire on the Cheshires position, which would last for the next three hours,[227] just as No. 9 Platoon moved into place:

> "No. 9 Platoon, extend to the left" Corporal Crooke jumped to life, his section extended on the left flank of the platoon and under the bank. Now what? "Forward" Corporal Crooke tried to take the bank at a bound but failed, sliding back into the road accompanied by the jeers of the men still in fours. Scrambling up and over the bank he raced after his section. This was going to be the real thing, at last. No more holding of dark and dismal streets. "Keep your extension!" he yelled excitedly. "Left incline," signalled Sergeant Arthur Raynor. Corporal Crooke repeated it to his section. They turned half left and doubled down the field. "Get down and make head cover!" Off came the packs and out came the entrenching tools. To the right the extended lines were coming down the field to take up a position alongside them. It looked fine, it was the soldiering he had been taught. Bullets began to whine over their heads. From along the line the rattle of rifle fire opened out.[228]

Once the platoon got into position and removed their packs, they were shelled by shrapnel and the position they were in was not good and they struggled to get into a good fire position:

> Where Corporal Crooke lay the ground was most uneven. He could obtain no field of fire and was unable to identify any of the targets upon which the remainder of the platoon were concentrating their fire. He crawled to the centre of the section but the ground there was just as bad. A terrific weird screaming noise passed overhead. Whatever was it? They looked at each other enquiringly. Word came down the line from Sergeant Raynor. "That is shrapnel and you are all right as long as you hear it screaming. It is passing overhead." From where he lay, Corporal Crooke could not see the gap and very little of the village. He decided to crawl his section forward to try and obtain a better field of fire. After several lengthy crawls the section obtained a good field of fire quarter left of their position, could get no frontal view and only a distant view to the right. The Germans were moving in batches across the open ground, quarter left of where they lay, and about 400 yards away.[229]

Captain Dugmore remained with the other two platoons of the company on or near the road and had made his headquarters near Lieutenant Grove's platoon to the right. About 800 yards

227 Simpson, *Cheshire Regiment the First Battalion at Mons and the Miniature Colour,* p. 29.
228 Crooke, Twenty Fourth August 1914 (An Impression), (*The Oak Leaf*, 2007).
229 Ibid.

to the right front of C Company was a coal mine occupied by two platoons of the Norfolk Regiment.[230]

By now both batteries of artillery were in action. 119th Battery RFA (less Lieutenant Preston's section) were to the rear right behind the Norfolk's reserve, B Company. 119th Battery had been given orders by Lieutenant Colonel Ballard to concentrate their fire on the advancing infantry once they were in range and in the open.[231] As they were engaging the advancing infantry they were engaged by counter battery fire from *Feldartillerie Regiment 40.* 'Some of the German shells that were meant for them fell short amongst the Norfolk reserve company.'[232] Lance Corporal Holland said 'it was agonising lying there, losing valuable men, and not being allowed to get a good whack at the enemy. C and D Companies lost a lot of men, and their retirement had to be covered.'[233] L Battery RHA to their left rear were engaged in counter battery fire and Gunner John Allan and Bombardier Perrett 'were busy bringing up ammunition and it was a very hot day in every sense. I don't know how long the action lasted but I remember a staff officer galloping up and shouting "Good old L!" On our way back, a farrier who was an old South Africa man told me we had fired more shells in one afternoon than the whole of the Boer War!'[234] L Battery had fired 'nearly all of its ammunition when the Brigade Major, Captain Hamilton-Grace; ordered the battery to retire. The guns were run forward about 20-30 yards to a hedge and extracted by single guns in succession (this running forward was the salvation of the battery, it could not have limbered up where it was). The position continued to be shelled long after the battery had left. The battery had fired a total of 450-500 rounds of ammunition'[235] Lieutenant Grenfell was sent off to look for Brigadier De Lisle; 'I went to the railway to look for De Lisle, and on approaching the brigade saw four artillery men swept off by a shell.'[236] Despite this the casualties for the battery had been relatively light with Lieutenant Marston and seven NCOs and men wounded and two missing. The battery had been subjected to fire only from shrapnel and not high explosive shells. The gun shields had provided effective protection to the detachments.[237]

Having got into position, the Cheshires machine gun section received its first order "gun numbers up," and at a range of 1800 yards engaged the Germans as they deployed in two direct columns from the wood immediately south of Quiévrain, and the upper part of the Bois de Deduit. 'The shells from the enemy's guns were soon bursting all about the section, and one of the guns was soon fired out of action. Several casualties occurred, but the shooting was indifferent and most of the shells burst beyond the position.'[238] 'Sergeant Barrow and Privates Spencer and Taylor's machine gun section[239] carried out their orders under heavy fire in a cool

230 Crookenden, *The History of the Cheshire Regiment in the Great War*, p. 8.
231 Lt. Col. C.R. Ballard, Account of Audregnies, p. 14.
232 Loraine Petre, *The Norfolk Regiment 1685-1918,* Vol II, p. 4.
233 *Belfast News Letter*, 12th November 1914 p. 6.
234 Hutton, *The Gunners of August*, p. 62.
235 TNA WO 95/1111: L Bty RHA War Diary, pp. 4-5.
236 Grenfell, Grenfell Family Papers (within Lyttelton Family Papers), 24th August, p. 38.
237 WO95/1111 - War Diary L Bty RHA p. 4.
238 Simpson, *Cheshire Regiment the First Battalion at Mons and the Miniature Colour,* p. 27.
239 8013 Sergeant Barrow, 7903 Private Spencer, 9327 Private Taylor.

and plucky manner worthy of all praise as the guns were necessarily exposed to heavy enemy artillery and rifle fire.'[240]

For the nuns in Saint Bernard's, the battle came to Audregnies at approximately 1215 when the shooting started, then shelling:

> We were going downstairs to the dining room, children were in the kitchen, they were a bit upset, but calm, we set up the dinner table. We realised that our best shelter was in the basement, on the ground, but still was not very safe: some of us went upstairs to get mattresses to fit as much as we can to the windows, except for the back ones...We pray, how can we do better when you're so close to real danger! Around 1300, the doorbell rang. When *Madame la Supérieure* is at the gate with another nun, an English medic was already trying to climb the wall; he was the first wounded, a bullet went through his cheek. He went downstairs with us because we couldn't move the ambulance, we put a mattress on the floor next to the kitchen; four others wounded arrived after him and we put them in hallways. *Madame la Supérieure* gives the signal for dinner...only to be interrupted a few minutes later when a casualty arrived, breathless. He received a shrapnel wound in his chest.[241]

At approximately midday, General Allenby arrived at Audregnies and his arrival did not go unnoticed. '2nd Lieutenant Roger Chance of A Squadron, 4th Dragoon Guards, saw the divisional staff arrive. "By God," he exclaimed, "it's the Bull himself." Captain Oldrey replied "we're for it now all right. Better get girthed-up." It would appear that General Allenby had ordered Brigadier De Lisle to put in a diversionary attack using any means he thought best, 'including mounted action if necessary.'[242] Brigadier De Lisle rode back to the village where he met Lieutenant Colonel Campbell and told him "I am going to *charge* the enemy and will tell the 4th Dragoon Guards, now in the village, to make an attack on the left. As soon as you see them debouch for the attack you will attack on the right with at least two squadrons." Lieutenant Colonel Campbell immediately ordered one of the squadrons in action to mount and formed up the other squadrons in the rear of some buildings ready to advance.[243] The Brigadier then went to meet Lieutenant Colonel Mullens of the 4th Dragoon Guards and ordered him 'to support the 9th Lancers with his regiment and to assume charge of the defence on the east of the river'[244] until his return. The 4th Dragoon Guards intention was to gallop to Baisieux in order to seize a house at the end of it, and thus to cover a further advance upon Quiévrain,'[245] Once the Brigade Commander had given his orders, he went to give the situation to General Allenby[246] who he met shortly afterwards.'[247] Lieutenant Colonel Mullens wrote:

240 Lt. Col. D.C. Boger, Mons, The Original Report of Lt Col D.C. Boger, p. 3.
241 *Annales du pensionnat Saint Bernard à Audregnies*, p.45, op. cit. in Jean Richez, *Un Champ de Coquelicots, La Bataille d'Audregnies le 24 Août 1914.*
242 Anglesey, *A History of the British Cavalry 1914-1919*, Vol. 7, p. 119.
243 TNA WO 95/1113/2: Lt Col. D.G.M. Campbell, Account of Audregnies, p. 1
244 Ibid., p. 21.
245 Edmonds, *Military Operations France and Belgium 1914,* Vol. I, p. 101.
246 Ibid., p. 21.
247 Brereton, *A History of the 4th and 7th Royal Dragoon Guards and Their Predecessors 1685-1980,* p. 312.

> At about 1330, as the Regiment was in *column of route* going to water under brigade arrangements, rifle fire was heard from the north west side of the town. I received verbal orders from the brigade staff to gallop my regiment out to the north of the town and to be prepared for a determined infantry attack. I had previously been informed that one regiment of the 2nd Cavalry Brigade was holding the north and north east of the town and I understood that the outskirts of the village were secure. I led my regiment along a narrow lane between a wall and high banks, was met by some rifle fire. I gave orders for the cottage to be seized, to cover the east of the lane. Two troops of B Squadron went forward but were swept by heavy rifle fire. Major Bridges then personally led one troop of his squadron to the cottages. His horse was shot under him, he was much shaken by being ridden over by the troop in the thick dust. He held on to the position with a few men under a very hot fire during the entire action. In order to help Major Bridges, I ordered Major Hunter to take up a position, but owing to extremely severe rifle fire his squadron had to take cover to the right flank. The machine guns were now in action at the head of the lane, range about 1500 yards. The squadrons had become separated and no further concerted action was possible. The order was received to withdraw to the south of the village. This was carried out without much further loss, the casualties amounted to 81.[248]

The first two troops from B Squadron which had tried to seize the cottages were led by Lieutenant R.G. Fetherstonhaugh and Lieutenant Sir A.E. Hickman. They were swept by heavy rifle and shell fire while trying to occupy the cottage, and were forced to take cover to the right of the lane. They eventually joined up with the 9th Lancers as they galloped north.[249] Private Dyer wrote:

> Had a rough time and had to gallop to a coal mine, where we sheltered behind a heap of rubbish…Lost many killed, wounded and prisoners, including Sir Alfred Hickman, Lieutenant Sanderson and many others. Caught Private Burgess's horse and found the sword hilt swimming with blood, also a coat and saddle. French interpreter blown to pieces here.[250]

C Squadron, under Major Bridges, wrote 'we were ordered to clear out the enemy from around the village [Baisieux]. Full of the spirit of the *arme blanche* and imagining that it was a matter of chasing away cavalry patrols, I debouched at the head of my squadron from the northern entrance of the village at a gallop, drawing swords as we went.'[251] Private Clouting from 4th Troop noticed, as they passed a corner in the road, who he thought was Brigadier De Lisle looking as they galloped, 'fanning out into the open fields beyond the village.'[252] Major Bridges went and, dashing up a lane between wire fences, on to a rise where there was a solitary

248 TNA WO 95/1112: Account of Audregnies, Lieutenant Colonel Mullens, 4th Dragoon Guards War Diary.
249 Rev. Harold Gibb, *Record of the 4th Irish Dragoon Guards in the Great War 1914-1918* (Canterbury, 1925), p. 6.
250 Pte H. Dyer diary (Property of the Royal Dragoon Guard's Museum), 24th August 1914.
251 Bridges, *Alarms and Excursions,* p. 81.
252 Van Emden, *Teenage Tommy,* p. 52.

cottage which seemed a likely *point d'appui,* but as he topped the rise he came under heavy rifle fire and *Umslopogaas* fell down on his nose with a broken leg. He felt like 'most of the squadron and machine gun section seemed to gallop over me.'[253] It is presumed that the main 4th Dragoon mounted action followed the same initial line of advance as the first two troops from B Squadron with the following squadrons also covering the ground as well to the west of the solitary cottage and Baisieux.

Lieutenant Colonel Mullens ordered Major Hunter, Officer Commanding A Squadron, to support C Squadron. Major Hunter gave a hasty squadron order and yelled to Lieutenant Chance (who was from Cambridge University UOTC[254]) and those in front: Gallagher, Archie Wright and Railston[255] but all they could hear was the 'whistle crack of bullets and the wheee-ump of shells.'[256] Lieutenant Chance followed his troop leader, 'who formed *troop in squadron columns* and we are off at the gallop, swords pointed…We spanned the un-metalled road, which runs straight, unfenced, through a stubble field dotted with corn stooks.'[257] Lieutenant Gallagher wrote:

> We were watering in Audregnies when the order came to mount and *charge*, I was at the head of the second squadron (A). It was quiet enough before that. We were dismounted in the village street, watering from buckets wherever we could find one. We jumped into our saddles and tore off down a narrow lane without in the least knowing where we were going or what was up. The dust was thick, so thick one could hardly see the man in front. We went off in a rush all right and rode down that choking lane with no other thought than keeping going. We had no order to draw sabres, and just galloped in a bunch. Before we had reached the end of the lane men began to fall. The bullets were coming from in front and seemingly from one flank, as well. More men fell, but we couldn't do anything save gallop. At the end the lane curved round a cottage to the right. I remember seeing Colonel Mullens, and Major Solly-Flood beside him, at the turn. Mullens cried, "Not there, not there!" but it conveyed no meaning to me. We dashed on after the leading squadron round the corner and into a very inferno of shell and small-arm fire. It was hot. No time to wonder what I was doing. Shrapnel was bursting right in amongst us and men falling every inch of the way, it seemed. Not far beyond the corner I saw a flash which seemed right in front of my eyes, and my horse went down. When I came round I was lying on my right side, with one leg under my dead horse. My head was bad. Alongside me was a French officer[258] who had been attached to us, a Count, someone said. He was dead. A bullet had hit him right in the centre of the forehead. All was quiet for a moment. Dead and, wounded lay all around, and everything seemed strangely still. Down the lane, I saw Major Tom Bridges ride out into view. [259]

253 Bridges, *Alarms and Excursions*, p. 81.
254 Brereton, *A History of the 4th and 7th Royal Dragoon Guards and Their Predecessors 1685-1980,* p. 307.
255 Lieutenant Spencer Julian Wilfred Railston. 18th Battalion, King George's Own Lancers, Indian Army, attached.
256 Brereton, *A History of the 4th and 7th Royal Dragoon Guards and Their Predecessors 1685-1980,* p. 313.
257 Ibid., p. 313.
258 Quilico is buried at Élouges.
259 Gallagher op. cit. in Coleman, *From Mons to Ypres with French,* pp. 357-358.

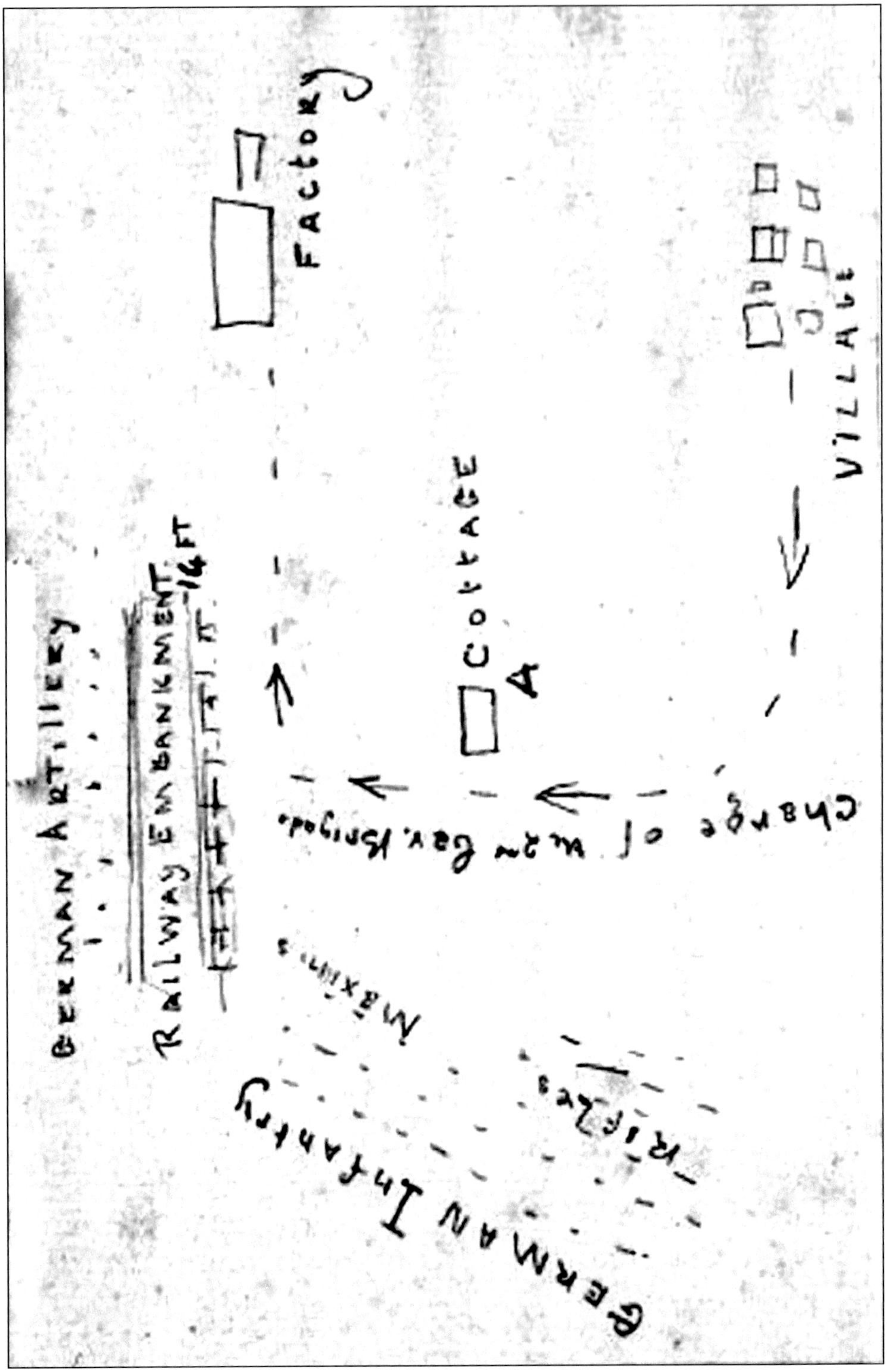


Map 15 Map from Captain Wright's Diary, 4th Dragoon Guards, 24th August 1914. (RDG Museum)

Captain Archie Wright of A Squadron wrote about the different effects of the machine gun and the rifle fire and how they suffered most of their casualties on leaving Audregnies for the cottages:

> By the time the 4th had left the village, the whole of the enemy's infantry and guns were brought to bear on them. A Squadron being the last to start and being in *column of section* had to face a tremendous fire and lost very heavily, the most casualties occurring on the way to cottage at 'A', where there were heaps of wounded horses and men. After leaving 'A' we came under Maxim fire but it was nothing like as bad as the infantry fire which came like hail. Just before reaching 'A', my pony landed on the top of three horses and men rolling in the dust, and I thought I was down too, but he slithered over them and regained his feet bearing me safely through without a scratch. On reaching the factory the remaining officers rallied their men, or what was left of their men and got them safely away. [see Map 15] The officers of A Squadron all of whom went through the 'Joy Ride' were; Major Hunter (commanding), Captain Sewell, Captain Hardress-Lloyd, Captain Wright. Mr Gallagher only wounded and taken prisoner. Lieutenant S.J. Railston (18th Lancers, Indian Cavalry) and Mr Chance, the junior subaltern, who had his haversack shot away and a collar badge broken. He kept quite cool and in fact everyone behaved very well as it was probably the hottest fire any cavalry has been under. The whole affair was of course quite futile.[260]

Lieutenant Chance who had earlier seen the "Bull" with Captain Oldrey later recalled:

> C Squadron went to the left and at the forward gallop to seize some cottages…We formed *Column of Troops* at the gallop, drawn swords, I rode at the head of my troop with my troop sergeant (a remarkable man) beside me…the harvest was just over, and this was open country, a field in which the corn was in stooks. We went full gallop down a dusty road into this field. I wasn't aware of it but there were artillery shells bursting on us…[261]

While A and C Squadron and the two troops of B Squadron were all engaged with the advancing Germans, the lane was being secured. The other two troops of B Squadron, under Major Hutchison, had come into dismounted action on the north outskirts of the village, and came under heavy shell fire.[262]

The 9th Lancer's *charge* was to be launched in the direction of the sugar factory on the axis of the Roman road, a position held earlier in the morning by the 3rd Cavalry Brigade. This was to coincide with the 4th Dragoon Guards who were to make the attack on the left. They were seen to debouch from the village of Audregnies.'[263] The dismounted squadrons which were engaging *Infanterie Regiment 72,* who were now advancing south from Quiévrain, were given the order to "cease fire and retire", which we did and were just mounted when our Squadron Leader said "we are going to *charge* the guns."'[264] Lieutenant Colonel Campbell 'came along and said we

260 Capt. A. Wright diary (Property of RDG Museum), 24th August 1914, p.3.
261 Sir Roger Chance recorded recollections, Liddle Collection, University of Leeds, op. cit. in Richardson, *1914,* (Barnsley, Pen & Sword, 2013), p. 52.
262 Gibb, *Record of the 4th Irish Dragoon Guards in the Great War 1914-1918*, pp. 7-8.
263 Anon., 9th Lancer War Diary, 24th August 1914, p. 21.
264 Cpl. H. Easton diary, 24th August 1914, p. 38.

were going to *charge*, order to mount and move off in squadrons.'[265] 'A and C Squadrons were immediately given the order to mount. Both squadrons formed up in rear of some buildings, B Squadron remaining dismounted till a little later, A Squadron led the way in *line of troops column*.[266] Corporal Easton saw Lieutenant Colonel Campbell give the signal to canter, a circular under arm movement, as the whole line cantered he saw to his left the trumpeter of the 4th Dragoon Guards, Trumpeter Jack Patterson who had been a big friend back in Canterbury 'where his parents kept a pub.'[267] By the time the *charge* was in full swing all three squadrons were taking part, but it was impossible to keep any formation on account of the terrific fire they encountered.[268] Lieutenant Colonel Campbell wrote in his report:

> I saw the 4th Dragoon Guards debouching from the village, and I at once led my two squadrons forward. The distance to the nearest enemy was from 1000 to 1200 yards. As soon as we appeared, all the enemy took cover behind corn stooks etc. so that it was very difficult to perceive an objective. We advanced under terrific rifle and artillery fire, at least three batteries must have been in action. Owing to no objective being discernible and on account of the terrific fire to which we were being subjected we swung somewhat to the right, and finally came into position on some high mounds of cinders to our right front.[269]

Captain Peek said that the Commanding Officer followed my [A] squadron and then the other two,[270] and was 'out in front with his trumpeter.'[271] As the Regiment moved forward, they 'had just one artillery gun firing behind us in support.'[272] This was the half section of Lieutenant Preston from 119th Battery RFA. Captain Grenfell formed his squadron in *line of troops column* and C Squadron moved off at a trot and rode knee to knee, and could see figures moving about in the distance "Lance engage," and the squadron galloped 'shouting and cheering.'[273] Captain Grenfell's squadron galloped forward under most "fearful fire and soon became a confused mass." They were opposed by artillery, rifle fire and machine guns and could do nothing. Captain Grenfell's one thought was 'how to get the squadron in hand and as I could not find my trumpeter, I blew my whistle all the way and cursed anyone I saw out of his place.'[274] As they set off, both regiments consisting of two sqaudrons from the 4th Dragoon Guards and three from the 9th Lancers led by the Commanding Officer galloped forward towards the advancing German Infantry. As soon as the advanced they…were heavily shelled and fired on from their left flank.'[275]

265 LCpl W. Hunt diary, p. 5.
266 Grenfell, Grenfell Family Papers (within Lyttelton Family Papers), B Squadron 1st, A Squadron, Captain Lucas-Tooth 2nd and C Squadron, Major Abadie. See LCpl W. Hunt diary, p. 5.
267 Anglesey, *A History of the British Cavalry 1914–1919*, Vol. 7, p. 121.
268 Anon., 9th Lancer War Diary, 24th August 1914, p. 22.
269 TNA WO 95/1113/2: Lt Col. D.G.M. Campbell, Account of Audregnies, p. 1.
270 Capt. R.G. Peek diary, 24th August 1914..
271 Cpl H. Easton diary, 24th August 1914, p. 38.
272 Ibid., p. 28.
273 Pte Wells diary, p. 2.
274 Grenfell, Grenfell Family Papers (within Lyttelton Family Papers), 24th August 1914, p. 25.
275 Account of the Action at Élouges by Lieutenant Colonel Charles Burnett 18th QMO Hussars.

> We were travelling too fast towards a very large brick works which the officers leading us soon saw, as we neared the works, that the guns were behind and that the whole of the brick works was enclosed behind a large wire fence about eight to 10 feet high. We were again signalled "*troops, right wheel*", but we were by this time too fast and too near to execute this movement.[276] We got shelled and then got hung up in some barbed-wire [sic], and wheeled round and collected ourselves at a railway embankment by a big coal yard.'[277]

The 4th Dragoon Guards on the left of the road were 'closely packed together and dense volumes of dust were kicked up, choking us and making it impossible to see beyond the man in front. We were galloping into carnage, for nobody knew what we were supposed to be doing and there was utter confusion from the start.'[278] They were brought up by agricultural barbed-wire strung across the line of advance, so that horses were being pulled up. Lieutenant Chance endeavoured to control his almost runaway steed one handedly. Sergeant Talbot went down in a crashing somersault and Lieutenant Chance was halted by the wire, and had to veer right "in disorder like a flock of sheep." It was then that he saw a trooper, crouched in his saddle *blasted to glory* by a direct hit. When they finally came to a halt they rallied behind a heap of slag where Captain Sewell appeared, whose horse was coughing foam and blood. "My God what a show!" he remarked.'[279] Private Clouting had been unseated and had made it as far as the embankment and managed to get himself another horse which had belonged to the 9th Lancers:

> I hit the ground at full tilt and with my sword still firmly attached by a lanyard to my hand, was lucky not to impale myself. Dazed, I struggled to my feet and can now recall only an odd assortment of fleeting thoughts and sights, a single image of chaos. A riderless horse came careering in my direction and, collecting myself, I raised my hand in the air and shouted "halt" at the top of my voice. It was a 9th Lancer's horse, a shoeing smith's mount and wonderfully trained, for despite the pandemonium, it stopped on a sixpence.[280]

Private Clouting rode through the field to his right where he saw the mineral railway, but just as he was about to cross the line, 'I caught a voice crying out, "Cronkie, don't leave me." I turned and saw Thomas Cumber, one of my own troop. He'd been brought down on the railway line, and there he lay, prostrate, with one side of his face smashed in and bleeding profusely. I pulled up, jumped down and struggled to get him on his feet.'[281] When Private Clouting got down to attend to 'Cumber he had apparently broken several ribs in the fall, and was in severe pain. I managed to pull up another loose horse and with difficulty helped him to mount before we followed the railway line back out of the action.'[282]

Due to the presence of wire, the 9th Lancers swerved to the right where it assembled in two parts, one under the embankment with Captain Grenfell, and the other under Captain

276 Cpl. H. Easton diary, 24th August 1914, p. 38.
277 LCpl W. Hunt diary, p. 5.
278 Van Emden, *Teenage Tommy*, p. 52.
279 Brereton, *A History of the 4th and 7th Royal Dragoon Guards and Their Predecessors 1685-1980*, p. 313.
280 Van Emden, *Teenage Tommy*, p. 53.
281 Ibid., p. 53.
282 Ibid., p. 55.

Lucas-Tooth on a high mound of cinders on the right front.'[283] On the large slag heap was two troops of A Squadron of the 18th Hussars. When the lancers arrived at the Hussar's location redoubled fire immediately opened from the enemy's guns and 'the locality became a miniature volcano.'[284] Lieutenant Colonel Campbell was with Captain Lucas-Tooth's squadron:

> It was here that a considerable number of men of the 4th Dragoon Guards became intermingled with the 9th Lancers. Cover was taken in a donga[285] running east from the mound, in which 60 horses and men were subjected to a terrific bombardment. The mound, as it commanded this donga, therefore became a very important tactical point to hold if the men and horses were to be safely extricated. Lieutenant Colonel Campbell directed Captain Lucas-Tooth to hold the mound until he could secure reinforcements and explain the situation to the general.[286]

B Squadron under Captain Grenfell eventually came to a house behind which they tried to take cover, but the house was soon blown down so they moved off at a trot to a railway embankment where they collected the debris.[287] Private Bertie Cook, a reservist from the 9th Lancers, later told a relative at Whitstable that he had lost two horses in the *charge* but found a third horse which carried him through to safety under the railway embankment where he met Captain Grenfell. [288]

> We had simply galloped about like rabbits in front of a line of guns; men and horses fell in all directions. Most of one's time was spent in dodging the horses. I am glad to say we managed to get the squadron together and when ordered to trot, although under a heavy fire, no one hesitated. I remember that on one occasion my regiment was ordered to trot in South Africa to save the situation, the thought of this flashed across my mind. The embankment fortunately sheltered us from an appalling shell fire, as of course it formed a splendid target which was accurately ranged on. Quite close by, I found the rest of the Regiment with very few officers and found myself in command. We assembled together under the embankment in very good order and sorted ourselves out.[289]

Corporal Taylor thought the position was a good one as it 'gave plenty of cover.'[290] The embankment that Captain Grenfell had sought refuge in was the location of Captain Leveson's B Squadron of the 18th Hussars. They were situated at the west end of the cutting.[291] Captain Leveson had watched the *charge* but they had passed out of sight and then between five and 10 minutes later, the remnants of the *charge*, a mob of men and horses, many wounded, poured into the cutting. He recognised Captain Sewell of the 4th Dragoon Guards and Captain Grenfell

283 Anon., 9th Lancer War Diary, 24th August 1914, p. 22.
284 Burnett, *The Memoirs of the 18th (Queen Mary's Own) Royal Hussars 1906-1922*, p. 23.
285 A Boer War term, usually dry, eroded watercourse running only in times of heavy rain.
286 Anon., 9th Lancer War Diary, 24th August 1914, p. 22.
287 Grenfell, Grenfell Family Papers (within Lyttelton Family Papers), 24th August 1914, p. 25.
288 *Whitstable Times and Herne Bay Herald*, 24th October 1914 p. 2.
289 Grenfell, Grenfell Family Papers (within Lyttelton Family Papers), 24th August 1914, p. 25.
290 Cpl. R.H. Taylor letter to Mr Stuart Gruber, 11th January 1973, p 3.
291 Maj. Charles H. Leveson letter to Lt Col Soppers, 7th July 1918.

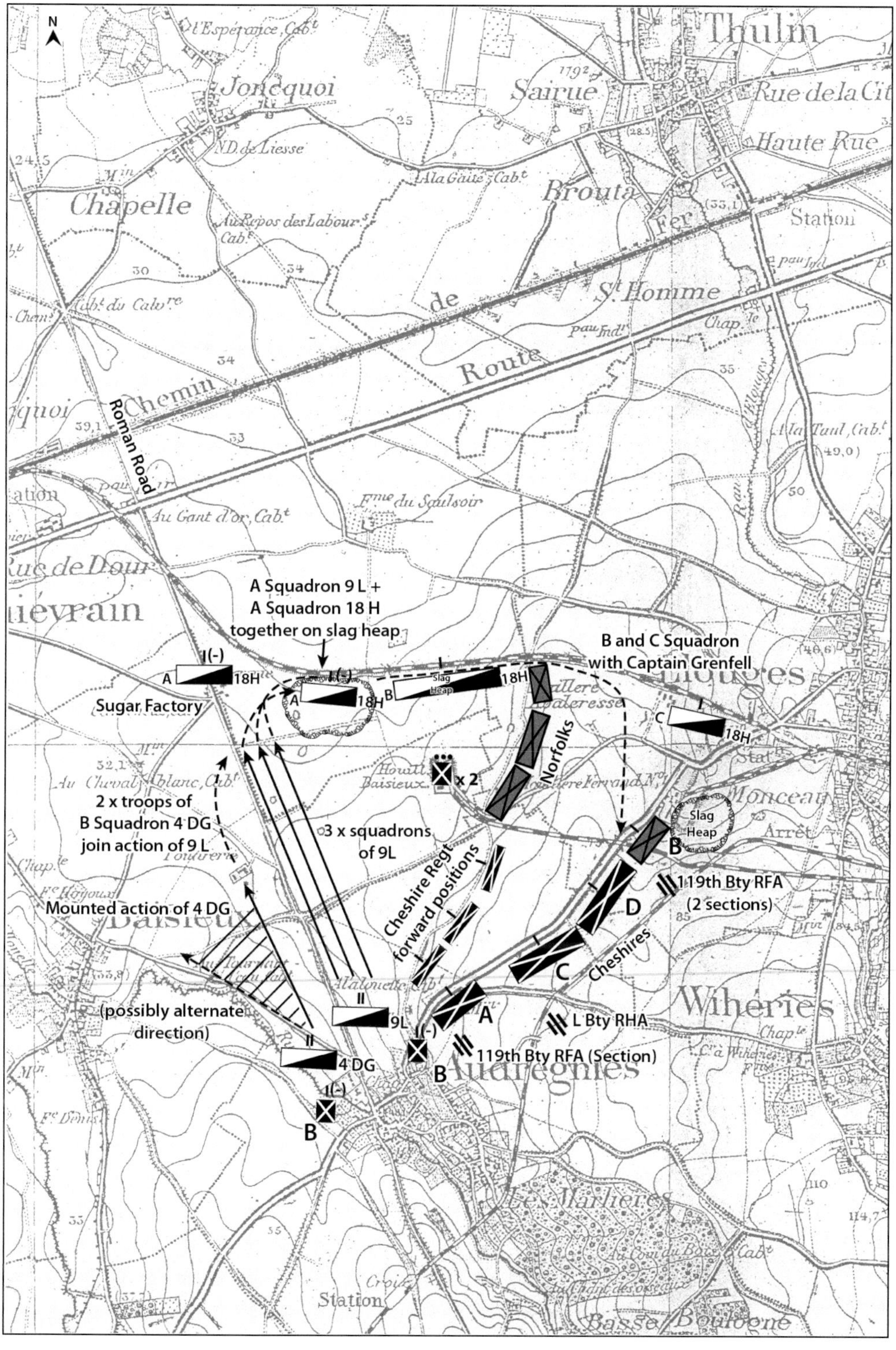


Map 16 Mounted actions of 2nd Cavalry Brigade. (Author)

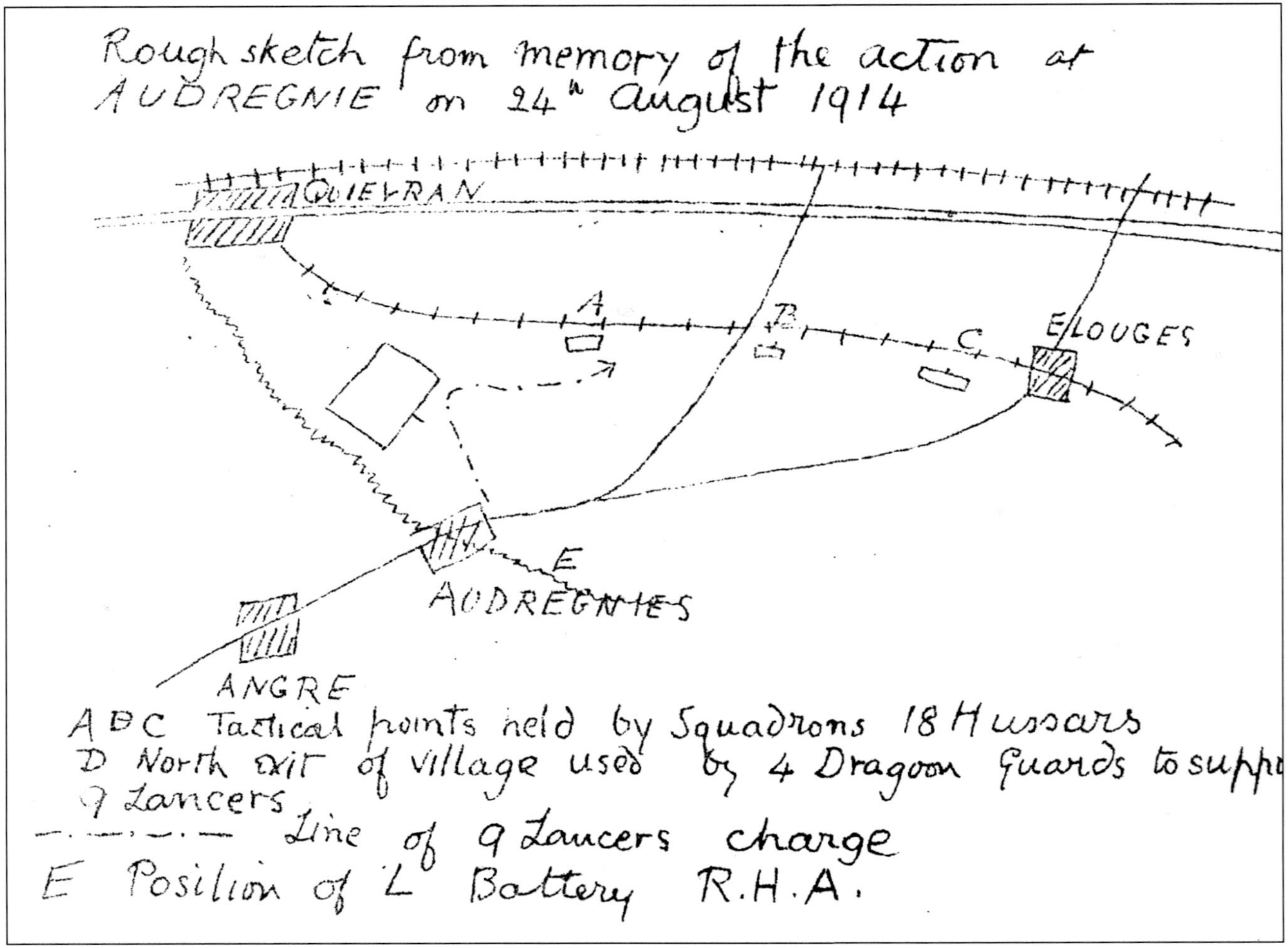


Map 17 9th Lancers: Rough sketch map derived from memory of the Action at Audregnies. (TNA WO 95/1113/2)

of the 9th Lancers and thought he saw Lieutenant Colonel Campbell of the 9th Lancers. The sheltering troops galloped down the cutting taking some of the 18th Hussars loose horses with them.[292]

The Cheshires, who had not long been in position, saw the cavalry to their fronts to the right front of D Company's advanced platoons. 'Momentarily they had to check fire so that the remnant of the cavalry who after the *charge* had been sheltering near some red sand hills in rear of the mineral railway which the enemy guns had shelled so effectively that horses and men were being sacrificed could get through.'[293] They also took the opportunity to adjust their positions. Driver W. Cryer, of 119th Battery 'said it was the most magnificent sight he ever saw...his battery was stationed at the foot the embankment, along the top of which ran the railway. After the *charge* the riderless horses careered madly along the railway, below which the battery was posted, screaming with pain or fright.[294] At the same time, soldiers of the 3rd Cavalry Brigade were to the north east of the mounted action of the lancers. It was a patrol from the 16th Lancers commanded by Lieutenant Dick Davies who had been detailed off 'to hold the ridge outside the village'[295] [Wiheries] and it was when Lieutenant Riddell went out to bring him in when 'he saw the *charge* of the 9th Lancers, which was held up by wire; a lot of their loose horses and those of the 4th Dragoon Guards came past us; one shot in eight places.'[296]

By 1200, *Infanterie Regiment 93,* having crossed the canal earlier in the morning, reached Quiévrain and were ordered to attack to the right of *Infanterie Regiment 72.* They reached Baisieux without opposition, but on leaving the town took artillery, machine gun and rifle fire from the heights west of Audregnies and the woods north of Angre.[297] The opposition *Infanterie Regiment 93* was experiencing was from the 3rd Cavalry Brigade. Earlier in the morning the brigade had moved at 0400 to a position of readiness centred on the sugar factory and the cluster of high slag heaps immediately to the east of it which lay approximately a mile and three quarters to the north of Audregnies on the Roman road.[298] Brigadier Gough posted the 16th Lancers to his front with a section of guns 'to take up a covering position.'[299] At 0730, the brigade retired through Baisieux to Angre, with the 16th Lancers acting as the advance guard[300] and had reached Rombies when it received its orders to return to the high ground in the vicinity of Audregnies.[301] The Brigade turned about with the 5th Lancers and 4th Hussars, while the 16th Lancers continued their retirement to Wiheries.[302] In anticipation, Lieutenant Horn took his Maxims from the wagons and moved them onto pack...something which he did not like and

292 Ibid.
293 Simpson, *Cheshire Regiment the First Battalion at Mons and the Miniature Colour,* p. 36.
294 *Yorkshire Post and Leeds Intelligencer* dated Friday 18th September 1914.
295 Lt R.A.J. Beech, *Diary of Lieutenant Beech,* 24th August 1914.
296 Ibid.
297 Zuber, The Mons Myth: A Reassessment of the Battle, p. 190.
298 Edmonds, *Military Operations France and Belgium 1914,* Vol. I, pp. 100-101.
299 Farrar-Hockley, *Goughie,* p. 125.
300 TNA WO 95/1134/2, 24th August 1914.
301 Edmonds, *Military Operations France and Belgium 1914,* Vol. I, p. 100.
302 TNA WO 95/1134/3, 24th August 1914.

he wrote in his diary "don't like "pack," as horses drawing limbers get dead beat, also guns get knocked about by passing vehicles on the road.'[303]

Once the Brigade was in position, Brigadier Gough sent out an officer patrol to make contact with the 5th Infantry Division at Élouges. It had been reported that gaps were forming so they started to move nearer and Brigadier Gough knew that Brigadier De Lisle was coming up on his left.[304] General Allenby had given Brigadier Gough orders to check the enemy's advance. The 4th Hussars were ordered to part [sic] the infantry, while the 5th Lancers crossed the stream and got up on the high ground to the left. The machine guns of both regiments were firing down the valley towards Baisieux. The guns of D Battery RHA had come into action on the hill behind.[305] At 1400, the 5th Lancers marched to Angre, where the Regiment came into dismounted action against German infantry in superior numbers.[306] As soon as *Infanterie Regiment 93* moved out of the town they 'took artillery, machine gun and rifle fire from the heights west of Audregnies and the woods north of Angre. The Regiment advanced in quick bounds, with 10 *Kompanie* swinging right towards Angre. II Battalion remained in brigade reserve. I Battalion had been committed to the left of II Battalion and advanced with 1 *Kompanie* and 2 *Kompanie* online, 3 *Kompanie* following in the middle and 4 *Kompanie* echeloned left. It too soon took shrapnel fire, but continued a rapid advance. The enemy was dismounted cavalry, which quickly vacated its positions.'[307]

The weight of the combined fire halted the Germans and the advance was 'checked temporarily'[308] but eventually they were forced to retire back through the village, where the Commanding Officer, Lieutenant Colonel Parker, was wounded.[309] The 4th Hussars were directed to gallop and seize the spur between the Honnelle and St Pierre rivers running out towards Baisieux. C Squadron was ordered to line the small wood half a mile north east of Angre while the remaining squadrons galloped across the enemy's front until they reached a sunken road running from Onnerjies to Baisieux, where they dismounted and sent the horses back up the ridges and extended the right of C Squadron. As the two squadrons crossed in front of Baisieux they came under intense rifle and machine gun fire from the village. The Regiment remained in position for the next two hours engaging the infantry as they advanced south. The regimental machine guns under Lieutenant North were in action with the other machine guns of the brigade on their left. At approximately 1430, the 4th Hussars were told to break off the action and retire. This was done with great difficulty owing to the heavy fire they were still receiving. During the action and retirement, the Regiment suffered 35 casualties and had 45 horses wounded or killed. Amongst the wounded were Lieutenants Faulkner and Bibby. All the wounded who were unable to ride had to be left behind as there was no other means of

303 Lt T.L. Horn, *Diary of the Regiment, 16th (The Queens) Lancers, 4th August – 18th October 1914*, 24th August 1914.
304 TNA WO 95/1153/2, 24th August 1914.
305 Ibid.
306 TNA WO 95/1134/2, 5th Lancers War Diary, 24th August 1914.
307 Zuber, *The Mons Myth,* p.190.
308 TNA WO 95/1134/2, 24th August 1914.
309 Col. J.R. Harvey & Lt. Col. H.A. Cape, '*The History of the 5th (Royal Irish) Regiment of Dragoons from 1689 to 1799, afterwards the 5th Royal Irish Lancers from 1858 to 1921* (Aldershot: Gale & Polden, 1923), pp. 237-238.

conveying them and they fell into the hands of the advancing Germans.[310] The 4th Hussars war diary noted 'casualties chiefly C Squadron. No artillery was employed against us and no patrols out in the direction of enemy who engaged with us…Retired through Roisin being shelled *en-route*.[311]

Bombardier Saville Crowsley from D Battery RHA wrote 'the right section under Lieutenant Maxwell took up a position north west of Audregnies and engaged German infantry advancing, hosts of them, and did great execution. The battery then retired further back and took up a position in a cornfield, got heavily shelled, difficult to get out of action.' As the section was trying to extricate itself, the centre section under Lieutenant Palmer was ordered to retire to cover the retreat of the other four guns, this was done. Bombardier Crowley was detached to Lieutenant Palmer as a signaller:[312]

> I was sent as signaller to this section to get into communication with the remainder of the battery which was a difficult task. I had to climb the house of the gate keeper at a level crossing and sit aside the gable of the roof before I could be seen by the other signallers. After an elapse of about 20 minutes, we received a message from the battery for the section to "limber up and prepare to advance at any moment." I repeated this order to Lieutenant Palmer, who thought they must be mad, but carried the order out when the signal was given, to move forward with the 16th Lancers to get round the German right flank. The two guns were halted in rear of the village. I had to assist Lieutenant Palmer to select a position, leaving our horses in rear of a large house with his horse holder. I cut down a wire fence in a few places so as to make it easy to get away, should he decide to move that way…One fell at our heels as we managed to just get clear at the corner of the wall surrounding the house. We then went back to the rear of the house and saw the colonel in charge of the cavalry [Lieutenant Colonel N.L. MacEwan]…Lieutenant Palmer told the colonel he would bring his guns into action at the top of the village, left me to bring orders should there be any. He did not stay in action long before the German artillery sent a very heavy fire at the guns so they had to retire to the rear of the village as it was impossible to stay in action. The right and left sections went into action in the open near Angre and, being completely missed by the fire of the German artillery, did great execution against an infantry advance. After a time, the left section under Lieutenant Walwyn was moved to the left to cover a valley and some dead ground on our left, firing with great effect, completely checking for a time a strong infantry advance up the valley. The right section under Lieutenant Maxwell was then moved still more to our left doing some good work against cavalry and infantry. The two sections between them fired 350 rounds with good effect.[313]

At the sugar factory, with the remnants that could be rallied from the 9th Lancers' mounted action, Captain Lucas-Tooth and A Squadron held the mound on their own as the General had not been found, and no reinforcements were sent. The enemy kept up an intense shell fire,

310 Capt. H.K.D. Evans, and N.O. Laing, *The 4th (Queen's Own) Hussars in the Great War*, (Uckfield: Naval & Military Press reprint of 1920 edition), pp. 4-5.
311 TNA WO 95/1134/4: 4H War Diary, 24th August 1914.
312 Hutton, *The Gunners of August 1914*, pp. 63-64
313 Ibid., pp. 63-64.

concentrating it mainly on the sugar factory and on the mound, and the rifle fire was also "very severe." There were many more horses than the ground could accommodate, and they were all now massed together. The fierce fire to which they were subjected caused a good number of them to stampede. A confused mob of riderless horses and perspiring footmen in pursuit was streaming away towards the south east.[314] When Lieutenant Colonel Campbell returned, he found the position being gallantly held. When the fire of the approaching infantry became too hot and the squadron was in danger of being surrounded, Captain Lucas-Tooth "withdrew his squadron with the greatest coolness under most trying circumstances."[315] Lieutenant Colonel Bennet also went to the factory where his squadron was and ordered Major Stewart to retire when he could do so in safety.[316] While Lieutenant Colonel Campbell had been looking for the General, he 'had met Lieutenant Grenfell and Captain Reynolds. He told them to rally as many men as they could find and disentangle the men of the 9th from among the men of the 4th Dragoon Guards in the donga.'[317]

During the *charge*, C Squadron was lead by Major Abadie. He had been unseated but had been given a horse by Sergeant Pickering who had "dismounted under heavy shrapnel and rifle fire and gave his horse to his Squadron Leader following the squadron until he secured a loose horse.'[318] This gallant act was particularly important as the Squadron Leader's presence was urgently required in rallying his men.[319] Corporal Taylor wrote about the *charge*:

> Horses and men were falling in great numbers, mostly horses losing their heads and getting out of control. My Squadron Leader Major Abadie came down but was able to mount on a spare horse. We galloped at full speed for about 1000 yards. Finally reaching an old town house which had been used for an observation post. Here the shells were bursting all round us, expecting every minute to see the house fall. Again, we got the order to form line. We were now only a matter of a few yards from their infantry, but as the shell fire was so murderous it was deemed advisable to retire by troop at 100 yards interval during the retirement the Regiment was broken up, a railway separating us. We reached a bridge over this railway with the roads running underneath and here we remained for some time awaiting further orders. Captain Francis Grenfell who was the senior officer took charge of us now being roughly 100 men we now changed our position coming into "dismounted Action." On the ridge of the railway here Captain Grenfell did some remarkably splendid work. Always cool, he put confidence into his men.[320]

During the *charge,* Captain Peek of A Squadron, 9th Lancers was thrown from his horse. Fortunately not much damage was done but *Joshua* got hit twice and threw him. Captain Peek was eventually found by a Hauptmann Rogge of *Infanterie Regiment 72* who left two of his men

314 Brig. Gen. C. Burnett, *The Memoirs of the 18th (Queen Mary's Own) Royal Hussars 1906-1922* (Winchester, Warren & Sons, 1926), p. 23.
315 Anon, 9th Lancers War Diary, 24th August 1914, p. 23.
316 Burnett, The Memoirs of the 18th (Queen Mary's Own) Royal Hussars 1906-1922, p. 23.
317 Anon., 9th Lancer War Diary, 24th August 1914, p. 23.
318 Backdated Military Medal Citation for Audregnies, *The London Gazette,* 11th October 1916.
319 TNA WO 95/1113/2: Lt Col. D.G.M. Campbell, Account of Audregnies, p. 3.
320 Cpl. R.H. Taylor letter of Sergeant 'Spur' R.H. Taylor, p. 3.

with him and his water bottle full of excellent wine.[321] A member of Captain Peek's troop later wrote a letter home on 11th September which appeared in *The Times* on the 18th:

> We have received the following letter, dated September 11, written to a friend in this country by a corporal in the 9th Lancers…I had a charmed life, horse shot under me and my saddle blanket drilled through…Lieut Peek [sic] is missing and several of our troop… It was magnificent but horrible. The Regiment was swept away before 1,000 yards was covered, and at 200 yards from the guns I was practically alone, myself, three privates, and an officer out of our squadron…A young chap in my troop had four horses killed under him within an hour…A peculiar feeling, that we were returning from Waterloo.[322]

Corporal Harry Easton was also captured. The 'German infantry had come from behind, their positions behind the German artillery, and were advancing in close order and had captured me and sundry other dismounted cavalrymen.'[323] Major Bridges during the *charge* received a heavy blow in the face when he was thrown by his horse. When he regained consciousness, he found himself, inside the cottage:

> Which held one or two Red Cross orderlies and some wounded, whose rifles had been piled in a corner. There was also an old Frenchman and his wife who had put up the shutters, for bullets were pattering against the walls. Stiff and sore, I got a man to help me on to a chair where I could see through the fanlight over the door. I could scarcely believe my eyes. Marching through the corn in open order and perfect formation, with fixed bayonets glinting in the sun, were line upon line of grey-green German infantry. The nearest could not have been 200 yards away. This sight galvanised me into action, and the back door being barricaded, I went through the open window like the clown in a pantomime.[324]

Major Bridges left the cottage, still dazed but managed to get himself another mount and made his way back towards Audregnies:

> Here I found rather a shamble of men and horses in the road. There was a chestnut horse with a wound in the shoulder standing patiently among the gooseberry bushes in the garden. I struggled onto his back and ambled off at a slow canter, pursued by a hot fire which, however, did not touch us. In front of me, I could see Farrier-Sergeant Old just disappearing into the village. I saw him do some very excellent work pulling wounded men under cover and have a hazy recollection of being helped into a house by him. Later, Old and I joined up again in the village, and made our way out of it along the railway line on to the hill behind. Here I rested in the garden of a little *estaminet* and could see various bodies of our cavalry collecting themselves in the distance.

321 Capt. R.G. Peek diary, 24th August 1914.
322 *The Times*, 18th September 1914.
323 Cpl. H. Easton diary, 24th August 1914, p. 39.
324 Bridges, *Alarms and Excursions,* p. 82.

The advance of the *Infantry Brigade 13, Infanterie Regiment 26 and 66* on the right of the Norfolks, was beginning to be felt. At 1340, 3 Battery, *Feldartillerie Regiment 40* and all of II Battalion moved into the *Infanterie Regiment 26* firing line, west of the Thulin-Élouges road.[325] From this position, the Regiment in support of *Infanterie Brigade 13*, would fire 233 shrapnel and 91 rounds of HE ammunition.[326] At approximately 1400, Lieutenant Colonel Ballard was getting concerned:

> I began to feel anxious, so sent Captain Robert Brudenell-Bruce to see what was going on. He came back very soon with serious news; there were no signs of our 5th Infantry Division, which had certainly left its original position; masses of German were within a quarter of a mile of our right flank; it looked as if we must be surrounded almost at once. Though the urgency of the moment had not given Captain Brudenell-Bruce time to reconnoitre for it turned out afterwards that his report was perfectly correct. Later on, we learnt that several messages from the brigade and division had failed to reach us. A minutes' talk with Captain Brudenell-Bruce was sufficient to show that the situation was bad, and I began to issue orders for a retreat.[327]

At the Norfolks battalion headquarters, Captain Thomas Bowlby of C Company informed Lieutenant Colonel Ballard with a message from Captain Luard of C Company that the German infantry were closing on his right flank,[328] and the leading troops were within a few hundred yards of their position. Elements of *Infanterie Brigade 13* (*Infanterie Regiments 26* and *66*) were seen advancing on Élouges and, in a short time, would be engaging the Norfolks. At 1430[329], Lieutenant Colonel Ballard ordered a general withdrawal to the south east and[330] sent his Adjutant Captain Cresswell, over to Major Alexander, the Commander of the 119th Battery 'with orders to limber up and gallop off at once.'[331] Lieutenant Colonel Ballard also despatched messages by cycle orderly at the same time as he sent his Adjutant, but the man was never heard of again. Having sent his orders by two different routes, Lieutenant Colonel Ballard was easier in mind, and felt free to organise his own withdrawal.[332] At approximately 1430, Captain Grenfell and some of his own squadron and C Squadron had wheeled around to the right and were sheltered amongst the slag heaps and had reformed by the bridge. It was here he spoke to Lieutenant Colonel Ballard and volunteered[333] to use his squadron of the 9th Lancers as rear party 'for 15 minutes while the Norfolks retired.'[334] The enemy were only 200 yards from the Norfolk's right flank. Lieutenant Colonel Ballard noticed that 119th Battery RFA were still firing and Captain Cresswell had not returned so went to inform Major Alexander himself to retire. When he got there, he 'found that Cresswell had been mortally wounded before he could

325 Zuber, *The Mons Myth*, p. 191.
326 Ibid., p. 191.
327 Lt. Col. C.R. Ballard, Account of Audregnies, p. 17.
328 Lt. Col. C.R. Ballard, Account of Audregnies, Rough War Diary, p. 4
329 TNA WO 95/1571/1: 1st Cheshire Regiment War Diary.
330 Ibid., p. 4.
331 Ballard *Rough War Diary*, 24th August 1914: "Body left under railway bridge", p. 6.
332 Crookenden, *The History of the Cheshire Regiment in the Great War*, p. 9
333 Lt. Col. C.R. Ballard, Account of Audregnies Rough War Diary, p. 5.
334 Ibid., p. 5.

give his message. 'I saw him lying on a stretcher, quite unconscious and at the last gasp; it was a bad shock for he was the best of my friends and a most valued Adjutant.'[335] Lieutenant Colonel Ballard sent another orderly to tell Lieutenant Colonel Boger of this, but he, too, failed to reach his destination. Lieutenant Colonel Ballard had struggled all day to get his messages through. He 'had previously sent five messages by orderly to brigade and divisional headquarters, but only one of them was received.'[336] 119th Battery RFA was positioned to the rear of the Norfolks reserve company on the high ground to the east of the colliery.[337] Lieutenant Preston's section had been detached for most of the day and was to the west at Audregnies. Major Alexander with his remaining two sections of four guns 'had been engaged in a duel with the German artillery, at first with two batteries near Quiévrain, of which one was silenced except for one gun.'[338]

As the afternoon had developed and the *rear guard* had withdrawn 'the Germans were able to bring up a battery to near Bois de Boussu, which enfiladed the 119th Battery position.'[339] The battery was also enfiladed by another battery on its right flank.[340]*Infanterie Battalions 26* and *66* were now advancing and 9 *Kompanie, Infanterie Regiment 72* were 'on the mining dumps 400-600 yards away.'[341] There was now concentrated fire from three batteries on the position of 119th Battery and considerable rifle fire from the infantry. A leutnant from *4 Battery Feldartillerie Regiment 40* wrote 'the first rounds strike with colossal effect; the poor fellows, we see ammunition caissons and men blown into the air…the effectiveness of our fire was frightful.'[342] By the time Lieutenant Colonel Ballard had given the order for the detachment to retire they were only capable of withdrawing one gun at a time.[343] 'Lieutenant Pollard, who had been trying to devise means to save his guns, came to where the lancers were resting, and put the matter before them. Captain Grenfell heard the lieutenant's request. 'We have no harnesses or ropes and cannot pull them out without it. Our horses, with their harnesses are further down the down the embankment, but the Germans have our range so exactly, that we cannot bring the horses up.[344] The wagon lines had been moved earlier in the afternoon to a hollow by the railway line by Captain John Colquhoun Walford, where they would be sheltered from enemy fire.[345] Captain Grenfell climbed carefully to the top of the embankment and surveyed the position.[346] Once he has ascertained the situation, Captain Grenfell found the battery commander, Major Alexander and said 'that he could rely on them to act as his escort or do anything that he wanted.'[347]

335 Lt. Col. C.R. Ballard, Account of Audregnies, p. 16.
336 Crookenden, *The History of the Cheshire Regiment in the Great War*, p. 9.
337 It is this statement which accurately positions the location of Major Alexander's two sections of guns.
338 TNA WO 95/1532: 5th Division Artillery War Diary, p. 13.
339 Ibid., p.13.
340 Unattributed 119th Battery account p. 73.
341 Ibid., p. 73.
342 Zuber, *The Mons Myth*, p. 192.
343 TNA WO 95/1532: 5th Division Artillery War Diary, p. 13.
344 *The Delhi Spearman*, August 1927.
345 Paul Oldfield, *Victoria Crosses on the Western Front August 1914–April 1915: A Guide to the Locations – From Mons to Hill 60* (Barnsley: Pen & Sword, 2014), p 25.
346 Prof. Albert Bushnell Hart, *Harper's Pictorial Library of the World War: Deeds of Heroism and Daring* (United Kingdom: ReInk Books reprint of 1920 edition), p. 13.
347 Anon., 9th Lancer War Diary, 24th August 1914, p. 16.

Just at this moment Captain Grenfell was wounded "I got hit by shrapnel. It felt as if a whip had hit me in the hand and leg, I think the artery was affected as the blood spurted out and my observer, Steedman, very kindly bound me up," Captain Grenfell found it amusing that in their training, the only place they had not learnt how to stop bleeding was the hand. 'We also had to put on a tourniquet and referred to the *Field Service Regulations* to find out how it was put on.'[348] Captain Grenfell had been affected by his wound. 'Things began to go round and round and I luckily remembered that in the wallet of the horse I had borrowed I had noticed a flask. This proved to contain a bottle of the best old brandy and my observer and I at once drank the lot. I now felt like *Jack Johnson*[349] instead of feeling a cripple.'[350] Once he had had his wound dressed, Major Alexander asked Captain Grenfell to find if there was an exit for his guns.'[351] To do this Captain Grenfell went out on his own and 'it was not a very nice job I am bound to say, I was relieved when it was finished.[352] The task 'meant leaving my Regiment on the embankment and riding out alone through the guns which were now out of action and were heavily shelled all the time to some distance behind where I found myself out of range of the shells.'[353] Once he had found the exit 'it was necessary to go back through the inferno as slowly as possible so as to pretend to the men that there was no danger and that the gun shells were more noisy than effective…the Battery Commander told me that the only way to save his guns was to manhandle them to some cover.[354] While Captain Grenfell was away another officer who he had spoken to was also returning to the battery when Corporal Taylor wrote that he had 'hardly reached his battery when a shell blew him to pieces.[355]

Captain Grenfell went back to his squadron and ordered them to dismount in front of their horses and called for volunteers. He reminded them that the 9th Lancers had saved the guns at Maiwand and had gained the eternal friendship of the gunners by always standing by the guns in South Africa and had great traditions to fulfil, as the Colonel had reminded us before they had left Tidworth.[356] Captain Grenfell had no problem finding volunteers from the soldiers of his own squadron and those of C Squadron who were intermingled with his own. 'Every single man and officer stated they were ready to go to what looked like certain destruction.'[357] Having selected the number he wanted and left the rest with their horses, he went up the hill again with his men 40-50[358] on foot.'[359] One gun was run back by the men of the battery and the 9th Lancers assisted in the running back of most of the guns and most of the wagons.[360] They 'formed the men in sections and doubled out to the guns. It was found one gun and a limber had to be left behind as the men were not sufficient, and therefore the sections went out a second time. The second time the sections went out the remaining gun and limber were brought in and also three gunners who

348 Ibid., p. 16.
349 Jack Johnson was the first African American heavyweight boxing champion (1908-1915)
350 Ibid., p. 17.
351 Ibid., p. 17.
352 Ibid., p. 17.
353 Ibid., p. 17.
354 Ibid., p. 17.
355 Cpl. R.H. Taylor letter of Sergeant 'Spur' R.H. Taylor, p. 4.
356 Anon, *9th Lancer Diary*, 24th August, p. 17.
357 Ibid., p. 18.
358 TNA WO 95/1532: 5th Division Artillery War Diary, p. 13.
359 *The Delhi Spearman*, August 1927.
360 Unattributed 119th Battery account p. 73.

were the only three who were forward to be left alive.'[361] 'This was carried out under a very heavy fire, and the guns had to be slowly turned around before we could guide them. We accomplished our object. We pushed one out over the dead gunners. I do not think we lost more than three or four men. One shell came around under the guns at which Eric Smith and two men were pushing. We were all knocked down but nothing further happened.'[362] 'All the guns were gotten out, except one limber and wagon which were damaged by the enemy's shells,'[363] while retiring.'[364] Corporal Taylor wrote that they left their horses behind 'one man to four:'[365]

> Six men were required for each gun. We extended out and ran into the open over very hard and stubble ground. Our brave Captain cheering us on as we went forth to do our duty. As we advanced on the guns, we met with another horrible thunderous fire but thank God we had not one casualty. A terrible sight met our eyes when we arrived at this spot, only four guns could be saved out of six and only one man alive and he had only just enough breath left to say "let me die, you cannot do anything for me." The remainder of the brave fellows had all fallen and were laying scattered about, their guns having performed their duties as brave and gallant men for King and country against such an overwhelming force. We limbered up and got the guns away as quickly as possible and thank God we were protected and guided safely through such a terrible time.[366]

In a letter home, Lieutenant Pollard wrote to his father recounting the part he has played at Élouges:

> We gave and received a terrific fire, and many experts say it was a very hot place indeed. When finally ordered away after about an hour of it, it was quite impossible to get horses near the guns, so I was sent down to ask some cavalry who were sheltering with our teams if they would help pull the guns out by hand. I found a most gallant captain and we collected volunteers, while the major started bringing down a gun with what men we had left. The captain and I then rushed up with more men, and we got away all the guns and most of the wagons as far as our sheltered teams. We then had to get the whole show away over a crest under a heavy fire, so I among others went up first to find the way. I couldn't find either of my horses at the moment, so I mounted a battery horse, and you would have shrieked with laughter to see me trying to kick a trot out of the obstinate old horse, who wouldn't leave the others, with shells bursting all round. I hadn't even a sword or a signalling flag to beat him with. However, by dint of huge kicks I got there and back, and then off we went at a steady trot. All got away except one wagon, which they dropped a shell on. Two wagons went straight over a railway line, jumping the hedge and little ditch. We then went through a village under fire, with the chimneys falling off the houses on us. The major and I were absolutely untouched; the captain got a bullet through each arm, very slight, but a shell

361 Maj. E.W. Alexander, Letter, p. 97.
362 Anon., 9th Lancer War Diary, 24th August 1914, p. 18.
363 TNA WO 95/1532: 5th Division Artillery War Diary, p. 14.
364 Unattributed 119th Battery account.
365 Cpl. R.H. Taylor letter to Mr Stuart Gruber dated 11th January 1973, p 3.
366 Cpl. R.H. Taylor letter of Sergeant 'Spur' R.H. Taylor, pp. 4-5.

> burst just over his head, and the shock hurt him a lot and knocked him flat, though the bullets, etc…all went on and missed him. Of the two other subalterns, one was with the baggage, poor fellow, and missed it all, while the other had a most splendid show with his own section, and unfortunately got hit three times. Although hit and riding on a limber, he stopped his guns and covered a cavalry retirement, finally getting both guns away safe.[367]

On receipt of his son's letter, Mr Alfred Pollard wrote to Captain Grenfell to thank him for 'having saved Geoff. from the bitterness of losing his guns.' Francis Grenfell wrote back to him while he was convalescing in London on 12th March 1915 having heard of Geoffrey's death on 24th October 1914 at La Bassée:

> My dear Mr Pollard,
>
> Your letter was the one I most appreciated of many very kind letters I have received. I have been very unwell, and so I hope you will forgive my not having written before, as I have been twice wounded, and lately had to undergo another operation, but am now on the right road, and hope soon to be back and at 'em again. I did not know your son, nor for some time what the battery was. It was our good fortune to be thrown by providence (after a good hard fight which threw us into complete confusion) behind a railway embankment, near the 119th Battery. They were occasionally firing and then, I believe, stopped. The brave way the two officers there behaved, and the dignified way the guns, still challenging, remained there, filled me with an admiration which I know will last a lifetime. No English regiment could have stood by without saying 'Can we give you a hand?' Had the senior officer done so he would not have been an Englishman. What we did was forced on us by the splendid example of the battery, which had been sat there by their two officers. The world is not curious for honour does not always go where it is due. Your son did much more, and deserved much more than I did, for I only followed his example. I can appreciate the great sorrow that has fallen on you and Mrs Pollard in the loss of a son who has done what we would all like to do – die for England. Please accept my greatest sympathy and gratitude for your kind letter.
>
> Yours sincerely,
>
> Francis Grenfell[368]

The casualties for the whole battery, including Lieutenant Preston's section, was two officers and 48 men killed or wounded and four men missing. Their horses had suffered terribly.[369] Sergeant Bert Walker, of the battery, wrote from hospital in Barmen, Germany to say that he has been 'wounded by shrapnel in the face and injured also about the body when the wheels of a gun carriage passed over him.'[370]

367 Pollard, *Two Brothers,* pp. 22-24.
368 Ibid., pp. 34-35.
369 Unattributed 119th Battery account.
370 *Manchester Evening News*, 26th October 1914.

Eventually, Captain Lucas-Tooth, who had been away to find Lieutenant Colonel Campbell, reappeared and took command. He brought the guns down under the embankment to where the teams had retired under cover. The drivers then limbered them up and withdrew them at the gallop. Battery Quartermaster Sergeant H. Morgan 'under heavy shell and rifle fire limbered up the guns section, and then brought up limbers and teams for other four guns, enabling them to be got away.'[371] For this he was recognised for his gallantry with the award of a DCM. Sergeant Davids and Turner of the 9th Lancers were also award the DCM for 'gallant conduct in assisting to save the guns of the 119th Battery RHA near Dour on August 24th, by manhandling them into shelter, only three gunners of the battery being alive.' Captain Walford was wounded twice[372] and his gallantry was also recognised with the award of a DSO for his actions at Élouges.[373] After the action, Major Alexander wrote in his report the 4th September 'I have the honour to send the following report on the assistance rendered by B and C Squadrons of the 9th Lancers to 119th Battery, RFA. B Squadron waited until all the battery had left and then retired. I consider Captain Grenfell's conduct most excellent and the help he and his men gave was most valuable. In my opinion he ought to receive the Victoria Cross for his action,'[374] Major Alexander was nominated by Lieutenant Colonel Ballard and was recognised for:

> Conspicuous bravery and great ability at Élouges on the 24th August 1914, when the *flank guard* was attacked by a German corps, in handling his battery against overwhelming odds with such conspicuous success that all his guns were saved, notwithstanding that they had to be withdrawn by hand by himself and three other men. This enabled the retirement of the 5th Infantry Division to be carried out without serious loss. Subsequently Lieutenant Colonel Alexander (then Major) rescued a wounded man[375] under a heavy fire, with the greatest gallantry and devotion to duty.[376]

Captain Lucas-Tooth gave the guns about 200 yards start and withdrew the Regiment in succession of squadrons in *extended order*.[377] When Lieutenant Allfrey returned to collect his horse, he found out that it had been shot and wrote 'so I go on foot, shoot at two Germans, 200 yards away with revolver, and they bolt…eventually get on to a transport wagon of East Surrey Regiment and so on to where I came across the remainder of the Regiment near St Waast(?).[378]

Captain Lucas-Tooth wrote 'as the German infantry was now closing in on the position there was nothing left but to get out with the guns in front of us. We eventually retired out of range and wandered about for some time looking for someone to give us orders and halted by a main road along which was marching an infantry column.'[379] At this point Captain Grenfell did not feel strong enough to command his squadron and so went to the ambulance to have his

371 *Western Mail*, 11th November 1914.
372 *The Standard*, 12th November 1914, p. 6.
373 *Western Mail* dated Wednesday 11th November 1914.
374 Alexander Report, 1654-5.
375 Lt. Col. C.R. Ballard, Account of Audregnies Rough War Diary, 24th August 1914: "For gallantry in bringing in Private Dack, Norfolk Regiment who was seriously wounded", p. 7.
376 *London Gazette*, 18th February 1915.
377 Maj. E.W. Alexander, Letter, p. 97.
378 Lt F. de V.B. Allfrey diary, 24th August 1914.
379 Anon., 9th Lancer War Diary, 24th August 1914, p. 16.

wounds attended to. He later wrote that "I never regretted anything more than being forced to leave my squadron." At approximately 1445, Lieutenant Colonel Ballard considered the task in hand, 'the heat was terrific, not a breath of wind, not a cloud in the sky. With the prospect of a long march in front of us, I felt much afraid that the men, who had been on outposts all night and on their feet since dawn, would straggle and be cut off.'[380] So, with 'a view to lightening their task, orders were given to dump on the ground all packs and equipment, keeping only rifles and ammunition.'[381] The heat of the day was also affecting Lieutenant Colonel Ballard. 'For a moment I felt that the heat would knock me out and I remember flinging away my collar and tie in desperate anxiety not to be left behind, which would mean falling into the hands of the enemy. Fortunately just then my groom and horse appeared and once, in the saddle, I felt all right.'[382] After putting Captain Cresswell's body under the railway bridge on the road, he gave the order for the battalion to retire. The battalion withdrew and 'the companies assembled in good order on the road north of Wiheries, but as that village was being heavily shelled I ordered them to sheer off to the east along a little valley that ran past the houses.'[383] However, not all the soldiers decided to remove their packs. Private Hurrell hung onto his. 'Most fellows threw their packs away…because the weight combined with the terrific heat got them down. The real reason I retained mine was that I carried several gold sovereigns and hated the thoughts of losing them and other things that were inside.'[384] He was also convinced that the pack had saved his life. 'I felt sure and knew it was that pack with all its contents that saved my life. My overcoat was riddled with bullets, my canteen had many holes and even a stray bent one inside. So, my ultimate conclusion was that my love for money had saved my life on this occasion, in spite of the fact that I wasn't rich.'[385]

As he retired, Lieutenant Colonel Ballard came across 'parties of stragglers which included several dismounted cavalrymen who told him that the 2nd Cavalry Brigade was retiring to the south and that they believed that the Cheshires were with them.'[386] Never at any time did Lieutenant Colonel Ballard doubt that Lieutenant Colonel Boger had not received his messages and, indeed, he thought he had taken every precaution to ensure that they got through, even though he had received no confirmation. He was also unaware that Lieutenant Briard's platoon of D Company on the far right had not received the orders to withdraw either. The German artillery had now found the correct range of the road and it was being bombarded by both high explosives and shrapnel. As the Germans were coming in on the flanks, they re-sited their 'machine guns in positions from which cross-fire could be brought to bear upon any target which presented itself. Any movement was greeted by machine gun fire, ever increasing in intensity.'[387] The only route between the companies and two regiments was the Élouges-Audregnies road. Any orderlies who made for the sunken road'[388] which was the 'the main artery of lateral communication was either incapacitated while crossing the

380 Lt. Col. C.R. Ballard, Account of Audregnies, p. 18.
381 Ibid., p. 18.
382 Ibid., p. 19.
383 Ibid., p. 19.
384 Pte R. Hurrell, Log of Round the World Cruise, pp. 36-36
385 Ibid., p. 37.
386 Ibid., p. 37.
387 Crookenden, *The History of the Cheshire Regiment in the Great War*, p. 9.
388 Ibid., p. 9.

open, or, having reached it, were caught by the concentration, of artillery fire in this awkward defile.'[389] The lack of ability to communicate had been compounded earlier by the removal of the battalion signallers to form a brigade signal section.[390] Any hope of establishing inter-company communication had been lost.[391]

Lieutenant Victor Briard. (<https://www.theislandwiki.org>/)

The Norfolks had withdrawn from their position, but D Company and the forward elements of the Cheshires at the colliery were still in position as Hauptmann Huber's *kompanie* were almost upon them. Captain Rich sent some men back to see what was happening to the battalion, but none of them had returned and his casualties were constantly increasing as his line had become enfiladed, and it had forced the platoons to retire to a fosse or dry ditch about 100 yards to the rear. At about 1600,[392] Captain Rich pressed in front and outflanked, withdrew his men yard by yard, disputing every inch of ground.'[393] Hauptmann Huber's *kompanie* was now only 600m from the colliery:

389 Crookenden, *The History of the Cheshire Regiment in the Great War*, p. 9.
390 McGuinness, *The Cheshire Regiment Forty Years on from Mons*, p. 170.
391 Crookenden, *The History of the Cheshire Regiment in the Great War*, p. 9.
392 TNA WO 95/1571/1, *1st Bn Cheshire Regiment War Diary*.
393 Crookenden, *The History of the Cheshire Regiment in the Great War*, p. 12.

> The 1 and 2 Platoons now followed, using the same movement formation, and although the enemy fire steadily intensified, they reached the mine head with few casualties. 9 *Kompanie* now recognised that the main enemy position was 600 metres to their front. The company deployed to both sides of the mine head and took up the fire fight. The leader of 3 Platoon was killed. The company butcher, who had left the field kitchen and picked up a rifle, was wounded. *Infanterie Regiment 26* was coming up on the left. The enemy had probably seen this and decided they needed to withdraw.[394]

Eventually Captain Rich gave the order "every man for himself." Captain Rich retired to the right with No. 14 Platoon and eventually escaped. He made his way back to the battalion to continue the fight. No. 12 Platoon of the Norfolk Regiment commanded by Lieutenant Bolton, with Sergeant Blackwell and about 25 men, retired through the cornfield until they reached the road. The *Infanterie Regiments 26* and *66* were now advancing without any severe opposition. The men from No. 12 Platoon formed up on the road and, in endeavouring to find the headquarters, halted in a wood. They were deciding where they should go when the enemy suddenly surrounded them and 'after a short resistance, they had to surrender.'[395] Private Hurrell was in the party of Norfolks that were captured:

> I wasn't there very long before I heard whistles blowing and shouting in a different language to my own and I soon found myself in the hands of the Germans. Two Germans soon picked me up and cut my equipment off me, they also took my jack knife and felt in all my pockets but didn't take anything out to my surprise. They performed all these duties while I had my hands above my head, and still the shots were whizzing past me. They also tried hard to break my gun in halves but couldn't do so. There I was led down the field where we met a few more of my battalion numbering about nine. There was one of the German soldiers who were with us could speak a little English and according to what he told us he was working in London last year. He told us lots about the war further on in the country and he also told us that they treated all prisoners of war very good in Germany. After stopping there, a short time we were all fell in between escorts and marched off.[396]

On taking his initial objective of the mine heads at the colliery, Hauptmann Huber had 'captured five officers and 30 soldiers and a machine gun. Two of the prisoners were French liaison officers who could not get away because their horses had been shot.'[397] The Norfolks other machine gun had been destroyed by a shell which knocked out the whole of his machine gun section and fatally wounded Lieutenant Harold Openshaw.[398] The soldiers were elements of the Norfolk's, No. 12 and 13 Platoon of D Company which had not received Lieutenant Colonel Ballard's order to retire. Lieutenant Briard's platoon had been on the extreme right and had been cut off, but the stout fight it put up checked the enemy for some time and eased

394 Zuber, *The Mons Myth,* p. 189.
395 Simpson, *Cheshire Regiment the First Battalion at Mons and the Miniature Colour,* p. 37.
396 Pte R. Hurrell Notebook 1, pp. 26-27.
397 Zuber, *The Mons Myth,* p. 189.
398 DOW 28th August 1914.

the situation for the rest of us.[399] Private Henry Grigglestone was with Lieutenant Briard at the time of his death and later wrote to his mother. 'I was in the same section as Lieutenant Briard was in charge of...he was directing operations and I stayed next to him. I saw him killed about two minutes before I was captured. I cannot tell you anymore, but all I can say is, "he died a hero."'[400] Lieutenant Colonel Ballard's rough war diary recorded that Lieutenant Briard was wounded and was taken prisoner and was seen talking to German officers late in the evening, so it is unclear at what point Lieutenant Briard lost his life. Once the objective had been taken a feldwebel from 9 *Kompanie* 'walked the battlefield later and counted 280 enemy bodies.'[401] Once Hauptmann Huber arrived at the mine head he realised that the main position of the Cheshires was further to his forward-right and now he had *Infanterie Regiment 26* to protect his left flank so he continued his advance and decided to join I Battalion on their attack on A and C Companies of the Cheshires.

While the 2nd Cavalry Brigade was reforming behind the Bois d'Audregnies at about 1430, several attempts were made by cavalry officers to persuade Captain Shore, with the left half of B Company, to retire under cover of the mounted troops but since he had not been ordered to do so by his own battalion headquarters, he had refused. At approximately 1445, Lieutenant Colonel Boger, concerned about the continued movement on his left, sent a cyclist orderly to Lieutenant Colonel Ballard to inform him of it. This orderly did not return and neither did three other orderlies who were sent at intervals afterwards. This was most likely because the Norfolks had already retired, and these men had run into *Infanterie Regiment 26* which was advancing from the north, and were either shot or captured. About this time, a mounted orderly galloped down the road shouting and shouted "the 2nd Cavalry Brigade will rally behind the wood" but none those who heard this had reason to connect it with a retirement.[402] At 1500, Captain Shore retired when given a direct order by a staff officer of the 3rd Cavalry Brigade.[403] Much to the consternation of Brigadier Gough, he had found that all his first-line transport had been sent to the rear by one of General Allenby's staff and no one knew where it was. These wagons contained all the spare ammunition and rations. They also contained all the maps of the Mons area which had not already been issued to the officers and as they withdrew they had marched off the edge of their map sheets and the rest of the navigation was done by guesswork.[404] At about the same time the Commanding Officer of the 4th Dragoon Guards gave orders that all the guns were moving behind the Bois d'Audregnies and that he was retiring and this party was to be *rear guard* and not delay and get cut off.[405] Having received 'definite assurance from another officer that the battalion had retired south east, Captain Shore then moved off in that direction. With about 70 men, he eventually found the Brigade Headquarters, the Bedfords, the Dorsets, and some details of the Norfolks and Cheshires.'[406] It is evident that everyone except the Cheshires knew of Lieutenant Colonel Ballard's withdrawal and everyone assumed that

399 Lt. Col. C.R. Ballard, Account of Audregnies, p. 18.
400 *BBC World* <www.bbc.co.uk/news/world-europe-jersey-28880397> (Accessed 5th July 2018).
401 Zuber, *The Mons Myth*, p. 189.
402 Crookenden, *The History of the Cheshire Regiment in the Great War*, p. 10.
403 Capt. J.L. Shore, Amplified Account, WO95/1571/1.
404 Farrar-Hockley, *Goughie*, p. 127.
405 Capt. J.L. Shore, Amplified Account, WO95/1571/1.
406 Ibid.

Lieutenant Colonel Boger had received his orders to conform. It appears that Captain Shore was the only officer who received any definite order to retire.[407] From the high ground north west of Élouges where the Norfolks had previously been, *III Battalion of Infanterie Regiment 26* could now see the withdrawing force 'in thick columns at 2000-2500 metres range south in the direction of Baisieux...Oberstleutnant Büstorff who was in the immediate vicinity was informed. He brought up first one battery into position on the hill, then a second. These batteries shelled the British artillery and withdrawing troops with crushing effect.'[408] By 1600, *Infanterie Regiment 93* was on the high ground and the woods west of Angre. The pursuit was finally broken and by 1730 *Infanterie Regiment 93* bivouacked in Quiévrain. During the day, their second in action of the war, *Infanterie Regiment 93* lost 14 killed and 77 wounded, most of the casualties coming from III Battalion.[409]

During the action at Audregnies, the 5th Infantry Division were withdrawing, but General Allenby was unsure how far they had moved. Lieutenant Colonel Barrow tried to establish contact with the withdrawing Infantry Division and to ascertain exactly where they were to their right. From his position, he made his way by the most direct route through Audregnies to where he thought the Infantry Division were likely to be. When he arrived in the village, he met Lieutenant Colonel Noel Birch, the Commanding Officer of 7th Brigade RHA 'I had penetrated only a short distance into the village, passing a dead horse and an overturned gun, when an officer came galloping around the corner of the street. He held up his hand and shouted out "don't go on. The Germans are just around the corner and they nearly got me." I needed no second warning and turned around and galloped away with him.'[410] However, not being deterred, 'I found my way on foot, revolver in hand, through the Audregnies wood, half expecting to find it swarming with Germans. I got through safely at last and was able to fulfil my mission.'[411] One presumes that General Allenby now had an accurate appraisal of where General Fergusson's division was now located. However, Lieutenant Colonel Boger knew little of what was occurring on his front or flanks and was not aware that Captain Shore had withdrawn on his left at approximately 1500 with the Cavalry Brigade and the Norfolks or that 119th Battery had withdrawn from his right at about 1445. He had not succeeded in getting in touch with D Company on the right or with Captain Shore's two platoons beyond Audregnies. He was still uneasy about the apparently unchecked advance of the Germans beyond the River Honnelle on his left flank. He decided, therefore, that his best course was to find Lieutenant Colonel Ballard, discuss the situation with him, and obtain his orders. Seeing that matters were coming to a crisis at approximately 1600, Lieutenant Colonel Boger left his headquarters accompanied by the Adjutant, Captain Tahourdin, under the command of Major Chetwynd-Stapylton and moved off up the road towards Élouges and towards the firing line. As Barrow later observed:

> I left the road and went towards the firing line to get a better view. I saw Captain Dugmore and told him to keep close touch with left. I could not see the company to the right of

407 Crookenden, *The History of the Cheshire Regiment in the Great War*, p. 10.
408 Zuber, *The Mons Myth*, p. 192.
409 Ibid., p. 190.
410 Barrow, *The Fire of Life*, and p.145.
411 Ibid., p. 145.

Captain Dugmore's (Norfolk Regiment). I went back the short distance to the road, close to where my right was, but saw no sign of any one of the Norfolk Regiment. I was fired at from about the railway line where the Norfolks had been and was hit in the hand.[412]

Major Chetwynd-Stapylton. (Cheshire Regiment Museum)

As he moved up the road, he warned Captain Dugmore that, owing to the continued advance of the German troops on the left flank, a retirement might be necessary. Captain Dugmore said he thought they could hold their own and he said that they hoped "to get some of their own back"[413] when the time came for the enemy to advance. He pointed out to the colonel that some of the Norfolks were still in position to his right front, but he could see nothing that was happening on his left.[414] Lieutenant Colonel Boger retraced his steps. On the way down the road, a cavalry officer galloped past me. I said "Are we cut off?" He pointed to the direction of the railway and galloped on. Lieutenant Colonel Boger told Sergeant Rothwell of No. 12 Platoon of C Company, who were lining the cutting to retire. He also signalled to another group which was crossing the road further to the south the direction in which to retire. He followed the first party and along with Sergeant Rothwell, who was subsequently wounded,

412 Lt. Col. D.C. Boger, Mons, The Original Report of Lt Col D.C. Boger, p. 2.
413 Simpson, *Cheshire Regiment the First Battalion at Mons and the Miniature Colour*, p. 34.
414 Ibid., p. 34.

and the section retired under the direction of Private Jordan[415] half right in the direction of Bois d'Audregnies.[416] Lieutenant Colonel Boger 'received a bullet through the foot, from the left flank, and one in the right side, and was rendered immobile.'[417] He knew for the first time that he was in danger of being completely enveloped on both of his flanks and he was alone on the battlefield, Captain Tahourdin, who had followed Lieutenant Colonel Boger when he left the battalion headquarters, had lost touch with him when passing an exposed part of the road that was swept by machine gun fire. In searching for Lieutenant Colonel Boger, he had ran into a party of Germans on the railway and was captured.[418] At the point, Lieutenant Colonel Boger realised he was on his own and that the situation had changed. He was now in command of his battalion and the decision to stay or withdraw rested with himself.

Once Hauptmann Huber's *kompanie* had taken the colliery and consolidated the position they continued their advance and joined in with the main battalion attack onto the centre of the Cheshires position. In the centre, moving in on A and C Companies of the Cheshires were 3 *Kompanie*, commanded by Hauptmann Magnussen, and 4 *Kompanie,* commanded by Hauptmann Rogge. Both these *kompanie*s were from I Battalion *Infanterie Regiment 72.* The two companies attacked at a rapid tempo and quickly reached assault distance…the signal was given for 'fix bayonets!'[419] As the Germans advance towards C Company and Captain Dugmore's position he ordered his men to preserve their ammunition and lie still and await the advance of the German infantry. The longer they waited, the more the casualties increased. Earlier in the action, Captain Jackson was seriously wounded by a shell which also killed Sergeant Walden and a private. Captain Jackson had been shot through the right shoulder and left knee and received two shrapnel wounds across the right ribs. One of the men took off his equipment and gave him a drink of water from his water bottle.[420] Seeing that they were being outflanked, a machine gun was deployed behind the old windmill (on the northern edge of Audregnies) at the side of which were a few trees and a small thin hedge. The range to the Germans was 900 yards. C Company opened fire when the enemy were about 800 yards from its front. When the German were at a range of approximately 500 yards to their front, they also received rifle and machine gun fire from their left front as they advanced to within 800 yards of the battalion. During the action, C Company Sergeant Major W.A. Francis was wounded and the enemy machine gun battery was enfilading the place where the Company Sergeant Major was lying. Privates Vaughan and Moore saw that he was lying wounded in an exposed position. They tried to carry him to safety but owing, to the heavy fire, the Company Sergeant Major told them to leave him and retire with the company. They retired a short distance but came back and again tried to move the Company Sergeant Major who then ordered the men to leave him.[421] By now, the ammunition was running low and Captain Dugmore endeavoured, without success, to get in touch with his reserve supply carried on the company mule, which appeared to have retired with

415 Crookenden, *The History of the Cheshire Regiment in the Great War*, p. 11.
416 Simpson, *Cheshire Regiment the First Battalion at Mons and the Miniature Colour,* p. 42.
417 Lt. Col. D.C. Boger, Mons, The Original Report of Lt Col D.C. Boger, p. 2.
418 Crookenden, *The History of the Cheshire Regiment in the Great War*, p. 11.
419 Zuber, *The Mons Myth,* p. 188.
420 Simpson, *Cheshire Regiment the First Battalion at Mons and the Miniature Colour,* p. 30.
421 144 Private J. Vaughan, and 6893 Private J. Moore. See Lt. Col. D.C. Boger, Mons, The Original Report of Lt. Col. D.C. Boger.

the support platoons of D Company. This shortage of ammunition, coupled with the continued and ever-increasing enemy pressure, caused Captain Dugmore to decide that the time had now come to move as the Germans were only 300 yards away.[422] At approximately 1630, he passed the order down to retire "individually from the right." He organised the men around him into two parties. He placed the first of 10 men under Lieutenant Grove's command and told him to withdraw to a position east of the Élouges-Audregnies railway to wait there for Captain Dugmore. The second party of eight men under Dugmore retired to a bridge on the mineral railway where he could obtain a good view. He ordered his men to line the railway cutting and called up Lieutenant Groves' party to join him, but the field of fire was unsatisfactory, so he ordered Lieutenant Groves to take a few men and make a further bound to a cottage away to the east, while he himself remained with his party to cover their retirement. [423] Captain Dugmore's smaller party had been augmented by a few stragglers, one or two of whom belonged to the Norfolks and 'offered their final resistance.'[424] The situation by 1700 had become distinctly worse and the enemy were advancing steadily. Nothing could stem the tide. When the Germans crossed the railway to the north of him, Captain Dugmore saw that the situation was hopeless and ordered the men to scatter and get away as best they could. The only soldier of his party that evaded capture was Private Sharples who had used a derelict transport wagon.[425]

The cottage on which Captain Dugmore ordered Lieutenant Groves to fall back turned out to be an *estaminet*, and he found Captain Rich and the remnants of a platoon of D Company who had withdrawn from their position on the right flank at the colliery had also made their way back there. In the absence of all other officers, the remainder of C Company had 'advanced 200 yards from the road. Corporal Harrap ordered the retirement. There were only about 30 men in this part of C Company's line able to retire. The rest were all killed or wounded.'[426] No. 9 Platoon, of C Company, under Sergeant Raynor, were still at their original position on the left of the Company when they received Captain Dugmore's order to retire.[427] Even to Corporal Crooke's inexperienced mind, it was obvious that the Germans were getting much nearer. He could not, however, see the attacking parties responsible for the fire. The shrapnel had ceased to pass over. "Retire individually from the right." Each man acted upon the order in turn and, taking up their packs, they started back up the hill. Farther up the field, other sections were going back and over the crest of the hills. It had been hot lying in the open with the sun blazing on one's back. Here and there a man stumbled and fell but most of the section managed to reach the road. Corporal Crooke relaxed, gasping under the shelter of the bank. In the road was some confusion. "Who had given the order to retire?" They did not have to wait long to find out as down the road came Sergeant Raynor. Corporal Crooke, the remainder of his section and the other men in the road, quickly went up on the bank. From where they were situated, the road turned over the crest of the hill and swung around a corner. Corporal Crooke was on the left of the line where the road led downhill. He never saw what happened at the other end of the line, nor could he say how far around the corner the line was extended, as that end was under the

422 Simpson, *Cheshire Regiment the First Battalion at Mons and the Miniature Colour*, p. 34.
423 Crookenden, *The History of the Cheshire Regiment in the Great War*, p. 11.
424 Simpson, *Cheshire Regiment the First Battalion at Mons and the Miniature Colour*, p. 36.
425 Crookenden, *The History of the Cheshire Regiment in the Great War*, p. 12.
426 Capt. J.L. Shore, Amplified Account, WO95/1571/1.
427 Crookenden, *The History of the Cheshire Regiment in the Great War*, p. 13.

platoon commander. Sergeant Raynor busied himself with the full length of the line, keeping everyone going. Fire was kept up on the Germans and as men came up the road from the left, they were put on the bank with the rest. To the right rear, fire opened out from some raised ground. Corporal Crooke judged it to be from the other platoon he had seen retiring over the hill crest. He wondered why they had gone so far back and had not stopped at the sunken road. Gradually the fire behind them died away, and they seemed to be alone in the road.[428]

Lieutenant Colonel Boger had been away from his headquarters for about an hour and Major Chetwynd-Stapylton, who did not suspect that the battalion's right flank was threatened, was more concerned about B Company and the significance of the security of Audregnies and the left flank.[429] Having had no news from Lieutenant Colonel Boger, Major Chetwynd-Stapylton left the position of the battalion headquarters to try and find him to get further orders. Before doing so, he told Lieutenant Campbell to get into touch with Captain Shore, from whom no message had been received, and who, it was assumed, had not left his original position. At approximately 1700, Major Chetwynd-Stapylton moved off up the road towards the right flank. At a bend in the road, he found No. 9 Platoon retiring. Sergeant Raynor went to meet him and asked, "who had given the order to retire?" Corporal Crooke glanced over his shoulder as he lay upon the bank. The Second-in-Command seemed to tower above him. It gave him a greater sense of security. He had kept his head well down because the bullets sounded so near. Seeing the major towering above him, seemingly oblivious to and completely unaffected by the hail of bullets, he felt much less apprehensive. The order to retire had all along been questioned. There did not seem to be any reason for it. It had not been followed up by any further instructions. Sergeant Raynor understood the major's question to infer that the retirement should not have taken place, and gave the order to advance again. Corporal Crooke and Lance Corporal Blake[430] mounted the bank ready to take the sections forward. "Bring them back, sergeant, it's no use." The Second-in-Command countermanded the Sergeant's order. Corporal Crooke slid hastily to the road, "things did hum up there."[431]

Major Chetwynd-Stapylton then returned to the battalion headquarters to discuss the situation in their centre with Captain Dyer. Major Chetwynd-Stapylton was still under the impression that Captain Shore's two platoons were continuing to hold Audregnies and hoped to withdraw those left in that direction. Captain Dyer agreed that a retirement was inevitable and started to withdraw A Company. Lieutenant Campbell, having been detailed by Major Chetwynd-Stapylton, set off towards B Company, accompanied by Lieutenant Matterson who had volunteered himself and his battalion scouts to go and join his old company [B]. Before they left, they had the difficult task of destroying *Trotter*, one of the Small Arm's Ammunition (SAA) horses which had been badly wounded by shell fire. 'Lieutenant Matterson said to Lieutenant Campbell "let's go and support the left." Lieutenant Matterson led the way, with Lieutenant Campbell about a yard behind him, and in passing an exposed gap, where the bank was low and exposed to fire, Lieutenant Campbell, a most popular young officer, was immediately shot through the head'[432] by machine gun bullets. At approximately 1730, having heard that

428 Cpl. W. Crooke, Twenty Fourth August 1914 (An Impression).
429 Crookenden, *The History of the Cheshire Regiment in the Great War*, p. 13
430 9708 Lance Corporal Blake, D Company.
431 Cpl. W. Crooke, Twenty Fourth August 1914 (An Impression).
432 Footnote: Temporarily buried where he was shot.

Lieutenant Campbell had been killed, Lieutenant Spencer-Jacobs, with the left platoon of A Company, tried to link up with Captain Shore at Audregnies. However, Lieutenant Spencer-Jacobs moved off to the left but could make little progress towards the village. A soldier of the Cheshires wrote that 'our fellows were grand under fire. Captain Dyer and Major Chetwynd-Stapylton were acting just if there was no such thing as bullets about.'[433]

Lieutenant Elliot's platoon of A Company were on the Élouges-Audregnies road, when it was pointed out to him that Private Millett was about 100 yards away laying wounded and trying to get back to the road but unable to do so and was still engaging the Germans. Lieutenant Elliot, noticed that Private Millett was completely exhausted, rushed forward, and dropped by his side, unfastened his equipment, and crawled back with Private Millett on his back, under heavy fire back to the sunken road where, but on reaching the bank[434] Lieutenant Elliot was shot through both feet.[435] His men removed his boots and bandaged his feet. Lieutenant Elliot, despite being wounded and in pain, took up his sword and a rifle and resumed his position with his platoon. Eventually, seeing that the position was hopeless, he ordered his platoon to retire, but was unable through loss of blood to retire with them, so he crawled to the *deserted cottage* where several men had taken cover. When he reached the cottage, he found that the wall that faced the Germans had no openings through which to fire, so the occupants inside decided to await the approach of the enemy, intending to fire on them as they entered the cottage. The door was slowly opened, and they were about to fire when, instead of the Germans, they saw Corporal Murdock leading a horse in. As he entered, he said "take care of this horse! They have killed the other one, but I am damned if they are going to get this!" He then walked out of the cottage, saying "they can kill me but not my horse." This horse was one attached to the SAA wagon with ammunition for the machine guns. Hauptmann Huber's *kompanie* was closing in on the Cheshires, 'who were probably unable to retreat across the open ground behind them and continued to fire from the *three houses*. Hauptmann Huber ordered another attack, with two platoons in the front and one in reserve, using fire and movement.'[436] The Germans were now getting ever closer and the position of the remaining machine gun made it ineffective. Lieutenant Elliot, knowing that capture was now inevitable, ordered Private Taylor[437] to bring the gun into the cottage. The breech block was removed, and the gun made unusable. In the meantime, Lieutenant Elliot tore up his maps into small fragments and threw them in out-of-the-way places in the cottage. He then made several attempts to break the blade of his sword so that it should not be surrendered to the enemy. At approximately 1800, as A Company was in the act of retiring, the men were fired on by two machine guns which had moved forward to a dip in the ground just as the forward troops of A Company had been withdrawn. Lieutenant Matterson came back and reported that Lieutenant Spencer-Jacobs was held up by the enemy between the two halves of B Company. As soon as he received Lieutenant Matterson's report, Captain Dyer drew his sword and called on the men near him to attack.

433 *Derry Journal*, 11th September 1914, p. 8.
434 TNA WO 95/1571/1: 1st Cheshire Regiment War Diary: '[C]arrying away a wounded man under intensely hot, he being shot through ankles when within 3 yards of the sunken road to which he eventually took this man.'
435 TNA WO 95/1571/1: 1st Cheshire Regiment War Diary: '[A]nkles witnessed by Corporal Oford.'
436 Zuber, *The Mons Myth*, p. 189.
437 9327 Private Taylor.

'Lieutenant Matterson, who was on the sunken road close behind Captain Dyer with four men, got through the wire and joined the front line. Captain Dyer gave the order to "advance and enfilade the enemy,"'[438] and Captain Dyer, with Captains Jolliffe and Massey and Lieutenant Matterson with 30 men of A and right half of B Companies, made a bayonet attack in the hope of covering the retirement of the remainder. Captain Dyer did not know that the battalion was completely surrounded and hoped that this manoeuvre would relieve pressure on Lieutenant Spencer-Jacobs and enable the remainder to make good their escape. The party advanced from the left of the *deserted cottage* and had reached the dead ground 800 yards away, on which there were a number of slag heaps on the left of the windmill. It was here that Captain Jolliffe was wounded by a shot through the shoulder. At this point, he realised he only had about 10 men left and Captain Dyer gave him permission to go back and get more, but within 100 yards a shot shattered his leg in two places.[439] The Spencer brothers rushed to his assistance and improvised two splints and stayed with him. It was here that Captains Massey and Dyer were also wounded, Captain Massey was shot through the forearm and Captain Dyer was severely wounded in the foot and thigh.[440] During this action there were many acts of individual personal gallantry: Corporal Fleet and Privates Riley and Drake, who 'were in the first line of the *charge* and after charging knelt in the open and continued firing rapid fire till both fell badly wounded.'[441] Sergeant Smith[442] of A Company 'led his platoon with, gallantry in the final *charge* on the advancing Germans'[443] and both Private Woodier and Private D. Thorp (a reservist)[444] also joined in the final *charge.* This gallant counter attack, practically a *forlorn hope,* was the means by which many wounded and other men were enabled to retire to the woods in the rear.[445] At the end of this brave action all but Lieutenant Matterson and 10 men had been shot down.[446] *Infanterie Regiment 72* reported that 'the British began waving white flags. A field grade officer, several other officers (including three captains) and about 200 unwounded enlisted men surrendered, and two machine guns were taken.'[447] Hauptmann Magnussen wrote in a letter home:

> It was wonderful! Everybody pushed forward with a will. The men were splendid! Even though some could barely crawl afterwards, you didn't notice this during the attack!' Hauptmann Huber reported '150 British raised their hands and surrendered. On the ground lay a senior British officer, supposedly the commander of a lancer regiment, who was dying of a stomach wound[448]. He asked for water; only one man in the company had any, but he willingly gave it up.[449]

438 Simpson, *Cheshire Regiment the First Battalion at Mons and the Miniature Colour,* p. 38.
439 Ibid., p. 38.
440 Ibid., p. 38.
441 Lt. Col. D.C. Boger, Mons, The Original Report of Lt Col D.C. Boger, p. 3.
442 9799 Sergeant W.J. Smith.
443 Lt. Col. D.C. Boger, Mons, The Original Report of Lt Col D.C. Boger, p. 3.
444 8261 Private F. Woodier.
445 Simpson, *Cheshire Regiment the First Battalion at Mons and the Miniature Colour,* p. 39.
446 Crookenden, *The History of the Cheshire Regiment in the Great War*, p. 15.
447 Zuber, *The Mons Myth,* p. 188.
448 The only Commanding Officer of a Lancer Regiment wounded on 24th August, was Lt. Col. A. Parker of the 5th Royal Irish Lancers. This officer's wound was not fatal and he was not captured.
449 Ibid., p. 189.

Hauptmann Magnussen. (*Das 4. Thüringische Infanterie-Regiment Nr. 72*)

By the end of the day, *Infanterie Regiment 72* would capture 1,144 prisoners.[450] When Hauptmann Rogge of 4 *Kompanie* arrived at the cottage on Lieutenant Elliot's position he had still not managed to break his sword. The sword had been carried by both his father and his grandfather but he was unable to destroy it before the enemy surrounded the cottage and a party with fixed bayonets demanded the surrender of the few Cheshires that remained. Lieutenant Elliot refused to surrender his sword except to an officer. Hauptmann Rogge came forward and received Elliot's sword, but seeing the weak condition he was in through loss of blood, returned it to him.[451] The actions of Lieutenant Elliot they day earned him the universal respect of his men 'he was spoken of by all the men in terms of the greatest praise,'[452] and it was Corporal Oford who later reported to Captain Shore, the senior surviving officer that Lieutenant Elliot had been 'left on the field.'[453]

No. 9 Platoon of C Company was still in the act of withdrawing when a drummer appeared over the hill top and was bent double. He was immediately pulled down under the bank and Corporal Crooke and Lance Corporal Blake began to bandage the wounds in his back. Before the task was finished Sergeant Raynor hurried down the road and said "fix bayonets, they're coming!" They let the drummer roll into the gutter with the others. Poor devil, they did not even fasten up his pants.[454] Just the sound of those words brought back memories of training and how

450 Ibid., p. 190.
451 Simpson, *Cheshire Regiment the First Battalion at Mons and the Miniature Colour,* p. 41.
452 Ibid., p. 51.
453 TNA WO 95/1571/1: 1st Cheshire Regiment War Diary.
454 Cpl. W. Crooke, Twenty Fourth August 1914 (An Impression).

good he had been at bayonet practice, Corporal Crooke had a swimming feeling in his stomach as he fixed his bayonet. On company training, this had been his special *forte*. He had always felt elated as they had fixed and charged with hearty yell. He turned to the chap near to him to see how he was taking it and saw the sweat trickling in lines down his cheek. Phew! He looked up the road. Sergeant Raynor stood, tense and rigid, peering over the bank. All seemed to be looking that way. It seemed to be less of a strain than staring at the top of the bank, waiting to see what would be coming over. Sergeant Raynor relaxed and went around the corner.[455]

It had been a long afternoon and just as Sergeant Raynor disappeared, one of the soldiers close to Corporal Crooke enquired if they had time for a cigarette, "what d'you think, corporal, will there be time for a draw before it starts up again?" The soldier was a reservist and Corporal Crooke had never taken any particular notice of him. His request sounded so startling that the youngsters around regarded him with interest. "Blimey!" thought Corporal Crooke, "fancy bothering about a smoke at a time like this!" He suddenly realised that he was very thirsty and that he had a water bottle. "Crumbs, they had been busy, no time to think of anything!""[456]

The German infantry were now getting closer to their position. The artillery fire was going over their heads and small arms fire was falling close by, at the same time as their own ammunition was running out. The Germans were again beginning to break cover from the ground on their left front. Casualties started to mount up and Corporal Crooke found the party running short of ammunition. He wondered how the other end of the line was doing. The sergeant came along but he was realising the same difficulty. In the pea field at Dour, the sergeant had anticipated their going into action and had drawn a generous supply of extra ammunition. These he had distributed, ordering the platoon to fill their pockets. There had been some grumbling at the additional weight. Corporal Crooke now wished they had brought even more. They were out of touch with the company and had no idea where the ammunition mules could be found. The reservist had an idea and got down from the bank. When he came back, he passed a few clips to each man and went for more.[457]

By now, Sergeant Raynor was talking to Captain Jones and Corporal Crooke could tell from the conversation and Sergeant Raynor's hand movements it was time to move. Captain Jones asked what they were doing. Sergeant Raynor explained the position. Almost immediately the observer, Private Wood reported "the people on our right rear are retiring," Captain Jones then asked for someone to go and find out why they were retiring, Lieutenant K.T. Frost the platoon commander of No. 9 Platoon volunteered for the task. Lieutenant Frost, was an officer of the *special reserve* from the 3rd Battalion. He went on his task but never returned. He was seen later by a wounded officer of the 4th Dragoon Guards, 'fighting like a demon, having refused to surrender.'[458] Although wounded several times, he refused to give in and death alone overcame his indomitable spirit.'[459] Later, he was buried by the Germans with full military honours out of

455 Ibid.
456 Ibid.
457 Ibid.
458 F. Simpson, *Cheshire Regiment the First Battalion at Mons and the Miniature Colour*, p. 52.
459 Bernard Rigby, *Ever Glorious – The Story of the 22nd (Cheshire) Regiment*, Vol. I (Chester: Cheshire Military Museum, 2007), p. 342.

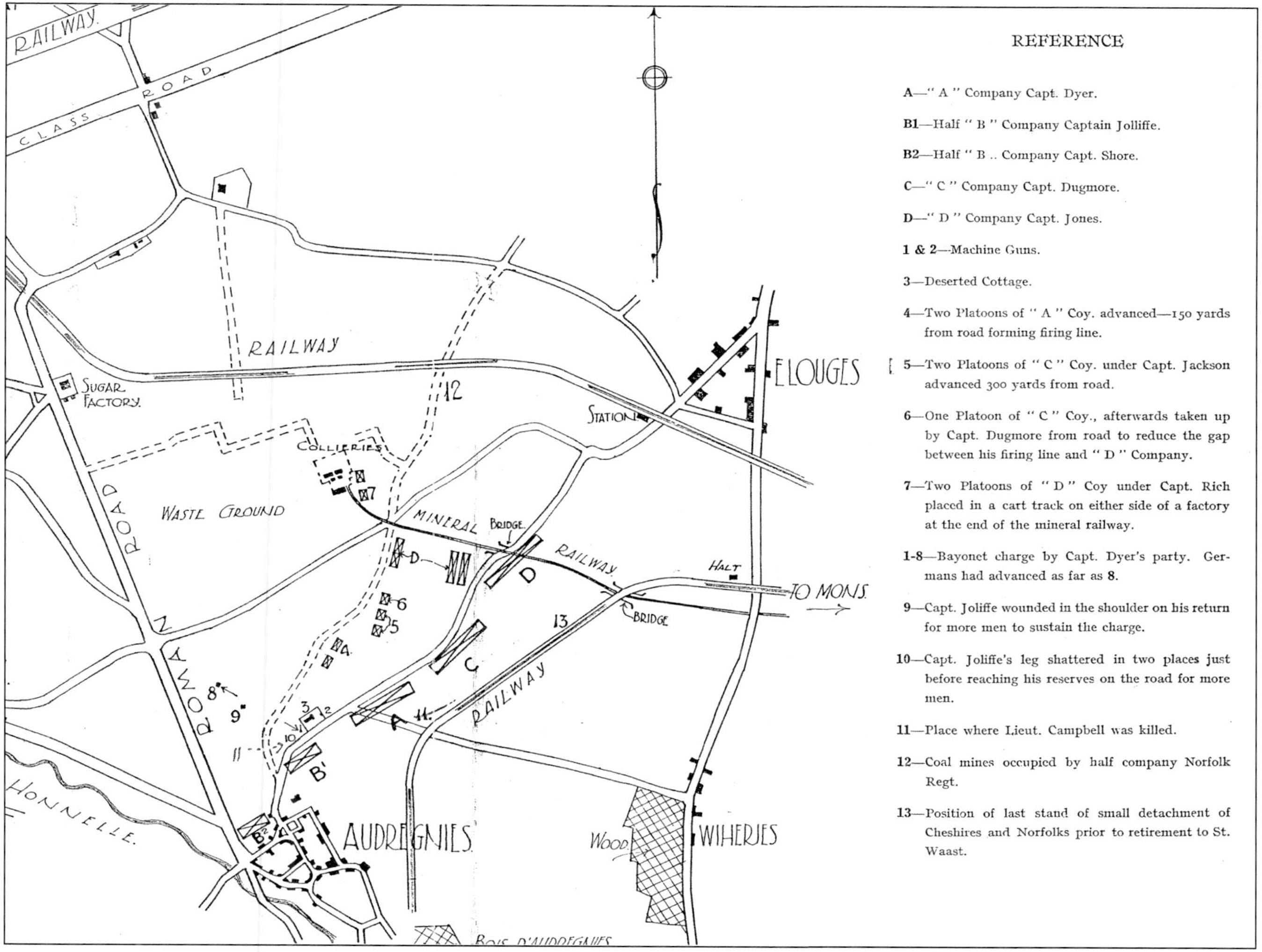


Map 18 Cheshire Regiment's final positions at dusk on 24th August 1914. Rendered by H.F. Davis. (*Cheshire Regiment and the Miniature Colour*)

respect for his gallantry.[460] Captain Jones at once ordered the men to retire, Corporal Crooke's account is most vivid:

> So, they stood awaiting the order. The captain and Sergeant Raynor at the foot of the bank on the opposite side of the road bent forward under the hail of bullets sweeping over. "For God's sake don't leave us!" cried the wounded. It was a strain to leave them, but they were safer there under the banking. The sergeant waved his left arm, the retirement began at that end. He waved to Corporal Crooke and that end followed. It was the last movement of the platoon. Corporal Crooke always liked to remember it was in perfect order, no undisciplined rush. Previously they had been retiring but had not known it. Now they knew they were retiring.[461]

As No. 9 Platoon moved off, the difficult decision to leave the wounded behind had to be taken. There were too many and they could not be got away safely. Even in the midst of the battle there were still civilians who had not been evacuated the evening before, Corporal Crooke saw a civilian man leading a child by the hand. As they moved forward, he lost sight of them. At the end of the field was a hedge but what a strain it seemed to reach it. Each time they went forward, their numbers were fewer. When about 20 yards away from the hedge, Corporal Crooke was wounded in the hand, and his rifle fell to the ground. Down he crashed too as 100 snarling whips cracked about his ears, the air around him seeming alive. The burst of fire slackened in a last despairing, frantic rush. Corporal Crooke burst through the hedge and slithered gasping and sweating to the railway metals below. A small group of dazed men, a dozen or so, stood between the lines. Corporal Crooke looked about for the man and child but could not see them.[462]

As they moved, the casualties increased. They made their way down to the railway. From his position he could see the Germans had already reached the same line. No more men came through the hedge. Corporal Crooke felt sick at heart, appalled at the sudden heavy losses of his section. All that remained of the platoon was the sergeant, himself and Private Wood. The rest of the party were men who had rallied to them in the road. A few minutes before the platoon had been holding its own, and now they were "a dazed, badly shaken remnant," Germans started to come down the railway. As they stood in the railway line, Corporal Crooke's thoughts were of the child he had seen in front of him. 'Did it go down under the hail of machine gun fire which had swept the platoon out of existence?'[463]

Sergeant Raynor now took charge of the situation. At this moment, Corporal Crooke noticed that Sergeant Raynor's cap had a bullet hole in it, and his own water bottle was now leaking. Sergeant Raynor noticed that Corporal Crooke was unarmed. "Where the devil is your rifle?" he asked sharply. So wild and frantic had been his last rush to the hedge, Corporal Crooke had forgotten to pick up his rifle which he had dropped when the bullet hit him. Hastily, he thrust his wounded hand behind him, in case he might be reprimanded for that as well. The sergeant led the way out of the railway, Corporal Crooke and the captain brought up the rear.

460 Simpson, *Cheshire Regiment the First Battalion at Mons and the Miniature Colour*, p. 52.
461 Cpl. W. Crooke, Twenty Fourth August 1914 (An Impression).
462 Ibid.
463 Ibid.

They turned down by the hedge lining the railway bank and set off in the direction of the Bois d'Audregnies. A burst of fire from the right drove them into some thickets. They dodged from thicket to thicket, evading the fire until they came to the edge of the wood. Corporal Crooke's water bottle had been hit by a bullet and the trickle of water down his leg caused him much concern until he discovered the reason.[464]

Once they had reached the wood, Sergeant Raynor went in first with his bayonet fixed. There was a path through to the far side of the wood which looked safe. Sergeant Raynor fixed bayonets and entered the wood, meeting a German patrol which cleared off at the sight of him. When Corporal Crooke followed, he found the sergeant and captain examining a cavalry pony which they declared to be English. The far end of the wood was still under shell fire, but that way seemed to lead to safety. The remaining members of the party, again reduced by casualties, penetrated the wood, coming to a well-defined path along which they proceeded. As they moved, the firing ceased and by the time they reached the end of the wood, all was quiet and peaceful. Corporal Crooke's hand was beginning to ache, but as he had used up his bandages on the drummer by the roadside, he could do nothing to it. He was sorely tempted to slip into the undergrowth and stay there. The sergeant called them all together and took stock.[465] The small group of men were not all armed and they had virtually no ammunition. Sergeant Raynor was doing his best to lead his men to safety. After he had returned from his reconnaissance, he felt that Audregnies on the other side appeared to be clear of enemy. Their party now numbered seven; four with rifles and three without: Corporal Crooke, Drummer Hogan and Captain Jones. They had 20 rounds of ammunition between them, five rounds for each rifle. Sergeant Raynor left the wood to reconnoitre, the others remaining just inside the wood until he returned to say that the way to the village in front seemed clear of the enemy. Across the fields they went, following a kind of cart track. Corporal Crooke felt more hopeful. At the entrance to the village the cart track emerged into a kind of cattle pen leading into a lane about 200 yards long. A gate barred the entrance to the lane and the pen was surrounded by a strong thorn hedge. As they approached the gate leading to the lane fire was opened upon them from the village end of it and from the gardens behind the houses. A lance corporal and the two privates sprang to the gate to return the fire. "Come out of it' yelled the sergeant, we shall be caught like rats in a trap." They broke through the hedge surrounding the pen and opened fire.[466]

When they reached Audregnies they quickly realised it was not clear of the enemy at all. It was at this point that Captain Jones considered that they might have to surrender, optimistically he thought to the French, "Have you a white handkerchief?" he asked. Corporal Crooke replied that he had a towel, "Keep it," continued the captain, "it will do to surrender to the French when we meet them." Knowing that Audregnies was now occupied and having no ammunition Sergeant Raynor decided it would be best to avoid the village and make for another wood. He collected his party in the field just outside the cattle pen to consider what their next step should be. It was useless to try and force their way through the village without ammunition. The sergeant decided that it would be better to make for a small wood about 400 yards away, quarter right from where they were standing. The captain did not mention a body of men he and Corporal Crooke had seen, so the sergeant was unaware of their position. As they started

464 Ibid.
465 Cpl. W. Crooke, Twenty Fourth August 1914 (An Impression).
466 Ibid.

off, Corporal Crooke moved off to the left of the party, the sergeant on the right. On passing the captain, the officer said "pass close to the right of where we saw them." Corporal Crooke nudged the drummer to follow him as he continued to peel off left. Soon he was close to the hedge that ran down the field and could no longer see the corner of the village. Captain Jones had seen a group of soldiers and had it in his mind that they were French. Corporal Crooke was hopeful, but not convinced, and was hoping that Sergeant Raynor would notice the captain's intention and call them beck. Vaguely he wondered whether the sergeant would notice the change of direction and call him in. The captain, the drummer and he should be peeling off quarter left, the sergeant and the three men with rifles quarter right. Would there be sufficient space between them before the sergeant noticed it and by the time, they reached the spot where he and the captain had seen that body of men? The captain had as good as indicated they were French, and he had seen them through his glasses. Corporal Crooke felt that they were remarkably quiet considering that the village was occupied by Germans. Were they French? Had the captain made a mistake? Corporal Crooke's mind boggled at the idea. If they were Germans what would he do when he came to the end of the hedge? Perhaps the captain thought that whilst they were being challenged the others would get away. Would he never speak? Down the hedge he went, his mind in a turmoil, his hopes oozing away with every step. At last the hedge came to an end. If he had had a rifle and ammunition he would have blazed madly around it, he was so worked up. He must have hesitated. Captain Jones discovered that they were not French but Germans hiding behind some corn stooks so he fired at them with his revolver and they immediately replied with a volley, which killed Captain Jones and Drummer Hogan (shot through left temple) and wounded Private Garrad in the stomach.[467] Private Woods ran back and hid in the cornfields, and Sergeant Raynor and Lance Corporal Blake ran for the belt of trees. A voice behind him ordered "straight on across the road corporal." Corporal Crooke went down the bank across the road, up the banking on the other side and into the field. Would nothing ever happen? He heard the empty cases roll into the road as the Germans reloaded. He tried to run but his legs refused to function, something seemed to go flop inside him. As he lay there, he seemed to have no sense of feeling, his mind worked in a dull rusty manner. Close to him he could hear someone coughing and vomiting. He watched some ants crawl over his wounded hand. The rifle fire slackened, then started up again. Corporal Crooke thought 'the others are up and diving for it, he tried to follow but everything just faded away.'[468]

When Corporal Crooke had regained his wits, he was being carried and someone was giving him red wine. It was at this point he knew he had been captured and he heard the familiar voice of Sergeant Raynor. He lay in the roadside, watching the Germans in a dim kind of way. He became interested in their numerals and noted that there were three different sets of numerals amongst them. How long he lay like that he could not say. He was aroused out of his stupor by a well-known voice which rasped out "well, if I had known you were living, I would not have bloody well surrendered!" There was Sergeant Raynor in the grip of some burly Germans, looking all hot and bothered for the first time that day. A German officer prevented him from being bayoneted for his outburst. Corporal Crooke's heart sank again. So, he had not got away after all. It transpired that when the rifle fire slackened the sergeant tried to take the

467 Simpson, *Cheshire Regiment the First Battalion at Mons and the Miniature Colour*, p. 43.
468 Cpl. W. Crooke, Twenty Fourth August 1914 (An Impression).

party on. "Who's going forward?" shouted the sergeant. Only Lance Corporal Blake responded and together they had raced for the small wood. The lance corporal tripped over a ditch and fell, losing his rifle. The sergeant turned back to help him, but the delay lost them ground. A squadron of German cavalry approached on one side and infantry on the other. They were surrounded and obliged to surrender. Once they were captured, they 'were roughly handled and searched, and Sergeant Raynor's maps were taken from him. The German officer then ordered Sergeant Raynor and Lance Corporal Blake to bring in the dead and wounded. It was then seen that the Germans had already secured one prisoner, Lance Corporal Woods, 9th Lancers, whom they had trussed up and tied to a tree.'[469] Once the small party of No. 9 Platoon had been captured the German commander was interested in Sergeant Raynor's ribbons. "What ribbons are they?" he enquired. "South Africa," replied the sergeant:

> He became a person of great interest and respect to all the Germans. They had seen him make his bold dash for freedom from under their rifles; had seen him turn back under their fire to help a comrade, and had accepted his grudging surrender, when without ammunition he had been obliged to capitulate to their tremendous superiority in numbers. Now they recognised him as an old and seasoned soldier.[470]

Sergeant Raynor went around with a few Germans and collected his party, reporting all accounted for, although Private A. Wood was lying behind a corn stook waiting for darkness to escape. The retirement was ended. The captain and the drummer were killed and Private Garrad, of D Company, and Corporal Crooke wounded. Sergeant Raynor and Lance Corporal Blake, after all they had endured, remained miraculously uninjured. Corporal Crooke and Lance Corporal Blake sat beside the mortally wounded Private Garrad. Corporal Crooke's wounds had been dressed and he did not feel so hazy, yet his heart and body ached. 'What a day, what an end to it!'[471]

Another small body who were unable to withdraw from Audregnies included 9461 Drummer C Baker, of Captain Jolliffe's half-company, who had been entrusted with the safe keeping of the battalion's miniature colour. The miniature colour that was carried into action had been made by the battalion wives in 1911. It was quarter size and was competed for by the best shooting company. The company that won it would use it as their company colour for that year. It was first competed for in 1912, and each subsequent summer. Captain Shore's B Company were the holders of the miniature colour when they went to war.[472] Seeing the position was hopeless, Baker rushed into a house in the village, climbed the staircase, and under the eaves hid the colour behind some straw. By signs he begged the occupiers not to give the colour to anyone but an Englishman. Baker had just got clear of the house when the Germans entered the village and took the little band of Cheshire prisoners.[473] Private Riley also of B Company was wounded and was taken to the *pensionnat* or treatment. While he was being treated, he took a nurse, Sister St Leon, into his confidence who in turn persuaded Monsieur Soudan the

469 Frank Simpson, *Cheshire Regiment the First Battalion at Mons and the Miniature Colour*, p. 44.
470 Cpl. W. Crooke, Twenty Fourth August 1914 (An Impression).
471 Ibid.
472 Crookenden, *The History of the Cheshire Regiment in the Great War*, p. 16.
473 Simpson, *Cheshire Regiment the First Battalion at Mons and the Miniature Colour*, p. 47.

*curé* to accept the responsibility of keeping it on behalf of the Regiment. Monsieur Soudan and Monsieur Alphonse Vallée, the local school master removed it from the cottage and hid it in the church behind one of the choir stalls. Later, Monsieur Dupont concealed it in a length of piping and bricked it up in the attic of Saint Bernard's, where it remained for the rest of the war. At the end of the war the battalion was only 12 miles from Audregnies and a colour party was sent to collect the miniature colour on 17th November 1918.[474]

At Saint Bernard's when all was quiet, from their perspective, the "Germans are the winners, but they have 2000 dead men and the English have 50. The English were firing three bullets while the German fired one." When it was over, *Madame la Supérieure* allowed the sisters:

> To take some fresh air in the garden but without going too far away from the veranda. We can see now some broken windows…and in the garden, bullets and shrapnel. Later in the afternoon at approximately 1630 the chaplain arrived to announce "the German's victory" and he told us that the Germans were now entering the village and that he had already got several Germans in his own home. "We just have to wait for them now." The Germans arrived in Audregnies singing and *Madame la Supérieure* went to the door. We could hear the noise of the march and we were all shivering because of the national victory songs, and the beautiful German music, so catchy, but it broke our hearts.[475]

On arriving in the village, the regimental commander of *72 Infanterie Regiment*, Oberst Fritz von Zehmen observed;

> As I rode to *I Battalion* after the battle, I was presented with an unforgettable view. On a green hill, the battalion colours fluttered gaily in the wind. The setting sun threw her rays on the Prussian eagle on its shining red background, under which camped a large group of prisoners, khaki-clad British mixed with a few French in their colourful uniforms, and in a ring around them stood our brave field-grey with bright eyes, proud of their success. At the bottom of the hill, hundreds of captured horses were assembled in perfect order. Over the whole scene stretched the blue evening sky with a few pink clouds, offering the painter the motif "After the Victorious Battle" that could not be improved upon.[476]

In a letter home, the commander of *III Battalion*, Major Freiherr Karl Grote, wrote 'it was wonderful! Everyone pushed forward with a will. The men were splendid. Even though some could barely crawl afterwards. You didn't notice this during the attack.'[477] At approximately 1800, two German officers introduced themselves and very politely, with a soft voice and full of respect, asked:

> "Do you have any wounded Germans?" We told them that we didn't, and they left. Meanwhile, with the help of Doctor Mailleux and François Jaspar, Dame Ste Asceline,

474 Crookenden, *The History of the Cheshire Regiment in the Great War*, p. 16.
475 *Annales du pensionnat Saint Bernard à Audregnies*, pp. 46-47, op. cit. in Jean Richez, *Un Champ de Coquelicots, La Bataille d'Audregnies le 24 Août 1914*.
476 Zuber, *The Mons Myth*, p. 190.
477 Ibid., p. 190.

> Dame Marie Felix, Soeur Sylvie and Soeur Euphenie carried some wounded men to the *L'Ambulance*. We put them at Saint Pierre so we can separate them from the Germans, in case some would come. Our men, Louis and Adolphe didn't show up. Adolphe ran away with his mother and children, he'll be back late in the evening, when we broke through the door. A German major introduced himself. He came on a horse and dismounted in front of the *L'Ambulance*. He was very polite, and just wanted to ask some questions, "do you have doctors, nurses, stretchers?" Before leaving, he told us that he had 60 wounded men, and then, respectfully kissed the hand of *Madame la Supérieure*. She hid her aversion and then discreetly wiped her hand. During the evening, only two wounded Germans were carried here. The Sainte Famille nuns have 50 of them.[478]

Smith-Dorrien's II Corps had again suffered heavy losses with 2,200 casualties to add to the 1,571 from the previous day. In total the corps had suffered 17% losses in its infantry strength in 48 hours and the 15th Brigade had lost approximately 30% of its fighting strength during the action at Élouges. [479] The Cheshire Regiment had started the day with 27 officers and 934 ORs. At the end of the day only six officers and 200 men paraded at Les Bavay. The battalion had suffered 73% casualties, [480] and of the 663 of the battalion who were made prisoners of war, one was the *plucky* Drummer W.F. Woods who had been so insistent on embarking with the battalion despite his age.

The news of the first actions of the BEF at Mons had made its way back to 10, Downing Street, and Herbert Asquith said to Margot 'bad news, the Germans have taken Namur, we've been driven back with the French, terrible fighting since Saturday...we shall have an awful list of casualties. I cannot understand why Namur could have fallen if it is a strongly fortified as we are told. The position now is very serious I must go and see Kitchener, then we have a cabinet.'[481] Margot could see that Herbert was 'terribly upset. It came like a thunderclap to me. The first time our fresh, keen, wonderful force were in battle, to have to retreat.'[482] Herbert told her that Lord Kitchener had 'cursed and sworn, and that he much feared that the French had been out-generalled by the Germans; and only wondered if our lot had been in any way cut off.'[483] Margot's diary recorded "a black day" and at lunch General Cowens said he thought they had lost 6,000 men, and if so "it is very good." Margot was appalled and asked if this was to be considered good, to which he replied "certainly, the losses my dear Mrs Asquith, will be tremendous in this war. I'm afraid the restless Frenchmen have done some folly."'[484] Herbert Asquith's always shared his thoughts and concerns with Venetia and told her about the telegraph which had arrived at 1030 from Field Marshal French which had taken an eternity to decipher 'and meanwhile we are all on tenterhooks, not knowing whether it is going to bring

478 Ibid., pp. 46-47.
479 Smith-Dorrien, *Memories of Forty-Eight Years' Service*, pp. 391-392.
480 TNA WO95/1571/1, *War Diary, 1st Bn Cheshire Regiment.*
481 Brock & Brock (eds.), *Margot Asquith's Great War Diary 1914-1916*, p. 23.
482 Ibid., p. 23.
483 Ibid., p. 23.
484 Ibid., p. 23.

the news of victory or retreat, or, worse than all, the names on the casualty list.'[485] The following day he wrote to her giving her more details:

> Delicious to get your letter this morning…we got news after midnight from French who had been fighting all day, but had got back to his new position. This morning there is another message from him which is pretty bad. The Germans harassed him all the way but were shaken off, not without considerable losses to the 2nd Army Corps and the cavalry: over 2000 in all. De Lisle's cavalry brigade…in charging some infantry, got entangled in wire and were "severely handled."…French's troops were in the best of spirits and quite ready to take the offensive, but the French resolved on a further retirement, and so our men have had to follow and are falling back on their original lines at Cambrai-Cateau.[486]

General Fergusson's flank guard action had been successful, although at a terrible cost to the Cheshire Regiment, which was never the intention. General von Kluck's enveloping action and his attempt to push the BEF towards Maubeuge had been halted for the time being in it tracks. The German Army had been advancing at a rate of approximately 25 kms a day since its had crossed the Belgium border nearly three weeks before, except while it took Liège. The soldiers of *Infanterie Divisions 7 and 8* had the opportunity to gather themselves together before the morning's engagements. Despite the gallantry of the officers and soldiers and the weight of three regiments of German artillery (potentially 18 batteries), by the end of the day the line of advancement south of the Mons-Condé Canal was little more that 5-6 kms. The stout resistance by the Cavalry Division and Colonel Ballard's flank guard was sufficient to cause the German advance to lose its momentum. Brigadier De Lisle wrote in his account of the day that "the enemy did not advance beyond the wire for four hours and gave time for the 5th Infantry Division to retire in good order."

There has been much post-war opinion as why General von Kluck did not *vigorously pursue*[487] the BEF. Had the BEF been effectively fixed, the final *coup de grâce* and the consolidation of the ground gained would have required the use of the reserve formations which were too far away to either give chase or take over the battle. The official German history of Mons suggests that the British had withdrawn south and that further pursuit was called off 'to avoid being pulled in the wrong direction.'[488] This does have merit as the plan for that day and the following day was still to drive the BEF towards Maubeuge. Others have attributed it to 'a total lack of enterprise and his obsession with the tactics of envelopment'[489] on General von Kluck's part. Others more harshly said that Generals von Kluck and Kuhl 'were just the sort of men to snatch failure from the jaws of victory.'[490]

485 Brock & Brock (eds.), *H.H. Asquith*, pp. 192-193.
486 Ibid., p 194.
487 French despatch, 8th September 1914: "I hoped, therefore, that his pursuit would not be too vigorous to prevent me effecting my object. The operation, however, was full of danger and difficulty, not only owing to the very superior force in my front, but also to the exhaustion of the troops.
488 Dunlop, Dunlop & Puttkammer, *The Battle of Mons, The official German Account,* p. 56.
489 David Ascoli, *The Mons Star, The British Expeditionary Force 1914,* p. 84.
490 Zuber, *The Mons Myth*, p. 198.

The reality was that despite General von Kluck's efforts, he had failed to fix the BEF and force them to accept battle at Mons. This enabled the BEF to disengage and move south which meant that the only method of pursuit now open to General von Kluck was the three divisions of the *HKK 2*, which, although they had been placed back under his command, were already committed elsewhere and did not effectively come under his command until late in the evening of the 24th August.[491] It might be argued that General von Kluck had won the battle at Mons, but the BEF had effectively slipped from his grasp and he would now have to pursue them again and force them to give battle. Another vital day had been lost. The battle at Mons and the result of the engagements on the previous day, the exact location and presence of the BEF was no longer in doubt *AOK 1* estimated it had engaged two to three divisions. Captured British and French orders gave clarity to the British intentions and General von Kluck now knew he was engaging the whole of the BEF and that his right flank was no longer under threat. With *HKK 2* under his command and control, knew they were now tasked with getting behind the BEF and cutting off their retreat.[492]

Little did General von Kluck know that General Haig had been taken ill that night after eating grapes 'poisoned by some powder which is dusted on the grapes to kill the insects.'[493] His doctor, Colonel Ryan, had seen him at 2300 and prescribed Sodium Bicarbonate solution which gave him instant relief.' This is more graphically described by his intelligence officer Brigadier John Charteris as 'immediate and volcanic!'[494] At 0400, Colonel Ryan found that he was "OK" and was requesting a horse. Colonel Ryan ordered him to travel by car.

491 Alexander von Kluck, *The March on Paris and The Battle of The Marne, 1914*, p. 56.
492 Robert Dunlop and Holger Puttkammer (eds.), *The Battle of Mons*, p. 63.
493 Haig to wife, 4th October 1914, op cit. in Ryan, *Haig's Medical Officer*, p. 21.
494 Charteris, *Field Marshal Earl Haig*, p 17.

# 11

# Aftermath

---

*My fingers were nastily gashed, but the bone was not damaged. I had a bullet through my boot and another through my sleeve and was knocked down by a shell, which did not burst but threw up a mass of dust in my face. My horse had also been shot. No one could say I had an idle day.*

Captain F.O. Grenfell

British casualties lay all over the battlefield as the 5th Infantry Division and the Cavalry Division withdrew. Their withdrawal was covered by the 1st Cavalry Brigade and by now General Allenby 'had discovered he had lost control over nearly all his brigades…as the horseman were already widely scattered and found themselves split up as they were drawn into operations to protect the flanks and rear…infantry brigades were retiring by parallel routes through a corridor 20 miles wide.'[1] The resulting move of the 5th Infantry Division was further to the east than expected which produced a large gap between themselves and the French and the remnants of the Cavalry Division covered the six mile gap during the night from St Waast to Saultain.[2]

Captain Jolliffe lay where he fell until about 1830 when the Medical Officer visited the various casualties. The Spencer brothers who rushed to Captain Jolliffe's assistance had remained with him. Captain Dyer was severely wounded in the foot and thigh. A soldier from the Cheshires saw Captain Jolliffe being picked out of a trench and carried away wounded. He had heard that 'Captain Dyer and Captain Dugmore were wounded. Several went on fighting until they collapsed. Immediately a man was laid out he was picked up and taken away. Many were brought to French hospitals or cottages,'[3] but some of the wounded lay out in the open until about 0700 next morning when they were removed to a Belgian Red Cross Hospital where most of them remained for about three weeks before being taken to Mons. On reaching Saint Bernard's at Audregnies, most of the wounded officers were separated. The prioress refused to let Lieutenant

1 James. *Imperial Warrior,* p 59.
2 *The Cavalry Journal, Vol. XII,* January to October, p 32
3 *Derry Journal,* 11th September 1914 p. 8.

Elliot retain his sword as she said "it was against the rules" but seeing he was attached to it she arranged that the parish secretary, Monsieur Georges Dupont, should take charge of it until it could be returned to him. He collected it after the war on a visit in 1919.[4]

Captain Jackson was left on the battlefield where he fell. Three German soldiers eventually found him and gave him some water. One of them took his map, paperwork, and wristwatch. Later, just as it was getting dark, he was attended to by a German officer and an orderly who dressed his wounds and covered him in straw. The following morning, he tried to attract the attention of German ambulances which passed close by but was unable to make himself heard. At approximately 1400, he was found by some French civilians who took him to the hospital in Audregnies where he joined Captains Dyer and Jolliffe and Lieutenants Elliot and Gallagher (4DG).[5]

The bodies of Captain Jones and Private Hogan were transported across a field to the right-hand side of the road entering Wiheries. Captain Jones was buried with his wristwatch revolver and equipment along with their broken rifles. The burial service was conducted by Private Randle, which was attended by Sergeant Raynor, Corporal Crooke, Lance Corporals Blake and Jones (9L) and Privates Garrad and Woods. At the end of the service the Germans fired a volley of three rounds over their graves. The Germans also made a small cross on which Sergeant Raynor wrote their names along with his own initials. In Captain Jones' possession was a silver match box and some money. These items were given to Lance Corporal Blake. Sergeant Raynor offered the Adjutant, Captain Tahourdin, the items later, but he declined to take them. The money was put to good use and was used to buy food for several prisoners during their captivity and the match box found its way home via Captain Lee Stewart. Private Arthur Wood who had been hiding in a field, eventually made his way back to England and when he reported to the depot on 5th March 1915, he made a statement to Colonel Neville and said that "two days later the people at the public house removed the Captain's body out of the grave, dug the grave deeper and washed his body and covered the body with a sheet and re-buried it. The daughter of the publican retained the captain's watch as a souvenir. The small cross was exchanged for a larger one about four feet high."[6] Private Wood's escape, like many, was facilitated by Miss Edith Cavell and on hearing of her later death he felt compelled to write to her mother:

> I escaped from the Germans after the battle of Mons and was hiding in the vicinity of that town when I got into communication with your daughter who arranged for me to get to Bruxelles and afterwards to go on from there to Holland. I was hiding in the hospital, of which your daughter was the matron, for five days and she treated me as my own mother would have done and proved herself to be the very best friend I ever had. I am not the only British soldier that your daughter befriended, there are four more in my own regiment, beside the men of the other regiments she has helped...[7]

4 Simpson, *Cheshire Regiment the First Battalion at Mons and the Miniature Colour,* p. 48.
5 Ibid., p. 48.
6 Ibid., pp. 45-46.
7 Rigby, p. 35.

Edith Cavell. (Author's Collection)

Lieutenant Colonel Boger was eventually captured and the Germans removed his revolver and field-glasses, but he was left where he was with other wounded soldiers. After dark, they could see the lights of Wiheries approximately 300 yards from where they lay. Lieutenant Colonel Boger asked if any of the other soldiers were able to walk but got no reply, but he did hear in the distance the faint calling of Sergeant Dowling who had said "his legs were smashed." Lieutenant Colonel Boger followed the fence line on his hands and knees to the nearest cottage and on entering the cottage he found it to be occupied by a young German officer. The German officer had Lieutenant Colonel Boger taken to another cottage where his wounds were dressed by a German doctor. He told them the positions of some of his other wounded soldiers including Sergeant Dowling. They then went out and brought them in. Later, Lieutenant Colonel Boger was taken by the young officer by car to the convent school in Wiheries which was being used as a temporary hospital, passing a German battalion which was on parade. It was here he was reunited with Sergeant Dowling. While at the hospital he and Sergeant Meachin managed to escape and hide in the village,[8] eventually finding their way to Bruxelles where they were assisted by Miss Cavell and her staff to continue to evade capture. Mrs Millicent Battrum was Nurse Cavell's assistant matron who had been with her for some years. In 1935 she wrote the following account on hearing of Lieutenant Colonel Boger's death in the *London Evening News:*

> Colonel Boger had been shot in the foot. He was lame and suffering much pain. I gave him chloroform, while a Belgian surgeon scraped his foot and extracted a bullet. A small

8 Simpson, *Cheshire Regiment the First Battalion at Mons and the Miniature Colour,* pp. 49-50.

bone had been broken. The Colonel was still wearing British uniform. We put him into the hospital telephone room and gave him a change of clothing. In his new guise, he looked just like a Belgian farmer. For safety's sake I took his identification disc from him and I have it still in my possession. We hid him in a room at the top of the building. He rarely left it for fear of falling into the hands of the Germans, but I myself took him into the city for X-ray treatment. He hobbled along with the aid of a stick and we rode in a tramcar with Germans all round us. Several times the Germans raided us. On each occasion we were able to smuggle Colonel Boger out by a back door and he walked about the streets until the danger was over. He remained with us till the beginning of December and then we got him into an English boarding house in the Avenue Louise. He had been there about three weeks when we fixed him up with a passport into Holland as a Romanian. We also provided a passport for one of his NCOs, Sergeant Meachin, who lived at Chester, and I obtained a passport too. The colonel, Sergeant Meachin and I all went by different ways to leave Belgium. I brought with me the colonel's dispatches, which I carried about for a long time in my clothing. Sergeant Meachin reached England, I believe, by a coal boat. I came via Holland. On reaching London I took Colonel Boger's papers to the War Office, and then I met his wife. I told her of her husband's escape and that she might expect to see him in a day or two, but instead she received a telegram saying he had been taken as a prisoner to Germany. He had been caught at the frontier.[9] Later, his health broke down and he was sent to Switzerland, and Mrs Boger was allowed to join him there. Just as he was about to be exchanged for a German officer, the Armistice came, and he was released.[10]

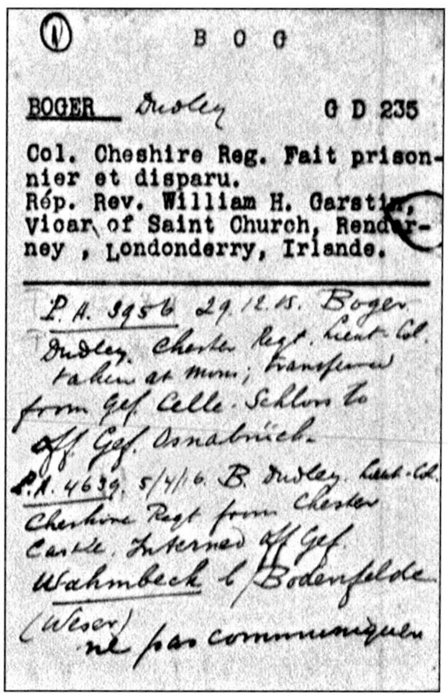
B O G

BOGER Dudley G D 235

Col. Cheshire Reg. Fait prisonnier et disparu.
Rép. Rev. William H. Garstin, Vicar of Saint Church, Renderney, Londonderry, Irlande.

P.A. 3956 29.12.15. Boger Dudley. Chester Regt. Lieut-Col. taken at Mons; transferred from Gef. Celle-Schloss to Off. Gef. Osnabrück.

P.A. 4639. 5/4/16. B. Dudley. Lieut-Col. Cheshire Regt from Chester Castle. Interned Off Gef. Wahmbeck b/Bodenfelde (Weser)

ne pas communiquer

Lieutenant Colonel Boger's International Red Cross POW postcard. (*Grand Guerre* <https://grandeguerre.icrc.org/>)

9 'On reaching Villevorde, his passport was seen to be not quite in order. He was ordered to appear before the commandant at Brussels and was interned at Ruhleben.' Ibid., p. 51.

10 *The Oak Tree*, 1935, p. 382.

Sergeant Meachin disguised himself as a fish hawker and succeeded in getting to Flushing and made it across the channel to Folkestone.[11] On 7th December, *The Liverpool Daily Post,* reported "Nantwich Soldier's Escape:"

> A Nantwich soldier, Sergeant Meachin, of the 1st Cheshire Regiment, returned home unexpectedly on Saturday. He was wounded at Mons by a bullet in the head and became unconscious after his wound had been dressed with a field dressing by Private Slack, another Nantwich soldier of the Cheshire Regiment. Later he fell into the hands of the Germans. When he had sufficiently recovered from his wound, he escaped from the German guard one night. The soldiers of the guard had drunk too much Cognac brandy. He procured civilian clothes from a French peasant, and was able afterwards, by passing as a refugee, to make good his escape to England.[12]

Another report regarding Sergeant Meachin was printed in *The Cheshire Observer* on 12th December 1914: "Sergeant Meachin's Escape:"

> Sergeant Frederick Meachin, of the 1st Cheshire Regiment, arrived at Nantwich last weekend, when his friends thought he was a prisoner of war in German hands. He is said to have had a sensational escape from the Germans, but he refuses to discuss the subject with reporters. He is the son of Sergeant F.J. Meachin, of Pepper Street, Nantwich, who is on active service with the 7th Battalion of Territorials. Sergeant F. Meachin wrote to his mother in September stating that he had been wounded in the head, and was in hospital, adding that he was quite deaf at the time of writing. According to a report now circulated, Sergeant Meachin recovered from his wounds, and when the German soldiers of the guard had imbibed too much Cognac brandy, he obtained some civilian clothes from a French peasant, and made his escape to England. He seems to have done a deed as daring as that credited to Corporal Glover, who says he was captured by the Germans, but after landing one a hefty blow under the chin he took to his heels and got away from his pursuers.[13]

Sergeant Meachin returned to the front and by 1917 was a Company Sergeant Major he was awarded the Distinguished Conduct Medal.[14] Another report was carried in the *Manchester Evening News* written by Private J. Burns of the Cheshires, who himself assisted to remove, under heavy fire, wounded men to places of safety, notwithstanding being wounded. He wrote from the prisoners' camp at Zertsh, Germany:

> Dear Mother, Do not worry, I am safe enough. I was wounded in the right foot by a shell on August at a place called Élouges, in Belgium, but am nearly better now. Of course,

11 Simpson, *Cheshire Regiment the First Battalion at Mons and the Miniature Colour,* p. 51.

12 *The Liverpool Daily Post,* 7th December 1914.

13 *The Cheshire Observer,* =12th December 1914.

14 *London Gazette,* 27th August 1917: "For conspicuous gallantry and devotion to duty. He led his platoon with great skill and dash after his officers had been wounded, and throughout the day he set an example of cheerfulness and gallantry which did much to encourage the men. He was invaluable in reorganising the company and making good the ground gained."

I have had it rough during the last month. When I was wounded, they brought me to a temporary hospital, and the Germans captured the place afterwards. I could not walk, so I could not get away was taken from Élouges and was put a hospital at Mons, and then sent to Rechlenhausen, and then to this place. I spent my 22nd birthday wounded in a German hospital. Very nice, wasn't it? Never mind, better days in store.[15]

From the Norfolk's, Privates Sheldrake, Hurrell and Grigglestone were captured as were Captain Peek and Corporal Easton from the 9th Lancers. Corporal Easton was made to advance with them for about 5 kms until we were gathered and placed in the company of German Military Police.'[16] Captain Peek was put in a captured Daimler by Hauptmann Rogge "as we were all very tired. He was a thorough gentleman, so different to many others we met later. At Quiévrain he had a small field tent erected for us and we slept well."

The following morning after breakfast, Hauptmann Rogge sent his subaltern back with us to hand us over to Hauptmann Magnussen at the Quiévrain Church. This subaltern was only a boy of about 18. A nice fellow and stopped all rude remarks from any of the German Army. At Quiévrain we found about 400-500 men, largely Cheshire Regiment who had been left behind to cover the retreat. Hauptmann Magnussen was really most kind and got us a couple of rooms in a house where we slept, and the good women fed is well. The dear old woman stripped her two beds, split the mattresses down for us to sleep on. The men were fed by means of a German field kitchen which is quite excellent and provides for about 200 at a time.[17]

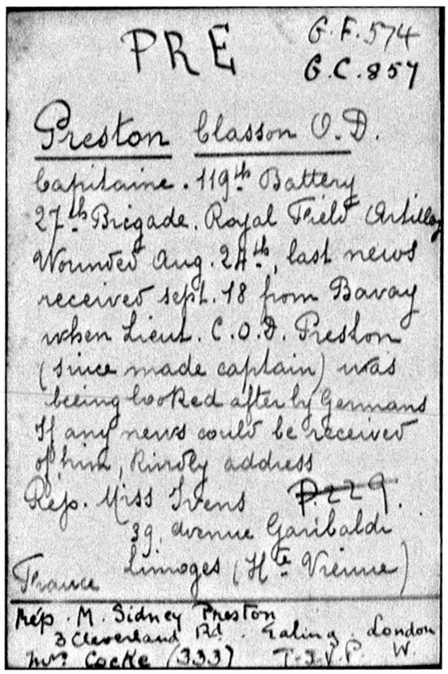
PRE G.F.574
G.C.857
Preston Classon C.O.D.
Capitaine. 119th Battery
27th Brigade. Royal Field Artillery
Wounded Aug. 24th, last news
received sept. 18 from Bavay
when Lieut. C.O.D. Preston
(since made captain) was
being looked after by Germans
If any news could be received
of him, kindly address
Rep. Miss Ivens P.229.
39. avenue Garibaldi
France Limoges (Hte Vienne)
Rep. M. Sidney Preston
3 Cleveland Rd. Ealing. London W.
No? Cocke (333) T.I.V.P.

Lieutenant C.O.D. Preston's International Red Cross POW postcard. (*Grand Guerre* <https://grandeguerre.icrc.org/> )

15 *Manchester Evening News*, 18th December 1914
16 Cpl. H. Easton diary, p. 39.
17 Capt. R.G. Peek diary, 24-25th August 1914.

The wounded Lieutenant Preston from 119th Battery RHA was also eventually captured, as were Sergeant Raynor and Corporal Crooke. Sergeant Raynor's gallantry was recognised with the award of the DCM. Private Henry Warr was captured and it was reported in his local paper 'H Warr, of the 9th Lancers, who was in the famous *charge* and had been missing since the end of August, was taken prisoner by the enemy. He has written saying that he is a prisoner at Munster, Germany, and is being well-treated by the Germans.'[18] Lance Corporal Doman (aka Dovey) of the 9th Lancers was hit in the back by shrapnel, and had been taken prisoner by Germans belonging to the *Infanterie Regiment 66.* Due to his wounds, he was taken to the German Hospital at Wiheries, where he joined about 40 other British soldiers, including a colonel [Boger] of the Cheshire regiment. He was in the hospital for just over four weeks during which time a plan of escape had been thought out by the colonel of the Cheshires. The civilian staff in the hospital brought them civilian clothes. On the morning of the 25th September while the sentry was having his breakfast:

> Thirteen of us, including the colonel, escaped over the walls of the hospital. We immediately broke up into parties of twos and threes, my one being composed of Sergeant Rothwell and Corporal Chapman of the Cheshires and myself. One of those who escaped, Bombardier Wiseman, RFA, 119th Battery, was unable to continue the flight on account of his wound, and sought refuge in the house of a civilian in the village, and he was still there a month ago, being tended by a Belgian doctor. Amongst those who remained in the hospital was Sergeant Barnard, 9th Lancers, wounded in left foot, Corporal Datlin 9th Lancers, wounded in the chest, Private Ackehurst, 9th Lancers, wounded in the left foot with two toes missing, Private Barlow, 9th Lancers, taken off the field sick, and Private Todd. Cheshire Regiment, unwounded. And there were also some men from the Norfolk Regiment…Having got clear of the hospital our party made headway for a large forest about a mile distant, where we hid for about five to six weeks, being fed by Belgian civilians who brought food to us at night. The first day we walked about 23 miles; and eventually arrived at a village called Tubize, where we stayed the night, putting up at the house of friends of the guide. The following morning, we started off again at 0700 passing a sentry on the main railway; we made our way to the canal that runs through Tubize to Bruxelles and walked along the side until we reached the capital, passing numerous sentries on bridges and railways. Having in our possession the address of an English lady in Bruxelles; a friend of the Colonel, we proceeded: at once to her house; we were hospitably received by Miss Cavell and put up for the eight. The next day our guide, Monsieur Ad------ after receiving our most grateful thanks, returned to Mons. Miss Cavell told us we should have to stay in her house until she could provide us with another guide, but as she found some difficulty in getting one, she endeavoured in the meantime to obtain a Belgian Passport from a certain lawyer, but this was refused. Among other things she told us that the colonel had arrived and left again, but that she had learnt he had been taken prisoner before he was able to get clear of Bruxelles. At last on the 23rd January, Miss Cavell informed us that she had secured a guide. We were taken by her on a car through Bruxelles and at a certain place we alighted and entered a cafe. Having ordered three beers, Miss Cavell placed the

18 *The Western Gazette* dated 6th November 1914.

> half of a card on one of the tables. Some minutes later a man entered, and upon noticing the half card on the table, placed a corresponding half beside it. This manner of procedure must have been arranged by correspondence, as the guide was unknown to Miss Cavell.[19]

Major Bridges, who was now south of Audregnies, had to shoot his wounded chestnut. He was sat by the roadside awaiting developments and from where he was, he could see the cavalry rallying on a hillside about a mile from where he was. The blow that he had received to his face "deprived me of the power of speech." Captain Grenfell passed him with the remnants of his squadron with a bleeding hand tied up in a bandana handkerchief and bullet holes in his clothes but very exhilarated. He told Major Bridges he had been joined by some of his men. He indicated to Captain Grenfell he would wait where he was for help to come his way. Expecting to be captured, he was surprised when a blue and silver Rolls-Royce driven by Lieutenant Sadler-Jackson of the 9th Lancers who was attached to the signals squadron came driving down the road looking for stragglers. Lieutenant Sadler-Jackson took Captain Bridges to the dressing station where he was pronounced "whole except for a splintered cheek bone and a slight concussion." He was given a hot drink and a bed of straw by two old ladies who seemed to be the last remaining locals. He slept until the morning having been woken during the night to see Uhlans in the moonlight questioning his *patronne.* In the morning, having found a stout stick, he said farewell to his hostess and made his way to the main road where he found a party of cavalry commanded by Brigadier Gough who had given him a spare horse and where eventually he was put into a car with the Assistant Quartermaster General Hambro. Major Bridge's wife, who had been working in the allied hospital in Bruxelles; had heard from the American Legations that her husband had been wounded and was missing. So, she set out for Mons in an ambulance flying a Turkish flag, accompanied by a Turk with supplies for the hospital, where she had hoped to find him. She had driven from Bruxelles to Mons through the German troops, eventually finding her way back to England via Ostend and getting on the last boat bound for England. It took Major Bridges another two days before he caught up with his regiment where he was informed that it lost 81 officers and men at Audregnies. He now collected all the stragglers he could find consisting of a miscellaneous commando of 150 men chiefly composed of 4th Dragoon Guards and 5th Royal Lancers where they eventually rejoined the Regiment and Brigade.[20]

For the 9th Lancers, the Regiment had been separated into two groups. The group commanded by Captain Lucas-Tooth was largely from of his own A Squadron, which had been at the mound at the sugar factory. It had suffered severely. In total 38 had been hit:

> It took days to find those who had had to escape on foot as best they might through their horses being shot. The German guns seemed to follow the Regiment all the afternoon with malignant fidelity as small knots of men left any cover which they had been able to find to run or gallop to rejoin the Regiment. Luckily the losses turned out to be much less than at first seemed possible, but they were heavy enough. Lieutenant Garstin was killed, Captain Grenfell wounded. Captain Edward Middleton, who stayed behind to succour some of the wounded, was captured by the Germans. On 25th August Major Beale-Browne took

19 LCpl J. Dovey POW Account.
20 Bridges, *Alarms and Excursions,* pp. 83-85.

> command of the Regiment during Colonel Campbell's absence to report to headquarters. The night was spent in a large field near Roulers. During the night, a further number of men joined up with the Regiment, but many were still missing. The men were thoroughly exhausted. At every halt they would bend forward on their horses' necks and fall asleep. Whenever there was time to dismount, as often as not in a lucerne field, for all north eastern France was lucerne and sugar beet, the horses were allowed to feed, but the men clutching the bridles in their hands would fall instantly asleep. When daylight came, the Regiment stood to, expecting to be in action at any minute, but though a battery was in action just in front they were not called upon. During this time, the rest of the Division was retiring to Le Cateau. At midday there was a long halt in a valley through which ran a delightful stream. Here the horses were watered and fed, and early in the afternoon the Regiment emerged on to a large plateau where it joined up with more cavalry, guns and a lot of transport. [21]

The majority of A and B Squadron were collected together by Major Beale-Browne at Ruesnes[22] where he spoke to the soldiers and told them 'that the *charge* was made to take the fire off the infantry who were retiring. He also read a message from Sir John French.'[23] The initial estimate on the casualties for the 9th Lancers had been one officer killed, Lieutenant Garstin. Four other officers wounded[24] and two captured.[25] Two soldiers, both from A Squadron, were killed with 22 wounded and 57 missing or as prisoners.[26] The 2nd Cavalry Brigade headquarters withdrew to Ruesnes with L Battery RHA, one and half squadrons of 9th Lancers, one squadron of 18th Hussars and two troops of 4th Dragoon Guards.[27] The remainder of the Brigade was found by Lieutenant H. Taylor-Whitehead who had been sent off by Brigadier De Lisle on patrol with Monsieur Leclercq and three men to Rombies…they found a few men of the Regiment, and under Major Solly-Flood, 4th Dragoon Guards together with other scattered portions of the brigade who had retired to Wargnies-le-Petit, amongst the party of 9th Lancers were Captain Wood, Captain G.F. Reynolds and Lieutenant F.L. Harvey with a few more men.[28] The total party of the 9th Lancers consisted of about 100 men mostly from C Squadron who had been collected together by the Commanding Officer. When Lieutenant Allfrey finally caught up with the Regiment, he found 'only a few there, and all very dismal.'[29] These elements of the 2nd Cavalry Brigade joined up with elements of the 3rd Cavalry Brigade to form a composite force under Brigadier Briggs.[30] Lieutenant Colonel Campbell told that he was to be recommended for the Victoria Cross, 'retorted "I want my squadrons back, not VCs or medals."[31] Major Home, from the Cavalry Division thought it was "a beautiful cavalry action. The men fought

21 Anon., 9th Lancer War Diary, pp. 24-25.
22 Sheppard, *The Ninth Queen's Royal Lancers 1715-1936*, p. 238.
23 LCpl W. Hunt diary, p. 6.
24 Capt. Grenfell, Capt Nash-Wortham, Capt. Porter and Capt. Montgomery.
25 Capt. Middleton (RAMC) and Capt. Peek.
26 TNA WO 95/1113/2: 9th Lancers War Diary.
27 TNA WO 95/1110/1-6: 2nd Cavalry Brigade War Diary.
28 TNA WO 95/1113/2: 9th Lancers War Diary.
29 Lt F. de V.B. Allfrey diary, 24th August 1914.
30 Sheppard, *The Ninth Queen's Royal Lancers 1715-1936*, p. 238.
31 Brereton, *A History of the 4th and 7th Royal Dragoon Guards and Their Predecessors 1685-1980*, p. 314.

splendidly," but as he got to his bed at a about midnight having had only half an hours sleep in the previous 48 hours asked himself the following questions 'why did we advance north only to retire? Were we short of guns? Perhaps it's part of a general plan, I hope so! It is poor comfort to the rank and file who know little except that they are retiring.'[32] Two days later at Le Cateau on the 26th August he also made a comment regarding the lack of artillery; 'it is no fun watching a battle, but without guns this sort of fighting is impossible.'[33] When he had observed an artillery section firing low air-bursts against infantry earlier in the morning he wrote "our artillery was excellent." It was not the lack of gallantry or skill of the gunners on the field of battle. It was simply that there were not enough and the batteries from both the 3rd and 5th Infantry's four brigades of artillery 'which, although within a few miles of the threatened sector did not fire a shot'[34] all day!

The two halves of the 9th Lancers would not see each other again for four days until they reunited on 29th August at Flavy-le-Meldeux where 'there was a joyous reunion in billets, cheered by the presence of pretty girls and the rumour that the "Russians are nearer to Berlin, than the Germans are to Paris."[35] Lance Corporal Hunt noted that the element of the Regiment with the Commanding Officer contained all the members of the band, with the exceptions of 'Evans, Geldard, and Cody who are wounded and prisoners. God help them.'[36] That evening they were told that they were to stay in the village and got a "decent stew of chickens and rabbits" However, while tending to a sore on his horse's withers, they got the order to "saddle up" as the Germans were entering the village. The Regiment got into dismounted action on the right flank. It was here that Sergeant Arthur Praeger[37] 'got the bowl of his pipe shot off, rather a close shave. We got the order to mount and retire and it was here that AP and myself went back for a fellow who came down in a ditch and his horse was laying on him. We got him out and just managed to get all three away safely, a near thing.'[38]

In the morning at Saint Bernard's, the Germans who had stayed the night bathed and left before 0600. They took with them the two wounded and most of the Germans who were at the *pensionnat*. During the night the nuns had had their first death, 'a Catholic for whom the priest gave the last sacrament. At the same time, a German sergeant asked the priest, with a gun in his hand, to go to the bell tower and take off the Belgian flag. Later they went to get some wounded English in the wood and fields nearby; the officer told the nuns that he had asked some people he met on his way but no one seems to have moved yet. *Madame la Supérieure* told him that "we can't go out ourselves and that people are afraid. He replied that with a Red Cross armband, the stretcher bearers won't need to fear for anything; he advised us to give them a bottle of fresh water because those poor guys are probably thirsty. What to do?…

32 Home, *Diary of a World War 1 Cavalry Officer*, p. 17.
33 Ibid., p. 17.
34 Gen. Sir Martin Farndale KCB, *History of the Royal Regiment of Artillery, Western Front 1914-18*, (Dorchester: Dorset Press, 1986), p. 22.
35 Sheppard, *The Ninth Queen's Royal Lancers 1715-1936*, p. 239.
36 LCpl W. Hunt diary, p. 7.
37 Died of Wounds 1-10-1914 buried Fere-En-Tardenois Communal Cemetery
38 LCpl W. Hunt diary, p. 8.

> Stretchers are made with ladders and old rugs and then the gloomy procession begins... There were 110[39] of them, about 40 of them to be honest were only hungry or had superficial wounds, but in which shape were the others!...and no surgeon. Monsieur Mailleux, who spent the night, did what he could, but he was only able to put bandages...We were short of everything: bandages, medicine. Events went faster and faster and the Red Cross didn't send anything in return to the survey that *Madame la Supérieure* had sent back to them. To finish the installation, we put a large rug in the small infirmary, mattresses in the gymnasium. We can now lie down about 30 of them. Around 1400, two carts arrived again, but really, we couldn't take this new burden. *Madame la Supérieure*, full of regrets, had to turn them down and they were sent to the *Sainte Famille*. She also wrote to the mayor to warn him about the current situation and tell him that we won't be able to feed all those people. That's also with those words that *Madame la Supérieure* talked to the community after dinner, while, however, encouraging people to be confident, dedicated and generous. Maybe we'll be short of bread at some point, but we have to believe in Saint Joseph to give us some.[40]

At 0700, Captain Grenfell left the Regiment. The officers "were very kind to me, the NCOs and the men came and shook me by the hand and gave me water from their water bottles. I cannot tell you how much this day, though a bad one, has increased my feeling of confidence and comradeship between me and my Squadron. The wounded Captain Grenfell was left by the roadside as the ambulance was full. He was picked up by a French staff officer who put him in his car and took him to Bavai. When he arrived at Bavai he met Bendor, the Duke of Westminster, who had volunteered for the RACVF, and Rivy. They took him to a French convent which was under Red Cross control and full of wounded. A civilian doctor and six nurses attended to him."

> Each one trying to outdo the other in kindness which was rather alarming. The difficulty arose as to how my leg should be attended to I suggested my trousers should be taken down but the senior Red Cross lady said that was impossible "*car il y trop de jeuennes filles*" (because there are too many girls) so my breeches were cut down my leg. The doctor took me to his house and put me to bed. I am bound to say I felt rather done. I got to bed at 2200 and at 2400 Rivy told me the town was to be evacuated. I hardly spoke to him but he told me he had arranged with Bendor to get me away. The doctor gave me some raw eggs and some coffee, and I left Bavai in Bendor's car about 0115. I cannot say how nice it was to find a friend on such an occasion. He took me to Le Cateau which we reached at about 0400 where I slept heavily in his bed.[41]

39 It is estimated that after Audregnies, St Bernard's treated 180 casualties. See *Historique – Le Couvent des Dames Bernardine* <http://www.foyernotredamedepaix.be/NDP02.html> (Accessed 27th August 2018).

40 *Annales du pensionnat Saint Bernard à Audregnies*, pp. 47-48, op. cit. in Jean Richez, *Un Champ de Coquelicots, La Bataille d'Audregnies le 24 Août 1914.*

41 Grenfell, Grenfell Family Papers (within Lyttelton Family Papers), 24-25th August 1914, pp. 29-30.

Shoe Smith Jack Friend and Lance Corporal Thomas Veness, who in their letters to their families said they would look after themselves sadly were both killed very early on in the War. Shoe Smith Jack Friend who told his family "not to worry" was killed in action three weeks later on the 7th September in the village of Le Montcel, having woken late and become detached from his squadron and entered the village which was occupied by German cavalry. His body was found 'riddled with bullets and thrown in a pond. Likewise, despite his best efforts to "look after himself," Thomas Veness was killed two months later on 18th October 1914 at Pont Rouge.

Lieutenant Gallagher, who had been unseated during the *charge,* had been crawling around on his hands and knees looking for the nearest shelter, which was a cowshed in the lane. Creeping inside, he found a wounded French interpreter and two wounded troopers:

> A moment later, a German officer and two German soldiers with bayonets on rifles came through the doorway. In the officer's hand was a tiny popgun of a pistol, which he kept pointed at each of the four of us as he went from one to the other. Reaching my corner, he stooped and relieved me of my revolver and my map case, the latter containing a notebook in which were an entry or two that I knew would hold his big round blue eyes. Running through my pockets, he came to a sovereign purse with seven sovereigns in it. This he tucked back in the pocket of my tunic, then stepped out the door to examine my notebook in the fading light. The moment his attention was well engaged, one of the German soldiers lost no time in extracting the sovereign-case and its contents from my pocket in a manner that left no suspicion in my mind that he intended replace it. A squad of 15 or 16 wounded prisoners mostly cavalry troopers or Cheshire Tommies were marched up from an adjacent house, hands in air. As they reached the door one man fell, a bullet through his arm maybe a chance shot. I saw Sergeant Hynes of my regiment in this lot. The slightly injured British soldiers were marched off to collect the dead and wounded, friend and foe. The more serious cases were taken to the convent in the village. The sergeant and myself were the last two to be moved. I was carried on the shed door. Before I was taken away, the German officer, who spoke no English, came over to where I lay and gave me first a drink of water, then a drink of milk. Stiffly and awkwardly, he reached down and shook me by the hand as he departed. I never saw him again. Not a bad sort, I suppose. Meant well probably. Sergeant Hynes had fared worse. One of his arms was black and blue from the blow of a rifle butt, delivered by a Hun for no better reason than that Hynes was the only one of a handful of wounded who had sufficient strength to sit up. Audregnies boasted two convents.[42] To one some 190 British wounded were taken, while an almost equal number of wounded German soldiers were placed in the other. [43]

Back at the Cavalry Division headquarters, "a jumble of reports" arrived saying that the 2nd Cavalry Brigade had been well-nigh wiped out. One dust-covered subaltern told Frederick Coleman that the Brigade was going out of the village in *column of sections* when it was attacked by German infantry, with the result that but 240 men out of the original 1,500 remained. Ninety of the 9th Lancers, 80 of the 4th Dragoon Guards, and 70 of the 18th Hussars were,

42 St Bernard and St Famille.
43 Gallagher op. cit. in Frederic Coleman, *From Mons to Ypres with French,* , pp. 58-60.

he said, all that was left of the command. The next report was brought in by Captain Francis Grenfell, of the 9th Lancers, who had been shot twice through the leg. He told me that the cavalry had charged a German infantry division well supplied with machine guns, and never reached a point closer than 800 yards to them. Grenfell and some of his lancers had that day saved the guns of the 119th Battery of RFA.[44] The troopers he met said the troopers themselves, told him we "could not see what we were charging either going or coming." The field across which they had to gallop was so plastered by all sorts of fire that to do more than simply gallop and keep clear of fallen and falling comrades was all that the men could do.[45] Four days after the action at Audregnies, Brigadier De Lisle issued a *Special Brigade Order* at Le Plessis on 28th August which read:

> I wish to express to the 2nd Cavalry Brigade my extreme pride and satisfaction with their conduct in the severe engagement at Audregnies on Monday, August 24th. The fight was necessary to save the 5th Infantry Division from an organised counter-attack during their retirement, and the object was achieved by the steady and gallant conduct of the Brigade. Major General Sir Charles Fergusson, commanding the 5th Infantry Division, thanked me personally for saving his division, adding that but for the Cavalry Brigade his division would have been destroyed to the last man. I especially wish to commend the true cavalry spirit of the 9th Lancers in daring to *charge* unbroken infantry in order to save neighbouring troops, and that of the 4th Dragoon Guards in the effective support given without hesitation or thought of danger. I intend to bring to the notice of high authority how greatly I value the devotion of my brigade. This to be read to all units on parade tomorrow.

Frederick Coleman was shown this order by one of the troopers of the 9th Lancers who had been with Captain Grenfell in the *charge*. He had managed to acquire of one of the original copies of the order, and proudly showed it to him as a souvenir of the event and said "It was hell, that *charge*, but I suppose it had to be done. Anyway, to read over that order made it seem to have been worthwhile,"'[46] and that was possibly the reason for its issue. Corporal Seward, of the 4th Dragoon Guards, sent his copy to his wife, who lived in Seaforth, Liverpool, as it paid 'tribute to the work of the cavalry after Mons.'[47] The 4th Dragoon Guards Regimental Medical Officer Captain Arthur Osburn RAMC, who had watched the *charge* had a somewhat more poetic impression:

> Over the brown masses of surging horsemen charging across the rather dreary plain beneath a lowering sky on that sultry afternoon came white feathery bursts of shrapnel. The threatening sky, the restless symmetrical movements, the whole scene reminded me in some strange way of Milton's description of the legions of dark angels practising for giant warfare with St Michael on the plains of hell.[48]

44 Ibid., p. 5.
45 Ibid., p. 8.
46 Coleman, *From Mons to Ypres with French*, p. 8.
47 *Dundee Courier*, 3rd October 1914.
48 Arthur Carr Osburn, *Unwilling Passenger* (London: Faber & Faber, 1932), p. 60.

News of the battle at Mons was slow to find its way back to England, and it would take over a month for the people of Cheshire to find out the detail of what had happened to their battalion at Audregnies. The detail contained in the papers was limited by the constraints of the DORA and on the following day, the 25th August the *Guardian* newspaper in Cheshire reported that 'British forces were engaged all day Sunday, and after dark, with the enemy in the neighbourhood of Mons and held their own and a great battle all along the line had taken place and that Namur had fallen, but it urged the British public not to attach too much importance to this reverse.'[49] The same newspaper on the 28th August, under the heading "Notes on the War" said 'the question is being raised in some quarters as to whether the censorship is being carried too far. We hear of fighting at Mons, and 2000 casualties but nothing else. It claimed the French papers were full of news, but all *The Times* has to say is "no doubt we will prevail."[50] On the 29th the *Chronicle*, carried the front page headline "Great Battle in Belgium" where it reported that Sir John French had admitted that the army had suffered 2000 casualties. It revealed that the British had fought a major battle at Mons and that the "prize riflemen and the cavalry had fought brilliantly against overwhelming odds," and on the next page showed a large accurate map of the battle area.[51]

On the 2nd September, in Jersey, the *Evening Post* reported "Jersey Officer Reported Missing." We regret to learn that one of the officers reported missing in the list of English casualties in France appears to be of Lieutenant E.F.V. Briard of the Norfolk Regiment. The missing officer is the elder son of the late Mr Ernest Briard & Mrs Briard of Bulwark House, St Aubin.[52] It is not clear when Private Grigglestone wrote his letter to Lieutenant Briard's mother, but the report gave her hope. In Cheshire it was not until the 4th September that the names of the casualties stated to appear in the papers and the *Guardian* published the names of 19 officers who had been captured including the names of Captains Dyer and Jolliffe, from the Cheshires, who were reported as prisoners of war.[53] The following day the *Chronicle* said that we finally got some idea of allied losses and said that the French losses were around 50,000 and the British losses were 10,000 and it reported the "appalling disaster that had overtaken the Cheshire Regiment with 18 officers reported missing, but with no mention of the enlisted men.'[54] On the 11th in the *Guardian* more details appeared with a list of 19 of the officer's names from the Cheshire Regiment including one missing, five wounded and six prisoners of war.[55]

On the 18th September, the headline in *The Times* was 'Gallant charge of the 9th Lancers' and there was the first of the grossly distorted stories of the action of the 9th Lancers. 'We have received the following letter, dated 11th September written to a friend in this country by a corporal in the 9th Lancers, who took part in the now famous *charge* at Toulin [sic] on 24th August:

49 *Guardian*, 25th August 1914.
50 Ibid., p. 34.
51 Ibid., pp. 37-38.
52 *Jersey Evening Post*, 2nd September 1914.
53 *Guardian*, 4th September 1914.
54 *Chronicle*, 5th September 1914.
55 *Guardian*, 11th September 1914.

Mons, Place Leopold, c. 29-30th August 1914: British prisoners marching towards the rail station to internment camps in Germany. (Philippe Yannart)

He [the colonel] says that we have earned more honour officially than any other crowd out here, and a few have been recommended for the VC. It is impossible to give it all but owing to fooling around and saving some guns and the 5th Infantry Division in the *charge* at Toulin in Belgium on the 24th August, several have been Mentioned in Dispatches. Perhaps you have seen an account of the *charge*, or you have seen the letter I sent you about it. I cannot give detail now but hope to live long enough to tell you personally. I had a charmed life – horse shot under me and my saddle blanket drilled through. We are worshipped by the 5th Infantry Division and cheered by them whenever they see us. Unfortunately, we lost several. Lieutenant Peek is missing and several of our troop. We rode absolutely into death, and the Colonel told us this morning that onlookers never expected a single 9th Lancer to come back. About 400 charged and 72 rallied afterwards, but during the week 200 more turned up wounded and otherwise.

You see the Infantry of ours were in a fix and no guns but four could be got round, so the General ordered two squadrons of the 9th to *charge* as a sacrifice to save the position. It was magnificent but horrible. The Regiment was swept away before 1,000 yards was covered, and at 200 yards from the guns I was practically alone, myself, three privates, and an officer out of our squadron.

Then the battery of four guns who had come to help us were out of action. The gunners were being mowed down. The 119th Field Battery were heroes to a man. Then we dragged their guns out of action and were finished. But on retiring the guns got the range and stormed us for about two miles, and we lost heavily. A young chap in my troop had four horses killed under him within an hour. The escapes were marvellous. We had no sleep for four nights afterwards, and I was hardly sane. A peculiar feeling, I had, that we were returning from Waterloo.[56]

The first eyewitness report of the Cheshires action at Audregnies appeared in the *Guardian* on 25th September. It was a letter written by Sergeant F. Tomkinson who was convalescing at Netley Hospital to his wife at 94, Greenall Road, Northwich and he said:

I had not been in action 10 minutes when I was wounded by shrapnel and knocked unconscious for a few minutes. I managed to crawl to safety with a handkerchief around my head to stop the bleeding…people who were under fire at Mons say that South Africa was a picnic compared to the present day…he felt he was dying and asked God to care for his wife and children…you cannot realise what it is to have men lying by the side of you getting shot and killed not a yard away, to see the shells bursting every second overhead and the cavalry getting shot off their horses in front of us.[57]

It was finally in this edition that the people of Cheshire had the names of those killed and missing from the Cheshires at Audregnies, as the paper carried a list of names of five names of those killed or wounded and a list of 601 of those thought to be missing or taken prisoner over a month after the action had taken place.

At the end of September, Victor Briard's widowed mother heard the news she had been waiting for:

Wounded and a Prisoner. We are pleased to state that information has been received in the Island that Lieutenant E.F.V. Briard of 1st Norfolk Regiment, who was reported to be wounded and missing on 25th August, is now reported to be a Prisoner of War. Needless to say, since the first news was received Mrs Briard has been passing through a most anxious time and her many friends will be pleased to hear that this suspense is ended, and that definite news has been received of her son. The extent of Lieutenant Briard's wounds are not known.[58]

The news coming back from the front was slow and by 25th March 1915,[59] 'unhappily there is no news as yet of Lieutenant Briard though it was very early in the war that he was reported wounded and a prisoner. Our great sympathy is with his mother in her prolonged suspense.' It was not until Monday 13th March 1916, that she knew the truth and that he had:

Died for His Country. It will be remembered that among the first list of casualties was the name of Lieutenant Ernest Felix Victor Briard, 1st Norfolk regiment, who was stated to be

56 *The Times*, 11th September 1914.
57 *Guardian*, 25th September 1914.
58 *Jersey Evening*, 25th March 1915.
59 *Jersey Evening Post*, 30th September 1914.

> wounded and a prisoner. However, no news has been received of him by his anxious family and a day or two ago Mrs Briard received notification from the War Office to the effect that Lieutenant E.F.V. Briard had been killed in action during the retreat from Mons on 24th August 1914. The War Office stated that they now have possession of his identification disc and that two Privates, now prisoners of war in the hands of the enemy, state that they were with him on 24th August during the retreat from Mons and that he was killed while leading his platoon between Dour and Élouges. The deceased, who was a pupil at Victoria College 1897-1900, was the eldest son of the late Mr Ernest Briard and of Mrs Briard of Bulwark House, St Aubin and was well known as a prominent member of the St Aubin's Swimming Club. To the bereaved mother and family, we tender our sincerest condolences. The demise of this promising young officer, who was but 25 years of age, will be a great loss to the country and to the army and the name of Lieutenant Briard[60] will be added to the roll of those of Jersey's sons who have died for their Country.[61]

The aftermath of the action of the 24th August would be felt by the families of the dead and wounded for the rest of their lives. For those who lived like 'Spur' Taylor, and who would return to his old Regiment for years to come, was something that would define him for the rest of his life. After the war in 1919, a solitary grave on the road to Élouges was found by the grave's directorate marked, "Unknown British soldier. Died 24/8/14."

> The man who buried him was interviewed, and showed the mission the photograph of a woman which was found in the man's right hand clasped against his heart. At the bottom of the card, which contained a cheerful message from the original, was the name of the hitherto unidentified man. When the work of the mission has been completed in close co-operation with the directorate of graves the public may rest assured that all that can be done has been done to trace the missing.[62]

It would be over a year before an honest account of the 9th Lancers mounted action was printed in *The War Illustrated* on the 9th of October 1915:

> On the 24th, our 5th Division was in a very tight place, and the cavalry was sent to its assistance, the 2nd Brigade reaching the scene of the action first. The Germans were advancing in great masses, so near the village of Audregnies, General De Lisle ordered his men to dismount and to open fire on them. They did so, but the enemy still came on in good order. The General then decided on a *charge*, and for this chose the 9th Lancers who, at the word of command, mounted their horses and rode steadily at the enemy. It was Balaclava over again. The squadrons rode to death, and the Colonel, so we were told, said that he never expected a single lancer to return. In face of a torrent of shot and shell

60 On 22nd August 2014, Phase 1 of the Belle Vue development, Jersey (35 lifelong apartments) by Andium Homes, were officially named Ernest Briard Crescent. The dedication ceremony was held on Friday 22nd August. His Excellency General Sir John McColl and Lady McColl attended along with the Bailiff, several parish and states representatives and members of Captain Briard's family.

61 *Jersey Evening Post*, 13th March 1916.

62 *Aberdeen Press and Journal*, 9th December 1919.

> from guns and rifles, they dashed on until they found themselves against two lines of barbed wire, where men and horses fell over in all directions. This ended the *charge*. The survivors were ordered to return into shelter, and out of more than 400 who had ridden out, only 72 at first answered their names, later some two hundred others turned up, but the Regiment had lost heavily. The lancers had drawn the enemy's fire and so had done something to help the harassed 5th Division.

For some, the story would run on a little longer before their story came to an end. On 19th February 1924 it was decided to exhume the 10 bodies of the officers and soldiers who were buried in Thulin Municipal Cemetery and relocate them to Cement House Cemetery, West-Vlaanderen, Belgium. The 10 bodies moved included six individuals who were killed or died of wounds on the 23rd-24th August 1914: Major John Boyd DSO, Lieutenant Harold Openshaw, (DoW on 28th August) and 6937 Private Clifton Baldry of the Norfolks. 1090 Sadler Corporal Thomas Denslow (9L), 7929 Private John Leggo, (1 DCLI) killed 23rd August and 5354 Sergeant Alexander Sutherland, (18H). For Private Gilbert Tustin, of the 9th Lancers and who was present at Audregnies, thought "the *charge* of the 9th Lancers was one of the most gallant episodes of the war," and when he died in January 1942 aged 55 and a friend told the *Gloucestershire Echo* that he 'remained cogently faithful in his belief in the superiority of the lance over the sword…'[63] Thus reminding us, that during the great pre-war lance debate and the focus on the opinions of Field Marshals Roberts, French and General Haig, that the soldiers had an opinion too!

Those who ultimately made the decision to take Britain to war were not free from the consequences and all suffered personal loss. The Prime Minister Herbert Asquith lost his son Lieutenant Raymond Asquith who, at the age of 37, was killed while leading the first half of 4 Company of the Grenadier Guards in an attack near Ginchy on 15th September 1916, at the Battle of Flers-Courcelette, when he was shot in the chest. Andrew Bonar Law, who had been the Conservative Leader of the Opposition in 1914, lost two sons in 1917. Lieutenant Charles Law, King's Own Scottish Borderers, was killed at the Second Battle of Gaza aged 20 on 19th April 1917 and later that year Captain James Law, serving with the Royal Flying Corps was shot down and killed on 21st September 1917. The Foreign Minister, Sir Edward Grey, had no sons, but his brother Lieutenant Charlie Graves MC served with the 4th Bn King's African Rifles. He was wounded and had to have his arm amputated at the fight at Kisii in British East Africa on 12th September 1914.[64] One of Charles' sons (Sir Edward Grey's nephew), Captain Cecil Graves, serving with the 2 Royal Scots was captured 26th August 1914 and interned for the rest of the war. The other son, Captain Adrian Graves MC*, served with the 40th Bn. Machine Gun Corps (Infantry) and was killed on 22nd March 1918, a loss that Sir Edward felt keenly.

For the Grenfell twins, the war had provided them with the opportunity they both had sought. For Francis, it gave him the chance to test his military prowess. For Rivy, it allowed him to escape the financial collapse of their joint estate for which he had been unwittingly responsible. It was an adventure they had willingly undertaken together, which had been facilitated by Francis with his family and social connections. Rivy, despite his military inexperience, was a willing

63 *Gloucestershire Echo*, 23rd January 1942.
64 *Kaisers Cross* <http://www.kaiserscross.com/188001/269501.html> (Accessed_12th June 2017).

and brave student learning at his brother's feet. Francis was awarded the Victoria Cross, which was gazetted on the 13th November 1914. The citation read: "For gallantry in action against unbroken infantry at Audregnies, Belgium on 24th August 1914, and for gallant conduct in assisting to save the guns of the 119th Battery, Royal Field Artillery, near Doubon the same day." A citation which, on first reading, seems somewhat bland, and lacks the detail found in fuller Victoria Cross citations that were to follow later in the War. After being evacuated for treatment, he heard that his twin brother Rivy had been killed in action on 14th September. Francis returned to France to resume command of his Squadron but was wounded again in the thigh at Messines on 31st October. He was evacuated to Bailleul before being sent home to recover in Dublin. He was eventually presented with his Victoria Cross by King George V at Buckingham Palace on 22nd February 1915. In April 1915, he rejoined the Regiment at Meteren, Belgium. It was during the Second Battle of Ypres on 24th May 1915 that he was shot in the back at Hooge, south of the Menin Road and died within the hour. He was buried in Vlamertinghe Churchyard but after the War he was moved to Vlamertinghe Military Cemetery. It is reported that his last words were for his squadron were "tell them I died happy, loving them all." Francis' own opinion on him winning the Victoria Cross was typically modest, he wrote, "I have been through so much. I have no great feeling of having achieved anything…I know so many who have done and are doing so much more than I have…any honour belongs to my Regiment and not to me." On reflection, as tragic as their two deaths might appear, it is difficult to imagine one living without the other!

## 12

# Analysis

## Training, Tactics and Doctrine

At the Battle of Jena on 14th October 1806, Napoleon made his decisive move against the Prussians and attacked their flanks, causing many of the enemy divisions on the flanks to flee the battlefield. With its flanks broken, the Prussian army was forced to withdraw and Napoleon had won another battle. In total the Prussian army lost 10,000 men killed or wounded, had 15,000 prisoners of war taken as well as 150 guns captured. Helmut von Moltke saw this as a defining moment in Prussian military thinking 'in one of those moments seemingly invented to demonstrate the changeover from one military era to another, they deployed far too slowly for the attack and said "solemnly, as if on the parade ground," they halted and formed line within rage of the French skirmishers in front of the village of Vierzehnheiligen.[1]

The resulting Prussian military thinking was established around the principle of *Auftragstaktik* in the *Exerzier-Reglement,* of 1888 and it was reinforced again in 1906. Clausewitz's doctrine stated that tactics should be delegated to the lowest tactical level and that junior commander's should take initiative had been long established, as had the fact that it was the enemy's flanks which were the main objective for attack and not the front. The *Exerzier-Reglements* had separated out drill from tactics and understood that 'everything depends upon the quick and independent actions of all involved, based on the concept of operations as well as the follow-up of artillery and ammunition supplies.'[2]

To enable the German army to train, by 1911 they had acquired 28 major training areas covering over 102,328 hectares of land. Each active army corps had its own dedicated training area. Additionally, there were three further training areas for the artillery including the extra-large area at Grafenwöhr. The training areas were designed to be large enough to allow live firing of both infantry and artillery without causing danger to the surrounding countryside and could facilitate exercises up to divisional level. Comparatively, the British Army had completed

1 Helmut Karl Bernhard von Moltke, *"Aus den Verordnungen für die höheren Truppenführer vom 24. Juni 1869" in Moltkes Militärische Werke, Zweiter Theil, Die Tätigkeit als Chef des Generalstabs im Frieden, ed. Preußischer Generalstab"* (Berlin: Ernst Siegfried Mittler und Sohn, 1900), p. 178.

2 Oberst Heeresleitung, *Die Abwehr im Stellungskriege, in Urkunden der Obersten Heeresleitung über ihre Tätigkeit 1916/1918, ed. Erich Ludendorff* (Berlin: E.S. Mittler und Sohn, 1921), p. 619.

its purchase of Salisbury Plain, consisted of 16,997 hectares of land by March 1900. Salisbury Plain also had areas allocated for small arms and artillery training.[3] Both Germany and Britain also conducted annual manoeuvres on a grand scale away from the main training areas each year which were attended and observed by each other, as indeed did France. Like the Prussian, at the Battle of Jena, 1806, the British Army also had had its *epiphany* in South Africa and on 7th July 1900, Major General James Grierson wrote from Pretoria to Arthur Bigge, Queen Victoria's Private Secretary:

> What a lot we have to learn from this war in every way! I think the first lesson is that we must have big annual manoeuvres and have our staffs properly trained. We don't seem to grasp anything higher than a division. And we must have staff Journey's to teach the control of armies in the field. If we take to the field with a force the size of this one against a European enemy and continue in our happy-go-lucky style of staffing and staff work, we shall come to most awful grief.[4]

By 1910, both the British and Germans had integrated the use of aviation into their manoeuvres and its use had highlighted both its strengths and weaknesses in reliability (50%)[5], observation and interpretation of what was being seen, as well as the difficulty of getting the information back to the troops of the ground quickly enough for it to be of use. The British also faced an additional challenge in that the 5th and 6th Infantry Divisions and the 3rd Cavalry Brigade were all stationed in Ireland, and with the exception of the 3rd Cavalry Brigade who came to Britain in 1910 to attend the Cavalry Division manoeuvres, the troops in Ireland exercised in isolation from the other four infantry divisions in England. The annual exercises in the Irish Command were only ever inter-divisional and the cavalry would provide troops to each side. In 1911, the main military manoeuvres were cancelled in Britain and Ireland as a result of the tension around the *2nd Moroccan Crisis* and industrial unrest in Britain. For the troops in Ireland, their training was also cancelled the following year as a result of an outbreak of foot and mouth disease. Ultimately, the troops of the BEF were trained and exercised, but it had been interrupted and the troops in Ireland did not benefit from the army level manoeuvres and were only able to use aviation in 1913 for the first time when five aircraft from No. 2 Squadron flew from England to attend.

France, Germany and Britain would all play out the prevailing political scenarios and tensions of the time. In 1906, for the French *Les Grandes Manœuvres,* in Langres,[6] over 30,000 soldiers of General Victor-Constant's 2nd Corps took part in the exercise designed to demonstrate the "Revenge" for the annexation of the Alsace-Lorraine. It lasted for three weeks. The choice of location was quite deliberate in that in 'case of tension with the German Empire, it would

3 Simon Batten, *Futile Exercise? The British Army's Preparations for War 1902-1914* (Solihull, Helion & Company, 2018), p. 21.
4 D. Macdiarmid, *The Life of Lieutenant General Sir James Grierson, p. 271,* op. cit. in Batten, *Futile Exercise?,* p. 22.
5 Batten, *Futile Exercise?,* p. 149.
6 Ibid., p. 165.

have been easy for the troops in exercise to join the strongholds of Verdun, Toul, Epinal and Belfort.'[7]

In Britain in 1910, the exercise was based around a fictional invasion of Britain and the two forces Red and Blue, which were commanded by General Haig (Red) and General Grierson (Blue). The scenario was that the Red force had crossed the frontier dividing Red from Blue between Wells-next-the-Sea and Hunstanton and the Red forces were rapidly advancing towards London and the Blue forces were to prevent the Red forces entering London.

In Germany the following year in 1911, *The Barrier Miner* carried the story from *Reuters:*

> German Military Manoeuvres. Over 100,000 men participating...Prince Friedrich Leopold of Prussia commands one army and General Freiherr von der Goltz...was representing tho defenders against, the so-called English invaders, retrieved an unfortunate position, his guards and Cavalry Division brilliantly capturing a hill at the lance's point. The Kaiser personally thanked the aviators. In one case, information was secured in 35 minutes which otherwise would have taken a strong force of cavalry four hours to get.'[8]

When comparing each country's annual manoeuvres, the numbers of troops is deceiving, in that numerically the conscript armies of France and Germany were much larger than Britain's volunteer army. The British Army Manoeuvres of 1910 consisted of over 50,000 exercising soldiers which, although few in comparison to the continental exercises taking place at the same time in France and Germany, constituted well over 50% of the British Army, and as such a greater proportion of the British Army had been exercised than their continental counterparts. In 1913, Field Marshal French's troops had numbered 38,000 in comparison to the 80,000 troops he would command as part of the BEF in 1914. The Blue Army of General Grierson of 1912, numbered 25,000 men which was much closer that the 36,000 men of II Corps which was commanded by General Smith-Dorrien.[9] Therefore, it might be concluded that a larger proportion of the BEF had been exercised that the French and German armies, and the size of forces commanded was more comparable to the forces they would command in war, but the troops of the Irish Command were under-exercised by comparison.

The Prussian Army and in turn the German Army had clearly started to develop its doctrine following Clausewitzian thinking. In Britain, despite the Army Reforms driven by Richard Haldane, the British Army throughout the Victorian period prior to the Boer War:

> Was distinctly averse to committing itself to any formal doctrine...a profusion of tactical ideas existed, meaning that tactics and training often varied considerably from battalion to battalion and new ideas and methods were localised. Tactics were influenced by a multitude of factors, including local combat experience in colonial actions, and attitudes of Commanding Officers...but the lack of overall doctrine in training meant that adherence to faulty, outdated concepts often continued unchecked...training was principally focussed on

7 *Fortifications* <http://fortifications.tourisme-langres.com/fr/langres-en-ordre-de-bataille_359.html> (Accessed 26th June 2018).
8 *Otago Daily Times,* 15th September 1911.
9 Batten, *Futile Exercise?*, p. 24.

> simple drill, with financial stringency and restrictions on manoeuvres meant that training at brigade level and above was a rare.[10]

Post-Boer War the *Army Council* also issued the *Field Service Regulations in* 1909. This in itself 'did not represent the creation of formal written doctrine'[11] as it failed to pull together the individual training manuals of each arm *Infantry Training 1905*, *Cavalry Training 1907* and *Field Artillery Training 1902 (amended 1904)* and did not give guidance on combined arms operation which resulted in a *tactically* sound but *operationally* weak army. The *Field Service Regulations 1909* reflected the perceived necessity to remain flexible in support of the plethora of different operations colonial policing might entail. In 1909, this was considered likely to be either back in South Africa, on the Afghanistan border with Russia or in Europe against the Germans so to that end the *Field Service Regulation* clearly stated that 'the fundamental principles of war are neither very numerous nor in themselves very abstruse, but the application of them is difficult and cannot be made subject to rules.[12] The *Army Council,* in response to criticism, expressed little concern as it clearly stated 'that methods should vary according to circumstances'[13] and, if the BEF was to be deployed, then Field Marshal French and GHQ would impose their authority. From the cavalry's perspective, the *magnetism of the charge* had not been carried forward from their own manual of 1907 and it placed the emphasis back on 'tactical flexibility and the independence granted to the cavalry by their rifle armament'[14] Erskine Childers noted the anomalies between the different publications and 'it is absolutely necessary to introduce clearness, consistency and harmony into the…manuals…at present the contradictions between these official manuals is a public scandal.'[15] With the exception of *Infantry Training 1911, Mobilisation Instructions* in 1912 and a revised *Cavalry Training 1912,* the *Field Service Regulations 1909*, would remain the final word on the conduct of war for the next five years.

The difference between the British and German development of its tactics and doctrine was simply down to focus and where they both thought they would likely to be conducting the next war. Germany's focus was a European war, and as such was that how they exercised and trained. For Britain, flexibility was the key, and it anticipated that its future operations would be in support of its Empire and not in Europe. It had yet to pull all its publications together and the *Field Service Regulations* were in need of another revision.

## IV Armee Korps (*Auftragstaktik)*

From the German regimental histories of the *IV AK,* commanded by Generalleutnant Sixt von Armin, there is strong evidence to suggest that his two infantry divisions (7 and 8) were well trained. Clear missions and objectives were set and initiative and trust was evident during the actions on the area of the canal between Quiévrain and Thulin. The *IV AK* had had the benefit of

10 Elgin Commission op. cit. in Spencer Jones, *From Boer War to World War, Tactical Reform of the British Army, 1902-1914* (Norman, Oklahoma: University of Oklahoma Press, 2012), p. 37.
11 Ibid., p. 53.
12 *Field Service Regulations 1909, Part 1,* p. 13.
13 S. Jones, *From Boer War to World War,* p. 54.
14 *Field Service Regulations 1909 Part 1,* p. 12.
15 Erskine Childers, *German Influence on British Cavalry*, (London: Edward Arnold, 1911), pp. 214-215.

marching and 'shaking out' since they had crossed the Belgian Border on 14th August at Aix-la-Chapelle. They had been together for 10 days on the march, and elements of the corps had seen action at Haelen, suffered their first casualties, shot down their first British aircraft and they had moved their soldiers who were struggling with the long hot marches to other duties. The corps had marched 25 kms most days and had reached the canal on the 23rd August, and at the end of their march from Silly and Ollignies they had attacked two of the three bridges they needed to cross and had moved south of the canal in two places. It was only the complexity of the crossing at Hensies and St Aybert with the two bridges that prevented the *IV AK* from crossing the canal despite the fact that the bridges were blown. Generaloberst von Kluck's assessment of the action was balanced and accurate in that he felt that the:

> *AOK 1* had had a successful day and that the British opposition on the canal had been "obstinate" and "fought excellently" in a battle where both sides had suffered heavy losses. He felt that *IV AK* had done particularly well and 'by the evening the *IV AK* had advanced to immediately north of the line Hensies-Thulin; showing a praiseworthy grasp of the situation, they had pushed on beyond the appointed end of the day's march and crossed the canal between Condé and St Ghislain,'[16]

The only piece of information that Generaloberst von Kluck did not have at the time that the BEF was withdrawing from its positions along the canal, and much of the ground that would be gained would be found to be either unoccupied or not contested as they advanced. On the morning of 24th August, at '0815 *Infanterie Regiment 72* was ordered to take Quiévrain. It deployed and entered the town, which they found had been prepared for defence, but when they arrived the BEF had left.[17]

## Conclusion

Generalleutnant Sixt von Armin's *IV AK* were well trained and gallantly led. They had delivered their tactics in accordance with *Exerzier-Reglements* 1906 and the officers and men who were for the most part (less *Infanterie Regiment 66*) in their first action of the war. The reserve men and officers were fully integrated into the regular units and they played a full participating role taking their own share of the casualties of the day. *IV AK*, as it crossed the Mons-Valenciennes road managed to get two *Feldartillerie Regiments* into action firing from both direct and indirect positions, who engaged in counter-infantry and battery fire. This was *IV AK's* second action and, unlike at Haelen, this action was fully supported by artillery throughout, with the guns being positioned and commanded in direct support of the advancing infantry. The final Cheshires position was encircled and enveloped by at least three infantry battalions. It would appear that *Infantierie Brigade 13* were particularly successful in crossing the canal with its supporting *Feldartillerie Regiment 40*, which might be attributable to the fact they were all based in Magdeburg and had trained and exercised together before.

16 Kluck, *The March on Paris and The Battle of The Marne, 1914*, p. 48.
17 Hippel pp. 31-32, cited in Terence Zuber, *The Mons Myth*, p. 185.

## BEF

The instructions that Lord Kitchener gave understood that they "must be prepared to put armies of millions into the field and maintain them for several years." He anticipated it would take time to recruit and train them and this he enacted on the 7th August with his "call to arms" as he immediately set about replacing the BEF that was about to embark with another army of 100,000 men who would be expected to serve a minimum of three years. Before Field Marshal French left, he gave him specific instructions and it limited him to:

1. Assist the French Government in preventing or repelling the invasion by Germany of French and Belgian territory and eventually to restore the neutrality of Belgium, on behalf of which, as guaranteed by treaty.
2. It must be recognised from the outset that the numerical strength of the British Force and its contingent reinforcement is strictly limited, and with this consideration kept steadily in view it will be obvious that the greatest care must be exercised towards a minimum of losses and wastage.
3. The gravest consideration will devolve upon you as to participation in forward movements where large bodies of French troops are not engaged and where your force may be unduly exposed to attack. Should a contingency of this sort be contemplated I look to you inform me fully and to give me time to communicate to you any decision His Majesties Government may come in this matter. In minor operations you should be careful that your subordinates understand that risk of serious losses should only be taken where such risk is authoritatively considered to be commensurate with the object in view.
4. A high courage and discipline of your troops should, and certainly will, have fair and full opportunity of display during the campaign, but officers may well be reminded that in this their first experience of European warfare, a greater measure of caution must be employed than under former conditions of hostilities against an untrained adversary.

It is against these instructions the Field Marshal French and his headquarters can be assessed as this was the *mission* and instructions he was given.

### Field Marshal French and General Headquarters

1. **Assist the French Government.** The BEF mobilised and embarked as per General Wilson's plan, as agreed with the French, less one infantry division, and managed to be in position to the left of the French Fifth Army before the first critical engagement with the Germans. This was achieved despite the delays and the initial questioning of the plan by the *Great War Council* on the 5th August. The BEFs initial positions were along the Mons-Condé Canal with the intention of advancing on the line of Soignies with two corps advancing with the Cavalry Division protecting its left flank and the 5th (Independent) Cavalry Brigade guarding its right flank. On the 21st August the timing of the advance had been given to General Lanrezac by General Joffre "I leave you absolute judge of the moment when your offensive movement should begin."

**Conclusion. Achieved**

2 & 3. **Minimum of losses and wastage.** The position of the BEF on the left of the French Fifth Army was on its exposed left flank and would be the subject of the planned and known intended German encircling movement, but the extent was unclear as was the line of the German advance. The German Army had started its advance on 4th August and Liège fell on the 14th August and Bruxelles had fallen on the 20th August. The British had taken up their start positions on the 22nd August without any clear indication of where the Germans might strike them first. Despite having no clear understanding of the overall strategic picture from either French or Belgian sources and despite the message from Lord Kitchener on the 21st August telling him "that the German sweep north and west of the Meuse seems definitely to be developing" and the message from the Military attaché in the Hague on the night of the 22nd-23rd August regarding 100,000 German troops in Liège on the 20th August.

4. **Caution.** The two main methods of gathering his own information was his cavalry and RFC. The role and purpose of the cavalry was well known by Field Marshal French having made a name for himself by commanding the Cavalry Division under Lord Roberts during the second phase of the Boer War. The use and role of the RFC had been exposed to him during the Army Manoeuvres of 1912 and 1913. He had observed that General Haig had been completely out-generaled by General Grierson and his use of aerial reconnaissance aircraft, and that General Grierson had almost perfect knowledge from air spotting of the movements of General Haig's troops and he had been "kept fully informed of their movements by his aeroplane scouts." Field Marshal French remarked "There is no doubt that the aeroplanes did extraordinarily valuable service, but...they failed to discover the 4th Division," so had not been entirely convinced but he also remarked that "The aerial work...had been the special features of these manoeuvres. The following year in 1913. This time the exercising Generals were Haig and Paget, under command of Field Marshal French with General Munro acting as the defender. Aviation again had played a major part in the manoeuvres with 30-40 aircraft being used and three balloons and HM Airships *Delta* and *Eta* had both communicated to each other and to the ground distances of 100-130 miles. If caution was to be exercised, then a degree of protection would be required:

> **Protection** Every commander is responsible for the protection of his command against surprise. A force can only be regarded as secure from surprise when protection is furnished in every direction from which attack is possible. The strength, composition, and disposition of forces detailed for protective duty must depend on circumstances, such as the nature of the country, the proximity, strength, and characteristics of the enemy; also, on whether the duty is to be carried out in clear weather, or in fog or darkness. The objects to be attained are, firstly, to obtain timely warning of any threatened attack, and, secondly, to ensure to the force protected sufficient time to prepare to meet the attack.[18]

When Field Marshal French arrived in Le Cateau the only factors to prevent him from using his cavalry and aviation to get a clear understanding of the strategic picture would have been

18 *Field Service Regulations 1909* p. 91.

the time and the weather. The first RFC reconnaissances were conducted on 19th August which had identified enemy cavalry, and General Allenby had sent out his own reconnaissance patrols. The cavalry moved forward in advance of the infantry divisions and provided a protective screen, but none of the cavalry had been thrown forward any significant distance to try and understand what lay much beyond the Mons-Condé Canal. After the initial patrols the cavalry occupied the line as per *Operation Order* No. 6: Thulin-Quiévrain–Baisieux–Audregnies–Élouges, south of the canal. Field Marshal French had a Cavalry Division at his disposal and, notwithstanding not wanting to waste horseflesh, did not use it as an expeditionary force asset. General Allenby had gathered information from his own division and the information collected by Lieutenant Colonel de Symons Barrow, who had made the phone calls from Mons station on 21st August which he passed on to Field Marshal French, to which General Wilson replied that "the information which you have acquired and conveyed to the Commander-in-Chief appears to be somewhat exaggerated. It is probable that only mounted troops supported by Jägers are in your immediate neighbourhood." However, the information from Lord Kitchener, General Allenby and the RFC showed that the German right actually extended much farther west than had been suspected.

## Conclusion

Field Marshal French, based on the information he had received on the 19th August, had not provided sufficient protection to the BEF. On the 23rd August, he was unaware of the exact dispositions of the German Army and did not react in sufficient time to redeploy his force to meet the flank attack on the BEF. Even though he had the means at his disposal and the underpinning knowledge and experience, he chose to ignore the information given to him by Generals Allenby and Henderson and deferred to the opinion of General Wilson, his Deputy Chief of Staff. Therefore, by not providing sufficient protection, he did not exercise the greatest "care must be towards a minimum of losses and wastage," and did not give the "gravest consideration…in forward movements where large bodies of French troops are not engaged and where your force may be unduly exposed to attack."

General French's headquarters issued three *Operation Orders* between 21st and 24th August. *Operation Order No. 5* was issued on 20th August by General Murray and *Operation Order* No. 6 was issued the following day on 21st August by Colonel Harper, late in the evening at 2355 when the location of the advancing German force was known, but is said that 'the movements of I and II Corps and 5th (Independent) Cavalry Brigade ordered for tomorrow in *Operation Order* No. 5 of 20th inst. will hold good except as regards outposts. *Operation Order* No. 7 was issued at 2025 on the evening of 24th August by General Murray which gave the instruction for the movement of the BEF the following day "The Army will move tomorrow, 25th inst. to a position in the neighborhood of Le Cateau. Exact positions will be pointed out on the ground tomorrow."

This meant that at the point it was decided to withdraw the BEF at sometime around 2300 on the evening of 23rd August and the issuing of *Operation Order* No. 7 at 2025 on 24th August that the withdrawal of the BEF and the engagement fought on the morning of 24th August were both executed without an *Operation Order* being issued by GHQ to provide detailed instructions. General Wilson stated that "between 2300 and 0300, we drafted orders and made arrangements for retirement to the line Maubeuge-Valenciennes." However, General Smith-Dorrien said when Brigadier Forestier-Walker returned from GHQ at 0300 "I naturally asked him for the plan of retirement, and was told that GHQ were issuing none, though he had gathered that the idea was for the I Corps to cover the retirement of the II, but that I was to see Haig and arrange a plan with him...There must have been some very good reason why four or five hours of valuable time had been lost by sending for staff officers instead of sending the order and plan for retirement directly the Chief had decided on it."

The following is an extract from the *Field Service Regulations of 1909,* Chapter 2 on *Intercommunication and Orders.* There is no specific chapter on command or headquarters.

> **Orders**. Operation Orders deal with all strategical and tactical operations, such as marches, protection, occupation of quarters, reconnaissance, and battle. They include such information regarding supply, transport, ammunition, medical, and other services of maintenance, as it is necessary to publish to the troops.[19] The object of an Operation Order is to bring about a course of action in accordance with the intentions of the commander, suited to the situation, and with full co-operation between all arms and units.[20] Orders for a possible retreat should always be thought out beforehand in case of need, but they should not be communicated to the troops before it becomes necessary to do so. They may be communicated beforehand, confidentially, to the higher commanders when considered advisable, but this should be rare.[21] Superior orders must be issued in sufficient time to enable subordinate commanders in turn to frame and distribute their own orders. In the case of a scattered force this may take a considerable time.[22]

Lord Kitchener recognised the gallantry of his officers and men, but understood they were inexperienced in European war and that they were not facing an untrained adversary. It was therefore critical that the instructions passed to Field Marshal French, as his intent, were passed down the chain of command and were fully understood by all his commanders. These instructions were issued on 8th August. On the 13th August, the 15th Infantry Brigade had been issued with a list of eight bullet points post-Liège. The last point was "Especially impress on all ranks that the 5th Division never surrender, we fight to the finish, everyone to the last man." This statement clearly did not support Lord Kitchener's instruction that the "greatest care must be exercised towards a minimum of losses and wastage." This message was repeated and subsequently reinforced by General Fergusson on 19th August and Brigadier Gleichen on 24th August. General Fergusson also said "and I myself will be with you to die in the last ditch if necessary; but remember! No surrender for the 5th Division, men we are up against it."

## Conclusion

Field Marshal French failed to convey Lord Kitchener's intent to the 5th Infantry Division and did not plan for a "retreat that should always be thought out beforehand." In not sending a message to II Corps he lost four to five hours planning time. This did not "allow sufficient time to enable subordinate commanders in turn to frame and distribute their own orders." Additionally, no *Operation Order* was issued by the GHQ for the critical 24 hour period of 23rd-24th August

19 Ibid., p. 27 para 1.
20 Ibid., p. 28 para 4.
21 Ibid., p. 32 para 15.
22 Ibid., p. 28 para 1.

as they "were issuing none…and I was to see Haig and arrange a plan with him." This is not to say that GHQ did not issue any *orders* during the period 21st and the 24th August. In fact it issued more than 30 sets of orders, 'many of them significant,'[23] but none of them were related to the retreat on the 24th August.

The operational planning conducted by General Wilson at GHQ was not connected with the withdrawal of the two corps and was possibly related to the movement of rear echelon elements to ensure the withdrawal route was clear. The delay in informing II Corps meant it had to withdraw while it was still in contact with the Germans thus losing the advantage of darkness.

## Flank Guard Action

### *Infantry*

"Remember that if you have no ammunition, you have your bayonets, if your bayonets get broken you have your fists. Fight to the last man, and I myself will be with you to die in the last ditch if necessary; but remember! No surrender for the 5th Infantry Division, men we are up against it." – General Charles Fergusson

"I shall always regret that I did not think of getting some of the lancers to take the order" – Lieutenant Colonel Ballard

"I have felt at times great soreness and regret that I was not informed that the army was in retreat" – Lieutenant Colonel Boger

*The subordinate commanders will, in turn, frame their own orders on receipt of the superior's order, of which only so much will be embodied as is necessary. Their orders should, however, be sufficiently full to enable those under them to appreciate the situation properly, and to understand how they may co-operate with others.*[24]

The analysis of the action sits somewhere between the two reflective statements of the Commanding Officers of the Norfolks and Cheshires. The *flank guard* action at Audregnies and at *Élouges on* the 24th August was about to find itself at the point of the encircling movement of von Kluck's *AOK 1.* The significance of this action was not fully understood by Field Marshal French, and in turn General Fergusson. Had this critical information been known; General Fergusson would possibly not have deployed elements of the 15th Infantry Brigade as a flank guard to the BEF without a formal independent command structure. The command of the *flank guard* was given to Lieutenant Colonel Ballard who had little recent operational experience (only seniority). He had served during the Boer War as a station commandant and he later became a staff officer in the Mounted Infantry Corps Mobile Column. The *flank guard* would also mean he would have to command a second infantry battalion and a battery of guns. Despite his experience, this was his first time in action and therefore it was critical he understood the mission he had been given beyond the command of his own battalion.

23 David Hutchinson, *Mons: An Artillery Battle,* (Warwick: Helion and Company 2018), p. 69.
24 *Field Service Regulations 1909*, p. 31 para 10.

General Fergusson and his staff, having established Lieutenant Colonel Ballard's seniority, gave him his orders for the *flank guard* action, although according to Lieutenant Colonel Ballard Colonel Romer had told him *rear guard.* Regardless of the possible confusion on the type of mission Lieutenant Colonel Ballard thought he had been given, Lieutenant Colonel Ballard presumed Lieutenant Colonel Boger had been briefed separately and therefore the instructions he gave Lieutenant Colonel Boger did not include anything other than his position and the defence of the length of road he had allocated to him. Therefore, the residual "no surrender" message had been embedded in Lieutenant Colonel Boger's mind, and that of his battalion. Lieutenant Colonel Boger was missing two key pieces of information. The first, for which Lieutenant Colonel Ballard was responsible (as he had been given it and he was the commander); was the exact nature of the mission (*flank* or *rear guard*) and the fact that the division was withdrawing. The second was a detailed knowledge of the limit to which he personally was required to obey any orders he had been given, especially if the situation changed:

> Notwithstanding the greatest care and skill in framing orders, unexpected local circumstances may render the precise execution of the orders given to a subordinate *unsuitable or impracticable.* Under such circumstances the following principles should guide an officer in deciding on his course of action. A departure from either the spirit or the letter of an order is justified if the subordinate who assumes the responsibility bases his decision on some fact which could not be known to the officer who issued the order and if he is conscientiously satisfied he is acting as his superior, if present, would order him to act.[25]

Although the "no surrender" spirit had prevailed, both Lieutenant Colonel Boger and his Second Command issued instructions for the battalion to withdraw. Captain Shore had been given orders by the Cavalry Brigade and Captain Rich had withdrawn from the north under his own initiative, eventually giving the order "every man for himself." Given the different responses to the desperate situation, the "no surrender" spirit had only been adopted elements of the Cheshires, particularly A and C Companies. At the point Lieutenant Colonel Boger realised that the Norfolks had gone, and the situation might be considered to have changed sufficiently enough that his orders were now *unsuitable or impracticable,* to invoke the provisions of the *Field Service Regulations* and he could withdraw on his own initiative without waiting for orders.

Lieutenant Colonel Ballard understood his obligation under the *Field Service Regulations* and when he withdrew he attempted to inform the division and the Cheshires 'should a subordinate find it necessary to depart from an order, he should at once inform the issuer of it, and the commanders of any neighbouring units likely to be affected.'[26] However, he did not get receipt of his messages and only sent runners and [27]cyclists. He later privately reflected 'no mounted officer was available, because Cresswell had been killed, Orr was missing, and the other mounted officers were busy collecting their own companies. I shall always regret that I did not think of getting some of the lancers to take the order, but at the time it did not strike me that our cyclists might fail to get through.[28] However, more publicly, when writing General Smith-Dorrien's

25 *Field Service Regulation 1909* p. 32 para ii.
26 Ibid., p. 32 para iv.
27 Lt. Col. D.C. Boger, Mons, The Original Report of Lt Col D.C. Boger.
28 Lt. Col. C.R. Ballard, Account of Audregnies, p. 21.

biography, he laid the blame at the change from an advance to a defensive operation and that 'signallers could have arranged a system of communication to keep the scattered units in touch with each other and with HQ. Nothing of the sort was done with the result that practically all messages had to be delivered by hand, and many of them went astray.'[29] He also justified the fact and said that they 'did not sacrifice themselves in vain…the whole German force had stopped their advance and halted for the night…saved the BEF from what might have been an awkward attack by overwhelming forces.'[30]

Boger's reflected thoughts were as follows:

> I have since seen it stated in print that we took part in a "*rear flank guard action*." I have felt at times *great soreness* and regret that I was not informed that the army was in retreat as it must have been already when we got into position. Definite orders could not have been expected in our isolated position, but a knowledge of the role the battalion was performing would have been of great value to me. From previous conversation with Sir Charles Fergusson at Dour I gathered, perhaps wrongly, that a stand to a finish on our line and vigorous counterattack was intended.'[31]

Lieutenant Colonel Boger also wrote back to Lieutenant Elliot later that month in response to a letter he had sent to him, 'we had no chance, no information, and no instructions, except to *guard the road*…I think they will say we did our best.'[32] Lieutenant Colonel Boger thought that they 'were merely a pivot point in the defensive position as they had been at Petit Wasmes and that they had other troops, our own or French in that direction and had no idea the army was withdrawing.'[33]

The truth is that he could have decided to withdraw his troops from the battlefield at any time, after the Norfolks had gone, and he was in command. This he eventually did; it was just too late. If he was unsure, he could have consulted his *Field Service Regulations*, which he should have been carrying and satisfied himself of any latitude he had. In the heat of the battle even when wounded, Captain Grenfell found time to consult his. 'We also had to put on a tourniquet and referred to the *Field Service Regulations* to find out how it was put on.'[34] The fact was that the *flank guard* commander had left the field of battle with some of his troops still engaged. History might judge Lieutenant Colonel Ballard poorly because as the metaphorical captain he did not go down with **his** ship, and Lieutenant Colonel Boger should have made his decision to withdraw earlier.

## Conclusion

It was Lieutenant Colonel Ballard's responsibility to ensure Lieutenant Colonel Boger clearly understood his mission. Notwithstanding Lieutenant Colonel Ballard's failure to personally do

29 Ballard, *Smith-Dorrien*, p. 157.
30 Ibid., p. 164.
31 Lt. Col. D.C. Boger, Mons, The Original Report of Lt Col D.C. Boger, The Hague, 20th May 1918, p. 3.
32 Crookenden, *The History of the Cheshire Regiment in the Great War*, pp. 17-18.
33 Lt. Col. D.C. Boger, Mons, The Original Report of Lt Col D.C. Boger, p. 2.
34 Anon., 9th Lancer War Diary, 24th August 1914, p. 16.

so; Lieutenant Colonel Boger was either insufficiently versed in the contents of the *Field Service Regulations* regarding the lexicon of *mission verbs* or did not understand what action was open to him regarding the changing of his orders if the situation changed and he was not able to discuss this with his superior commander. If the Cheshire's direction was not to surrender – at any cost – then this was clearly not followed, as 677 surrendered.

## Artillery

Post-Boer War, introducing the lessons learnt, the introduction of new equipments, and the supporting direction, training and adjustments to establishments was a longer process than that for the infantry and cavalry. The *Field Artillery Training* manual was issued in 1902 and was amended in 1904 when the QF 13 and 18 pounders were introduced. Direction for the use of artillery was given in the *Field Service Regulations 1909*, but the technical solution to firing from covered positions was not solved until 1910. The next edition of the *Field Artillery Training* was not issued until 1914 after the war had started. Additionally, to address the command and control issues at divisional level, the appointment of Commander Royal Artillery (CRA) did not take place until 1912, and the appointment of Brigade Major Royal Artillery (BMRA) was not created until 1913. The final piece that was missing was the creation of the divisional ammunition columns which were only formed in 1914, and indeed some were only formed 10 days before embarkation.[35] This tempo of development left the artillery lacking doctrine, constant direction, and a deficiency of technical equipment and their command structure above regimental level 'had little experience of handling artillery at this level.'[36]

Notwithstanding structural and technical issues, the prevailing debate was the merits of *direct* fire or *indirect fire* from concealed positions. The firing from concealed positions had been encouraged since the end of the Boer War, as a result of seeing how effectively it had been used against them by the Boers and in 1902 General Sir Charles Warren said to *The Elgin Commission* said that 'concealment of guns both on attack and defence is now a matter of primary importance.'[37] In the same year the artillery issued the *Field Artillery Manual,* old habits were difficult to eradicate and Lord Roberts had been disappointed in 1903 'to find the guns much exposed…on the whole there was practically little attempt at concealment.'[38] By 1906, as a result of the introduction of the new artillery pieces the QF 13 and QF 18 pounder in 1904, the *Field Artillery Training* manual was amended in 1904. In 1906, General Ian Hamilton, GOC Sothern Command remarked "that the methods of 1904 are to an extent already obsolete."

The last publication published on tactics by the artillery was the *Field Artillery Training 1906,* however the *Field Service Regulations of 1909* added its weight to the direction being given centrally. The *Field Service Regulations of 1909*, certainly advocated a level of aggression:

> The advance of the firing line must be characterised by the determination to press forward at all costs…it will be absolutely necessary for the troops to whom the role of wearing down the enemy's resistance is allotted to act with vigour. No half-measures will succeed…

35 Farndale, *History of the Royal Regiment of Artillery, Western Front 1914-18*, p. 2.
36 Ibid., p. 4.
37 Elgin Commission, 2:66 op. cit., Spencer Jones, *From Boer War to World War,* p. 135.
38 Jones, *From Boer War to World War*, p. 133.

> this will call for as much self-sacrifice and devotion on the part of these troops as will be required from those taking part in the decisive attack.[39]

It also encouraged the use of concealment and care when siting the guns to ensure they could be moved quickly:

> In distributing the artillery, the combination of its fire with that of the infantry in the close defence, and also the importance of artillery support to counterattacks must be considered. Guns should usually be concealed as much as possible…The first consideration in selecting a position for the artillery is, that it shall be able to open fire on an enemy at long range, and thus compel his infantry to assume an extended formation at the greatest possible distance. The second is that it should be possible to withdraw without difficulty.[40]

It also saw that the artillery in close proximity to infantry had a positive effect on morale:

> The advance should be covered by all the artillery available, which should at the same time keep a careful watch for the appearance of the enemy's reserves, so that they may be crushed without delay. The action of the artillery should be characterised by boldness. The moral effect of batteries advancing in support of the infantry may decide the issue when success or failure hangs in the balance.[41]

This did not answer the conundrum of finding the balance between concealment, which would guarantee their own security and protection, and the use of direct fire in close proximity to the infantry and the *moral effect* it would have.

The policy of firing from concealed positions waxed and waned post Boer-War. When lessons were fresh it was at its most dominant but most difficult to achieve. In 1907, the Inspector General of Forces complained that there was an absence of uniformity and requested that the General Staff make an official announcement 'regarding the merits of direct versus, indirect fire.'[42] This note was not actioned and it was noted in his report the following year that different commands chose opposing methods. The introduction of the QF 13 and 18 in 1904 with its gun shields enabled the guns to fight more safely out in the open. The British guns suffered from technical difficulties which, due to financial constraints remained unresolved before the beginning of the war. The gun platforms were unstable and the gun needed to be relayed between rounds. The fuse on each round also had to be manually set. These technical problems and the time it took to prepare concealed positions greatly reduced the artillery's ability to get quickly into action and slowed down its rate of fire. By 1910, General French was becoming concerned and noted 'my opinion is that our artillery compared with the French *rafale* tactics is slow in ranging and in opening fire for effect, and that the ever-growing complication of our method is tending to surpass the capacity of the average battery commander.'[43] To overcome

39 *Field Service Regulations 1909 Part 1*, p. 138.
40 Ibid., p. 96.
41 Ibid., p. 149.
42 TNA WO/163/13: IGF Report op. cit. in Jones, *From Boer War to World War*, p. 140.
43 Ibid., p. 139.

the technical difficulties of engaging targets in both the *direct* and *indirect role,* a new sighting system for the QF 13 and QF 18 pounders was introduced. The Number 7 Dial Sight and the Number 3 Director (survey instrument) were designed to make it easier for the occupation of covered gun positions.[44] Despite the introduction of this new equipment, there was still no supporting doctrine outlining its use. The following year, in 1911, it was noted that in the absence of formal artillery doctrine, that French tactics had been observed being adopted on manoeuvres without official sanction.[45] These tactics were exclusively '*direct fire* and from open positions.'[46] The lack of consensus, and a level of uncertainty persisted over the correct doctrine to be used,[47] and consequently there was a variety of tactical ideas in circulation, with individual officers being left to choose between them...and the use of covered positions was never fully codified...much responsibility was devolved onto the artillery commander as to how to fight his guns.[48] The success or failure of the battery in action 'was often dependant on the degree of enlightenment of the officer in charge.[49]

There were at least five different artillery actions on the morning of the 24th August fought at Élouges and Audregnies by L Battery, RHA (see Map 14) and 119th Battery, RFA and the success or failure of these early actions was very much dependant on a battery commander's own thoughts on the merits of *indirect* fire from concealed positions or firing *direct* from open position in close proximity to the infantry they were supporting. Lieutenant Preston's section occupied two different positions. Firstly he deployed *"500 m east where it subsequently moved from a half cock position north on the Wiheries-Audregnies road,"* and then he moved his position *"south west along the road until they came into action in the open just alongside the end house of the village where two field tracks met in a fork, heavy ploughed land."* L Battery occupied three positions, and fired from two firstly, *"L Battery RHA came into action having joined the 2nd Cavalry Brigade from Wiheries at first light. The battery deployed south of Élouges and east of the E in Élouges,"* later it moved when *"Brigadier De Lisle then sent L Battery to the high ground between Audregnies and Élouges."* The decision for them to finally withdraw was taken by Lieutenant Colonel Ballard, who told Major Alexander that his four guns were to retire and L Battery were told to retire once they had nearly fired all their *"ammunition by the Brigade Major, Captain Hamilton-Grace."* Lieutenant Preston was required to retire after his isolated position came under *direct fire.* At this point in the battle, both batteries of artillery were ordered to retire, which left the Cheshire Regiment with no supporting fire for the next three hours while the battle continued and neither of the batteries who had previously been in action were re-supplied and sent back to support Lieutenant Colonel Boger. Notwithstanding the fact that Lieutenant Colonel Ballard thought the Cheshire Regiment was withdrawing, it would have been apparent from the noise, that the battle was still taking place and there were soldiers still on the battlefield.

L Battery RHA, on the 24th August, came in and out of action on two occasions without difficulty, and their casualties amounted to no more than 10, with no fatalities. Both elements of 119th Battery RFA suffered heavy casualties, a total of 54 men of which 11 were fatal. The

44 Gen. Sir Martin Farndale KCB, *History of the Royal Regiment of Artillery: Western Front 1914-18*, p. 2.
45 TNA WO 163/18: IGF Report 1911, pp. 495-496 and Farndale, p. 139.
46 Ibid., p. 115.
47 Ibid.
48 Ibid., p. 157.
49 Ibid.

manpower was sufficiently depleted to necessitate support from the 9th Lancers to extricate the remaining four guns. This would indicate that the reserve company of the Norfolk Regiment who were in the sunken road 300 yards to their front had already retired. The guns and limbers were placed to the rear and there were two gallantry awards for this action in addition to Major Alexander's Victoria Cross; a DCM for Battery Quartermaster Sergeant H. Morgan who 'under heavy shell and rifle fire limbered up the guns section, and then brought up limbers and teams for other four guns, enabling them to be got away,'[50] and a DSO for Captain Walford who was wounded twice[51] and his gallantry was recognised for his actions at Élouges.[52] There is no explanation as to why a party of men commanded by Captain Walford and BQMS Morgan did not come forward and assist their own battery? For his gallant action, Lieutenant Preston was mentioned in despatches and promoted to captain while he was a prisoner of war.

In all the artillery actions fired in support of the action at Élouges and Audregnies, the guns fired from *exposed positions* and the battery commanders chose not to fire from concealed positions. The lack of clear artillery doctrine and the lateness of the introduction of technical solutions left a degree of autonomy with the commanders, as to the gun position to be adopted. This, when supported by the *Field Service Regulations 1909,* possibly influenced the artillery commanders towards firing from open positions in close support of their infantry. It would appear that both the Major Hon. Sclater-Booth and Major Alexander (and Lieutenant Preston) all favoured firing in this way. The only difference between the two commanders was the fact that Major Alexander had not considered how he would extricate himself if the position became untenable, which clearly was not the case with L Battery "the guns were run forward about 20-30 yards to a hedge and extracted by single guns in succession (this running forward was the salvation of the battery, as it could not have limbered up where it was).

The firing from open positions might also have been the preferred *modus operandi* for all the artillery in the 5th Infantry Division and since they had trained in isolation in Ireland, it is likely to have prevailed throughout. Later that month, at La Cateau, it was noted that of the three infantry divisions deployed that it was "the artillery of 5th Division who chose to occupy forward positions, ostensibly to inspire the infantry.'[53] Also, when comparing casualties at La Cateau, 'the 5th Divisions guns followed the line of the *Field Artillery Training,* and although offering strong support also suffered serious casualties, whereas 3rd Division's guns took the concealed route preferred by the *Field Service Regulations*.'[54]

## Conclusion

Prior to the morning of the 24th August, neither battery commander had had the opportunity to fight or exercise alongside their infantry before and neither had been subjected to enemy rifle or artillery counter-battery fire. Given the opportunity to fight the action again they both might have chosen (especially 119th Battery who could have moved the guns back 300 yards to

50 *Western Mail*, 11th November 1914.
51 *The Standard*, 12th November 1914.
52 *Western Mail*, 11th November 1914.
53 Richard Holmes, *Riding the Retreat: Mons to the Marne 1914 Revisited* (London: Pimlico, 2007), p. 179.
54 Shelford Bidwell & Dominick Graham, *Fire Power: The British Army-Weapons and Theories of War 1904-1945:* (London: Leo Cooper, 2004), p. 68.

the position of the railway line in the hollow where their limbers had been placed) to have done it differently. What is not in doubt is the gallantry and aggression of the batteries in support of their infantry. Their choice of tactics was a decision of the unknown, it was just unfortunate that they were not able to stay in action longer, from concealed position and be re-supplied with ammunition once theirs had been expended. The withdrawal of artillery from the battlefield at Audregnies was at best premature since there were still troops in action for a further three hours who were left without support, which was the sole *raison d'être* of the artillery. The artillery engagement and support at Audregnies was made to work at a tactical level. The debate over the fire positions to be adopted on this occasion was possibly academic. The fact that the infantry were left on the field of battle with no artillery support, when the four brigades of artillery belonging to the 3rd and 5th Infantry Divisions, who were only a few miles away and did not come into action at all on the 24th August, was a failure of the CRA, which was compounded by poor communications and as yet an underdeveloped doctrine. Had the weight of power of the four unused brigades been brought to bear against the enveloping movement of *AK IV*, the result would have been significantly different, and the casualties incurred by the Cheshires would have been marked less.

## Cavalry

"The present training of cavalry shows tendencies that may lead to the useless sacrifice of our available cavalry force in war" – General Sir Charles Douglas, 1913[55]

"In no circumstances, however, does the C-in-C wish the Cavalry Division to be seriously engaged until he is ready to support it" – General Wilson

"I am going to *charge* the enemy and will tell the 4th Dragoon Guards, now in the village to make an attack on the left. As soon as you see them debouch for the attack you will attack on the right with at least two squadrons" – Brigadier De Lisle

Engagement, where the absorption of the contest, the extended formations adopted by the infantry, and the exhaustion entailed by the continued strain of battle combine to render artillery and infantry particularly susceptible to sudden and unforeseen attacks by mounted action.[56] The attacking troops will remain as long as possible at the trot; they will increase the pace to a gallop in sufficient time to permit the charge being made with the necessary momentum.[57] The charge usually at about 300-500 yards distance from the enemy, he will give the command "LINE WILL ATTACK" the pace will be slightly increased and lances bought to the engage… the charge should not be ordered, therefore until the line is about 50 yards distant from the enemy…On the command "CHARGE one cheer will be given.[58] The artillery and machine guns…their duty is to prepare the way for the cavalry and to support it…the commander should separate the mounted attack from the fire attack so that the latter is not masked up to the

55 Anglesey, *A History of the British Cavalry 1899-1913*, Vol. 4 (London: Leo Cooper, 1986), p. 422.
56 HMSO, *Cavalry Training 1912*, p. 229 para 1.
57 Ibid., p. 278 para 5.
58 Ibid., p. 279 paras 6-8.

moment of collision. This can be carried by…moving away from each other.[59] He must arrange to reconnoitre beforehand all ground over which the cavalry might have to act, and to take such steps as may be possible to make it more suitable for the movement of cavalry e.g. opening gates, cutting wire fences, ramping ditches and so forth. His orders must be clearly given, objectives clearly pointed out to his subordinates, his force duly detailed accordingly in accordance with these objectives and moved and deployed under cover, before he launches his attack.[60]

General Allenby clearly sowed the seed of a mounted attack to Brigadier De Lisle, who did not need much encouraging. Whether that was General Allenby's intent is difficult to assess since he was known not to finish his sentences, and did 'not convey exactly what he means.'[61] General Allenby was still attached to old-style cavalry tactics despite facing up to the realities of modern warfare, 'ignoring what he had seen and learnt in South Africa, still hankered after traditional cavalry warfare.'[62]

The mounted attack took place with the 9th Lancers in the lead supported by the 4th Dragoon Guards. The direction of attack was north from the village of Audregnies towards Quiévrain using the line of the Roman road as the axis of advance. The enemy had just been seen by Lieutenant Colonel Campbell "who could see long lines of infantry advancing east from Quiévrain. I at once ordered one squadron to take up a fire position and fire was shortly after opened on us, the range to the nearest troops being 1200 yards." The infantry of the Cheshires and Norfolks including Captain Shore's B Company were in position, and the artillery were engaging the enemy from three locations: L Battery RHA to the rear right of the 9th Lancers at Audregnies along with Lieutenant Preston's section from 119th Battery RFA, with the remaining guns of the battery under the command of Major Alexander to the south west of Élouges. To the front of the 9th Lancers were the squadrons of the 18th Hussars deployed along the line of the mineral railway east to west and there were no standing troops north of the mineral railway. The nature of the ground to the north of the cavalry position was familiar to both regiments as they had withdrawn across it earlier in the morning. The 4th Dragoon Guard's supporting action was in the direction of Baisieux and, during their initial *charge* two troops became embroiled amongst the troops of the lancers. In many publications, the axis and the direction of the 4th Dragoon Guards has been taken from the diary account of Private Clouting (and others) who was caught up with the lancer action and attributed their personal direction as that as the same as that of the main regimental movement, but this is incorrect. The official history of the war, written by Edmonds records this part of the action accurately as two separate regimental mounted actions. However, technically three separate mounted actions took place if you count Lieutenants Fetherstonhaugh and Hickman initial action as being separate from the main 4th Dragoon Guard charge towards Baisieux, and the 9th Lancer action as a single charge.

It would appear that although the 4th Dragoon Guards were to support the 9th Lancers, their mission was different as Lieutenant Colonel Mullens "received a verbal order from the brigade staff to gallop my Regiment out to the north of the town and to be prepared for a determined infantry attack." Major Bridges thought "we were ordered to clear out the enemy from around the village, full of the spirit of the *arme blanche* and imagining that it was a matter of chasing

59 Ibid., pp. 268-269 para 2-3.
60 Ibid., pp. 240-241 para 4.
61 Batten, *Futile Exercise?*, p. 114.
62 James. *Imperial Warrior, p. 49.*

away cavalry patrols," whereas for the 9th Lancers, the objective was further north. As both regiments deployed from Audregnies, the 9th Lancers "A Squadron led the way in *line of troops column*...Captain Grenfell formed his squadron in l*ine of troops column* and the 4th Dragoon Guards, Lieutenant Chance followed his troop leader, "who formed *troop in squadron columns.*" At no point did any of the squadrons of either regiment form LINE or the word *CHARGE* was given. Corporal Easton's references to charging the guns and *charge* cheering would appear to be case of conflagration of the story as a result of being retold over time. Those who were charging said "we were galloping into carnage, for nobody knew what we were supposed to be doing and there was utter confusion from the start"..."We are going to charge the guns"..."moved off at a trot and ride knee to knee and could see figures moving about in the distance "lance engage," and the squadron galloped 'shouting and cheering.' *Therefore, technically, no charge took place and would be more accurately described as a mounted action.*

## Conclusion

The launch of the mounted action was premature, as the German infantry were 1200 yards to the north. The mounted attack was in the same line as the supporting fire, from L Battery, Lieutenant Preston's section from 119th Battery and the Maxim Guns of the 9th Lancers and 4th Dragoon Guards. This masked their view and they were not best able to provide covering fire. The ground was not suitable for a mounted action and the presence of wire fences was known before the mounted action by either the 9th Lancers or the nuns in the *pensionnat.* No attempt had been made to prepare the ground prior to the deployment or the positions of either the artillery or cavalry adjusted to give them the best opportunity of success. Despite the focus on the mounted action being brought to a halt by the wire fences, no cavalry managed to cross the line of the mineral railway which is where the German infantry were at the point of execution, and therefore the cavalry did not make physical contact with the German infantry. The railway provided a more significant obstacle to the cavalry and, even if it had managed to cross the railway, it is difficult to imagine how they would have wheeled and formed line to effect a mounted *charge.* The effect on the enemy might be best judged by the fact that of the four infantry and the two artillery regiments, none of them mention it in their regimental histories. There is only the single reference by *Feldartillerie Regiment 74* of "*1000 metres to the left a dismounted cavalry squadron practiced flag signals towards the south.*"

On two separate occasions prior to leaving at Tidworth, Brigadier De Lisle demonstrated and practised mounted cavalry charges: one, Regimental. For Queen Mary on the 8th August and a second one on the 14th August as a whole brigade on his final inspection. From a cavalry perspective, if ever there was an example of how the Brigade Commander thought he would operate, clearly this was Brigadier De Lisle's expectation of the war he was about to embark upon and he used it on the first opportunity presented to him. The mounted action was conducted by elements of a single brigade, General Allenby did not look to use or support the actions of the 2nd Cavalry Brigade and 3rd Cavalry Brigade with either of his other two brigades, and neither did he consider using the batteries of uncommitted RHA guns to support the 2nd Cavalry Brigade's mounted attack. Therefore, despite the whole of the Cavalry Division being in the locality, it was limited to two small Cavalry Brigade actions. The reality was that General Allenby from the outset had never gripped the brigades under his command and had "failed to win their liking or their confidence." As a result, the Division was a collection of four independent brigades, with a somewhat critical and suspicious allegiance to Divisional Headquarters. This status quo, the fluid situation and poor communications created an almost impossible task 'to handle this unwieldy formation in circumstances of the utmost difficulty and danger, into which they were plunged at once without any opportunity to settle down,.[63] For much of the following period, Brigadier Sir James Edmonds thought that General Allenby and his staff 'never knew where their brigades were.'[64]

The personal relationship between General Allenby and Brigadier Gough typified the situation. Brigadier Gough later wrote in February 1930, 'I had been so occupied and so confined to my own problems and owing to the faulty command system of that stupid man Allenby we were kept in such ignorance of the entire situation.'[65] He claimed to have not known the whole story of what had been going on in 1914 until he read Smith-Dorrien's memoirs.'[66] On the 26th August, instead of seeking direction from General Allenby, Brigadier Gough phoned GHQ asking for further orders, to which General Wilson told him 'you are on the spot. Do what you like, old boy.'[67] On the 27th August, when Brigadier Gough was asked by Brigadier Chetwode why his Cavalry Brigade was miles from where it was supposed to be in support of I Corps, he replied that 'he was getting as far away from the Bull as possible.[68] Later he explained his action saying 'I felt compelled to safeguard my own brigade.'[69]

Doctrinally, it is difficult to see where the mounted action initiated by General Allenby conforms other than:

> The characteristics of the arm often allow but little time for consideration. Rapid decisions must often be made under most unfavourable conditions and executed at once without detailed instructions or explanations. In many cases it will be impossible for the cavalry commander to gauge with any degree of accuracy, the strength and dispositions of his adversary.[70]

The German infantry were 1200 yards away, so they had time. The moment of consideration and the adjustment of the troops had been replaced by the daring and dash of the cavalry, which resulted in no discernible military effect on the Germans. Major Beale-Browne had told the soldiers after the attack "that the *charge* was made to take the fire off the infantry who were retiring." The Special Brigade Order was correct in that the *flank guard* action "was necessary to save the 5th Division from an organised counter-attack during their retirement," but it is difficult to reconcile "but for the 2nd Cavalry Brigade his division would have been destroyed to the last man." The statement regarding "the true cavalry spirit of the 9th Lancers in daring to *charge* unbroken infantry in order to save neighbouring troops, and that of the 4th Dragoon Guards in the effective support given without hesitation or thought of danger," is correct, but

63 Wavell, *Allenby*, p. 129.
64 Brian Gardner, *Allenby* (London: Cassell, 1965), p. 75.
65 Farrar-Hockley, *Goughie*, p. 352.
66 Ibid., p. 352.
67 Gen. Sir Gough Hubert, *The Fifth Army* (London: Hodder & Stoughton, 1931), p. 32.
68 Gardner, *Allenby*, p. 75.
69 Ibid., p. 72.
70 HMSO, *Cavalry Training 1912*, p. 230 para 299.

it is just difficult to specifically attribute the mounted actions effect on the overall result of the day. De Lisle wrote in his account of the day "the *charge* was well led and gallantly executed by all squadrons. The actual effect was marred by a wire fence between the squadrons and the cavalry. The moral effect was complete." Captain Osburn wrote that the Commanding Officer of the 4th Dragoons did not agree with his Brigade Commander's assessment and said he was 'indignant, sorely grieved, wondering who had ordered his squadrons into this disastrous affair. One subaltern complained that De Lisle "had lost half his brigade for no reason."'[71]

## Wire Fences

Historically, the *charge* at Audregnies has become famous more for its misleading reports and dramatic artwork that appeared in newspapers and periodicals, showing the lancers charging the guns then the detail of the action itself. It is difficult to be sure where this corruption started, but is then likely to be a combination of reasons which included the restrictions of the DORA, which stated that: "no person shall by word of mouth or in writing spread reports likely to cause disaffection or alarm among any of His Majesty's forces or among the civilian population." This sentence alone prevented the accurate reporting of early actions of the war in France and Belgium and ensured that the early reports erred towards the positive at a time when the country and the press was desperate for news from the front. The fragments of information which slowly made their way back from the front or were carried in the French press were remarkably accurate, and as the story grew the picture developed. The artwork around Captain Grenfell's Victoria Cross citation was numerous and exaggerated, possibly conforming to an image of how the artists perceived the action to have been and corrupting the interpretation of his citation from "For gallantry in action against unbroken infantry at Audregnies, Belgium on 24th August 1914, and for gallant conduct in assisting to save the guns of the 119th Battery, Royal Field Artillery, near Doubon the same day" i.e. to somehow read the charging of guns?

For the following 100 years, historians took the opportunity to point out the errors in the subsequent artwork and in particular the most famous of pictures painted by Richard Caton-Woodville (which was donated by Colonel Christopher Peto, in 1978 and hangs in the National Army Museum), called "The First Victoria Cross of the European War, Captain Francis Grenfell, 9th Lancers at Audregnies, 24th August 1914," which in itself was technically an inaccurate title as this excluded the Victoria Crosses won the previous day." The first two Victoria Crosses were won on 23rd August by Lieutenant Maurice Dease and Private Sidney Godley from the 4 Royal Fusiliers.

> This action was later compared to the Charge of the Light Brigade since it demonstrated great bravery but accomplished little. Later in the day, Grenfell and his men helped to drag away British guns which were in danger of being captured. In this painting, the artist appears to have combined the two events. Although not the first action of World War One (1914-1918) for which the Victoria Cross was awarded.[72]

71 Anglesey, *A History of the British Cavalry, 1914-1919*, Vol. 7, p. 124.
72 *National Army Museum* <https://collection.nam.ac.uk/detail.php?acc=1978-09-22-1> (Accessed 20th August 2018).

Recovering the Guns. (Author's Collection)

These misleading images were also supported by poetry which compared the *charge* of the 9th Lancers to the *charge* of the 21st Lancers at Balaclava. Sir William Watson wrote in the *The Times*, and it was carried in many other newspapers including the *Manchester Evening News* on Saturday 5th September 1914:

**Charge of the 9th Lancers**

MELINITE, lyddite, darkened heaven,
*But straight at the guns the Lancers rode*
*By the light of the rage that in them glowed*
*Straight at the guns, the deadly Eleven*
*That had raked and shelled them seven times seven.*
*With never a halt or a needless word*
*With never a screen from the shattering breath*
*Of a myriad iron throats of death*
*At the cannon in ambush our horsemen spurred,*
*Fiercely, grimly their fathers' sons*
*And slew the gunners beside their guns,*
*And captured the cannon, the roaring Eleven,*
*That deafened the earth and darkened the heaven.*
*Then their dauntless remnant came*

*Out of the hurricane, out of the flame,*
*Covered with smoke and dust and fame.*

*Shout, you shires, with a chorus sent*
*Ringing from Caithness right to Kent,*
*From far Northumberland down past Devon!*
*Shout for your heroes, Britain's sons,*
*Who stifled the breath of the thundering guns.*
*The courage that lifted their hearts shall leaven*
*All who go forth in England's name,*
*Born to o'ercome as these o'ercame,*
*And winnow the earth with the flail of Heaven.*

The presence of wire and fences was an issue for the Germans and British alike. It was a hazard the cavalry had encountered during the Boer War and squadrons were issued wire cutters to remove them. With the exception of exercising on Salisbury Plain, the 9th Lancers would have encountered wire and fences during the summer manoeuvres of 1911 and 1912 when they returned to England. Neither of these major exercises took place on military training areas which would have been cleared of wire. The cavalry had been seen to be removing wire by Lieutenant Owens, and Lieutenants Norman and Riddell from the 9th and 16th Lancers had been sent out on patrol to cut wire. Prior to the mounted action, Captain Grenfell stated "I at once reconnoitred the ground with my glasses and saw there was a good deal of wire." The 9th Lancers would now advance north over ground they had already withdrawn over and occupied for the previous 24 hours. The threat to the cavalry horses was known in Audregnies and "the order has been widespread through the village to take off all wire fences that separated the meadows to allow easier troops movements." Major Horn on his first reconnaissance patrol reported that "country very much wired and very like England in many places." While in position with D Battery RHA, Bombardier Crowley "cut down a wire fence in a few places so as to make it easy to get away, should he decide to move that way." The fact that the cavalry got "entangled in wire" was known to Herbert Asquith almost immediately the following morning. Even the chancellor knew the story as when he was visiting sick and wounded soldiers at Albany Road Hospital in Cardiff, David Lloyd George asked a soldier what his regiment was to which he replied "I was with the 12th Lancers" to which the chancellor said "were you in the *charge* against the barbed wire?" No, said the bed-ridden lancer, "that was the 9th Lancers."[73]

On the 28th September 1921, Major A.H. Burne from the Royal Artillery and a friend visited the area around Quiévrain, Audregnies and Élouges and said that "there was no sign of any wire fence near the *sucrerie de carachette* or anywhere else in the neighbourhood." He said this had been confirmed by five local men who were in the vicinity.[74] The reason for this statement is unclear, and has only served to add confusion to the story. The weight of evidence from both British and German sources would suggest that this statement can be safely

73 *Western Mail*, 1st October 1914.
74 Van Emden, *Teenage Tommy*, p. 57.

disregarded. Interestingly the presence of wire fences and the impact it had on the cavalry *charge* is not mentioned in Edmonds' official history![75]

**Conclusion:**

The presence of wire was never disputed and its presence was known prior to the mounted action serving as a hindrance to the cavalry as they advanced towards the guns. The wire fences for the most part would appear not to be barbed, but simple livestock fences of a ribbon type construction thicker than seen in England. The cavalry did not cross the line of the mineral railway even in the areas where there was no wire. The mineral railway served as a far greater barrier to the advancement of the cavalry than the presence of wire. The focus on the presence of wire has been over-emphasised as a contributing factor in the stalling of the intended cavalry action, as a result of the misleading illustrations carried in the popular press. It was a hindrance to both the German and British infantry and cavalry alike. The British cavalry *fatalities* remarkably low considering the weight of small arms and artillery fire they were subjected to. The continued alternative narrative of the cavalry being caught in wire is an observation as to the inaccuracies of artwork has only served to provide a barrier to the known military facts, and neither the lancers nor dragoons ever claimed to have "charged the guns." Even if the line of the cavalry advance had been free from wire, it is highly unlikely that the 9th Lancers would have been able to successfully get more than 600 horses across the mineral railway line and wheel into line to conduct a formal cavalry *charge* in the face of an advancing infantry battalion supported by artillery. Had there been other significant mounted actions by the cavalry elsewhere or later in the war, it is highly likely that the same story would have been re-told. The presence of wire was not unique to Audregnies and cavalry moving at speed over open countryside would at some point hit either a sunken road, a wire fence or railway line which would either disrupt or halt a mounted action moving at speed. The lack of further mass cavalry actions has allowed this story to sit in isolation and appear unique.

**Summary**

For the BEF and its commanders, Mons and Audregnies were the first engagements of the war it seems a little trite judging them against the manuals and regulations of the time, with the benefit of hindsight. The observations made are specific to the actions of the regiments involved in the actions discussed in this book and do not encompass the broader actions of the day. In truth, none of the senior commanders were holding operational appointments they had held before and despite all the lessons learnt post-Boer War by the Army as a whole, they still needed to be learnt by the individuals concerned. Both General Allenby and Brigadier De Lisle were wedded to *arme blanche*, and it would only be the coming campaign that showed how the cavalry might be more effectively used within the context of the modern battlefield.

75 There is no specific mention of wire fences in Edmonds, *Military Operations France and Belgium 1914*, Vol. I, p. 101.

For the most part, in the first 48 hours of the strategic battle, Field Marshal French's headquarters was ineffective, and neither he or GHQ commanded the battle effectively. The battle was fought by two Corps Commanders with a series of independent brigade actions. It was entirely *reactive* and dictated by the actions of the advancing Germans and the withdrawal of General Lanrezac. After the Cavalry Division's participation in the actions on the 24th August, and for the following period, even before the separation of his division into two separate forces (1st and 2nd Cavalry Divisions) on the 6th September it is difficult to see to what extent General Allenby actually commanded his whole Cavalry Division. The only adjustment to the initial deployment positions before the battle was the allocation of 19th Infantry Brigade to General Allenby to covered the far-left flank and the loan of Brigadier Haking's 5th Infantry Brigade from the 2nd Division to fill the gap between General Smith-Dorrien's two divisions, so in effect all the commanders fought their battles with the troops they had at hand. The overall lack of strategic understanding in the first 24 hours did not permit Field Marshal French's headquarters to concentrate their troops where they were required once the mission had changed from an *advance* to a *withdrawal* and the engagement of the BEF and *AOK 1* was therefore a *meeting engagement.* Any success that was achieved at Audregnies and Élouges was though the training, professionalism and gallantry of the junior officers and soldiers and the overall success of the day was achieved at a tactical and operational level.

The action at Audregnies was fundamentally flawed as it was not in keeping with the direction given in the *Field Service Regulations 1909:*

> When the object is to act as a covering force, or to gain time, a commander will be much influenced by the strategical situation and the nature of the country in which he is operating. The delaying power of a numerically inferior force is greatly affected by ground. When a force is occupying a strong position, which cannot be turned or can only be turned by a wide movement through difficult country, its delaying power is very great; and where a series of such positions exist, a comparatively small force, acting on the general principles… of the action of a rear guard.
>
> On the other hand, if such a force accepts battle in a position which is liable to envelopment, or in a country and under conditions where an enemy has liberty to manoeuvre, it can extricate itself only under cover of darkness, or by a successful counter-attack.
>
> When an enemy has liberty to manoeuvre, the passive occupation of a position, however strong, can rarely be justified, and always involves the risk of crushing defeat; under these conditions a delaying force must manoeuvre, so as to force an enemy to deploy as often as possible, but should rarely accept battle.[76]

Regardless of the formal nomenclature: *flank guard, rear guard* or *flank-rear guard,* the commander's intent was ultimately to gain time for the two corps to withdraw. No consideration was given as to what would constitute or necessitate withdrawal and how or when it would take place when the order was given. Ultimately, the aftermath of Audregnies and the dispersion and loss of control of the Cavalry Division was the battle at Le Cateau, when on the morning of the 26th August, General Allenby rode to General Smith-Dorrien's headquarters at Bertry 'with

76 Ibid., p. 155.

the news he lacked the cavalry to keep the Germans at bay and that, if Smith-Dorrien did not shift his men before dawn, "there will be another Sedan." Having established that the soldiers of II Corps were too tired to move, General Allenby said, "in that case I do not think you will get away," to which General Smith-Dorrien replied "I'll fight it out."[77]

77 James. *Imperial Warrior*, pp. 61-62.

# Appendix A

## 9th Lancer's Casualties 24th August 1914

### Regimental casualties (Squadron unknown)

| No. | Rank | Surname | Status | Sqn | 21L | PoW Camp |
|---|---|---|---|---|---|---|
| 5125 | Pte | Jarvis | K | | | |
| 4786 | Pte | Jones | K | | | |
| 30 | Pte | King | W | | | |
| 581 | Pte | Laverty | K | | | |
| 860 | Pte | Linder | K | | | |
| 563 | Pte | Lyons | P | | | Münster |
| | Capt | Middleton | P | RAMC | | Unknown |
| | Capt | Montgomery | W | 7DG | | |
| 537 | Pte | Phillips | P | | | Dülmen |
| 4590 | Pte | Phyall | P | | | Soltau |
| | Capt | Porter | W | | | |
| 53 | Pte | Rittey | K | | | |
| 4969 | Pte | Tuckey | W&P | | | Döberitz |

### A Squadron, 37 casualties

| No. | Rank | Surname | Status | Sqn | 21L | PoW Camp |
|---|---|---|---|---|---|---|
| 537 | Pte | Ackehurst | W&P | A | | Suder Zollhaus |
| 4462 | Pte | Barlow | P&S | A | | Döberitz |
| 531 | Sgt | Barnard | P | A | | Wahn Schiessplatz |
| 319 | Pte | Bentley | P | A | | Rennbahn (Münster II) |
| 4423 | Pte | Bowdle | W | A | | |
| 4076 | LCpl | Bullinger | M | A | | |
| 3400 | Pte | Bumstead | P | A | | Soltau |
| 4745 | Pte | Busk | P | A | | Soltau |

| 4034 | LCpl | Cardy | P | A | | Sennelager |
|---|---|---|---|---|---|---|
| 2441 | Pte | Clancey | W&P | A | | Soltau |
| 3133 | Bdsm | Cody | P | A | | Dülmen |
| 1431 | Pte | Course | W | A | | |
| 2391 | Cpl | Datlin | W&P | A | | Döberitz |
| 4147 | LCpl | Dorman | W&P | A | | |
| 2199 | Pte | Earl | W&P | A | | Soltau |
| 4526 | Pte | Fitzgerald | P | A | | Limburg-Lahn |
| 1600 | Bdsm | Geldard | P | A | | Sennelager |
| 1695 | Sgt | Goodwin | P | A | | Cellelager Hanover |
| 550 | Pte | Grigabe | W&P | A | | Döberitz |
| 1701 | Pte | Guy | P | A | | Soltau |
| 4529 | Pte | Hollings | K | A | | |
| 4477 | LCpl | Lang | P | A | | Erfurt |
| 4525 | Pte | McKnight | K | A | * | |
| 5010 | Pte | Mills | P | A | | Lippspringe |
| 4847 | SSgt (F) | Moxon | P | A | | Soltau |
| | Capt | Peek | P | A | | Gütersloh |
| 939 | Pte | Richardson | P | A | | Sennelager |
| 5121 | Pte | Robinson | P | A | | Soltau |
| 3649 | Pte | Rowlands | W&P | A | | Münsterlager |
| 1125 | Pte | Small | W | A | | |
| 4822 | Sgt | Tyte | W&P | A | | Scharnhorst Magdeburg |
| 4024 | Pte | Wall | P | A | | Döberitz |
| 3741 | LCpl | Wallis | P | A | | Scharnhorst Magdeburg |
| 4653 | Pte | Warr | P | A | | Soltau |
| 3929 | LCpl | Webb | W | A | | |
| 4464 | Pte | Winter | M | A | | |
| 4406 | LCpl | Wood | P | A | | Sturboat bei Celle Hanover |

**B Squadron, 26 casualties**

| No. | Rank | Surname | Status | Sqn | 21L | PoW Camp |
|---|---|---|---|---|---|---|
| 4788 | Pte | Brock | W&P | B | | Wittenberg |
| 4152 | Pte | Cole | P | B | | Soltau |
| 5099 | Pte | Conway | M | B | | Limburg-Lahn |

| | | | | | | |
|---|---|---|---|---|---|---|
| 2753 | Pte | Cowler | P | B | | Münster |
| 121 | Pte | Cox | P | B | | Sennelager |
| 3420 | Pte | Cross | P | B | | Hakenmoor (Stroken) Hanover |
| 4560 | Pte | Dark | K | B | | |
| 1090 | Cpl | Denslow | K | B | * | |
| 4629 | Pte | Dove (aka Doman) | P&E | B | | Soltau |
| 4025 | Pte | Duggan | M | B | | Reserve Lazarett-Münster |
| 35 | Cpl | Easton | P | B | | Soltau |
| 3168 | Tptr | Evans | P | B | | Wittenberg |
| 1194 | Pte | Fletcher | P | B | | Soltau |
| | Lt | Garstin | K | B | | |
| | Capt | Grenfell | W | B | | |
| 3381 | Pte | Hooper | W | B | | |
| 1308 | Pte | James | M | B | | |
| | Capt | Nash-Wortham | W | B | | |
| 628 | Cpl | Oliver | W | B | | |
| 4484 | Pte | Prosser | W | B | | |
| 4027 | LCpl | Scott | K | B | | |
| 4117 | Pte | Smith | W | B | | Wittenberg |
| 4452 | Pte | Stephen | P | B | | Sennelager |
| 4028 | Pte | Suckling | P | B | | Grossesmoor Schwege Moorzentrale |
| 5126 | Pte | Velvick | K | B | | |
| 161 | SS | Wyness | P | B | | Sennelager |

**C Squadron 15 casualties**

| No. | Rank | Surname | Status | Sqn | 21L | PoW Camp |
|---|---|---|---|---|---|---|
| 528 | Pte | Barnes | K | C | | |
| 2189 | Pte | Clarke | P | C | | Soltau |
| 4041 | Pte | Clay | W | C | | |
| 4462 | Pte | Cullen | W&P | C | | Grosses Moor Schwege Moorzentrale |
| 2493 | Pte | Fiernan | P | C | | Hanover |
| 2194 | Pte | Freestone | W | C | | |
| 2196 | Pte | Gibling | P | C | | Döberitz |
| 4784 | Sgt | Holloway | P | C | | Sennelager |

| | | | | | | |
|---|---|---|---|---|---|---|
| 4291 | Sgt | Pickering | P | C | | Schudermahl |
| 4810 | Pte | Pritchard | W | C | | |
| 1362 | Tptr | Reeves | W | C | | |
| 4990 | Cpl SS | Smith | W&P | C | | Döberitz |
| 4963 | Pte | Streek | K | C | | |
| 5075 | Pte | Tebboth | P | C | | Sennelager |
| 4547 | Pte | Walton | M | C | | |

Research originally commenced by Mr Stuart Gruber

K killed or died of wounds
W wounded
P prisoner of war
S sick
E escaped
M missing (not pow)

## Appendix B

### British and German Casualties, 24th August 1914

| Regiment | Killed or DoW | | Wounded | | Missing/PoW | |
|---|---|---|---|---|---|---|
| | Offrs | ORs | Offrs | ORs | Offrs | ORs |
| 9th Lancers | 1 | 14 | 4 | 18 | 2 | 57 |
| 4th Dragoon Guards | | 9 | | | | 65 |
| Cheshire Regiment | 6 | 59 | | | 14 | 663 |
| Norfolk Regiment | 4 | 51 | 4 | 83 | | 167 |
| 18th Hussars | 1 | 18 | | | | |
| L Battery RHA | | | 1 | 7 | | 2 |
| 119 Battery RFA | | 11 | 1 | 37 | 1 | 4 |
| **Total** | 12<br>**1,304** | 162 | 10 | 145 | 17 | 958 |

| Regiment | Killed or DoW | | Wounded | | Missing/PoW | |
|---|---|---|---|---|---|---|
| | Offrs | ORs | Offrs | ORs | Offrs | ORs |
| Infanterie Regiment 26 | 2 | 20 | 4 | 108 | | 14 |
| Infanterie Regiment 66 | 1 | 3 | | 22 | | |
| Infanterie Regiment 72 | 2 | 32 | 2 | 216 | | |
| Infanterie Regiment 93 | | 14 | | 77* | | |
| Feldartillerie Regiment 40 | | | | | | |
| Feldartillerie Regiment 74 | 3 | 9 | | 49** | | |
| **Total** | 8<br>**564** | 78 | 6 | 472 | | |

* The majority were in III Battalion 1 offr and 32 Ors KIA and 48 wounded.
** All (except for one) from III Battalion.

## Appendix C

## Honours and Awards, 24th August 1914

Names of Individuals whose names were brought forward and recommended for gallantry awards for Audregnies and Élouges.

| | | | | | |
|---|---|---|---|---|---|
| | Maj | Alexander | VC | Élouges | 119th Bty |
| | Lt | Allfrey | | * | 9L |
| 8013 | Sgt | Barrow | DCM | | Cheshires |
| | Lt Col | Boger | DSO | | Cheshires |
| | Maj | Bridges | | | 4DG |
| | Lt Col | Campbell | | | 9L |
| | Maj | Chetwynd-Stapleton | MiD | | Cheshires |
| | Lt | Crossley | | * | 9L |
| 4997 | Sgt | Davids | DCM | | 9L |
| | SSM | Durant | Med de Mil | | 9L |
| 9863 | SSM | Ambrose | Med de Mil | | 9L |
| | Capt | Dyer | DSO | | Cheshires |
| | Lt | Elliot | MiD | DSO? | Cheshires |
| | 2Lt | FL Harvey | | * | 9L |
| 9877 | Cpl | Fleet | | | Cheshires |
| | Capt | Fraser (CIH) | | * | 9L |
| | Capt | Grenfell | VC | * | 9L |
| | 2Lt | Harvey DH | | * | 9L |
| | Capt | Hornby | DSO | | 4DG |
| | Lt | Jacobs | MiD | | Cheshires |
| | Capt | Jolliffe | DSO | | Cheshires |
| | Capt | Jones | | | Cheshires |
| | Capt | Lucas-Tooth | DSO | | 9L |
| | 2Lt | Martin-Smith (Int Corps) | | * | 9L |
| | Lt | Matterson | MiD | | Cheshires |
| 6893 | Pte | Moore | MiD | | Cheshires |

| | | | | | |
|---|---|---|---|---|---|
| | BQMS | Morgan | DCM | | 119th Bty |
| | 2Lt | Norman | | * | 9L |
| 4291 | Sgt | Pickering | MM | | 9L |
| | Lt | Preston | MID | | 119th Bty |
| | Lt | Randall | MiD | | Cheshires |
| 4277 | Sgt | Raynor | DCM | | Cheshires |
| | Capt | Reynolds GN (21L) | | * | 9L |
| | Pte | Riley | MiD | | Cheshires |
| | SSM | Sharpe | | | 4DG |
| 9799 | Sgt | Smith | DCM | | Cheshires |
| | 2Lt | Smith | | * | 9L |
| 7963 | Pte | Spencer | MiD | | Cheshires |
| | 2Lt | Straker | | * | 9L |
| | Sgt | Sutherland | Med de Mil | | 18H |
| | Capt | Tahourdin | MiD | | Cheshires |
| 9327 | Pte | Taylor | MiD | | Cheshires |
| | 2Lt | Taylor-Whitehead G | | * | 9L |
| | Pte | Thorpe | DCM | | Cheshires |
| 5001 | Sgt | Turner | DCM | | 9L |
| 144 | Pte | Vaughan | | | Cheshires |
| | Capt | Walford | DSO | | 119th Bty |
| 8261 | Pte | Woodier | DCM | | Cheshires |

* Present at the saving of 119th Bty RFA's guns.

## Bibliography

### Archival Sources


#### War Diaries, The National Archives (Kew)

| | |
|---|---|
| TNA WO 279/47 | Report on Army Manoeuvres, 1912. |
| TNA WO 279/52 | Report on Army Manoeuvres, 1913. |
| TNA WO 95 | 1st Cavalry Division, 1st Signal Squadron Royal Engineers. |
| TNA WO 95/1110/1-6 | 2nd Cavalry Brigade. |
| TNA WO 95/1111 | L Bty, RHA. |
| TNA WO 95/1112 | 4th Dragoon Guards (Account of Audregnies Lieutenant Colonel Mullins). |
| TNA WO 95/1113/2 | 9th Lancers (Lieutenant Colonel D.G.M Campbell, Account of Audregnies). |
| TNA WO 95/1113/2 | 9th Lancers. |
| TNA WO 95/1134/2 | 5th Lancers. |
| TNA WO 95/1134/3 | 16th Lancers. |
| TNA WO 95/1134/4 | 4th Hussars. |
| TNA WO 95/1135 | 4th Cavalry Brigade. |
| TNA WO 95/1139/1 | E Battery RHA. |
| TNA WO 95/1153/2 | 3rd Cavalry Brigade. |
| TNA WO 95/1531/2 | 27th Bde, RFA. |
| TNA WO 95/1532 | 5th Artillery Division, Divisional Troops. |
| TNA WO 95/1535 | 59th Field Company, Royal Engineers. |
| TNA WO 95/1548/1-7 | 13th Infantry Brigade. |
| TNA WO 95/1560/1-3 | 14th Infantry Brigade. |
| TNA WO 95/1564/1 | 1st Duke of Cornwall Light Infantry. |
| TNA WO 95/1571/1 | 1st Cheshire Regiment (Captain J.L Shore, Amplified Account). |
| TNA WO 95/1571/1 | 1st Cheshire Regiment. |

#### Her Majesty's Stationary Office (HMSO)

HMSO *Cavalry Training 1912.*
HMSO *Field Service Regulations 1909 (amended 1912), Vol I.*
HMSO *Great Britain and the European Crisis.*
HMSO *Regulations for Mobilisation 1912.*
HMSO *The First Belgian Grey Book.*

**Personal Diaries and Letters**

Alexander, Maj E.W. Letter property of 9/12L, Derby Museum Collection (#2089/5).

Allenby, Field Marshal Liddle Hard, Sir Basil and Edmonds, Brigadier Sir James Liddle Hart Centre for Military Archives, Papers of Field Marshal Allenby, Sir Basil Liddle Hard and Brigadier Sir James Edmonds.

Allfrey, Lt F de V.B. Diary property of Mr Jimmy Meade.

Anon. 9th Lancer Diary. Property of Malcolm Wright.

Ballard, Lt Col C.R. Account of Audregnies Rough War Diary, property of the Norfolk Regiment Museum.

Ballard, Lt Col C.R. Account of Audregnies. Property of the Norfolk Regiment Museum.

Beech, Lt R.A.J. Diary property of QRL NY Museum.

Boger, Lt Col D.C. Mons, Original Report by Lt Col DC Boger (The Hague, 20th May 1918).

Brigade correspondence NWHRM 12/8. Property of the Norfolk Regiment Museum.

Burnett, Lt Col C. Account of the Action at Élouges by Lieutenant Colonel Charles Burnett 18th QMO Hussars.

Clarke, Pte W. Diary of Private William Clarke, property of the 1st Queen's Dragoon Guards.

De Lisle, Brig Sir H. Account of Audregnies.

Dovey, LCpl J. POW Account. Property of the 9/12L, Derby Museum Collection (#2089/28).

Dyre, Pte H. Diary property of the RDG Museum.

Easton, Cpl H. Diary property Liddle Collection, University Library at Leeds University (LIDDLE/WW1/POW/056/05).

Friend, Shoe Smith J. Letter to Mother, property of 9/12L, photocopies held at Derby Museum, originals are the property of Mr Hitchcock.

Grenfell, Capt F.O. Grenfell Family Papers (within Lyttelton Family Papers); NL/GRE/16/9; Francis Grenfell account of First World War.

Grenfell, F.O. and R.N. GRE/16/5, Grenfell Family Papers (QMUL, within Lyttelton Family Papers); Captain Francis Grenfell booklet on his observations on Germany and the German Army.

Horn, Lt T.L. Diary of the Regiment, 16th (The Queens) Lancers, 4th August-18th October 1914.

Hunt, LCpl W. Diary property of Mrs Marjorie MacMullen.

Hurrell, Pte R. Log of Round the World Cruise (1936). NWHRM # 6586.

Hurrell, Pte R. Notebook property of the Norfolk Regiment Museum. NWHRM #6585.1

Lamb, Lieut. A.J.R. Diary property of the 1st Queen Dragoon Guards.

Leveson, Maj Charles H. Letter to Lt Col Soppers, 7th July 1918.

Marden, Lt B.J.N. Diary of Lieutenant Basil Marden, property of the 9/12L, Derby Museum Collection (#2009-11).

Norman, Lt C.W. Letter to Mr Stuart Gruber, 29th March 1973.

Owens, Capt H.B. The Private Papers of Captain Henry Barton Owens (IWM 4788) dated 24th August 1914.

Peek, Capt R.G. Diary of Captain Grenville Peek, property of the 9/12L, Derby Museum Collection.

Sheldrake, Pte R. Diary (Zwickau, Saxony and Millbank Hospital) property of the Royal Norfolk Regiment Museum.

Sheldrake, Pte R. Prisoner of War Notebook (1915) property of the Royal Norfolk Regiment Museum.

Taylor, Cpl R.H. Letter of Sergeant 'Spur' R.H Taylor. Property of Colonel Patrick Lort-Phillips.

Taylor, Cpl R.H. Letter to Mr Stuart Gruber, 11th January 1973. Property of Mr Stuart Gruber.

Wells, Pte Diary property of the 9/12L IWM Collection (18542).

Wright, Capt. A. Diary property of the RDG Museum.

**Electronic Sources**

Bingham, Adrian *Harmsworth, Alfred Charles William, Viscount Northcliffe* entry <https//encyclopedia.1914-1918-online.net/article/harmsworth_alfred_charles_william_viscount_northcliffe>

Clark, Andrew The Army Council and Military Medical Administration, *British Medical Journal*, No. 1, 20th February 1904) <https//www.jstor.org/stable/i20279576>

Anon, *A Review of Public Events at Home and Abroad for the Year 1914* <https//www.gutenberg.org/files/46471/46471-h/46471-h.htm>

Baker, Betsy Hague Peace Conferences (1899 & 1907), *Oxford Public International Law* (Oxford, Oxford University Press, 2009) <www.opil.ouplaw.com>

Chapman-Curry, Ian *Vengeance Denied* <www.vaguelyinteresting.co.uk/vengeance-denied/>

Connell Jr, Joseph E.A. *Ulster Covenant* <https//www.historyireland.com/20th-century-contemporary-history/the-1912-ulster-covenant-by-joseph-e-a-connell-jr/>

May, Karen Could Captain Scott have been saved? Revisiting Scott's last expedition? (*Aurora Journal*, Vol. 32, No. 4, June 2013) <https//isobelpwilliams.com/2012/02/16/could-captain-scott-have-been-saved/>

Farnell, Kim *A Brief Biography of Alan Leo* <http//www.skyscript.co.uk/Alan_Leo.html>

Elliott, Malcolm *Opposition to the First World War: The Fate of Conscientious Objectors in Leicester* <www.le.ac.uk/lahs/downloads/05_7799_vol 77_Elliott.pdf>

Pearsall, Mark *Enemy Aliens in Great Britain* <https//blog.nationalarchives.gov.uk/enemy-aliens-great-britain-1914-1919/>

Mackrell, Sue Radical Leicester in the First World War: Resistance, Opposition and Non Co-operation <www.storyofleicester.info/cityheritage/atwar/worldwari/>

Fowler, Tom Newport Docks Dispute <www.radicalwales.org>

**Unpublished Thesis**

Teagarden, Ernest Merle The Haldane Army Reforms, 1905-1912 (Unpublished. Ph.D. dissertation, Western Reserve University, 1962).

**Publications and Periodicals**

Crooke, Cpl. W., Twenty Fourth August 1914 (An Impression), *The Oak Leaf Journal*, 2007.
McGuinness, Maj J.H., The Cheshire Regiment Forty Years on From Mons, *The Oak Tree Journal*, 1954.
Seligmann, Matthew S., *Naval Intelligence from Germany: The Reports of the British Naval Attachés in Berlin, 1906–1914* (London, Navy Records Society Publications, 2007).
*The Cavalry Journal The Cavalry Journal* Vol. XII, January to October, London, Royal United Service Institute, 1922).
Various *The Delhi Spearman: 9th Queen's Royal Lancers Regimental Journal*, 1927-28.
Various *The Vadette: Journal of the 21st (Empress of India's) Lancers*, 31st March 1915.
Wood, Prof Robert W., A New Departure in Photography, *The Century Magazine*, 1910.
Wood, Prof Robert W., Photography by Invisible Rays, *The Photographic Journal*, 1910.

**Printed Sources**

Albertini, Luigi, *The Origins of the War of 1914* (New York: Enigma Books, 2004).
Andreopoulos, George and Selesky, Harold E., *The Aftermath of Defeat, Societies, Armed Forces, and the Challenge of Recovery* (New Haven, Connecticut: Yale University, 1994).
Anglesey, Marquess of, *A History of the British Cavalry, 1816-1919, vol.4 1899-1913* (London: Leo Cooper, 1986).
Ascoli, David, *The Mons Star, The British Expeditionary Force 1914 (*London: George G. Harrap and Company, 1981).
Asquith, Margot, *Margot Asquith's Great War Diary 1914-1916, The View from Downing Street* (Oxford: Oxford University Press, 2014).

Ballard, Brig C.R., *Smith-Dorrien* (London: Constable, 1931).
Baring, Maurice, *A Year in Russia* (New York: E.P Dutton and Company, 1907).
Barrow, Gen Sir George de Symons, *The Fire of Life* (London: Hutchinson and Company, 1942).
Bascomb, Neal, *Red Mutiny: Eleven Fateful Days on the Battleship Potemkin* (London: Houghton Mifflin Harcourt, 2007).
Batten, Simon, *Futile Exercise? The British Army's Preparations for War 1902-1914* (Solihull: Helion and Company, 2018).
Baxter, Dolly, *Suffragette the Diary of Dollie Baxter, London 1909-1913* (London: Scholastic, 2003).
Beazley, Ben, *Four Years Remembered, Leicester During the Great War* (Derby: The Breedon Books Publishing Company, 1999).
Beckett, Ian, *The Army and the Curragh Incident, 1914* (London: The Bodley Head for the Army Records Society, 1986).
Benary, Oberstleutnant Albert, *Königlich Preußisches Magdeburgisches Husaren Regiment Nr. 10 im Weltkriege 1914/1918* (Königsberg: Verlag Bernhard and Graefe, 1934).

Bickers, Robert and Tiedemann, R.G., *The Church Militant: Armed Conflicts between Christians and Boxers in North China* (Lanham: Rowman and Littlefield, 2007).
Bidwell, Shelford and Graham, Dominick, *Fire Power: The British Army-Weapons and Theories of War, 1904-1945 The British Army-Weapons and Theories of War, 1904-1945* (London: Leo Cooper, 2004).
Bilbrough, Ethel M., *My War Diary 1914-1918* (Cambridge: Cambridge University Press, 2014).
Blake, Robert, *The Unknown Prime Minister, The Life and Times of Andrew Bonar Law 1858–1918* (London: Faber and Faber, 2011).
Bloem, Walter, *The Advance to Mons: The Experiences of a German Infantry Officer* (Solihull: Helion and Company, 2004).
Bonham-Carter, Violet, *Winston Churchill: An Intimate Portrait* (United Kingdom: Smithmark Publications, 1997).
Bostridge, Mark, *The Fateful Year England 1914* (London: Penguin, 2014).
Bradley, Profs Anthony W. and Ewing, Keith D., *Constitutional and Administrative Law* (London: Longman, 1998).
Brereton, John M., *A History of the 4th and 7th Royal Dragoon Guards and Their Predecessors 1685-1980* (York: Published by the Regiment, 1982).
Bridges, Lt Gen Sir T., *Alarms and Excursions: Reminiscences of a Soldier* (London: Longmans Green and Company, 1938).
Brock, Michael and Brock, Eleanor, (ed.) *H.H. Asquith Letters to Venetia Stanley* (Oxford: Oxford University Press, 1985).
Brough Scott, John, *Galloper Jack* (London: Racing Post Books, 2012).
Buchan, John, *Francis and Riversdale Grenfell: A Memoir* (London: Thomas Nelson and Sons, 1920).
Bülow, Fürst Bernhard von, *Fürst Bülows Reden nebst urkundlichen Beiträgen zu seiner Politik* (Berlin: G. Reimer, 1907).
Buttar, Prit, *Collision of Empires: The War on the Eastern Front in 1914* (Oxford, Osprey Publishing, 2014).
Burnett, Brig Gen C., *The Memoirs of the 18th (Queen Mary's Own) Royal Hussars, 1906-1922, including operations in the Great Wa*r (Winchester, Warren and Sons, 1926).

Callwell, Maj Gen Sir C.E., *Field-Marshal Sir Henry Wilson Bt. GCB, DSO: His Life and Diaries* (London: Cassell and Company, 1927).
Osburn, Arthur Carr, *Unwilling Passenger* (London: Faber and Faber, 1932).
Cassar, George H., *The Tragedy of Sir John French (*University of Delaware Press, 1985).
Chambers, Ian, *The Chamberlains, the Churchills and Ireland, 1874-1922* (New York: Cambria Press, 2006).
Charteris, Brig Gen John, *Field Marshal Earl Haig* (London: Cassell and Co., 1929).
Chesney, Capt G.T., *The Battle of Dorking Reminiscences of a Volunteer* (London: William Blackwood and Sons; 1871).
Childers, Erskine, *German Influence on British Cavalry* (London: E. Arnold, 1911).
Childers, Erskine, *Riddle of the Sands: A Record of Secret Service* (London: Smith, Elder and Co, 1903).

Church, Randolph S., *The Churchill Documents, Vol. 4: Minister of the Crown, 1907-1911* (Hillsdale, Michigan: Hillsdale College Press, 2007).
Churchill, Winston S., *The World Crisis, Vol 1* (London: Odhams Press, 1938).
Clark, Christopher, *Kaiser Wilhelm II A Life in Power* (London: Penguin Books, 2009).
Coleman Richard P. and Neugarten, Bernice L., *Social Status in the City* (San Francisco, Jossey-Bass, 1971).
Coleman, Frederic, *From Mons to Ypres with French: A Personal Narrative* (London: Sampson Low, Marston and Company, 1916).
Colvin Lt Col F.F. and Gordon, Capt E.R., *Diary of the 9th (Q.R.) Lancers During the South African Campaign 1899 To 1902* (South Kensington: Cecil Roy, 1904).
Connolly, Sean, *Oxford Companion to Irish History* (Oxford: Oxford University Press, 1998).
Creagh, Sir O'Moore and Humphris, E.M., *The VC and DSO: A complete record of all those officers, non-commissioned officers and men of his majesty's naval military and air forces who have been awarded these decorations from the time of their institution, with descriptions of the deeds and services which won the distinctions and with many biographical and other details* (London: Standard Art Book Company, 1924).
Crookenden, Col A., *The History of the Cheshire Regiment in the Great War* (London: W H Evans and Co, 1938).
Cross, Rupert *Punishment, Prison and the Public, An Assessment of Penal Reform in Twentieth Century England by An Armchair Penologist* (London: Stevens and Sons, 1971).

Dedijer, Vladimir, *The Road to Sarajevo* (London: Macgibbon and Kee, 1967).
Donnell, Clayton, *Breaking the Fortress Line 1914* (Barnsley: Pen and Sword Military, 2013).
Donnell, Clayton, *The Forts of the Meuse in World War I* (Oxford: Osprey Publishing, 2007).
Donnelley, Paul, *Assassination!* (London: Dataday Publishing, 2012).
Doughty, Robert A., *Pyrrhic Victory: French Strategy and Operations in the Great War* (Cambridge, Massachusetts: Harvard University Press, 2008).
Douglas, Roy, *History of the Liberal Party 1895-1970* (London: Sidgwick and Jackson, 1971).
Duffy, Stephen M., *The Integrity of Ireland Home Rule: Nationalism, and Partition, 1912-1922* (Vancouver: Fairleigh Dickinson University Press, 2009).
Dunlop, John K., *The Development of the British Army1899-1914* (London: Methuen, 1938).
Dunlop, Robert and Puttkammer, Holger (eds.), *The Battle of Mons: The official German Account* (London: Robert Dunlop, 2015).
Dunn, Capt J.C. *The War the Infantry Knew 1914-1919* (London: Abacus, 1988).

Edmonds, Brig Gen Sir James E., *Military Operations France and Belgium 1914, Vol. I* (London: Macmillan, 1922/1934).
Edwards, John, *Remembrance of a Riot: The Story of the Llanelli Railway Strike Riots of 1911* (Llanelli: Llanelli Borough Council, 1988).
Elliot, Brian, *Blériot Herald of an Age* (Stroud: Tempus Publishing, 2000).
Elvert, Jügen, *Northern Ireland Past and Present* (Stuttgart, Franz Steiner Verlag, 1994).
Emmerson, Charles, *1913 The World before the Great War* (London: Random House, 2013).
Ensor, Robert C.K., *England 1870–1914: The Oxford History of England* (Oxford: Oxford University Press, 1936).

Esher, Reginald Brett, 2nd Viscount, *Journals and letters of Reginald Viscount Esher, 1870*-1903 (London: Ivor Nicholson and Watson, 1934).
Esherick, Joseph W., *The Origins of the Boxer Uprising* (Los Angeles, Berkeley and Los Angeles, California: University of California Press, 1987).
Evans, Capt H.K.D. and. Laing, N.O., *The 4th (Queen's Own) Hussars in the Great War* (Naval and Military Press reprint of 1920 edition).

Farndale, Gen Sir Martin KCB, *History of the Royal Regiment of Artillery, Western Front 1914-18* (Dorchester: Dorset Press, 1986).
Farrah-Hockley, Anthony, *The Life of General Sir Hubert Gough, Goughie* (London: Hart-Davis MacKibbon, 1975).
Fergusson, Sir James, *The Curragh Incident* (London: Faber and Faber, 1964).
Foley, Robert T., *German Strategy and the Path to Verdun: Erich von Falkenhayn and the Development of Attrition, 1870-1916* (Cambridge: Cambridge University Press, 2005).
French, Field Marshal Viscount of Ypres, *1914* (London, Constable and Company, 1919).

G Gardiner, Alfred *Prophets, Priests and Kings* (London: Alston Rivers, 1908).
Gardner, Brian, *Allenby* (London: Cassell and Company, 1965).
Geiss, Imanual *July 1914: Selected Documents Outbreak of the First World War* (New York: Charles Scribner's Sons, 1968).
Gertrude Colmore, *The Life and Death of Emily Wilding Davison* (London: Women's Press, 1988).
Gibb, Rev. Harold *Record of the 4th Irish Dragoon Guards in the Great War 1914-1918* (Canterbury: Harold Gibb, 1925).
Glaser-Gerhard, Dr Ernst, *Das Altmärkische Feld-Artellerie-Regiment Nr. 40 im Weltkriege 1914-1918,* (Aus Deutschlands großer Zeit Band 53. Zeulenroda Bernhard Sporn 1932).
Glasmeier, Heinrich, *Geschichte des Kürassier-Regiments von Driesen Nr 4* (Oldenburg: Stalling, 1932) translated by Anne-Eline Taylor.
Gleichen, Brig E., *Infantry Brigade 1914: The Diary of a Commander of the 15th Infantry Brigade, 5th Division, British Army, During the Retreat from Mons* (Driffield: Leonaur, 2007).
Gleichen, Lord E., *A Guardsman's Memories: A Book of Recollections* (London: Lord Edward Gleichen, 1932).
Godwin-Austen, Alfred R., *The Staff and the Staff College* (London: Constable and Company, 1927).
Goldstone, Jack A., *The Encyclopedia of Political Revolutions* (Washington DC: CQ Press, 1998).
Gooch, George P. and Temperley, Harold, *Great Britain, British Documents on the Origin of the War, 1898-1914* (London: HMSO, 1928).
Gooch, John, *Britain and the Boer War: The Aftermath of Defeat* (New Haven, Connecticut: Yale University Press, 1994).
Gough, Gen Sir Hubert, *Soldiering On: Being the Memoirs of General Sir Hubert Gough* (London: Arthur Barker, 1954).
Gough, Gen Sir Hubert, *The Fifth Army* (London, Hodder and Stoughton, 1931.
Grey, Lord E., Viscount of Fallodon, *Twenty-Five Years 1892-1916* (London: Hodder and Stoughton, 1928).

Grey, Viscount of Fallodon, Harris, Sir Charles, Frank Heath, Sir H. and Schuster, Sir Claud, *Viscount Haldane of Cloan, O.M.: The Man and his Work* (London: Humphrey Milford, , 1928).
Gröner, Erich, Dieter Jung, Martin Maass, *U-boats and Mine Warfare Vessels: German Warships 1815–1945* (Annapolis, Maryland: Naval Institute Press, 1991).
Gruson, Oberst Ernst, *Das 4. Thüringische Infanterie-Regiment Nr. 72 in der Flandern-Schlacht. Oktober 1917* (e.V.), Torgau 1922).

Haldane, Richard B., *Army Reform and Other Addresses* (London: T. Fisher Unwin, 1907).
Haldane, Richard B., *Before the War* (London: Cassell and Co., 1920).
Haldane, Richard B., *Richard Burdon Haldane: An Autobiography* (London: Hodder and Stoughton 1929).
Hamilton Gibb, Maj A., *Gun Fodder, The Diary of Four Years of War* (Boston, Massachusetts: Little, Brown, and Co., 1919).
Hampden, Gordon, *The War Office* (London: Putnam, 1935).
Hankey, Maurice, *Government Control in War* (Cambridge: Cambridge University Press; 1945).
Hart, Prof Albert Bushnell, *Harper's Pictorial Library of the World War. Volume X, Deeds of Heroism and Daring* (London, ReInk Books 2018 reprint of 1920 edition).
Harvey; Col J.R. completed to 1921 by Cape, Lt.-Col. H.A., *The History of the 5th (Royal Irish) Regiment of Dragoons from 1689 to 1799, afterwards the 5th Royal Irish Lancers from 1858 to 1921* (Aldershot, Gale and Polden, 1923).
Hawes, James, *Englanders and Huns The Culture-Clash which Led to the First World War* (London: Simon and Schuster, 2014).
Hawes, James, *The Shortest History of Germany* (London: Old Street Publishing, 2017).
Hazlehurst, Cameron, *Politicians at War, July 1914-May 1915, A Prologue to the Triumph of Lloyd George* (London, Jonathan Cape, 1971).
Heeresleitung, Oberste, *Die Abwehr im Stellungskriege, in Urkunden der Obersten Heeresleitung* über *ihre Tätigkeit 1916/1918, ed. Erich Ludendorff* (Berlin: E.S. Mittler und Sohn, 1921).
Hertslet, Sir Edward, *The Map of Africa by Treaty* (London, Cass, 1967).
Higdon, Tom G., *The Burston Rebellion* (The Eye Press, 1984).
Hikins, Harold, *The Liverpool General Transport Strike* (Liverpool: Toulouse Press, 1980).
Hippel, Konrad von, *Erinnerungsblatt des ehem. Königl. Preuß. Torgauer Feldartillerie-Regiments Nr. 74* (Berlin: Oldenburg i.O, 1928).
Hogarth Milne, J., *Great Britain in the Coronation Year: Being a historical record of the crowning of Their Imperial Majesties King George the Fifth and Queen Mary* (London: W.H. Allen, 1914).
Holmes, Richard, *Riding the Retreat: Mons to the Marne 1914 Revisited* (London: Pimlico, 2007).
Holmes, Richard, *The Little Field Marshal: A Life of Sir John French* (London: Cassell and Company, 2007).
Home, Brig Gen Sir Archibald, *Diary of a World War 1 Cavalry Officer* (Tunbridge Wells: D.J. Costello Publishers, 1985).
Horsfall, Jack and Cave, Nigel, *Mons 1914* (Barnsley: Pen and Sword Book, 1999).
Hurd, Archibald, *The Merchant Navy, Vol. II* (London: John Murray, Albemarle Street, 1924).
Hussey, Brig A.H. and Inman, Maj D.S., *The Fifth Division in the Great War* (London: Nisbet, 1921).
Hutchinson, David, *Mons: An Artillery Battle* (Solihull: Helion and Company, 2018).

Hutton, John, *The Gunners of August 1914, Baptism of Fire* (Barnsley: Pen and Sword, 2014).

James. Lawrence, *Imperial Warrior: The Life and Times of Field Marshal Viscount Allenby 1861-1936* (London, Weidenfeld and Nicolson, 1993).

Jeffery, Keith, *Field Marshal Sir Henry Wilson: A Political Soldier* (Oxford: Oxford University Press, 2006).

Jeffery, Keith, *The Military Correspondence of Field Marshal Sir Henry Wilson, 1918-1922* (London: The Bodley Head, 1985).

Jones, Max, *The Last Great Quest Captain Scott's Antarctic Sacrifice* (Oxford: Oxford University Press, 2003).

Jones, Spencer, *From Boer War to World War, Tactical Reform of the British Army, 1902-1914* (Norman, Oklahoma: University of Oklahoma Press, 2013).

Kaplan, Temma, *On the Socialist Origins of International Women's Day* (London: Feminist Studies, 1985).

Keir, Sir David Lindsay, *The Constitutional History of Modern Britain* (London: Adam and Charles Black, 1938).

Kennedy, Paul, *The War Plans of the Great Powers 1880-1914* (London: Allen and Unwin, 1979).

Kluck, Alexander von, *The March on Paris and The Battle of The Marne 1914* (London: Edward Arnold, 1920).

Koburger, Charles, *The Central Powers in the Adriatic, 1914–1918: War in a Narrow Sea* (London: Greenwood Publishing Group, 2001).

Korfes, Otto, *The German 66th Regiment in the First World War* (Stroud: History Press, 2016).

Leask, Anthony, *Putty. From Tel-El-Kebir to Cambrai: The Life and Letters of Lieutenant General Sir William Pulteney 1861-1941* (Solihull: Helion and Company, 2015).

Lepsius, Johannes Mendelssohn-Bartholdy, Albrecht and Thimme, Friedrich, *Die Grosse Politik der Europäischen Kabinette, 1871-1914. Sammlung der Diplomatischen Akten des Auswärtigen Amtes, im Auftrage des Auswärtigen amtes* (Berlin: Deutsche Veragsgesellschaft für Politik und Geschichte, 1922).

Lewis, Geoffrey, *Carson: The Man Who Divided Ireland* (London: Continuum, 2006).

Lewis, Peter, *British Aircraft 1909-1914* (London: Putnam and Co., 1962).

Lloyd-George, David, *War Memoirs of David Lloyd-George* (London: Odhams Press, 1938).

Lloyds News, *Lloyds ABC of the War, A Complete Reference Book of Facts and Figures which all should Know* (London: Hodder and Stoughton, 1914).

Locker, William A., *Lloyd George by Mr. Punch with an Introduction* (London: Cassell and Company, 1921).

Loringhoven, Hugo Frh von Freytag, *Preußisches Kriegsministerium, Exerzir-Reglement für die Infanterie (signed 1888)* (Berlin: Ernst Siegfried Mittler und Sohn, 1889).

Friedrich, Philipp Johann Freytag, *Das Exerzier-Reglement für die Infanterie vom 29. Mai 1906 Kriegsgeschichtlich Erläuter* (Berlin: Ernst Siegfried Mittler und Sohn, 1906).

Ludendorff, Gen, *My War Memories 1914-1918* (London: Hutchinson and Co, 1920).

Ludwig, Emil, *July 1914* (London and New York: G P Putnam's Sons 1929).

Ludwig, Emil, *Kaiser Wilhelm II* (London: GP Putnam's Sons, 1926).

Lytton, Constance, *Prisons and Prisoners Some Personal Experiences* (London: Heinemann, 1914).

Maccoby, Simon, *English Radicalism: 1886-1914, Vol. 5-1914* (London: Psychology Press, 2001).
Macdiarmid, Duncan, *The Life of Lieutenant General Sir James Grierson* (London: Constable, 1923).
MacDonogh, Giles, *The Last Kaiser: The Life of Wilhelm II* (New York: St Martin's Griffin 2001).
MacMunn, Lt Col G.F., *Horse Mobilisation, The Army Review,* Vol V, No. 2, October 1913).
Magnus, Sir Philip, *King Edward The Seventh* (London: John Murray Publishers, 1964).
Mallmann Showell, Jak P., *The U-Boat Century: German Submarine Warfare 1906-2006* (Annapolis, Maryland: Naval Institute Press; 2006).
Marreco, Anne, *The Rebel Countess* (London: Weidenfield and Nicolson, 1967).
Martin, Rudolf E., *Deutschland und Englander Ein offense Wort an den Kaiser* (Berlin 1980).
Massie, Robert K., *Dreadnought: Britain, Germany, and the Coming of the Great War* (New York: Random House, 1991).
Maurice, Frederick, *Haldane 1856-1915* (London: Faber and Faber, 1937).
Maurice, Maj Gen Sir F., *Forty Days in 1914* (London: Constable and Co., 1920).
Maze, Paul, *A Frenchman in Khaki* (London: Heinemann 1934).
Miles, Hallie E., *Untold Tales of Wartime London: A Personal Diary* (London: Cecil Palmer, 1930).
Moltke, Helmut Karl Bernhard von, *"Aus den Verordnungen für die höheren Truppenführer vom 24. Juni 1869," in Moltkes Militärische Werke, Zweiter Theil, Die Tätigkeit als Chef des Generalstabs im Frieden, ed. Preußischer Generalstab"* (Berlin: Germany Ernst Siegfried Mittler und Sohn, 1900).
Morgan, Ted, *Churchill: The Rise to Failure 1874-1915* (London: Jonathan Cape, 1983).
Morris, Anthony J.A., *The Scaremongers: The Advocacy of War and Rearmament* (London: Routledge and Kegan Paul, 1984).

Nicolson, Harold, *King George The Fifth: His Life and Reign* (Garden City, New York: Doubleday and Company Inc, 1953).
Nicolson, Harold, *King George V* (Pennsylvania: Trans-Atlantic Publications, 1984).

Oldfield, Paul, *Victoria Crosses on the Western Front August 1914-April 1915: A Guide to the Locations – From Mons to Hill 60* (Barnsley: Pen and Sword, 2014).
Owen, Edward, *1914: Glory Departing* (Ashford: Buchan and Enright, 1986).

Packer, Ian, *Liberal Government and Politics, 1905-15* (Basingstoke: Palgrave Macmillan, 2006).
Palmer Alan and Veronica, *The Chronology of British History* (London: Century LTD, 1992).
Pankhurst, Emmeline, *My Own Story* (New York: Hearst's International, 1914).
Pankhurst, Estelle Sylvia, *The History of The Women's Militant Suffrage Movement 1905 1910* (New York: Source Book Press 1970).
Pankhurst, Estelle Sylvia, *The Suffragette Movement, An Intimate Account of Persons and Ideals* (Philadelphia: Wharton Press, 2010).
Pegler, Martin, *Soldiers' Songs and Slang of the Great War* (Oxford, Osprey Publishing, 2014).
Pelling, Henry, *Popular Politics and Society in Late Victorian Britain* (Basingstoke: Palgrave Macmillan 1979).
Petre, Francis Loraine, *Napoleon's Conquest of Prussia 1806* (London: Pickle Partners Publishing, 2011).

Petre, Francis Loraine, *The Norfolk Regiment 1685-1918 Vol II* (Norwich: Jarrold and Sons.1924).
Picart, Caroline Joan, Smoot, Frank Blodgett, Jayne, *The Frankenstein Film Sourcebook* (London: Greenwood Publishing Group, 2001).
Piper, Leonard, *Dangerous Waters: The Life and Death of Erskine Childers* (London: Hambledon, 2003).
Pollard, Alfred, *Two Brothers: Accounts Rendered* (London: Sidgwick and Jackson, 1917).
Purvis, June, *Emmeline Pankhurst A Biography* (London: Routledge 2003).

Radford, Mark, *The Policing of Belfast 1870-1914* (London, Bloomsbury Academic, 2015).
Raleigh, Walter, *War in the Air* (Oxford: Clarendon Press, 1922).
Reid, Walter, *Architect of Victory: Douglas Haig* (London: Birlinn, 2006).
Repington, Charles à Court, *Imperial Strategy* (London: John Murray, 1906).
Repington, Charles à Court, *Vestígía: Reminiscences of Peace and War* (London: Houghton Mifflin Company, 1919).
Richardson, Matthew, *1914: Voices from the Battlefields* (Barnsley: Pen and Sword, 2013).
Richez, Jean, *Un Champ de Coquelicots, La Bataille d'Audregnies le 24 Août 1914* (Privately published).
Rigby, Bernard, *Ever Glorious: The Story of the 22nd (Cheshire) Regiment* (Chester: W H Evans, 1982).
Risio, Maj A.J., *Building the Old Contemptibles, British Military Transformation and Tactical Development from the Boer War to the Great War, 1899-1914 (*BiblioScholar, 2012).
Robertson, William, *Soldiers and Statesmen, 1914-1918* (London: Cassell, 1926).
Robinson, Douglas H., *Giants in the Sky: History of the Rigid Airship* (Yeovil: G T Foulis and Company, 1973).
Rose, Norman, *Churchill An Unruly Life (*London: I B Tauris and Co., 2009).
Rosen, Andrew, *Rise Up, Women! The Militant Campaign of the Women's Social and Political Union, 1903-1914* (London: Routledge Library Editions, 2012).
Ryan, Alfred P., *Lord Northcliffe* (London: Collins St James's Place, 1953).
Ryan, Alfred P., *Mutiny at the Curragh* (London: MacMillan, 1956).
Ryan, Eugene, *Haig's Medical Officer: The Papers of Colonel Eugene 'Micky Ryan* (Barnsley: Pen and Sword, 2013).

Scales, Lillie, *A Home Front Diary 1914-1918* (Amberley Publishing, 2014).
Schubert, Gustav, In Frankreich Kriegsgefangen, meine Erlebnisse auf dem Vormarsch der 1. Armee durch Belgien und Frankreich sowie in der Französischen Kriegsgefangenschaft (Magdeburg, 1915).
Scott, Robert F. and Huxley, Leonard, *Scott's Last Expedition, Vol. I* (New York: Dodd and Mead, 1913).
Sheppard, Maj E.W., *The Ninth Queen's Royal Lancers 1715-1936* (Aldershot: Gale and Polden, 1939).
Simpson, Frank, *Cheshire Regiment the First Battalion at Mons and the Miniature Colour* (Chester: W H Evans, Sons and Company, 1929).
Skennerton, Ian D., *Lee-Enfield Story: A Complete Study of the Lee-Metford, Lee-Enfield, S.M.L.E. and No.4 Series* (Privately published, 1993).
Smith-Dorrien, Gen H., *Memories of Forty-Eight Years' Service* (London: John Murray, 1925).

Somervell, David C., *The Reign of King George the Fifth an English Chronicle* (London: Faber and Faber, 1936).
Sommer, Dudley, *Haldane of Cloan, His Life and Times, 1856-1928* (London: George Allen and Unwin, 1960).
Spears, Brig Gen Edward L., *Liaison 1914: A Narrative of the Great Retreat* (London: William Heinemann, 1930).
Spender, John A., *The Life of the Right Honourable Sir Henry Campbell-Bannerman* (London: Mifflin Company, 1924).
Stewart, Capt P.F., *The History of the XII Royal Lancers (Prince of Wales's)* (Oxford: Oxford, University Press, 1950).
Strachan, Hew, *The First World War* (London: Simon and Schuster, 2003).
Strachan, Hew, *The First World War, Vol. 1, To Arms* (Oxford: Oxford University Press, 2001).
Strachan, Hew, *The Outbreak of the First World War* (Oxford: Oxford University Press, 2004).

Tanner, Michael, *The Suffragette Derby* (London: Robson Press, 2013).
Taplin, Eric L., *Near to Revolution: The Liverpool General Transport Strike of 1911* (Liverpool: Bluecoat Press, 1994).
Taylor, Alan J.P., *The First World War: An Illustrated History* (London: Hamish Hamilton, 1963.).
Taylor, Andrew, *Bonar Law* (London: Haus Publishing, 2006).
Taylor, Sally, *The Great Outsiders: Northcliffe, Rothermere and the Daily Mail* (WandN, 1996).
Terraine, John, *Mons: The Retreat to Victory* (London: Leo Cooper, 1991).
Thompson, John L., *Fleet Street Colossus: The Rise and Fall of Northcliffe, 1896–1922* (Edinburgh: Edinburgh University Press, 2006).
Thomson, George M., *The Twelve Days, 24 July-4 August 1914* (London: Secker and Warburg, 1975).
Thornton, Andrew, *Old Contemptibles. Men of the British Expeditionary Force on 1914: The Cavalry* (Exeter: CreateSpace Independent Publishing Platform, 2016).
Ticknor, Caroline, *Glimpses of Authors* (Cambridge, Massachusetts: Houghton Mifflin, 1922).
Trotsky, Leon, *My Life: An Attempt at an Autobiography* (London: Penguin Books, 1970).
Tuchman, Barbara, *August 1914: The First Month of the First World War* (London: Constable and Co., 1980).
Twells, Brex, *Scare-Mongerings from the Daily Mail 1896-1914 – The Paper that Foretold the War* (London, Forgotten Books reprint, 2017).

Urban, Mark, *Generals: Ten British Commanders Who Shaped the Modern World* (London: Faber and Faber, 2005).

Van Emden, Richard, *Teenage Tommy: Memoirs of a Cavalryman in the First World War* (Barnsley: Pen and Sword Military, 2013).
Vormann, Wolfgang von, *Infanterie-Regiment Fürst Leopold von Anhalt-Dessau (1. Magdeburg.) Nr. 26.* (Oldenburg: Verlag Stalling, 1926).

Waller, Philip J., *Democracy and Sectarianism Political and Social History of Liverpool, 1868-1939* (Liverpool: Liverpool University Press, 1981).
Warner, Philip, *Field-Marshal Earl Haig* (London: The Bodley Head, 1991).

Warnes, David, *Russia: A Modern History* (London: Bell and Hyman, 1984).
Watson, Maj Philip, *The Last Charge, of the 9th/12th Royal Lancers* (Kettering: Crest Publications, 2016).
Wavell, Gen Sir Archibald, *Allenby, a Study in Greatness: The Biography of Field-Marshal Viscount Allenby of Megiddo and Felixstowe* (London: George G Harrap, 1940).
Westlake, Ray, *Kitchener's Army* (Staplehurst: Spellmount, 1989).
Whitmarsh, Andrew, *British Army Manoeuvres and the Development of Military Aviation, 1910-1913, War in History* (London: Sage Publications, 2007).
Wile, Frederic W., *The Assault Germany before the outbreak and England in Wartime: A Personal Narrative* (Indianapolis, Indiana: Bobbs-Merrill, 1916).
Wilhelm, Kaiser II, *My Memoirs 1878-1918* (London: Cassell and Company).
Wilkinson, Alan, *The Church of England and the First World War* (London: SPCK, 1978).
Wolmar, Christian, *Engines of War How Wars Were Won and Lost on the Railways* (London: Atlantic Books, 2012).
Wyrall, Everard, *The Die-Hards in the Great War Vol. 1* (Uckfield: Naval and Military Press reprint of 1926 edition).
Wyrall, Everard *The History of The Duke of Cornwall's Light Infantry, 1914-1919* (London: Methuen, 1932).

Yarmolinksy, Abraham *The Memoirs of Count Witte* (Garden City, New York: Doubleday, 1921).

Zuber, Terence *The Mons Myth: A Reassessment of the Battle* (Stroud: History Press, 2010).

# Index

## PEOPLE


Abadie, Major Eustace 47, 114, 195, 236
Ackehurst, Private 272
Acland, Lieutenant A.C. 139
Adam, Monsieur Felix 89
Addison, Mr 115
Alexander, Major 215, 220, 238–240, 243, 299–300, 302
Allan, Gunner John 222
Allenby, General 54–55, 66–68, 77, 91, 115–116, 119, 123–127, 129, 152, 156–157, 161, 165, 181, 183, 186, 200–201, 223, 234, 247–248, 266, 292, 302–304, 308–310, 319, 324, 326, 330
Allfrey, Lieutenant Frederick de Vere Bruce 88, 121, 196, 213, 243, 274, 316, 319
von Armin, Generalleutnant Friedrich Sixt 65–66, 116, 212, 288–289
Armstrong, Lieutenant Pat 200
Arnim, Oberst Louis von 173, 212
Asceline, Dame Ste 63, 262
Asquith, Prime Minister Herbert 25–26, 31–32, 53, 61–62, 263, 283, 307
Asquith, Mrs Margot 263
Asquith, Lieutenant Raymond 283

Baker, Squadron Sergeant Major Harry 31, 261
Baker, Mrs Joan 31
Baker, Drummer C 261
Baldry, Private Clifton 283
Ballard, Lieutenant Colonel Colin Robert 75–76, 184, 203–206, 212, 215, 222, 238–239, 243–244, 246–248, 264, 294–296, 299, 319, 321
Barlow, Private 272, 311
Barnard, Sergeant 272, 311
Barrow, Lieutenant Colonel George de Symons 19, 67–68, 91, 123, 125, 157, 222, 248, 292, 316, 321
Basil, Lord Basil 115
Battrum, Mrs Millicent 268
Bayly, Lieutenant Charles 143
Beale-Browne, Major 196, 273–274, 304
Beauchime, Colonel 106
Beech, Lieutenant Rowland 152, 186
Bendor, the Duke of Westminster 51, 276
Bennet, Lieutenant Colonel 236
Bethmann-Hollweg, Chancellor von 20, 27, 33
Betts, Private Reginald 137
Bibby, Lieutenant 234
Bigge, Arthur 286
Bingham, Brigadier 148
Birch, Lieutenant Colonel Noel 248
Blackwell, Sergeant 246
Blackwood, Lord 115, 203, 213
Blake, Lance Corporal 252, 255, 260–261, 267
Bloem, Hauptmann Walter 93, 117
Boger, Lieutenant Colonel Dudley 136, 163, 198–199, 203–207, 209, 239, 244, 247–250, 252, 268–269, 294–297, 299
Bolton, Lieutenant 212, 246
Bonham-Carter, Lieutenant I.M. 143, 186, 194
Borchert, Reserve Leutnant 189, 192
Bowes, Colonel William 79
Bowlby, Captain Thomas 238
Bowly, Captain W.A.T. 114
Boyd, Major John 283
Briard, Lieutenant Ernest Felix Victor 216, 244–247, 279, 281–282
Briard, Mr Ernest 279, 282
Briard, Mrs 279, 281–282
Bridges, Major Tom 35, 49, 56, 122, 132–133, 135, 220, 224–225, 237, 273, 302
Briggs, Brigadier 274
Brinckman, Hauptman 53
Brook, Major Victor 51
Brooke, Geoffrey 138
Brudenell-Bruce, Captain Robert 238
Bulk, Corporal 39, 188
Bulmer, Fred 133
Bülow, General von 95, 99–100, 119
Burgess, Private 224
Burne, Major A.H. 307
Burnett, Lieutenant Colonel 60

Burns, Private J. 270
Büstorff, Oberstleutnant Adolf 189, 217, 248

Campbell, Lieutenant Colonel David 60, 164, 203, 212, 219, 223, 228, 230, 233, 236, 243, 252, 274, 302
Capel, Arthur 68
Carter, Private 143, 169, 186, 194
Caselli, Private Tom 48
Caton-Woodville, Richard 305
Cavell, Miss Edith 267–268, 272–273
Chance, 2nd Lieutenant Roger 29, 48, 50, 70, 131, 138, 144, 153, 181, 223, 225, 227, 229, 277, 296, 303
Chapman, Corporal 272
Charteris, Brigadier John 265
Chetwode, Brigadier Philip 124, 127, 304
Chetwynd-Stapylton, Major 163, 248–249, 252–253
Childers, Erskine 288
Churchill, Winston 20, 32
Clarke, Private William 179, 200
Clarke, Theodore 68
Clouting, Private Ben 123, 129, 132–133, 224, 229, 302
Coleman, Frederick 187, 277–278
Colvin, Lieutenant Colonel Forrester Farnell 46
Cook, Private Bertie 107
Corballis, Lieutenant 123
Cowans, Sir John 32, 263
Cresswell, Captain Francis 212, 238, 244, 295
Crooke, Corporal Walter 137, 221, 251–252, 255–256, 258–261, 267, 272
Crossley, Lieutenant Frank 84, 106, 114, 131, 188, 213
Crowsley, Bombardier Saville 235
Crowley, Bombardier 235, 307
Cryer, Driver W. 233
Cumber, Thomas 229

d'Amade, General 161, 186
Darrock, Mr George 67
Datlin, Corporal 272, 312
Davids, Sergeant 243
Davies, Lieutenant Dick 233
Davies, Reggie Lieutenant 186
De Lisle, Brigadier Henry de Beauvoir 49–50, 60, 72, 103, 119, 122, 130, 200–201, 203, 213, 222–224, 234, 264, 274, 278, 282, 299, 301–303, 305, 308
Dease, Lieutenant Maurice 305
Denslow, Sadler Corporal Thomas 283
Doman, Lance Corporal 272
Done, Major H.R. 212, 215
Donop, Sir Stanley von 32
Douglas, General Sir Charles 71, 108, 114, 301
Dowling, Sergeant 268
d'Amade, General 161, 186
Drake, Private 254
Drummond, General 161
Dugmore, Captain 209, 221, 248–251, 266
Duke of Wellington 52, 150
Duke of Westminster 48, 51, 276
Dunn, Captain James 105, 323
Dupont, Monsieur Georges 262, 267
Duquesne, Monsieur 203
Durant, Squadron Sergeant Major Hugh 51–52, 191–192
Dyer, Captain 209, 224, 252–254, 266–267, 279

Easton, Corporal Harry 80, 195, 228, 237, 271, 303
Edmonds, Brigadier Sir James 55, 302, 304, 308
Edwards, Mr Raoul 150
Eisenhart-Rothe, Oberstleutnant Sigismund von 168
Elliot, Lieutenant 102–103, 136, 253, 255, 267, 296
Emmich, General von 53, 94

Faelligen, Oberleutnant 167
Faulkner, Lieutenant 234
Feldmann, Landwehr Feldwebel 110
Felix, Dame Marie 89, 263, 281
Fergusson, General Sir Charles 112–113, 163, 186, 198–201, 203–205, 207, 248, 264, 278, 293–296, 324
Ferte, Captain P.B. Joubert de la 111
Fetherstonhaugh, Lieutenant R.G. 224, 302
Fiske, William 56–57
Fitzgerald, Lieutenant Colonel Brinsley 86
Fitzgerald, Admiral Charles 36
FitzGerald, Captain 'Pat' 97, 169
Fleet, Corporal 254
Flint, Lieutenant Robert 169
Foch, General 22
Fonck, Cavalier Antoine 19
Forestier-Walker, Brigadier 180–181, 293
Fort, Paul 94, 97
Francis, Sergeant Major W.A. 250
Fraser, Major Henry 105
Fraser, Lieutenant William 47, 195
French, Field Marshal, Sir John 22, 32, 55, 61, 69, 72–73, 85–86, 95, 98–99, 102–103, 107–109, 112, 118, 124, 126–127, 129, 141–142, 144–146, 156–158, 161, 173, 179–181, 263, 274, 279, 283, 287–288, 290–294, 298, 309
Freytag, Leutnant 143, 168, 170–171, 186
Fricke, Leutnant 189
Friend, Private Jack 50, 58, 72, 277

Frost, Lieutenant K.T. 256

Gallagher, Lieutenant 169, 225, 227, 267, 277
Garcia, Albert 31
Gardner, Alfred 34–35
Garrad, Private 260–261, 267
Garstin, Lieutenant Charlie 85, 89, 114, 130–131, 177, 188, 191–192, 213, 273–274
Gibb, Private Arthur 43
Gill, Lieutenant W.T. 154, 174
Gleichen, Brigadier 75, 102, 126, 135, 154–156, 204–205, 293
Glover, Corporal 270
Godley, Private Sidney 305
Goltz, General Freiherr von der 287
Gorton, Colonel Edward St George 32
Goschen, Sir Edward 20, 27, 34
Gough, Brigadier Johnny 55, 137–138, 180, 200, 233–234, 247, 273, 304
Gow, Private 171
Grand Duke of Württemberg 42
Graves, Captain Adrian 283
Graves, Captain Cecil 283
Grenfell, Lieutenant Riversdale "Rivy" 47–48, 50–51, 60, 69, 72, 81–82, 84–85, 88, 97, 105–107, 114–115, 120, 122, 130, 134–135, 138, 147, 161, 164–165, 191–192, 200, 213, 222, 236, 276, 283–284
Grenfell, Captain Francis O. 47–51, 59, 72, 80–82, 84–85, 88–89, 105–106, 110–111, 114–115, 120, 122, 130, 132, 134–135, 138, 147, 161, 164–165, 177–178, 187–189, 191–192, 212–213, 228–230, 236, 238–240, 242–243, 250, 266, 273, 276, 278, 283–284, 296, 303, 305
Grey, Sir Edward 19–20, 32, 237, 262, 283
Grierson, Lieutenant General Sir J.M. 32, 54, 71–73, 105, 108–109, 112–113, 125, 286–287, 291
Grigglestone, Private Henry 247, 271, 279
Groener, General Wilhelm 39
Grote, Major Freiherr Karl 262
Grove, Lieutenant 203, 221, 251
Gunton, Sam 57

Haig, General Douglas 22, 32–33, 35, 54–56, 62, 71–73, 105, 124–125, 129, 145, 156–158, 172–173, 180–182, 201, 265, 283, 287, 291, 293
Haig, Lady 73
Haking, Brigadier 172–173, 309
Haldane, Richard 22, 26, 32, 35, 43, 50–53, 287
Hambro, General 273
Hamilton, Sir Ian 222, 297, 299
Hamilton, Johnnie 32
Hamilton, General Hubert 173
Hamilton-Grace, Captain 222, 299
Harmsworth, Alfred 31
Hankey, Colonel Maurice 32
Hardress-Lloyd, Captain 227
Harper, Colonel G.M. 126, 292
Harrap, Corporal 251
Harvey, Lennox 50, 83
Harvey, Douglas 83
Harvey, Lieutenant F.L. 274
Henderson, Brigadier Sir David 72, 143, 157, 292
Hermens, Leutnant 109–110
Hickman, Lieutenant Sir Alfred E. 224, 302
Hildebrandt, Generalleutnant Georg Karl August 146
Hippel, Oberst Konrad von 174
Hoensbroech, Leutnant Lothar Grafen von und zu 133
Hogan, Private 259–260, 267
Holland, Lance Corporal G. 206–207
Holscher, Oberleutnant 109
Home, Major Archibald 68, 79, 91, 103, 108, 119, 156, 274
Hope-Johnstone, Major 114
Horn, Major 307
Horn, Lieutenant Trevor 138, 169, 233
Hornby, Captain Charles 121, 132–135
Hottois, Madame 203
Howard, Captain Henry 67
Huber, Hauptmann 216, 245–247, 250, 253–254
Huguet, Colonel 145
Hunt, Lance Corporal William 88–89, 97, 106, 114, 122, 135, 146–147, 178, 195–196, 275
Hunter, Major 169, 178, 224–225, 227
Hurrell, Private Reginald 60, 73, 76–77, 91, 100–102, 111, 125–126, 137, 155, 198, 216, 219, 244, 246, 271
Hutchison, Major 227
Huxtable, Sergeant Ernest 174
Hynes, Sergeant 277

Jackson, Captain 163, 209, 221, 250, 267
Jagow, Gottlieb von 20
Jaspar, François 57, 262
Jaurès, Jean 23, 36
Jolliffe, Captain 209, 254, 261, 266–267, 279, 316
Jones, Captain 209–210, 256, 258–260, 267
Jordan, Private 250
Jouhaux, Léon 23

Kaczmarek, Hussar 203
Kartes, Leutnant 110
King Charles II 25
King Edward VII 51
King George V 88, 284, 327

Kitchener, Field Marshal Lord 25–26, 32–33, 37, 51–53, 56, 58, 61–62, 85, 89, 91, 108, 112–113, 263, 290–293
Kleist, Major von 93
Kluck, Generaloberst von 41–42, 64, 93, 95, 109, 115, 117, 119, 135, 143, 146–148, 152, 182–183, 185–186, 194, 264–265, 289, 294
Knaths, Hauptmann 93
Knauff, Major 109
Koebbling, Leutnant 109
Kortes, Leutnant 110
Kuhl, General 264
Kunzmann, Reserve Feldwebel 192
Küster, Kűrassier 133
Kotz, Feldwebel 134

Lamb, Lieutenant A.R.J. 100, 141, 150, 200
Lanrezac, General Charles 22, 97–99, 118–119, 124, 126–129, 141–146, 148, 177, 290, 309
Law, Captain James 283
Law, Andrew Bonar 283, 322
Leclercq, Monsieur 97, 274
Ledebour, Leutnant Freiherr von 173
Leggo, Private John 283
Leibold, Mrs Martina 31
Leman, General Gérard 53, 94
Lemmon, Sergeant R.J. 216
Lettory, Monsieur 97
Leveson, Captain 189, 230
Luard, Captain C.E. 212, 238
Lucas-Tooth, Captain Douglas 48, 82–83, 103, 134, 229–230, 235–236, 243, 273
Ludendorff, General Erich 27, 53
Ludlow, Colonel Edmund 67
Lyle, Lieutenant G.C. 207

MacClure, Don Raúl Edwards 150
MacDonald, James Ramsay 30, 62
Macdonald, Lieutenant 69
Macdonogh, Colonel George 67, 79, 144–145
Magnussen, Hauptmann 250, 254–255, 271
Mailleux, Doctor 262, 276
Mapplebeck, Lieutenant G.W. 111
Marcard, Major von 53
Marden, Lieutenant B.J.N. 83, 87–88, 90, 95, 97, 103, 106, 113–114, 121, 134–135, 178, 196
Marques, Lorenzo 61
Marston, Lieutenant 222
Martin-Smith, Julian 115
Massey, Captain 254
Mather-Jackson, Lieutenant Henry 85, 188, 192, 213
Matterson, Lieutenant Cuthbert 188, 252–254, 316
Maurice, Lieutenant Colonel F.B. 173
Maurice, General Sir Frederick 40, 43
Maxwell, Lieutenant 235
Maze, Paul 23, 154, 157, 161
McCartney, Sergeant 213, 220
McGillicuddy, Captain R.K. 130
McHale, Private Timothy 58
McKenna, Reginald 59
Meachin, Sergeant Fred 210, 268–270
Meufel, Hauptmann 217
Middleton, Captain Edward 273
Miles, Hallie 46
Millett, Private 253
Moltke, General Helmuth Graf von 27, 35, 39–41, 64, 93, 99, 115, 150, 183, 285
Monck, General 25
Montgomery, Captain Joseph 115, 311
Moore, Private J. 250
Morgan, Sergeant H 243, 300
Mullens, Lieutenant Colonel Richard 89, 134, 223, 225, 302
Munro, General 291
Murdock, Corporal 253
Murray, General Sir Archibald 32, 73, 102, 124, 144–145, 157–158, 292

Naessens, Victor 94
Nash-Wortham, Captain 82–83, 164, 177, 191–192, 195
Neville, Colonel 267
Newson, Lieutenant 210
Norman, Lieutenant 194, 307
North, Lieutenant 234
Northcliffe, Lord 31, 34–35

O'Melia, Corporal 198
Oford, Corporal 255
Old, Farrier-Sergeant 237
Oldrey, Captain 223, 227
Openshaw, Lieutenant Harold 246, 283
Orr, Major 207, 212, 295
Osburn, Captain Arthur 278, 305
Otton, Private Albert 46
Ott, Hauptmann 53
Oven, Oberst von 53
Owens, Lieutenant Harry 194, 307
Oxley, Colonel 172

Paget, General 291
Palmer, Lieutenant 235
Pankhurst, Emmeline 37, 59
Parker, Lieutenant Colonel 81, 234
Peek, Captain Roger 83–84, 96–97, 105, 114–115, 121, 228, 236–237, 271, 280
Perkins, Private Sidney 103

Perrett, Bombardier 222
Petavel, Major 167
Peto, Colonel Christopher 305
Picard, Lieutenant 19
Pickering, Sergeant 81, 236
Plessen, Generaloberst Hans von 183
Pollard, Lieutenant Geoffrey 78, 135, 239, 241
Pollard, Mr Alfred 242
Pope Pius X 117, 213
Porter, Captain Mark 60, 72, 167, 196
Praeger, Sergeant Arthur 81, 275
Preston, Lieutenant C.O.D. 213, 219–220, 222, 228, 239, 242, 272, 299–300, 302–303
Price, Major 139
Prince Friedrich Leopold of Prussia 287
Prince Louis of Battenberg 26, 32, 54
Prince of Wales 25, 329
Prince Rupprecht of Bayern 42
Princess Mary 60

Queen Victoria 37, 286

Railston, Lieutenant S.J. 225, 227
Randall, Lieutenant 210, 317
Randle, Private 267
Ranke, Herr Robert von 19
Raynor, Sergeant Arthur 221, 251–252, 255–256, 258–261, 267, 272, 317
Reeves, Jack 97, 196
Regan, Sadler Corporal Edward 134
Reich, Leutnant 94
Reichenau, Generalmajor Paul von 173
Reuß, Leutnant von 170, 186
Reynolds, Private William 191
Reynolds, Captain Guy 47, 81
Reynolds, Captain Gerald F. 46–47, 81, 201, 274
Rich, Captain 210, 212, 244–246, 251, 295
Riddell, Lieutenant Jack 195, 233, 307
Riedel, Generalleutnant Johannes 42, 146
Riley, Private 261
Rittmeister, Hans von Puke 203
Roberts, Field Marshal Lord 32, 35, 69, 291, 297
Robertson, General 67
Rogge, Hauptmann 236, 250, 255, 271
Romer, Colonel 204–205, 295
Romilly, Captain 139
Rosebury, Lord 26
Rothwell, Sergeant 249, 272
Ryan, Colonel Eugen 'Micky' 71, 73, 105, 265

Sadler-Jackson, Lieutenant 273
Sambrook, Private 159
Sanderson, Lieutenant 224
Savile, 2nd Lieutenant 159
Schacht, Leutnant 170, 186
von Schlieffen, Field Marshal Alfred 27, 35–36, 39–41, 64, 70, 183
Schubert, Gustav 159
Schüßler, Generalmajor Georg von 59
Schwerer, Antoine 54
Sclater-Booth, Major Hon. Walter 201, 300
Seldte, Reserve Leutnant 168–169
Semeral, Major 219
Sewell, Captain 227, 229–230
Sheldrake, Private Robert 24–25, 28–30, 56, 63, 75, 90–91, 102, 112, 125, 137, 155 218
Shephard, Captain G.S. 186, 194
Shore, Captain 52, 205, 209–210, 247–248, 252–253, 255, 261, 295
Smith, Sergeant W.J. 254
Smith, Lieutenant Eric 122
Smith, Julian 115, 178
Smith-Dorrien, General Horace 73–74, 105, 108–109, 112–115, 127, 129, 156–157, 160–161, 172, 180–182, 184, 194, 201, 263, 287, 293, 295, 304, 309–310
Snelling, Corporal Percy 84
Solly-Flood, Major 134, 225, 274
Sordet, General 119, 124
Soudan, Monsieur 261–262
Spears, Lieutenant Edward 19, 21–22, 31, 38, 78, 98–99, 129, 141–142, 144–145, 179, 181
Spencer-Jacobs, Lieutenant 253–254
Spiers, Private Harold 59
Stanley, Venetia 26, 32
Stewart, Major 236
Stewart, Captain Bertrand 68, 123
Stewart, Captain Lee 267
Straker, Lieutenant Ian 85, 114–115, 188, 191–192, 213
Stumpff, General Karl von 217
Sukowski, Frederick 31
Sutherland, Sergeant Alexander 161, 198, 283
Swallow, Lieutenant 132

Tahourdin, Captain 248, 250, 267
Taylor, Corporal R.H. 'Spur' 147, 178, 195, 201, 222, 230, 236, 240–241, 282
Taylor, Private 253
Taylor-Whitehead, Lieutenant H. "Bunny" 83, 114, 274
Tempest-Hicks, Lieutenant Charles 137–138
Thiele, Leutnant 207, 213, 215
Thornhill, Lieutenant 67
Thorp, Private D. 254
Thorpe, Private F. 212
Thũmmel, Hauptmann 173
Todd, Private 272

Tomkinson, Sergeant F. 281
Tulloch, Lieutenant Colonel 154
Tunnicliffe, Corporal 188
Turner, Sergeant 243
Tustin, Private Gilbert 283

Ullmer, Feldwebel 110

Vallée, Monsieur Alphonse 262
Vaughan, Colonel John 67, 180, 250
Veness, Lance Corporal Thomas 49, 277
Victor-Constant, General 286
Villain, Raoul 23
Voigtlander, Musketeer Hermann 171

Walden, Sergeant 250
Waldenstrom, Knut Otto 67
Walford, Captain John Colquhoun 209, 239, 243, 300
Walker, Sergeant Bert 180–181, 242, 293
Walwyn, Lieutenant 235
Ward, Private 169
Ward, Lieutenant Colonel Bertram 165
Warr, Private Henry 272
Warren, General Sir Charles 297
Waterfall, Lieutenants Vincent 143
Watson, Sir William 306
Wavell, Field Marshal 55, 66
Weatherby, Major 156
Wells, Private Alfred 97
Westphal, Acting Officer 109
Wetherall, Major 198
Wieblitz, Trumpeter 110
Wile, Frederic 33
Wilson, General Henry 32–33, 35, 38, 41, 49, 54, 67, 73, 96, 98–100, 124–127, 143, 158, 179, 187, 290, 292, 294, 301, 304, 322, 326
Wincker, Leutnant 189
Winter, Private Charles 103
Wiseman, Bombardier 272
Wood, Private Arthur 256, 260, 267
Wood, Captain 83, 274
Woodham, Captain 171
Woodhouse, Jack 138
Woodier, Private 254, 317
Woods, Drummer W.F. 75, 263
Woods, Lackey 178
Woods, Lance Corporal 261
Wright, Captain Archie 72, 89, 121, 169, 225–227
Wussow, General Friedrich von 53

Zehmen, Oberst Fritz von 262

**PLACES**

Aachen 64–66, 116
Afghanistan 69, 288
Africa 29, 54–55, 69, 83, 131, 191, 203, 222, 230, 240, 261, 281, 283, 286, 288, 302
Aibes 120
Aiken 99
Aix-la-Chapelle 64, 70, 289
Alsace 19, 23, 40, 286
Amesbury 80, 82–83
Amiens 32, 72, 85, 101, 103, 105
Angre 186, 197, 200–201, 203, 233–235, 248
Antwerp 32, 95, 100, 115, 119
Arlon 39
Ath 121, 123, 132, 145–146, 194
Audregnies 57, 63, 127, 138, 141, 146, 150, 152, 178, 183–184, 186–187, 196–197, 200–201, 203–207, 209–210, 212–215, 217, 219–221, 223, 225, 227, 232–235, 237, 239, 244, 247–248, 250–253, 259, 261–262, 267, 273, 277–279, 281–284, 292, 294, 299–303, 305, 307–309
Austria 37, 54
Avesnes 142

Bailleul 284
Baisieux 127, 138, 201, 203, 209, 223–225, 233–234, 248, 292,
Balaclava 145, 282, 306
Base Camp No. 3 103
Basecles 146
Battice 19
Bavai 172, 186, 276
Beetz 110
Belfast 54, 56, 60, 62, 73, 75, 77, 85, 102
Belfort 287
Belgium 19–20, 23, 27, 33, 39–40, 57–58, 61, 69–70, 79, 87–93, 95–96, 115, 118–120, 122–123, 127–128, 135, 137–138, 264, 269–270, 279–280, 283–284, 290, 305
Berlin 20, 27, 33, 96–97, 106, 275
Bertrix 126
Bievre 126
Binche 116, 119, 124, 138, 148, 150
Bismarck 27
Bois d'Audregnies 247, 250, 259
Bois de Boussu 135–136, 154, 239
Bois de Deduit 222
Bois du Boussu 184
Bois la Haute 134
Bonnet 119, 172, 201
Boulogne 72, 87, 89–90, 95, 97, 103, 114–115
Boussu 135–136, 154, 184, 239
Braine-le-Comte 123

Bray 137–138, 148
Brillecourt 121
Broich 64
Bruxelles 40, 49, 53, 100, 111, 115–117, 119, 121–122, 129, 143, 267–268, 272–273, 291
Bulford 60, 82
Busigny 102–103

Café du Croissant 23
Cavalry School, Sangor, India 46, 67
Cambrai 186, 264, 326
Cambron 132
Canal d'Antoing 173–175, 184
Canterbury 52, 80, 228
Casteau 132, 134, 146
Cement House Cemetery, West-Vlaanderen, Belgium 283
Charleroi 105, 123
Charleroi canal 123
Charring Cross 72
Château Brison 146
Chester 204, 269, 328–329
Chievres 146, 152
Chimay 142
China Seas 54
Combrie Castle 66, 72
Condé 127, 130, 144, 173, 182, 289
Condé Canal 119, 127–129, 138, 143, 146–148, 152, 172–175, 188, 264, 290, 292
Condé sur Escaut 127
Craigavon 63
Curragh 25, 45, 78

Dierst 110
Dinant 108
Doubon 284, 305
Dour 135, 137, 154, 171, 184, 198, 203, 205, 243, 256, 282, 296
Dover 32, 72
Dover Straits 32
Driefontein 203
Dublin 54, 75, 78, 284
Dusseldorf 64

East Dereham 24
Egypt 26, 32, 43
Eldern 85
Élouges 127, 138, 152–153, 177, 184, 186, 189, 193, 196–197, 201, 203–207, 209–210, 212–213, 217–218, 220, 234, 238, 241, 243–244, 248, 251, 253, 263, 270–271, 282, 292, 294, 299–300, 302, 307, 309
England 24, 26, 28, 33, 36, 47, 50–51, 54, 67, 70–71, 85, 91, 105–106, 108, 114, 127, 137, 242, 267, 269–270, 273, 279, 286, 307–308
English Channel 41
Epinal 287
Erquelinnes 119, 144
Estreux 165

Fauroeulx 115
Flanders 40, 87, 92–93, 95, 99
Flavy-le-Meldeux 275
Florence 23
Folkestone 37, 270
Fontaine L'Sogne 119
Fort de Loncin 94
Frameries 130, 172
France 20–21, 23, 26, 31–32, 36, 38–40, 42, 54, 57, 59–61, 79, 88–89, 92–93, 95–96, 102, 109, 115, 135, 274, 279, 284, 286–287, 305
Frenière 142

Geete 110
Gembloux 105, 111
Gemmenich 20
Genappe 111
Genoeis 85
Germany 20, 23, 25–28, 30–31, 33, 35, 38–39, 42, 50, 54, 61, 72, 89, 96, 242, 246, 269–270, 272, 280, 286–288, 290
Gette River 99
Ghislenghien 123
Ghlin 130
Gibraltar 29, 54
Ginchy 283
Givet 108, 118, 177, 179
Givry 116, 120, 127, 130
Givy 137
Glasgow 54, 76
Gommignies 125–126
Grammont 143, 146
Grand Ring 115, 120–121
Great Britain 20, 28, 31, 34, 73
Grevenbroich 57, 64

Haelen 109, 289
Hal 117, 123, 146, 150
Hanin 156
Hannity 154
Harchies 173–176, 184
Harmignies 119, 121, 127, 138
Harveng 115
Harwich 53
Hastiere 179
Hastifcre 177
Hauts de Meuse 39
Hensies 152, 176, 181–182, 184, 199, 289

Herstal 64, 70
Holland 32, 40, 222, 267, 269
Holywood Barracks, Belfast 56
Honnelle 234, 248
Hornu 184
Horse Guards Parade 21
Houillères Baisieux 209
House of Commons 30, 59
Huddersfield 48
Hyde Park 37, 73

India 32, 35, 43, 46–47, 67, 69, 75, 77, 91, 125, 181, 195, 321
Ireland 45, 54, 56, 63, 73, 76, 286, 300
Irish Channel 85

Jemappes 130, 146, 152
Jersey 54, 216, 279, 282
Jeumont 101, 103, 105–106, 120
Jurbise 146

Kimberley 203
Köln 42, 53

La Bassée 242
La Bout en Haut 121
La Haine river 139, 156, 169, 171, 189
La Hamaide 146, 153
Land's End 77, 85
Landrecies 142
Langres 286
Le Cateau 102, 107, 142, 150, 180, 186, 274–276, 291–292, 309
Le Havre 66, 68, 72, 78–79, 90–91, 100, 102, 105, 129, 141
Le Montcel 277
Le Petit Crépin 139
Le Pommereuil 101–102, 112, 125, 204
Leighton Buzzard 51
Lens 123, 146, 148
Leny 186
Les Bavay 263
Les Herbieres 127, 139, 153
Lessines 123
Leuze 150, 194
Liège 32, 40, 42, 49, 53, 64–66, 69–70, 85, 87, 94, 137, 145, 183, 264, 291, 293
Lille 115, 150
Llanelli 59
Lock No. 3 174
Lock No. 5 139, 148, 154, 165, 200
London 19–20, 22, 32, 34–35, 51, 54, 67, 112, 129, 135, 143, 158, 242, 246, 268–269, 287
Londonderry 74–75
Lorraine 23, 40, 42, 286
Louvignies 132
Löwen 134
Luxembourg 33, 39, 42

Maastricht 40
Magdeburg 42, 59, 80, 116, 167, 289
Maiwand 240
Malta 54, 204
Marlière 167, 186
Maubeuge 32, 35, 41, 49, 68, 79, 103, 106–107, 119, 143, 145–146, 179–180, 183, 186, 264, 292
Maurage 119
Mediterranean 54
Messines 31, 284
Mettet 142
Meuse 39–40, 53, 64, 70, 85, 95, 98–100, 113, 118–119, 124, 177, 179, 291
Millen 85
*Ministère de la Guerre* 21–22
*Monceaux Halte* 198
Mons 24, 57, 63, 108, 119–124, 127–130, 132–134, 138–139, 141, 143–144, 146–148, 150, 152, 156–157, 172–175, 182–185, 187–189, 194, 196, 200, 206, 216–217, 247, 263–267, 270–273, 278–282, 289–290, 292, 308
Mons Salient 157, 184
Moselle 39
Mount Vesuvius 184
Mullingar 75
Munster 272

Namur 100, 118, 137, 177, 179, 263, 279
Nantwich 270
Natal 155
Netherlands 40, 64
Neuf Château 39, 126
Newhaven 54
Nimy 119–120, 127, 130, 148, 150, 157
Nivelles 111, 123
No. 8 Rest Camp 91
North Elmham 24, 28, 102
North Sea 39, 77
Norwich 29–30, 47, 56, 77, 102
Notre Dame 132
Nottingham Forest 56–57

Obourg 119, 148, 150, 157
Obrechies 101, 103, 106–107, 109, 115
Olligniés 146, 289
Onhaye 177
Onnerjies 234
Orange River 203
Ormeignies 132

Ors 102, 125, 263
Ottignies 111

Paadeberg 203
Paliseul 126
Paris 20–21, 23, 31, 70, 78, 85–86, 185, 187, 275
Park View 24
Paturages 172, 184
Peronnes 137–138
Peruwelz 194
Pervez 105
Petit Wasmes 163, 296
Philippeville 141, 179
Pissotiau 139
Pompeii 184
Pont de Briques 95
Pont Rouge 49, 277
Pont-a-Celles 123
Poplar Grove 203
Pretoria 286
Punjab 46

Queenstown 54
Quiévrain 126–127, 138, 148, 156, 165, 173, 178, 182, 184, 186, 197, 199–200, 203, 206–207, 210, 212–213, 215–219, 222–223, 227, 233, 239, 248, 271, 288–289, 292, 302, 307

Rawalpindi 46
Rechlenhausen 271
Recquignies 106
Remouchamps 19
Rethel 78–79, 97
Rhine 42, 64
Rivage 173, 184
River Geete 109–110
River Honnelle 248
River Meuse 40
Roisin 186, 235
Rombies 186, 233, 274
Rouen 101
Roulers 274
Rouveroy 120
Ruesnes 274
Rummen 109
Russia 33, 39, 288

Sachsen 65
Salzwedel 109
Sambre 108, 118–119, 142–144
Sardon 139, 167
Sars-la-Bruyere 156–157
Saultain 266
Scilly Islands 77
Scotland 28, 54, 73
Serbia 33, 37
Sergueux 105
Silly 25, 146, 171, 289
Soignies 118, 121, 123, 127, 132, 143, 146–147, 290
Somaliland 204
South Africa 54–55, 69, 83, 131, 191, 222, 230, 240, 261, 281, 286, 288, 302
Southampton 41, 54, 58, 62, 66, 72–73, 80, 82–85, 91, 95
Southwold 53
Spiennes 130
St Aubin 279, 282
St Waast 243
St Aybert 152–154, 165, 200, 289
St Ghislain 127, 138, 146, 148, 152, 182, 289
St Pierre river 234
St Symphorien 115, 182
St Waast 266
Stambruges 146
Stavelot 19
Stettin 57, 64
Stockholm 51
Strasbourg 42
Switzerland 269

Termonde 115
Thulin 118, 127, 138, 147, 150, 152–153, 156, 164–165, 167, 171, 173, 177–178, 181–182, 184, 186–187, 189–192, 194–197, 200, 203, 207, 212–213, 217–218, 238, 283, 288–289, 292
Tidworth 43–44, 46–47, 49, 51, 57–60, 68–69, 80–82, 85, 95–97, 240, 303
Tirlemont 100, 110
Tongres 99
Toul 39, 287
Tournai 150, 158, 194
Transvaal 203
Tubize 123, 272

Valenciennes 119, 152, 161, 165, 179–180, 186, 189, 194, 196, 206, 215–217, 289, 292
Vatican 117
Verdun 39, 127, 287
Vierzehnheiligen 285
Vieux Reng 115
Ville Pommeroeul 127, 130, 139–140, 152–153, 156, 158–160, 164, 167–168, 173, 182, 217
Villers 138
Vise 64
Vitry-le-François 31
Vosges 39
Vusigny 103

Waasbroek 117
Walcourt 177
Wallonia 87, 92, 95
Wargnies-le-Petit 274
Wasmes 163, 184, 205, 296
Waterloo 34, 85, 103, 237, 281
Weedon 77
West Africa 54
Whitstable 230
Wiheries 195–196, 206, 209, 213, 233, 244, 267–268, 272, 299
Woëvre 39

York 31, 67, 75, 321–322, 324, 326–328, 330

Zertsh 270

## MILITARY FORMATIONS

**Armies**

Belgian Army 49, 92, 99, 109, 115

*British*
British Army 32, 36, 43, 49–50, 119, 128, 136, 152, 181, 194, 285–287
British Expeditionary Force (BEF) 22, 32–33, 35–36, 41, 43, 45, 53–56, 58–59, 61–62, 67, 72, 81, 87, 89, 91, 95–97, 103, 108, 113, 115, 117–119, 123–124, 127, 129, 135, 138, 141, 143–146, 148, 150, 152–153, 156, 158, 164, 173–174, 177, 180, 182, 184, 186, 194, 199–200, 204, 207, 215, 263–265, 286–292, 294, 296, 308–309
Indian Army 67, 91

*French*
Third Army 181
Fourth Army 38–39, 118, 126, 177, 181
Fifth Army 38–39, 107, 118-119, 127–129, 141, 144-147, 179–181, 183, 186, 290–291

*German*
*AOK 1* 40, 42, 57, 64, 69–70, 92, 95, 99–100, 105, 113, 119, 146, 150, 182–183, 265, 289, 294, 309
*AOK 2* 27,40, 42, 69, 99–100, 119, 194
*AOK 3* 42, 119

**Corps**

*British*
I Corps 54, 71, 119, 127–129, 148, 150, 180–182, 187, 201, 292–293, 304
II Corps 54, 105, 108, 127, 129, 138, 148, 150, 153, 156, 158, 165, 172, 180–182, 184, 187, 200–201, 263, 286-287, 293–294, 310
Royal Flying Corps (RFC) 111, 123–125, 143, 156, 158, 179, 283,291–292

**German**

*II AK* 146, 173
*III AK* 152, 65, 93, 109–110, 115–117, 146, 150, 152–153, 159, 167–169, 171, 173, 181–182, 185, 207, 213, 215–217, 248, 262, 288–28, 301
*IV AK* 65, 93, 109–110, 115–117, 146, 150, 152–153, 159, 167–169, 171, 173, 181–182, 185, 207, 213, 215–217, 288–289, 301
*VII AK* 142, 179 270
*IX AK* 69, 93, 109–110, 115–117, 146, 150, 152–153, 159, 167–169, 171, 173, 181–182, 185, 207, 213, 215–217, 248, 262
*X AK* 142, 179, 270
*Heereskavalleriekorps 2* (HKK 2) 99, 132, 134, 150, 183, 207, 265

*French*
Fifth French Corps 177
French Cavalry Corps 108, 119, 124, 144

**Divisions**

*British*
1st Division 54
2nd Division 54
3rd Division 40, 54, 115, 126, 130, 172–173, 181, 275, 301
4th Division 54
5th Division 54, 71, 112, 126–127, 130, 135, 138, 152, 172, 181, 184, 186–187, 189, 194, 198, 200, 203, 234, 238, 243, 248, 264, 266, 275, 278, 280, 286, 293–294, 300–301
6th Division 286

*French*
84th French Territorial Division 152, 186, 194

*German*
*Infanterie Division 7* 42, 146, 152–153, 158, 182, 184, 203, 217, 264
*Infanterie Division 8* 146, 173, 182, 184, 199, 215, 217–218, 264
*Kavallerie Division 9* 132–133

**Brigades**

*British*
1st Cavalry Brigade 141, 189, 200, 266
2nd Cavalry Brigade 49, 71, 80, 103, 106, 114, 119, 135, 152–153, 186, 196–197, 200–201, 207, 210–211, 224, 231, 244, 247, 274, 277–278, 299, 303–304
3rd Cavalry Brigade 54, 116, 201, 227, 233, 247,

274, 286, 303
4th Cavalry Brigade 55, 148, 152, 154, 165
5th (Independent) Cavalry Brigade 115, 119, 124, 127, 290, 292
5th Brigade 172, 181, 309
7th Brigade 248
13th Brigade 138, 184
14th Brigade 139, 153–154, 156, 165, 171, 184
15th Brigade 70, 75, 90–92, 100, 105, 112, 125, 135, 152, 154, 156, 163, 172, 184, 198, 205, 263, 293–294
19th Brigade 161, 165, 184, 186–187, 200, 309

*German*
*Infanterie Brigade 11* 53
*Infanterie Brigade 13* 42, 59, 152, 158, 171, 184, 194, 212, 238
*Infanterie Brigade 14* 53
*Infanterie Brigade 15* 173
*Infanterie Brigade 16* 117
*Infantry Brigade 13* 238
*Kavallerie Brigade 13* 132

**Units**
*British*
2nd Dragoon Guards 141, 150, 178–179
4th Dragoon Guards 49, 72, 89, 97, 119, 121–123, 132–134, 161, 169, 192, 195, 210, 220, 223, 226–230, 233, 236, 247, 256, 273–274, 277–278, 301–304
5th Dragoon Guards 178
6th Dragoon Guards 148, 153–154, 165, 173–174
11th Hussars 31, 67, 122, 142, 191
15th Hussars 124, 127
18th Hussars 58, 60, 153, 178, 186, 189, 197–198, 200–201, 206, 210, 230, 233, 274, 277, 302
19th Hussars 124, 127, 161, 169
21st King George's Own Central India Horse 47, 195
9th Lancers 43, 46–47, 49–50, 59, 68, 71–72, 80, 82, 85, 87, 89–90, 92, 95, 97, 103, 105, 107, 109–110, 113–114, 116, 119, 121–123, 130, 134–135, 138, 146–147, 153, 156, 161, 164–165, 173, 177–178, 184, 186–187, 189, 192, 194, 196, 200, 212–213, 223–224, 229–230, 232–233, 235–238, 240, 243, 261, 271–275, 277–279, 282–283, 300, 302–308
12th Lancers 47, 77, 84, 307
16th Lancers 44–45, 67, 137, 152, 195, 233, 235, 307
18th Lancers, Indian Cavalry 227
21st Lancers 46, 80, 89–90, 105, 306
2nd Life Guards 154
2nd Argyll and Sutherland Highlanders 161, 165
1st Bedford Regiment 75, 154, 163, 172, 247
1st Cameronians 165
1st Cheshire Regiment 56, 70–71, 74–75, 77, 100, 102, 112, 136, 154, 156, 163, 174, 184, 188, 198–199, 203–207, 209–210, 212–213, 215–216, 221–222, 233, 244–245, 247, 249–250, 253, 255, 257, 263–264, 266, 270–272, 279, 281, 289, 294–295, 299, 301–302
1st Dorset Regiment 75, 154, 163, 247
1st Duke of Cornwall's Light Infantry (DCLI) 138–140, 147–148, 153–154, 156, 159–160, 164–165, 167–171, 173, 184, 187, 283
1st East Surrey Regiment 153, 243
2nd Manchester Regiment 156, 167, 169, 171, 187, 198, 205
1st Middlesex Regiment 121, 165, 174
1st Norfolk Regiment 25, 29, 56, 60, 62, 73, 75–76, 85, 92, 100–102, 111–112, 125, 137, 154, 156, 163, 184, 198, 203–204, 206–208, 210, 212, 216–217, 220–222, 238–239, 245–249, 251, 272, 279, 281, 283, 294–296, 300, 302
2nd Royal Scots 283
2nd Royal Welsh Fusiliers 105, 165

59 Field Company, Royal Engineers 156, 169
119th Battery 78, 135, 204–205, 207–208, 213, 215, 217–219, 222, 228, 233, 238–239, 242–243, 248, 272, 278, 284, 299–300, 302–303, 305, 317

Royal Automobile Club Volunteer Force (RACVF) 129, 276

*German*
*Husaren Regiment 3* 148, 152
*Husaren Regiment 8* 132, 152, 159
*Husaren Regiment 10* 109, 116, 156, 203
*Kürassier Regiment 4* 132–134

*Infanterie Regiment 26* 66, 93, 109–110, 116, 143, 152, 158–159, 167–169, 171, 184, 189–190, 194–195, 207, 213, 217–218, 221, 238, 246–248
*Infanterie Regiment 66* 42, 59, 64–66, 70, 85, 93, 99, 109, 117, 152, 159, 168–169, 171, 184, 189–190, 192, 194–195, 207, 212, 217–219, 238, 272, 289
*Infanterie Regiment 72* 199–200, 202, 213, 215–216, 219–220, 227, 233, 236, 239, 250, 254–255, 262, 289
*Infanterie Regiment 93* 173, 175, 199, 233–234, 248

*Feldartillerie Regiment 4* 168–169, 171
*Feldartillerie Regiment 40* 189, 194, 217–218, 222, 238–239, 289
*Feldartillerie Regiment 74* 174–175, 199–200, 207, 215, 218, 303

*Pioneer Battalion 4* 85, 169, 171, 199

## MISCELLANEOUS TERMS

Army Act 44
Army Council 61, 108, 288
Balkans War 28
Bank of England 51
*Cavalry Training 1907* 288
*Cavalry Training 1912* 288, 301, 304
Entente Cordiale 35, 54, 89–90
*Field Artillery Training 1902* (amended 1904) 288
*Field Artillery Training* 1906 297
*Field Service Regulations Part 1 of 1909* 198, 240, 288, 293, 295–297, 300, 309
*French Plan XVII* 35, 38–39, 187
Harland & Wolff 77
House of Commons 30, 59
Imperial Defence Conference 22
*Infantry Training 1905* 288
*Infantry Training 1911* 288
*Mobilisation Instruction 1912* 288
Official Secrets Act 31
*Operation Order 7* 127
*Operation Order No. 5* 115–116, 119, 126, 292
*Ordre Particulier No. 15* 118, 126
Red Cross 23, 58, 63, 192, 237, 266, 269, 271, 275–276
*Remount Manual* 44
*Schlieffen Plan* 36, 39–40, 64
Scotland Yard 28
*The Moltke Plan* 40
*Three-Year Service Law* 23
*War Council* 32, 54, 290

**Conflicts**

Balkans War 28
Battle Cannae 39
Battle of Jena 285–286
Battle of Mons 120, 133, 185, 267
Battle of Ypres 284
Boer War 28, 60, 203–204, 212, 222, 287–288, 291, 294, 297, 307–308
Burmese Expedition 204
Relief of Mafeking 122
Second Battle of Gaza 283

**Publications**

*Belfast Telegraph* 60
*Bugerwelzyn* 70
*Chronicle* 279
*Evening Post* 279
*Gloucestershire Echo* 283
*Guardian* 26, 47, 81, 279, 281
*Kölnische Zeitung* 170
*La Patriote* 115
*Le Vengeur* 36
*London Evening News* 268
*Manchester Evening News* 270, 306
*Mercantile Advertiser* 58
*Northampton Mercury* 77
*The Barrier Miner* 287
*The Cheshire Observer* 270
*The Elgin Commission* 297
*The Liverpool Daily Post* 270
*The Singapore Free Press* 58
*The Times* 31, 35, 37, 112, 237, 279, 306
*The War Illustrated* 282

**Vessesls**

*Britannic* 77
HM Airship *Delta* 291
HM Airship *Eta* 291
*HMS Amphion* 53, 77
*Königin Luise* 53
*Minneapolis* 77
*Sentinel* 72
SS *Armenian* 80, 87
SS *Massilia* 75, 77
SS *Oronsa* 75
SS *Welshman* 80–81, 87–88